Carol Lynley:
Her Film & TV Career in Thrillers,
Fantasy & Suspense

by Tom Lisanti

BearManor Media

Orlando, Florida

Carol Lynley: Her Film & TV Career in Thrillers, Fantasy & Suspense
© 2020 Tom Lisanti. All Rights Reserved.

No portion of this publication may be reproduced, stored, and/or copied electronically (except for academic use as a source), nor transmitted in any form or by any means without the prior written permission of the publisher and/or author.

Published in the USA by
BearManor Media
1317 Edgewater Dr. #110
Orlando, FL 32804
www.BearManorMedia.com

Softcover Edition
ISBN: 978-1-62933-633-6

Printed in the United States of America

Table of Contents

Acknowledgements	ix
Foreword by Nelson Aspen	xiii
Preface	xvii
Introduction	xxvii
1. The Early Years: Child Model to Teen Idol	1
The Light in the Forest; Shirley Temple's Storybook; Alfred Hitchcock Presents	
2. A Sex Kitten Purrs…Briefly	55
The Alfred Hitchcock Hour; Shock Treatment	
3. She's Not There	97
Bunny Lake Is Missing	
4. Terror in Dunwich	127
The Shuttered Room	
5. Suave Spies to Invading Aliens	153
Danger Route; The Man from U.N.C.L.E.; The Invaders; Journey to the Unknown; Shadow on the Land; The Smugglers	
6. Murder in the Rough	201
Once You Kiss a Stranger	
7. What's a Bippy?	217
The Maltese Bippy	
8. On the Run with the Immortal	233
The Immortal (TV-movie and series)	
9. A Foul-Mouthed Hooker in a G-Rated Comedy	247
Norwood	
10. Vampires and Druids and the Blob! Oh, My!	267
Weekend of Terror; Mannix; Crosscurrent; Beware! The Blob; The Night Stalker; Night Gallery; The Sixth Sense	
11. Hell, Upside Down	315
The Poseidon Adventure	

12. Bad Girls, Harried Heroines, and Disaster Divas — 353
Orson Welles' Great Mysteries; The Magician; The Evil Touch; The Elevator; Death Stalk: If It's a Man, Hang Up!; Quincy, M.E.; Flood; Bad Georgia Road; Kojak

13. Welcome to Fantasy Island! — 429
Fantasy Island (TV-movie and series)

14. Remake It Again, Sam — 451
The Cat and the Canary

15. Imperiled from the Earth to the Moon — 467
Having Babies II; Hawaii Five-O; Cops and Robin; The Beasts Are on the Streets; The Shape of Things to Come

16. Soaps to Suspense — 503
The Best of Friends; Willow B: Women in Prison; Judgement Day; Balboa; Vigilante; Hotel; Tales of the Unexpected; Hammer House of Mystery & Suspense

17. High Rise Horror — 541
Dark Tower

18. Some Memories Are Better Left Buried — 549
Blackout

19. From Rampaging Rats to Hideous Demons — 565
Night Heat; Monsters; Spirits; Howling VI: The Freaks

20. Three Cons and a Kid — 575
Neon Signs

21. Final Act — 587
Vic; A Light in the Forest

22. Film & TV Credits — 599

23. "Carol Lynley for the Block": Select Game Shows, Talk Shows, and Other Appearances as Herself — 607

Bibliography — 657

End Notes — 681

Select Index — 709

To my parents, Vincent and Joan Lisanti, who launched my Carol Lynley obsession when, on my twelfth birthday, they brought me to the drive-in to see *The Poseidon Adventure*

Acknowledgments

My deepest gratitude to the all the people who contributed to this book starting with those who graciously spoke with me or wrote to me about knowing or working with Carol Lynley over the years— MacKenzie Allen, Arledge Armenaki, the late Stephan Chase, Alex Cord, Gene deRuelle, Matt Dotson, John Goff, Monika Henreid, Olivia Hussey, Howard Kazanjian, Margaret Kenney, Tom Kibbe, Marc Kolbe, Harry Langdon, Jr., Alan J. Levi, James Polakof, Tina Sinatra, Howard Wexler, and Jeffrey Wolf. Several of them shared interesting back stories on the films and TV shows they worked on with Carol.

A special thank you goes to Carol's brother Daniel Jones Lee for his comments and for clearing up many false items written about Carol's childhood. And special mention to Arledge Armenaki and Alan J. Levi for sharing with me their video copies of *Blackout* and *Judgement Day*, respectively.

A huge thanks goes to the wonderful and multi-talented TV host/writer/singer/actor Nelson Aspen for composing the Foreword. We met back in the late nineties due to our love for Carol Lynley. I will never forget walking up the path to the front door of his house in Los Angeles and hearing through an open window him singing, "The Morning After" while at the piano. We have remained friends ever since.

My deepest appreciation goes to Carol's dear friends Marlin Dobbs and James Radford who I was put in contact with by Lee Pfeiffer from *CinemaRetro* magazine, always a supporter of mine. Thank you, Lee! Marlin shared with me many aspects of her career which he learned firsthand and for opening his vast collection of Carol Lynley photographs to me. I will forever be grateful. We have shared many conversations since. And thanks to James for connecting me to Marlin and for sharing his expertise on *The Poseidon Adventure*.

I am profoundly grateful for the following for their continued support:

My longtime friend writer/blogger Shaun Chang for his continued insights and detective skills. I always value his input. We can chat for hours about sixties starlets.

Jak Castro who kindly allowed me to use portions of his interview with Carol Lynley from 2003.

George Carpinone for sending me stories about Carol that he uncovered for his research on the adorable Sandra Dee and for gifting me with magazines from Carol's teenage modeling days.

David Paris, from Down Under, for kindly providing me research articles within minutes about Carol's work in Australia and contacting me with any new Carol video sightings on YouTube.

Jim McGann my webmaster. I will forever be your servant.

A huge shoutout to my friend and former co-worker, Lis Pearson, who not only watches our cats, Teddy and Maxie, but re-edited this entire manuscript! She is meow-velous!

My friends with a special shout out to Stephen Bowie, Michael Carroll, Thom Chavez, Teressa DeTurris, Matt Fletcher, Kathleen Germann, Bill and Diane Hay, Clyde Jones, Pete Kaiser, John Kelly, Judy and Rick Kiefer, Jeanne and Tony Koproski, Phil Lindow, Steve Newell, Alan Pally, Jose Reina, Kevin

Winkler, and especially Ernie DeLia who has put up with everything Carol Lynley.

My late father Vincent Lisanti, my mother Joan, my siblings Joe, Lorraine, and Donna who had to live with me and my obsession with Carol for years. Even though they probably never heard of Carol Lynley, I will add my nieces and nephews Emily, Vincent, Kelly, McKayla, Christina, Samantha, and Sean. Lastly, my nephew Joey Nicolo who knows his share of my royalties comes with the price of being the keeper of my ashes when I am gone.

I couldn't have written this book without using the vast collections of The National Film Information Service at the Margaret Herrick Library in Beverly Hills; the General Research Division at The New York Public Library, The Paley Center for Media (where I watched Lynley's' four 1973 appearances on *The Tonight Show Starring Johnny Carson*), and the Billy Rose Theatre Division at The New York Public Library for the Performing Arts, with a special thanks to librarian Jeremy Megraw and photographer Martin Parsekian. Also, the Facebook tribute pages *The Poseidon Adventure: The Movie (1972)* and *The Poseidon Adventure 1972* for all the fun facts, articles, behind-the-scenes photos, and trivia they have shared with fans. They were a major source of information.

Finally, a huge thank you to the fabulous Carol Lynley. After over a year of writing to her, she finally agreed to speak with me about her career, but only if the book was not touted as a biography. We spoke twice by phone. Her winsome personality and infectious laughter made the time go by in a flash as we talked about aspects of her career. Since we were on the record, I think she was bit more reserved than when speaking to friends or fans at autograph conventions but I am appreciative of the time she gave me. Carol also corrected some of the erroneous things that were written about her over the years, which required me to make major revisions to the manuscript, so I am happy to be able to set the record straight.

Through Carol's film and TV appearances she has brought joy into my life since I was kid. I could never have imagined that I would not only one day speak and meet her but also write a tribute book about her. I will forever be a fan.

Unfortunately, Carol died on September 2, 2019 before this project reached fruition and we could talk one last time. I am still saddened by her death and so disappointed that she never got to see this book. She was looking forward to it. Here is hoping she would have approved.

Foreword
by Nelson Aspen

As an entertainment journalist for over a quarter century, I often remind people that "fan" is just an abbreviation for "fanatic." It certainly applies in my case when it comes to Carol Lynley. Anyone who knows me, even casually, also knows that she is my "favorite movie star" just as they would know my eyes are blue or that I am a marathon runner. Oh yeah ... and there's that enormous *Poseidon Adventure* tattoo on my leg.

What makes someone a fan? What undefinable, magical chemistry exists between the Adored and the Adorer? As evidenced in Tom Lisanti's book which you are about to enjoy, when it comes to Carol Lynley fans, it may be mysterious but it's not unique. There are a lot of us out there, most introduced to her vulnerable luminosity in *The Poseidon Adventure* back in the 1970s.

Given my tastes in art, music, literature and style, I always contended that I was "born too late" ... even in my devotion to Carol's career. After all, her greatest fame as a Teen Model and young leading lady came in the years before she was forced to climb up Irwin Allen's Christmas tree.

I was an obsessed 14-year-old when I first met Carol at the Stage Door of NYC's Music Box Theater after a matinee performance of *Absurd Person Singular*. A year later, we had a long lunch together at the tony Metropolitan Club after my Dad arranged a meeting with her agents to discuss further theatrical opportunities. Those never manifested, but a wonderful, unusual 40+ year friendship did!

Over the decades, Carol and I shared countless meals, marathon phone conversations and spectacular adventures. We've worked together on camera for my TV news outlets…she has done staged readings of dramatic works I've authored and has appeared in several of my books. We've walked red carpets and shared the stage at Film Festivals. I even perform a musical tribute to her in my cabaret shows, which any audience who has ever idolized a celebrity always enthusiastically appreciates. She was funnier than you'd guess and possessed a knack for humor and storytelling that was a testament to her Irish roots. You could drop a name ("Jimmy Farentino," "Ernie Borgnine," "Ronny Neame," "Francis Albert [Sinatra]," "Ollie Reed," "Rip 'The Ripster' Torn," "Too" [Tuesday Weld]) and sit back knowing you were in for a treat.

Carol's career spanned the second half of the 20th Century and her body of work, while not always critically remembered, is an important reflection of those eras. She was literally the face of All-American Teenage pulchritude in the '50s … the modern, sexually unleashed young woman of the '60s … a free-spirited, fresh-faced '70s chick … and ultimately (my favorite incarnation) the smart but sultry MILF of the '80s. In the decades after that, she evolved into one of Filmdom's most reliable preservationists: always happy to recount her memories and impressions of the great artists with whom she worked and loved. She loved movies and loved being a part of the movie business. Ironically, Turner Classic Movies finally wised up and planned their first "Carol Lynley Tribute Night" for the same week she passed away, September 3, 2019.

Just what is it about Carol Lynley that has captivated me for a lifetime? I can't put my finger on it, but my 90-year-old mother who has witnessed this relationship develop has always said, "I've never been surprised at all. What's not to love?" If you're holding this book in your hands, chances are you've felt that, too.

Nelson Aspen
September 9, 2019
www.nelsonaspen.com

Nelson Aspen and Carol Lynley, ca. 1990s. Courtesy of Nelson Aspen

Preface

I have been fascinated with actress Carol Lynley since I was twelve years old. With her long blonde hair, bluest of blue eyes, delicate porcelain complexion, soft voice, and a permanent look of slight bewilderment, she had a cool screen quality that I found appealing. From trying to escape a sinking upside-down ocean liner, to searching for a missing daughter who may or may not exist, to being haunted by visions in a spooky mansion, to being taken hostage while on a river kayaking trip by prison escapees, she simply riveted me with these lady in peril roles. The look of terror on her face always struck me as more real than acting. It probably did others as well since she was often cast in this type of role beginning in 1965 in the thriller, fantasy, and suspense genres, though Lynley played a myriad of parts throughout her career.

Every pubescent boy in 1973 wanted to see *The Poseidon Adventure* and I was no different. I was captivated by the TV commercials and desperately wanted to see the movie. My family rarely took us to indoor movies but we frequented the drive-in during the spring and summer months often beginning in 1968. My favorite movies were *The Boatniks, Beneath the Planet of the*

Apes, and *Skyjacked*, but that would soon change. When my birthday rolled around on May 11, 1973, *The Poseidon Adventure* was still playing in theaters across the country five months after it premiered. Guess what I received for a present? However, it was almost derailed when my parents' friends, Anthony and Pauline Evangelista, stopped over during the day with their sons, Louis and Vinny, who were a bit older than me. I remember showing them my *Mad* magazine that lampooned *The Poseidon Adventure* as *The Poopsidedown Adventure*. But my heart literally stopped when I heard their parents ask mine to go out that night. Thankfully, my mother declined due to my birthday plans. So, to my utter relief, later that warm Saturday night, off to the drive-in we went.

I was too excited for words and got to sit in the front seat between my mom and dad while my brother and sisters settled down in back. The sun went down, and the movie began. I was immediately drawn into the drama as it began to unspool introducing the passengers and crew hours before the New Year's Eve countdown. Of course, I knew what was in store for all and sat there waiting anxiously for the big moment. Then it came. As the ocean liner began to roll over after being hit by a 90-foot tidal wave, I was spellbound. I had never seen anything like it. My heart was racing as the people in the ballroom began to reach out desperately for anything to grab on to, as the ship began to tilt. "Hold on Linda," Mike Rogo yelled to his wife. It was to no avail as they, Belle, Nonnie, Manny, Reverend Scott, Susan, Robin, and the rest all began tumbling down as the ocean liner began to capsize. It is the best piece of trick photography, stunt work, and special effects for me to this day.

After that capsizing scene, I sat mouth agape for the rest of the movie as the passengers and crew made their way up to the bottom of the boat–climbing, swimming, crawling their way to reach freedom. The movie was tense, exciting, shocking (they killed off major characters in horrific ways!), tender, and funny. I loved all the characters but the one that got the most sympathy from me was the hippie singer Nonnie clad in hot pants and go-go boots. She was the lone character who expressed sheer terror continually regarding their predicament. I could relate, as I was petrified just watching in a parked car.

When the movie ended, it was like I just awoke from a dream. First thing

I asked my mother was "who was the pretty blonde playing Nonnie?" She said, "Carol Lynley. She was in that vampire movie [*The Night Stalker*] that I told you not to watch last year." I was hooked.

Then one Saturday night the following year NBC-TV was broadcasting a Glen Campbell comedy called *Norwood* from 1970. He played a returning G.I. who wanted to get out of his sleepy hometown and make it as a vocalist on some hayseed radio show. At a local roller rink, he meets up with shady Grady who tells the naïve boy that he has connections to the show and all Norwood needs to do is drive one of his cars to New York City unaware it is hot. When Norwood shows up the next day, he finds there are two cars and a passenger sitting in it named, "Yvonne Phillips and she is a dandy." For me that was an understatement.

A pretty, sun-drenched blonde with short hair in an orange mini dress Yvonne was a ball of fire eating her can of peaches as the duo began arguing their way across the country. Unfortunately, after Norwood runs a stop sign and the duo are chased by an inept deputy and his sheriff, he gives the stolen car to Yvonne who drives off to find her "cannonball" Sammy Ortega in Illinois and disappears from the movie. I watched until the end to see who the actress was, and I was stunned to see it was Carol Lynley. Carol Lynley!?! The same Carol Lynley who has long hair and a hippie look in *The Night Stalker* and *The Poseidon Adventure*? It could not be. Here she looked completely different playing such an animated, amusing role so far removed from the almost-catatonic Nonnie. But it was her.

From that moment on I tried to catch every movie and TV show Lynley appeared in. I would scour the *TV Guide* to plan my week's viewing. If Carol turned up during the daytime on *The Hollywood Squares* or a talk show, I would feign illness that day to stay home from school. It only worked a few times as my mom began to catch on. If Carol turned up in primetime, I would beg to watch her on the color television and if I was overruled, I would retreat to my bedroom where I had my own portable black-and-white TV. If one of Carol's movies appeared on the *Late Late Show* (as *Harlow* and *Bunny Lake Is Missing* often did) I would try to keep myself awake or set my alarm to get up (remember this was pre-VCR days). Luckily, many of her films were regular features on the *ABC-TV 4:30 Movie* where I was introduced to teen queen Carol and sex kitten Carol and lady in peril Carol.

As an adolescent during the seventies I was a shy outsider who never really fit in with the boys in my neighborhood. I always felt like one of the 'misfit toys' from the TV Christmas special, *Rudolph the Red-Nosed Reindeer*. I sucked at and disliked playing team sports, except kickball. While my brother and friends could recite the roster of the New York Yankees and Mets' teams, I could regurgitate the complete filmographies of Carol Lynley, Pamela Tiffin, and Yvette Mimieux; recite every cast member from the *Beach Party* movies; and name all of Elvis Presley's leading ladies. However, it was Lynley who stood out for me the most. I began a scrapbook of clippings on her tearing out her picture or magazine/newspaper articles on her wherever I saw them. Hence, I became an avid reader of *The National Enquirer*, *The Star*, and *Rona Barrett's Hollywood* and *Gossip* magazines. The paparazzi snapped photos of Carol out and about with many different men (including David Frost, Dan Klosterman, Glenn Ford, Jack Haley, Jr., and her close pal, Fred Astaire) making her great fodder for these gossip rags.

I would spend hours at my local and then college libraries doing research on Carol's career. I remember getting excited every time I would discover a new acting credit or learn Carol placed on a promising newcomer poll as if I just won the lottery. I wrote to the "Problem Line" and TV columns of our local newspaper *Newsday* with questions asking if there was a movie sequel to *Peyton Place* and who sang "The Morning After" in *The Poseidon Adventure* with only the goal to get Carol Lynley's name and hopefully a picture in the paper. Recently, I learned I was not the only fan doing this. My fascination became so acute and my family so aware that once on vacation in Shawnee, Delaware I was up past midnight watching *The Shuttered Room* in our timeshare condo. My mom and her friend Claire Prettitore were having tea when Claire turned towards the television and said, 'Is that Carol Lynley?' My mom looked up and said, "Yes, Tom stays up to all hours to watch Carol Lynley movies and pro wrestling." The latter is for another discussion.

Preface

> **Q.** I have a $10 bet with my family that there was a sequel to the movie "Peyton Place." If there was, can you tell me who played in it and how it did at the box office?
> —T.L., North Bellmore

My question to "Problem Line" published in *Newsday* on May 15, 1979. By the way, there was no bet.

My family and friends were perplexed by my fascination with Carol Lynley. She was not a sex symbol along the lines of Raquel Welch or Farrah Fawcett or an Oscar winning actress of the Golden Age—so why her? Looking back, I think it was because she had a unique quality that touched me and specifically because she was not the typical actress of the time I should idolize. She was different and so was I, dealing with my sexuality. I think obsessing on someone else was a way of not having to face my own issues. Carol was an underdog and I was rooting for her to succeed even more than she did.

In 1975, the airwaves in the New York metropolitan area were filled with TV commercials for the hit Broadway play *Absurd Person Singular*. I remember the announcer exclaiming something to the effect of, "Come to the Music Box Theatre to see Geraldine Page, Carol Lynley, and Fritz Weaver in Alan Ackbourne's *Absurd Person Singular* the longest running comedy on Broadway!" The closest I came was in junior high school when our class was taken to see the musical *Raisin* and our bus passed the Music Box with my face plastered against the window hoping to see a glimpse of Carol's name on the marquee. Yes, I was a complete dork.

Being a Carol Lynley fan though during this period had its frustrations and I had so many questions back then. Why were there so many gaps in her credits? Why didn't she follow up *The Poseidon Adventure* with another big theatrical release? I would learn over the years that while some of these hiatuses were inactivity by Lynley's own choosing, they were taken at the most inopportune times. These stops and starts greatly affected her career as she seemed to be always making a comeback. Her career was also hampered by delayed television broadcasts (*The Smugglers* and *The Evil Touch*) and film distribution problems sometimes preventing U.S. audiences the chance to see some first-rate performances on the big screen (*Cotter* and *The Cat and the Canary*). Also like most actors, her career included frustration with not getting parts she desired, missed opportunities, and bad role choices due to misguided agents, love affairs, or money. In some past film reference books, Carol has been called "underrated" and having "untapped talent." This is true, but she did have a few opportunities that she unwisely passed on that may have propelled her standing in Hollywood even further. Even so, Carol plowed through and still was able to muster a commendable body of work and a career lasting more than forty years - a true accomplishment for any working actress.

In 1995, I had written an article on Carol for my friend Louis Paul's fanzine *Blood Times*. He and his then wife thought it was quite good and suggested I send it to her to see if she would give me an interview. One day, I came home and was stunned to hear Carol Lynley on my answering machine saying she received my lengthy "book" on her and would be happy to talk with me. I was elated to say the least. This resulted in an article for *Filmfax* magazine. Since then, I have met Carol in person at an autograph show and found her simply delightful. She is witty and fun. In 2010, she agreed to talk to me again about the making of the movie *Harlow* for my book *Dueling Harlows: Race to the Silver Screen* and provided lots of backstage stories and anecdotes.

With the advent of the Internet, I discovered there were many fans of Carol Lynley out there. *The Poseidon Adventure* alone due to its cult status made her iconic in the eyes of mostly men in my age range who were enthralled by the movie. Carol, however, does have her share of female fans as well. My fascination with her introduced me to Nelson Aspen and we have remained friends since the late nineties and more recently to new Carol admirers via Facebook, Twitter, and Instagram.

Carol Lynley was able to break free from her teenage idol persona and play adult parts in various genres but with an emphasis in the thriller/fantasy/suspense/horror genres She was usually cast as the victimized heroine terrorized by everything from psychotic relatives to werewolves and the Blob, from murderous convicts to nature's beasts gone wild. Most fans of these genres do not realize how prolific Carol was going from theatrical features (*Bunny Lake Is Missing*, *The Shuttered Room*, *Beware! The Blob*, *The Cat and the Canary*), to made-for-TV movies (*The Immortal*, *Weekend of Terror*, *The Night Stalker*, *Death Stalk*, *Flood)*, to television guest appearances (*Alfred Hitchcock Presents*, *The Man from U.N.C.L.E.*, *The Invaders*, *Journey to the Unknown*, *Night Gallery*, *The Evil Touch*, *Fantasy Island*) and back again for over twenty years.

Her performance in *Bunny Lake Is Missing* was hailed by film historian Mark Jancovich who, writing in the journal *Palgrave Communications* in 2017, went on to call Carol "one of a small group of young female stars who would become associated with the 1960s prestige horror film (Mia Farrow, Audrey Hepburn, Lee Remick and Katherine Ross), and she would also go on to appear in a number of horror films and television projects."[1]

It is interesting to note that despite Jancovich's assessment and the acknowledgement that she played the lady in peril in many films and TV shows, Lynley did not consider herself to be a Scream Queen or a horror film actress ("Though some of my films turned into horrors but that's another story,"[2] she quipped with a laugh). Carol remarked,

> I feel most of the things I did were not horror but thrillers and suspense films. To me, horror films feature monsters and mutations with icky make-up and special effects. As for my films, except for *The Night Stalker* and *Beware! The Blob* most of my films fall into the thriller/suspense genre. *Bunny Lake Is Missing* is a mystery-thriller. *The Shuttered Room* is a thriller with a horrific ending, and *The Cat and the Canary* is more of a mystery-suspense film.[3]

Her lack of true "horror" movies may have diminished her stature as the damsel in distress with fans of these genres and hopefully *Carol Lynley: Her Film & TV Career in Thrillers, Fantasy & Suspense* will elevate her based on her body of work. Not a biography per Carol's wishes, it is a career retrospective highlighting Lynley's appearance in the titled genres peppered with brief anecdotes and comments from interviews with her specifically for this book and past published sources. It features behind-the-scenes stories from actors, directors, producers, and cinematographers that worked with Carol Lynley. Also included is a filmography and list of her guest TV episodes. The last chapter contains a detailed list of Carol's appearances as herself in a variety of programs including talk shows, game shows, award shows, and radio broadcasts. It has been thoroughly researched but is by no means complete as it is exceedingly difficult to track down these appearances. I did the best I could using numerous sources.

As I began putting the finishing touches on this book, Carol suddenly and unexpectedly died in her sleep on September 2, 2019. It was a few days before Turner Classic Movies finally was going to show her some love with the primetime "Starring Carol Lynley." Aired were *Bunny Lake Is Missing* and *Blue Denim* featuring two of her finest and most well-received performances. I was on vacation when I learned of her death and was shocked and saddened like many. Shaken, it took about a day before I could respond to many inquiries received via my social media outlets. More surprising to me were some flippant and dismissive obituaries written about her particularly the one in *The Washington Post*. Carol was ignorantly described as "a film actress whose best-known role was as a ditsy, shrieking lounge singer in the 1972 disaster movie *The Poseidon Adventure*" and that "known for her pert good looks, she soon moved to Hollywood and became a minor star in mostly minor films."[4] Carol was much more than that to her legion of fans and my aim with this book is to prove that.

I hope to present a well-written, entertaining history of Carol's career from her progression from teenage ingénue to adult actress but with the focus on her genre work with back stories on the making of these films and TV shows. I hope my goal in shining a light on Carol Lynley's underrated genre appearances and why she deserved a tribute book is achieved for her devoted fans and for casual moviegoers who only remember her from *The Poseidon Adventure*.

Introduction

In the late fifties and early sixties, Carol Lynley was part of a contingent of teenage blonde actresses who were all the rage with young movie fans. Mostly former adolescent models with shapely figures and perky personalities, these pretty nymphets were Hollywood's version of what the All-American girl should be. They were light years away from the buxom platinum blonde bombshells who came before them and ruled the fifties. Led by Marilyn Monroe, she and her counterparts Jayne Mansfield, Mamie Van Doren, Barbara Nichols, Diana Dors, Sheree North, and Joi Lansing oozed overt sex appeal on and off the screen. But that was soon to change though Marilyn would remain at the top until her death in 1962.

The shift in popularity between these two distinctive types of blondes began with Carroll Baker. In 1956, the sex-filled *Baby Doll* (1956) made the flaxen-haired actress a star. Based on an original screenplay by Tennessee Williams, Baker was simply scintillating as Baby Doll Meighan, the childish nineteen-year-old bride of much older Karl Malden, a cotton gin owner.

Baby Doll sleeps scantily clad in a crib-like bed and sucks her thumb driving her lecherous husband into a sexual frenzy. Though married, he cannot lay a hand on her until she is "marriage ready" as he vowed to her father. Newly arrived competitor Eli Wallach forces Malden out of business and in a fit of desperation he burns down his rival's cotton gin. Vowing revenge, the tempestuous Sicilian focuses his charms on Baby Doll hoping to seduce the nubile girl and get her to confess her husband's crime.

An overnight sensation due to *Baby Doll*, Carroll Baker won raves from the critics with her natural ease in the part culminating with a Golden Globe Award for Most Promising Newcomer – Female and an Academy Award nomination for Best Actress. And she was greeted as a newfound sex symbol. In the days of the busty platinum blonde sexpots, Baker represented a new more attainable male fantasy come to life. But the role had its downside typecasting the actress who vowed not to play anymore similar type parts.

With Baker holding steadfast to her convictions and abandoning these types of roles, she opened the door to a new batch of Baby Dolls—Sandra Dee, Tuesday Weld, Yvette Mimieux, Carol Lynley, Connie Stevens, Diane McBain, and Sue Lyon. They ruled Hollywood from 1959 (the year the Barbie Doll was first released and which many felt the doll was modeled on) to 1964. They were the "It" girls of the time, especially with younger audiences as they essayed the virginal teenager, the knocked up good girl, or the innocent looking nymphet who could be naughty or nice in glossy overwrought melodramas or romantic comedies such as *The Restless Years, Blue Denim, Gidget, Hound-Dog Man, Imitation of Life, Because They're Young, A Summer Place, Where the Boys Are, Tammy Tell Me True, Parrish, Claudelle Inglish, Return to Peyton Place, Susan Slade, Lolita, The Light in the Piazza, If a Man Answers, Bachelor Flat, Palm Springs Weekend, Diamond Head,* and *The Pleasure Seekers* that have pop cinema appeal today.

The resemblance between these baby doll blondes was so great that in 1977 writer Diane White reflecting on the sixties jokingly asked, "Could the average person differentiate among Sandra Dee, Tuesday Weld and Carol Lynley without the aid of fingerprints and dental charts?"[5]

Tuesday Weld, Carol Lynley, and Sandra Dee grace the cover of *Movie Life* magazine December 1960.

Though most film historians will forever include Carol in this category of actresses due to the obvious physical similarities, the actress surprisingly did not consider herself part of this group—shades of Andrew McCarthy who was always distancing himself from the eighties' Brat Pack. Carol stated, "I was never Gidget. I never was a teenage sex-kitten. I had a theatrical background before I went into film."[6] This is true and some of the others went directly from modeling to motion pictures, but there is no denying Carol was comparable in looks and became quite popular with the same teenage audience. And in some producers' minds and for most moviegoers they were interchangeable.

Carol does stand out though because where some fell victim to typecasting, she escaped due to her versatility. She had the talent, insistence, and smarts to tackle a variety of roles from the ingénue in *Blue Denim* and *Hound-Dog Man*, to a teenage murderer on *Alfred Hitchcock Presents*; from a fairy-tale heroine on *Shirley Temple's Storybook*, to a neurotic starlet on *General Electric Theater*. You never would find Sandra Dee, Connie Stevens or Yvette Mimieux playing such varied roles early on due to the teen screen personas their studios or managers were trying to create for them. However, years later Lynley did muse, "Sometimes I think I should have given in to typecasting. I'd be richer and more famous."[7] Perhaps, but her fans most probably are glad she did not.

After taking a break from Hollywood to get married and have a daughter, Lynley, vowing no more teenage roles, was able to graduate to the "sex kitten" beginning with the comedy *Under the Yum Yum Tree* (1963) as a college coed living platonically with her boyfriend. Next came *The Cardinal* (1963) followed by *Shock Treatment* (1964) as a manic depressive and *The Pleasure Seekers* (1964). Shaking her ingénue image completely, Lynley posed semi-nude in *Playboy* and then played sex goddess Jean Harlow in the Electronovision production *Harlow* (1965).

The late sixties were a time for change and none of these blonde baby dolls unfortunately were able to sustain their early movie star popularity due to the shifting social mores of the time. By 1967, many young people had totally rejected the fifties and early sixties' morality foisted on them. It was a time of free love, experimenting drug taking, and protesting in the streets. This new open attitude was reflected by their preferences in fashion, music, and movies. Of the latter, out were Elvis Presley, beach party musicals, Troy Donahue, Annette Funicello, Gidget, and Tammy. In were Peter Fonda, biker flicks, Raquel Welch, acid trips, screen nudity, a rise in independent filmmaking with a new breed of leading men led by Dustin Hoffman, and more.

Carol Lynley, ca. 1963. *From Marlin Dobb's Collection*

This new phase of late sixties Hollywood particularly hurt Sandra Dee and Connie Stevens so associated with that Eisenhower period based on the virginal ingénues they played. Their big screen careers came to a grinding halt. Carol Lynley, who had wisely resisted typecasting, was able to carve out a successful though underrated film and TV career working in the thriller/fantasy/suspense genres usually playing the lady in peril. It was her excellent turn as the unhinged mother searching for her child who may or may not exist in Otto Preminger's cult thriller *Bunny Lake Is Missing* (1965) that was the start. She quickly followed up with another convincing performance as a vulnerable newlywed who inherits an old millhouse with something lurking in the attic in *The Shuttered Room*. These two performances established her as a reliable actress to play harried heroines in film, made-for-television movies, and TV shows. However, as with most actors, she craved more varied parts in different genres.

Carol Lynley, ca. 1968.

Her other fellow blondes took different career paths sometimes not of their own volition. Though Tuesday Weld continued turning down box office hits (i.e. *Bonnie and Clyde, Bob and Carol and Ted and Alice, True Grit*, etc.), she became a highly respected actress taking quirky roles in independent films through the early nineties and even scoring an Academy Award nomination for her performance in *Looking for Mr. Goodbar*. Diane McBain found herself unjustly mired in low-budget drive-in movies before the sixties even ended. Sue Lyon bounced from studio productions to foreign films due to her erratic private life. Only Yvette Mimieux tried the lady in peril route like Carol appearing in the thriller/suspense/horror genres with her motion pictures (*The Time Machine, Dark of the Sun, Skyjacked, Jackson County Jail*) and made-for TV movies (*Death Takes a Holiday, Devil Dog: Hound of Hell, Snowbeast*). However, except for her short-lived TV series *The Most Deadly Game*, Mimieux shunned episodic television unlike Lynley who was the only one who essayed dramatic roles in all three with an equal amount of felicity.

Carol Lynley, ca. 1972. *From Marlin Dobb's Collection*

Bunny Lake and *The Shuttered Room* led Carol Lynley to many memorable ladies in peril roles culminating on the big screen as terrified pop singer Nonnie Parry in *The Poseidon Adventure* and heiress Annabelle West who must survive the night in a mansion with a psycho on the loose to collect her inheritance in *The Cat and the Canary*. On the small screen Carol's standout roles included the mischievously droll Annie Justin looking for justice for the false imprisonment of her finance but needing continuous rescuing by agents Solo and Napoleon on *The Man from U.N.C.L.E.*; scarred psychologist Elyse Reynolds who may or may not be working with the aliens on *The Invaders*; determined Sylvia Cartwright the finance of racecar driver Ben Richards whose blood contains anti-aging cells in the TV-movie *The Immortal*; Gail Foster the encouraging girlfriend of reporter Karl Kolchak investigating a series of murders committed by a modern day vampire in the TV-movie *The Night Stalker*; fragile fashion designer Gail Sumner who is experiencing murderous visions in a rented home on *The Sixth Sense*; trophy wife Cathy Webster kidnapped on a rafting trip by escaped cons in the TV-movie *Death Stalk*; oblivious super model Suzy Martin harassed by a stalker in *If It's a Man, Hang Up!*; various imperiled women on *Fantasy Island*; and an adulterous husband-killing wife done in by her vanity on *Tales of the Unexpected*, among others.

Some may say that Lynley's career turn playing the put-upon heroine in the thriller/fantasy/suspense/horror genres was out of necessity because in the latter half of the sixties female leads in the big movies were going to the likes of Natalie Wood, Jane Fonda, Raquel Welch, Faye Dunaway, and others. However, the fact is that if Lynley did not have the talent to play these victimized women so well she would not have been sought out and cast so frequently.

Arguably, if Lynley would have embraced playing roles in these genres, she could have made a bigger name for herself. However, during her most active period, she had the frustrating habit of taking time off to travel or accepting roles on the stage. You cannot fault an actress for wanting some down time or the desire to play more challenging roles which is what the theater offered, but it was detrimental to her film and TV career. She seemed to be always making a comeback. One could imagine what Lynley's career would have been if she fully accepted being a "suspense/thriller film actress." The fact that she did not and yet she still was able to amass a commendable body of work in these genres is testament to her talent.

So, what qualities did Carol Lynley possess that made her the perfect lady in peril that perhaps her rivals lacked in one way or another? Author and film historian Susan Day of the web site *Ghost Hunting Theories* suggested that it was a combination of traits. She remarked that Carol had "huge blue eyes and delicate features that made her seem quite child-like. She was the ideal candidate for movies about women being stalked and tormented because of her extremely feminine and delicate manners and cultured speaking voice being an ideal counterpoint to a rough and angry male character."[8]

Jeremy R. Richey writing in the journal *Soledad* noted, "Unlike other sixties icons like Tuesday Weld and Ann-Margret who exuded a strong animal-like electricity, the sullen and quiet Carol Lynley had a real enduring icy calm about her. This was never more apparent than in *The Shuttered Room* where [David] Greene's camera seems fixated on her lovely face, as if he is waiting for her cool features to suddenly transform into something completely different, but no less captivating."[9]

Carol had that appealing quality of beauty, voice, and poise, coupled with a slight look of permanent bewilderment with a tilt of her head that made her a perfect choice for playing the harried, vacant-eyed heroine, or terrified lady in peril, or the naive innocent. Carol sometimes could be criticized for being a bit too blank-faced and flat-voiced, but it turned out to be an advantage for her when playing the heroine who may or may not be unstable (i.e. *Bunny Lake Is Missing*; episodes of *Run for Your Life*, *The Invaders*, *Mannix*, *Orson Welles' Great Mysteries*, *The Evil Touch*, etc.). And she had the talent to always make the audience feel compassion for her character. For instance, Carol took the hapless Nonnie in *The Poseidon Adventure* and made her arguably the film's most sympathetic character (and gay icon as she would learn years later) due to her understated performance despite the frustrations of the audience with her helplessness. You wanted to reach into the screen and be the one to guide her to safety. It was a combination of the real fright in her eyes (Carol suffered from acrophobia) and the vulnerability she projected as a petrified Nonnie made her way through the bowels of the upside-down ocean liner. That is not to say she was not able to act other type roles effectively. She could, as exemplified by a range of parts in the seventies from a gun moll, to an adulterous wife, to a psychotic killer in a variety of genres.

Carol Lynley, ca. 1976. *From Marlin Dobb's Collection*

Commenting on her acting technique regarding playing a variety of roles, Carol shared,

> I'm a natural actor. I think it's because I started as a child, I have no fear of it [and] actually kind of get off on it. I get a little tingle, I love it. Even if I must cry, scream or yell a little or whatever. It's not difficult for me … and I just do it. I don't have to work myself up in a rage and I don't have to get into a fight with somebody. I respect my other actors and take very good care of my other actors because I want them to feel comfortable with me. And I feel like, in turn they do, and that makes my life easier. Some people must talk themselves into it. In the end nobody cares what you do, it's the end result that matters. Some people have a problem exposing themselves like that.[10]

Carol Lynley's success in genre roles has been discussed elsewhere though not in detail. A chapter on her was included in the 1978 book *Scream Queens: Heroines of the Horrors* by Calvin Thomas Beck. Nicely illustrated, her career in horror and thrillers were celebrated (particularly *Bunny Lake Is Missing*, *The Shuttered Room*, and *The Night Stalker*). Other noted actresses profiled in the book who made their mark in those genres included Fay Wray, Laura LaPlante, Bette Davis, Joan Crawford, Anne Gwynne, Hazel Court, Faith Domergue, Shelley Winters, Patty McCormack, Yvette Vickers, Martine Beswicke, and Barbara Steele. The book *Terror on Tape* included a profile on Lynley too. Author James O'Neill remarked about the actress, "Classy and talented, she graced a number of genre roles with her cool beauty."[11] Lynley also has her own dedicated pages on a number of web sites including *The Terror Trap* (http://www.terrortrap.com).

Carol Lynley, ca. 1980. *From Marlin Dobb's Collection*

Carol worked consistently for many years with the bulk of her success from 1964 through 1984. Her career slowed down in film and on TV during the latter half of the eighties. Though she successfully fought typecasting earlier in her career, she was not able to overcome it now. In the minds of producers, she would always be the fragile, porcelain-skinned, beleaguered heroine and there were not many of those roles for women over forty whose faces began to show the ravages of time. Though Carol undoubtedly excelled as the lady in peril, she proved over the years that she had the ability to play varied roles, but the opportunities did not arise on primetime network television or in major feature films at this point. Still looking lovely, she then found intermittent work in low budget independent movies or films that went straight to video in the thriller/fantasy/suspense/horror milieu. During this time, Carol achieved two standout moments leaving the lady in peril far behind. She was chilling as a mother from hell who is dismayed when her grown daughter returns home looking for her missing father in *Blackout* (1988) and so entertaining as a greedy, two-bit, gun-toting thief, partnered with Barbara McNair, on a cross-desert crime spree in *Neon Signs* (1996). Both these performances proved she had the talent to excel playing complicated tough-as-nails women when given the opportunity. It is a shame she was not given more chances to showcase her talents.

1.
The Early Years: Child Model to Teen Idol

Carol Lynley was born Carole Ann Jones on Feb. 13, 1942 in New York City to Frances Felch and Cyril Roland Jones. "My father was from County Kerry in Ireland … my mother was born in Boston and her father was an American Indian. He was Iroquois."[12] Her parents were separated when she was two, and she and her younger brother Daniel, who was born in 1943, resided with their mother in New York City.

Frances (who would go on to marry three more times) worked as a waitress to support herself and her children. Carol used to see her father Cyril once a week but he walked out of his children's lives for good when she was eight ("It's not that we didn't get along, I just never knew him."[13]). The family first lived in the Highbridge section of the Bronx. When Carol was seven years old, they relocated across the river to Inwood in upper Manhattan.

Hearing of what was written in the past about Carol's childhood in Inwood including that she was part of a street gang that made zip guns; stole money from a local charity; and that she donned her communion dress on weekends to get her Irish neighbors to give her a dollar for luck, her brother Daniel Jones Lee said laughing, "Inwood was a working class neighborhood. People worked in the garment industry, for the transit system, etc. It was not particularly dangerous. We went to Catholic school and I am sure Carol never even saw a zip gun."[14] With regards to the Communion dress scam, Daniel bluntly stated, "That's bullshit."[15] Obviously, a very creative press agent fed these stories to the media to make Carol's rise from humble beginnings more dramatic.

When asked what Carol was really like as a child, Daniel replied, "She was a very ordinary Irish Catholic girl. There wasn't anything unique about her. She just really clicked when she got into modeling and acting." First, though, were dance lessons.

Margaret Kenny, who worked in magazine publishing for years and who is now a published writer, was a childhood classmate of Carol's. Back then she was known as Peggy McKoy and she shared, "I was a student at Good Shepherd School in the Inwood section of Manhattan. I met Carole Ann Jones there when I was in the sixth grade and she was in the fifth. We both attended the MacLevy School of Dance on Dyckman Street. Carol took ballet classes and I took tap. She was an extremely talented ballerina … and was quite precocious.

"At Christmas, the [dance] school did a holiday pageant with all the different level classes participating," continued Kenny. "Carol did a performance of 'Popo, the Puppet' and was the star of the show. It was the first time Carol performed 'on pointe' and she never made a mistake. After the show, Rhonda Lee, the ballet dance class teacher, complimented Carol on her performance. In a dramatic gesture, Carol swept her hand over her forehead and said, 'Popo, the Puppet is branded on me.' Once Carol became a successful teenage model, her mother transferred her to New York's Professional School … I never saw Carol again."[16]

Reminded of "Popo, the Puppet" and Rhonda Lee, Carol said laughing, "I remember Rhonda very well because she bought me by ballet shoes. She took me to an ice-skating rink in New York City because she believed ice skating would strengthen my legs for the pointe work. I have always been grateful to her. Everything was just so chaotic at that point in my life and I was just trying to stay above water."[17]

Daniel Jones Lee remembered appearing on a local television show called *The Sidewalks of New York* and thinks Carol appeared as well. When she was almost ten, Carol auditioned and beat out over 100 other youngsters to make an appearance on the TV program *Prize Performance*. This was a talent variety show on CBS that ran in the summer of 1950. Hosted by Cedric Adams with judges Arlene Francis and Peter Donald, each week four child performers would compete, and that week's winner would go on for a chance to win the grand prize of a $500 scholarship. Carol did a ballet to the "Toy Trumpet." She admitted a few years later, "I was rather uninspired in the performance. I was so busy watching myself on the television monitor."[18] Not surprisingly, Carol did not win.

Meanwhile Frances Jones was working in a Midtown restaurant near the Garment Center. Per Carol's brother, "One day, my mother showed a picture of Carol to some of the regulars who would come in. They thought that she should give modeling a shot. They suggested some photographers to see if there was any interest. I think Carol got like three jobs that first week."[19]

Carol shared on the local Los Angeles TV chat show *Joan Quinn Etc.* in 1992, "My mother got me a job modeling clothes for an Eskimo catalog. They sort of put dark makeup on me—it's a very strange life. On the way home we had to take the subway up to Inwood which is the northern part of Manhattan. Somebody had told my mother about a modeling agency—it was by the subway stop. We just went up and I've worked ever since."

Work came so quickly that it took reportedly another five weeks for the busy child to sit and pose properly for professional photos for her modeling book. It was here that Carole Jones became Carolyn Lee. When asked if he knew why the name change, Daniel replied, "It was just cooked up by an agency. I still go by Daniel Jones Lee but I don't know why specifically they chose Lee. It was just a generic name."[20]

Modeling soon consumed Carol's life and her mother's. Since her daughter was a minor and was booking so many jobs, Frances left her job as a waitress to accompany Carol on her assignments. Daniel remarked, "There is no way you can have a kid at that age running around the city going to modeling jobs by herself. It became obvious quickly that my mother was going to have to quit waitressing. She never really had a regular job after that until Carol was about eighteen. Carol became the breadwinner for the family. There was one point where Carol reached an awkward age and she was in between dress sizes that they wanted her to model. She couldn't work for a time. I acted and got a job as an understudy on a Broadway show earning eighty-four bucks a week and we were living off that. We were both working kids and my mother was basically a professional mother."

When asked if he saw any changes with Carol as her modeling career took off, Daniel replied, "She became a kind of businesswoman. When she was between the ages of twelve and fourteen, she was in the adult swim. She didn't spend a lot of time with other kids. Modeling wasn't a cutthroat business amongst the other models it was the mothers who were competitive. She was a contemporary of Tuesday Weld and Sandra Dee."

Any rivalries among the trio were in the minds of others. Commenting on Tuesday and Sandra, Carol exclaimed,

> Tuesday is great! I've known her since I was ten years old. She is just a unique and terrific person. I was never as close to Sandy [Sandra Dee] as I was with Tuesday because we grew up at the same time although I am a year and half older as she always reminds me. I did like Sandy and her family though as well.[21]

Daniel Jones Lee knew the two models as well and reflected how different their lifestyles were. He remarked, "I remember going to dinner at Sandra Dee's home. Her stepfather was Eugene Douvan and they lived in a hotel. It was so unusual to me as the catering staff came up to their apartment and served us dinner. I went over to Tuesday Weld's house once. She lived down in the Village. Tuesday had a bad reputation and I remember Carol saying that Tuesday was kind of fast or something like that. When someone asked Carol about something Weld did, Carol said, 'I'll just leave it to the local authorities.' They stayed friends for years and I saw her when Carol was living up in Malibu."[22]

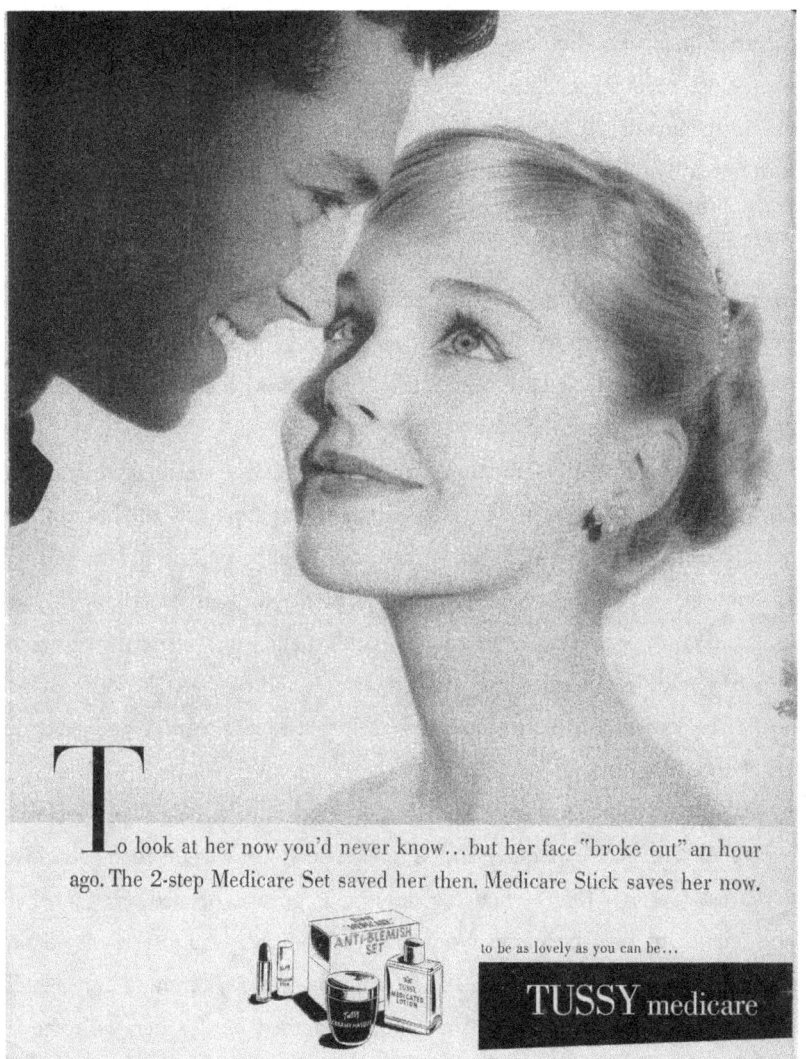

Carol Lynley in a print ad for Tussy Medicare in *Co-ed Magazine*, September 1957.

Daniel admitted feeling left out with his mother focusing most of her time and energy on Carol. He revealed, "When Carol's career really got going, they didn't quite know what to do with me. My mother always said that Carol decided and was adamant that they weren't going to farm me off. We stayed together but it was definitely a strange relationship—not a normal one. We were close to our grandparents and would spend a lot of time with them in Massachusetts. My grandfather was a great guy. We'd go up there in the summer and on holidays."[23]

In 1978, Carol was asked if any of her childhood modeling days stood out for her and she shared, "I remember … doing a hat job for this guy named Max. He had old-fashioned lighting that took forever, and he put me up on this stool and to keep me from squirming, he'd give me a wad of $100 bills to count."[24] Max must have read a then quote from the young model who announced that where the money goes, she follows.

Two years into her modeling career, Carol began getting work as an extra on TV ("I got into more shows where more people saw the back of my neck than anything."[25]) and then at age twelve landed a role in the touring production of Moss Hart's *Anniversary Waltz* with Leif Erickson, Phyllis Hill, and Andy Sanders. Carol loved Moss Hart and owes her acting career to him. She said, "He hired me to play a short, fat and ugly girl, he kept saying he didn't know why. Moss was lovely; he felt that I had potential and gave me my chance."[26]

It was at this point that she learned that another Carolyn Lee was registered with Actors Equity and Carole Ann Jones was deemed too close to actress Carolyn Jones—hence a name change was needed. Her mother wanted her to use the name Nora O'Flynn but her daughter insisted on retaining Carol as her first name. Carol said, "I was born a month-and-a-half after Carole Lombard died and my mother named me for her, with the 'e' in Carol. Moss made up the Lynley and took the 'e' off Carole. I don't know why."[27] Carol, though, always used her legal name on her passport because she felt Carole Jones was a sweet name.

Carol Lynley, Leif Erickson, Andy Sanders, and Phyllis Hill in the stage production *Anniversary Waltz*, ca. 1954. *Photo by Fred Fehl, Billy Rose Theatre Division, The New York Public Library for the Performing Arts*

Modeling remained Carol's highest priority. She did a lot of TV and print ads for Coca-Cola that lasted for about a year though she was never officially the "Coca-Cola Girl." By the time Carol was in her mid-teens, this delicate beauty, along with her friends Sandra Dee and Tuesday Weld were reportedly the highest paid teenage models in New York (earning over $60 per hour) appearing in many fashion spreads and print ads. *Pageant* magazine remarked that Carol's "prettiness evokes visions of sugar plums and fairy godmothers." She graced the covers of many publications including *Cosmopolitan* and *Seventeen*. Many young girls during this period wanted to be her. *Los Angeles Times* writer Charles D. Rice contributed Carol's success to the fact that her looks gave her the advantage to "look like an enchanting child of ten or a stunning young woman in her 20's."[28]

For a Lane Bryant print ad touting their new children's clothing line, Carol worked, with of all people, the future Emmy award-winning comedy writer Bruce Vilanch. He recalled their shoot in a 2020 online talk show *Game Changers* with Vicki Abelson and said, "There was me and another sort of Jewish-looking kid … we were on like a couch and in between us was

Carol Lynley who was a Shiksa goddess looking gorgeous. The message was if you put your fat Jewish kid in Lane Bryant clothing ... they will attract this gorgeous goddess beauty." Though some today may find the idea of this ad offensive, Vilanch does not and is still on the hunt for a copy of it.

Because of her looks, Carol was not considered a child model for very long. She explained, "I was doing adult modeling at thirteen. They smeared some makeup on me and made me look eighteen. Why, I was only twelve or thirteen when I did a *Seventeen* cover, and I looked the perfect age for the job."[29]

With Carol being at the top of her profession, of course she had many rivals, some more admiring than others. Actress Diane McBain (a future Warner Bros. contract player) revealed in her memoir, "Even as a teenager, I had admired Carol. I wanted to look like her, in fact. We were modeling at the same time. She graced the cover of *Seventeen Magazine* while I was doing cover shoots for *True Love* and *Modern Romance*. I thought she was the most beautiful girl I had ever seen."[30] Laurel Goodwin (Elvis Presley's leading lady in 1962's *Girls! Girls! Girls!*) remarked years later, "I had to constantly live with the 'Carol Lynley image,' which kind of bothered the hell out of me. We were slightly of similar type and age group. Carol was in every magazine and on every cover. I was in *Seventeen* also but not on the cover."[31]

Being perhaps the first teenage "super model" did have its drawbacks in terms of nutrition. Per Jill Zimmerman writing in *The Humanist*, "According to *Seventeen*, Carol Lynley ... 'came prepared for every photo shoot in the 1950s with a head of lettuce, a pound of seedless grapes, and three green peppers,' her food for the day.'"[32]

Daniel confirmed that Carol had weight issues and revealed, "She surely did struggle with her weight. It was a point of contention as she was always eating these dietetic foods from that time. They were always trying to fatten me up but there was never anything fattening in the house as to keep her from overeating. It was something she struggled with for a long time."[33]

Modeling brought Carol fame but it had its downside. Spending countless hours with her mother affected their relationship in a negative way. While other kids had normal childhoods with time away from their parents in school and then playing with other kids their age, Carol was tied to her mother for many hours per week and interacting with other adults. Her brother opined, "My mother identified so much with Carol she couldn't deal with a teenager wanting to assert her independence. That put a strain on their relationship for sure." Teen models Sue Lyon and Tuesday Weld also went through the same. It became so bad between Tuesday and Mrs. Weld that she began telling people her mother had passed when she hadn't. Years later, Weld's mother wrote a daughter dearest type book entitled *If It's Tuesday…I Must Be DEAD!*

By the mid-fifties, the acting bug seemed to have taken hold of Carol. Some feel it is very easy to progress from modeling to acting but Lynley disagreed and explained years later, "In the first place, if you look good in stills, that doesn't necessarily mean you look good when you're moving. In the second place, you've got to work on your voice no matter what kind of voice you have."[34] The fact that Lynley concentrated working on stage and live television no doubt helped her perfect these qualities before making the leap to the silver screen.

The young model kept busy learning her craft in live TV dramas. At first, she was in supporting roles such as the adoring girlfriend of a boy (Clay Hall) struggling to mature in "Grow-Up!" on *Goodyear Playhouse* and a financially struggling economics teacher's brilliant daughter who doesn't want to go away to college in "Cracker Money" on the *Kaiser Aluminum Hour*. Both were televised in 1956. Her good notices led to lead roles on TV. Hollywood took notice too and came a-calling, but the headstrong young girl did not want to go west before she established a solid reputation as a fine actress.

There was one misstep during this time. She was ridiculously cast as a young Japanese girl in "The Big Wave" on *The Alcoa Hour*. It was adapted by Pearl S. Buck from her novel and was one of the first TV productions to be shot in color. Joining Carol was an esteemed cast including Hume Cronyn, Rip Torn, and Robert Morse all embarrassing themselves immensely, no doubt. They slapped a black wig on the blue-eyed blonde and did not even bother trying to slant her eyes. The things they got away with in the fifties and sixties.

Daniel shared, "I went to watch many of Carol's early television appearances. It was the early days of live TV and it was very interesting. I did a couple of shows and had some lines on *Mr. Peepers*. Carol got some excellent parts early on. One of the reasons was because as kids we were always watching old British movies on TV. Carol picked up an English accent easily. I am sure this helped her."[35] This may also explain why as an adult, Carol worked in London much more so than her American contemporaries of the time.

Returning to the stage, Carol Lynley made her Broadway bow in Graham Greene's *The Potting Shed* playing Dame Sybil Thorndike's American granddaughter. Directed by Carmen Capalbo, it was a mystery thriller about the son of two famous Atheists who is still traumatized by an event that took place in his family's potting shed when he was fourteen. Though he cannot remember the incident, it still haunts him to this day and affects his relationship with his wife. He decides to uncover the mystery once and for all. The drama received almost unanimous praise and played sold out crowds during its twelve-week run at the Bijou Theatre and then moved to the Golden Theatre for the remainder of the season.

Recalling her experience doing the play, Carol shared, "Mr. Green used to come backstage and talk to me ... I just burbled away, having no idea who he was. I knew he'd written the play but I didn't know anything else about him, didn't know he was one of the great literary personalities of our time. He didn't act important."[36]

Playwright George S. Kaufman's wife Leueen MacGrath was also in the cast and he would visit during rehearsals. Per Carol, "Kaufman was quite bombastic ... he and Graham Greene ... used to watch from the back of the theater. Kaufman would shout, 'Rubbish!' and stalk out. Everybody was always kind of nervous around him."[37]

As for her fellow actors, Carol said, "The cast was British except for me. It was during the run of that show that I learned to speak properly. With a distinguished cast headed by Dame Sybil Thorndike, you couldn't help but learn ... She used to talk to me about acting. She told me I should be in films because I had a face that was perfect for the camera."[38]

Carol also explained she got the hang of stage acting by observing her director and fellow actors. It was a process she continued while making movies to help her improve. She revealed,

> I had learned a great deal from the director Carmen Capalbo, but it took me three months before I could do the part properly. I watched the principal actors. In the beginning, I didn't know why I had a laugh or didn't have a laugh. Sometimes I would get the reaction I wanted but I didn't know why. Then at the next performance, I would try something else, at the next something else again, until I finally I learned what I was doing to shape—or not shape—a particular audience reaction. That is why the stage is so creative. You can watch and learn.[39]

The Potting Shed was nominated for three Tony Awards including Best Play and Carol received a Theater World Award for one of the year's Most Promising Personalities along with Peggy Cass, Bradford Dillman, George Grizzard, Jason Robards, Cliff Robertson, and Pippa Scott, among others. She also landed on the cover of *Life* magazine in an article entitled "Busy Little Career Girl." She now achieved her goal solidifying her prowess as an actress and was ready to tackle the movie business. Her then agent Neil Cooper had previously set up meetings with several studios including Columbia Pictures whose executives were eager to sign Carol to a contract but at the time she was not ready.

Walt Disney saw Lynley on the cover of *Life* and wanted to sign her to a picture deal too but was only able to retain the actress for one film with her agent rejecting an option for a second. Other studios were also pursuing the young actress, but after making her decision, she remarked, "They all talk long contracts, MGM, Columbia, but they don't want me to be myself. They want to glamorize me ... talking about the type of make-up they'll have me use, the way they'll do my hair. Whatever quality I have, it's me and I don't intend to change it at all. Mr. Disney is wonderful about leaving me the way I am in *The Light in the Forest*."[40]

Though Carol was high on doing *The Light in the Forest*, her mother reportedly wanted her to turn it down. Lynley explained, "She didn't think it was big enough for me. I thought it was much better for me to take a part where I didn't have too much to do and learn something about making movies before jumping in and biting off more than I could chew."[41] In some aspects Carol was wiser than her years.

The Light in the Forest was directed by Herschel Daugherty (his first feature after working steadily in television) and based on the classic Conrad Richter novel. Carol's first film role was a sort of junior lady in peril colonial-style. She was an indentured servant girl to a family whose patriarch was a brute and always threatening her.

Carol's brother Daniel recalled, "It was our first experience in Hollywood. She was decidedly not impressed staying at the Chateau Marmont. Carol felt New York was the center of the world. If I remember correctly, they shot a lot of the movie in Big Bear. She got to know James MacArthur whose mother was Helen Hayes. He was a fine young man and staying at the Chateau Marmont too. I remember he would be at the pool and Carol would be watching him from our window. As far as I know they were not romantically linked. She then got into the Hollywood world as she called it."[42]

Carol admitted that she had a lot of adjusting to do going from stage to the big screen especially when getting into her character before shooting a scene. She explained at the time,

> They play music to put you in the mood and you try to grow into the part before the camera starts, while the powder man is slapping you in the face with the powder puff … and the wardrobe mistress is pulling you this way and that, and the lighting man is switching things all around, and the person you're supposed to be talking to isn't even around, and that great big camera is staring

right down your throat. I thought I'd die. When we were making *Light in the Forest* it was not only the heat. That was maybe 100 degrees, but they started off shooting last scenes first and half the time I didn't know what I was doing. I got so nervous trying to do what they wanted. I was eating like a horse. You know compulsive eating. I took on 20 pounds.[43]

Despite her trepidation, Carol proved to be a professional and would adapt quickly to the quirks of filmmaking. Her nervousness and binge-eating would be a thing of the past. She would have to wait awhile before the movie was to be released as Walt Disney decided it would be one of the studio's summer attractions in 1958.

The scuttlebutt on Carol from the set of *The Light in the Forest* was so good that she was named a 1957 Hollywood Deb Star even before her picture was released. This accolade was bestowed on her by the Hollywood Makeup Artists and Hair Stylists Guild. She shared that year's honor with fourteen other promising newcomers including Joan Blackman, Dolores Hart, Diane Jergens, Ruta Lee, Jana Lund, and Joyce Taylor. Each actress was introduced on the arm of a promising male actor in the manner of a coming out ball. Recalling the ceremony, which she claimed she would never forget, Carol said a brief time afterwards, "I was introduced to a Hollywood glamorous audience as one of the deb stars of the year. I wore a long evening dress but was so fat and clumsy that I tripped walking up the ramp. My hair was straight, and I had pimples. I felt miserable."[44]

Despite Carol's insecurities, producer Pandro S. Berman was courting the young actress (after a successful screen test opposite Leslie Nielsen) to play the female lead (Debbie Reynolds reportedly declined the part) in the MGM comedy *The Reluctant Debutante* with Rex Harrison and Kay Kendall as her parents. He and the studio were determined to sign her, as was Walt Disney who wanted Carol for another film. She, however, returned to New York. Per her brother, "She was in love with the theater and the idea of being an *actress*.

She considered theater to be more valid than films. I am sure she felt that her stage career gave her legitimacy that movies didn't."[45]

It was thought Carol would play a supporting role in the Broadway play *The Dark at the Top of the Stairs* by William Inge. But instead director Joshua Logan chose her (after she had auditioned several times) to play the much bigger role of an unwed teenager who gets pregnant by her boyfriend (Burt Brinkerhoff) and has an abortion in *Blue Denim* by James Leo Herlihy and William Noble.

Since the play did not go into rehearsals until January 1958 with a two-week tryout in Philadelphia in February, MGM gave up on the actress and cast Sandra Dee in *The Reluctant Debutante* instead. This seemed not to have bothered Lynley in the least since she was not happy with this film assignment and revealed, "When I saw my MGM test for *The Reluctant Debutante*, I could have cried. It was awful. All the make-up they put on me! From now on I do my own."[46]

While waiting to gear up for *Blue Denim*, Lynley played two disparately different characters on television and received raves for both in part due to the top-flight directors she worked with. She made her first foray into the world of suspense in "The Young One" on *Alfred Hitchcock Presents*. It was one of the earliest TV dramas directed by future Academy Award nominee Robert Altman. Airing in December 1957 during the middle of the third season, it was one of the series' few episodes up to that point in time to have a teenage character as the main protagonist.

Regarding the novice director, Carol said enthusiastically, "I liked him and thought he was terrific. He was intelligent and knew what he was doing. He was delightful to work for because he knew what he wanted. He told you and you did it."[47]

Carol also had praise for the series' producer Joan Harrison and remarked, "Looking back, I realize what a precedent she set for me and particularly other girls, who only saw women as homemakers, or teachers … She made an impression on me as a powerful career woman."[48]

The episode opened with the typical Alfred Hitchcock banter as he introduced his audience to his gift shop containing an assortment of items ranging from a revolver to poison mushrooms that could be used in knocking off anyone you wish to make disappear from your life. He ended by saying, "As for tonight's story, I won't tell you whether or not any of these weapons are used. You will have to watch and see."

Carol played Janice, an angel-faced teenage charmer bored with small town life and living with her overprotective Aunt May (Jeanette Nolan). At the local honkytonk, she attracts the eye of a handsome motorcycle riding hep cat named Tex (Vince Edwards) by dancing provocatively around him (Carol is light on her feet) angering her boyfriend Stan (Stephen Joyce) who storms out. When Tex initially rejects her, a waiting Stan takes Janice home where she is confronted by her worried Aunt May. Janice puts on a good show lying about her whereabouts and tries to sweet talk her aunt who sees through the ruse. An argument ensues, and Janice becomes annoyed and insulting towards May. She returns to the club where Tex is still drinking at the bar. He is smitten, and she feeds him her tale of woe convincing him she wants to run away to experience life. He knows she is trouble and is warned off by the sheriff who promises to stop by to check up on her, but it doesn't stop Tex from walking her home. After some prodding, she "reluctantly" lets Tex in and keeps him there until the right moment. As the sheriff drives up, Janice rips her blouse and smashes a lamp to the ground as she runs screaming out of the house into the sheriff's arms. When they enter the home, they find Tex standing next to a dead May lying at the bottom of the staircase. Janice fingers Tex and the sheriff believes her until Stan reappears. He admits he returned to see Janice and found her aunt dead on the floor proving her niece is the murderer as she breaks down into tears.

The episode ends with Alfred Hitchcock who quipped, "Well, she had me fooled. After all, anyone who would bludgeon her elderly aunt can't be all bad."

Burt Brinkerhoff and Carol Lynley as teenagers dealing with an unwanted pregnancy in the stage production *Blue Denim*, 1958. *Photo by Friedman-Abeles, ©Billy Rose Theatre Division, The New York Public Library for the Performing Arts*

Carol loved playing this schizophrenic bad seed with a double personality—one nice and sweet and the other a unfeeling killer. She was striking in the role. Her Janet comes off as spoiled and self-centered with a hint of a temper underneath and had viewers wondering it this cutie could really stoop to murder? The critics were impressed. Larry Wolters of the *Chicago Daily Tribune* commented that she played "the baby-faced brat with a real streak of meanness and hardness … persuasively" and Elizabeth L. Sullivan, of the *Daily Boston Globe*, wrote that Lynley gave a "remarkable performance." Portrayals like this helped Carol overcome goodie-goodie stereotypes and proved she had the range to play varied roles unlike some of her blonde contemporaries of the time.

Not everybody was happy with Carol's appearance on *Alfred Hitchcock Presents*. Per the actress at the time, "My grandmother saw the show and she was very upset—my family comes from Boston—she didn't like the idea of my playing a murderess at all but it brought me a lot of attention."[49]

Carol next beat out over thirty other young actresses to star in the comedy with music *Junior Miss*, the Christmas offering of *Du Pont Show of the Month*. It was directed by Ralph Nelson who had just won an Emmy as Best Director for "Requiem for a Heavyweight" on *Playhouse 90*. It would be one of the first shot in color on the stages in Hollywood.

The TV show was based on the original stories by Sally Benson that was turned into a Broadway play in 1941 and included five new songs by Dorothy Fields and Burton Lane. A pig-tailed precocious Carol Lynley played the mischievous thirteen-year-old Judy Graves with Joan Bennett as her bewildered mother, Jill St. John as her older sister, and Suzanne Sydney as her partner in mischief. Judy imagines her father is having an affair with his boss' daughter and schemes to fix the gal up with her uncle resulting with the firing of her father. Originally cast as Mr. Graves was Bob Cummings who later withdrew unhappy with the size of his role in a revised script. He was replaced by Don Ameche who sings the title song at the end of the show. Carol sang too and though her range is limited, she does well enough with the few songs she is given.

The show received reviews along the lines of "a bit of fluff" and "amusing," while Carol continued her streak of receiving positive notices for her performance. John Crosby of the *New York Herald Tribune* found her "lovely and appealing" and Bob Bernstein in *The Billboard* felt the entire cast was "excellent ... with Carol Lynley in full command as the omnipresent teenager."

Despite her fine notices, Carol was not a fan of this special or her vocalizing. When asked about *Junior Miss*, she remarked a few years after it aired, "Oh, I'd rather forget about that one. My reviews weren't so bad, but this show wasn't so much. We all sang too, just about got through it. Don Ameche had a real voice, but none of the rest of us did."[50] At the time, the sixteen-year-old probably could not have imagined that fourteen years later she would be playing a singer in *The Poseidon Adventure* and it would become her most iconic role.

Watching *Junior Miss*, one could easily see if Carol played the Hollywood typecasting game her career could have gone the Sandra Dee route of Gidget's and Tammy's. She had just the right amount of perkiness and was not cloying like some actresses in these roles. However, Lynley had the foresight to buck this and keep her fans guessing on what type of character she would play next.

Two months later, Carol opened on Broadway in *Blue Denim*. As high schooler Janet Willard, Lynley's character discovers she is pregnant after going all the way with her immature teenage boyfriend Arthur Bartley (Burt Brinkerhoff). Her revelation shatters the idyllic basement life he has horsing around with his wise-cracking friend Ernie (Warren Berlinger). With his help, the couple finds an abortionist. Act two picks up with the aftermath and how the young couple deals with their feelings for each other and the reactions from their distracted parents who discover what happened.

Choosing to do the play proved to be a wise career move by Lynley though it took a toll on the actress. She revealed that it was "exhausting" and she had "such a terrible time ... onstage eight times a week going through all that emotional tension and disturbance, and the misery of that poor little girl with all her problems."[51]

Blue Denim was almost universally praised by the critics and Carol received kudos for her sincere sympathetic performance as a sweet teenager who struggles with the decision to have an abortion and the repercussions from it. Brooks Atkinson in the *New York Times* raved that "Carol Lynley's glowing, round-faced, eager Janet is honest and winning." Cyrus Durgin of the *Daily Boston Globe* went even further with the compliment commenting, "Equally telling is the superb performance of Carol Lynley ... This is acting of such smoothness and deftly sustained characterization that is seems altogether real." Carol was quick to share the success she had with the part with her director and exclaimed, "Josh Logan was wonderful and helpful."[52]

Blue Denim was groundbreaking and propelled Carol to acting stardom but there came a responsibility to it that she was unprepared for especially while starring in such a controversial play. Carol recalled, "I was fifteen when I did it on Broadway ... I was a virgin at the time and knew nothing whatsoever about sex—I came from a rather sheltered background—and every night I'd portray this pregnant girl who's going for an abortion. People would come up to me and talk about teenage sexuality!"[53] Audiences still sometimes cannot separate the actor from the role they are playing.

Daniel confirmed that his sister was peppered with these questions about sex and it annoyed Carol to no end. He shared, "I saw the play and was backstage a fair amount. It was a good meaty play and Carol did a very fine job. Movie magazines were a big thing then and there were always people coming to the house. They would always ask her questions about teenage sexuality and abortion. She would reply, 'I don't know. I am just an actress and not an expert on teenage sex lives.' She was so frustrated always being asked about it. She wasn't prepared from her real life experience to comment on any of it."[54]

With her excellent reviews for *Blue Denim*, which was a bona fide hit, Lynley was now considered one of the most talented teenage actresses around. Her future in show business looked extremely bright, but still the teenager stated many times that acting was not her main priority in life. Getting married and having lots of children is what she truly desired per her press interviews, but work seemed to have kept her too busy to even find a boyfriend let alone a husband. Her success on Broadway again made the actress a hot property.

Following her stage success, *The Light in the Forest* finally opened in early July 1958.

In the movie, top-billed Fess Parker (of TV's Davy Crockett fame) played Del Hardy a scout for the Royal American Regiment. He acts the intermediary between the British and the Lenape (dubbed the Delaware Indian tribe by the White man) in 1764 Pennsylvania. A treaty is signed giving the Delaware rights to their land and a promise that no White man will attack them in exchange for the ceasing of Indian raids on settlers and the return of all captured Whites. This included bare-chested True Son (James MacArthur), the adopted son of Chief Cuyloga (Joseph Calleia), who considers himself Indian and refuses to leave. However, Cuyloga has given his word so back the boy must go much to his chagrin. The first thing the hostile youth does is to attack Del who quickly disarms him. He lets True Son's cousin Half Arrow (Rafael Campos) come along on the trek bringing wise words from Cuyloga that helps True Son accept his fate.

Poster art for *The Light in the Forest* (Buena Vista, 1958).

After being reunited with his father Harry Butler (Frank Ferguson), True Son now Johnny Butler with his Mohawk haircut returns to his home. Waiting on the porch is the Butler's Indian hating neighbor Myra Elder (Marian Seldes) and Carol Lynley as her indentured servant girl Shenandoe who flees in fear of Johnny. She was orphaned after Indians attacked and killed her family. Waiting upstairs is Johnny's mother Myra (Jessica Tandy). She is loving but strict and lays down the law to her son that he will speak English and read from the Bible.

Carol's first line is at a party the Butler's throw to reintroduce Johnny to his family and friends. Myra's husband Wilse Owens (Wendell Corey) provokes the boy and forces Shenandoe to admit that Indians scalped her parents and little sister. She once again flees from Johnny.

Sweet Shenandoe is also afraid of the hard-drinking Wilse who tries to kiss her and then pressures her to steal Johnny's Indian clothes or else he will sell her indentured service contract to someone else. He uses the garments as target practice on a scarecrow before Johnny takes them back. A contrite Shenandoe mends the bullet holes in them as best she can and confesses that she took them before explaining that she is trapped too being almost a slave to the Owens. This scene, as the two attractive youths commiserate about their situations and wish they were free like the forest denizens around them as they trail a deer, is quite touching. Later at a party thrown by the Butlers and Milly Elder (Joanne Dru) so Johnny can meet young people, a jealous Shenandoe serves drinks while eyeing Johnny dancing with a girl. He gets a piece of cake with a ring. Prodded to give it to the girl he likes best, he chooses Shenandoe but won't kiss her and she runs off yet again. A drunken Wilse follows and punches out Johnny claiming the boy attacked him. Shenandoe follows Johnny back to their spot in the forest and tells Johnny to ignore Wilse or he will grow up to be a hateful man just like his uncle. Del then gets an idea from Milly to have the Butlers buy the land in the forest that Johnny loves, so the boy can settle there. A coy Shenandoe tells him that she wishes she could help him build his log cabin, but she will be free by then and hopefully married to some nice boy. The sly girl gets Johnny to say that he wants to be that boy and when he goes to kiss her, he lands a peck on the cheek. Frustrated, Shenandoe closes her eyes and kisses him full on the lips. Carol's first screen kiss. This sweet scene is interrupted by gun shots and shouts that the Indians are attacking.

Johnny runs off to see what is going on and finds Half Arrow who came with Little Crane to see his White wife who gave birth to their child. Wilse Owens came upon them and shot Little Crane (Eddie Little Sky) killing him. He goes to shoot Half Arrow, but Johnny knocks him down. His cousin is about to scalp him when Shenandoe arrives on the scene and begs them not to. Johnny wants her to come away with him back to the Delaware but she tearfully pleads for him to remain with his family. Thinking he cannot resist the beautiful girl; Johnny surprisingly opts for his Indian family and runs off with Half Arrow.

Along a riverbank, Johnny strips out of most of the White man's clothes and throws them into the water. Feeling liberated, he and Half Arrow celebrate his being an Indian again but the mention of Shenandoe brings sadness upon Johnny. He admits the thought of her now reminds him of his murdered friend, Little Crane. Things go from bad to worse when the Delaware decide to avenge the death of Little Crane and attack the settlers. Johnny diverts some river rafting settlers from a second ambush and is to be burned at the stake by the tribe. Cuyloga steps in and saves his son. However, he disavows True Son banishing him to live with the Whites as Johnny Butler and to never return.

Brought back to his home by Del, they immediately run into Wilse who defends his killing of Little Crane. He goes to fist fight Del but Johnny steps in instead. Wilse beats up the boy as a wild-eyed Shenandoe ("Hit him!") cheers Johnny on. With instructions from Milly and Del, Johnny gets the best of Wilse. The movie ends with Johnny and Shenandoe together in the forest at the spot of their future home.

The story was much more adult than expected coming from Disney studios. Both the Whites and Indians are portrayed fairly and shown in a positive and negative light. The story captivates and enthralls. James MacArthur's conflicted Johnny holds the movie together and he delivers a believable performance. The audience will immediately feel for his situation. Fess Parker as Del is understated and good. His character takes a step back and lets Johnny deal with his new surroundings. Surprisingly, the female characters are no stereotypes. Jessica Tandy's Myra Butler is stern and expects Johnny to follow the rules of the home and immediately embrace being White. However, she comes to understand his predicament and respect his Indian upbringing. Joanne Dru's Milly is no meek preacher's daughter. She can coyly manipulate a man without him knowing, while coaching another on how to fist fight.

Wilse Owens (Wendell Corey) menaces his indentured servant Shenandoe (Carol Lynley) when she overhears his plot to hurt young Johnny Butler in *The Light in the Forest* (Buena Vista, 1958).

Shenandoe evolves from a frightened fawn afraid of the Owens and Johnny, to gaining her confidence enough to kiss Johnny on the lips and yell for Johnny to pummel Wilse in during their altercation. Her shouting "hit him" with a blood thirsty look in her eye is not what you would expect in a Disney movie. Her face is expressive even when she does not utter a line. The actress remarked, "I find if you're quiet and everyone else is noisy, people notice you. They feel sorry for you."[55] This worked here and would again years later in *The Poseidon Adventure*.

Despite these positive attributes, the movie received mixed notices. Though Bosley Crowther of the *New York Times* found it to be "wholesome in an outdoor, simple way," he added that it was on "about the 12-year-old level." Marjory Adams of the *Boston Globe* called it "a pleasing, moderately exciting, and beautifully photographed adaptation."

Carol, though, impressed the critics with her performance. Adams found Lynley to be "sensitive-faced" giving a "sympathetic performance." Nora E. Talor of *The Christian-Science Monitor* commented, "The adults, however brightly shining, are secondary to the young stars" and that "Miss Lynley's portrayal ... should win her larger roles in future." Geoffrey Warren of the *Los Angeles Times* found the two young leads to be "real charmers with more than their share of talent."

Come awards season, Carol received a Golden Globe nomination for Most Promising Newcomers – Female (she, Joanna Barnes and France Nuyen lost to Linda Cristal, Susan Kohner, and Tina Louise) and she placed second for Best Juvenile Performance of the Year in *Film Daily's* Famous Fives behind Patty McCormack in *Kathy O*. Carol was also nominated for the Photoplay Gold Medal Award for Most Promising Actress. The magazine's readers voted for their favorites from a list of nominees provided by the editors and staff writers. Sandra Dee triumphed that year ironically for her performance in *The Reluctant Debutante*, the film Lynley passed on. Other nominees included Molly Bee, Hope Lange, Tina Louise, France Nuyen, Jill St. John, Connie Stevens, and Diane Varsi. The annual *Screen World* voted Carol one of 1958's Most Promising Personalities. Also honored were Stephen Boyd,

Stuart Whitman, Carolyn Jones, John Gavin, Diane Baker, William Shatner, James Darren, and Molly Bee, amongst a few others.

Though *The Light in the Forest* did not match the grosses of Disney's animated films, it earned a respectable $2 million domestically.

With her emerging fame as an actress, it was around this time when Carol decided to concentrate on acting fulltime and let the modeling drift. Remembering her time as a model since she was a child, the outspoken teenager was in a reflective mood when she revealed in a lengthy interview in *Seventeen*,

> Some days I think it is wonderful some days I think it's terrible. When I was twelve, I had a terrible time, my weight was changing, my face was breaking out. I was gaining weight and I kept thinking they were all picking on me. They—photographers, editors—were only telling me what was wrong, but that was my adolescence. Sometimes girls ask me about modeling. I tell them to get an agent. I don't know much about it really. I happen to have made a lot of money at it because I had a certain type of face that was wanted but that's about all. I don't know why any young girl would want to do it. I wouldn't put my daughter to work as a child. You see them trundling around at four going from one job to another. It's hard on a child. Start when you're seventeen. Then you can really appreciate it. Before that, you make money, it comes in, it goes out, you don't have any idea about its real value. If girls knew all the work involved—even though you can make a lot of money at it if you are successful—they wouldn't want to do it. I'm making so much that I'm embarrassed when I present the bill at the end of a session. I can make as much in a day modeling as I can in a couple of weeks on salary as an actress.[56]

This interview caused quite a stir with Carol's teenage female fans. She bared her true feelings and what was reported in print put off some of her faithful supporters. It received some love but surprisingly the feedback was more negative as readers voiced their disappointment to the magazine:

"The article was very good. All my friends and I have read it at least three times," K. T., Ridgely, MD.

"I have often admired Carol Lynley ... and have thought of how wonderful it would be to be in her shoes. But after reading this article ... I have but four words for Carol, 'You're missing so much,'" C.V., Mount Clemons, MI.

"I feel sorry for Carol Lynley after reading her thoughts. She seemed to be unhappy and highbrow, although she has everything a girl could want," R.C. Indianapolis, IN.

"I was disappointed and amazed. I always thought Carol to be a sweet, normal teenager ... Your article brings out her selfish traits and conceited attitude," I.M., West Babylon, NY.[57]

This article and its reaction just proved how tough it is to be a teenage idol adored by millions when you just consider yourself to be a working actress and don't behave or express your thoughts the way the public feels you should. As the adage goes you can't please everyone.

Carol could be seen on TV taking quick advantage of the publicity *The Light and the Forest* and *Blue Denim* brought her. She received a lot of press for starring opposite another teen idol, Sal Mineo, in "The Vengeance" the debut episode of the new CBS-TV anthology series *Pursuit*. Lynley has a nothing role as the pretty nice girl who falls for Mineo's juvenile delinquent just released from reformatory school trying to "go straight." However, he is harassed by a detective (MacDonald Carey) whose son was crippled in a street fight with him and by two gang members who are afraid he will give them up for a murder they committed that he witnessed. The show received wildly mixed reviews.

Carol then made her first of many appearances in the fantasy genre with her guest turn in the almost universally praised "Rapunzel" on *Shirley Temple's*

Story Book. It was her first lady in peril role in the fantasy genre. Former child movie star Shirley Temple, then in her early thirties, introduced each episode and usually sang a song. This was an extremely popular TV show at the time for adolescents. Carol's episode, one of the most fondly remembered, was directed by the busy James Neilson who worked in television almost exclusively in the fifties before making films (many for Walt Disney) in the following decade.

Series' producer Alvin Cooperman revealed that after he read the "Rapunzel" script he thought, "What we need for this role is an 18-year-old actress with 30 years of acting experience." He continued, "But that's what I say every time we cast a Storybook. I can give these ingénues fame and a future—but I just can't find enough of them."[58] He then went on to praise his casting choice of Carol Lynley. "Carol is only 16, but she has six years of experience … She looks her age but acts way beyond the experience she could possibly have garnered in her young life. And oh, does she look like a princess!"[59]

Carol wore a reportedly twenty-five-foot white blonde braided wig that made her look like a "fallen angel," as she was once described, to play Rapunzel the young maiden kept prisoner in a castle's tower by a wicked witch (scene stealing pre-Endora Agnes Moorhead) who snatched her at birth. A lonely Rapunzel's singing attracts handsome smitten Prince Peter (Don Dubbins) who searches the barren Forest of Evil for her. After spying the witch calling out "Rapunzel, Rapunzel, let down your hair" and climbing up to the tower room, he does the same after she departs. It is immediate love at first sight, but fear seeps in when the young couple see a dark outline of the witch on her broom flying past the moon. Despite the dramatics, you cannot help but chuckle as this almost mirrors the opening of Moorehead's TV series *Bewitched* some six years later. This also raised the question that if the witch could fly why did she have to climb up Rapunzel's hair and not just fly into the tower room on her broomstick?

Sensing their love, the witch cuts Rapunzel's golden locks and casts a spell on the prince blinding him. Of course, true love wins out and the witch is banished as the Forest of Evil blooms with flowers and life now that she is gone.

The Witch (Agnes Moorehead) strikes fear into the fragile Rapunzel (Carol Lynley) in "Rapunzel" on *Shirley Temple's Storybook (*NBC-TV, 1958).

Carol enjoyed working with Agnes Moorehead immensely and remarked in author Charles Tranberg's Moorehead biography *I Love the Illusion* that she "was feisty, witty, direct and very professional; just a fabulous lady [and] a private person, she never volunteered information regarding her private life. I think she was one of the all-time great Grande Dames of Hollywood."[60]

The show and Carol received excellent notices. The critic in *The Hartford Courant* raved, "This Grimm Brothers fairy tale is the best in months on this series. Story is enhanced by the playing of Carol Lynley ... and Agnes Moorehead." John P. Shanley of the *New York Times* commented, "There was impressive make-believe in the performances of Carol Lynley [and] Don Dubbins." One pan came from Harry Harris of *The Philadelphia Inquirer* who wrote, "Carol Lynley portrayed Rapunzel ... with all the blonde heroine blandness of a junior Kim Novak." Overall, though, "Rapunzel" was another TV triumph for the young actress.

The young actress brought the right amount of innocence and ingenuity to the story book Rapunzel and is convincingly frightened and terrorized by the witch throughout. These were qualities Carol would use numerous times as an adult actress in many ladies in peril roles to come. However, tired of being the witch's prisoner, her Rapunzel musters the strength to fight back due to her love for the prince and shows true courage whereas some of her later roles did not.

Arguably, her best scene is before she meets Prince Peter when she confesses to the witch that an indescribable sensation has taken over her from head to toe, which makes her sing. Carol believably conveys that Rapunzel has stirrings of love for the first time, which she has never experienced before. Her leading man was reliable TV actor Don Dubbins who lacked charisma in the part. It would not be the last time Carol was saddled with less than inspiring young actors to play opposite.

On the motion picture front, despite her hesitation, Carol listened to her agent and signed a picture deal with 20th Century-Fox. The agreement included some unusual perks for a newcomer including permission to do television whenever she wanted, and a Broadway show every other year; the right to continue residing in New York; and the right to receive paid roundtrip airfare for herself and her mother every time she had to come to Hollywood.

Her first assignment for the studio was *Holiday for Lovers* (1959), based on the Broadway stage play, which unfortunately proved to be an undistinguished comedy when released. Directed by Henry Levin, the plot concerned two over-protective parents who jet off to Brazil, with Carol as their younger hip-talking teenage daughter ("What's rockin'? Roll?") in tow, when they think her older sister has fallen in love with her college professor (Paul Henreid) while attending school in Brazil. Reportedly, Bing Crosby, Gene Tierney, and Suzy Parker were originally announced as the leads. Clifton Webb (whom Carol found to be "a kind and gentle soul"[61]) wound up as the father, Jane Wyman stepped in as the mother when second choice Joan Fontaine became ill, and though Diane Varsi and Diane Baker were reported as Parker's replacement, it was Jill St. John who took the part of the sister.

Robert Wagner (right) visits Gary Crosby and Carol Lynley on the set of *Holiday for Lovers* (20th Century-Fox, 1959)

Respected veteran actor Paul Henreid was impressed with Carol Lynley while making this movie. His daughter Monika Henreid remarked that her father said that "Carol was wonderful to work with ... she was truly a professional, knew her lines, brought ideas, and discussed dialogue and scene study."[62] Monika also met Carol at her mother's dance and etiquette classes she taught in Beverly Hills. Carol and Brandon deWilde attended their Trophy Ball and Monika found Carol to be "darling, quiet, shy, and absolutely lovely."[63]

Carol developed a warm bond with Jane Wyman, whom she felt acted as a real mother should. Their friendship lasted for years. Per Nelson Aspen, there were two women Carol would call on Mother's Day every year—Jane Wyman and later Nelson's mom.

For Carol, her happiest memory making *Holiday for Lovers* had nothing to do with the cast but with Robert Wagner. She recalled,

> The first time we met we were filming and RJ came on the set while I was in front of the camera. I could see him out of my sideline. I went, '*Oh, my God! Oh, my God! It's Robert Wagner!*' He then came over and asked me to do some awards ceremony with him. I shouted, '*Yes, yes of course!*' I had the biggest crush on him for years.[64]

Presented in Cinemascope, *Holiday for Lovers* was touted as a colorful, picturesque travelogue, but is frustrating since the cast never left the Fox back lot (and it shows) as stock footage is used liberally. Rear projection is incorporated for the exterior scenes of the cast and is as phony-looking as they come. For a family comedy, it also contains a horrible chauvinistic cringe-worthy scene where Lynley's character gets a good old-fashioned spanking over the knee by her military crush (a pudgy Gary Crosby) whom she just met in Brazil. Daddy is at first aghast, but clueless mommy thinks he is just showing that he cares. To make matters even worse, they then allow their barely eighteen-year-old daughter to give up her college aspirations to marry the jerk! Welcome to the fifties. On the plus side, it is fun to see a nimble Carol play a wisecracking teenager for laughs.

Fox, meanwhile, bought the rights to *Blue Denim*, but did not immediately offer the film to Lynley, much to her chagrin. Reportedly, the studio was looking at three other actresses they had picture deals with—twenty-one-year-old Diane Varsi, twenty-three-year-old Lee Remick, and twenty-five-year-old Hope Lange to essay the part of the pregnant high schooler. Wiser heads prevailed though and the teenaged Lynley got to reprise her role. Even so, this did not stop the vocal actress from venting to the press, "I'd have thought they were crazy if they hadn't chosen me. When you've created something, you don't want to see someone else do it—not after you put half a year's work on it."[65]

A Cinemascope black-and-white production, *Blue Denim* was directed by Philip Dunne with a watered-down screenplay by Dunne and Edith Sommer based on the stage play. Downplaying the will-she-or-won't-she get an abortion, the film touted itself as an emotional frank drama about the communication gap between teenagers and their parents.

According to Dunne writing in his memoir, the forced new ending is the only interference he received from the studio. He wrote, "I was blessed with an able collaborator on the screenplay in the person of Edith Sommer. The picture, very daring for its time, was concerned with teenage pregnancy; Edie was something of an expert on teenagers having written a successful Broadway play on the subject: *A Roomful of Roses*."[66]

Cast opposite Lynley was Academy Award nominated child actor Brandon deWilde (*Shane*, *Member of the Wedding*). According to biographer Patricia McLean writing in *All Fall Down: The Brandon deWilde Story*, "Brandon's first onscreen and offscreen romance was with Carol Lynley." She added that due to Brandon's lack of a driver's license, the young couple would double date with Brandon's friend. He would drive the deWilde's family car, a yellow 1958 Oldsmobile 88 convertible.[67] Carol's brother remembered her going out on "these movie magazine dates with Brandon. I think they were more friends though than a romantic couple."[68] Perhaps their shared experiences as child actors with atypical upbringings bonded them.

A story about misunderstood youth, top billed Lynley as Janet and deWilde as Arthur are touching and very believable as naïve teenagers who go all the way with major consequences. Arthur is shy and soft-spoken. He is also heartsick as the movie begins because his family put his ill dog down while he was at school without telling him. They wanted to "spare" him the pain. This only angers the boy more to their surprise. Arthur takes out his frustrations with his wisecracking friend Ernie (Warren Berlinger). In Arthur's basement they talk tough, drink beer, smoke cigarettes and play poker. Neighbor Janet, a frequent visitor to the man cave, is sweet on Arthur who downplays his attraction. When sharing their first kiss, the inexperienced pair bump noses. Outside, after inviting Janet to his basketball game, an awkward Arthur hems and haws before Janet says, "It's no good if you ask" before planting a kiss on his lips and then running off.

Both teens share distracted parents they cannot relate to. Janet's widower father Prof. Willard (Vaughn Taylor) tries to mold his daughter into the image of his virtuous dead wife who Janet refuses to imitate and exclaims, "She must have been an angel or a saint or something, but I'm not!" Arthur's retired military dad Major Malcolm Bartley (MacDonald Carey) thinks the army will make a man of Arthur who wants to be "a somebody," while his ditzy mother Jessie (Marsha Hunt) is obsessed with planning her daughter's wedding. After Arthur confirms that they are going steady, Janet follows him into his darkened basement when he goes to retrieve a compact, she accidentally left behind. She admits that she has never been with a boy sexually. After boasting that he has with other girls, teary-eyed Arthur breaks down and admits that he too is a virgin. They then innocently make fumbling love.

The movie then jumps three months and a terrified Janet knows she is pregnant but has not told anyone. At their high school spring dance, Arthur follows her to the library where she is looking at a book about pregnancy. Janet than tearfully cries, "but they don't tell you how to stop it!" This is such a heartbreaking moment and Carol's best in the movie. Arthur pressures Ernie to help them find an abortionist though the words "pregnant" and "abortion" are never uttered. Though Ernie bragged about helping a friend with the same problem, he admits he lied and only heard of the story. Aghast and calling it murder, Ernie nevertheless comes through with the information. Weak-willed Arthur lets Janet go alone after stealing money from his father's checking account when he and Ernie cannot raise the funds themselves. After his sister's wedding, a guilt-ridden and upset Arthur confesses to his dumbstruck parents after they confront him about the missing money. With a furious Prof. Willard in tow, Arthur and his father race to find Janet to prevent the operation. Bartley beats the secret whereabouts of the doctor's office out of Ernie's contact. They arrive in the nick of time and take the drugged girl home. Letting his daughter decide what she wants to do, Janet bravely and selflessly decides to have the baby and stay with an aunt out of town. Not wanting to ruin Arthur's life to become "a somebody," she asks that he not be told. However, Ernie spots Janet leaving and tells Arthur who decides to be by her side for the necessitated happy Hollywood ending ... or was it?

Arthur (Brandon deWilde) and Janet (Carol Lynley) share a tense moment in *Blue Denim* (20th Century-Fox, 1959). *Billy Rose Theatre Division, The New York Public Library for the Performing Arts*

Carol and producer Charles Brackett defended the ending in the press after the movie opened and elaborated that now these teenagers, who are not yet adults, will have grown-up responsibilities as parents. Both adolescents and adults flocked to the movie and made it one of the studio's biggest hits of 1959. Tender was the word for Carol, as that is how many reviewers described her performance. For example, "tender and poignant" wrote Bosley Crowther in the *New York Times* and "tender and beautiful" wrote Hedda Hopper in her syndicated column. The reviewer in *Variety* wrote, "Carol Lynley repeats her stage role with the same éclat and sensitivity." Even more complimentary was Marjory Adams who raved in the *Boston Globe*, "Carol Lynley is the most effective member of the cast … She is dignified, sweet, frightened, and brave by turns. It is a portrayal that breaks your heart." The international press also praised Lynley. The critic in *The Jerusalem Post*, for instance, called her "a young actress of remarkable emotional depth and power."

Carol once again made *Film Daily's* Famous Fives for Best Juvenile Performance – Female. She placed fourth with her *Blue Denim* performance after Sandra Dee in *A Summer Place*; Millie Perkins in *The Diary of Anne Frank*; and Janet Munro in *Darby O'Gill and the Little People*. She was also nominated again for a Golden Globe for Most Promising Newcomer – Female. However, the second time around did not prove the charm and she was irrationally overlooked. Winners were Angie Dickinson (who should have not even been nominated since she was no newcomer with over nine prior films to her credit beginning in 1955) in *Rio Bravo*; Stella Stevens in *Say One for Me*; Tuesday Weld in *The Five Pennies*; and Janet Munro in *Darby O'Gill and the Little People*. Carol arguably deserved that fourth slot over Munro but since the Press was made up of foreign correspondents a non-American usually always snuck in. Other nominees were Diane Baker in *The Best of Everything*, Yvette Mimieux in *Platinum High School*, and Cindy Robbins in *This Earth Is Mine*.

Today *Blue Denim* is dated in terms of the teenagers' naiveté, but the performances by the actors still make the film well-regarded. For example, years later the TV critic from the *El Paso Herald-Post* wrote, "Curiously touching soaper about a young couple faced with an unwanted pregnancy. Carol Lynley does an outstanding job." The critic of *The Austin American Statesman* raved, "A seemingly dated plot … is given new life by the extremely talented young actors who portray them with such poignancy. Every young person should tune in."

Blue Denim was still being praised for its daringness in 2018. Film historian Julie Kirgo, who wrote the liner notes to the Twilight Time Blu-ray release, opined, "*Blue Denim* remains dignified and touching. It's a period piece, certainly, with all its period's flaws. But guess what? Nowhere here do we have the suggestion of sin, or of religious condemnation of any kind. These kids are in a tough situation—but no one ever slags them off as bad or evil or even, really, transgressive. They're just human. And that conclusion puts *Blue Denim* in a uniquely nonjudgmental place. Would—could—any movie on this subject today be quite so broad-minded? Sadly, we fear not."[69]

*****

Carol Lynley's third film released in 1959 was *Hound-Dog Man*. It was produced by Jerry Wald and directed by Don Siegel (later known for his gritty movies with Clint Eastwood). With Elvis Presley in the army after scoring four box office hits including *Jailhouse Rock* and *King Creole*, the studios were desperate to discover the next handsome young rock 'n' roller who could fill the void. One contender was Philadelphia native Fabian Forte who had a pleasant but not strong singing voice. What he did have in abundance was charisma and dark smoldering good looks, so Fox signed him to a long-term picture deal.

Hound-Dog Man was a laid-back homey tale, based on the novel by Fred Gibson, where nothing much happens. It was Fabian's first movie and they paired him opposite one of their most popular teenage actresses, Carol Lynley. Well, that is what they *should* have done. Instead, a pert Lynley is a small-town girl, who favors the charms of an older scalawag named Blackie (Stuart Whitman) to that of Fabian's teenage lay about who likes to spend his days with his younger brother (Dennis Holmes) and Blackie "a huntin'-and-a-fishin." Fabian has eyes for another (the awkward Dodie Stevens) causing Carol's adolescent fans to scratch their heads in bewilderment, no doubt.

Reviews were kind with critics describing the movie as "folksy," "warm," "amusing," and "pleasant." Even the *New York Times* cottoned to it for its "mighty pretty color scenery and friendly rusticity," The entire cast does well in their roles including Fabian who sings a few songs nicely. Despite the positive reviews, director Don Siegel surprisingly revealed years later, "It could have been very good, if it had been done the way it should have been by Sam Peckinpah, who is of the west and knows it well … He would have done it the way it should have been done: small."[70]

The box office take was disappointing compared to what the Elvis Presley films were grossing at the time. The misleading poster art with Fabian and Lynley prominently featured led teenagers to believe that they were the film's major romantic couple. Perhaps once word got out, the youngsters stayed away?

Poster art for the motion picture *Hound-Dog Man* (20th Century-Fox, 1959).

Producer Jerry Wald had a different take on it back then. He thought older moviegoers were uninteresting in seeing it, putting the blame on Fox's marketing campaign for "slanting the advertising away from the romance between Carol Lynley and Stuart Whitman and fastening it all on Fabian."[71]

Despite the less than stellar grosses, the movie continued to buoy Lynley's standing amongst teenage moviegoers and she so impressed producer Jerry Wald that he was determined to get the reluctant actress to star in *Return to Peyton Place* the sequel to his 1957 hit.

Carol made a few television guest appearances during 1959. The most notable that garnered her much press was "Deed of Mercy" on *General Electric Theater*. It reunited her with "Rapunzel" director James Neilson and co-star Agnes Moorehead. Carol, however, was no innocent maiden this time as she played neurotic Barbara Clark. A well-respected Hungarian scientist (Carl Esmond) picks up a hitchhiking Barbara, who is headed to Hollywood to find fame, and befriends her. Thinking she can gain notoriety quickly; Barbara accuses the man of indecent behavior towards her after they are in a car crash not caring that she could ruin his career. A vacationing reporter (Ronald Reagan who also hosted the series) stumbles upon the scene and is determined to prove the man's innocence.

Cecil Smith, the then *Los Angeles Times*' entertainment editor, was hired to play a small role of a journalist. He described James Neilson as "a quietly master at his trade (and of the buttoned-coat tie-knotted school of directing rather than the open bloused ranters)."[72] He watched some of the scenes with the stars and remarked that Lynley played her villainous role "softly, indirectly, with enormous effectiveness."[73] The actress defended her character as most actors do when playing the villain. Carol felt that Barbara was "an ambitious young girl" and "doesn't realize the harm she's doing as she connives … I don't think the character is mean—just opportunistic."[74]

By this time, Carol Lynley was one of the most popular teenage actresses of the period. With this fame, Whitman Publishing, hopefully with her authorization, used her image as a standup paper doll (popular with little girls back then) complete with twenty-eight costume changes for her fans to purchase and dress her up.

Lynley was also splashed across all the movie magazines of the day including *Photoplay, Modern Screen, Motion Picture, Teen Screen, Movie Stars, Screen Stories*, and more. They published outrageous stories about her looking for love and her romances with early co-stars James MacArthur and Brandon deWilde. She was regular fodder for these magazines for the next six years with tales of her marriage and divorce; her return to single life; and her *Playboy* pictorial, which really ruffled the feathers of Hollywood's old guard. Article titles included, "Will Carol Ever Say Yes?"; "Can There Ever Be a Nice Way to Say I Don't Love You;" "Love Is the Ginchiest…the Craziest…the Greatest…Especially When Carol Lynley and Brandon deWilde Get Together!;" "Carol Lynley Reveals Ten Ways Guaranteed to Kill Your Guy;" and "Love Is a Simple Thing, But…" Later headlines blared, "My Baby Taught Me Love;" and "What Made Carol Lynley Pose Nude?". This was part of the job no actor could avoid especially ones with studio contracts or picture deals. Even if an actor, pressured by studio public relations men, cooperated with these gossip rags they still were prone to printing exaggeration or downright falsehoods sometimes supplied by the stars' own publicity people.

One of Hollywood's most powerful columnists was Louella Parsons. Every newcomer had to kowtow to her and Carol was no exception. She recalled her humorous first encounter at the gossip maven's home when brought there by her press agent,

> Louella had this big house in Beverly Hills. There were a few people in attendance, and they split to leave me alone with her to do our interview in this room. She then fell asleep as she was talking to me. I didn't want to be rude and wake her up so I sat there. She was out cold. Then I thought, 'Oh, God maybe she's dead.' This went on for about an hour. Finally, my press agent came into the room and I leapt out of my chair towards him. We left and I didn't make anything of it because she was so famous.[75]

To Carol's relief, Louella was not dead. She lived for another twelve years and long enough to take Carol to task for something the actress did in 1965 that the columnist did not approve of in the least—not that Lynley could have cared less what she thought.

With much fanfare, it was reported in all the columns that Carol was going to reunite with Fabian to play romantically involved college students in the comedy *Daddy O* written by Garson Kanin and starring Gary Cooper. However, after Cooper took ill, the movie was reworked by screenwriters Tom and Frank Waldman to fit the talents of replacement Bing Crosby as a self-made millionaire, who after his wife passes away, decides to enroll in college to earn a degree. Now called *High Time* (1960), Blake Edwards was brought in to direct. However, the production hit another snag when Lynley refused to do the movie. She commented, "I think it's time I began playing grownup parts. It's not that I don't like Fabian. I do. He's a grand boy and a fine actor and we're good friends. But teaming with him would mean I'd have to play a sub-deb again."[76] Carol held to her convictions and was replaced by Tuesday Weld.

The mainstream press got *High Time* right but sometimes they were no better than the Hollywood columnists reporting rumors and gossip from press agents as facts. It was announced that Carol turned down a leading role opposite Elvis Presley in *Wild in the Country*. In the next few years, her name would be mentioned as being considered for such movies as *One, Two, Three*; *Bon Voyage*, *Honeymoon Hotel*; *The Young Lovers*; *Lilith*; and *The Glory Guys*, among others. The press reported that she landed the female lead opposite Troy Donahue in *My Blood Runs Cold* but was replaced by Joey Heatherton. Carol was unaware she was up for any of these films or that she had turned any of them down. She stated,

> Sometimes producers would compile a list of actors who they like or are thinking about for a role. If they come to you then they are seriously considering you. If they don't contact you, an actor can never know they were on the list. It is totally not

true that I turned down *Wild in the Country*. I would never have turned down an Elvis Presley movie! Are you kidding!?! I never even heard of *My Blood Runs Cold* so whatever was written is untrue.

I don't dwell on this stuff but [currently] I only remember turning down … *Snow White and The Three Stooges* because it was ridiculous. Carol Heiss who was an Olympic ice-skating champ at the time did it. The movie bombed—no surprise.[77]

Around this time and for the next decade items would be planted in the press with Carol's name attached to movies that never came to be. One of the most interesting projects was called *High Heels* that producer Jerry Wald failed to get off the ground. It was the story of a trio of Roaring Twenties taxi dancers to be played by Carol Lynley, Tuesday Weld, and Jennifer West.[78] How campy would that have been? Wald did eventually get Lynley and Weld into the same movie and Carol would dance the tango on screen as well in another.

In 1960, the trade magazine *Motion Picture Exhibitor* released its annual Laurel Awards. There was no ceremony and editors voted the top five to ten films and actors/directors/producers in several categories. Carol was voted the fifth Top New Female Personality of the year. She placed behind Jane Fonda, Joan O'Brien, Luana Patten and Tuesday Weld, and before Haya Harareet, Cindy Robbins, Joan Blackman, Leslie Parrish, and Donna Anderson.

It seems Carol's newfound fame made her want to take more control of her choices. Her brother conferred and said, "She wanted to assert her independence from my mother more. I am sure of that. She wanted to do some little play that wasn't even Off-Broadway and everybody was at her asking why you are bothering with this. She thought doing live theater would keep her credibility as an actress."[79]

The play in question was called *Answered the Flute* by Sam Robins and sponsored by the nonprofit group Studio Three. Carol played the teenaged daughter of a composer who pressures him to complete a symphony he has been working on for children. Among the cast was Burt Brinkeroff, Lynley's co-star on stage in *Blue Denim*. It was scheduled to only run for six performances at the Finch Theatre.

Carol explained one significant thing happened while doing the play and revealed to columnist Hollis Alpert why she cut her long beautiful blonde mane, "On my way to the theater, I suddenly got that now or never feeling and I went into the dressing room and snipped off most of my hair. I was a little shaky about it at first, but now I'm not at all sorry."[80] Impetuous to say the least, but perhaps it was a rebellious action against the adults who had been controlling her career?

Publicity photo of Carol Lynley in *The Last Sunset* (Universal, 1961).

Carol's new short 'do though was perfect for her next movie. She accepted the role of fifteen-year-old Missy, who transforms from a child to woman on a cattle drive from Mexico to Texas, in the soapy 1961 western *The Last Sunset* (working title *Day of the Gun*) starring Rock Hudson and Kirk Douglas, whose production company Brynaprod, S.A. produced the movie for Universal Pictures. It was directed by Robert Aldrich and adapted by Dalton Trumbo from the novel *Sundown at Crazy Horse* by Howard Rigsby. Recalling how she landed the movie, Carol stated, "I went to Kirk Douglas' house to meet him and Bob Aldrich. We had lunch and I got the job. I was seventeen years old and had never really been out of this country. I got down to this tiny town in Aguascalientes, Mexico and looking at my window from where I was staying saw endless open space, which coming from New York was foreign to me."[81]

Filmed entirely on location in Mexico (per Carol she spent three months in Aguascalientes and another three months in Mexico City[82]), this was a troubled production. Screenwriter Dalton Trumbo took his fair share of the blame in many interviews he gave at the time and acknowledged Kirk Douglas' rightful frustration with him. Blacklisted, he never thought he would get screen credit and worked haphazardly on the screenplay between writing scripts for the higher profile films *Spartacus* and *Exodus*. However, when the film was in trouble during shooting, he did go down to Mexico to try to fix things with the script. One of the problems he faced was that once Hudson was cast, he had to beef up his role and drop the plot of a romantic triangle with the outlaw and mother and daughter.

Kirk Douglas also clashed with director Robert Aldrich who purportedly campaigned to direct the western. After being hired, he reportedly came to Mexico with an entourage of writers who were working with him on other projects. As head of the production company, Douglas ordered them to leave and his relationship with the director remained frosty. Aldrich forever bad mouthed the movie. In interviews he said the experience was unpleasant and shooting began before the script was ready.

Carol was aware of all this on-set strife and recalled,

> I knew that the fighting was going on but because I was so young—I was a simple seventeen-year-old—nobody talks to you. I just adored and worshipped Kirk—I was crazy about him! So, I never paid too much attention to anybody who said a negative word about him. I thought he was just the greatest and I still do. Kirk was multi-lingual and spoke Spanish too, so he was always chatting away with the crew. He did not just speak Spanish but was able to think in another language.
>
> I liked Dalton Trumbo and he was still blacklisted at the time. We were literally in the middle of nowhere and this tiny plane would fly in to pick up people. I would be standing there and Dalton who was a very tall guy with a mustache would get off. He was imposing but would come in to do what he was supposed to do and then leave. He didn't stick around too much. I knew that Kirk and Bob Aldrich weren't getting along but that wasn't surprising because they both were hyper males.[83]

Carol impressed those she worked with during the making of the movie. Harsh conditions in the desert were a far cry from the modeling studios and Hollywood soundstages she was used to. Kirk Douglas praised Carol and remarked, "She's a real craftsman…[and] a perfectionist. That was a rugged film and Carol is going to come in for a lot of praise when it is released."[84]

Besides Carol's admiration for Kirk Douglas, she also had fond memories of Rock Hudson who also avoided the turmoil. She said fondly,

> I liked Rock Hudson a lot. I used to hang out with him. He was enormous—very tall—but a sweet guy and professional. They had to send for a bigger horse for him because he was in pain from riding the first smaller one they gave him. At the end of the

day, I would have dinner with him and his friend. I knew that something was up between them. I wasn't that sophisticated at the time, but I knew there was something a bit off kilter there.[85]

Remembering Jack Elam and Neville Brand who played cowhands, Carol said with a laugh, "They shared the honeymoon suite at the local hotel. I used to have dinner with them every night and then they would send me home to my mommy. They were quite a pair."[86] The actress also hit it off with the crew. There was one person she remembered most and said,

> I had a friend named Gabriel who I believe was the still photographer. I talked with him a lot since he was one of the few from the Mexican crew who spoke English. We were in the middle of nowhere and he would ask me to take my sunglasses off because the guys wanted to see my blue eyes. I'd take them off and they would yell, 'Azul! Azul!'[87]

Daniel Jones Lee revealed that Carol's mother was with her the entire time and that he flew down there too. He recalled, "I went during the summer after school. I brought my cat with me and had to get it shots first. I know it was a stupid idea to travel with a cat. We stayed at a hotel in Mexico City for quite some time while they were shooting the interiors at the studio. I got to meet Rock Hudson. I just wandered around Mexico City. I was free to do whatever I pleased. Carol was working virtually every day. I remember one day I was on the set while filming outdoors. Carol had on her sunglasses. The crew would come up and ask to see her eyes. She was forever taking those glasses on and off so people could look at her blue eyes."[88]

In *The Last Sunset*, Carol's Missy is the immature teenage daughter of drunken cattle rancher John Breckenridge (Joseph Cotten) and his wife Belle (Dorothy Malone). They are about to embark on a cattle drive from Mexico to Texas when along comes Belle's former lover, black-clad outlaw Brendan O'Malley (Kirk Douglas), on the run from a murder charge and pursued by Deputy Dana Stribling (Rock Hudson). Breckenridge is having trouble hiring hands to make the cattle drive and, to Belle's consternation, O'Malley volunteers to join up for one fifth of the herd. Desperate, Breckenridge agrees but they are still short one man. When Stribling shows up, O'Malley promises to turn himself in once they cross the border if he works the cattle drive too. Just before they are to depart, a drunken Breckenridge is killed at a local cantina, leaving the two adversaries to help the ladies get the cattle to their Texas destination. Along the way screenwriter Dalton Trumbo throws every cliché at them including dust storms, marauding Indians, predatory cowboys, and romance as Dana falls for the widow and a now more grown up Missy for the charming but older O'Malley. However, what the poor gal does not know is that he is her biological papa! After he has shared a romantic dance with Missy, a vision of loveliness in her mother's yellow dress, and a kiss, Belle tells him the truth when her daughter confesses her love for O'Malley. Stunned and ashamed, the outlaw does not believe her until he sees her on the dock just before his showdown with Stribling. They go through with it, despite the protestations of Belle and Missy, and O'Malley is shot dead. When the Deputy picks up his gun, he finds that it was unloaded.

Lobby card for *The Last Sunset* (Universal, 1961) with Carol Lynley and Kirk Douglas.

When *The Last Sunset* opened, the Freudian western was not as well received as expected considering all the talent involved. Mae Tinee of the *Chicago Daily Tribune* blasted the movie and wrote, "The script is overblown and idiotic, the entire film so inept that it's downright ludicrous." Most of the other negative notices were not so scathing. Some critics of the day such as Philip K. Scheuer did understand that Trumbo was aiming for an unconventional type western and remarked in the *Los Angeles Times*, "its screenplay combines unexpected flashes of poetic prose with just-what-you'd-expect-'em-to-say."

Carol begins the movie as an awkward tomboyish baby-faced teenager who only has Mexican cattle hands for friends and slowly progresses to a lovely young lady by the end, all fresh-faced and enchanting. She does an impressive job playing this transformation, as the audience watches the young girl mature before their eyes. Lynley is simply radiant when she emerges wearing that yellow dress for the first time to meet up with Douglas as equals rather than adult and child. She not only takes his breath away but that of the audience's as well.

Marjory Adams of the *Boston Globe* found Lynley "eager and lovely in her role" and Philip K. Scheuer commented, "Miss Lynley ... projects a winsome warmth that is like a welcome shaft of sunlight through the storm clouds." Not all was favorable as she, Kirk Douglas, Rock Hudson, and Dorothy Malone "won" The Harvard Lampoon Movie Worst Award for Worst Performance by a Cast in Toto. This would not be the last time she was singled out by the satirical magazine. As a consolation, around this time readers of *Seventeen* voted her one of the top five Female Stars of the Future along with Sandra Dee, Tuesday Weld, Annette Funicello, and Connie Stevens.

Its initial mediocre reviews may have hindered the grosses considering the box office appeal of the two leads and its name supporting cast. Though the movie took in $3 million at the box office, it fell short of its budget.

The Last Sunset grows on you in repeated viewings and you appreciate it being an atypical film of its genre. The performances all hold up quite well. Television does not do the movie justice and it really needs to be seen on the big screen or in its original ratio format to appreciate fully Ernest Haller's majestic cinematography.

When it was released both Dalton Trumbo and Robert Aldrich dismissed the film and seemed to abandon ownership of it. Today, the western is held in higher regard. Historians appreciate that Trumbo was trying to deliver a more psychological western rather than the standard shoot 'em ups. Former Film Forum staff member Brynn White thought so and eloquently opined in *Film Comment*, "*The Last Sunset* has more to do with the elemental intermingling of earth, wind, fire, and water than its John Wayne heritage. Partaking equally of chaos and classicism, it becomes a spectacle of body movements amidst sandstorm-torn terrain, of character dynamics vanishing into and emerging from the night's shadows."[89] This is just one example of the more positive reviews the movie has received since being rediscovered in the 2000's.

Carol walked away from *The Last Sunset* with an ability that she did not have going in. She explained,

> One day, my friend Gabriel said to me, 'No mas English.' I said, 'What?' He replied, 'We are going to teach you to speak Spanish.' I first said no because I didn't want to do that. He wouldn't take no for an answer. Gabriel told me that he and the crew would give me fifteen different words a day and nobody will speak English to me. I cried, 'Gabriel, please no!' He said firmly, 'No, we have decided. This is how it will be.' They started off with easy phrases like what I wanted to eat or I have to go to the bathroom. I had a radio in my hotel room and listened to that as well. In three weeks, I was speaking Spanish and still do.[90]

*****

During this period, Carol was dating Fox publicist Mike Selsman whom she met at the premiere of *Blue Denim* almost a year prior. Since he worked in the publicity department at Fox their paths crossed again and the two became serious.

The actress' romantic life did not bother 20th Century-Fox so much. What irritated the studio heads (and producer Jerry Wald) was that they wanted her to star as Allison MacKenzie in *Return to Peyton Place*, the planned sequel to *Peyton Place*.

In 1957, Wald and Fox had a tremendous success with the movie *Peyton Place* based on Grace Metalious' novel. It revealed the dirty secrets of the small New England town of Peyton Place and unmasked its residents as hypocrites. Lana Turner starred as Constance McKenzie, newcomer Diane Varsi was her illegitimate daughter Allison, Hope Lange was victimized Selena Cross from the wrong-side-of-the-tracks, and David Nelson was Selena's wealthy boyfriend Ted Carter.

The movie made millions and scored a boatload of Academy Award nominations. With such a hit on their hands, Jerry Wald encouraged Metalious to pen a follow-up, *Return to Peyton Place*. He originally thought the cast would reprise their roles for the sequel but hit a snag when Lana Turner asked for a huge amount of money and Diane Varsi walked away from Hollywood and her Fox contract. The casting roundelay began immediately, not helped by the fact that Wald kept changing his mind about which screenplay he was going to use.

Anna Maria Alberghetti, Lee Remick, and Diane Baker were announced for Allison at various times. Baker looked to be the frontrunner. In February 1960, Fox released an elaborate press piece complete with photos of the new cast members. Baker was listed as Allison and Lynley was to play the new role of Jennifer, a rich spoiled Boston socialite who marries recent law school graduate Ted Carter (Dean Stockwell) to the chagrin of her new mother-in-law Roberta (Joan Crawford). Jealous that Jennifer keeps her son living in Boston and only spends weekends with her in Peyton Place, she prepares to bump off the bride. However, Jennifer is no bubbleheaded blonde and turns the tables.[91] This and other reported storylines featuring Suzy Parker, Trevor Howard, and Terry Moore never came to be. A writers' strike also interfered and pushed back the making of the movie.

In a revised script approved by Jerry Wald, Lynley's Jennifer was out.

Perhaps souring on Diane Baker, the producer wanted Carol as Allison instead. However, Carol did not want to play her and it was reported that she turned it down because she did not want to reprise a role created by another actress. Carol confirmed this was half true and explained,

> I turned it down because I was back in New York and I was tired of flying back and forth all the time. I also wasn't crazy about the script. It had nothing to do about another actress at all. Jerry Wald got me on the phone and convinced me to take the part. He literally talked me into it.[92]

Carol was more surprised that Diane Baker wanted the role of Allison. "I knew Diane and had no idea we were up for the same part," admitted Lynley. "She is a fine actress. We did a press tour together once. She was somebody I never really got to know very well but she was always around ... she was like just [pause] *there*."[93]

Allison MacKenzie (Carol Lynley), with her publisher Lewis Jackman (Jeff Chandler) by her side, defends her trashy novel *Samuel's Castle* at a town hall meeting in *Return to Peyton Place* (20th Century-Fox, 1961).

Joan Crawford should have been one of Carol's co-stars but she withdrew from the production (reportedly miffed that Fox had the audacity to cast her daughter Christina Crawford in a small role in *Wild in the Country*). Her part as steely-eyed Roberta Carter was taken by Mary Astor (delivering a brilliant chilling performance that should have earned her an Oscar nomination) with Luciana Paluzzi as her hated Italian daughter-in-law Raffaella married to her attorney son Ted (Brett Halsey the real-life ex-husband of Paluzzi). Other actors playing characters from the original film included Eleanor Parker as Allison's mother Connie; Robert Sterling as Connie's husband Mike Rossi; and Tuesday Weld (with her hair dyed brown because she and Lynley looked too much alike) as Allison's best friend Selena Cross.

Carol had one life changing experience while filming *Return to Peyton Place* and she revealed to authors Lillian and Helen Ross, "In the middle of making the picture I got married [to Mike Selsman], so I look back on the picture through a sort of haze … the day of my scene with Tuesday Weld was the day of my wedding. I was married at 9:15 in the morning and then I went back to the set and did the scene with Tuesday 22 times. Acting isn't easy."[94]

With regards to her marriage, Carol admitted in many interviews thereafter she only married to get away from her mother. When asked his take on it, Carol's sibling responded, "Yes, that is pretty much true. She didn't put it quite so bluntly to my mother then but it was a common assumption. But she did tell people while she was growing up that she wanted to get married and have five kids. She was always saying that even to the press. Soon as she got married and had one kid, she wasn't interested in marriage any longer."[95]

Asked his opinion of Selsman, Daniel added, "I met him maybe three times. He was fine but I really didn't have a strong opinion about him one way or the other. He was a movie executive type—very show business."[96]

In *Return to Peyton Place*, young author Allison MacKenzie, who flits around like a flighty teenager at the beginning of the movie, is elated when a New York publishing company purchases her manuscript. Heading to New York solo, the novice writer is in for a rude awakening when publisher Lewis

Jackman (Jeff Chandler) helps turn her innocent tome into a scandalous book called *Samuel's Castle*. It is a disguised look at her hypocritical small town including their treatment of rape victim Selena Cross. The residents' reaction is outrage, as her own mother Connie finds it "cheap and dirty and vulgar." Disgusted matron Roberta Carter calls it a "lurid piece of trash," tosses it in the garbage can, and bans it from the high school library in between trying to break up son Ted (Brett Halsey) and his new wife (Luciana Paluzzzi), an Italian model. Already repulsed by her daughter, Connie then discovers that Allison is in love with her older married editor and berates her even more causing Lynley's Allison to cattily retort, "What you're afraid is like mother like daughter." Infuriated, Connie slaps Allison who flatly responds, "I hate you for that," in one of the film's many melodramatic moments. Tuesday Weld gets her big scene too and does equally badly when Selena relives the "whole dirty story of Selena Cross" recanted in Allison's novel. With her new beau ski instructor Nels (a wooden Gunnar Hellstrom) reading it aloud, Selena flips out when he gets to the passage of her sexual assault by her stepfather. Thinking Nels is her rapist, she clocks him with a fire poker before fleeing like a lunatic into the night.

The story culminates in a town hall meeting where Roberta leads her cronies to ban Allison's book and to fire her stepfather Mike Rossi as principal due to his reinstatement of it. Jackman stands up for *Samuel's Castle* as do the other young people including Roberta's son Ted. They sway their fellow residents to reinstate the book and Mike. A humiliated Roberta stubbornly holds on to her narrow-minded views chastising her neighbors for their decision, which she vows they will regret, and exits wounded, but with her head held high. The movie then cuts to Jackman saying goodbye to Allison as she stands on a hillside overlooking Peyton Place deciding to remain there. The original ending had an even worse fate for Roberta who dies in a house fire when Ted rushes in and must make a choice to save his bride or his mother. This was unnecessary and the decision to excise it was correct. The movie's topic of censorship still resonates today and despite all the soap opera trappings and stilted acting prior, the town hall meeting is quite stirring with the cast at its best here.

Excited about the sequel, novelist Grace Metalious filmed a promotional newsreel with its leading lady Carol Lynley. It was described in *Vanity Fair* as "creepy" due to Grace who was found to be "awkward, bloated, and tired."[97] Carol added that Metalious was "a little discombobulated ... and verklempt."[98] Even so, the author was able to convince Jerry Wald to hold the premiere at the Colonial Theater in her hometown of Laconia. The only cast member to attend was Jeff Chandler along with Fox contract player Ina Balin.

Despite the hoopla and anticipation, *Return to Peyton Place* was reviled by the critics and arguably contains a less-than-stellar performance from Carol. Everything seems to be working against her. She is a bit listless and stoic throughout and speaks with a monotone voice. Her new short hairdo that was so cute in *The Last Sunset* was styled differently and made less flattering here as Carol attested to. It was not a favorite look of hers on camera. The actress who charmed in *Blue Denim* and *The Last Sunset* was nowhere to be found. Partial blame can go to director Jose Ferrer for not getting her to lighten up in the role not counting the earlier scenes. Surprisingly, Carol only had praise for her director and remarked, "He was nice and extremely professional—he got on with it. He had a beautiful speaking voice. I didn't know him that well, but I enjoyed working with him."[99]

Most of the younger cast Ferrer directed is equally disappointing and they all seem to be competing to see who can give the worst performance— Gunnar Hellstrom wins hands down closely trailed by Luciana Paluzzi. This all contributes to making *Return to Peyton Place* one of those Bad Movies We Love until this day.

Despite the drubbing the film received (Judith Crist laughingly wrote in *TV Guide*, "There are enough soap suds to pollute the Mississippi along with the mind."), moviegoers flocked to the sequel propelling it to become Fox's highest earning movie of the year with a $4.5 million gross. With her top billing, it was another feather in Lynley's cap with Fox. Her negative reviews aside, theater owners judged Hollywood actors based on the amount of coin they brought in and Lynley had an excellent year. In December, she came in fourth in the *Motion Picture Herald*'s yearly Stars of Tomorrow poll. She trailed Hayley Mills, Nancy Kwan, and Horst Buchholz, but placed ahead of Dolores Hart, Paula Prentiss, Jim Hutton, Juliet Prowse, Connie Stevens, and Warren Beatty - who should have asked for a recount. Bad enough he came in tenth but to trail behind Connie Stevens!?! That was adding insult to injury.

Another award Lynley was up for in 1961 but surely glad she lost was the Sour Apple given out by the Hollywood Women's Press Club for being the least cooperative of all film and television personalities. She vied for the prize with Warren Beatty, Bobby Darin, Doris Day, Paul Newman, and Tuesday Weld. They were all bested by Natalie Wood who took home the trophy. Seeing Lynley on this list is not surprising since she seemed to have done her best to keep her nuptials a secret from the prying press.

These awards were probably all moot to Carol because, by all accounts, she was trying to make a sincere go of it as a housewife in Queens and took a respite from movie acting. This would not be the only time she took a break from show business at the wrong moment. The box office success of *Return to Peyton Place* made her a hot property and she missed out on taking advantage of the momentum it brought her. Luckily for her fans, Carol got bored quickly and wanted to act again. Perhaps to help, her husband accepted a new job as a publicist working for Arthur Jacobs' publicity agency in Beverly Hills and it was "California here we come!"

2. A Sex Kitten Purrs... Briefly

Now settled in posh Beverly Hills, Carol Lynley should have returned to the big screen but she arrived pregnant. She confessed to columnist Bob Thomas, "I was miserable the whole time I was gone. If the experience taught me anything, it is that I am entirely unsuited to be a housewife. My husband agrees with me."[100]

Not letting her pregnancy be a deterrent from working, Lynley made a TV appearance in the Emmy-nominated CBS comedy special *Henry Fonda and the Family*. It was written, produced, and directed by comedic heavy weights Bud Yorkin and Norman Lear. Fonda was the audience's guide as it spoofed situations that affected families all based on statistical analysis accumulated from government home surveys. Among the lookers were Dick Van Dyke, Cara Williams, Paul Lynde, Dan Blocker, Spring Byington, and the boyishly cute Michael J. Pollard teamed with Lynley as a young married teenage couple expecting a baby. Their sketch had the pair surprisingly sharing a double bed, still a rarity during this period on television. The show aired on February 6, 1962 without any musical numbers or commercials except for "dental health messages" from the American Dental Association. As anticipated with that creative pedigree, the show delivered the laughs with humorous facts buoyed by the splendidly game cast in a sort of pre-*Laugh-In* way. In some segments, they are seated and just throw out fun facts and witty barbs toward the camera. This is Carol's sole variety show-type appearance and she handles her comedy sketch quite playing an expectant mother driving her young husband crazy in the middle of the night with her cravings and comical demands.

Daughter Jill Selsman was born in March 1962. Despite being a loving mother based on all accounts, Carol was itching to act. Episodic television is where she was able to exercise her pent-up passion playing a varied array of characters from a nun, to a beauty queen, to a murderous twin, to a deaf teacher. These roles gave her the acting challenge she relished.

Carol Lynley's former home on Benedict Canyon Drive in Beverly Hills. *Photo by Tom Lisanti, ca. 1981*

First up for the actress during the 1962-63 TV season was a return to Alfred Hitchcock's reformatted show. CBS asked the director if he would be willing to expand his half hour anthology series to an hour. He agreed and *Alfred Hitchcock Presents* was re-christened *The Alfred Hitchcock Hour*. Lynley's episode was reportedly the first one to be filmed, though it was the sixth one aired.

"Final Vow" was directed by Norman Lloyd who also produced the series and had a long association with Alfred Hitchcock. Prior, he was the associate producer of *Alfred Hitchcock Presents* and as an actor worked for the director in *Saboteur* and *Spellbound*, among others. The episode was written by the prolific Emmy Award-winning Henry Slesar most famous for his stint as head writer for the daytime serial *The Edge of Night*. This episode plays as a straightforward crime drama, though having the protagonist be a conflicted novitiate nun elevates the story. It is also boosted from a sympathetic performance from Carol and a genuinely surprise ending, making it well worth watching.

Carol's leading man was Clu Gulager and she remarked, "I always liked Clu but I was never quite sure what he was talking about. He had a speech pattern that was very different from mine. He is quite a good actor but I always had to lean over a little bit to understand what he was saying. As a person, he couldn't have been nicer."[101]

Regarding Hitchcock, Lynley said, "I never did meet him. I was somewhere and he was at a table nearby. He kept looking over at me and circling around. I was told later that he decided I was too young [for his film *The Birds*], which I was."[102]

In this episode, Carol perfectly projects the anguish Sister Pamela endures as she doubts her calling. Before making her final vow, she agrees to visit a former pupil, Wormer (Don Hanmer), of an elderly, sick nun to pick up a gift he has for the convent. Unbeknownst to the nun, he is now a criminal and the present is a priceless Donatello statue of St. Francis. At the bus depot, a thug named Jimmy Bresson (Clu Gulager) runs off with it after naive Pamela sets down her bag. He is apprehended without the stolen object, but Pamela cannot positively identify him. She then decides to leave the order and do her own sleuthing. Lynley is good and plays Pamela with a bit of hesitancy as the nun is treading in new waters foreign to her. Getting a job at the factory where Bresson works, she attracts him immediately. To the chagrin of a jealous girlfriend, Bresson invites Pamela to a party at her apartment. Catching Pamela snooping, Bresson's girl suggests she visit a pawn shop where she may find her stolen item. However, it is a set up. Bresson, in cahoots with the shop owner, threatens that after he sells the statue to his fence, he is going to kill the terrified young woman. In a surprise ending, the fence turns out to be Wormer who convinces the thief that the statue is worthless. He regains it from Bresson and exits with a shaken Pamela. He drives them back to the convent where she has decided to remain a nun.

The show oddly opened with an introduction by Alfred Hitchcock seen learning the art of tattooing as he practices on a side of raw beef steak. How this relates to the episode is anybody's guess. It closed equally strangely with Hitchcock about to tattoo a living customer—a cow. He explains since billboards across the U.S. highways are being torn down, placing ads on cows who graze roadside will be the new thing.

 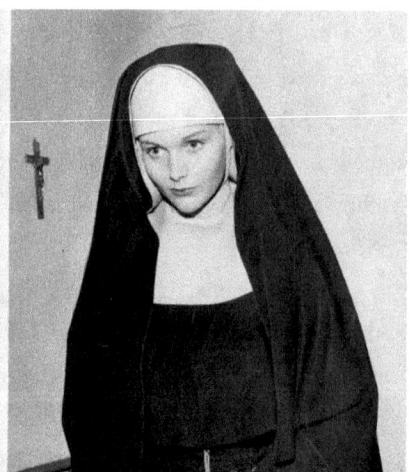

Publicity photo of Carol Lynley in and out of her habit as Sister Pamela in "Final Vow" on *The Alfred Hitchcock Hour* (Universal Television, 1962).

"Final Vow" (called "offbeat" and "intriguing" by the TV critic in *The Atlanta Constitution*) is notable in Carol Lynley's genre career because it is her first adult TV role as the harried heroine. Her Sister Pamela takes a bold step to leave the confines of her convent life to go back into the real world to reclaim the stolen artifact. Carol projects both strength and vulnerability as she gingerly ingratiates herself with Gulager's thug to find out what he did with the statue. However, Pamela gets in over her head and a man needs to rescue her as was usually the norm back then. Carol excels in the part even in scenes without uttering a word. For instance, when realizing Jimmy is going to kill her, she projects fear with her facial expressions gaining the audience's empathy. Some actresses can go over the top with the look of terror in their eyes, but Lynley always played it more subtlety than most. This is a quality truly needed for successfully playing these types of parts.

Up next for her was "Whatever Happened to Miss Illinois?" on *Alcoa Premiere*. A reporter (Anthony George) investigates the life of a beauty queen (Lynley) who placed first runner up in the Queen of America pageant. She finds that her title does not help her much as an aspiring disillusioned model in New York City.

During the first season of *The Virginian*, a new ninety-minute western from Universal Television, Carol appeared in "The Man from the Sea" reuniting with director Herschel Daugherty from her first movie *The Light in the Forest*. However, her character was far removed from the sweet Shenandoe as here she was cast as an unstable miss keeping to the actress' desire to not get typecast as the wholesome ingénue. The series was loosely based on the novel *The Virginian, Horseman of the Plains*. It starred James Drury as the title character who only went by the moniker the Virginian and was the tough foreman of Shiloh Ranch which was owned by Judge Garth (Lee J. Cobb). Other ranch denizens included cowhands Trampas (Doug McClure) and Steve Hill (Gary Clarke) and Garth's niece Betsy (Roberta Shore).

Lynley's fellow guest stars were Tom Tryon and Shirley Knight - who would all soon have a major connection to Otto Preminger's *The Cardinal*. Playing twins, Carol is Judith the vivacious and outspoken one, while Knight's Molly is mousey and timid. They come to Medicine Bow to settle down. Molly opens a shop while Judith only dreams of traveling the world. A handsome lusty sailor named Kevin Doyle (Tryon) arrives and is interested in Molly but she spurns him. He then turns his attention to Judith who agrees to marriage but only if he murders her sibling. Judge Garth is suspicious of the sisters and investigating their background uncovers the truth about Judith.

Carol next received some of the best reviews of her career for her co-starring role opposite Peter Falk in "A Rage of Silence" on *The Dick Powell Theatre*. He played Martin a lonely deaf mute with behavioral issues and she was Elise who was also deaf and a teacher of sign language. Well-adjusted and effervescent, she helps Martin become a functioning member of society and even gets him a place to stay in the same boarding house. They begin spending time together outside the classroom as the volatile Martin's temperament begins to wane. However, he mistakes Elise's compassion and friendship for love unaware that her boyfriend Don (Fred Beir) intends to marry her. Jealous when she leaves Martin to spend time with Don, the enraged Martin flips out and violence ensues when he trails them to the seashore.

The episode's director Don Taylor called Lynley, "a pro. Very easy to work with. She's excellent."[103] The ending especially shows how difficult it is being deaf and unable to communicate in an emergency as Lynley's frantic Elise tries to get some of the beach denizens to help Don who is being pummeled by Martin. Even when the police arrive, they are at first stumped by Elise's behavior and obviously have no training to deal with the hearing-impaired. It most likely was an eye-opening episode for the day and brought attention to the problem.

In the *Los Angeles Times*, Cecil Smith found Carol to be "excellent" as the good-hearted teacher and Rick Du Bro writing in the *San Bernadino Sun* found her part "well-acted." He went on to describe this hard-hitting drama as "the kind of compassion and art one finds in a Nelson Algren skid row story." Carol received the most adulation from TV critic Percy Shain who raved in the *Boston Globe*, "The casting coup of the year—Peter Falk as a volcanic-tempered handyman, Carol Lynley as a sweet-natured teacher, and both members of that closely bound fraternity of deaf-mutes—turned a modest script into tense, seething drama ... These were magnificent portrayals of Emmy Award stature, made even more vivid by the fact that not a sound could pass through either's lips." A few months after Carol's episode aired, Shain slammed the Emmy Award nominating committee for overlooking "A Rage of Silence" and other deserving programs. In the Best Actress in a Dramatic Series category, he called the five nominees' performances "ordinary" and felt Lynley and some others deserved to be honored instead for their "vivid portrayals."[104]

*****

Deaf teacher Elise (Carol Lynley) instructs student Martin (Peter Falk) how to sign unaware that he has fallen in love with her in "A Rage to Silence" on *The Dick Powell Theatre* (Four Star Productions, 1963).

Producer Jerry Wald again wanted Carol for one of his featured films. He cast her as the small town sweetheart of restless Kenny Baird (Richard Beymer) who falls for an aging exotic dancer (a miscast Joanne Woodward in a role meant for Marilyn Monroe and needing someone with va-va-voom appeal) in *The Stripper* (1963) based on the William Inge play *A Loss of Roses*. It was an undemanding part and basically a waste of Lynley's talent.

Curtis Harrington was the Associate Producer on this. Its working title was the same as the play's *A Loss of Roses*. Prolific television director Franklin J. Schaffner was hired to helm his first motion picture and the screenplay was adapted by Meade Roberts (whom Harrington described as "the most intensely neurotic writer I had ever met."[105]). Roberts' prior movie script credits included the acclaimed stage play adaptation *Summer and Smoke* (1961). The movie had a few problems. Leading lady Joanne Woodward's breasts were too small to make a believable striptease artist (no surprise there) so they had to be augmented with a cast of her own breasts worn on top of the real ones. More impactful was the sudden, unexpected death of Jerry Wald before the movie was completed. With Wald no longer alive, there was no one to go up against Fox studio head Darryl F. Zanuck who thought the movie was too downbeat and took it out of the hands of its director. He forced the cutting of a few musical numbers (that Harrington said gave the movie "a slightly fanciful air"[106]) and a pivotal moment wherein Woodward's character attempts suicide by cutting her wrist with chards of glass. Harrington described it as "a disturbing, brilliantly acted scene, absolutely the dramatic high point of the film. Without it, the attitude of the characters at the end of the film made no sense."[107]

Not finished with screwing around with the movie, Zanuck then changed the title to the more exploitative *The Stripper*. Even with its new moniker and Woodward's fake tits, the movie received mediocre reviews and was not able to draw the masses. When mentioned, most critics felt that Lynley was wasted in her small role. Oscar winning designer Travilla, though, received an Academy Award nomination for Best Costume Design – Black and White. He lost to Piero Gherardi for Federico Fellini's 8½.

Carol was saddled with a nothing role that saw her wander in and out of the movie mooning over Beymer's character. She looked lovely in Travilla's creations, however, it was not an acting stretch in the least and did not further her career.

Although 20th Century-Fox was in the financial doldrums due to the cost overruns on the historical epic *Cleopatra*, they continued to hold Carol to the terms of their picture deal. Explaining her pact with Fox, Carol said, "Every time I was unavailable, or expressed disinterest, or had other things to do [including having a baby], they extended it for six months. It went on like that."[108] Despite what was reported in the media, she added, "I never had a picture deal with Columbia Pictures or Otto Preminger—he was not a picture deal kind of guy."[109] True, but Preminger was known for putting novice actresses (Jean Seberg, Jill Haworth, Barbara Bouchet, and Faye Dunaway) under personal contract so he could control their careers.

On the upside, Carol was still free to pursue work at other studios and landed two high profile roles at Columbia Pictures. She first auditioned for producer/director Otto Preminger, who was casting the highly sought after roles of priest Stephen Fermoyle and his ill-fated younger sister Mona, in his religious epic *The Cardinal* - based on the novel by Henry Morton Robinson. Carol got it, beating out Ann-Margret, Dolores Hart, Shirley Knight (who was offered but turned down the role of Mona's bigoted sister Florrie), and Pamela Tiffin. Tom Tryon was cast in the male lead over Robert Redford, Bradford Dillman, and Stuart Whitman, among others. Though the movie was loaded with characters, Mona had a few standout dramatic scenes that any young actress would have loved to play.

Carol though began filming *Under the Yum Yum Tree* first when producer Frederick Brisson chose her (over Ann-Margret and Tuesday Weld) for the female lead opposite Jack Lemmon. One actress who was chagrined that she did not get the part was Columbia contract player Stefanie Powers. She bemoaned, "I was a little bit frustrated with Columbia because they had given certain roles to other actresses who weren't under contract that I would have been right for, one of which was the movie version of a play I had gone to San Francisco to do, *Under the Yum Yum Tree*."[110]

Lynley's deal was completed when Brisson and Preminger were able to work out the shooting schedules for her on each movie. In *Yum Yum*, the role of a coed experimenting with living together platonically with her boyfriend was in complete juxtaposition to the melodramatic role of Mona. It was a perfect choice to show Hollywood how versatile she could be.

Lynley was now filming two movies simultaneously and to make it even more difficult she had to dye her hair black (wigs did not work) for *The Cardinal* and bleach back to blonde for *Yum Yum*. Recounting how the brunette look came about, Carol revealed that Preminger wanted her to have black hair and quoted him as saying, "'you are too pretty. We've got to dull you down. And after we finish, we will turn you back into a blonde. If all your hair falls out, we will buy you a wig.'"[111] Luckily, that was not necessary.

Life magazine published a story about Carol making both films with photos of her rehearsing the "sinuous tango" she performs in *The Cardinal* and having her hair dyed. Commenting on her natural flaxen hair, Carol said, "I look more ethereal ... but black brings my eyes out and gives me character."[112] Surprisingly, *Life* did not give Lynley the cover, but the following year she did grace the cover of one of its rivals, the *Saturday Evening Post*.

Under the Yum Yum Tree (1963), directed by David Swift and based on the Broadway play, was the beginning of Carol's progression to adult roles. The five character play, set in a single attic apartment in San Francisco's Telegraph Hill, was expanded to include perhaps a dozen or so speaking roles and extended the action to the UCLA campus, the Beverly Hills Hotel Crystal Room, a supermarket, and the exterior of the vast apartment complex. The latter was built on a huge soundstage, called Villa d'Este, but the cast and crew dubbed it the "Sin Bin."[113]

Carol played Robin a perky, enterprising college coed who tries living platonically with her boyfriend David (Dean Jones) to see if they are marriage compatible while staving off the lecherous advances of her playboy landlord Hogan (Lemmon). Commenting on working with the talented Jack Lemmon, Lynley raved during filming, "I find him marvelous, very creative, and so funny that I laugh all the time. Such people give a tremendous lift; when they create, you begin to act creatively too."[114] Tina Sinatra who was a fan of Carol's and worked with her years later in *Fantasy Island*, asked Jack Lemmon, who stated many times his dislike of the film and the character he played, about the actress since this was her favorite Carol Lynley movie. Per Tina, he replied, "I adored her."[115] Nice to know he did not hold his opinion about the movie against her.

Freddie Brisson launched a huge publicity campaign touting the beautfil blonde actress as the "Yum Yum Girl" following in the tradition of Clara Bow as the "It Girl" and Ann Sheridan as the "Oomph Girl." Despite her teenage protestations about not being the glamorous type and shrugging off cheesecake photos, the adult Carol Lynley willing accepted a complete makeover for the role with Don Feld designing her costumes appropriate for a college coed. It was reported that he was given a $25,000 budget just for Lynley's wardrobe alone. She had sixteen costume changes. He used the color of ice cream for each outfit: "a pistachio coat, a peach nightgown, a lime sherbet robe, a custard shift, a caramel car coat…"[116] George Masters created the "Yum Yum Coif," as it was publicized, for the actress. Her hair was longer now (just short of her shoulders) and he framed her fuller face with a more slimming lacquered hair style with the sides flipped up and no part coupled with "double rows of black false eyelashes [with her fair complexion]; red pouty lips."[117] When asked at the time what she thought of her new look, Carol confessed, "It's nice. I have a better figure now and I am older. I love it."[118]

The result of all their efforts truly paid off. Arlene Dahl described Carol as "a Botticelli angel (slender version) come to life with her blonde hair, translucent skin, and baby-blue eyes."[119] Moviegoers who hadn't seen Carol on screen since *Return to Peyton Place* were in for a pleasant shock. After the opening credits featuring James Darren singing the title tune while a couple dances under a prop tree on a bare soundstage, the live action shifts to David and Robin lying on the campus grounds under a Yum Yum tree. The first thing you notice is how Carol fabulously blossomed into adulthood—wholesome but playful and sexy. She projects the perfect quality for the audience to believe why her boyfriend wants to put a ring on her finger and why her lecherous landlord wants to seduce her.

Robin (Carol Lynley) listens intently to her landlord Hogan (Jack Lemmon) unaware of his lecherous designs on her in *Under the Yum Yum Tree* (Columbia, 1963).

As David proposes marriage, Robin protests and touts her outrageous plan to live together without having sex to see if they have "character compatibility." He thinks it is a wacky idea but reluctantly agrees to give it a shot. Surreptitiously, Irene (Edie Adams), Robin's professor and aunt, is vacating her apartment and the coed goes to look. The owner of the complex is a pushy, fast-talking, lech named Hogan (Jack Lemmon) who only rents to nubile young ladies. As Robin peers around corners and up and down stairs, the director and cameraman Joseph F. Biroc take full advantage and she is shot in some exploitative camera angles for emphasis. Robin mentions a roommate but does not say it is a man. Intrigued to have two beauties, or so he thinks, living across the hall, Hogan agrees and leases her the space. After he discovers that her roommate is a he and not a she and learning of Robin's crazy scheme, the rest of the movie has Hogan doing his best to sabotage it in quite a comical matter. His goal is to be the one to deflower the virginal beauty and not David. Looking on is his envious gardener Murphy (Paul Lynde) who lives vicariously through Hogan's playboy lifestyle and his bossy, disapproving wife and Hogan's maid, Dorcas (Imogene Coca).

The movie climaxes with David's drunken seduction plot. Not surprisingly, nobody climaxes since this is an early sixties sex comedy where everybody remains chaste. Fed up with the frustrating living situation, he sets out to seduce Robin with a little help from mezcal, romantic music, and poetry by E. E. Cummings. David gets his beloved pie-eyed ("When you get used to it, it tastes just like fruit juice," exclaims Robin grabbing the bottle). However, feeling guilty and realizing he is a trustworthy guy, he runs off into the night allowing the peeping Hogan to get his shot with the inebriated and frisky Robin.

The next morning, Hogan insists he had sex with someone. Actually, he blacked out while making a pass at Irene who delivers the most chauvinistic speech about marriage ever to come from the lips of a woman ("Darn his socks!?! Forgive her when she is a boob!?!") courtesy of the fantasy of male script writers. Irene leaves to marry her colleague while it is wedding bells too for Robin and David. Hogan is also abandoned by Dorcas and a disappointed Murph ("You're still aces with me," he quips) and vows now to only rent to men until a van of nubile coeds drives up looking for apartments quickly changing his mind. In the play, Hogan changes his philandering ways and proposes marriage to Irene.

Carol had some wonderful moments here, most notably her drunk scene where her boyfriend plots to deflower her. She gets some good laughs as she jokes throughout the planned seduction and then starts making aggressive advances on the stunned David, but critics mostly commented on her looks than comedic skills when the film was released in October of 1963. Margaret Harford of the *Los Angeles Times* called Carol "a peaches-and-cream beauty." Marjory Adams of the *Boston Globe* found her to be "young and attractive." Bosley Crowther commented, "Carol Lynley is surprisingly nimble and basically wholesome as the girl." The critic in *The Baltimore Sun* found Carol and Dean Jones to be "consistently appealing." Charles Moore of *The Atlanta Constitution* homed in more on overall performances and remarked, "It is just plain funny from start to finish without a false note being struck by the cast."

Under the Yum Yum Tree itself received mixed reviews. When critics did not find the sex comedy to be funny, they called it "smarmy," "offensive," and the critic in *Newsday* even quipping, "A Yum Yum tree grows in the gutter." With descriptions like that of course the moviegoers came in droves. Budgeted at $1.5 million, it brought in $5.0 million at the box office and was the 15th highest grossing movie of that year turning quite a profit to Columbia and producer Freddie Brisson.

What is ironic about the subject matter is that a few years later young couples shacking up without the benefit of marriage became almost the norm making *Under the Yum Yum Tree* instantly outdated. Good thing it came out when it did.

Carol revealed that it was after the making of *Under the Yum Yum Tree* when she was confronted by columnist Hedda Hopper about a vicious rumor making Carol out to be a homewrecker. She recalled,

> I always liked Hedda even though I had various interviews with her where you got nowhere because she already had the story in her head. One day while I was living in Beverly Hills, Hedda called me. She said, 'Well Carol I have a tip that you've been in Palm Springs with Freddie Brisson [who was married to Rosalind Russell].' I replied, 'Hedda, number one, I was not in Palm Springs with Freddie. Number two, I am a Catholic girl and I do not hang out with other people's husbands. And I have never been to Palm Springs in my life.' She seemed to appreciate the fact that I told her the straight story. It was the last time I ever spoke to her. Also, I knew Rosalind Russell. She was loved by everyone and I thought she was wonderful. I don't fool around with other people's husbands.[120]

*****

Carol Lynley had a much different filming experience on *The Cardinal* due to volatile director Otto Preminger who had one of the worst reputations with actors in Hollywood. Recalling her impressions about Preminger, Carol opined,

> Otto was a cineaste and I think he saw the end result before it was actually filmed, which most people really into cinema do. And he would lose his temper with the execution of it. He could tell you what he wanted done. He needed it done instantly. If you could not translate that instantly, he had no in-between. He'd go from very charming to Mount Vesuvius ... if you couldn't execute his ideas instantaneously that would create tension.[121]

What he did for the Jewish people with his movie *Exodus* in 1960, Preminger tried to do the same for Catholics with *The Cardinal* (1963). It traced Father Fermoyle's (Tom Tryon) elevation from Boston priest to Cardinal and the tribulations he faced along the way in a span of thirty years and goes from Boston to Vienna and Rome. Lynley plays Fermoyle's youngest sister, Mona, who, after her strict Irish Catholic family rejects her Jewish fiancé Benny (John Saxon) who refuses to convert after a failed attempt, runs off to become a dancehall prostitute. The unwed Mona ultimately dies in childbirth when her brother makes the difficult choice to save the baby and not the mother. Haunted by his decision, Fermoyle takes a sabbatical to teach a college course in Vienna where one of his students (Romy Schneider) pursues him romantically. He eventually rejects her and returns to the priesthood. Preminger was so impressed with Lynley's acting that he also offered her the role of Mona's daughter, Regina. Carol once joked that she was probably the only actress to ever give birth to herself on film.

It is well known that Tom Tryon did not get along with Otto Preminger who bullied the actor throughout the shoot. It was reported in one scene Tryon was so nervous holding a coffee cup and saucer that due to his shaking they had to fastened it to his arm so he would not drop it. When asked why she thought the director cast Tryon over more experienced actors and what it was like for him filming *The Cardinal*, Carol responded,

I don't know why Otto cast Tom. I think somewhere along the line though Otto realized he had made a mistake, but it was too late to correct without spending a lot of money. I loved Tom. But there was something in his psyche that was willing to be verbally beaten up like that by Otto. I'd think how come he doesn't say, 'Fuck it! Shove it up your ass, Otto!' But I'm from New York. I used to ask people around me why Tom just doesn't quit. Otto already had so much film on him and he was the centerpiece of the movie that it would have cost Otto at least a million dollars to start all over again with another actor. That is something actors instinctively understand. I suspected that Tom must have known that and he had some power. However, he kept taking the abuse and of course that made Otto go in deeper.[122]

Tryon was not the only actor who had problems with "Otto the Ogre," as he was nicknamed. Describing a scene when Otto would lose his temper, Carol shared,

On the set, it had to be done his way. If not, he would start getting agitated. Then when he got agitated you could see the veins start to pop on his quite bald head. When I would see that, I would think, 'Oh, God!' Then he'd turn bright red and start shouting and the actor would just fall apart. Otto's idea of a joke when the actor was quivering was that he'd come up to them and yell into their ear, 'relax!' The actor would fall apart even more. People were led away by assistants quite a lot.[123]

As Mona's daughter Regina, Carol had one scene in Rome and it was her first trip abroad. She was in Europe for a total of two days. She said at the time, "I spent a day and a half in Rome, one hour in Paris, a half-hour in Milan, six hours in Copenhagen, and an hour and a half in Greenland. Every

Father Fermoyle (Tom Tryon) tries to persuade his errant taxi dancer sister Mona (Carol Lynley) to come home as her lover Ramon (Jose Duval) looks on in *The Cardinal* (Columbia, 1963). *Billy Rose Theatre Division, The New York Public Library for the Performing Arts*

place we stopped I got out of the plane and looked around."[124] Air travel has come a long way since then and the actress would spend a lot more time traveling around Europe in the years ahead.

Carol came away from *The Cardinal* unscathed by Preminger. Most critics felt Carol did fine in her dual roles, but some thought she was a standout. Marjory Adams of the *Boston Globe* found her "touching as the little sister, and … radiant as the illegitimate but beloved daughter." The critic in the *Monthly Film Bulletin* raved that Lynley was "superb as tormented lover and sleazy tango-dancer." Perhaps, the most complimentary came from Richard Roud who remarked in *Sight and Sound*, "Certain seemingly conventional scenes in *The Cardinal* deserve to become anthology pieces: a vulnerable and surprisingly moving Carol Lynley confessing the sin of lust to her priest brother. The scene gains its emotional intensity by the subtle variations in pitch and volume—the confessional whisper that bursts out passionately and is then quickly repressed." Mona then runs out into the night and is not seen until months later.

Another powerful scene with Lynley is when Fermoyle confronts a tarted up Mona and her Latin lover at a dance hall after they perform a lusty Tango. He begs his sister to come home since her absence is breaking their mother's heart. While drinking a beer, she sarcastically asks if he will hear her confession. When her brother refuses, she agrees to come home and requests if she could bring Jose to meet their mother. "He drinks and gambles a lot, but you can tell her he is *a Catholic*. He is also a Spic." When her brother mentions Benny, Mona begins to break down but pulls herself together, forcefully tells her brother that she is through with his God and goes back to the dance floor. Throughout the movie, Carol convincingly runs a gamut of emotions from sorrow that her family will not accept her Jewish boyfriend, to happiness when he agrees to convert, to desperation when he decides to remain in his religion and she confesses to her brother that they had sex, to bitterness after she has run away and become a prostitute. Her desperate cry of "Stephen!" in her last scene, as Mona is being wheeled into the delivery room after her brother instructs the doctors to save the baby and not the mother, is haunting. *Variety* even had Carol on its short-list for a possible Best Actress Academy Award nomination. Alas, it did not come to be.

Like *Under the Yum Yum Tree*, *The Cardinal* was a box office smash placing sixth on the list of highest grossing movies of 1964. Both movies were even recognized come awards season. *Under the Yum Yum Tree* received Golden Globe nominations for Best Comedy and Best Actor - Comedy/Musical for Jack Lemmon. *The Cardinal* surprisingly won the Golden Globe for Best Drama and was named one of the Ten Best Films of the Year by the National Board of Review. John Huston won the Golden Globe for Best Supporting Actor but fellow nominees Tom Tryon for Best Actor – Drama and Romy Schneider for Best Actress – Drama did not. Huston was also nominated for an Academy Award as was Otto Preminger for Best Director. He also received Golden Globe and Directors Guild nominations. *The Cardinal* received an additional four Oscar nominations in the technical categories (color cinematography, art direction, costume design, and film editing). The surprise omission was for Jerome Moross' exquisite score that Preminger used intermittently throughout the movie. Author and film music historian Royal S. Brown opined that the exclusion of Moross's "warm, varied, and understated score" from the list of nominees was "one additional proof of how just far afield Hollywood has tended to be in its musical judgement."[125]

*****

Carol Lynley was now at the pinnacle of her movie stardom. However, it came with a price—the collapse of her marriage to Mike Selsman. She confessed, "I want to be a glamorous movie star who can act. I'm not a housewife. I tried it and found it just wasn't for me."[126] This resulted in a bitter divorce and child custody battle, which the press had a field day covering. While Carol refrained from saying anything too negative about her husband, Selsman could not help himself. He remarked in just one of many interviews he gave at the time, "She was an entirely different girl when I married her. She has now become the complete movie star. If that's what she wants, I do not wish to stand in the way of her unhappiness."[127]

Asked his observations about the marriage, Lynley's brother opined, "I would only say again that Carol did an about face telling everybody she wanted to get married and have a lot of kids. She then decided she wanted to be a working actress instead. That is about all I know in terms of their relationship. I saw Carol infrequently by that point. They were separated for a while before they divorced but he still came around. I know one time her car had nearly bald tires. Without even asking her, Mike just took the car and bought new tires for it."[128]

When the dust cleared, Carol reportedly had to give Selsman $25,000 in community property and received from him a modest monthly amount for child support. At that time, her husband was not the only relation that disappeared from her life—so did Carol's mother.

Recalling what transpired between them, David Jones Lee recounted, "As I said, my mother was a professional mother. There is a natural tension between a woman and her teenaged daughter. Add on top of that a professional tension between them. As a child working many hours per day, the mother becomes the director, the handler, the business adviser, the manager. It's a recipe for disaster. My mother couldn't let go and kept calling Carol's agents working around her. She'd talk to different people and say, 'You should tell Carol this. You should tell Carol to do that.' It came to the point where Carol decided to break off all contact with my mother, but not at first with the rest of the family. That was a very difficult period for my mother. It was horrible. I was living at home and had to listen to her for years after. Carol kind of erased my mother from her life."[129]

Perhaps due to the stress of her divorce and the issues with her mother, Carol may have unknowingly rubbed a few of her co-stars the wrong way. Regarding the actors she worked with in *The Cardinal*, Jill Haworth commented, "The only person I did not like was Carol Lynley. I just did not understand people who couldn't get over themselves."[130] Writer Peer J. Oppenheimer remarked that Carol had a "reputation for being 'tough, preoccupied, and egotistical.'"[131] This personality issue would rear its head again for Carol with another co-star when making *The Pleasure Seekers*.

Personal interactions aside, based on her performances in *Under the Yum Yum Tree* and *The Cardinal* and their box office success, Lynley was named one of 1964's Stars of the Future – Female in the All-American Screen Favorites Poll. Voters included newspaper and magazine editors; theater owners; and the working press. Lynley placed fourth behind Patty Duke, Annette Funicello, and Elke Sommer, and ahead of Jill St. John and Tippi Hedren.

Carol did better in another poll. Writing for *Woman's Day*, columnist Hollis Alpert contacted several producers and studios executives asking them to rank which actors and actresses they thought would be filmdom's next superstars. The list of eight wildly differed from the list submitted from movie magazine editors where Connie Stevens, Richard Chamberlain, Ann-Margret, and Suzanne Pleshette top lined. The biggest surprise in the studio big wig poll was that Carol Lynley was the highest-ranking actress behind James Garner, Steve McQueen, and Albert Finney, and ahead of Hayley Mills, Romy Schneider, Peter O'Toole, and George Peppard.[132]

An anonymous movie executive explained why he thought Lynley ranked so high and opined, "The money pictures are going her way. She has a dramatic part in *The Cardinal*, has a good comedy in *Under the Yum Yum Tree*, and is being starred at Fox in *Shock Treatment*. She's developed a considerable amount of faith in her abilities."[133] Alpert added, "This honey-blonde girl of twenty-one has a quality of niceness, an air of seriousness about her work, and improves from picture to picture."[134]

Lynley was by this time far from a newcomer, but this demonstrates that the motion picture world still recognized her talent and potential. They had tremendous faith in her and were waiting for that one key role that would catapult her into super stardom. Unfortunately, 20th Century-Fox did not come through for her.

Carol was now in high demand based on her well-received performances and the financial success of *Under the Yum Yum Tree* and *The Cardinal*. A few projects announced (including Columbia Pictures wanting to reteam her with Dean Jones in a remake of the Rita Hayworth musical *Cover Girl*) never reached fruition and one lead role Carol auditioned for in the comedy *Goodbye Charlie* went to Debbie Reynolds.

Instead, the more mature Carol played up her new sex kitten image in two less than successful Fox films, the thriller *Shock Treatment* and the colorful romantic travelogue *The Pleasure Seekers*. Carol was not forced by the studio to make either and remarked, "I don't remember why I did *Shock Treatment*, but I had no objections to it. And I had absolutely no objections in doing *The Pleasure Seekers* whatsoever because it was filmed in Spain and I speak Spanish—need I say more?"[135]

Shock Treatment (1964) was Carol's first foray into big screen suspense. Fox bought the rights to Winfred Van Atta's novel of the same name soon after it was published in 1961. Studio head Darryl F. Zanuck's son Richard was a producer at the time and he commissioned a screenplay because the story, set in a mental health institution, intrigued him. It was on track to go before the cameras, when the senior Zanuck halted all production due to the financial behemoth *Cleopatra* that almost bankrupted the studio.

When production resumed a year or two later, the younger Zanuck was now in charge and he handed the project to producer Aaron Rosenberg and his production company Arcola Pictures with 20th Century-Fox distributing. Rosenberg felt the book had the makings for a fine suspense picture because it had "fantastic characters and an interesting background."[136] Sydney Boehm was hired to write a new screenplay. A former reporter, he visited a mental facility while working on the script and spent the night in a ward on two separate occasions. Commenting on his massive rewriting of the script, he said, "I wouldn't have tried to make a movie, following the novel. It was completely unbelievable. This is unbelievable enough. But if it's done right it could draw a big audience."[137] Unfortunately it did not.

Denis Sanders was chosen to direct. He won an Oscar in 1954 for Best Short Subject for his UCLA filmmaking master's thesis *A Time Out of War* and only had two features under his belt, *Crime and Punishment USA* (1959) with George Hamilton and the well-received *War Hunt* (1962) with John Saxon and Robert Redford. Having never worked on a thriller, a gung-ho Sanders enthusiastically commented, "We are not making a message picture. This is a great picture for a director ... This is just one hell of a yarn. The purpose is to thrill and shock the audience."[138]

The producer employed three actors (Stuart Whitman, Carol Lynley, and Roddy McDowall) who had picture deals with Fox— that was perhaps the reason why freelancing actor Anthony Perkins lost out on the lead role, for which he reportedly campaigned. If true, he would have at least brought the film some notoriety and more interest by the public to boost its box office grosses. Stuart Whitman was a fine journeyman's actor but really had no mass or cult following. Here he played a struggling actor named Dale Nelson, hired to feign insanity and get committed to a nut house so he could learn where crazy gardener Martin Ashley (McDowall) had stashed the loot he stole after murdering his employer. Lynley was another patient and, after a four-year absence from the big screen, Lauren Bacall was lured to play the facility's head doctor Edwina Beighley. It was a role like ones played by other older actresses who had gone the thriller route at this time such as Bette Davis and

Carol Lynley as manic-depressive Cynthia Lee Albright in *Shock Treatment* (20th Century-Fox, 1964).

Joan Crawford in *Whatever Happened to Baby Jane?* and Olivia de Havilland in *Hush...Hush, Sweet Charlotte*.

Ironically, the exterior scenes at the mental institution were filmed outside the grounds of Fox studio's administration office buildings where no doubt many a nut was employed. Another interesting fact about the movie was that for 1963 it cast several African American actors including Ossie Davis, Pauline Myers, and Lili Clark in varied non-stereotypical roles such as psychiatrists, technicians, and inmates.

Briefly recalling the movie, Carol remarked,

> I liked working with Lauren Bacall. It was an honor. Stuart and I had known each other forever. It was always a pleasure to work with him. I don't remember too much about Denis Sanders other than him being there. Nothing about him stands out that much. I think this was the first time I worked with Roddy. We worked together so much over the years that we had this running gag. He would come to makeup or I would and he'd say, 'Oh, God not her again!' He was joking, I *think*!?![139]

Carol as Cynthia Lee Albright pops up as one of the patients being bussed to the looney bin. On board is also Dale, using the name Arthur, who has gotten committed as planned. He is immediately attracted to Cynthia no doubt due to her fragile blonde beauty, which sticks out like a sore thumb amongst the busload of crazies. She panics though when he touches her. After the new patients are settled in the hospital, Arthur searches for Cynthia to apologize.

Cynthia is next seen under hypnosis as Dr. Walden (Pauline Myers) questions her about the past and Dr. Beighley and other doctors observe from behind a one-way mirror. A frantic Cynthia does not want to remember what happened to her. She rolls her eyes and thrashes her head trying to fight the memories. With her disheveled blonde mane being tossed around, Lynley looks like she is performing an Ann-Margret musical number. It is no wonder why the critic in *Variety* described her as "a Lustre Crème lunatic." Beighley finally has had enough and the doctor brings Cynthia back to the present.

After rushing out of a dance social, Cynthia reveals to Arthur her troubled background with a kindly father who died young leaving her with a stern mother who forbade any interactions with boys. Even seen walking and talking with one she considered 'cheap.' The woman warped her poor daughter's mind so much that as an adult Cynthia Lee freaks out by the mere touch of a man. This is Carol's big scene in the movie and she is touching. Though Arthur tries to prevent it, Cynthia then undergoes a round of shock treatment. Afterwards, Cynthia becomes quite inconsequential to the plot. At the denouement, Arthur and Edwina follow an escaped Martin back to his employer's house where he digs up the loot. However, it is revealed to be just burnt ashes - to the horror of Edwina who loses her mind over it since she was counting on it for research funding. Cynthia is last seen being released with Arthur from the institution while the crazed Dr. Beighley is now interred as the prize patient.

Shock Treatment was not received well by the critics or moviegoers alike. Jerry Goldsmith's "creepy" score received the most praise. Despite what Denis Sanders and Aaron Rosenberg promised, the film is not that terrifying or suspenseful. For thriller fans, it disappoints though it does keep you mildly interested despite being able to guess what is going to happen before the characters do. Reviewers were harsh. "A bad movie that will drive you right out of the theater," quipped Margaret Harford in the *Los Angeles Times*. Other adjectives used to describe the movie from critics around the country included "tasteless," "hokey," "silly," "depressing," and "distasteful."

Boxoffice, which tried to find the good in any movie, did here as well and called it a "tense drama" and "entertaining from its shock value." Howard Thompson, of the *New York Times*, found the acting "not bad" and offered, "Minus the spooky music, the general tone of bland sensationalism, and a pat, almost farcical ending, this slick picture might have made a genuinely suspenseful chiller."

Japanese promotional ad for *Shock Treatment* (20th Century-Fox, 1964) with Carol Lynley and Stuart Whitman (center) and Roddy McDowall and unidentified actor in (upper left).

The film's biggest problem was a lack of suspense. Stuart Whitman plays the lead in a too macho heroic fashion registering not a hint of him losing his mind when committed to the asylum. The role needed a more sensitive actor such as Anthony Perkins who would have kept the audience more on edge to see if he would succumb to the treatments imposed on him by the wicked Dr. Beighley. As for Carol, the adoration most critics had for her as a teenager was fading and she received some harsh reviews. The film was a major letdown after the success of her two previous movies.

A weak box office tally was most likely due to the tepid reviews and the subject matter, which kept mainstream moviegoers away. The more adventurous also did not come either probably because the movie was not exploitative enough. *Shock Treatment* grossed less than $1 million. Its box office chances were also hurt by the similarly themed and titled film *Shock Corridor* from director Samuel Fuller that was released a few months prior in 1963 to better reviews and has developed a cult following over the years.

*****

Next up for Carol was the romantic travelogue *The Pleasure Seekers*. One of the most popular and frivolous subgenres in Hollywood history was the 'three girls looking for romance' movies. It hit its zenith with the 1954 Academy Award-winning *Three Coins in the Fountain* from 20th Century-Fox and directed by Jean Negulesco. A trio of young women (Dorothy McGuire, Maggie McNamara, and Jean Peters) living in Rome set out to-trap-themselves-a-man. The movie was such a hit that Fox decided to remake it ten years later as *The Pleasure Seekers* with the same director but with the locale shifted from Rome to Madrid. It follows the typical pattern where lovelorn girls get boys, lose boys, and get boys again for a happy ending. Despite the predictable plot, *The Pleasure Seekers* is just so well produced by David Weisbart, with gorgeous overly made-up gals and handsome guys in front of beautiful Spanish scenery accompanied by a catchy musical score making it one fun film.

In *The Pleasure Seekers*, Ann-Margret plays Fran, a sardine–loving dancer and singer who falls in love with a poor, but proud, Spanish doctor (Andre Lawrence). Carol, in primo sex kitten mode, is Maggie a pouty newswire secretary who thinks she loves her boss (Brian Keith) who has a steely-eyed wife (Gene Tierney, a last minute replacement for Dina Merrill) while ignoring American playboy reporter Pete (Gardner McKay). Pamela Tiffin is Susie the naïve tourist ("I know everything about Spain but Spanish.") who catches the eye of notorious rich Spanish cad Emilio LaCayo (Tony Franciosa).

With the casting locked, gossip maven Louella Parsons weighed in and cattily wrote in her column, "I must say that my young friend, Richard Zanuck [20th Century-Fox's studio head], is a brave boy for he has set Carol Lynley, Ann-Margret, and Pamela Tiffin—all in the same picture. Doesn't Richard know how ambitious this trio of cute dolls is? While the exteriors will be done in Spain, interiors will be done in Hollywood. I personally think the attempt at scene-stealing will go on all over the place. The free-for-all—or film, if you insist, starts right after the first of the year."[140]

As the cameras began to roll in Spain, the actors' frustrations and unhappiness began to immediately emerge from the set. Most of the major players were contractually bound to appear in the movie and showed up to fulfill their obligations and collect their pay checks. And most went on record regarding their negative feelings towards the script. Ann-Margret and Gardner McKay were most vocal about their displeasure and said so to the press. It should be no surprise then when Pamela Tiffin stated, "Making *The Pleasure Seekers* was strange. Nobody connected with anyone. When working people are very competitive or are only after money, it is agony to work with them because they bring their hang-ups to the set. I tried to make friends with Ann-Margret and Carol Lynley. But I think both of them at that time weren't interested in friendship with another woman. Carol was especially reserved and aloof. In retrospect, I recall she just had a baby and therefore was entitled to be private."[141]

Carol was a bit surprised that Pamela felt that way and her feelings toward the movie were different because she was excited to be working in Spain.

Roommates Maggie (Carol Lynley) and Susie (Pamela Tiffin) primp before attending Susie's first Madrid party in *The Pleasure Seekers* (20th Century-Fox, 1964).

Exploring the country and working with Brian Keith, who she liked immensely, were the highlights for her. She then added,

> I liked Pamela and Ann-Margret. Gardner McKay was alright. He was sort of there. I didn't spend a lot of time around him off-set. While we were working, I didn't have any problems with him whatsoever. Jean Negulesco was very flamboyant. He had been making movies since the late thirties and he had a kind of old-fashioned gentility to him. He treated his actresses, and actors, with a European charm.[142]

The Pleasure Seekers is pure candy-coated kitschy entertainment. Though Pamela Tiffin steals the movie with her ditzy character trying to outmaneuver Franciosa's master player when it comes to the game of amor, Carol has two standout moments. The first is when her Maggie accompanies flighty Susie to her first Spanish party and a frustrated Maggie tries to school her friend on the caddish ways of Emilio who is in attendance with a date. Both actresses are visually stunning here (Tiffin with her hair in a French Twist and wearing an elegant black dress with a sparkling black-and-white patterned wrap around her arms and Lynley wearing a lovely powder blue sparkling dress with matching shawl) and play off each other quite well.

Much later in the film, before Maggie can wallow in the sadness of her brokenhearted friends who have decided to return to the States, she is invited to a party by her boss Paul. She gets dolled up in a beautiful skintight beige dress with black embroidery, which came from the noted Spanish fashion designer Cristóbal Balenciaga. Carol added, "That is why the dress looked so good. Jean Negulesco knew Balenciaga. The costume supervisor took me to their fashion house where they created the dress for me. I met the designer and he was great."[143]

Hosted by his friend, the "party" is a swanky get together where married men go with their beautiful young mistresses. The sneaky couple is unknowingly trailed by Paul's wife Jane who watches the cozy duo in their cab from behind and then crashes the festivities uninvited. Like the ladies' room showdown in *Valley of the Dolls*, Jane confronts Maggie about her feelings for Paul. The scene builds with intensity as Maggie continues brushing her hair as Jane digs into her until the secretary explodes. She flings her hairbrush at the wall and stands up to confront Jane. Maggie accuses Jane's indifference to her husband as the cause for his wandering eye and says she pities her. A furious Jane slaps Maggie across the face and sneers, "How dare you feel sorry for me you little tramp." Jane rushes out of the party with Paul trailing after her. Pete comes to Maggie's rescue and escorts her out. Carol recalls shooting this catty scene with Gene Tierney, one of the movie's most memorable, and said,

> I was in awe. *I am going to do a scene with Gene Tierney! Wow!* I grew up watching her movies on TV and seen almost all her work. I thought she was wonderful. I had to be mean to her and I found that difficult because it is not in my nature. But of course, the part called for it. She was quiet and quite thoughtful but she seemed a bit sad. When we were shooting the scene, an AD came up to me and said, 'Carol, I hope you don't mind but we have given Miss Tierney the same dressing room that you have.' I exclaimed, 'No I do not mind, are you kidding!?!' When it came to the part where she slapped me, *she really slapped me*! I don't get hit a lot but getting slapped by Gene Tierney is not bad.[144]

Lynley then gets her big moment and plays drunk just as amusingly as she did in *Under the Yum Yum Tree*. No doubt it was even more difficult here considering she was acting opposite the stiff Gardner McKay. On the steps where a statue of Don Quixote is displayed, an inebriated Maggie rehashes the night and says, "She called me a little tramp." She admits she fell in love with Paul but wiped his wife Jane right out of her mind. Remorseful and depressed, Maggie clutches Pete and wants his advice on what to do next. Pete drives her home and as they pull up in front of her house, she finishes the sad tales of Fran and Andres, and Susie and Emilio. "Nice girls," she says. "Really rather nice—what happens to us? We all crash into flames." She then bemoans that even the voyeur across the alley is not interested in them any longer. "We're too old for him," she exclaims before collapsing into Pete's arms. Maggie asks Pete to kiss her and as he makes his move, she passes out cold.

Jane Barton (Gene Tierney) confronts her husband's secretary Maggie (Carol Lynley) after catching them in a romantic clinch in *The Pleasure Seekers* (20th Century-Fox, 1964).

Reviews for *The Pleasure Seekers* were mixed. Most critics praised Daniel L. Fapp's colorful cinematography of Spain and the Prado's art masterpieces that looked glorious in Cinemascope; Lionel Newman's musical score (which surprisingly scored an Academy Award nomination); and the Flamenco dancing by the renowned Antonio Gades. What transpired in front of the beautiful Spanish scenery was not as well received by the critics of the day. Reviewers who did like the movie used words like "diverting," "pleasant," "frothy," "enjoyable," and "appealing" to describe it. Many negative reviews were also received in sometimes a cruel but witty manner, such as "Film is aimed at the cliché seekers," per Mike McGrady of *Newsday*.

All three actresses are made up and styled gorgeously in *The Pleasure Seekers*. Ann-Margret shakes her wild mane, sings, and dances extremely well. Her dramatic scenes however, particularly when she cries or makes the attempt, are laughable. Carol pouts prettily as a secretary whose only visible job duties seem to be making coffee and dusting off her boss's desk—so much for that college paid education. If Negulesco wanted to be more "with-it 1964," she should have been a reporter. Carol does though fare better acting-wise than Ann-Margret due to her ladies' room confrontation and her drunken scene near the end. Pamela Tiffin has the most rounded part and juggles the dramatic, comedy and romantic scenes quite well. She also gets the most talented leading man (Franciosa) and the best exterior scenes in Spain.

When all is said and done, Jean Negulesco's updated trio of cuties was not far removed from their fifties' counterparts. As the critic of *The Times of India* so rightfully noted, "The good little girls play at being bad, talk glibly about last year's problems, but settle for that thin gold band every time, bless their conventional little hearts."[145]

The Pleasure Seekers wound up grossing an estimated $2.0 million domestically - barely breaking even. An additional $1.2 million worldwide gross helped it generate a small profit. In comparison, *Three Coins in the Fountain* reaped $5 million in the U.S. alone and was one of the Top Ten highest grossing films for 1954.

The disappointing box office take was caused by Fox, which planned to release *The Pleasure Seekers* in mid-January 1965 with a big launch premiere. However, problems arose at the studio. Notre Dame filed an injunction against Fox charging the studio "had illegally misappropriated the name, symbols, and prestige of the university" in the movie *John Goldfarb, Please Come Home*. It was a confusing, unfunny comedy about Notre Dame's football team going to Fawzia, a fictitious Middle Eastern country, to play an exhibition game and forced to lose on orders from the CIA. The movie was supposed to open in over 200 theaters across the nation. Fox had to pull it and offered *The Pleasure Seekers* as a replacement. Most theaters accepted, so *The Pleasure Seekers* snuck into theaters without fanfare or promotion. In fact, ads for *John Goldfarb* were still running because it was too late to remove them. This move severely hurt the box office chances of the movie, which unfortunately was the innocent victim of the lawsuit between Fox and Notre Dame.

An interesting side note to *The Pleasure Seekers* is that three years later David Weisbart produced another three-girl movie called *Valley of the Dolls*. Though it was reported that Ann-Margret was considered for Neeley O'Hara, Carol Lynley was not a contender for the role of Anne Welles, which was surprising considering that the character in the book was a blonde blue-eyed model. Carol had the perfect glacial beauty and modeling background to bring the character to life. Asked what her relationship with Weisbart was like, Carol answered, "It was great! I remember him quite well. He was extremely polite and well-spoken. He told you what he wanted and I had no problems with him whatsoever. I didn't know anything about *Valley of the Dolls* perhaps because I was working on something else at the time."[146] Considering that they got along quite nicely, it is mind boggling why Weisbart didn't think of Carol for his camp classic. She would have been perfect for icy Anne. However, by that time she had been spending most of her time in London and perhaps out-of-sight, out of mind?

After *The Pleasure Seekers* completed production, Lynley purposely stayed unemployed because she needed the break. She commented, "I used to fret when I wasn't working. But no more."[147] She revealed she spent her down time caring for her daughter Jill, buying antiques, and "just loafing."[148] She also made the occasional talk or game show appearance (i.e. *Girl Talk*; *The Celebrity Game*, *You Don't Say!*) no doubt to keep her face in the public eye.

It was during this period when she was introduced to new director in town, Roman Polanski, with whom she became close friends (per Polanski writing in his 1984 memoir they were briefly lovers). The Polish filmmaker was riding high due to the success of his movie *Knife in the Water* (1962) and was making the studio rounds. Recounting her first meeting with him, she said in *People* magazine,

> Roman Polanski asked me out on a date. He wanted to go to Disneyland. I don't know how Federico Fellini got into the act. Roman spoke little English, Fellini spoke Italian, and I was speaking French and Spanish. Then we went on this ride where you get into a boat and go through a tunnel with these dolls and hear, 'It's a small world after all.' Roman loved it. Fellini and I had to go on it with him four times.[149]

Reportedly, Polanski wrote his classic psychological horror film *Repulsion* (1965) with Carol in mind. He even named his antagonist after her. Lynley was offered the movie but was purportedly turned off by the script and heeded the misguided advice of her agent not to do it. Catherine Deneuve stepped in instead. It would not be the last time her agent steered her in the wrong direction and Carol admitted one of her biggest faults was staying loyal to him. She revealed that she changed agents only a few times throughout her career.

After about five months of inactivity, Carol made a return to television after a two-year absence from the small screen. She accepted the role of a young American girl who volunteers as a Red Cross nurse behind enemy lines at the Battle of Verdun in the WWI drama "The Fliers" on *Bob Hope Presents the Chrysler Theatre*. Her co-stars included John Cassavetes as a renegade American pilot of the French Escadrille and Chester Morris (whom she worked with on Broadway in *Blue Denim*) as his commanding officer.

Commenting on the show back in 1965, Carol said it was Emmy nominated writer David Rayfiel's script that impressed her because her role "ranges from tender scenes of romance to the shattering brutality of war."[150] Reflecting on that, Carol added, "I've just been lucky, but I've never before been faced with the shock of anything remotely resembling battlefield casualties."[151]

"The Fliers" was well-received, with the critic from the *New York Daily News* raving that "it is an exciting and romantic chapter from 1916" and a "robust drama." As for the performances, they found Cassavetes "excellent as was Carol Lynley ... and Chester Morris."

The actress next received much publicity from two print publications. She was one of the main contenders chosen by *The Philadelphia Daily News* in February 1965 to be Hollywood's next Love Goddess and to follow on the heels of Marilyn Monroe. Each day one actress was given a full page spread in the newspaper. Others vying for the crown were Ann-Margret, Carroll Baker, Sandra Dee, Mia Farrow, Sue Lyon, Suzanne Pleshette, Lee Remick, Jill St. John, Elke Sommer, Connie Stevens, and Tuesday Weld.

Becoming more provocative and perhaps in a major attempt at winning that Love Goddess mantle, Carol graced the pages of Hugh Hefner's *Playboy* magazine the following month. Taking her sex kitten persona to the highest level, she posed semi-nude in a pictorial entitled, "Carol Lynley Grows Up" discreetly baring her breasts and derriere. Reportedly, Carol personally chose Sam Shaw (a talented photographer who shot the iconic photo of Marilyn Monroe with her skirt blowing up while standing on a subway grate used to promote *The Seven Year Itch*) to take the pictures. It was a daring move for the time, but she did it under advisement from her agent who felt it would help her progress to adult roles and leave the ingénues to Sandra Dee and Connie Stevens. If the goal was to jettison her teenybopper fan base, it worked.

Her pictorial was published in March 1965 shortly before producer Bill Sargent was looking for his new Jean Harlow. Coincidentally, Lynley's photo spread appeared four months after Carroll Baker, slated to play Jean Harlow for producer Joseph E. Levine, disrobed for the magazine. The Hollywood establishment was not surprised with Baker's nudie pictures, after her sexy role in *The Carpetbaggers* and her appearance at a press conference in a see-through dress, but they were shocked about Lynley's even though the photos were tastefully done. The pretty actress was taken to task with Louella Parsons leading the charge calling her, "young and foolish."[152]

Having to defend herself in constant interviews, the free-spirited Lynley frankly admitted she posed because she just wanted to and felt just wonderful wearing not a stitch of clothing. At the time she asked, "What's all the excitement about? It's only skin."[153]

Carol's family was not surprised about her decision to disrobe. Per Daniel Jones Lee, "We understood that Carol was trying to jettison that teenage Barbie doll image. She wanted to be taken seriously as an adult actress. I never brought it up to her when we spoke. It was strictly a career move."[154]

Considering Carol's earlier aspirations to be taken seriously doing theater, it seems out of place for her to go the nudity route to achieve that same goal. It is hard to determine what affect, good or bad, this had on Lynley's career. She had already progressed to adult roles (*Under the Yum Yum Tree*, *The Cardinal*, *The Pleasure Seekers*) unlike some others of her ilk, so it was not necessary. Whatever effects it had; it was a courageous choice. Prior to March 1965, most actresses who disrobed for the magazine were usually aspiring unknown starlets who became Playmates (i.e. Stella Stevens, Teri Hope, Joan Staley, Yvette Vickers, Delores Wells, Marianne Gaba, etc.), fifties blonde bombshells who exuded sex (i.e. Marilyn Monroe, Kim Novak, Jayne Mansfield, etc.), or more free-spirited European sexpots (i.e. Anita Ekberg, Elsa Martinelli, Brigitte Bardot, Elke Sommer, etc.). Not many already established American actresses took their clothes off in print.

Lynley became a bit of a trailblazer and she was followed by many an actress into the pages of *Playboy*. Diane McBain admitted in her memoir that Carol was the reason she agreed to pose nude for *Playboy* despite her trepidation. She revealed, "I went ahead with the shoot. After all, Carol Lynley, whom my mother thought looked just like me in *Under the Yum Yum Tree*, was a *Playboy* centerfold [*sic*] a couple of years before and the exposure hadn't hurt her career. Carol was still working in spite of her nude photos, maybe even more than before. So, I surmised the photo session was worth a try."[155]

Despite her satisfaction with the photo shoot, McBain had a change of heart and cancelled (though the pictures surfaced years later). She quipped, "Forget what Carol Lynley did, I didn't want anyone under my yum yum tree."[156] Though McBain backed out and had her pictorial squashed, others did not, including Sherry Jackson, Sharon Tate, Joanna Pettet, Barbara McNair, Lana Wood, and Alexandra Hay who appeared semi-nude in *Playboy*. Years later, Carol was still defending her decision to pose nude and remarked,

> I still cannot believe the hoopla that surrounded that pictorial. My agent suggested I do it because it would be good for my career. Growing up in Manhattan, I'm very liberal so I agreed. It was very tame—before they started to show pubic hair. I firmly believe there is no evil in nudity.[157]

In contrast to her exposing her half-naked body, also at this time Carol revealed her more intellectual side when she was the guest writer for the vacationing Arlene Dahl who had a weekly syndicated newspaper column. It usually focused on women's issues from fashion, to health, to beauty. Carol wrote about how important it is for women to be able to converse and to learn the art of conversation. How a woman should be able to "listen, speak, give knowledgeable opinions, respect the other person's opinions."[158] To achieve this ability, Carol strongly recommended to Dahl's audience, "Read everything you can get your hands on: daily newspapers; the weekly news magazine, the bestsellers, and an occasional classic. Take a half hour a day to read for fun and knowledge. You'll be surprised to see how it can change your life."[159] It is not surprising that this was the advice Carol advocated since she was an avid reader for her entire life.

*****

While Lynley's bare breasts and shapely derriere were being ogled across the country by horny teenage boys and *Playboy*'s more mature subscribers, Bill Sargent was about to begin shooting his $1.5 million Electronovision black-and-white production of *Harlow* starring Dorothy Provine in the title role. This was not to be confused with producer Joseph E. Levine's elaborate big budget color production also called *Harlow* starring Carroll Baker for Paramount Pictures.

Electronovision was like shooting a live TV show or stage production employing multiple cameras getting all the angles simultaneously and in sequence. The chosen shots were then transferred by cable to a mobile station for recording on a modified motion picture camera. Kinescope tape was used then transferred in the film laboratory to 35mm prints

Sargent's *Harlow* featured a script by screenwriter Karl Tunberg, an Academy Award nominee for *Tall, Dark and Handsome* and *Ben-Hur*, and was to be directed by Alex Segal who directed many a live TV drama during the fifties. The cast also included Efrem Zimbalist, Jr., Hurd Hatfield, Barry Sullivan, Hermione Baddeley, Michael Dante, and Judy Garland as Mama Jean. It played up Harlow's start as a bit player in Laurel and Hardy films and other movies; her home life with a grasping mother and ner'er-do-well stepfather; her discovery and rise to stardom in *Hell's Angels*; her doomed marriage to ill-fated studio executive Paul Bern; her love for the fictitious William Mansfield (a disguised William Powell); and her death.

Dorothy Provine was pushed out as Harlow by Bill Sargent who was not happy with her performance and was now desperate to recast since he was in a race to beat Levine's movie to the silver screen. According to a friend, Jayne Mansfield campaigned mightily for the part to little avail.[160] To find a replacement, Bill Sargent reportedly had an artist go through the Players Directory and draw Harlow's platinum-blonde tresses on each actress who might be right for the part. When he came to Carol, they thought they found the perfect fit and offered her the role. Though she stated that she knew nothing of Jean Harlow or of the rival movie, she accepted to get the chance to work with Judy Garland as her mother. Alas it was short-lived and by the time rehearsals were through so was Garland to Lynley's surprise and dismay. Ginger Rogers was brought in as a last-minute replacement as Mama Jean.

Japanese magazine ad for Carol Lynley as Jean Harlow in *Harlow* (Magna Pictures, 1965).

Despite the free promotion rival producer Joe Levine's outrage brought to Sargent's *Harlow* and the publicity Lynley herself drummed up with her notorious *Playboy* pictorial, the movie only played most theaters seven days or less. It did better business at drive-ins, no doubt because the indiscriminate teenage audience really did not care what film was showing on the screen. At the time of big screen epics filmed in Technicolor and Cinemascope, the poor production values offered by Electronovision (akin to watching a live early fifties variety show or soap opera on Kinescope) doomed its box office chances. Critics attacked the movie from all fronts pointing out "extraneous noises, gaffers' shadows, fluffed lines, and focusing errors." Kathleen Carroll of the *New York Daily News* described *Harlow* as "a crossbreed, something like watching a drama on a TV set with poor reception." Karl Tunberg's dialogue was called "atrocious" and Segal's direction "rambling."

Not surprisingly, most of the reviews for the movie (from the Hollywood trades, to the major national newspapers, to even smaller cities' local papers) were scathing: "worst movie of the year" (*Film Quarterly*); "cheap, lusterless and excruciatingly dull" (*New York Times*); "contender for all-time worst" (*Cue*); "looks terrible and sounds worse" (*Saturday Review*); and a "tasteless, tawdry screen biography" (*Oakland Tribune*).

As for Lynley, some critics were sympathetic to the fact that this *Harlow* was such a cheap rushed production and gave her credit for a valiant effort. Her reviews though were all over the place, which is not surprising since Carol had no time to prepare. Her notices ranged from "Miss Lynley, faced with the challenge of depicting a performer who is admittedly a bad actress, is equal to the demands of her role." (Larry Jonas, *Film Daily*) to "Carol Lynley, playing the title role, [is] a first-rate actress with far more talent than Jean Harlow herself ever displayed." (Gerald Ashford, *San Antonio Express/News*)

Despite the drubbing it took in 1965, *Harlow* is not that bad and somewhat entertaining, especially for Lynley's fans and for moviegoers unfamiliar with the real Jean Harlow (her fans should stay away). Carol does have some really good moments mostly when chastising her ne'er-do-well stepfather or butting heads with Efrem Zimbalist, Jr.'s pompous William Mansfield. Carol's projects a gentler side of Harlow in her scenes with Ginger Rogers and Hermione Baddeley.

As *Harlow* was in the throes of completion, Carol Lynley's name, unbeknownst to the actress no doubt, was on Paramount's list of actresses considered to play opposite Elvis Presley in *Paradise, Hawaiian Style*. The character of Judy Hudson was the main love interest for Elvis' amorous flyboy. She is an ace pilot too, but because she is a woman has a tough time getting hired. Needing to support herself, she becomes the office manager for Elvis' charter service but pretends to be married to keep him at bay. Other contenders listed were Yvette Mimieux, Sandra Dee, Pamela Tiffin, Ann-Margret, Elizabeth Ashley, and Tuesday Weld. According to a Paramount studio memo dated June 24, 1965, "they are either unavailable or far out of reach on price. Most of this list ranges from $50,000 to $250,000."[161] Newcomer Suzanna Leigh was cast instead, undoubtedly on the cheap.

Carol did mention a movie she turned down at this time and shockingly revealed, "I passed on *Fantastic Voyage*. Raquel Welch, who I got to know later and liked very much, did it. Filming conflicted with *Bunny Lake Is Missing* and I wanted to do that. I think I made the right decision there."[162]

It is unfortunate that Carol was not able to take that *Fantastic Voyage*. Though the role was merely decorative especially compared to the dramatic role of Ann Lake, the film was well-received and a box office hit. And who knew Carol had a hand in helping to catapult Raquel Welch to stardom? It is too bad she could not have done both movies but you cannot fault her for taking a lead role opposite acting legend Laurence Oliver in the least. It is what almost any young aspiring actress of the day would have done.

3. She's Not There

After *Harlow* wrapped, Carol Lynley almost immediately jetted off to London to work with producer/director Otto Preminger again. Alhough she was too expensive for Elvis, Carol was not for Preminger and was rewarded with Oscar winner Laurence Olivier as her leading man in his newest movie, *Bunny Lake Is Missing*. It was based on the novel of the same name by Merriam Modell writing under the pen name of Evelyn Piper. This was a mystery suspense tale about an unstable young woman who reports the disappearance of her four-year-old daughter who may or may not exist. The film catapulted Lynley out of the Baby Doll blonde brigade and made producers begin to look at her as a talented leading lady adept at playing the beleaguered heroine.

It took Otto Preminger almost six years to finally get *Bunny Lake Is Missing* into production. Reportedly, Preminger's niece brought the book to his attention and he purchased the screen rights in 1958 for $75,000. Preminger remarked, "I bought it because it was a good suspense story, but it had weaknesses, especially in the solution."[163] In the book, the illegitimate child turns out to be real and was kidnapped by the headmistress of her nursery school in cahoots with the grandmother. Preminger abhorred this ending and wanted something more sensational. He then went through a litany of writers including Walter Newman (*Ace in the Hole*; *The Man with the Golden Arm*); Charles Beaumont (*Queen of Outer Space*); novelist Ira Levin ("I thought I liked it [his script] then I decided it wasn't right,"[164] said Otto); Academy Award winner Dalton Trumbo who wrote the screenplay for Preminger's epic *Exodus*; and playwright Arthur Kopit.

During this entire period when it looked like the movie might go into production, it was a comedy of errors as columnists of the day, led by Hedda Hopper, reported who was going to star in Preminger's movie. In June 1960, Hopper announced that Lee Remick and John Saxon were wanted by Otto Preminger for his "next picture *Bunny Lake Is Missing*."[165] There was a lull after this when Preminger announced that he was moving ahead with *Advise and Consent* before *Bunny Lake*. In July 1961, Hopper was at it again and reported that George Maharis, who appeared in *Exodus* and was starring on TV's popular *Route 66*, was going to be the leading man and the movie would be shot entirely in New York.[166] Polly Bergen let it be known that she would "love to do *Bunny Lake Is Missing*."[167] Hopper shortly after struck out again announcing that Carroll Baker had won the role of the mother.[168]

In August 1961, Otto Preminger announced that his next movie after *Advise and Consent* would be *The Cardinal* and promised that *Bunny Lake Is Missing* starring Lee Remick "would definitely follow."[169] It didn't. His WWII epic *In Harm's Way* came next. In June 1963, it was reported in the *Los Angeles Times* that prolific TV director Jeffrey Hayden was preparing *Bunny Lake Is Missing* for the big screen to star his wife Eva Marie Saint in the lead.[170] There is no indication that Preminger gave up the rights to *Bunny Lake*, even temporarily, so this item is a bit odd and no source is credited. Finally, in late 1964, *Bunny Lake Is Missing* was confirmed to go before the cameras the following spring. Hedda Hopper reported that Robert Shaw was cast in a key role and she speculated that the role of the mother's brother would be played by Robert Redford who lost out on *The Cardinal* because he was too young.[171] As usual, she was wrong on both accounts.

Frustrated with the screenplays submitted, Preminger decided to take a new tactic and explained, "Gradually I came to the conclusion that what it needed was a novelist's approach rather than a scriptwriter's. I wanted a whole new job of character invention … So I sent the book to Penelope Mortimer. I admired her novel *The Pumpkin Eater* very much. She came up with just what I wanted. Of course, she isn't a scriptwriter, but her husband John is, so I put them to work on it together."[172]

Despite what had been published previously, Preminger seemingly only had one actress in mind to play the mother. Living nearby, the director would invite Carol Lynley over for dinner. The actress relayed to producer Eckhart Schmidt in a featurette on the *Bunny Lake Is Missing* Blu-ray in 2006,

> One night he told me I must come over to meet John and Penelope Mortimer. I went, and he said, 'They are writing a movie for you called *Bunny Lake Is Missing*.' They told me the story … It had been a book, which I had no idea. It happened. Columbia at the time wanted Jane Fonda who just came off a movie called *Cat Ballou*. Otto was … adamant that I do it because it was written for me. Three months later I am in London shooting it.[173]

After Preminger passed on Fonda, Columbia Pictures pushed Ann-Margret as the mother. Meanwhile, Stella Stevens who had a Columbia picture deal campaigned for the role. Preminger held firm and only wanted Lynley for the part

In 1979, film critic Joe Baltake wrote a piece on models-turned-actresses that may indicate why Preminger felt Carol was exactly right for the role of Ann Lake. Baltake opined, "The reserved 'fashion model' actress—usually a glacially beautiful blonde—has always fulfilled an important (and often unappreciated) role in movie storytelling. Her icy manner and cool exterior immediately indicate good breeding and, therefore, provides plotlines with a veneer of glamour. Carol Lynley, Suzy Parker, Millie Perkins and Tippi Hedren are a few examples of former models who have successfully adapted their qualities of superficial worldliness to the dimensions of the big screen.

And filmmakers have made effective use of their unemotional ways ... by contrasting these qualities with the violence, vulgarity and venality of their storylines. Historically, critics have been harsh ...disregarding their shrewd knowledge of the camera. (A model, by virtue of her knack for 'manipulating the camera, is a natural born scene-stealer.)"[174]

Carol Lynley as the desperate Ann Lake whose daughter has disappeared (or has she?) in *Bunny Lake Is Missing* (Columbia, 1965).

It was those qualities that were needed to keep the audience guessing on the state of Ann Lake's mental health. However, also required was an actress who could simultaneously elicit sympathy from the audience and keep them at arm's length as to her trustworthiness. It is what was required to make *Bunny Lake Is Missing* work successfully as a mystery. Arguably, neither Jane Fonda nor Ann-Margret had those traits. Carol Lynley was the perfect choice for the part.

Though elated to win the role of Ann Lake, it did come with some stress. Carol admitted,

> My movie daughter was about four and my daughter was about four in real life. Before we started shooting, I went to a psychiatrist because I wasn't sure how I would handle it. I was afraid to do it because I was afraid if I made it reality it would come true. He said, 'No, that is absolutely not true. There is that separation between reality and fiction.[175]

Per Carol, Preminger was considering Columbia's choice Ryan O'Neal and Keir Dullea to portray her sibling Steven. After she mentioned to Otto that Keir looked remarkably like her own brother, he was cast and with their resemblance easily passed as the too-close-for-comfort siblings. When filming at the nursery school, the actors compared their looks. Carol recalled,

> There was a big mirror at the top of this staircase. In between camera setups, Keir and I stood in front of it to examine our faces because there are amazing similarities. We stood side by side in front of it and I said, 'Yes, I can see it. Where is your father from?' He said he was born in America but his grandfather was from County Kerry in Ireland. I replied, 'Really!?! My father is from there.' He is actually from Cahersiveen a small town there. Staring at our faces, mine is a bit rounder and his narrower. We figured it out and are related—probably second or third cousins. The south of Ireland is very rural. His grandfather came from the county next door where my father was born.[176]

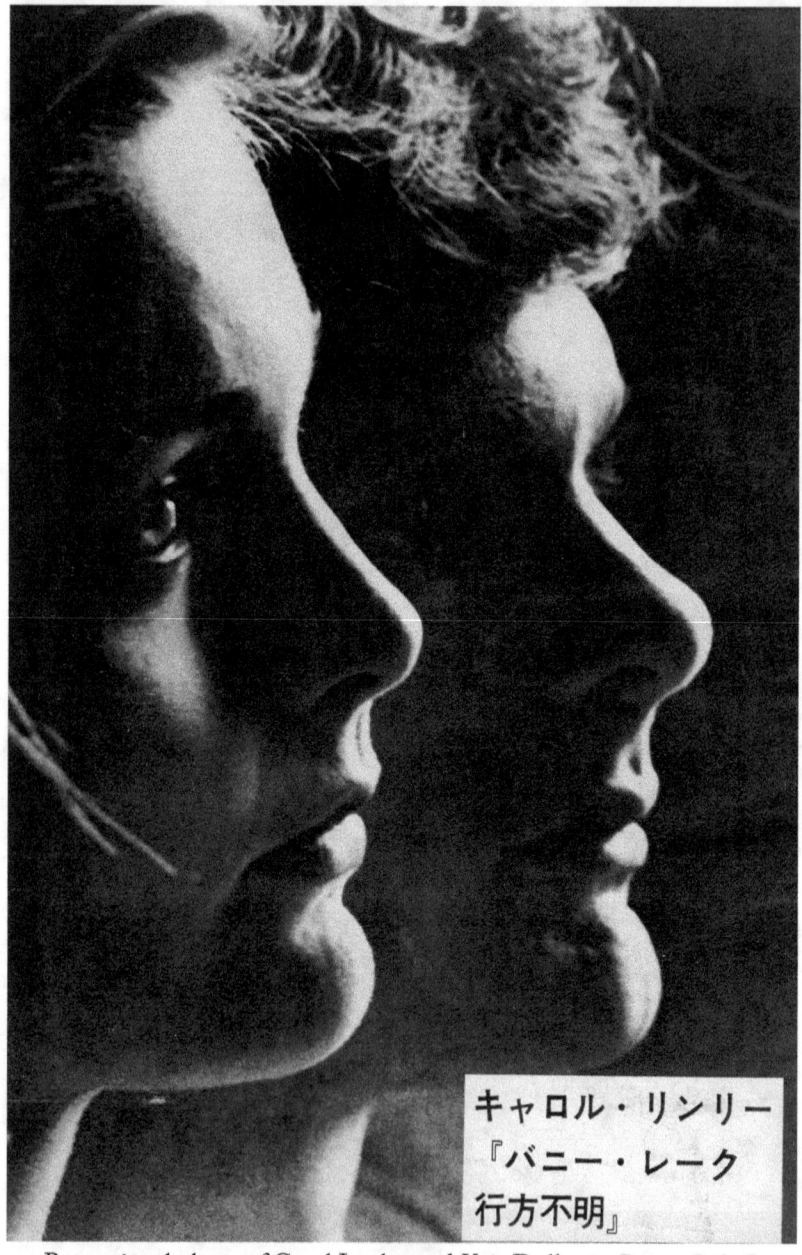

Promotional photo of Carol Lynley and Keir Dullea in *Bunny Lake Is Missing* (Columbia, 1965).

Although the novel is set in New York, Preminger wisely had the writers shift the locale to London with the American mother newly arrived to live with her brother, a wire service journalist. Cast in the supporting role as the lead police inspector was top-billed Laurence Olivier. Per Preminger, "I sent the script to his agent and Larry liked it. The part is quite unlike anything he has ever done, and it happened to come at a time when he was not acting."[177] Olivier hadn't made a film since 1962's *Term of Trial*.

Preminger then surrounded his leads with esteemed British character actors as potential suspects including Noël Coward as the Lake's new landlord (per Otto, "He liked the part—it's short and showy"[178]); Martita Hunt as the retired founder of the nursery school; and Anna Massey as the harried head mistress. Others cast included two-time Tony Award nominee Clive Revill in his first major film role as a detective; Finlay Currie as a doll maker; and the rock group The Zombies as themselves seen on a TV screen in a pub.

As he did with his most recent films such as *Exodus*, *The Cardinal*, and *In Harm's Way*, Preminger insisted on shooting exteriors and interiors on location. He did not want to use sets built on a soundstage, if possible. Among the locations used as background were an actual nursery school (during Easter vacation); Scotland Yard; the offices of Cunard Steamship; Trafalgar Square; the Soho district; the DuMaurier home in Hampstead; and Carlton Terrace Mews, two blocks from Piccadilly, which was used for sets and offices.

Before he left for London to finally begin shooting the long-awaited *Bunny Lake Is Missing*, Otto Preminger joked, "I have had this story for such a long time that Bunny Lake isn't missing, she's almost been legally dead."[179] More serious was his explanation on his past approach to filmmaking and how he was going to do the same with *Bunny Lake*, "I work very closely with the writer on the script until the whole form is in my mind—subconsciously. But no shots are ever preconceived; I pick the angles on the set. The script outlines only the master scenes, but I stick to them once I approved. And I don't let actors change the lines, either."[180] The latter became a problem for Keir Dullea who kept going up on his lines due to nerves.

The actor had some admitted troubles working with Otto the Ogre.

Despite the stories he heard about Otto, he did not think it would happen with him. Preminger's outbursts and sarcasm rattled the young actor from day one. He became so upset that he retreated into himself not speaking to his co-stars for most of the shoot. After receiving advice on how to handle Preminger from visiting friend Irvin Kershner, who directed Dullea in *The Hoodlum Priest*, the actor finally stood up to his tormenting director.

When asked what he thought of Carol Lynley, the actor said, through his agent, that he liked working with her, but disliked working on the movie. The only good thing, he said, that happened during the shoot was he found out that Stanley Kubrick wanted him for his next motion picture, *2001: A Space Odyssey*.[181]

Opining about the way Dullea was treated by Otto Preminger, Carol commented hesitantly,

> Give me a second here. I had no problems with Otto whatsoever. As a director, he knew what he wanted and I gave him what he wanted. We got along fine. My theory, and I may not be correct, is that Otto was a bit harsher with men. I think the male does not acquiesce as much as the female. I'm couching my words here but trying to be fair. The funniest thing that Keir has said to me about working with Otto was that it took about three years for his voice to become lower again. That gives you an idea of the anxiety he felt in dealing with Otto. Keir didn't really have any personal problems with Otto, it's just that Otto was sometimes combative. The difference between Keir and Tom Tryon is enormous. Tom was nowhere near as good an actor as Keir. Otto took advantage of that. Being the better more confident actor, Keir was able to handle Otto well—and it was a lot to handle.

Keir had a difficult role. But quite honestly, he was just marking time after he got *2001: A Space Odyssey*. His acting was wonderful in that too when you consider he had nobody to act with for most of the movie.[182]

Carol also sets the record straight that she never once heard Noël Coward say on the set "Keir Dullea, gone tomorrow" to the actor or anyone else for that matter. "Noël was a polite and compassionate man," stated Carol fondly. "I doubt he ever said that. I think it has stuck because it is a nice rhyme. He never said a bad word about Keir."[183]

Laurence Olivier had not been on screen in a few years. He was doing *Othello* on stage when he accepted the part of the police official, however, it was with the stipulation that there would be no screaming from Preminger when he was on set. The director, for the most part, kept his promise. When asked what it was like for her to work with Olivier, Lynley proclaimed,

> It was like getting handed a box of chocolates. He was wonderful! Most people think he was a stiff British actor, but he was the complete opposite. He was a jokester and a punster. He insisted we call him Larry. I grew up watching his movies, so I was in complete awe of him so much so that I first couldn't act. Otto asked me what my problem was. I told him that I was awed working with Olivier. He looked at his watch and said, 'Ve break for lunch now. I give you an hour to get over it.' I did, and the movie turned out great. I learned a lot about acting from watching Olivier, Noël Coward, and Martita Hunt.[184]

Carol recalled in *The Washington Post* that one of her favorite pastimes when filming was just sitting with Oliver and Coward between takes or set-ups and listening to the raconteurs share stories of years gone by. She felt like "the most privileged person alive. There was only one subject Oliver and Coward never discussed: Vivien Leigh. Otherwise they reminisced easily about everything they'd ever done in the theater—and they covered just about everything anybody else had done. Their sense of the continuance of their art impressed me enormously."¹⁸⁵

Det. Newhouse (Laurence Oliver) learns Ann (Carol Lynley) and Steven Lake (Keir Dullea) are not spouses but siblings in *Bunny Lake Is Missing* (Columbia, 1965).

While in London filming, Carol had another pastime and his name was David Frost, a popular journalist, television host, writer, and comedian in Great Britain. He was mostly known in the U. S. for being the host of TV's critically acclaimed but short-lived variety series, *That Was the Week That Was.* The couple had to meet discreetly, per David Frost, because Otto Preminger expected "his young actresses to live like nuns and get bags of sleep during the period that they had the signal honor of being under his command."¹⁸⁶

However, the sly lovers did get caught by her director and Frost revealed in his autobiography, "[O]ne morning on the set, [Preminger] questioned Carol about why the skin on her chin was peeling slightly. 'Sunburn,' she replied quickly. 'Looks more like Frostbite to me,' barked Otto. Carol blushed, and thus was spared one of Otto's legendary temper tantrums. Her open-mouthed amazement at his omniscience was sufficient reward for the great man."¹⁸⁷

Carol's dalliance with Frost outlasted the filming of *Bunny Lake Is Missing*. However, it was on and off for over the next fifteen years or so. They would reunite with the columnists having the couple on the verge of marriage only to see them drift apart once again.

Newspaperman John Crosby of the *New York Herald Tribune* visited the shoot when the company was filming in the Little People's Nursery. Commenting on filming up and down the corridors and in the classrooms and small cramped offices, Preminger said, "It's a challenge. I can't do what I want. I can't change things to suit myself. It gives the actors a feeling of reality."[188] This comes through on screen adding to the suspense. Carol remembers shooting in the nursery quite well. She recalled,

> We shot almost everything in continuity except the nursery school scenes. They were at the beginning of the movie, but we filmed them towards the end of the shoot. That was the only time that Otto could get the school. It was a real school and those were actual nursery school kids. The teachers were all real teachers except for Anna Massey, Adrienne Corri, and, of course, the fabulous Martita Hunt. She was wonderful in everything she did. Just to be around Martita was incredible.
>
> One of my favorite scenes was when I am going up the steps looking for Bunny as the children come down the staircase. It worked out wonderfully. Otto needed all the children who were really getting released for the day. You know how children are involved in themselves but they were like 'What is that? Who are these people?' The kids were on their normal schedule and we were working with that schedule. When I started the scene with the staircase, I was tired and quite run down but I knew it was the end of filming so I kept on going. Otto said now you walk up the steps. I said okay and then suddenly there was a sea of children. He never told me about them coming down the staircase. Obviously, I have been around children all my life and it worked

out greatly. I didn't mind it at all. The kids kept on moving because they were getting ready to go home.[189]

Since the movie was shot on location and a good portion was set at night, the shoot required many days of difficult overnight filming. Carol stated,

> The hours were rough. It was six weeks of night shooting, six days a week… At night we would go into Larry's dressing room where he had a butler who would keep him supplied with ice cold Coca-Cola's and endless supply of violets. We would try to keep ourselves awake because with that kind of night shooting if you go to sleep you are dead in the water because you can't wake up. If you do, you are groggy. This was not a movie I could be very groggy in. I had always worked a lot with English actors. The way most work is that you get on with it. You do it … I'm a day person and not a night person. But when you are working with Laurence Olivier and Noël Coward and you have these great scenes to do, it's not difficult at all.[190]

This does not mean that it was all moonlight and roses for Carol making this movie. She also had her issues, albeit minor ones, with the director who sometimes threatened to replace her with his newest protégé, Barbara Bouchet. However, she did not let his outbursts get the best of her.

Academy Award winning art director Lyle Wheeler worked with Otto Preminger on seventeen films and he opined about the director and his reputation as an ogre, "Like many men … Otto's got a short fuse. On the set, he ignites easily. But boom! And it's all over with. In private … he's one of the most charming, urbane, cultured men you could meet. This stuff about his being a terror has now become a legend, and Otto's too much of a showman not to perpetuate the legend. But underneath it all, he's about as hard as cotton."[191]

Carol shared stories showing the disparate nature of Preminger's personality. Playing cruel jokes on his actors one minute, and then showing affection and interest in their personal lives the next. She remarked to Eckhart Schmidt, "In the scene [in the basement] of the hospital where I run into the room where they are using mice for all these experiments, which was kind of scary, Otto locked me in there and shut off the lights. I am yelling, 'Let me out! Let me out!' He thought it was a great joke. He laughed his head off and thought that was really funny."[192]

A pleasanter experience for Carol making this movie was to meet and speak with the esteemed actor Finlay Currie who played the owner of the doll shop. Carol recalled at the time,

> I was introduced to him around midnight and he said, 'Carol would you come into my dressing room and we can go over the lines?' I said, 'Of course, Finlay.' I went in and...he said, 'Carol, you know I have just done a matinee and evening performance. I am eighty-four years old and if I forget my lines they will say I am losing it.' In between set-ups, I would go over the lines with Finlay. He'd tell me stories about doing Shakespeare in 1911 traveling across the United States. He was just wonderful. He said to Otto, 'I only request one thing. I have to shoot this sitting down because I have just done a matinee and evening performance and I am eighty-four years old. Dear Otto, may I shoot this sitting down?' Otto said, 'Of course.'[193]

Besides helping Finlay Currie with his lines, Carol had to also concentrate on shooting their logistically difficult scenes, as well as others with her in action, and explained,

> [This] scene when I go get the doll was shot in a doll store. It was from the Victorian time and had no electricity. They had a generator outside and I am holding this lamp, but I was tethered to the camera, which was on the same cable. The camera and I

are going in tandem. If I went too fast, they couldn't see me, and I was worried about tripping on the cable. If you notice in the scene, I look down quite a bit because the cable was down at my feet. It worked beautifully. I was the one moving the most. Otto did a lot of tracking shots. When doing that you have to work with the camera. You can't go ahead of it. You can't lag behind it. The camera guy takes his movements off your movements and you work together.

The movie had great photography [from] Denys Coop...[It] had a rhythm to it and starts out on the slow side. Then it starts to pick up and in the last half of the movie all hell breaks loose. It takes your breath away—at least I think so. The long shots, which there were a lot, and tracking shots had my body rhythm—how fast I ran and when I slowed down. What I did. That's what happens with that kind of a movie. The speed of the movie takes some from the rhythm of the actor.[194]

The last three weeks of filming took a toll on Carol due to an illness. However, being a total professional, it did not deter her from shooting or making suggestions to help the movie. She said proudly,

When I break the window and get into the house ... It was written as the lines but it was my idea to do it as when I talked to him [Steven] like we were children ... obviously he had a fixation on us when we were both children. I talked to him like he was four and I was three. It unnerved Keir, but it worked.

On the swings, Otto said, 'What nursery rhyme do you want to do?' I said 'Here We Go around the Mulberry Bush' because I used to do that as a kid. Denys Coop had something built off the swing so as the swing goes up, he and I went up together. The swing got quite high and I thought one of us is going to get killed. It worked; it really did work."[195]

Before Columbia Pictures released *Bunny Lake Is Missing*, the producer showman in Otto Preminger reared its head. He tried to do ape what Alfred Hitchcock did with his film *Psycho* to entice the public. The press campaign announced that the doors to the theater would be closed once the movie began. Ad copy read "No one admitted while the clock is ticking!" Based on the film's box office receipts, they needed not worry that there would be many latecomers.

Per Carol not all that was shot made it into the final print. She revealed, "There was a great scene between Olivier and Coward where Noël's character's homosexuality is fully revealed as he makes an overt pass at Olivier. They played the scene well, but the studio balked and demanded the scene be cut. Otto put up a fight but eventually bowed to the pressure."[196] Columbia did allow Preminger to push the boundaries with this movie and it is considered one of the first where a character actually says the word abortion. Adding the homosexual angle may have been too much for the studio to risk including.

Columbia Pictures and Otto Preminger threw a huge, star-studded premiere in New York City at the Victoria Theater. Besides Preminger and his two leads, Carol Lynley and Keir Dullea, attendees included Barbra Streisand, Roman Polanski, Tennessee Williams, Richard Rodgers, Paula Prentiss, Robert Morse, Jill Haworth, Jill St. John, Roddy McDowall, Burgess Meredith, Candice Bergen, Ossie Davis, Ruby Dee, and the novelist Evelyn Piper. A post-reception was held at the discotheque Arthur and was televised nationally on *The Merv Griffin Show*. That night Otto and his actors received kudos and congratulations from the invited guests and even a rave from Earl Wilson who wrote, "I always leave my seat to check with my office. But this was so full of suspense; I could never leave my seat."[197]

Bunny Lake Is Missing opens with an ingeniously inspired title design by the esteemed Saul Bass who worked on many Alfred Hitchcock films as well as Otto Preminger's *The Cardinal*, among others. Here a roughish hand rips away strips of jagged black construction paper to reveal the credits underneath. This is enhanced by the haunting theme music composed by Paul Glass that featured what sounds like a child's musical recorder to chilling effect. The last credit shown reads, "Produced and Directed by Otto Preminger," next to a cutout of a child. The hand then pulls the paper, crumbling it into a ball.

Poster art for *Bunny Lake Is Missing* (Columbia, 1965).

Commenting on the meaning of his title design, Saul Bass said, "One of the two key protagonists in the film is a deeply emotionally disturbed person … The opening reflects this psychotic state of mind. The peeling away of layers of paper is a metaphor for the peeling away of layers of mystery in this film...The symbol, a child torn out of paper, relates to the child's absence and to there seeming to be no proof of her existence."[198]

After the title credits for *Bunny Lake Is Missing* end, the audience sees a man walking through a backyard and picking up a white teddy bear - a child's swing still in motion. The viewer learns the man is Steven Lake (Keir Dullea) and he is having his belongings moved from Frogmore Court to a new residence. Next, a young blonde woman in a nondescript raincoat emerges from the First Day Room at the Little People's Nursery School. The puzzled woman wanders the lower level, opening doors, only to find nobody behind them until she stumbles on a German cook in an apron who grumbles about the teachers and her homemade junket. Introducing herself as Ann Lake, she says her daughter Bunny is in the First Day Room and she cannot find anyone to notify, which does not surprise the woman. Ann is late to meet the movers, so the cook volunteers to look in after Bunny until her teacher comes down and Ann dashes out.

Ann lets the moving men into the new apartment and gets a phone call from Steven who says his editor assigned him to cover a possible student protest at the Congolese embassy. Once the movers depart, Ann begins to unpack when she is startled by the flamboyant TV personality Horatio Wilson (Noël Coward), her neighbor and landlord, and his Chihuahua named Samantha. His aggressive, albeit friendly, demeanor ("poet, playwright, and dropper of alcoholic bricks") unnerves his new resident and she leaves to do her shopping. After unpacking her purchases including a child's box of candy, which she hides, Ann rushes out to pick up Bunny.

At the nursery school, Ann waits with the other mothers when a parade of kids come marching down the stairs to a cacophony of voices. Bunny is not among them and a perplexed Ann begins her search of the classrooms, but her daughter is nowhere to be found and neither is her teacher who left early to visit the dentist. When confronting the perplexed teachers, she is constantly told that the "fours have all gone home." One finally suggests that Bunny may be down in the cafeteria for lunch. She isn't there either. Ann then goes to the frazzled head mistress Elvira (Anna Massey) who is dealing with the walk-out of the German cook. When told of the missing Bunny, Elvira suggests they ask her teacher. "Miss Daphne went home with a toothache," an exasperated Ann yells as she reaches for the telephone.

Ann calls Steven and soon the pair is searching the nursery from top to bottom. They discover the private flat of dotty retired founder Ada Ford (Martita Hunt) who enjoys interviewing children about their dreams and nightmares for a book she is writing. Ada joins the unsuccessful hunt calling out for Bunny. When she overhears Ann call her crazy, she retorts, "Don't you think we all are, to one degree or another?" Later when Ada learns the Lakes are not a married couple but siblings, she quips, "curiouser and curiouser." With Ada's approval, Steven calls in the police despite Elvira's objections. Scotland Yard Superintendent Newhouse (Laurence Olivier) arrives on the scene. He quickly learns the cook had told Miss Daphne there was one child, a baby boy, in the First Day Room. He surmises that during that ten-minute span Bunny may have wandered out. Ann asks, "You must think I am a terrible mother for leaving her that way." That thought may have already crossed the mind of some moviegoers, no doubt. Newhouse replies, "No, Mrs. Lake. I don't know anything about you yet."

These search scenes at the school are masterfully shot as Preminger has his camera going up and down staircases, peering in and out of closets and rooms with doors opening and closing all with children's voices in the background as their day progresses without the slightest knowledge of the goings on amongst the adults. Newhouse then learns of the family connection between Steven and Ann, and that Bunny is illegitimate. Neither Lake can produce a snapshot of Bunny, so Newhouse sends Sgt. Andrews (Clive Revill) and Steven to the flat to fetch her passport while Newhouse escorts Ann to the police station. They then rush off to the Lake's apartment as the mystery deepens when learning that all the Bunny's belongings are gone. There is not an ounce of proof that the child exists, other than the word of the Lake's. Starting to doubt that Bunny is real, Newhouse asks Ann to think deeply about who saw Bunny and to provide a list. Ann soon realizes what the inspector is implying and begins to freak out. Pulling herself together, she remembers the candy she hid in the cupboard to play hot-and-cold with Bunny and gives it to Steven who drives off to show the police.

Newhouse returns to the nursery school to speak with Ada Ford. The retired teacher gives him an intriguing bit of information that when alone with Steven earlier, he admitted that during her childhood his sister had an imaginary friend named Bunny Lake. In her opinion, he was more worried about the fragile state of his sister than the child. Steven arrives to learn that the school has no record of Bunny's registration. Speaking with the inspector, Steven reveals that their father was killed in the war and that their mother was a fanatical believer of the afterlife. Ann was protected by her brother who convinced her not to marry the boy that impregnated her.

Newhouse returned to the Lake's home and rescues Ann from the drunken Wilson who has been coming on to her in perhaps the movie's most ridiculous scene. Coward just cannot pull it off. Newhouse escorts Ann to a pub to get some food inside her. There, on a TV, the rock group The Zombies are seen singing. Ann admits to having an imaginary playmate called Bunny. When Newhouse asked what happened to her, Ann responds matter-of-factly, that Steven decided it was time to send her to heaven and "He had read about this Buddhist funeral ceremony they have each year in Japan for broken dolls. So, we dug a grave in the garden, and then we buried her after burning all of her things." An irate Steven then bursts in and Newhouse states he is going home - not believing the Lake's story.

A hysterical Ann dissolves into tears as a poignant Carol has the audience genuinely believing Bunny Lake exists. You want to reach out and help her find her daughter. However, the next scene turns on the dime as does Ann's demeanor. While Steven is bathing, a glacial Ann walks in and sits at the edge of the tub and the duo share a cigarette. This scene is so casually well-played that it raises the question if they are an incestuous couple and are making up Bunny Lake? The actors deserve kudos for keeping moviegoers guessing.

Ann then discovers, in Steven's jacket pocket, a forgotten ticket to retrieve Bunny's doll from a repair shop. Believing this is the proof she needs for

Newhouse, she runs out into the night and is overwhelmed and engulfed by Swinging London nightlife as crowds throng the streets. Ann finally makes into the shop, which is stacked with all types of dolls from floor to ceiling. Showing the kindly doll maker (Finlay Currie) her ticket number, he gives her a kerosene lamp and tells her to look in the basement. Retrieving the doll, she bolts upstairs.

SPOILER

There she runs into a wild-eyed Steven. He burns the doll and knocks out his sister. Ann awakens in the hospital and is desperate to leave. Steven meanwhile has driven back to Frogmore where the Lakes first resided. He opens the trunk and there is a sleeping Bunny Lake (played by Suky Appleby whom Carol said, "We were all aware of protecting Suki and not exploiting her in any way. I loved her. She was a sweetheart. Nobody wanted to interrupt her growing process."[199]). He carries the little girl inside and continues burning her possessions. Ann, who has snuck out of the ward, has arrived and is horrified by Steven's actions as she watches from the window. When Steven takes off his tie to strangle the girl, Ann breaks in and begins distracting her psychotic brother by playing childhood games like hide-and-seek and singing nursery rhymes such as "Here We Go 'Round the Mulberry Bush." She also gets her brother to reveal how he kidnapped Bunny and how he made it looked like she was not real. Ann tries to keep Bunny away from her brother but he is determined to off her because his sister "likes her better." The nightmare continues until Newhouse (who remembered that Ann said her ship docked four nights ago while Steven insisted it was five) and his men come in as Steven pushes Ann on a swing ("Higher! Higher! Higher!"). The insanity finally ceases as Ann carries Bunny Lake ("Now that you exist," says Newhouse) back home.

As usual with his movies, Otto Preminger's *Bunny Lake Is Missing* received wildly mixed reviews upon first release. Almost half the critics dismissed it outright, some even despising it. You can just hear the hissing emanate from the *New York Times*' Bosley Crowther who wrote, "Nothing outside of a new script could save this phony film." Critics who liked it heralded it along the lines of "brilliant suspense story," "tremendously suspenseful," and "it will keep you glued into your seat until the end," and some considered it one of Preminger's best movies since *Laura*.

Respected film critic Andrew Sarris of *The Village Voice* was the movie's biggest champion. He wrote, "I can understand critics and readers reacting violently to even moderate praise of Preminger, but the fact remains that Preminger's mise-en-scène in *Bunny Lake Is Missing* is the most brilliant I have seen all year. The movie is a pleasure to watch from beginning to end, but there are really no characters to consider in Preminger›s chilling world of doors and dolls and deceits and degeneracies of decor." Years later, Sarris was still screening it for his Columbia University film students and called it one of Preminger's "four masterpieces of ambiguity and objectivity."

Det. Newhouse (Laurence Olivier) takes a frazzled Ann (Carol Lynley) to a pub while his men search her apartment in *Bunny Lake Is Missing* (Columbia, 1965).

Carol gave it her all to get moviegoers to fill theater seats. She did the television talk show route and a promotional tour throughout the U.S. including stops in Miami and Dallas. In Houston, there was even a 'win a date with Carol Lynley' contest. Readers of the *Houston Post* were asked to select who they thought was the most handsome player on the University of Houston football team. The winner was to have the honors of an all-expense paid date with the actress.

Not everyone associated with the movie was its champion. Considering the way Preminger treated him and feeling it hurt his performance, Keir Dullea understandably commented, "Nobody ever gave the performance of his career in a Preminger film. No actor ever peaked with him. How could you?"[200] However, he was arguably wrong. Preminger directed Maggie McNamara in *The Moon Is Blue* and Sal Mineo in *Exodus* to Academy Award nominations. Their careers never reached that pinnacle again. And even Dullea's co-star Carol Lynley garnered some of the best reviews of her career for *Bunny Lake*. Fans, critics, and even the actress herself feel it was her finest moment on the silver screen. Of course, there were some naysayers, but those the critics who were impressed praised Carol fervently:

> "Carrying much of the film on her shoulders, Carol Lynley, as the mother shoved into a state of near hysteria from almost the beginning, is outstanding. Bordering on exhaustion, she fights to find the strength to cope calmly (and at the end alone) with the dangers and uncertainties that beset her." (Robe, *Variety*)
>
> "Carol Lynley carries the burden in Otto Preminger's *Bunny Lake Is Missing* [and] does wonderful." (Jesse H. Walker, *New York Amsterdam News*)
>
> "Miss Lynley quite possibly gives her best performance to date." (Al Ricketts, *Pacific Stars & Stripes*)
>
> "Carol Lynley does a supremely good job of acting as the distracted mother." (Kate Cameron, *New York Daily News*)

"The performances ... are strong ones. Carol Lynley achieves the ambivalent attitude the director wants; we never know to believe her or not." (Linda Deutsch, *Ashbury Park Evening Press*)

"Carol Lynley and Keir Dullea take the leads and perform their roles with emotional effectiveness. Miss Lynley's part ... is poignantly handled." (Marjory Adams, *Boston Globe*)

"The deliberately controlled rhythm of the film ... is subtly engrossing and so are the performances. Carol Lynley neatly confuses the viewer as the baffled mother..." (Richard L. Coe, *The Washington Post*)

"This is the era of spine-tingling films, and *Bunny Lake* hardly lets your spine rest. It's the best film Otto Preminger has made in a long while, and in a fine cast Carol Lynley and Keir Dullea are excellent." (Florence Somers, *Redbook*)

"As the distraught mother she [Carol Lynley] is very clever in keeping the viewer busy guessing as to whether she is, or is not, telling the truth." (Frank Morris, *The Globe and Mail*)

"Preminger has cajoled, bullied, or frightened ... a fine, distraught performance from Carol Lynley ... The distance between Miss Lynley's acting in the gruesome quickie *Harlow* and in *Bunny Lake Is Missing* can be measured in light years." (Emerson Beauchamp. *The Evening Star*)

Despite these raves, Lynley was snubbed come awards time and failed to score Academy Award or Golden Globe nominations. Carol rightfully lamented, "I was terribly disappointed when it was first released. Critics seemed to be reviewing Otto's personality rather than the film itself. I put my heart and soul into that film. Also, Columbia Pictures lost faith in it and instead pushed *The Collector*."[201] The latter received Academy Award nominations for leading actress Samantha Eggar, director William Wyler, and its adapted screenplay. It is a shame Columbia Pictures did not tout Lynley. She certainly had the notices to back it up. The film's failure at the box office coupled with some truly negative reviews from critics who did not like the film most likely caused the studio to think it would be wasting its money promoting it. However, a full-page ad did run in the January 28, 1966 edition of *Variety* with a still of Carol fleeing from the hospital. In the lower left corner was the movie's logo and centered at bottom was a quote from columnist Vernon Scott that proclaimed, "Carol Lynley deserves an Oscar nomination."

Arguably, Scott was correct and Lynley did deserve an Academy Award nomination for her performance. Watching the movie, Carol keeps her character's motivations a mystery for most of it. First, she is distraught and frustrated that her daughter is missing and the police are beginning to doubt her existence. Then she seems mentally unbalanced being coddled by her overly protective brother in a relationship that seems incestuous, especially when Ann nonchalantly sits in the bathroom while her brother baths nude. Once Ann is confronted with the horrifying truth, she then pulls herself together knowing she is the only one who could save her daughter since the police do not believe Bunny exists. Carol makes this transition from victim to heroine wonderfully believable. It is the most compelling performance of Carol's career.

Oscar nominations should have also gone to Paul Glass for his original musical score with its haunting opening theme and especially to Denys Coop for his masterful black and white cinematography. He expertly used shadows and light with his camera peering around corners to create a creepy effect. Coop did receive a BAFTA nomination, as did the movie's art direction, which was odd since it was mostly filmed in real locations. *Bunny Lake Is Missing* was also nominated for an Edgar Allan Poe Award for Best Motion Picture but lost to *The Spy Who Came in from the Cold*.

As a minor consolation, Carol's admired performance was acknowledged by the Hollywood Makeup and Hair Stylists Guild. At their 1966 Hollywood Deb Star Ball, they bestowed a special award to Carol "as the former Deb

Star to most fully realize the potential she showed when presented at the Ball (1957)."[202] Lynley was no doubt honored for her splendid performance and because she was the first Deb Star to act opposite someone of Laurence Olivier's stature and hold her own.

Perhaps one of the reasons the film did not draw the movie going public (it grossed less than $1 million in the U.S.) was due to its misguided trailers. In the one widely shown, Otto Preminger, à la Alfred Hitchcock, speaks directly to the audience. However, he does so in a dull monotone fashion even when pushing his gimmick that no one would be allowed to enter the theater once the movie started. He is on screen more than his cast though the Zombies get touted a lot. A second trailer features the Zombies on a bare set singing their hit song "Just Out of Reach" with the lyrics changed to "come on time" to drive Preminger's point across. In both trailers the Zombies overshadow the cast and story. Why Preminger thought this mildly popular group would draw fans is its own mystery. The final trailer was a straightforward one about the disappearance of a little girl who may or may not exist. However, the deadpan narrator sounds like he is straight out of *Dragnet* and sucks all the life out of it. Watching it, you would think *Bunny Lake Is Missing* is just a routine police procedural movie. None of the trailers captured the essence of the movie and downplayed all the suspense and chills.

Based on comments from small town movie exhibitors in *Variety*, the movie could not draw customers due to the subject matter and the fact that their moviegoers wanted motion pictures shot in color. Columbia's *Ship of Fools*, out at the same time, was also floundering in rural America:

"Black and white scope not good for my set up." (S.T. Jackson, Jackson Theatre, Alaska)

"My customers were missing also." (Jesse J. Gore, State Theatre, Oklahoma)

"Moderately successful attempt to thrill. All in all, okay." (Arthur K. Dame, Scenic Theatre, New Hampshire)

A few years after *Bunny Lake Is Missing* all but disappeared from the theaters, it began airing on television. TV critics were giving it a revisionist look and more appreciated what Preminger set out to do with the movie. The *Toronto Daily Star* called it "a good thriller." Some even singled out Carol for praise. The reviewer in *The Courier-News, Bridgewater, NJ* raved, "A real suspense thriller with a surprise ending. Carol Lynley does an excellent job." The review for the syndicated *TV Scout* column proclaimed, "Carol Lynley may surprise you by the depth of her performance … She is even able to hold her own against the formidable talents of Sir Laurence Olivier." Joe Brugger in *Idaho State Journal* found the role of the harried Ann Lake, desperately searching for Bunny, "tailor-made for Lynley, the script and twists are noticeably English and exceedingly well-done."

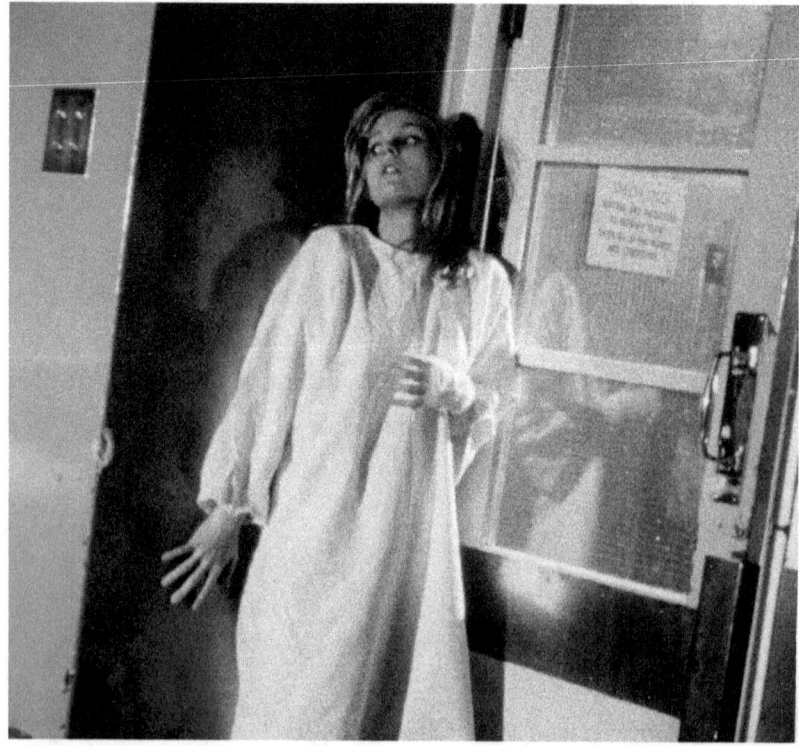

Ann (Carol Lynley) desperately tries to escape from the hospital in *Bunny Lake Is Missing* (Columbia,1965).

Author Ivan Butler wrote one of the first critical books about horror movies simply called *The Horror Film* in 1967 and then a revised version retitled *Horror in the Cinema* in 1970. He was a respected voice in the field. He called *Bunny Lake Is Missing* "an intriguing if implausible mystery story." Then he went on to heap praise on the finale, "culminating in a whirling shouting climax on a swing, build up to a most satisfying pitch of horror."

Critic Judith Crist reviewed the movie for *TV Guide* and remarked, "Otto Preminger's *Bunny Lake Is Missing* starts off as a straightforward mystery about the disappearance of a little girl who may or may not exist. Then it develops into a game of psycho, psycho, who's got the psychosis … the film is distinguished with fine performances." The *Movies on TV* review (culled from syndicated newspaper TV reviews) read, "*Bunny Lake Is Missing* is a first-class mystery drama filmed with an excellent cast headed by Keir Dullea, Carol Lynley, and Laurence Olivier. Carol Lynley goes through one nightmare after another as a harried young mother who enlists the aid of Scotland Yard to find her missing daughter. Her brother (fascinatingly played by Keir Dullea) joins his sister in her search despite the fact that police inspector Laurence Oliver begins to doubt that Bunny Lake ever existed. The surprise ending is played for chills, so be forewarned."

In 2004, the Feminist Press, an imprint from the City University of New York, re-released a soft cover edition of the original novel with a photo of Lynley in the movie on the cover with a quote from the actress, "The distraught, gutsy and hip mother I played in *Bunny Lake Is Missing* is my all-time favorite role." Ann Lake has become a "badass" among today's feminists. As explained by Sarah Khan on the web site *Cinefilles: Real Girls. Reel Talk*, "It's Ann who first figures out the twist after a shocking betrayal and then goes on to walk the thin line between revealing the truth and saving her life … she uses her mind to come up with wily ways to distract the bad guy in order to buy herself time to think of a more solid plan; she shows no fear, just pure gumption throughout the movie."[203]

By the 2000s, *Bunny Lake Is Missing* got its revenge. While *The Collector* has faded from memory for a lot of film fans, *Bunny Lake* has gained in stature. Most film critics and cineastes consider the peculiar but fascinating *Bunny Lake Is Missing* one of Preminger's best films of all-time and one of the most criminally overlooked movies of the sixties.

J. Hoberman of the *New York Times* reviewed the movie when released on Blu-ray in 2015 and perfectly explained that critics in the sixties who disliked the movie focused on individual points rather than reflecting on the entire movie. After praising the two leads ("Keir Dullea and Carol Lynley … make a striking pair of possibly incestuous siblings"[204]), he opined, "As noted by hostile contemporary reviews, the movie has its share of logical inconsistencies, although to dwell on them is to ignore its deliberate ambiguities and considerable panache. *Bunny Lake* is full of Expressionistic, if not surreal, touches: a nursery packed with demonic children, a wall of glaring African masks, a spooky doll hospital. Nor does the movie lack tension."[205]

With *Bunny Lake Is Missing* on streaming platforms during the COVID-19 pandemic, Rick Lattanzio of IndieWire.com promoted the thriller to film lovers. He remarked that the film "is probably most famous for its final 20 minutes, a cascade of nonsensical psychological hairpin turns that merge to become a quite stunning pile-up car-crash of 'is this really happening?' moments. That's the ghoulish fun of this unhinged movie, which provides the most toxic brother-sister codependency plot this side of Shakespeare or Hitchcock's darkest nightmares."[206]

He concluded with, "Preminger, here, didn't quite have Alfred Hitchcock's precision, losing his way on the road to a story of warring, sickening psyches that just ends up coming across as bafflingly, unforgettably weird. Which is exactly the reason to watch this, quite frankly, fucked film. From the set design to the cinematography to the performances, there is a general air of madness permeating every nook and cranny of *Bunny Lake Is Missing*, so it becomes a fun, evil little game to play 'I spy' with all the ways director Otto Preminger tried to paint a breakdown into all the corners."[207] Carol no doubt would have been tickled with Lattanzio's take on the movie if she was here to read it.

Carol felt vindicated with all these later admiring reviews and reassessments of the movie now touted as Preminger's brilliant overlooked masterpiece. It has become a cult classic in many circles. There are numerous screenings of it in art houses, film festivals, and museums. Carol remarked,

> *Bunny Lake* was a slow starter. It really wasn't that successful when it first came out. Now it is a major cult movie and recognized for what it is. It's a class act. Otto was a class act as a filmmaker. The other actors were class acts.[208]

Despite it not getting the full regard it deserved at the time, the one thing *Bunny Lake Is Missing* did was that it made Hollywood take a fresh look at Carol Lynley. She proved she could truly act and carry a motion picture. It elevated her from the Sandra Dee's and Connie Stevens', and she became for a period quite in demand to play the lady in peril or psychologically disturbed heroine based on the splendid work she did in *Bunny Lake*. Her next role was undoubtedly due to this movie. Preminger's film also began Carol's long relationship with the British entertainment industry. Over the years, the Brits provided Carol with some of her best lady in peril roles on film (*The Shuttered Room*, *The Cat and the Canary*) and television (*Journey to the Unknown*, *Orson Welles' Great Mysteries*, *Thriller*, *Tales of the Unexpected*, *Hammer House of Mystery and Suspense*).

Concluding her thoughts on *Bunny Lake Is Missing*, Carol remarked, "I see the movie from time to time and am always knocked out by it—it's just fabulous. It had a great part for me and just a great movie so well made."[209]

Another happy note is that though they never worked together again, Carol and Otto Preminger remained friends. She recalled warmly,

> I had dinner with Otto once near my birthday. He said I am going to give you a present. I am going to give you French. He arranged for me to take classes with this instructor ... and I did for almost two years. I speak French a little now but am fluent in Spanish. It was such a lovely gesture. Towards the end, Otto became famous for being famous rather than for his

movies, which was wrong. His movies are brilliant. Sometimes when they reviewed his movies, they reviewed him and not the movie. At one point he called me up and said, 'You must stop this immediately.' I said, 'What do you mean?' He said, 'You are saying nice things about me. *You are going to ruin my reputation! You must stop it now!*' I said, 'I'm so sorry Otto, but I do feel that way.' I have very fond memories of him.[210]

4. Terror in Dunwich

Back in Hollywood after filming wrapped on *Bunny Lake Is Missing*, the always unreliable Hedda Hopper announced that Carol Lynley was to go right into production of *End of a Wild, Wild Summer* opposite Alain Delon. After that she was purportedly scheduled to work for Otto Preminger again in the comedy *Genius* by Patrick Dennis about an egocentric movie director who terrorizes everyone who works with him.[211] Sounds like the Otto Preminger story. Neither came to pass—too bad, because if true, she and Delon would have made one sexy couple.

Director John Ford wanted Carol for the role of a young missionary in his China-set *7 Women* but MGM pushed Sue Lyon. The normally obstinate director accepted Lyon in exchange for full financing and carte blanche in casting all other roles.[212] This would not be the last time Lynley and Lyon were considered for the same parts. During the latter part of the sixties, Sue became Carol's new Tuesday Weld and Sandra Dee in the similar looks department. They both sported long straight blonde hair and did resemble each other a bit. Not sure how Carol felt, but it bugged Lyon who resented it. Reportedly, when fans mistook her for Lynley, Lyon would reply. "I'm not—I'm nobody."[213]

The one missionary role that Lynley should have played was in 20th Century-Fox's *The Sand Pebbles* opposite Steve McQueen. It was reported in various press items that the film's director, Robert Wise, was in negotiations with the studio to have Carol play the part, but ultimately newcomer Candice Bergen was cast.[214] Carol though refuted this and said, setting the record straight, "I never had anything to do with this movie and don't know where this rumor came from. I would have *loved* to have worked with Robert Wise."[215] Carol actually deserved *The Sand Pebbles*. Unlike other actresses with deals with Fox such as Diane Baker, Tuesday Weld, Pamela Tiffin, Barbara Eden, Millie Perkins, and Juliet Prowse whose options were dropped; Fox held Lynley to her contract to the bitter end. The least they could have done was reward her with a lead opposite someone of McQueen's stature in an epic after paying her dues working in medium-budget movies opposite less than charismatic leading men (i.e. Richard Beymer and Gardner McKay).

Instead, Lynley returned to the small screen in a highly publicized guest role as a mentally unbalanced young woman who takes on different identities on the Emmy-nominated TV series *Run for Your Life* starring Ben Gazzara as lawyer Paul Bryan whose doctor tells him that he only has two years left to live. He decides to travel the world (via the studio's backlot) doing things he never got the chance to try before. The series was in the vein of *The Fugitive* but without the law in hot pursuit of the hero. Carol remarked,

> Ben Gazzara was a wonderful actor and fun to be around. You never knew quite what he would say. He had an adventuresome sense of humor. He used to hang out with Fernando Lamas who would come visit him on the set. The two of them were free and easy—I mean that verbally. Beyond that I have no idea.[216]

It was reported at the time that Carol wanted to break free from frustrated or psychotic women roles and play the sweet, romantic girl next door again.[217] Carol said that is far from the truth. "I always considered myself lucky to have been offered very good parts that were complicated and you had to work to play them."[218]

Publicity photo of Carol Lynley in "In Search for April" on *Run for Your Life* (Universal Television, 1966).

In "In Search of April," Carol played the seemingly carefree April Martin who meets Paul at Mardi Gras in New Orleans. They spend the entire night together though he senses something is off with her. Unbeknownst to them, they are spied on by a man (Don Rickles) costumed as a creepy Bugs Bunny. He turns out to a private eye hired by a former paramour to find her. The next morning April has mysteriously vanished from the French Quarter. April's real name is Margaret and is suffering from a psychological disorder, making her take on other identities. Per her wealthy family, she was in a happy mood upon her return from New Orleans, unlike when she came back from Miami all sullen and afraid. Her doctor has convinced her reluctant parents to let her go on these journeys. When Paul tracks her down to her home, he finds a subdued fragile young woman who does not remember him – a far cry from the one he spent time with in New Orleans swimming, dancing, and drinking.

After receiving advice from Margaret's concerned doctor, Paul heads back to New Orleans and on the train runs into the unstable girl - now a vivacious woman named Kathy from North Dakota. Paul retraces their steps from the first visit, but nothing seems to trigger her memory. Paul catches the private eye questioning Kathy and later tracks him down to learn that, as Dorothy, she witnessed a murder in Miami. The killer named Dan finds a confused Kathy in her room who does not remember him or what happened in Miami. Paul bursts into Kathy's room just in time to save her from being suffocated by Dan. After the police leave, Margaret immerges remembering her time as Dorothy in Miami and the other women she pretended to be. Returning her home, the doctor thinks this breakthrough is a sign of a full recovery for her. Though Paul promises to visit her again, Lynley as Margaret never made another appearance on the show.

The fast moving "In Search of April" holds the viewer's interest - buoyed by the performances from Gazzara (always good) and the stylishly costumed and coiffed Lynley, who is quite convincing as this fragile disturbed young woman. *The Hartford Courant* called the episode, "confusing and suspenseful, with a good cast."

Carol looks smashing in living color coming soon after the black-and-white *Bunny Lake*. There her hair was pulled back into a ponytail held by a bow for most of the movie and she wore a dowdy raincoat over a nondescript skirt and blouse befitting her character. Since then, she had let her hair grow even longer and wore it straight as she had during her *Blue Denim* days. However, she was no longer an adolescent and her face had lost any remnants of baby fat. Now, her high cheek bones were on full display and, coupled with the flattering eye makeup, she was strikingly beautiful in this episode.

With that forever vacant look in her eyes, Carol was perfectly cast as the mentally unbalanced heiress. Her best scenes are when she is her true self Margaret and Gazzara's Paul goes to her home. As he talks to a family member, the fragile Margaret is a vision of loveliness in the distance, peering questionably at him from behind the branch of a tree. Later when he speaks with her, Lynley is quite believable projecting fascination and puzzlement as her Margaret is curious about their time together. When Paul describes their night in New Orleans, Margaret says, "I've never been," but then quickly pauses after realizing she was there based on what she just learned.

Carol followed this up with her second appearance on the *Bob Hope Presents the Chrysler Theatre* anthology TV show and her second time working with director Stuart Rosenberg. In the soapy "Runaway Bay," written by Tom Mankiewicz and Ben Masselink, she played a young woman named Miranda Woodland who returns to her small town after finding only unhappiness and disappointment in New York City. She causes immediate problems for her former boyfriend (Sean Garrison) who is now married to another, but Miranda wants him back. Her widowed mother (Lola Albright) wishes to be treated as a sister rather than parent and offers no words of wisdom. Only a local artist (Robert Wagner) tries to make Miranda take accountability for her own actions and life choices. The TV reviewer in the *Pittsburgh Post-Gazette* remarked, "Beautiful Carol Lynley, photographed like a million dollars in color, decorates the scenery in this routine drama. *Peyton Place* fans will be served with a full hour of trials and tribulations."

*****

Shortly after, it has been reported that Carol followed in the footsteps of her character Ann Lake and, with her child in tow, relocated to England due to the work offered her there. However, Lynley clarified that she never fully deserted Hollywood, having places to live in three different cities. "I did London-New York-LA for about fifteen years. At one point [during the early seventies] I used the Chateau Marmont as a place to stay in California but then took an apartment because of my daughter. In whatever city I got work, my apartment is where I would stay."[219]

Although at this time in her life the free-spirited actress did not want to be tied down with a permanent home, she came to regret that decision. She reportedly felt that she should have been wiser and purchased a house during the seventies when the real estate prices in Los Angeles were affordable. She claimed it was one of her biggest mistakes.

Career-wise, the reason it seemed that Lynley stopped working while living in London was because her next feature film and first made-for-TV movie were not released until 1968, causing a gap between acting credits. Both were made in 1966, but for several reasons their distribution and broadcast dates were delayed. This was a recurring problem that seems to have vexed her career.

Carol's sole theatrical venture in 1966 was the medium-budget *The Shuttered Room,* originally a Seven-Arts and Troy-Schenck International Production, which made it to the big screen—eventually. Reportedly, she signed for the movie while making *Bunny Lake Is Missing* and was again cast as the lady in peril. This time though terrorized by something monstrous living in the attic of an old millhouse she has just inherited and a lascivious distant relative who has taken the term 'kissin' cousins' to heart. Carol excelled in her role as the vulnerable newlywed and rose above the quality of the problem-laden script.

The movie is based on a short story credited to H.P. Lovecraft and his publisher August Derleth. However, it was written by Derleth, a respected writer in his own right, after Lovecraft's death. According to historian Charles P. Mitchell who wrote *The Complete H.P. Lovecraft Filmography,* the tale was published in 1959 and was thirty pages in length. He reported, "It was one of sixteen works crafted by August Derleth based on fragmentary notes, concepts and ideas by H.P. Lovecraft. Derleth tried to copy Lovecraft's style concepts faithfully, but very little actual Lovecraft prose appears in these posthumous collaborations."[220]

Carol was cast as Susannah Whately Kelton with Academy Award nominee and perennial supporting player Gig Young upped to male lead as her sophisticated older husband Mike Kelton. The movie was American financed and supposedly set on an island off the coast of Maine but was actually shot in England with a British crew and supporting cast all sporting American accents including Oliver Reed as Lynley's brooding, violent cousin Ethan and the esteemed Flora Robson as her overprotective Aunt Agatha.

Carol admitted to author Robert Sellers that she was immediately attracted to burly hell raiser Oliver from the get-go, "I noticed right away he was a very sexually attractive man and very masculine. He made a point of being masculine. He was also very plain-spoken and very gentlemanly. He couldn't have been nicer."[221]

Ken Russell, who had been directing short films and television productions since 1956, was hired to direct his first theatrical motion picture. He and Oliver Reed had worked together on *The Debussy Film* in 1965 and developed a friendship. It was because Russell was hired that Reed accepted the role in *The Shuttered Room*. The screenplay was by first time screen writer D.B. Ledrov and Nathaniel Tanchuck, a prolific TV writer whose last film was the low budget *Married Too Young* in 1962.

Exteriors were to be shot on locations approximately two hours from London by car. "An abandoned lighthouse near Dover's White Cliffs was pressed into service as Aunt Agatha's citadel from which she controls the village nestled below. An ancient millhouse near the Roman town of Colchester in Essex became the property inherited by Susannah and Mike."[222] The millhouse would create quite the controversy at the end of the shoot. Carol added, "We shot most of this in the countryside and just a few scenes on a soundstage."[223]

Ethan (Oliver Reed) torments his newly arrived cousin Susannah Whately Kelton (Carol Lynley) in *The Shuttered Room* (Warner Bros. – Seven Arts, 1967).

On the first day of filming in April 1966, cast and most of the crew reported to work. According to Carol,

> We were all together and were told that Ken Russell had quit but I never knew why. We were supposed to start shooting the next day. I turned to Ollie and asked, 'What are we going to do?' He said, 'Let's give it a try.' And we did.[224]

The next day the producers introduced the new director, David Greene. His prior experience was only in television and, as with Ken Russell, this would be his first theatrical feature. Carol opined with a laugh,

> David was quite an extraordinary person. He was extremely tall with a beard. He used to twirl the ends of it and then put them into his mouth to chew on while he was talking to you. You could not take your eyes off him.

> He told us he had been living in Rome and dropping acid for several years. On his first day he threw the entire script out—adios. He said, 'We will make this up as we go along. And you'll make up your part Carol. Ollie and Gig will make up their parts.' That is what we did. Every morning we would get to the set and say, 'Well, how is the story going to go today?' I'm not a screenwriter and neither were Ollie or Gig. You normally get a script and follow it with some deviations but not much. This started from nothing and having the responsibility to contribute to your character was a bit daunting. Ollie and I went with it though.[225]

When asked if she knew why it was decided that the movie should be set on an island off the coast of New England instead of where it was filmed, Carol laughed and said, "Beats me! I thought it was weird. We filmed in Kent which was in south England and it was so lovely. It is one of the most beautiful parts of the world."[226] This served absolutely no purpose to the story. The beautiful Cornish coast and hills were blatantly not America. It also caused some hazardous filming situations. Per Carol,

> We had trouble when Gig and I were riding in this big American car. Thank God he was driving and not me. Since we were supposed to be in the U.S., we were driving on the wrong side of the road—which is not a good idea. We had a walkie-talkie, which Gig had control of as well. The AD would say over the walkie-talkie, 'OK, now go.' They would clear the roads so we wouldn't meet any traffic literally coming at us. Every so often though a car would sneak by and Gig would have to quickly pull over to the other side of the road. We would then wait for another all clear and once again start driving on the wrong side of the road, do our dialog, and then rapidly move to the right side of the road.[227]

Newcomer Judith Arthy from Australia was cast as Oliver Reed's ill-fated slutty girlfriend. She recalled her experience making the movie and stated, "Everyone had an American accent. I'm a chameleon with accents. When I'm with Englishmen, I sound English and when I'm with Americans I sound like an American. I remember Gig Young would say to Oliver Reed, 'Why do you always sound like Louis Armstrong?'"[228]

The hard-drinking tough guy may not have thought he sounded like Armstrong but admitted a few years later that the time when he was "most plastered" was during the making of *The Shuttered Room*. He surprisingly remembered, "It was my birthday party. I can't remember it all that well, but we were in this pub. There was a huge coal bucket which we filled with 12 bottles of red wine, and I went round and tipped quadruple measure of everything that was in that bar into it, plus a jar of cocktail cherries to round it off. Everyone on the crew had to drink 12 sips straight out of the bucket. We had three bucketsful of the stuff in the end—and then we went on to pints of bitter. I remember my man Reg [his valet, bodyguard and driver] drove me into a hop field and I got out and wanted to die. I felt so ill. I think it was the last time in my life that I threw up. Then I fell asleep in the car… When I woke up, we found our way to a café off the Motorway, and everyone was staring at me. I said to Reg, 'See what it is to be a famous star? They all recognize me!' He said, 'It's not that. Your shirt tail is hanging out, and you're all covered in mud and puke!' But I always said that wine should be drunk, not sipped."[229]

Gig Young was not as rowdy as Reed and when asked her opinion of him, Carol replied cautiously,

> I want to be nice about this because Gig wasn't a bad guy at all. He was simply too old to play my husband. Nobody was more aware of it than him. I had been around older people my entire life and it never mattered to me at all. Gig would always come up to me and pinch my skin to see how fast the wrinkles came back. I know—it was weird. I think that he was more aware of

Mike Kelton (Gig Young) and his wife Susannah (Carol Lynley) climb the winding staircase to the home of Susannah's aunt in *The Shuttered Room* (Warner Bros. – Seven Arts, 1967).

the age difference between me and him than I was. It made him uncomfortable and he didn't seem like a happy guy. Oliver and I and everyone else went out of our way to make him feel at ease. What can I say—it didn't help.

I saw Gig a couple of times after we finished the movie. I always liked him and he never gave me any reason to dislike him except I had lunch one day at the Russian Tea Room in New York with his former agent. He asked me about Gig and I said, 'He was very private and I didn't get to know him that well.' He then said, 'I have to tell you something, Carol. He just committed suicide.' The worst part is that he had just married a young woman in her early thirties and shot her first before killing himself. I have never quite forgiven him for that. If you want to off yourself that's your privilege, but you don't off the person sleeping next to you. They had only been married a brief time."[230]

Whatever his true feelings about *The Shuttered Room*, Gig Young kept them hidden from the press and he boasted to the *Los Angeles Times*, "Oh, it's a departure for me—I'm strictly the leading man."[231] He also went on to talk about Dame Flora Robson and why she accepted the role. Per Young, "She said, 'I'll do it on one condition—that it will be in good taste morally!' I'm afraid she'll be shocked."[232] This last comment was about an attempted rape of Susannah by her kissin' cousin Ethan. Young probably hoped lascivious scenes like this would draw the more adventurous moviegoer since he had an added stake in the thriller. It was reported that he took a reduced salary in return for 5% ownership in the movie once it reached the one-million-dollar mark in box office revenue.

Young was involved in one peculiar set incident where moviemaking intersected with real life. Young's Mike Kelton was steering a boat towards a dock where he was supposed to rendezvous with Lynley's Susannah. As described by columnist Harrison Carroll, "As he neared the banks, a barge suddenly bore down on him out of the fog. Behind the barge, a speedboat suddenly turned a searchlight on the scene. Men started to jump off the barge. One of them swam up and clambered aboard with Gig."[233] The police were in pursuit of river pirates who stole crates of cognac off a dock. The actor had to prove to the police official who he was. After he did, Carroll reported that the officer replied, "Just like in the movies, eh, Mr. Young?'"[234]

Other than the run-in with the law, filming of *The Shuttered Room* remained low key - until almost the end. First, the romance between Oliver Reed and his lovely co-star became public just before shooting wrapped. The couple then became fodder for all the gossip rags. A few years after they broke up, Carol revealed, "We had a wild affair. They had to drag me out of his bedroom all the time. My hairdresser would rap on the door and shout, 'Carol. Carol.' We were notorious."[235]

The bigger story however that brought the movie unwanted notoriety had to do with the finale. This was set in the old millhouse that is accidentally set aflame. Instead of using a model, the film company purchased the condemned 130-year-old Hardingham Mill with all intentions of burning it to the ground. When the locals discovered what was afoot they went public with their protest. They were outraged that one of the few remaining mills in the area was going to be destroyed. The owner was going to have to pay out of his own pocket to have the structure demolished. He defended his decision to sell it instead to the movie company and said, "The fact that the old mill is going might shock some people but it's not worth preserving."[236]

Gig Young backed the owner's decision to sell the dilapidated structure to the producers and commented, "And then we came along and offered real money for its use, and burned it to the ground saving him more money. But nobody wanted to print the truth on that matter. It was much better to call American movie makers mercenary destroyers of English history."[237] Carol confirmed this was all true but, unlike Gig Young, was not happy about the entire situation. She admitted,

> I didn't like to see it burn and it made me feel extremely uncomfortable. I didn't quite understand why they did it and would have preferred if they hadn't. People sometimes think the actors have more say than they really do. Nobody asked me my opinion so I had no part in the decision. We were filming as it was aflame. When Gig and I get in the car at the end he drove out of there like crazy. The mill was really burning and the embers were falling all around us. The more hazardous it was the better it was for the shot so you go with it. It was sad though.[238]

As a footnote, many books state that Lynley also played her mad sister. However, historian Charles P. Mitchell revealed that the part was played by actress Celia Hewitt who confirmed via email that she did work on this movie. Carol tried to set the record straight to the best of her recollection,

> When David Greene began shooting the scenes with the crazy sister, there was another actress playing her. I do not remember who she was. Then at one point, he decided that he didn't like that and wanted me to do it, so I did. When I look at the final print of the movie, what I think David Greene did was that he intercut the sister scenes between the other actress and me. Why he did this I do not know.[239]

With this added information, it is a good bet that during the final reveal when Susannah discovers her sister in the attic it was Carol playing both parts.

The Shuttered Room opens with a chilling and truly scary prologue photographed from the point-of-view of someone or something frightening a blonde four-year-old girl in her bed shortly after her mother has just tucked her in. This was a stylish technique David Greene successfully used throughout the movie to give it an added eerie touch. Her screams awaken her parents who quickly run to her. The father tries to guide the intruder back up to the attic while the mother cowers in fear as the audience never sees what it is. The credits then roll as tree-lined images are seen from a moving car's windshield with a reflection of the beautifully angelic-looking Carol Lynley sitting in the passenger seat underscored by Basil Kirchin's jazzy theme atypical for a gothic thriller. Once the opening titles cease, she yells, "Stop the car!" The woman is Susannah Whately who, with her older New York sophisticate husband Mike Kelton (Gig Young), is returning to her childhood home of Dunwich on an isolated island off the Maine coast after a twenty-year absence. She was sent away as a small child after the death of her parents. A haunted Susannah knows that something horrible happened to her there, so she is hesitant to complete the trip. Mike leaves it up to his new bride and they continue onward.

Spanish poster art for *The Shuttered Room*.

All the villagers the couple encounter on the way to Susannah's ancestral home are unwelcoming oddballs led by a brute of a cousin named Ethan (Oliver Reed) the leader of a gang of local toughs from the village where "black, weather-board houses, wild stagnant marshes and a tower in ruins give it an atmosphere of almost medieval gloom."[240] Mike is even warned by blacksmith Zebulon Whately to take his young wife back to New York or face the Whately curse. As he removes his welder's mask, he is missing an eye that seems to have been lost in a violent struggle.

Meeting his cousin unnerves Ethan who races through the island until he comes to a creepy dilapidated lighthouse. Atop is an old woman "bedraggled, hair streaked with grey, and with a wild-looking bird for company as she looks out over her domain."[241] Ethan yells to his Aunt Agatha (Flora Robson), "Who is Susannah Whately?" The look on her face freezes, as she stands and summons him up.

Arriving at the abandoned Whately home, with an adjacent millhouse, a chill goes through a frightened Susannah. They find the interior covered in cobwebs. Ethan comes around to let the couple know that Susannah's Aunt Agatha wishes to see her. Instead of taking them by a paved road, Ethan spitefully leads them via a dirt path up hills and through bushes. What better way to showcase Lynley's shapely legs, as her stockings tear on the trek? Susannah instantly remembers Agatha who is genuinely happy to see her niece but is scared for her safety. She tries to persuade her husband to take Susannah back to New York City immediately, telling him that all Whately's are doomed, but the skeptical couple is determined to reopen the home as a weekend getaway. This is all observed by Ethan's slatternly girlfriend Emma (Judith Arthy) who is obsessed with Susannah's fine hosiery.

Back at the millhouse, Mike unpacks while Susannah senses a strange presence and an eye appears looking through a knothole on the wall. Susannah decides to take a walk and is spotted by Ethan and his friends who stalk her. She is chased to the end of a pier where Ethan grabs and kisses her just as Mike arrives. The toughs back off, and Mike escorts his shaken wife home.

That night while the couple sleeps, Emma, who stole a pair of Susannah's silk stockings, is mauled to death by something monstrous. Agatha arrives to take the thing back to the attic and is relieved to find the Kelton's unharmed and asleep in their bed. However, she inadvertently drops a glove.

The next morning Mike finds the glove and ventures into town to buy supplies. Susannah gets reacquainted with her childhood room and furnishings. Lynley does extremely well in these scenes enacting a sense of trepidation as Susannah hesitantly roams the house fearful that something is watching her. Director David Greene really builds the suspense as Susannah is drawn to the attic. She enters and is secretly watched as she notices a bed, dirty blankets, and an old stuffed animal. Spooked, Susannah leaves and goes for a walk outside.

As Mike drives back, he is ambushed by Ethan and his ruffians who want to drive his brand-new car. They then begin to rough him up and get the best of him until Mike unleashes his martial arts skills taking them down in the most ridiculous scene in the movie. Ethan meanwhile has slipped away. He finds Susannah alone and makes unwanted sexual advances. As he begins to force himself on her, she gets away and runs back to the house. Taking refuge in her old dollhouse, the lascivious creep finds her. She heads for the darkened shuttered room followed by Ethan. Needing light, he sets a stuffed teddy bear on fire and out of the shadows emerges the hideous scratching resident. A startled Ethan staggers backward and falls to his death dropping the bear that sets the millhouse ablaze.

Meanwhile, Mike stops at Agatha's house where she reveals the truth of what is in the mill's attic. He rushes to his wife's rescue. Susannah comes almost face to face with the attic dweller who is fascinated with the beautiful woman. "My sister," she gasps as Mike arrives. The couple escapes as the flames intensify. Outside they run into Agatha, who with Mike, go in to rescue Susannah's sister. Agatha though tricks Mike and locks herself in the attic with the demented girl feeling it is better for all if they perish. Mike and Susannah drive off with the millhouse in flames behind them.

It was reported that *The Shuttered Room* screened for Seven-Arts big wigs in November of 1966. They were so pleased with the movie and with Lynley that they offered her a two-picture deal.[242] However, soon after the film (along with two other Seven-Arts productions *The Fox* and *The Vengeance of Fu Manchu*) became a victim of the then merger between Seven-Arts and Warner Bros. Its fate remained in limbo for months and it sat on the shelf as the two companies hammered out an agreement. *The Shuttered Room* was finally released in the United Kingdom in the summer of 1967. It would be another six months or so before it would get a U.S. release in early 1968. This did not bode well for Gig Young's pocketbook since he took a percent of the gross in exchange for a reduced salary. He bemoaned that it "might be a lost cause."[243] Unfortunately, he was proved right.

Moviegoers in Great Britain got to see the movie first and critics were not overly impressed. Notices were in line with Ian Wright of *The Guardian* who called it "a gothic tale … superior to Hammer but poor Hitchcock." David Greene was commended for adding original touches to the film with the camerawork and an experimental jazzy musical score by Basil Kirchin, but they felt he was defeated by a weak script or no script per Carol. The film's chilling opening was particularly praised by the British Film Institute that remarked, "The imaginative opening sequence, with a subjective camera retreating in front of an unseen attacker, creates an atmosphere of tangible but undefined terror." *The Times of India* reviewer praised the cinematography by Ken Hodges and remarked that the movie was "beautifully and cleverly photographed."

Hodges, who previously worked with Oliver Reed on *The Jokers*, particularly did an awesome job shooting Carol who arguably never looked lovelier on film. She is also clad in some stylish suits designed by Hylan Booker. An African American former G.I., Booker was stationed in England and remained there after his tour of duty was completed in 1958. He went to London's Royal College of Art in England and became a dress designer. His star rose quickly in London and his fashions were coveted by many resulting in his own shop. Women's suits were his specialty. *The Shuttered Room* is his only film credit.

Susannah (Carol Lynley) and Mike (Gig Young) discover the thing in the attic in *The Shuttered Room* (Warner Bros. – Seven Arts, 1967).

In America, *The Shuttered Room* began rolling out in late January 1968. In some theaters, it topped a double bill with *The Vengeance of Fu Manchu* starring Christopher Lee. The studio unbelievably did not take advantage of putting stunning Carol Lynley on its movie poster but instead used a silhouette of the deranged attic dweller attacking a man with the tag line, "Sleep one night in the house with the shuttered room and you may never want to sleep again…" Other countries were wiser and used Lynley's beauty to lure ticket buyers.

As in the UK, the film received widely mixed reviews from the U.S. critics. *The New York Times*, in particular, cruelly trashed the movie. Some critics rightfully wondered why the producers did not just set the movie in the Cornish Coast of England where it was filmed rather than have the beautiful landscape pretend to be an island off the coast of Maine. It was a concession to Americans that did not have to be, and it did nothing to improve the box office.

There were positive reviews though. Joseph Gelmis in *Newsday* commented that it was directed "with gusto by David Greene" and thought it an "above-average … unseen-terror yarn." Marjory Adams of the *Boston Globe* also praised David Greene and said he "directed the picture with an admirable amount of suspense and a definitely hysterical pace." Her main objection with the movie was that "no sensible couple would have behaved so foolishly as Gig and Carol."

One of the most favorable mainstream reviews was published in the *Independent Film Journal*. Their critic raved that the movie "will come as a pleasant surprise to thriller fans … the picture is a beautifully produced and exquisitely color-photographed tale of diabolic possession and an apparent family curse, which surround a young woman who returns to the scene of her childhood to claim her property." Carol received a backhanded compliment from the journal, "The acting is generally good, with Miss Lynley's usual flat-voiced delivery and somnambulistic beauty oddly effective." The reviewer for *Boxoffice* delivered Carol a compliment without a dig and commented, "Gig Young and Carol Lynley have starring roles but his performance is somewhat routine compared to hers, which makes the most of the screenplay."

Carol and Oliver Reed had differing opinions about the film as well. Back then, Reed admitted that it is "so bloody awful I didn't even see it myself."[244] Carol, on the other hand, was impressed. She remarked, "Considering how the film was put together I thought for sure this was going to disappear off the map. It was such a mess. When I first saw it at a screening at Warner's, I was amazed how good as it was. I don't know who cut it but they did a pretty good job."[245]

Susannah (Carol Lynley) watches helplessly as her ancestral home goes up in flames in *The Shuttered Room* (Warner Bros. – Seven Arts, 1967).

The Shuttered Room earned less than $1 million dollars in the U.S. It disappeared from theaters after a week though in some places it stuck around reduced to the bottom of a double bill with the Academy Award winning *Bonnie and Clyde* or *Rosemary's Baby*. However, it seemed the movie had legs and would not die. In the spring and summer of 1970, it was the second feature paired with *They Shoot Horses, Don't They?* (making it a Gig Young double-feature) in some areas and led a drive-in triple bill with *The Haunted*

House of Horror (one of the films AIP reportedly wanted Lynley for) and *The Crimson Cult* starring Christopher Lee.

The delayed release of *The Shuttered Room* arguably hindered Carol's career. If distributed in late 1966 or early 1967 when it should have been, the movie would have been a timely follow-up for her after *Bunny Lake Is Missing*. She looked fabulous in the picture and gave another extremely effective performance. It would have kept her name alive with moviegoers and the one-two punch of these movies, where she excelled as the lady in peril, could even have put her in contention for *Rosemary's Baby*. It has been reported over the years that Jane Fonda, Tuesday Weld, Julie Christie, Sharon Tate, Patty Duke, Joanna Pettet, and Elizabeth Hartman were all talked about for the lead role before Mia Farrow surprisingly won the part. One can easily see Carol as the tormented Rosemary especially after her turns in *Bunny Lake Is Missing* and *The Shuttered Room*. Perhaps if the latter had screened in theaters the studio or producers would have considered her especially since she was friendly with its director Roman Polanski. Alas, it was not meant to be though there is no doubt Carol would have been wonderful as Rosemary.

The Shuttered Room made its primetime television debut in November 1970 and critics still could not decide if they liked it or not. For example, the reviewer for *The Hartford Courant* wrote, "Despite the lack of originality, it is well photographed, chilling and not for the faint of heart."

About the same time Ivan Butler in his tome *Horror in the Cinema* raved, "A really believable and terrifying 'thing-in-the-attic' raises this conventionally shaped thriller well into the region of superior horror, despite some gratuitous violence. The introductory sequence is a masterly exposition of terror. Carol Lynley looks unnervingly vulnerable, and Flora Robson grandly eccentric."

The mainstream critics were not overly fond of *The Shuttered Room* and neither were true Lovecraft fans and historians because it did not stay true to its origins. Charles P. Mitchell remarked in his book, "*The Shuttered Room* is a film that merely uses the trappings of a Lovecraft story to depict a creepy and atmospheric setting. In actuality, segments of the picture, mostly in the first half, are rather effective and rather good. Unfortunately, it then switches more to a juvenile delinquent plot which becomes repetitious and rather tedious. By the time the plot returns to the main story, it robs it of any supernatural or fantastic elements, rendering the story rather hollow and empty by the conclusion. A few viewers may write the film off as a total loss, but it does manage to capture the flavor of Lovecraft in a few excellent scenes, however briefly."[246]

What Michell was addressing in his commentary was that in the original story the thing-in-the-attic was really a thing—a half-human, half-amphibian creature who sustains itself by first feeding off wildlife and then graduates to people when accidentally released by the mill's inheritor Abner Whately. This makes sense that since it is not fully human how could it survive living in a rundown mill with no heat or electricity? Mitchell points out that making the creature Susannah's madden sister makes the story implausible. How does she endure all these years chained up? And are viewers led to believe that no one in the village ever saw Aunt Agatha make her regular trips to the mill and questioned her on it?

More of Mitchell's criticism was heaped on the Ethan character. "Ethan, of course, believes he should inherit the millhouse, but since it is abandoned and rumored to be haunted, the property does not seem to be of much value to him. At times Ethan is civil and well mannered, and then abruptly he acts like a rowdy brute. There seems to be no reason for his abrupt shifts."[247] These are all valid points. Carol admitted the cast and the director were making it up as they went along, so it should come as no surprise there was a loss of continuity with the characters' motivations and actions.

Author and film historian Don G. Smith opined in his book that *The Shuttered Room* was "a dull disappointment." He specifically faulted the screenplay, the "brassy" musical score, and Gig Young who he rightly states, "Irritatingly smirks throughout [and] does not make a very sympathetic male lead." His most praise was reserved for Oliver Reed and especially Carol Lynley whom he felt "is appropriately fragile and vulnerable."[248]

Despite plot improbabilities and criticisms from true Lovecraft aficionados, the film found renewed interest in the seventies and eighties (one critic felt it was a successful mix of thriller and Hammer-styled horror) and developed a cult following of horror film fans due to the H.P. Lovecraft connection and especially admirers of Lynley. It became one of three films, along with *Bunny Lake Is Missing* and *The Poseidon Adventure*, the lovely blonde actress is most remembered. The movie became a popular staple of syndicated television. *The 4:30 Movie* broadcasting in the New York City metropolitan area on ABC-TV was extremely popular and ran the movie at least once or twice a year for almost the entire decade. Print ads with Carol prominently featured were placed in *TV Guide* and other television magazines. For years it sent chills down the spines of children and teenagers, just home from school, who needed a break before it was homework time.

The movie became synonymous with Carol who is believably confused and on edge throughout. At times it seems her Susannah is on the verge of an emotional breakdown raising the suspense factor. Despite her uneasiness, her husband keeps abandoning her and making her susceptible to the clutches of her brutish cousin or whatever is mysteriously lurking in the attic forcing Susannah to face the reality of her situation alone. Carol handles the role perfectly, plus her beauty is stunning. She carries most of the movie on her talented shoulders with sinister support from Oliver Reed and a gripping atmosphere thanks to David Greene. It is no surprise then why it became so popular in syndication.

Carol Lynley's appearance in *The Shuttered Room* has left favorable impressions on people who saw it long after it was released. In his 2002 novel *EXploZion!*, author Ross Wells had his film-loving protagonist reminisce about Carol and the film while driving. He wrote, "As Gabriel cruised, he remembered a curious little film which he had seen in 1968, *The Shuttered Room* ... which starred the absolutely gorgeous blonde-haired and porcelain-faced actress Carol Lynley. The tale concerned a dreamy-eyed young woman, played by the vivacious Lynley, one of the dream blondes with whom he was fascinated during his youth." As for the pairing of Carol with the older Gig Young, Wells described them as an "odd couple, dreamy Lynley and unimpressive Young." He then goes on to explain the plot of the movie while continuing to praise Carol, confirming that it is one of her most memorable roles.

Carol is still receiving praise for her performance. Jeremy Richey, while reviewing the movie in the journal *Soledad*, rightly attested in 2019 that this is one of Lynley's most memorable roles remarking, "The biggest coup of the film is the magical lead performance by underrated sixties icon Carol Lynley. Lynley, one of the most heartbreakingly beautiful women of the period, is extraordinary in the demanding dual role of the passive and lonely Susannah and her crazed twin sister Sarah."[249] Carol's fans would heartily agree.

5. Suave Spies to Invading Aliens

Carol's next film assignment took her back to Universal Television in LA for a new phenomenon—the made-for-television movie. Though they became almost synonymous with the ABC network due to the success they had with their *ABC Movie of the Week* programs beginning in 1969, it was NBC-TV who launched them. Most of these aired under the umbrella of the *NBC World Premiere Movie*.

In the summer of 1966, *The Smugglers* (working title *Package Deal*) went into production. Despite that she leased a townhouse on Montpelier Street in London close to the famed Harrod's department store, Carol accepted the offer to co-star with the esteemed Shirley Booth. Asked by columnist Sheila Graham why she decided to settle in London, Carol replied at the time, "It was a question of being out of work in Hollywood or being out of work in London. And I preferred being out of work in London."[250] But that decision did not stop her from taking a job in Hollywood and she assured Graham, "I'll fly right back."[251]

Fresh off the cancellation of her hit TV-sitcom *Hazel* that earned her two Emmy Awards, Shirley Booth was tapped to star in this suspense tale. She played a dotty little old lady on a driving tour of Europe with her beautiful stepdaughter (Carol Lynley) now mending a broken heart. The duo becomes dupes of a smuggling ring and become embroiled in intrigue and murder. Carol's Jo is more lighthearted than her previous ladies in peril. Jo realizes that the two are being used and perhaps are in danger. Although Jo is still lovelorn over a broken romance, she is having a rollicking time with her stepmother and ignores any bad vibes she is sensing around them.

Some sources state the movie was filmed on location in Europe while others refute that. Clearing up the confusion, Carol firmly stated, "We shot this on Stage 14 on the Universal lot only. I didn't know at first it was being made for television."[252]

Co-starring with Booth and Lynley were Kurt Kasznar, David Opatoshu, Donnelley Rhodes, Charles Drake, and Gayle Hunnicutt in an early role. Also cast pre-*Bonnie and Clyde* was Michael J. Pollard who had co-starred with Lynley before on TV in *Henry Fonda and the Family* and on the big screen in *The Stripper*. The movie was produced and directed by Norman Lloyd who had previously worked with Carol on *The Alfred Hitchcock Hour*. With his work in the field of suspense, Lloyd seem to be a perfect choice to helm this.

Carol has the most memories of Shirley Booth and remarked,

> I was fascinated by Shirley. I knew who she was and knew she was an incredible actress. However, on a one-to-one level, I never quite understood her. She was very lively and nice. Every so often though she would break out into song and I could never understand why. I never said anything because she was *Shirley Booth*! Her Oscar-winning performance with Burt Lancaster [in *Come Back, Little Sheba*] is just wonderful. I did enjoy working with her because she was so talented and unusual.[253]

Despite the time and effort that went into making *The Smugglers*, NBC decided not to air the movie for unknown reasons and it was shelved for now, despite the star power of Booth and Lynley.

*****

The restless actress then returned to London. Unfortunately, she had nothing much to show work-wise for the next year except for making an appearance as herself on the TV special *David Frost's Night Out in London* and a co-starring role in *Danger Route* (1968), a serious spy thriller in the vein of *The Quiller Memorandum*.

It should not have come as much of a surprise to Carol's fans that she would purposely reach a loll in her career. Just two years prior, after appearing in five straight movies, she hinted at this and was quoted as saying, "I find that working so hard has been good for me. It certainly keeps me from ever getting bored, but pretty soon, I'm going to be due for a rest."[254] In actuality, Lynley had been working non-stop since she was ten years old, modeling and acting, so she was certainly entitled to take a break. However, it was bad timing again on her part to take a sabbatical at this moment. With *Bunny Lake Is Missing* failing at the box office, she needed a hit to follow it up with. She delivered an impressive performance and should have been looking for another worthy film project. Hollywood was churning out some important movies in 1966 and 1967. Carol had not yet hit super stardom to remove herself from the film capital. Actresses of her level still had to play the game of being seen and noticed to remind the studios that you were available. Though she claimed she never abandoned Hollywood, producers may have thought otherwise.

Carol though kept the London press beat active. While there, reporters had a field day guessing what her next movie would be. Per Mike Connolly, still striking out with his predictions, Carol signed a contract to star opposite James Mason as a drunken barrister in producer Anatole de Grunwald's *Stranger in the House*. She was to play his teenage daughter who begs his help in defending her boyfriend, falsely accused of murder. The movie was later made as *Cop-Out* with Geraldine Chaplin in the role meant for Lynley.

Director/writer Noël Coward announced to the press that Carol Lynley would be his *Pretty Polly* for Universal Pictures.[255] They worked well together previously on *Bunny Lake Is Missing*, so this seemed quite plausible. The film, based on his short story "Pretty Polly Barlow," is about a shy, young girl who accompanies her wealthy spinster aunt to Singapore. When the older woman unexpectedly dies, Polly is free to grow from a girl to woman when she falls for a local boy. Coward was replaced by director Guy Green and his script tossed, though he did get a story credit. With Coward out so was Lynley, and Hayley Mills got the part in the movie, re-titled *A Matter of Innocence*.

The U.S. press was also in on the speculation and the most outrageous claim came from columnist Earl Wilson who announced to his readers, "Carol Lynley will be a motorcycle moll for American International in *Devil's Angels*."[256] She didn't and Beverly Adams hopped on instead.

The one British movie Carol did appear in was *Danger Route*, based on a novel titled *The Eliminator* by Andrew York. It was an Amicus Productions film and released through United Artists. It was produced by Max J. Rosenberg and Milton Subotsky and shot almost entirely on soundstages at Shepperton

Jocelyn (Carol Lynley) has a deadly surprise waiting for secret agent boyfriend Jonas Salk (Richard Johnson) in *Danger Route* (United Artists, 1968).

Studios. Seth Holt, most famous for his Hammer Studios' thrillers *Taste of Fear* (1961) and *The Nanny* (1965) starring Bette Davis, was chosen to direct and he was an appropriate choice but was hampered by an overly complicated script and a limited budget.

Richard Johnson is top billed as Jonas Wilde, a British secret service agent licensed to kill ("He is a weapon," the tag line proclaimed due to his killer karate chop) who wants to resign. Besides its leading man who bore an uncanny resemblance to Sean Connery, the only other thing that made this similar to the James Bond series was a bevy of pretty lasses—Carol Lynley (using a believable, lilting British accent), Barbara Bouchet, Sylvia Sims, and Diana Dors. There are no exotic locations (the marina scenes were done in-house with a phony backdrop), outrageous gadgets, or humorous banter to be found. Even Wilde's drink of choice, Bacardi on the rocks, is not as hip as Bond's martini shaken not stirred.

Asked why she accepted such a small role, Carol reflected and replied, "I think I wanted to work with Seth Holt. It was a name I had always heard of and really didn't know too much about but was curious. I liked working with him a lot."[257]

It was reported that *Danger Route* (working titles *People Who Make No Noise Are Dangerous* and *I Call Karate*) was a troubled production. Milton Subotsky called it "a doomed film."[258] The movie went into production on February 20, 1967 under the novel's title *The Eliminator* and the screenplay was by Meade Roberts (who also scripted Lynley's movie *The Stripper*). Writer Robert Stewart was credited for supplying special material. Max Rosenberg also revealed it was a problematic shoot and shared that one day "David Chasman, who was the head of UA productions in the UK at the time, came out to the set and he and Milton got into a fight—I don't know about what. And I think David, who was quick off the mark, called Milton an idiot. Anyway, Milton came to my flat that night with a letter addressed to David saying, 'I am not an idiot. I am a member of MENSA [the high IQ Society].'"[259] Rosenberg wisely convinced his partner (who he claimed lived in "cuckoo land") not to send the note.

Danger Route opens with a brassy song by Lionel Bart and belted out by British singer Anita Harris, doing her best Shirley Bassey imitation, over the title credits. Lynley enters the film clad in a mod sixties mini dress as a market researcher who rings the doorbell of Jonas Wilde. The audience has already learned that he is an agent for the British secret service just returned to London after an assignment in the Caribbean. His cover in England is as the owner of a boatyard in the Channel Islands where he works with yachtsman and fellow agents Brian Stern (Gordon Jackson) and Peter Ravenspur (Maurice Denham) who lives in a farmhouse close to the marina. Wilde's working unit is invaded by Mari (Barbara Bouchet), a beautiful American, claiming to be Ravenspur's long-lost niece from California, but is suspected by Jonas to be a British spy. Unbeknownst to Wilde, someone in the secret service wants him dead and arranges for him to eliminate a Czech defector being held by the Americans. They are hoping that either the agent in charge named Lucinda (Sam Wanamaker) will kill him or, if Jonas succeeds in his mission, a woman they have in place will finish the job.

Lynley's market researcher is named Jocelyn and she playfully asks him questions about his purchasing habits. It turns out she is actually Jonas' live-in girlfriend, who is happy to see him. Tired and burned out, Jonas talks of retiring to Majorca with her. His superior Canning (Harry Andrews) communicates with him via coded messages placed in the want ads. Jonas sees a message but acts on it early. To the consternation of Canning's wife Barbara (Sylvia Sims), he invades their home on a night of a dinner party to resign. Canning says he will pass it on to the higher ups, but they have one last mission for him—to take out that Czech scientist being held in a safe house by the Americans. Wilde returns home to Jocelyn who is hosting a bunch of zonked out friends and informs her that he must leave the next day to sail a boat down to another harbor for a client.

Carol is missing from the rest of the convoluted movie as Jonas completes his mission to assassinate the scientist with the help of an unsuspecting housekeeper (Diana Dors) only to discover that Canning is missing, and that Stern is a double agent who has killed Ravenspur and then Mari before Jonas eliminates him. Returning home, Wilde comes to the realization that Stern had to have inside help. After fixing himself a drink, he finds Jocelyn casually soaking in the bathtub. Clad in her robe, she nonchalantly emerges from her toilette. Jonas then tells her that he knows she was working for Stern and she replies cavalierly, "It pays well. And that's what drives us, isn't it—all the lovely loot." Jocelyn then informs Jonas that she poisoned his ice cubes that he habitually has with his Bacardi and now his body will soon be slowly shutting down leading to death. Wilde embraces her and then points to the dead fish floating in his aquarium where he dumped the cubes. Trapped in his grip, Jocelyn says, "You can't Jonas. You were in love with me." He replies, "I still am," as the camera pans left to the fish tank and, in shadow on the wall behind it, the audience see Jonas deliver a deadly karate chop to her neck. The missing Canning turns up alive and blackmails Wilde to remain an agent or he will have to answer for the murder of Jocelyn.

Danger Route was released throughout Great Britain in November 1967. Milton Subotsky was not happy with the finished movie and elaborated, "A spy story that came out at near the end of the spy cycle. Director ill. Cameraman changed during production. Only the actors came out of it well."[260]

Director Seth Holt (who died of a heart attack three years later making his next movie) does a deft job keeping the action moving though the plot becomes confusing and some scenes are outright uninteresting. This is more the fault of the script than director. Like his producer, Holt detested the spy movie and remarked, "It's dreadful. I scarcely saw it finished. I had a very difficult schedule. I was waiting between one and another and I needed the bread."[261]

Critical reaction was mixed. Penelope Mortimer in *The Observer* called it "a small-scale British thriller quietly and ably directed by Seth Holt" and that Lynley "is cute up until that last swipe that breaks her neck." Richard Roud in *The Guardian* found the movie to be "a reasonably satisfying piece of work, in spite of somewhat messy construction."

In the U.S., *Danger Route* did not screen until winter/early spring of 1968 – during the time *The Shuttered Room* was playing. As with that movie, this too sometimes wound up on the bottom of a double bill paired with *Attack on the Iron Coast*. Critics either followed the plot and liked it or were totally lost. For example, Howard Thompson of the *New York Times* remarked, "What hoists *Danger Route* to the level of pretty good pulp melodrama is the incisive dialogue, especially the clipped direction of Seth Holt, who gathers it all up at about mid-point, and hurls it at the camera." On the other end of the spectrum was Edgar Driscoll, Jr. of the *Boston Globe* who described the movie as being "hazy ... long on murder and mayhem and short on the whys and wherefores." He did find Carol to be "lithe and lovely" matching the reviewer in *Variety* who called her "pretty."

Johnson is stiff and glum throughout the film except in his scenes with Diana Dors that are fun with him pretending to be a working-class guy on the make. Evoking mod mid-sixties London with her wardrobe and hair styles, Carol looked gorgeous and is a visual highlight in her brief appearance. Second billed, she is missing from almost three quarters of the film. Having the baby-faced blonde emerge as the double-crossing agent was a nice twist at the end (though a cheat since her character is never fully developed and there is not a hint to make the audience suspicious) and viewers can tell Carol relished playing the final scenes. Leonard Maltin thought so too and wrote in *Leonard Maltin's Movie and Video Guide*, "Appearance (in both senses of the word) of Lynley and Bouchet give a little boost to typical secret agent tale with several plot twists."

As with *The Shuttered Room*, *Danger Route* too did not make a dent at the U.S. box office and brought in less than $1 million dollars. And just like with that thriller, it has grown in stature over the years especially with fans who like their sixties spy movies more serious than spoof. In 2009, director Quentin Tarantino even chose it as one of his favorite genre movies to air when he hosted a week of programming on the now defunct cable network TRIO. When told this, Carol exclaimed, "I would have loved to have appeared in one of his movies! I think he is an extremely talented director."[262]

Danger Route would prove to be Carol's swan song while living in London. Her name was bandied about in the press for two important American movies though while there. It was reported that Warren Beatty saw photos of Lynley from *Harlow* and liked her thirties-era look enough to consider her for *Bonnie and Clyde* but ultimately felt she looked too young for the part. That is as far as it went despite what many reference books allege. Per Carol, "For the record, I never met with Warren Beatty to discuss *Bonnie and Clyde*, nor did I ever see the script. Believe me; if this role was offered, I would have taken it in a second."[263] And probably unbeknownst to her, she was on producer Lawrence Turman's short-list to play Mrs. Robinson's daughter in *The Graduate* along with Natalie Wood, Ann-Margret, Jane Fonda, Tuesday Weld, Carroll Baker, Sue Lyon, Lee Remick, Suzanne Pleshette, Elizabeth Ashley, Yvette Mimieux, Pamela Tiffin, Patty Duke, and Hayley Mills.[264] Katherine Ross got the part and an Academy Award nomination.

Personally, Lynley seemed to be enjoying spending more time in England simply focusing on herself. According to an interview she gave to writer Victor Davis, she settled on King's Road where she contemplated opening a stall in the Chelsea Antiques Market. She called this period her "first real break from celluloid into reality."[265] Carol confirmed this was the reason she stayed in London for that long. Working since she was a child; it is understandable that the twenty-four-year-old actress wanted some time to concentrate on herself and her daughter.

Despite her lack of work, columnist Alex Freeman reported in January 1967 that Carol was determined to build an acting career in Europe.[266] Shortly after, Earl Wilson reported that Vittorio de Sica proclaimed that "the new Carlo Ponti film will show Carol Lynley parading semi-nude down Rome's Via Veneto."[267] It never happened—on film at least.

*****

Carol returned to living in Los Angeles fulltime sometime during the summer of 1967. She moved back into her tony Beverly Hills home but sold it a few months later, trading in the hubbub of the city for the tranquility of Malibu. She rented a house there but not in the Colony, which was home to the rich and famous. Among her celebrity neighbors in her part of Malibu were actors Larry Hagman (who would come a-calling for a favor soon), Burgess Meredith, and Bobby Darin.

Reflecting on living abroad, Carol commented to columnist Dick Kleiner upon her return, "For the first time in my life I was on my own, really on my own. I had to stand on my own two feet. I did things there that I never could have done here. A friend of mine gave a party for Princess Margaret and I was the hostess."[268]

In an interview with columnist Vernon Scott two years later, the actress went even further on why she left for a time and what about Hollywood drove her away. She stated matter-of-factly,

> England was a good place to get away from it all and to escape trapping myself in a typical Hollywood setting. The move helped me to expand as a person, and when I returned I made the decision to live in [Malibu]. This way I can work in motion pictures or do a TV show without becoming part of the scene. Women in this town can lose their identity. It's dehumanizing. I look at some of the actresses and wonder if there is a real person inside. I am not going to become one of those hard actresses.[269]

Although it seems living in London was a maturing process for the young actress, her career had changed. Being off the silver screen for so long (as they say in Hollywood, you are only as good as your last movie) may have hurt her stature with film producers. Movie magazines wrote much less about her (which Carol was happy about remarking, "I like to date and go out, but I don't like the publicity that goes with it."[270]) and her female teenage fan base had grown up and moved on. Also, Hollywood was a-changin' with the rise of the independent producer and the studios cutting back on their film production. Whereas some of her contemporaries such as Yvette Mimieux,

Diane McBain, Mimsy Farmer, Susan Strasberg, and Sandra Dee lowered their standards from earlier in the decade and now took jobs in B-movies for American International Pictures, Carol never did.

Lynley would remain off the silver screen until the spring of 1969 though she was purportedly up for one important movie that came to light in the press. According to columnist Alex Freeman, Carol was seriously considered for the role of the nineteen-year-old babysitter opposite Burt Lancaster as *The Swimmer*, but at age twenty-four was reportedly deemed too old for the part (as compared to *Bonnie and Clyde* where she looked too youthful).[271] Newcomer Janet Landgard was cast instead. No wonder Lynley felt stymied.

In an interview she gave to *Newsweek* at this time, Carol shared her thoughts on why she was having a tough time finding good movie roles. It was a problem that vexed Tuesday Weld and Yvette Mimieux as well. *Newsweek* speculated that while they were still trying to shake their ingénue personas and land that standout cinematic vehicle, others, such as Faye Dunaway due to *Bonnie and Clyde*, soared by them to the top. Carol felt no animosity towards Dunaway and commented, "There hasn't been any American actress terribly successful for ages. She has been presented with great style and ability in an unusual film and that's enough. She's broken out of the mold."[272]

Opining on why she was having difficulties, Carol felt she was typed as the ingénue no doubt due to when she arrived on the Hollywood scene - about the same time as Tuesday, Yvette, Sandra Dee, and Connie Stevens. She stated,

> I can't fit into stereotypes. I'd love to work with Fellini or Fred Zinnemann—they put the actor in natural situations and ask him to perform naturally. If I walked through the door tomorrow, I would be considered exciting. But when a person has been in this business a long time, people lose interest. They think of you as you were four years ago. I've only started to come out of this young girl thing in the last year or so. I'll be at my most successful at 26 or 28.[273]

Despite the challenges she faced, Carol was pleased that she was free of her contractual binds to 20th Century-Fox. "I was not interested in picture deals or anything like that," she revealed today. "My agent negotiated that pact with Fox that included six-month extensions if I couldn't do a movie for whatever reason. I made seven films for Fox when it ended. My then intention was to make movies all over."[274]

Though she may not have realized it at the time, and despite her frustrations about not getting lead roles in big movies like she did prior in the decade, 1967 is when a new more interesting phase of Carol's career began. With her *Playboy* pictorial and appearances in two thrillers and a spy adventure film, boys and men began to take more notice of her. She had matured into a beautiful woman with an angelic face who projected the perfect qualities to portray the terrorized innocent, bewildered by her predicament or the mentally distressed woman who may or may not be victimized in genres favored by males. This is where most of the dramatic film and TV roles Lynley would be cast in for the next twenty years or so.

Carol excelled as the frightened, unbalanced, fragile heroine, so it is not surprising to learn that she was a fan of actress Vivien Leigh. She commented, "I've always admired the inspired edge of light insanity she brought to her work. That slightly-bananas quality fascinates me."[275] This also can be said to the qualities Carol brought to some of her characters and why she was a popular choice to play these types of women.

Television offered Carol opportunities in late 1967 and 1968 that the big screen did not. She made guest appearances playing various roles on three popular fantasy-type television programs—an avenging headstrong young woman in a spy spoof; a psychologist captured by aliens who may or may not be abetting the series' hero in a sci-fi adventure; and a blank-faced mannequin come to life in a supernatural anthology—plus a young woman on the run when mistaken for a bank robber in a cop show and a resistance fighter who sacrifices love in a serious tele feature set in the near totalitarian future. Purposefully or not, Carol accepted off-beat lady in peril roles that provided an acting stretch for her. Commenting on her succession of TV roles, Carol said,

> I think what most people don't realize is that I *had* to work. I had to not only support myself but my daughter too. I didn't receive any help from anyone unfortunately. I would have liked it but wasn't able to. I had to keep working to educate my daughter and put her through school and then college. I didn't have an easy time of it. I didn't have the luxury of turning down scripts and did most of what was offered to me.[276]

Napoleon Solo (Robert Vaughn) meets the troublesome Annie (Carol Lynley) in the two-part "The Prince of Darkness Affair" on *The Man from U.N.C.L.E.* (MGM Television, 1967).

Her first TV show guest episode to hit the airwaves was *The Man from U.N.C.L.E.* It offered a comedic lady in peril role for Carol, whose character was a continuous thorn in the side to the U.N.C.L.E. agents. The series was originally conceived by James Bond creator Ian Fleming as *Solo*, a show about ace agent, Napoleon Solo, who worked for a United Nations law enforcement unit. The show was renamed before airing and became one of the biggest hits on television during the 1964-65 season. The series really found its footing during the latter half of that season and the beginning of the next. Audiences were glued to their sets, as the show safely stylized their fantasies (handsome virile men and gorgeous women entangled in all sorts of fantastical espionage) and fears (THRUSH a Cold War-like conglomerate of enemy agents).

U.N.C.L.E.'s top agent was Napoleon Solo (Robert Vaughn) aided by Russian Illya Kuryakin (David McCallum), both who took orders from the fastidious bureau chief Mr. Waverly (Leo G. Carroll, who followed actor Will Kuluva as Mr. Allison in the pilot). Influenced by the wonderful technological space age gadgets on display in the Bond films, *The Man from U.N.C.L.E.* was a true delight for young viewers, especially boys and men as a number of sexy starlets including Senta Berger, Yvonne Craig, Danielle de Metz, France Nuyen, Luciana Paluzzi, Diane McBain, Anna Capri and many others could be seen on the program. The show was so popular that a number of two-part episodes were re-edited, padded with new footage or outtakes and rushed into theaters. During the show's first two years on the air, fans could see their favorite U.N.C.L.E. stars on the big screen in *To Trap a Spy* (1965), *The Spy with My Face* (1965), *One Spy Too Many* (1966) and *One of Our Spies Is Missing* (1966). Unfortunately, as the series began to become more of a spoof than a dramatic show by season three, the quality of the program suffered. A new producer was brought in for season four returning the show, if not to its full glory, something close. However, by then the fans had slipped away (the change in timeslot did not help matters) and U.N.C.L.E. mania had waned.

With much fanfare, Carol Lynley guest starred during the fourth and last season in the two-part episode "The Prince of Darkness Affair," directed by the prolific and talented Boris Sagal ("He had a wonderful sense of humor,"[277] recalled Carol). It was his first and only time working on the series. The teleplay was by Dean Hargrove who was considered one of the series' most popular writers as he successfully blended nonstop action with humor in his scripts. This episode is one of his best. It aired on October 2 and 9, 1967 and rivaled some of the earlier well-received ones.

Reportedly, the episode was one of the series' most costly and used approximately eighty elaborate sets ranging "from an African village and plush Persian palace to a Greek island stronghold and the new U.N.C.L.E. headquarters with its electronic compute marvels." Jungle scenes were shot on MGM's backlot, already constructed for many of its Tarzan movies. Unfortunately, there is some obvious sloppy editing and continuity gaffes (i.e. an unconscious and bound Solo at end of Part 1 only to be neither at the beginning of Part 2; disappearing and reappearing ID badges; etc.) that should have been caught and corrected.

Many actresses that worked on this series found David McCallum to be utterly charming and approachable unlike Robert Vaughn. BarBara Luna commented, "As for acting with him [Vaughn], he is not unpleasant to work with, just aloof."[278] Kathy Kersh noted, "I respected him very much as an actor, but he was rather pompous and a bit full of himself."[279] Sharyn Hillyer who had a recurring role on the series as agent Wanda commented, "Robert Vaughn was nice and friendly enough, but he kept to himself. He was professional, but he wasn't much fun."[280]

Statuesque blonde Thordis Brandt had a small role as Miss Zalamar the enamored assistant to bad guy Luther Sebastian in Carol's episode. Recalling the making of it, Thordis found both lead actors distant. She said, "Robert Vaughn and David McCallum kept to themselves. Neither one socialized with me on the set."[281]

When asked her opinion of her co-stars, Carol commented,

> I liked David McCallum a lot. Robert Vaughn too and I always got along beautifully with him. He was aloof and reserved like some actresses have said, but that was just the way he was.

When you got to know him and spend time talking with him, he was absolutely terrific. I kind of brushed by Bradford Dillman when I was younger and living in New York. He was a quiet guy—well-mannered and nice. And he was a very good actor.[282]

A pistol-packing Annie (Carol Lynley) proves she means business in the two-part "The Prince of Darkness Affair" on *The Man from U.N.C.L.E.* (MGM Television, 1967).

In "The Prince of Darkness Affair," THRUSH is after a ray generator called the Thermal Prism invented by Dr. Kharmusi (John Dehner). Mr. Waverly recruits wanted master criminal Luther Sebastian (Bradford Dillman), hiding out as a member of a religious sect called The Third Way on a remote island, in aiding agents Solo and Kuryakin in retrieving it from Kharmusi's home and fortress in exchange for immunity. Clad in a striped blue mini dress,. Carol Lynley as Annie is styled stunningly here and is a knockout in her opening scene - shopping at an outdoor market in Tehran (you won't find ladies dressed like that there any more) and flirtingly eyeing Solo who cannot but help ogle her back. When she, accompanied by the knife-throwing Hassan Aksoy (H.M. Wynant), discovers that Napoleon is an U.N.C.L.E. agent and that Sebastian is working with them, she is miffed but still determined to bring Sebastian to justice because "my fiancé Hugh Winslow of the Bakersfield's Winslow's is in a Turkish prison because Sebastian framed him for a murder *he committed*. I've spent a whole year collecting evidence. I must free my poor Hugh from that awful prison." The episode's running gag is that Hassan is one of four brothers of Hugh's cellmate, also framed by Sebastian, and as one is killed off another takes his place (all played by Wynant).

Kharmusi's double-crossing wife Azalea (Lola Albright) knocks off the first brother and takes Solo to her home where her husband is expecting him as a potential buyer of the Prism. However, he knows from the get-go that Solo is an U.N.C.L.E. agent. While Kuryakin and Sebastian fight, climb, and crawl their way into the safe, Annie (clad in a super short minidress to rival that of Uhura's on *Star Trek*) shows up pretending to be Solo's wife. She thinks by ratting out Napoleon she can make a deal with Kharmusi for Sebastian, but the doctor has no idea who he is. Annie then pulls a gun on him only to find the bullets have been removed. Taking her to his control room, they watch as all hell breaks loose with Kuryakin rescuing Solo and Azalea from Kharmusi's sand trap and Sebastian cracking the safe to snatch the prism. He shoots Kharmusi dead and, as programed, his fortress explodes shortly after the five of them escape. Part I concludes with Napoleon, Illya, and Annie tied up on a boat after they have been double-crossed by Sebastian (who planned the entire operation), Azalea and the Third Way followers. Sebastian plans to control the balance of power in the world after he launches the Thermal Prism into space. After a bound Annie tells Sebastian and Azalea they are "strange, really strange," Sebastian quips, "I have no idea who you are but I have a feeling you deserve whatever happens to you." They hop off the boat and send it at full speed toward the U.N.C.L.E. boat that Mr. Waverly is on and a torpedo is launched to counter it. The episode closes with a bound Solo trying to break free and climbing up to the bridge only to fall and hit his head rendering him unconscious.

The second half of "The Prince of Darkness Affair" gives Lynley much less to do and she only has one or two good scenes. It opens with a rehash of the end of Part I, but instead of Solo climbing up the ladder and falling, he miraculously breaks his bounds and frees Kuryakin and Annie. They jump off the boat and swim away from it before it explodes to smithereens. This is such an easily spotted blooper and it is amazing that no one in production picked up on it. The continuity folks and editors were truly asleep at the wheel.

At U.N.C.L.E. headquarters, Waverly blames Annie for putting the mission in jeopardy and wants her gone. Illya thinks she can cause no more harm just as the alarms go off. Agents catch Annie trying to sneak into an equipment room after her debriefing and she tries to double-talk her way out of it, berating them for not doing enough to find Sebastian while her poor Hugh is still rotting away in that Turkish prison.

Solo tries to track down Sebastian by visiting his estranged wife (Julie London) and then going undercover as a member of the Third Way (white hair and all to fit in). Annie, meanwhile, has hooked up with another Aksoy brother and they follow Kuryakin to a theater where they are captured by Azalea and her Third Way followers. Brought to Los Angeles, Azalea puts the disguised Solo in charge of watching her prisoners. They leave when a group of female Third Way members arrive for a celebratory party, however Sebastian has ordered them to be gassed. Solo escapes while Sebastian, discovering that Azalea has a tracking device on her, ejects Hassan's brother from the car into Los Angeles freeway traffic in revenge. He then takes them to a downtown office building which is a front for his missile silo where he intends to launch the Thermal Prism into space. A third brother appears and lends Solo a helping hand as he tricks Sebastian's uncooperative wife into revealing where he is. While brother number three keeps Sebastian and his cohorts at gunpoint, Solo tries to diffuse the rocket. Sebastian knifes the brother and then he and Solo scuffle resulting in the madman being pushed into the rocket as it takes off only to explode on entry into space. Azalea and the others are rounded up.

The episode concludes with Annie receiving unwelcome news about Hugh from Hassan's freed brother Aksoy who was imprisoned with him. Hugh won't be returning to her, but she goes off with Aksoy instead after a bit of matchmaking from Solo.

"The Prince of Darkness Affair" was well-received at the time of its initial broadcast. The *TV Scout* column called it "a must for all super-spy fans." It still holds up all these decades later and *Man from U.N.C.L.E.* fans consider this episode a highlight of season four and one of the better episodes of the entire series. For instance, on the web site TheManfromUNCLE.org it was described as "like a throwback to season two, very fast moving and the most expensive for the series."

In a role that could have been annoyingly cloying in the hands of the wrong actress, Carol gives an amusing performance as Annie. Her character stubbornly perseveres even though she finds herself in more dangerous situations than expected and the brothers sent to help her keep getting killed off. Although she continues to muck things up for the U.N.C.L.E. agents, you cannot help but love her determination to get justice for her fiancé, plus Carol is a knockout in the skimpiest of mini dresses. This is a type of character that can be quite irksome in a spy adventure, but Carol played her with such a playful, innocent touch that she is a highlight of the episode.

In 1968, the episode was restructured into the feature film with the uninspired title *The Helicopter Spies*. The editing gaffes were corrected (most notably there was now a shot of Solo slipping out of the ropes that bound his hands on the boat), some special effects sequences were enhanced, and a few newly shot scenes with Julie London as Sebastian's man-hungry ex-wife, seen with several shirtless men in her boudoir (in the TV version she is solo with Solo), were added. The film never played in U.S. theaters, but was released internationally. It was received warmly in Hong Kong by the *South China Morning Post* whose critic commented, "Not since *The Spy in the Green Hat* have the men from UNCLE been so good, which is to say a lot. *The Helicopter Spies* is slick, well-made and, at times, wryly original." The *Monthly Film Bulletin*'s review included, "Against a variety of low budget sets, and with minimal direction, the cut-price mini-Bonds mechanically perform what is required of them, while Carol Lynley as a mini-skirted all American avenger … [shows] desperate determination in the face of impossible odds."

Critics in the United Kingdom were not so generous. Richard Roud of *The Guardian* wrote, "The *Helicopter Spies* is another in *The Man from U.N.C.L.E.* series, sillier and duller than usual." Tom Milne of *The Observer* found *Helicopter Spies* to be "easily the worst of *The Man from UNCLE* series, and surely the very last gasp of the moribund spy and secret agent cycle." It wasn't. There was one more to come from the *U.N.C.L.E.* franchise and many more spy films from others to follow.

*****

As with *Star Trek*, the science fiction series *The Invaders* only received middling ratings during its one and a half season run. It developed a minor cult following after it was cancelled. However, unlike *Star Trek* that found new audiences in syndication, *The Invaders* all but disappeared from the air waves making its unavailability more of a draw for its fervent fans. Carol Lynley has the distinction in appearing in the episode that changed the premise of the series for its remaining time on the air.

The Invaders was created by Larry Cohen who sold the idea to ABC-TV even without a pilot. He envisioned the series airing two days a week in half-hour installments with a cliffhanger like with the network's *Batman*. That idea was rejected and ABC brought in prolific producer Quinn Martin (*The Untouchables*; *The Fugitive*) and his production team. This would be his first foray into science fiction. With this team in place, Cohen had no control of the series' direction and was only able to offer suggestions. Unhappy with the outcome, it was the catalyst for Cohen to go into film production where he could maintain control as producer/director/screenwriter.

Describing the premise of the series, producer Alan Armer explained to the media, "They're here among us now … in your city … maybe on your block. They're invaders … alien beings from another planet … but they look just like us! Take a look around. Casually. No sense letting them know you're suspicious. The new neighbors across the street. The substitute teacher. That too-pretty secretary in your husband's office. Any one of them might be an invader from outer space."[283]

The Invaders premiered January 10, 1967 on ABC. Overworked architect David Vincent (Roy Thinnes) pulls over to the side of a deserted country rode to rest his eyes when he is awakened by a piercing sound from above and is astonished to see a flying saucer landing. He contacts the police, but they do not find anything where Vincent thinks he saw the UFO set down. A young attractive couple is also in the area and as they deny seeing or hearing anything, Vincent notices that their hands are mutated with their pinkies jutting out at an odd angle. With nobody believing his story, Vincent searches for proof thinking the fate of the world rests in his hands. He meets a sympathetic hotel owner (Diane Baker) who believes him but then he discovers that she is one of the aliens from a doomed planet now here to take over the Earth to survive. Since they can take on human form, the aliens plan to infiltrate all aspects of society until they control Earth. He is told not to fight the inevitable.

This set the tone for the remainder of the first season and the ratings climbed as our hero combats the aliens while trying to prove their existence to doubting humans. Over time, viewers learn that besides the misshaped pinky, some aliens glow when they need rejuvenation to keep their human form and that they have no pulse or heartbeat. When *The Invaders* returned for the start of its second season on September 5, 1967, the ratings began to decline quickly. The audience became weary with the series, as each episode seemed to follow the same formula, where the people David puts his trust into turn out to be aliens while the humans think he is nuts. Trying to inject life into the series and increase viewership, writer Barry Oringer delivered the episode, "The Believers" where David finally meets several other people including Lynley's character who also know that the aliens are among them. Considered to be one of the series' best episodes, "The Believers" was directed by Paul Wendkos (his eighth episode of the series). Explaining this new direction, producer Alan Armer remarked, "We made the change because David Vincent's plight seemed such a hopeless one. His task was so huge that we felt the viewer was becoming frustrated and despairing of his success … With 'The Believers' we introduce seven allies, some in prominent positions, and the viewer feels there is a chance. It becomes a bit more of a contest … Under the new format Vincent has friends who bring him into the story, whom he can touch bases with, who have contacts and are capable of helping with research and investigation."[284]

Another reason for the change was due to his leading man. Armer went on to explain, "In the past it was hard for Roy Thinnes to play scenes with 'people' who had no emotions or with humans who felt either pity, skepticism, or scorn for him. We had to work hard to keep this from becoming a series cliché. Carol Lynley…joins the group and we are hoping to have her back again if her schedule permits."[285]

Carol especially enjoyed doing this episode due to Roy Thinnes whom she called, "a sweet man and I mean that in a positive way. He was a sensitive guy and was a good actor. I liked him a lot."[286]

When asked if she liked playing these ambiguous characters, she answered proudly,

> Producers just offered me those kinds of roles. It is hard to say this out loud—I had a very pretty face, but I was a much better actor than that. I think people realized that and that is why I was given those kinds of roles. I had the ability to do them well.

I had the presence and security. I knew what I was doing and most people around me knew what I was doing. However, I also was always willing to listen to anybody who had a suggestion or wanted me to do something another way.[287]

An uneasy David Vincent (Roy Thinnes) puts his trust in Elyse Reynolds (Carol Lynley) to help him escape from the aliens in "The Believers" on *The Invaders* (Quinn Martin Production, 1967).

"The Believers" begins with Thinnes' David Vincent meeting with a small group of people who also believe in the aliens' presence. After their clandestine gathering in which industrialist Edgar Scoville (Kent Smith), by telephone, has agreed to fund their operation, the group, except for David, is gunned down by the aliens who have uncovered their whereabouts. He is rendered unconscious and taken to an indoctrination center. Under hypnotic interrogation, David counters their hypnosis and divulges nothing. They then set up another ruse to get him to reveal the whereabouts of the Believers and fail again

While in the center's cafeteria, David meets lovely clinical psychologist Elyse Reynolds (Carol Lynley) who is being held prisoner. She confides to a distrusting David that the aliens are using her to learn more about the psyche of humans in the face of disaster. Still suspect of her intentions, David allows her to lead him to a vent where they make their escape. While hiding out in a hotel, David tries to ditch Elyse but, after pleading her case - that she wants to help defeat the invaders and that with her brother dead she has no family to return to - he reconsiders, agreeing to take her to meet the remaining Believers.

After returning from an encounter with a Prof. Hellman (Rhys Williams), Elyse breaks down and confesses that her sixteen-year-old brother was killed by the aliens when they abducted her. That night they learn Hellman is dead. Once again, David's suspicions of Elyse arise, especially after a secret rendezvous with Believer Bob Turin (Anthony Eisley) and his wife Mary (Maura McGiveney) in a motel ends with a surprise ambush by the aliens leaving Mary dead. David sets a trap for Elyse and she falls for it. He then forces her to confess her true involvement with the aliens. She begs forgiveness claiming that they are holding her brother prisoner and she is being forced to help them track down the Believers. David, however, has proof that her sibling really did die in the car wreck when they grabbed Elyse. Realizing that she was duped, Elyse breaks down in tears. After escaping from another group of aliens, David brings Elyse to the remaining five Believers where she pledges her loyalty to stop the aliens at any cost.

Elyse Reynolds was a standout role for Carol. Acting peculiarly throughout, you are never quite sure of Elyse's motives and intentions. The question of her loyalty remains a mystery and that is due to Lynley's utterly convincing performance that keeps the viewer and our hero guessing. She is particularly sympathetic when she cries over the realization that her brother is dead but the viewer is still not assured that she is a dedicated Believer.

TV historian Stephen Bowie called this episode one of the series' best and commented on his blog, "Carol Lynley turns in an excellent performance as Elyse, and a suspenseful finale in a deserted bus station represents director Paul Wendkos' best work for the series. But it is Barry Oringer's teleplay that takes *The Invaders*' grim tone and its paranoid outlook to a new level. The script contains multiple tricks and betrayals, and like Vincent the audience is never certain if Elyse can be trusted. Vincent's reluctance to become emotionally involved with her gives viewers a rare look at the toll that his lonely, alien-hunting existence has taken on him …Vincent acknowledges the stepping up of his war in a speech to Elyse in which he urges her to carry on if he is killed."[288]

It was not surprising to Lynley's fans that she was good in this role, but it was shocking to them seeing her extremely short haircut ala Mia Farrow in *Peyton Place*. Carol told the press, "It was just an impulse that made me have it cut. Believe me, it was not temperament. The last time I had it this short was when I was 18 years old."[289] It takes quite a bit getting used to and not the most flattering, but as it grew out, Lynley never looked better - as evidenced in *Once You Kiss a Stranger* and *Norwood* to be filmed the following year.

Lynley and some of the other guest stars were wanted to reprise their roles on the series now that David was part of a group combatting the aliens. Though Kent Smith became a regular and appears in the remaining episodes and Anthony Eisley, as Bob Torin, turns up one more time in "Ransom," Carol, as Elyse, did not. When asked if she was invited back, Carol replied, "I certainly didn't turn anything down. I might have been working on something at the same time though."[290] Unfortunately, viewers never got to learn if Elyse remained committed to David and the Believers. It is too bad because the emotionally scarred Elyse could have added extra tension to the drama.

Inspector Erksine (Efrem Zimbalist, Jr.) tries to help the troubled Lynn Hallett (Carol Lynley) after she is charged with armed robbery in "False Witness" on *The F.B.I.* (Warner Bros. – Seven Arts Television, 1967).

Filmed prior, though it aired five days after *The Invaders*, Carol turned up with long hair, looking ravishing in "False Witness," an action-packed episode on *The F.B.I.* (one TV critic found it to be "an absorbing" hour), which based its stories on real life cases. Lynley's beauty worked against her playing Lynn Halpert, a small-town waitress with a criminal record and a mistrust of authority figures. The glamorous actress looks a bit out of place behind the counter at a greasy spoon dive. That said, she emotes quite well in the part and convincingly conveys Lynn's desperation and skepticism.

Before shooting began, Carol did some research to get inside the mind of the character, so alien to her, and headed over to the Sunset Strip. Even though she was just a few years older than the hippies who hung out on the famous thoroughfare, Carol was a mother and working actress and had no connection to this new breed of young people. She explained in 1967,

> I wanted to figure out what makes the 'hip set' tick so that I could properly portray a disenchanted young girl who had fallen so out of step with the world—so insecure that she allows herself to be drawn into a robbery plot. I made an interesting discovery while mingling with the so-called way-out types ... Many of the girls are exactly like the role I wanted to portray, but they are not the hippies they seem. Most are from good backgrounds, quite a few are smart secretaries during the day and merely gravitate to the Strip ... It's almost as though they are leading double lives ... It is all terribly unreal. The search for 'kicks' is too intense, the atmosphere too contrived to be spontaneous.[291]

The episode begins as Lynn Halpert is mistakenly identified as the getaway driver in a bank robbery. When a wounded guard dies, and a murder charge is added to her list of crimes, she escapes the lecherous advances of her "concerned" boss and skips town with her ex-con boyfriend Mike James (Peter Deuel breaking away from his sitcom persona) and heads to Los Angeles. Though the evidence is stacked against her, Inspector Erskine (Efrem Zimbalist, Jr.) believes in Lynn's innocence and works with the crime lab to prove it. His hunch pays off and the F.B.I. closes in on the real bank robbers. Meanwhile on the run, Lynn hesitantly agrees to help Mike and his former cellmate rob the box office of the Long Beach Auditorium. She wisely backs out just before the federal agents close in and arrest Mike and his buddy. After being cleared of all the charges held against her, Lynn decides to remain in LA to offer moral support to Mike who, as the epilog indicated, was convicted of conspiracy to commit armed robbery.

Interestingly, *The Invaders* and *The F.B.I.* would be the only two Quinn Martin TV shows Lynley would ever appear in. Even during the seventies when she was at her height of doing guest stints on TV, appearing in many crime dramas, she was surprisingly never cast in any of his popular detective series such as *Dan August, Cannon, Banyon, The Streets of San Francisco*, and *Barnaby Jones*.

*****

Carol's new shorn locks were not a hit with the producers of her next TV show, *Journey to the Unknown*. This was an anthology series filmed in England about the supernatural - co-produced by 20th Century-Fox Television and Hammer Films who reportedly invested $3 million into this venture. Joan Harrison who had nine years' experience in the realm of fantasy and suspense as producer of *Alfred Hitchcock Presents* and *The Alfred Hitchcock Hour* was co-Executive Producer. Her goal for the series' viewers was "to scare. I think there is no point in not hitting the nervous system as far as one can ... I think people rather like to be frightened sometimes, as long as they are entertained as well."[292]

Explaining why they chose to film in Britain, Harrison said, "This kind of series really is very well set in England, which has always been known for its mystery. Secondly, there is the benefit of the quota to combine American actors with good English character actors."[293] Harrison also admitted that another reason was due to the "cheap labor costs, it's possible to film almost twice as long on the same budget. This permits the attention to detail and reshooting that promises to give *Journey to the Unknown* almost movie like quality."[294]

Harrison's producing partner was Norman Lloyd. They had worked together on the Alfred Hitchcock TV shows. Describing *Journey to the Unknown*, Lloyd remarked, "It was a suspense series, but with a mystic element in the stories. It was made at Boreham Wood Studios, and the experience of working there was exciting. The physical facilities—the sets, the wardrobe that was available to you, the locations—the looks of those places—were outstandingly good."²⁹⁵

When the actress arrived in merry ol' England the producers were taken aback with her short 'do. She was still beautiful but for the character of Eve the mannequin who comes to life they envisioned her with long blonde locks. Carol was immediately given a fall to emulate the hair she had shorn off, but it obviously looks like a wig. Carol said with a laugh, "They did give me that fall to wear but no one said that they didn't like my short haircut!"²⁹⁶

Window dresser Albert Baker (Dennis Waterman) and his lady love Eve (Carol Lynley) a mannequin who comes to life in "Eve" on *Journey to the Unknown* (20th Century-Fox Television/Hammer Films, 1968).

Carol's mane was the least of Joan Harrison's worries. She shared what it was like trying to shoot a TV show with many exterior scenes in England and remarked, "Although this series managed to show a fair amount of the countryside, it is not likely I would attempt to film much of another series outside, because it means waiting for the weather all the time. With the tight schedule of a television series, it is impossible to wait for the weather, so, unless you shoot them in the studio, there is no chance for the glamour scenes like people lying on the beach. Filming in London itself is not so bad, because you can always shoot interior locations when it is raining."²⁹⁷

Carol had nothing but praise for Joan and stated, "She was always a pleasure to work with. Her sets were always professional."²⁹⁸

American Robert Stevens was a veteran Emmy Award winning director of many suspense TV shows in the fifties and sixties including *Suspicion*, *Alfred Hitchcock Presents*, *The Twilight Zone*, and *The Alfred Hitchcock Hour* and a natural fit to helm this episode.

Two mannequins were created in Carol's likeness. She recalled,

> Before I went to London, I was sent to Fox to meet with John Chambers who did the makeup for *Planet of the Apes*. He created a plaster mask of my head and my face. It was not a simple thing to sit through and easy to get spooked by it. John knew what he was doing so that made me feel more comfortable. He was friendly and patient. Once the mask dried and they took it off me, you can see the resemblance. It was kind of freaky. When I got to London to shoot the episode, they had the two dummies with the mask and my hair already assembled.²⁹⁹

It was reported that during filming one of the mannequins kept falling apart causing production delays. An expert had to come in and stated that he had to "retool … the actress wasn't temperamental—the dummy was."³⁰⁰

Describing what it was like playing a mannequin, Carol remarked, "At first it was difficult for me because I couldn't talk. Dennis Waterman would have these long speeches and he would be speaking to me. I was always looking like I know what you mean but can't reply because I am a mannequin. I was terribly limited in what I could do."³⁰¹

Lynley commented on making *Journey to the Unknown* back in 1968 and was impressed with the visual aspects of the episode. Some of the scenes with Waterman and her were shot in soft-focus to give it a dream-like quality. "I must say that although I was shocked at first seeing the rushes, I began to enjoy it. That soft lighting! I felt like Doris Day. I mean everybody's got a wart somewhere and all that was screened out.[302]

Carol is practically mute the entire time in "Eve," as a living doll in the mind of lonely lad Albert Baker (Dennis Waterman), who wishes his life were a romantic fantasy like in the movies. A shoe salesman at a department store, he transfers to a lower paying job in the window dressing department when one night while walking past the store's exterior Eve comes to life and beckons him to join her. On his first day as a trainee, Albert sneaks into the window to see Eve who holds his hand. He then makes sure to work on every display where Eve is placed, while his boss Mr. Royal (Michael Gough) attires the lovely dummy in stylish evening gowns, mini dresses, and furs. Albert, meanwhile, fantasizes about their romantic times together out on the town in London. Their idyll ends when a panicked Albert learns that the store is replacing all its mannequins with newer models. While trying to sneak a fur-draped Eve out of the store, he is caught by his boss who is pushed by Albert off the second-floor balcony to his death.

Albert and Eve hide out at his place but run off to the country due to his nosy land lady (Hermione Baddeley). They stay with a hippie artist friend named George (Errol John) who feels sorry for the disturbed Albert after he introduces the mannequin as his girlfriend, Eve. When he confesses killing his boss accidentally, George tries to get him to face the truth that Eve is just a dummy. Eve, however, suddenly talks telling him that she is real and Albert is not the crazy one. The more Albert begins to think Eve is not alive the more she kisses him and confesses her love for him. When Albert overhears George talking to the police, he grabs Eve and they flee. They meet up with two drunken motorcycle ruffians. Thinking they are going to rape Eve; Albert jumps to her defense. A fight ensues, and Albert is stabbed. As he lays dying, he dreams of his time with Eve as he crawls over to his love and dies in her arms. As the thugs look down, they are dumbstruck as real tears flow from the mannequin's eyes. Was Eve just a figment of a lonely demented young man's mind or did she really come alive?

Carol Lynley is solely featured in this promotional print ad for the TV series *Journey to the Unknown. Billy Rose Theatre Division, The New York Public Library for the Performing Arts*

Though "Eve" was the tenth episode produced, it was chosen by ABC-TV to be the series' debut, most likely due to Lynley's name value as a draw for viewers. The network promoted the hell out of this and print ads of Carol appeared in *TV Guide* magazine and local newspapers throughout the U.S. The actress even went on a fifteen-city tour to help sell the series to the public. To interest viewers even more, the show was touted as being a cross between Alfred Hitchcock's shows with *The Twilight Zone*.

Despite the wig, Carol is looks wonderful in this and is nicely paired with Dennis Waterman, who is just terrific. Carol is effective as well. Using only her eyes and facial expressions, she relays Eve's feelings from lust for a mink fur that Albert offers her, to pure pleasure about being with him as the duo frolic together, to panic knowing the police will be after them. Reviews in general were mixed from fair to excellent, with many critics praising the high production values, exquisite photography, and superior writing. The critic for *The Hartford Courant* remarked that it "was beautifully done" and "the plot is not strong on either suspense or mystery, but the dialogue and characterization is excellent." The reviewer in *The Evening Press, Binghamton, NY* concurred remarking "The opener offers fewer chilling moments than the advance publicity … However, the glossy on-location photography of mod London …compliments a tale which proves daydreams can get out of hand."

Ben Gross of the *New York Daily News* particularly loved it, and raved, "The story was projected with such delicacy, that viewing it became a moving experience. Dennis Waterman made a touching figure and Carol Lynley, as Eve, won all hearts … An outstanding production."

More praise for the actors came from the critic in *Variety* who remarked that Waterman and Lynley "sensitively played" their roles. Though Percy Shain of the *Boston Globe* felt the story was weak, he praised the actors and commented, "One must say Carol Lynley made a very lovely dummy and Dennis Waterman had the proper forlorn and introverted look for a lonely boy … Their scenes together, fragmented and idealized like a dream, had an ethereal quality quite in keeping with the context." Donald Kirkley of *The Sun* also found a lot of fault with "Eve" but thought Carol played her role "sweetly and naively." The *New York Times* raved that "Dennis Waterman gave an inspired performance … and Carol Lynley provided the radiance of face necessary for the moments when her suitor brought the mannequin to life." Speaking of Carol's face, she shared, "I've been called a female Paul Newman. Not derogatively, of course. It's just that I have the same good facial bone structure he has."[303]

Decades later, Carol was still getting fine notices for this episode. Writing in her Joan Harrison biography *Phantom Lady*, author Christina Lane opined that Carol gave "a consummate performance that telegraphed the series' avant-garde, psychedelic hue."[304]

This episode had a lasting effect on songwriter/musician Richard Carpenter. He revealed that it was the inspiration for the song "Eve" that appeared on The Carpenters' first LP entitled *Offering* in 1969. Carpenter composed the music and the opening lyrics. He continued with the melody and John Bettis contributed the rest of the lyrics. It was never released as a single.

Journey to the Unknown aired on Thursday night opposite *Dragnet* and the first half of *The Dean Martin Show* on NBC and *The CBS Thursday Night Movie*. Ratings were respectable at first but began to go downhill almost immediately despite critical praise. This journey was short-lived and ended after airing its allotted seventeen episodes.

*****

Though TV was keeping her busy, Carol was disappointed that it did not offer actresses much of a range in roles. She commented to Vernon Scott, "There are only a limited number of things a girl can play in a television series. If you're in an adventure series based on a strong male role, the actress is limited in what she can do. And westerns are worse. The woman usually remains at home wringing her hands until her men show up. Then she'd better be quick with the bandages and tears … I won't consider a series unless the role is just right. And there's something else. A participation in the profits and control over what I am doing. Otherwise you're dead."[305]

Carol confirmed that she said this and held to her conviction. She stated,

> I am an intelligent woman. Pretty blondes are not supposed to be. [That is probably why she was never cast as the ditzy dumb bimbo.] I knew back then that an actor had to have a voice in the creative process to protect themselves and partake in the financial gains. Actors, especially women, were not supposed to think this way. Nowadays, it is customary practice.[306]

Carol was ahead of her time regarding her outlook on doing a series. Actresses of the day were just to be satisfied with having a job, leaving all decision making to the men. Her wanting a say about production and partial ownership of a project was wise but her foresight may have hindered her chances for becoming a series regular. The television industry was not yet ready to allow this unless you were of a Lucille Ball-type stature.

Next up for Carol was a guest star turn on *The Big Valley*. Despite what she said about westerns, the actress probably accepted the part because it was a woman's role out of the western norm. She got to gamble, ride horses, and shoot 'em up along with the men.

In "Hell Hath No Fury" Carol portrayed poker-playing Dilly Shanks who falls for series regular Lee Majors' Heath Barkley. Dilly, an Annie Oakley type who can shoot and play a mean game of poker, is also the leader of a gang of stagecoach robbers alongside her three brothers. She comically tries to go straight, but when Heath rejects her marriage proposal she returns to her criminal ways. At the end, she sacrifices her life to save Heath's.

The *Pittsburgh Post-Gazette* critic raved, "Carol Lynley, as the tough, gun-shooting leader of a small band of outlaws, adds excitement to the entry." He added, "It's mostly Miss Lynley's show." However, the reviewer for *TV Scout* found her "not totally believable … playing an aggressive young lady who leads an outlaw band." And some diehard fans of the series agree. They are not impressed with Carol's light-hearted approach and felt it was not a fit for this western. She is lively and is a burst of energy when she is on screen but her performance is schizophrenic. It seems she was trying to reach a balance between being a bit quirky and unrefined when it comes to the matters of the heart and hardened due to her life of crime. Though Carol makes Dilly an interesting character, she unfortunately does not make her sympathetic hence her heroic death is not the tear-stained moment it should have been. Director Virgil W. Vogel should take some blame for not reeling Carol in a bit to play Dilly less broadly. She is also not helped by the ill-fitting fall she was forced to wear to give Dilly long hair. Carol's best scene is her confrontation with Heath's mother played by acting giant Barbara Stanwyck. Perhaps knowing she was going to be emoting opposite such a powerhouse, Carol is more subdued here. She convincingly essays the usually confident Tilly letting her insecurities get the best of her when confronted by the formidable Victoria Barkley.

Lynley next snuck in her only proposed feature film during this time. However, the modern-day western *Cotter* with Don Murray and Rip Torn was undeservedly shelved. The film offered her a change of pace lady in peril role and considering her previous comments on the parts offered to her on TV, it is no wonder she may have jumped at the chance to play a battered wife.

This was an independent production with the odd working title *The Narrow Chute*. Producers Studio was a rental lot owned by Fred Jordan. This was his first production. Interiors were shot at the studio and exteriors on location in Solvang, California. Paul Stanley was hired to direct. A prolific TV director who was nominated for a Director's Guild Award for an episode of *Mission: Impossible* in 1966, this was his second theatrical feature after *Cry Tough* in 1959. The screenplay was by actor/writer William O. Gordon who has just scripted the war movie *Sergeant Ryker* starring Lee Marvin. Shooting began the first week of December 1967.

In the film, Carol played the emotionally dramatic role of Leah. She was the drab, lonely wife of the small town's resident, rowdy saloon owner Roy (Rip Torn) who is having an affair with his busty bar maid Shasta (Sherry Jackson). Roy's childhood friend Cotter (Don Murray) comes roaring into town in a stolen car. An alcoholic, half-Sioux Indian working as a rodeo clown, his inaction due to his drinking accidentally caused the death of a cowboy as shown in the film's opening scene. He not only loses his job but is run out of the rodeo by the other cowboys. As a guilt-ridden Cotter tries to face the realities of what he has done and remain sober, despite the coercing from party-loving Roy, he is befriended by the equally damaged Leah and they form a sweet bond. Then the wealthy owner of the car Cotter "borrowed" is found murdered and the $50,000 he had on him missing. All fingers point to Cotter, and with racial tensions high, Roy provides protection from the local law enforcement and the incensed towns folk. However, debt-ridden Roy believes his buddy really did steal the money and is out to find where Cotter hid the loot to take for himself. Cotter now needs to prove his innocence. The state police find the real culprit. Cotter then punches out the manipulative Roy before leaving town with Leah.

DVD cover art for the unreleased theatrical feature *Cotter* (1968) starring Don Murray, Carol Lynley, Rip Torn, and Sherry Jackson.

All of Carol's scenes are with Torn and Murray (for whom she had nothing but praise), but one of her best is at the end when a newly empowered, though battered, Leah confronts Roy's wanton mistress, Shasta. Leah is on her way out of town to start a new life, sans Roy, and stops by the saloon to drop off a house key to her replacement. Shasta is taken aback by Leah's bruises. She advises Leah to have a doctor "look after your face." As Leah walks out, Shasta asks, "What should I tell Roy?" Leah cattily responds, "Whatever you've been telling him since you came here, Shasta. He seems to like it."

The movie is a nice character study, well-acted by all the principals, though perhaps an actor with some Native American blood should have been cast in the lead instead of Murray. Burt Reynolds comes quickly to mind. It didn't matter because the movie was never released theatrically for unknown reasons even to Carol who commented, "I don't know either. I've never seen it and nobody let me know what happened to it. Quite often the actors are never told."[307]

Considering some of the low-quality films that wound up on the silver screen in 1968, it is perplexing why this one, though a bit slow at times, was not distributed. It is unfortunate because Carol is well-cast as the scarred Leah. Using a convincing Southern accent and her beauty toned down (she has less makeup on and wears a fall, which works for the character), Lynley delivers a truly believable and poignant performance. The scene where Leah and Cotter are sitting at her kitchen table and Leah is questioning him about his past, has a nice spark to it. Cotter makes the dowdy Leah come alive, something that her husband tries to squash with his drinking and domineering attitude. Though Leah is a sort of lady in peril, it was in a domestic drama rather than a suspense film or thriller giving Carol the chance to break away temporarily from those genres.

With the new more appropriate title *Cotter*, the movie was sold directly to television five years after it was completed. It turned up in syndication in Canada airing in August 1973 and the U.S. beginning in early 1974. Of the few sources that reviewed it, notices were mostly positive such as one that called it a "spirited drama." In *Leonard Maltin's 2015 Movie Guide*, the reviewer remarked, "Good cast in fair script that fares best in creating small-town atmosphere."

*****

It was back to the small screen for Carol with a supporting role in the controversial made-for-TV fantasy/science-fiction film *Shadow on the Land*. It was directed by Richard C. Sarafian and created by Sidney Sheldon, best known for his lightweight sitcoms *The Patty Duke Show* and *I Dream of Jeannie*. Screen Gems allotted a $1 million budget and a twenty-seven-day shooting schedule. This was higher than average, since the studio and ABC-TV had a lot of faith in this production.

Shadow on the Land (working title *U.S.*) was the story "of an American dictatorship and the attempts of an underground (Society of Man) organization to overthrow it." This was the pet project of actor Jackie Cooper who at the time was also the head of Screen Gems' West Coast production. It was a proposed pilot for a weekly TV series. Cooper cast himself to attract other actors to take roles and he was able to get John Forsythe (cast against type as the villain), Gene Hackman, Janice Rule, Michael Margotta, and Carol Lynley (a last minute replacement for an unnamed actress who dropped out just before filming began) to come aboard. The male lead was played by the relatively unknown Canadian actor Marc Strange.

1968 was a volatile year in American history with protests raging against the Vietnam War and the U.S. government. It all came to a head with the violent clashes between protestors and the police during the Democratic Convention that summer. Of course, the network was wary of the violent *Shadow on the Land*, which portrayed America as a totalitarian state. The president is replaced with The Leader and citizens cannot work, travel, learn, read, etc. without permission from the leadership. The Bill of Rights is rendered null and void wiping out freedom of speech, press, and religion. Members of the Society of Man are trying to fight back and overthrow the dictatorship.

Jackie Cooper knew the material was going to push people's buttons, but he said, "I know we're in an advertising medium, but I think we're also obligated to say something good once in a while. There were two scripts and several rewrites done before *Shadow on the Land* went before the cameras ... and very little remains of the politics of how the dictatorship came about."[308]

When asked why *Shadow on the Land* didn't sell as a series despite the watering down of the more controversial aspects, Cooper (a self-described progressive Democrat) replied, "The networks evidently felt it was an attack on our government, or were worried about the Republicans. I don't know. We even audience-tested it three times, and each time a big percentage said the film shouldn't be shown on the air. I guess they voted for Wallace."[309]

Shadow on the Land aired on the *ABC Wednesday Night Movie* on December 4, 1968 a few weeks before Christmas day. With Congress dissolved and a dictator now leading the nation due to an unexplained national emergency, an organization called the Society of Man emerges to try to take back the country and restore democracy. Maj. Shepherd "Shep" McCloud (Marc Strange) is a member of the fascist Leader's International Security Force but he is also secretly a member of the Society. Lynley played Abby, a beautiful well-known actress who masquerades as Shep's girlfriend. After Shep helps hide abducted army officer Lt. Colonel Andy Davis (Jackie Cooper) at the mission run by Davis' priest brother (Gene Hackman), Shep immediately rushes off to Abby's apartment knowing he is being followed. Heading out to a party, duty now calls. She strips off her mini dress to a black bra and matching panties before slipping on a frilly blue robe. Shep fills her in on the night's happenings, just as ISF agents arrive to question her. They depart believing the two have been together for the entire night. It is here that the audience finally learns how the U.S. wound up with a dictator, as Shep says, "Riots in the ghettos. Panic in the press. Every unthinking fool who had so much as a used car wanted to vote in some strongman to protect it. But you fight hunger with food, not force, not power. That's what the national emergency was about. That's what Operation Hammer is about. More power to the Leader." Shep and the Society of Man are afraid that the Leader will create another national crisis and frame the Society emboldening their stranglehold on the country even more.

Abby then begins to wax nostalgic for the time, a few years prior in New York, Shep was dating her best friend and encouraged her to keep acting. He cuts her trip down memory lane short and instructs her to go to the mission the next day if things go awry. Nervously smoking, she then informs him that her boyfriend Charlie proposed, but she knows they cannot wed until her assignment working with Shep comes to an end. She wonders if it ever will.

Carol, looking cute with her short haircut, only has these few scenes in the movie. Even so, she delivers a sincere performance and is quite poignant when she tells Shep about her marriage plans that may never come to fruition due to her cover as his paramour.

If a network had picked up the pilot as a series, Jackie Cooper pictured "a chase every week with our hero and his friends winning back a little bit of the country in each episode."[310] Sounds like the fantasy aspects would have been played down making the series more in the vein of *The Fugitive* or *Run for Your Life*, rather than science-fiction. He ended the interview by suggesting that the show would have probably found a buyer if it, "Had been turned into another *Man from U.N.C.L.E.* with a foreign power threatening the United States."[311]

Shadow on the Land earned a disappointing 13.7 rating and a 25 share. *Then Came Bronson* was the season's highest rated made-for-TV movie with a 24.8 rating and 40 share as comparison. After its initial airing, the movie literally disappeared from TV screens only turning up sporadically in syndication during the seventies. It has never been released on VHS or DVD. At the time some reviewers thought it too farfetched to ever occur in the U.S., but with what has happened in American politics beginning with the election of 2016, the TV-movie proves it was way ahead of its time.

Shortly after *Shadow* aired, NBC surprisingly decided to take *The Smugglers* starring Shirley Booth and Carol Lynley out of mothballs and air it on December 24, 1968 on the *NBC Wednesday Night Movie*. Obviously, the network dumped it during "dog week" (the holiday season with typically low viewership) because they had no faith that it would attract a big audience and needed anything original to fill the time slot.

The Smugglers awkwardly blends suspense, violence, and comedy. It is much more lighthearted than what you would expect from the title credits featuring a foreboding musical theme by Lyn Murray and the film's tense opening scene with a hotel owner named Anton snitching to the police about a smuggling operation going on at his hotel in Austria. He is overheard by his shrewish wife Anna (Ilka Windish) who runs to warn her lover Harry (Charles Drake) who is the smuggler. He now needs a new plan to get a statue full of contraband to neighboring Italy. Along come nosy, advice-giving Mrs. Hudson (Booth) and her stunning stepdaughter Jo (Lynley). They are on a driving tour of Europe to help Jo get over a lost love. From the get-go, it feels as if the pair has wandered into the wrong movie as they jovially banter with each other about the inn's lack of modern plumbing and other incidentals. The actresses have nice chemistry and play off each other quite well. Booth is a bit hammy and over the top but amusing, while Lynley is more reserved despite the silly facial expressions she makes when her stepmother says or does something outrageous. Over dinner, Harry enthralls Mrs. Hudson about Alla Rosa, a picturesque town just across the border in Italy. Due to his enthusiasm, the gullible ladies decide to visit the town and agree to deliver the valuable statue to his friend Willie (Kurt Kasznar) the caretaker at the Alla Rosa Castle and the intrigue begins.

Booth and Lynley continue to be the best things here (even upstaging the pretty countryside footage of Italy and Austria sparingly shown) and make all their scenes fun, despite the macabre surroundings and crimes being committed around them. They get in too deep with the smugglers and their lives are put in jeopardy as they accept Willie's invite to stay at his castle, whose inhabitants also include the creepy Michael J. Pollard as a quasi-Italian halfwit named Piero. Anna shows up with a wounded Harry and Willie keeps them in hiding so his guests do not run into them. Knowing Willie is uncomfortable with the smugglers staying at the castle; Piero suffocates the injured Harry and strangles Anna. Willie then sweet talks the naïve Mrs. Hudson, to a suspicious Jo's chagrin, into taking his crates of apples (actually the bodies of Harry and Anna) with them to the train station to be delivered to a friend in Naples. There is also an unnecessary subplot with Willie trying to buy the castle, on behalf of "a friend," from Alfredo Faggio (David Opatoshu) who is the owner's crooked attorney with an equally greedy young lover (Gayle Hunnicutt). Faggio becomes involved when he and his car are inadvertently hijacked by Sergeant Rossi (Rico Cattani) to follow the ladies. Donnelly Rhodes, using a laughably phony stereotypical French accent, is handsome and virile as police detective Antoine Cerret, the ladies' hero who makes Jo swoon and comes to their rescue.

Jo (Carol Lynley) and her stepmother (Shirley Booth) are naive tourists being used to transport stolen goods in *The Smugglers* (Universal Television, 1968).

When broadcast day finally arrived for *The Smugglers* after a long slog, it still could not get a break. Halfway through it was interrupted by news of Apollo 8 when it became the first American spacecraft to reach the orbit of the moon. What did air pulled in a 13.7 rating the same as *Shadow on the Land* but its share was a bit higher at 30. It did not get a full broadcast on NBC until June 1, 1970.

Critics did not pay much attention to *The Smugglers*. *Variety* called it "strictly Grade B international crime stuff" and found Booth and Lynley "in roles far beneath their talents." They do buoy the movie and when either is not on screen it falls completely flat. Director Norman Lloyd just could not successfully mesh the light comedy moments with the intrigue and delivered a rather disjointed film.

The Smugglers never became a fan favorite, although after repeated viewings it grows on you due to the pairing of the talented Booth and Lynley. They are able to project a warmth between their characters and you do care what happens to them. The film aired in syndication during the seventies and eighties and then disappeared like many made-for-television movies.

*****

Carol Lynley returned to the espionage game in early 1969 guest starring on Robert Wagner's hit TV series, *It Takes a Thief*. They previously appeared together in the melodramatic episode "Runaway Bay" on the *Bob Hope Presents the Chrysler Theatre* in 1966. Wagner starred here as Al Munday, an urbane cat burglar extraordinaire, sprung from prison and indoctrinated into spying by becoming a member of the SIA, an elite government force, where he reports to agent Noah Bain (Malachi Throne). Lynley's episode entitled "Boom at the Top" was directed by Paul Stanley (who she worked with previously on the movie *Cotter*) and aired during the second half of the show's second season. It also reunited her with Barry Sullivan who played her shady step daddy in *Harlow* and Roddy McDowall who she co-starred with in *Shock Treatment*. Both would go on to work with Carol several more times.

Regarding her crush on Robert Wagner, Carol commented fondly,

> I worked with RJ a few times. He is professional and a joy to know as a human being. I think he is rather special. We have another connection. My hair stylist Joe who I have been going to for over forty years only cuts men's hair. I don't like the smell of beauty shops. Joe has been cutting RJ's hair just as long. Joe says RJ always asks for me when he goes in and from time to time, we run into each other. I just think he is the best![312]

Publicity photo of Carol Lynley (wearing an unnecessary long fall) and Robert Wagner in "Boom at the Top" on *It Takes a Thief* (Universal Television, 1969).

Carol's haircutter's full name was Joe. T. Torrenueva but friends called him "Little Joe." He began his career working for Jay Sebring who was murdered along with Sharon Tate and others by the Manson Family. After he became the hair stylist to the stars, a story about him appeared in *TV Guide* a few months after "Boom at the Top" aired. He described his Beverly Hills establishment as "an artistic tonsorial parlor" because most of his clients were "artistes."[313] With Carol being his only female client, she was pictured getting her hair cut by him along with Robert Wagner, and Bill Bixby and Brandon Cruz of *The Courtship of Eddie's Father*. Back when the average price for a man's haircut was roughly $6, Joe was charging a $35 consultant fee for the first visit on top of the $20 fee per cut thereafter. For $50, he would come to the actor's house or on set dressing room.[314] In 2007, Joe received national attention for giving that infamous $400 haircut ($150 plus traveling expenses) to then presidential candidate John Edwards.

"Boom at the Top" became newsworthy and made the entertainment columns because the exquisite fashions worn by Lynley and the models were created by esteemed Cuban designer Luis Estevez who played himself. He boasted that due to budget restrictions, he created the clothes in three hours by altering costumes taken off the rack of Universal Studio's wardrobe department. For Carol he designed a beautiful aqua gown that had "a floor length cape (the better to hide a fur), a wrap shirt with Velcro (for fast removal) over a black leotard for action."[315] It was the perfect design for the occasion, as it also hid a rope so she could shimmy down to the apartment below without being noticed. Carol did not remember the gown but she had fond memories of its creator. "I knew Luis before we did the TV show," she related. "I liked him a lot and since I speak Spanish, with a Mexican accent, we chatted away while filming."[316]

In this suspenseful episode, Mundy's mission is to catch a thief—a pickpocket who stole the wallet of an SIA agent containing a business card with a microdot that has valuable national security information on it. The SIA throws a lavish fashion show featuring designs by Luis Estevez which they know will draw the crème de la crème of society, hoping their thief cannot resist such wealthy pockets to pick and jewels to snatch. Mundy is distracted by Lynley's Michelle, a beautiful blonde guest who plays hard to get because she is a fur thief scoping out Estevez' creations and Roger (Roddy McDowall) a former prison pal working as a waiter. On top of this, Mundy must break the fail-safe mechanism of a bomb-laden briefcase, containing plans for a Polaris missile, shackled to SIA traitor Robert Benjamin (Barry Sullivan) who crashes the party seeking Munday's help. He threatens to blow the joint if Munday rats him out after the case is accidentally activated by his foreign cohorts led by France (Will Kuluva).

When Benjamin notices his wallet is missing containing his SIA card, Mundy suspects it was taken by Roger but it was stolen by Michelle who also snatched jewels and a $50,000 fur jacket. She hid them under her gown and cape along with a rope so she could shimmy down to the apartment below without being noticed. However, Mundy quickly realizes she is the thief and follows. Caught red handed, Michelle reluctantly agrees to help Munday in exchange for a diplomatic passport so she can flee the country.

Mundy begins audio taping the fashion show on his reel-to-reel recorder leaving Michelle to make sure no one goes near it and then returns to diffuse the bomb. Roger bursts into the study thinking there is something valuable in the case. He pulls a pistol that goes off hitting Benjamin and then runs off, only to bump into Michelle who overhears about the bomb. Mundy clears out the fashion show guests and has Michelle turn on the tape recorder to trick Benjamin into thinking all the hostages are still in attendance. Just as Munday releases the handcuffs, France and his cohorts, who have been staked outside all night, enter to steal the briefcase. Thinking Munday has diffused it, they take it not knowing he just switched the color indicator lights.

At the fadeout, Noah Bain informs Munday that the foreign agents' embassy was blown up. Munday covers for injured Benjamin keeping his traitorous scheme a secret. Noah wants to know if Munday retrieved the microdot as originally missioned. He says yes as he introduces him to Michelle wearing one of Luis Estevez's flowing gowns accessorized by the stolen jewelry and the white fur jacket. Munday negotiates all that plus the diplomatic passport for Michelle in return for the microdot. As an enraged Noah exits to arrange the passport, a seductive Michelle aske Alex if he believes in love at first sight. When he replies no, the relieved girl says, "Neither do I" as Alex turns on some seductive music. Michelle then adds, "but let's see what develops," as they kiss on the moonlit balcony.

The critic for the syndicated the *TV Key Staff Previews* was one of the few who actually reviewed the episode and proclaimed in *The Morning Herald*, "Easily one of the best shows of the series so far. Not a scene is wasted during the hour as Al comes across a gallery of petty and grand thieves, reluctant conspirators, and determined foreign agents … It's all as slick as TV's slick series can be, and the attractive guest list includes Carol Lynley, Barry Sullivan, and Roddy McDowall."

The episode is wonderfully edited with scenes from the high-end fashion show accompanied by musician Earl Grant (who died shortly after filming this in a car accident) on the organ, intercut with the tense scenes of Wagner's Munday trying to diffuse the bomb and having to deal with Lynley and McDowall's pair of thieves. Carol is fine but the part was not much of an acting challenge and producers yet again were not happy with Carol's short hair, unnecessarily making her wear an obvious long blonde fall. Even still, despite her sophisticated loveliness, Carol was rarely cast in these glamorous type roles so it is a special treat to see her so elegantly clad. She and Wagner have good chemistry and would be paired again next in the 1971 TV-movie *The Cable Car Murder/Crosscurrent*.

6. Murder in the Rough

The press was calling it a comeback in late 1968 when Carol Lynley returned to making films in Hollywood. She had not made a major studio produced film since *Bunny Lake Is Missing* in 1965. *The Shuttered Room* and *Danger Route* were produced independently, and distribution rights picked up by Warner Bros. and United Artists, respectively. Lynley worked almost non-stop appearing in a thriller, a horror movie spoof, a road comedy, and a made-for-TV sci-fi adventure, which received the most acclaim. Her roles were varied, giving her an acting stretch.

It was a bit of a surprise when it was announced that Lynley was cast as a homicidal psychopath in an unofficial remake of Alfred Hitchcock's *Strangers on a Train*. She had played unhinged characters before but none so evil as here. Following in the footsteps of other former teenage idols such as Troy Donahue in *My Blood Runs Cold*, Sal Mineo in *Who Killed Teddy Bear?* and Tuesday Weld in *Pretty Poison* who wanted to shake up their on-screen personas, perhaps Carol did too. "I thought the role was great and jumped at the chance to play such an unstable character," she admitted.[317]

In Carol's case, she plays an enticing, mini-skirted, baby-faced heiress who entraps unsuspecting and vulnerable golfer Paul Burke into a bizarre reciprocal murder scheme in Warner Bros. – Seven Arts' entertainingly over-the-top *Once You Kiss a Stranger* directed by Robert Sparr. A two-time Emmy nominated editor; he began directing Warner Bros.' television series in 1959 with an emphasis on westerns such as *Lawman*; *Bronco*; and *Cheyenne*. His first feature was the independent beach party knock-off *A Swingin' Summer* (1965) that introduced Raquel Welch to moviegoers, followed by the Clint Walker western *More Dead Than Alive* (1969). In between were episodes of *77 Sunset Strip*; *Batman*; *The Rat Patrol*; *Star Trek*; and others. He seemed an odd choice to direct this suspense tale, he was no Hitchcock, but the studio must have had faith in his abilities.

The lovely but psychotic Diana (Carol Lynley) emerges from the surf in *Once You Kiss a Stranger* (Warner Bros. – Seven Arts, 1969).

An interesting side note is that Robert Sparr's Assistant Director was Howard Kazanjian who would go on to work with Alfred Hitchcock on *Family Plot* and then as producer on *Raiders of the Lost Ark* and *Return of the Jedi*. He went to UCLA film school where he became good friends with George Lucas. After graduation, Howard began getting work as the Second Assistant Director on such films as *Finian's Rainbow* and *The Great Bank Robbery*. Asked how he landed First Assistant Director on *Once You Kiss a Stranger*, he responded, "I had recently returned from Mexico [working] on *The Wild Bunch*. Dutch Meyer, head of physical production, suggested I meet with Robert Sparr and Robert Goldstein. If I recall correctly, the film did not start out as a Warner Bros. – Seven Arts full production, although we did shoot on the Warner Bros. lot and used all their equipment."[318]

Once You Kiss a Stranger... (as it was officially called in the opening title credits) went through various working names while being filmed in the summer of 1968. Among them were *You Can't Win 'Em All*, *Sudden Death*, and *The Perfect Set-Up* before *Stranger* was settled on. All these phrases were uttered by a character in the movie. Per Kazanjian, "The script I have dated July 11, 1968 was titled *You Can't Win 'Em All*. However, I do remember conversations, or perhaps earlier drafts that I don't have, titled *Sudden Death*. Blue pages [colored pages are used to depict revisions to a locked script] came through dated July 31 through August 8. One of those pages had the title *You Can't Win 'Em All* and underneath that title was *Violent Summer*."[319] The studio was having a tough time deciding on what to call this film.

Perhaps one reason for the revolving door of titles was to distance itself from the source material. Under the screenplay credit for Frank Tarloff (Academy Award winner for *Father Goose*) and Norman Katkov is listed "Suggested by a Patricia Highsmith novel." It is obviously her classic *Strangers on a Train*. Highsmith did not know they were remaking the movie and never saw it. She remarked, "God knows, it was certainly done behind my back—Strangers on a Golf Course."[320] It is a wonder how the studio got away with doing this without the author's knowledge or consent. Another mystery is that Mann Rubin reportedly delivered a final script with the title *Once You*

Kiss a Stranger. It is unclear what became of his screenplay and why he did not receive writing credit but was listed as Associate Producer. However, per Howard Kazanjian, he does not recall Rubin ever setting foot on the set or on location. Perhaps the credit was in concession for using some of his script?

The film was budgeted at an estimated one million dollars with a filming schedule of thirty days. Interiors were shot on the Warner Bros. studio soundstages and exteriors were shot at the Calabasas Country Club and in Malibu. It opened with a shot of a bikini-clad Lynley emerging from the ocean and chasing off a little girl, claiming it was her beach. In real life the same thing happened per Howard Kazanjian who explained, "Lucien Ballard, who was the Director of Photography on *The Wild Bunch* whom I had just finished working with, walked down from his home and told us this was his beach and we couldn't shoot there. Our production manager spoke with Lucien. I don't know if they paid him off, or convinced him that the beach, sand, and ocean were not his."[321] However the ironic situation was handled, it was settled and shooting commenced.

Carol recalled this incident as well and added,

> He [Lucien Ballard] wouldn't let us film there because we are showing his house. I thought, 'God, someone must have given him a tough time for him to do this.' We had to stop so my makeup man Perc Westmore and I had to climb up this big hill to get back up to the road. We then had to climb down on the other side of this guy's house. I didn't know it, but Perc was ill at the time. He died shortly afterwards.[322]

Filming was moved to another spot on the beach where the house would not be seen. This was one of the many trials director Robert Sparr had to endure. Commenting on his boss, Kazanjian wrote, "I got along fine with Robert, but I believe our relationship was strictly business since I don't remember the smiles and friendship as with other crews. I recall it was a challenging shoot for a small picture. I do think he was under pressure to get a rather intricate story shot within budget and allowed days. Besides several sets on the stage, we did have a long drive to Calabasas, Malibu, and the streets of LA. But he didn't rush his cast and did find time to work with them."[323]

Carol also did not form a bond off-camera with Sparr whom she found to be "very busy and authoritative. I was in almost every scene so I had a lot of work to do. He was excellent about moving the production on even when unexpected things happened that slowed down the process. But I really never got to know him or much about him."[324]

Another trial for the director and his AD was Robert Goldstein who according to Kazanjian "was present from time to time."[325] However, when he was on set, it seems he had one demand that he would not let go of. Normally, a producer wants his latest flame in a picture but Goldstein was determined on having a car get its closeup. According to Howard, "Throughout the production Robert Goldstein had (or was given) a new Jeep (cannot remember the model) that needed to be prominent in the movie. Other than Carol and Paul's cars and the police tailing vehicle, there was no place to showcase the Jeep. Goldstein asked me multiple times to show the car. While we were at the golf course, he brought the vehicle to the location asking me to place it where it was visible. I told Robert we're way out on the green and other than golf carts, it was impossible to showcase the car. He parked the vehicle in front of the club house closest to the course and asked both Robert Sparr and me to try to include it in the shoot. There is one shot where one sees several cars, but if someone was standing nude next to it one couldn't tell."[326]

"The next day a driver was to bring the Jeep to another location," continued Howard. "Parked in the Warner Bros. garage at night, the driver started the car, and putting it in gear, it jumped forward smashing into two prototype picture cars to be used in someone's commercial. It smashed the front of both. I never knew the damage to the Jeep as we never saw it again."[327]

Pro golfer Jerry Marshall's (Paul Burke) bad luck continues when he meets the looney Diana (Carol Lynley) in *Once You Kiss a Stranger* (Warner Bros. – Seven Arts, 1969).

Regarding all the golf scenes filmed at the country club, Kazanjian confirmed that Paul Burke, Phil Carey, and Peter Lind Hayes were all golfers offscreen, so no stand-ins were needed when they were teeing off or when they were on the green. He did add though, "We did have a pro on the set that could help them with their stance or swing. Also. the professional could hit the ball into the hole when wanted. We had hundreds of extras [watching the golf action]. Many were the standard Warner Bros. extras I had seen and used many times before."[328]

As for the cast, the two leads seemed to be private people. Per Kazanjian, "Paul Burke and Carol Lynley kept to themselves. Carol was professional, cooperative, and easy to work with."[329] Martha Hyer was a bit more outgoing. "She was an old-time professional actress I had seen many times on the screen. She was married at the time to producer Hal B. Wallis, whom was a legend himself. Often, I would meet her in the make-up department and watch her get made up while I offered her breakfast and we would converse."[330]

As for Carol's feelings about her castmates,

> I liked Paul Burke very much. We had a tough filming schedule. He was easy going and a good actor so you could work with him and he works with you. He had an even-tempered personality at least when I was working with him. At the end I am in a dune buggy and try to run poor Martha Hyer over on the beach. She was such a good sport about it—*she really was!*[331]

It was reported that during the making of this film, Carol was being romanced by Frank Sinatra coming off his breakup with Mia Farrow. Photos of the pair began appearing in the gossip rags of the time including *Photoplay* and *Modern Screen*. Howard Kazanjian was unaware of this and shared, "As an Assistant Director, you and your second assistant should know where your cast is always. They are either in their dressing rooms just outside the stage door, at lunch, or sitting on the set somewhere. There was one time we were ready for Carol and I asked my assistant to have her make-up checked and bring her onto the set. He came back and said she is not in her dressing room, on the stage, or outside the stage itself. I went looking for her. There were several separate sets on the Warner Bros large soundstages. I stumbled on Carol and Frank Sinatra sitting closely to each other in a restaurant booth in the corner of one. This was the first and only time I saw Sinatra in person. I didn't know it but he was romancing her, I was told later. I let Carol know that we were ready for her. Frank asked if everyone else was on the set. I said they were and left. Carol followed shortly thereafter."[332]

Lynley's relationship with the singer eventually ended and the breakup was amicable. Years later, Carol remarked in J. Randy Taraborelli's book *Sinatra: Behind the Legend* that she found him to be "spectacular, intelligent, and sensitive; interested in art, literature, music."[333] They also shared a love of reading and for five years thereafter Lynley received every book released by Random House courtesy of Sinatra's pal publisher Bennett Serf. Describing her passion to writer Richard Freedman, Carol said, "I'm a great reader—I've been reading non-stop since I was 4. I do so much flying … [so] I get the chance to go through the complete works of any author I get hooked on."[334]

No matter what they titled the movie to hide the connection, *Once You Kiss a Stranger* is a rip-off of Alfred Hitchcock's classic movie (hence getting "Stranger" in the title) with, per Judith Crist, a "sport and sex switch on Hitch."[335] In the original, victim Farley Granger's game was tennis while Robert Walker was a subtler protagonist who pulls Granger into a quid-pro-quo murder pact after a chance meeting on a train. Granger wants a divorce from his two-timing wife, so he can marry another while Walker wants his father dead. Drinking on the train, Granger plays along, but nutty Walker does strangle the wife and expects Granger to reciprocate.

In this remake, Paul Burke's pro golfer wants his cocky number one rival done away with. Lynley is a psycho chick who wants her psychiatrist bumped off so she can run off to Europe instead of the padded cell he wants her committed to. They meet at the bar of a swanky country club, but it seems it was deliberate on Lynley's part rather than chance as in the original. Carol admitted,

> I was kind of aware of the other movie but I had never seen it. For me it was like good news and bad news. I wasn't trying to imitate Robert Walker and I didn't know who he was. Why? I don't know. If I had known I was playing my friend Bobby Walker's father, I think I could have done more.[336]

One of Carol's favorite scenes was when she knocked off Carey. She remarked, "The original script called for me to strangle Phil first. He is a big, tall guy. I couldn't even reach his neck let alone wrap my fingers around it. So, I said to the director, 'can't I just club him to death with a golf club only?'"[337] The answer was no. Instead, Lynley's character ran him over first with a golf cart before she clobbered him with the iron. Carol admitted that not only had she never held a golf club in her hand before, but also had never been on a golf course either.

Kazanjian too remembers the issues with filming the murder scene and wrote, "There was some discussion about this and if I recall correctly we did shoot several ways."³³⁸ Strangling Carey's character matches how the wife was killed off in the original *Strangers on a Train* so that is probably why it was written that way in the new script. However, based on the physical size difference between the two actors, the wiser choice of running him over first was more realistic and served its purpose.

Carol looks lovely throughout the movie and is shot and lit in the most flattering way by prolific cinematographer (and sometimes director) Jacques Marquette. His credits ranged from fifties B monster movies, to mid-sixties beach films, to the Elvis Presley musical *Frankie and Johnny* plus many TV shows. He previously worked with Robert Sparr on his western *More Dead Than Alive*. Remembering the Director of Photography, Howard Kazanjian commented, "Jacques Marquette was very professional and fast—very fast. He was also fun to work with. He always was smiling or had a joke to tell. I did not realize at the time all the work he had accomplished in his career and wish we had worked together again."³³⁹

Poster art for *Once You Kiss a Stranger* (Warner Bros. – Seven Arts, 1969).

Unfortunately, tragedy struck before the movie opened in 1969. Robert Sparr was hired to direct his next movie, the United Artists western *Barquero* with Lee Van Cleef, and while scouting locations in Colorado on July 11, 1969, the helicopter he was riding in crashed - instantly killing the pilot. Sparr and his cameraman, Gerald Finnerman, survived the initial impact, but a few weeks later the director died of his injuries and never saw the release of his last movie.

In *Once You Kiss a Stranger* subtlety is thrown out the window as Lynley's petulant Diana is an obvious wacko from the get-go as she emerges bikini-clad from the ocean and terrorizes a little girl playing on the sand in front of her beach house. Diana though has other troubles including a dotty old auntie named Margaret (Kathryn Givney) that will not give her money to go off to Europe and a shrink Dr. Haggis (Whit Bissell) who wants to send her back to the loony bin. What is a nut job to do? Go country clubbing, of course. There, the devious lass watches Jerry "Second-Place" Marshall (Paul Burke) choke on his winning putt, causing a sudden death match with his rivals arrogant Mike Wilson (Phil Carey) and amiable Pete Martin (Peter Lind Hayes).

That night, at the country club's bar, the depressed, married Marshall rejects Diana's obvious come-ons after phoning his wife Lee (Martha Hyer) and assuring her that he wants her by his side. However, after Lee rejects his offer still sore that he cheated on her previously, Jerry invites Diana into his room when she shows up at his hotel door in a slinky mini dress. Wanting to get her into the sack, he plays along as she goes on about a hypothetical double murder scheme involving her shrink and his rival. Jerry chalks up her ramblings to drunken foolishness but after a night of love making (secretly taped by a hidden video camera [reportedly a Panasonic model NV-8100 reel-to-reel videotape recorder] in her oversize handbag, nat'ch) Diane sneaks out when hearing Wilson's voice. Stalking him as he rides through the golf course with his date, Diana slinks up to the big lunk when his insulted paramour bolts. Before he knows it, the seductive miss is running him over with a golf cart before bludgeoning him to death with Jerry's putter.

The next morning Diana phones Jerry and nonchalantly confesses while devouring a hamburger (murder must give her an appetite) but he thinks it is a joke. The sudden death match tees-off without the missing Wilson and Jerry stumbles upon his body in the rough.

Jerry's Marshall's wife Lee arrives but he leaves her and heads to the police station where he finds a waiting Diana. She again proudly admits to the killing and expects Marshall to return the favor by offing her meddling doctor. The cunning gal also discloses that she used his golf club that has the victim's dried blood on it and has no problem framing him for the murder. When he threatens to spill all to Lt. Gavin (Stephen McNally), Diana shares with him their lovemaking pictures ("Smile, you're on *Candid Camera*.") and that she has a video ("Home movies—it's a hobby of mine.") she would love to show his wife. Diana then tells the detective on duty that she is the head of Marshall's fan club and that her idol has something to tell Lt. Gavin while waiving her photos in the golfer's face. As the detective goes to get Gavin, Jerry says, "What the hell are you trying to do to me?" The demented Diana replies, "Helping you confess, remember?" Marshall states forcefully, "You must be out of your mind!" Diana responds matter-of-factly, "Well, I *know*. I have known ever since I was thirteen years old. That's the year my mummy and daddy died. That's the year they started sending me away to institutions." She goes on to explain the situation with her aunt and her doctor who wants to lock her up for good and how Marshall is going to kill him. Knowing Diana is insane, Marshall is forced to flee before Gavin returns.

Back at his hotel room, Marshall's amorous, robe-clad wife Lee (with a lacquered bouffant hairdo and an exposed shoulder) is anxiously waiting to celebrate their reconciliation. A frazzled and confused Jerry almost ruins it, but Lee succeeds in seducing her husband. Meanwhile, Dr. Haggis visits Diana's aunt to inform her that she will need to commit her psychotic homicidal niece to another institution. Diana drives up and hides until the doctor departs. She then slaps her bedridden aunt around until the frightened woman admits that the doctor was there to get her consent to commit Diana.

An intense Marshall returns to the police station and lies to Gavin that he was alone the night Mike was killed. Disbelieving the golfer, Gavin has him tailed. Jerry, driving a beige Torino, easily detects the big unmarked cop car that is practically right on top of him and then speeds away losing him. He then spots Diana in her red convertible and follows her into a parking lot. When she walks away, he searches for his golf club in the back seat. Diana catches him and says, "Even *you* wouldn't think that I was dumb enough to leave the putter there. You'll get it back when you've done for me what I did for you." The golfer loses his temper and starts to strangle Diana. He lets go and she states that is proof enough that he has the killer instinct. She expects him to off Dr. Haggis that night after her group therapy session promising to leave the door unlocked for him.

A hesitant Jerry follows through and arrives at the office building as Diana watches from the café across the street. Calling himself Mr. Davis, he approaches the doctor seated at his desk with the intent to strangle him. He backs down and Dr. Haggis determines that he came with the intent to harm. Jerry is next seen leaving the building and the detectives who discovered his car there are trying to figure out why he went there in the first place. Clad in what looks like a pastel, multi-colored muumuu, Lee arrives at the country club bar to find an inebriated Pete who tries to assure her that her husband is not cheating on her again.

The next day a happy Diana goes to her scheduled appointment with Dr. Haggis. Expecting to find his corpse, she practices shocked looks on her face in the waiting room mirror. However, she is in for a real surprise, when after opening the door, she finds the good doctor alive and flees from the office. She heads home and begins doctoring the video tape to make it sound like Jerry was planning to kill Mike Wilson. He is at the country club where the sudden death playoff is reconvening as is Lee having lunch with Pete's wife. Jerry emerges victorious just as Lee gets a call from Diana to meet her at the pro shop. Diana reveals to the disbelieving Mrs. Marshall that Jerry killed

Mike and that she has the murder weapon and the dropped cigarette lighter in her possession. Once Jerry does that small favor for her, she assures Lee that she will return the incriminating items. Lee confronts her husband who explains all and she knows he may be an adulterer but not a killer. Just then Lee gets a phone call and it is Diana playing her doctored audio making it look like Jerry planned the murder.

Jerry runs off and Lee thinks he is going to kill Diana. She arrives at Diana's Malibu beach pad and is relieved to find her alive until the psycho tells her it is Haggis, not her, that he must kill. After escaping a harpoon attempt on her life, Lee is chased down the beach by the wild-eyed lunatic in a dune buggy. Watching zaftig Lee, clad in a hideous, frilly brown dress with white polka-dots trying to run in the sand is funny and more so that Diana keeps missing such a big target as she. The vehicle crashes into a rock flipping over. A stunned Diana crawls out while Lee escapes and heads to Haggis' office where she finds her husband holding a paperweight. Jerry did not kill the doctor; he confessed and called Gavin. The last scene has the police escorting demented Diana off to jail while the little girl from the beginning is playing on the sand.

Once You Kiss a Stranger opened in the late fall of 1969 after her next picture *The Maltese Bippy* and after the broadcast of her TV-movie *The Immortal*. In some areas, it went out on a double bill with *Frankenstein Must Be Destroyed* starring Peter Cushing. It did not play theaters in New York City until April 1970. It is not a great movie and production-wise is one step above the made-for-TV films of the era though it is nicely shot on location. Robert Sparr just could not seem to get his cast in check. Paul Burke is stoic and a bit dull as the hero (though he looks simply fine shirtless) while Martha Hyer is horribly costumed and totally shrill. Phil Carey is appropriately cocky and obnoxious as Burke's chief rival but Stephen McNally is deadly monotoned as the police detective. Luckily for them, Carol Lynley saves the movie and is *the* reason to watch. She completely enthralls the viewer right from the beginning as she rises out of the ocean à la Ursula Andress in *Dr. No*, pulling off her snorkeling mask to shake the water off her stylish short 'do, and then jarringly harpooning a child's beach ball while hissing, "Stay off of my beach!" In her colorful pad (whose design is reminiscent of TV's *The Brady Bunch*), she goes after her pussycat with a butcher knife for sipping milk from her glass. She then preens in front of a video camera the ahead-of-her-time gal has hooked up to her TV (years before video recording became commonplace) and then drives off in her convertible as the haunting title song (sung by Dick Addrisi of the Addrisi Brothers pop group) plays over the opening credits.

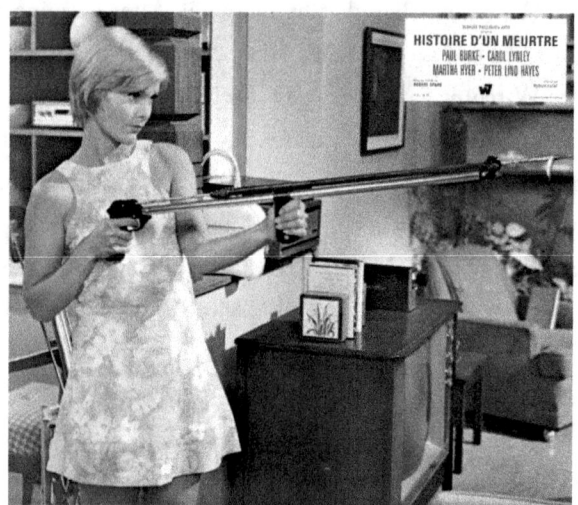

An agitated Diana (Carol Lynley) aims her harpoon in *Once You Kiss a Stranger* (Warner Bros. – Seven Arts, 1969).

From that point on Lynley owns the movie. She is totally engaging as she captivates the audience with her exquisite sex kittenish looks and over-the-top performance. She goes from being amusingly playful instructing the disapproving butler about poisoning her old aunt (taking a bite from her toast Diana quips, "Not enough arsenic."), to impatient haranguing her TV watching invalid aunt (she purposely steps on the cord cutting off the power), to seductive getting the resistant Marshall into bed, to manipulative as she prods him to kill her doctor, to complete nuttiness as she slaps around her bedridden aunt and tries to run down Marshall's wife. Lynley is having so much fun as the emotionally disturbed Diana that you can't help but cheer for her as she makes life hell for a Burke's somber hero and Hyer's blowsy wife (described amusingly by the *Motion Picture Examiner* as being "bouncy, flouncy, and beruffled."). However, that was not the true intent of the movie. More charismatic actors were needed to play the golfer and his wife to keep the viewer rooting for them and not for Lynley's Diana.

Despite Carol giving it her all, *Once You Kiss a Stranger* was not a hit and disappeared from theaters quickly. Comparisons to Alfred Hitchcock's original were inevitable and critics had a field day disparaging the film. In one of the most negative reviews the movie received, the critic from *Boxoffice* commented, "Why someone would want to remake Alfred Hitchcock's classic *Strangers on a Train* is anybody's guess, and putting Carol Lynley in the role first played by Robert Walker makes it even more of a mystery... [It features] pallid direction...[a] cliché-ridden script and amateur night performances."

Mixed reviews for the film were spread out amongst the pans. Some critics even recognized what Carol's fans knew - that she was having a ball playing a gorgeous homicidal loon (Bob Geurink of *The Atlanta Constitution* described her character as being "a Loch Ness monster in a bikini"), so far removed from her usual lady in peril or innocent ingénue roles. Roger Greenspun of *The New York Times* noted, "Carol Lynley seems more interesting than her role." John Mahoney of *The Hollywood Reporter* remarked, "Miss Lynley is quite good as the mean little chick." Kathleen Carroll of the *New York Daily News* remarked, "It is so ridiculously contrived. Even Miss Lynley's first-rate performance doesn't help."

One of Carol's best notices came from Don Gordon of the *Hollywood-Citizen News*, who raved that her portrayal "is an interesting piece of acting. There is nothing quite so chilling as a cold-blooded beauty—psychotic and amoral—bludgeoning a golf pro to death with a heavy putter. And afterwards she's so cool. Even flippant, to the point of being amusing."

A few years later, the movie received the designation of "Bomb" in *Movies on TV*. However, its actual printed review did not suggest such a poor rating, "*Once You Kiss a Stranger* is a glossy but empty look at the country club set and their intrigues. Paul Burke suffers as the hero, while Carol Lynley, looking terrific, rolls her eyes as an unstable Miss bent on using men."

Despite being aided by some great psychedelic poster art with a bikini clad Lynley front and center, the movie failed to draw an audience. Television did not treat the film any better as it got only intermittent air play over the years, usually in overnight time slots, and it was never released on home video. Thankfully, it is now available as a burn-to-order DVD through the Warner Bros. Archive Collection and fans can relish over and over one of the most entertaining performances of Lynley's career.

Asked what he thought of *Once You Kiss a Stranger*, Howard Kazanjian replied, "I don't recall my thoughts when first viewing the movie. I did see it again recently and was taken back at how sick and evil Lynley's character was."[340] Indeed.

7. What's a Bippy?

Carol Lynley next snared the female lead in the haunted house spoof *The Maltese Bippy* starring Dan Rowan and Dick Martin. On paper, playing the lady in peril (or was she?) opposite two of small screen's most popular comedic actors no doubt seemed like box office gold. Alas, as the adage goes nothing is ever a sure thing.

In 1968, comedians Dan Rowan and Dick Martin ruled the airwaves as hosts of the enormously popular TV variety series *Rowan and Martin's Laugh-In*, the No. 1 rated TV show on the air. Seeing how well-known Rowan and Martin had become due to their hip, irreverent TV show, every movie studio in Hollywood wanted to cash in on the comedians' popularity hoping the duo would repeat their success on the big screen as well. 20th Century-Fox courted the duo but they wanted to do a *Laugh-In* type of movie complete with big name guest stars such as John Wayne, Sammy Davis, Jr., and Jack Lemmon. Another studio pushed a feature with an original story but it had to include the duo's co-stars from *Laugh-In* in supporting roles. They dismissed both of these offers, wanting to distance themselves as far from their TV success as possible. Instead they signed a three-picture deal with producers Robert Enders and Everett Freeman at MGM with the comics keeping 50% control.

It was agreed by all that these movie projects "are conceived to veer as far as possible from the *Laugh-In* TV image."[341]

Despite what the public thought, this would be the second theatrical feature to star Rowan and Martin. Ten years before *Laugh-In* came along, the duo starred in the forgettable western spoof *Once Upon a Horse* (1958) co-starring Martha Hyer and Nita Talbot. The guys played a pair of inept desperadoes who want to go straight after one last heist. When asked about this movie while making *The Maltese Bippy*, Dan Rowan replied, "There really isn't much of ourselves in it."[342]

An old-fashioned mystery, haunted house spoof originally titled *The Maltese Bippy* (but quickly changed to *The Strange Case of...!#%*) was chosen to be their first feature. Explaining how this project first started out, producer Robert Enders said, "I knew there was a big market for a Rowan and Martin movie. I found out that a property producer Everett Freeman had written entitled *The Incredible Werewolf Murders* was still available and asked Dan how'd he like to watch Dick turn into a werewolf. He broke up. Then I asked Dick how he'd like to watch Dan watching him turn into a werewolf. They both broke up."[343]

Ray Singer was brought in to do rewrites on Freeman's original script. Though he did not receive credit, the *Los Angeles Times* reported that Stanley Ralph Ross (who scripted numerous episodes of *Batman*, among other TV shows) was brought in to write special material for Rowan and Martin. Commenting on the screenplay, Dick Martin oddly liked "its pastoral setting. The houses are right across the street from the fresh air and greenery of a cemetery in Flushing, N.Y."[344] This courtesy of sets built on stage 26 at MGM studios.

Norman Panama was slated to direct. The three-time Academy Award nominated screenwriter had turned director in the fifties and two of his best films starred Danny Kaye—the comedies *Knock on Wood* and *The Court Jester*. His last film was the Tony Curtis/Virna Lisi comedy *Not with My Wife, You Don't!* in 1966. Based on his experience with comedy spoofs and working with comedians, MGM thought he would be a good fit with Rowan and Martin.

Having a lot of faith in the comic duo's drawing power, MGM gave the film a budget of $2.5 million (a hefty sum for that time) and enlisted some talented people to work behind-the-scenes including many Academy Award winners—cinematographer William H. Daniels, art directors Edward C. Carfagno and George W. Davis (who dubbed their style for Martin's house set "mod-Victorian"[345]), make-up artist William Tuttle (who designed the wolf man makeup especially for Martin), and composer Nelson Riddle.

When it came time to cast the other roles, the comedians were adamant that none of their TV co-stars would appear. They did not want to draw any connections to *Laugh-In* despite its success. Holding firm, the duo rejected a major push by MGM for Goldie Hawn to co-star. Their loss was her gain, as *Laugh-In*'s most popular ditzy comedienne went on to appear in *Cactus Flower* and win an Academy Award. Needing a leading lady to play the "damsel in distress," the role was offered to Ann-Margret. Her then agent Alan Carr felt the movie was in the vein of *Abbott and Costello Meet Frankenstein* and aimed at eight-year-olds. He revealed he hung up on them and said, "Their offer opened at $250,000 ... They went up to $400,000. It was very hard to say no."[346] But no is what he said.

Despite Carr's feelings, several actresses wanted this role. In a surprise decision, the producers chose winsome Carol Lynley. The actress appeared with the duo on *The Tonight Show Starring Johnny Carson* in late 1968 so perhaps she made an impression on them? Though the pretty blonde excelled at playing the lady in peril, she had not appeared in a movie comedy since *Under the Yum Yum Tree* in 1963. Though she proved her adeptness playing light comedy with that film and *The Pleasure Seekers*, producers, even on TV sitcoms, never thought to cast her so it was somewhat shocking that she was selected to co-star opposite two of the biggest TV comedy stars of the day. But since her terrorized character acts as more of the "straight man," a comedienne was not a must.

It was not the script or the opportunity to co-star with Rowan and Martin that made Carol accept the role. It seems some of that hefty dough offered to Ann-Margret came Carol's way as she confessed, "I was talked into doing this film, against my better judgement, by my agent and manager. They negotiated, which for me at the time, was a very good salary. That's why I did it."³⁴⁷

Publicity photo of Carol Lynley in *The Maltese Bippy* (MGM, 1969).

Others cast in supporting roles included Mildred Natwick (recent Academy Award nominee for *Barefoot in the Park*) as Martin's chatterbox housekeeper; acclaimed theatrical actor Fritz Weaver as the vampire-like neighbor (when asked what he remembered most about this movie he replied that it was voted one of the ten worst movies of the year); scintillating Julie

Newmar (Catwoman from TV's *Batman*) as his ghoulish sister; Dana Elcar and Robert Reed (just prior to joining TV's *The Brady Bunch*) as police detectives; and lovely Jennifer Bishop as a real estate agent.

Filming began in late February 1969. The set used for Dick Martin's house was the same as Judy Garland's in *Meet Me in St. Louis*. As an homage to *Laugh-In*, the names on the headstones in the cemetery are of former 'Sock-It-to-Me' victims. This was an idea of Rowan and Martin's and the only thing in the movie related to their TV series. Even the characters the comics play are atypical for them. Dan Rowan explained, "On TV, I'm the reasonable, sane, intelligent guy and Dick is the goof, interested in broads. But in the movie, he's reasonable and settled and I'm a fast-talking con man, not too bright. I'm a nudie film producer and Dick's my partner who's against that stuff and about to quit me."[348]

Reportedly, the shoot was easy going and fast. Dick Martin attributed this to "an awful lot of good planning and very little self-indulgence on the part of the producers, director, cameramen, and players."[349] It was also a bit free-wheeling, with the comics allowed to ad-lib on occasion, though the duo had distinctly opposite work habits. Rowan liked to rehearse and spend time off by himself or conferring with the director about the next scene to be shot. Martin meanwhile would be clowning around with cast and crew. He liked to improvise, if he could, and just wing it. Dan Rowan commented, "It's easier that way, of course, and Dick always likes to take the easiest way. Dick and I ... have opposite views—politically, socially, morally. The only thing we see eye to eye on is the act and how to do it."[350]

Carol confirmed that the comedy duo shared opposite personalities. She commented,

> I liked Dick tremendously; he was sweet and easy-going. We stayed friends after the movie ended for many years and I knew his wife Dolly. He was so charismatic and such a loving person towards everyone.

Dan Rowan was not a lot of fun. He had a rough edge to him and you never quite knew what was going to happen. I am bad with people like that. I am always professional when it comes to doing my scenes and interacting with all the actors, but if I am having trouble with somebody off-camera you do not see me hanging around. I am gone. I did not think that Dan was a happy person. He always seemed mad. Why? I don't know because quite honestly, I never got to know him that well to make any judgement on why he was like that. Dick was just the opposite. I never knew how Dick handled that guy but he obviously did.[351]

As for some of her female co-stars, Carol continued,

I would see Julie Newmar around in New York where I used to take dance classes a lot. When I was working on Broadway there was a place a lot of the actors used to hang out either before or after their shows and I would see her there too. I would think, 'Wow, that is a tall woman.' I was young at the time. Working together she was very professional. I can't say I got to know her well. Now Millie [Mildred Natwick] I adored.[352]

Due to a rushed production schedule and to help Rowan and Martin settle into their characters, it was reported that *The Maltese Bippy* was filmed in continuity. Carol confirmed this and when asked if that helps the actor with their performance, she responded with a laugh, "It depends—it definitely did with *Bunny Lake Is Missing*. With *The Maltese Bippy* not so much. What can I say?"[353]

Not only was the movie shot this way to help the comics, but because two editing teams "were splicing double-time to meet the fast deadline for a final cut."[354] This may have helped keep the filming on track but it also inflated the budget as some actors who should have worked for a week or two were paid for the entire run.

What's a Bippy?

Sam Smith (Dan Rowan) catches coed Robin Sherwood (Carol Lynley) snooping in the cellar in *The Maltese Bippy* (MGM, 1969).

Purportedly, Elvis Presley visited the set a few times. He was a major fan of *Laugh-In* and wanted to make an appearance. He discussed this with Rowan and Martin. As usual, Elvis' greedy manager Col. Tom Parker sabotaged it. About Elvis making a cameo, Dick Martin said, "We dig that. But we don't dig Elvis' salary."[355]

Another distinctive aspect of this shoot was that Nelson Riddle composed his musical score from the script rather than the finished movie. He reportedly created different themes such as love moods, horror moods, etc. Ten days after the final cut was delivered, he recorded his score with a 52-piece orchestra. Since *The Maltese Bippy* was the only film in post-production at MGM, it seemed the entire studio from sound engineers to marketing experts worked on this at a lightning pace to get it into theaters in June.

During filming, the movie's title kept changing. It went from *The Incredible Werewolf Murders*, to *Who Killed Cock Robin?*, to *The Coogle Affair*, and then back to *The Strange Case of...!#%*. At some point, after filming wrapped, MGM reverted the title back to *The Maltese Bippy*. Some felt the changes were all a just publicity stunt to keep people talking about the movie. Rowan and Martin, however, hated the title *The Maltese Bippy*. They thought it was too reminiscent of their TV series. No doubt it was selected just for that reason and to capitalize on the catchphrase from *Laugh-In* that was sweeping the nation. At least once a show, Dick or Dan would utter, "You bet your sweet bippy." Sounding suggestive, kids across the nation started using the phrase for a brief period. What's a bippy? Audiences were never told though Dan Rowan claimed that bippy "is a coined word of Dick's and mine."[356]

Filming ended six days ahead of schedule. Director Norman Panama credited this feat to "four days of rehearsal ahead of time" and "the world's best and fastest cameraman [William Daniels, who photographed 90% of Garbo's pictures, at her request] and Dan and Dick, who are unbelievable."[357] To celebrate, Rowan and Martin threw a haunted house wrap party catered by Chasen's one of the top Hollywood restaurants. For publicity purposes, the comedy team claimed that they had a Maltese Bippy locked up in a medieval chest and that they would reveal the contents. When the chest was finally opened, out came only a puff of smoke. It was reported that Dick Martin then said, "Sorry, but when exposed to air the Maltese Bippy disintegrates."[358]

The Maltese Bippy was shot and edited in ten weeks, which for a major studio production was lightning fast. It was ready for release in fourteen and a half weeks. Producers wanted the movie saturated in theaters across the country just in time for students' summer vacation. With this being MGM's only release until November's *Goodbye Mr. Chips* starring Peter O'Toole, the studio threw all its weight behind it with a media blitz. The studio's ad campaign played the movie up as a horror spoof rather than an old-fashioned mystery in a haunted house thinking that would attract more ticket buyers.

The highly awaited film had its West Coast premiere at Pacific's Picwood Theatre in Los Angeles on June 5, 1969. It was televised on *The Joey Bishop Show*, the late-night competition to *The Tonight Show Starring Johnny Carson*. It also featured a roasting of the comic duo. Guests attending included the comedy team's TV cast mates Goldie Hawn, Ruth Buzzi, and Arte Johnson plus their TV producers Ed Friendly and George Schlatter. Other celebrities in attendance were Greer Garson, Edward G. Robinson, Buddy Hackett, Greg Morris, Dick Smothers, and Anne Baxter, among others. Not surprisingly, considering her feelings about the movie, Lynley was nowhere to be found.

The following night *The Maltese Bippy* had its East Coast premiere at the Boyd Theater in downtown Philadelphia. Of course, Rowan and Martin were in attendance as were Ruth Buzzi, Alan Sues, lovely statuesque Inga Neilsen, Henry Gibson, and Dave Madden.

Cast and crew were also sent out on the road across North America to promote the movie. Even *Laugh-In* cast mates that Rowan and Martin adamantly did not want cast in the movie pitched in. Dick Martin said, "In Toronto and all the other major cities on our tour, we've scheduled a local premiere of our movie the night before the *Laugh-In* appearance. For smaller cities we'll have our producers and some of the *Laugh-In* kids make an appearance, and for real smaller cities we're sending our make-up man out on tour. He can go on local TV and demonstrate how he puts on a cute werewolf face."[359]

To pique viewer interest, the producers even had a fifteen-minute featurette made to show moviegoers what went on behind-the-scenes during filming. It was broadcast on June 19, 1969 on *The CBS Thursday Night Movie* after that night's feature *The Hellions*.

As *The Maltese Bippy* opens, there are a few false starts, including an epic about Irving the Horrible, before a tuxedoed Dan Rowan and Dick Martin saunter onto a white, barren set and banter amusingly about the credits as they are displayed on screen with Dan playing straight man to Dick's dim bulb who is bored waiting for the movie to begin with all the names that scroll by. He even asks if there is a happy ending with him and Rowan walking off into the sunset. Then the story begins with scheming producer Sam (Rowan) overseeing the shooting of his latest nudie film *Lunar Lust* starring his friend Ernest (Martin) and an underage bikini-clad dippy starlet (Pamela Rodgers who would go on to become a regular on *Laugh-In*) playing the Queen of the Moon. As Sam directs her to make love with Ernie, the leading man keeps interrupting the scene with his strange urge to howl like a wolf foreshadowing what is to come.

After the vice squad raids them, Ernie dissolves his partnership with Sam and returns to his house next door to a cemetery in Flushing, Queens. Besides his meddling housekeeper Molly (Mildred Natwick) who is constantly at odds with Sam, his oddball boarders include Robin Sherwood (Carol Lynley), a mini-skirted college coed who carries a human skull around with her, and introverted musician Axel (Leon Askin). His real estate agent Joanna (Jennifer Bishop) also keeps traipsing through the house with prospective buyers.

That morning a clawed and mutilated body was discovered in the graveyard, so two police detectives, Lt. Crane (Robert Reed) and Sgt. Kelvaney (Dana Elcar) are on the scene to investigate. Living next door to Ernie are his creepy, suspicious Hungarian neighbors Mr. Ravenswood (Fritz Weaver), his flighty sister Carlotta (Julie Newmar) who thinks Ernie is her long-lost love Prince Igor, and their burly housekeeper Helga (Eddra Gale). Ernie, however, thinks he is the killer due to his incessant dreams of being a werewolf.

Carol sprightly plays the damsel in distress role. Her Robin (a biology major at the local university) is seen driving up to the house in a red convertible where she runs into the police officers exiting her home. When questioned by Crane why she is not living on campus, she replies, "I'm exercising my right of dissent." He asks from what and she glibly quips, "Sit-ins, stand-ins, love-ins—every kook on campus wants to have a private sleep-in with me." When she retreats to her room, she pulls out a camera and begins snapping away at Ravenswood's dog wearing a talisman around its collar revealing that biology is not the only thing she is studying. Robin goes back and forth from being a terrorized victim (she and Ernie are spooked during a rainy night, find a secret passage that leads to a crypt in the graveyard adjacent to the Ravenswood house where they learn of their plot, and then chased by Ernie after he is hypnotized to eradicate her after the Ravenswood's uncover her true identity), to deceitful when she presses attempted murder charges against Ernie even though she knew he was not under his own free will.

Though the Ravenswood family pretends to be a pack of werewolves who threaten to eat an unconscious Sam in front of Ernie, they are actually in cahoots with his psychiatrist Dr. Strauss (David Hurst) to scare Ernie off because his house is the hiding spot for a 101-carat diamond called the Excalibur. Robin finally confesses to Ernie that she is the daughter of the man who found it and it was stolen by the former owner of his house who hid it somewhere in its confines. Sam, Ernie, and Robin think it is in the body of a man they found in the dumbwaiter and attempt to cut him open. It all comes to a surprising comical finale with different endings. As the trio are about to cut into the body that they discovered in the basement, a gun-toting Ravenswood and Carlotta show up to steal the diamond. Carlotta then shoots her brother, but she is gunned down by Strauss who in turn is killed by Ernie's real estate agent Joanna who dies from a knife in the back thrown by Helga. As the behemoth is about to carve the body herself to retrieve the diamond, she is shot just as Lt. Crane arrives with the police and housekeeper Molly who had been kidnapped by the Ravenswood's. Crane reveals he represents the Motion Picture Production Code and arrests the comic duo for excessive violence on film.

Outraged over the "cop out" ending, Dick presents his tale of how the movie should end with the butler (Arthur Batanides) doing it even though there was no butler in the film. He turns out to be Robin's father—the rightful owner of the diamond. But when he goes to shoot Ernie, Robin jumps in front of the gun and dies in his arms. Hating that ending, Dan's version has Molly as the killer because she was in love with him. Trying to shoot herself in the head, she misses twice killing the guy who shot Helga and another of Ernie's phony tenants before being taken off in police custody. The end credits role as Sam and Ernie walk off holding hands into the sunset just as Dick Martin asked if they would at the beginning of the movie.

Trying to be as zany as the television series to appeal to its young fans, *The Maltese Bippy* begins promisingly with funny one-liners delivered by the two comedians, even addressing the audience directly, as they goof on the film's opening credits. Unfortunately, this comical pace does not continue, and the movie turns into a conventional haunted house mystery spoof with the two leads morphing into a poor man's Abbott & Costello but not nearly as funny. The film continues in a straightforward manner with some amusing moments until the ending and again reverts into a madcap comedy that audiences expected from Rowan and Martin.

Director Norman Panama described *The Maltese Bippy* as a "contemporary action-adventure-romantic-horror-melodramatic comedy."[360] That is probably why it disappointed because it was trying to be everything to everybody and fully pleased mostly no one. Prior to the opening, the confident director predicted, "Audiences are going to enter theaters preparing to laugh their heads off. It was the job of us involved with *The Maltese Bippy* to make sure they are not disappointed."[361] Unfortunately, of the few who ventured out to see it, most were.

Ernie Grey (Dick Martin) and Robin (Carol Lynley) are rattled by strange noises in *The Maltese Bippy* (MGM, 1969).

Surprisingly, the critics were not too cruel with reviews ranging from "lightweight entertainment," "breezy summer fare," and "a very funny film," to "cheapens everything it touches" and "lame spoof." Gannett News Service critic Bernard Drew quipped, "It is wild and silly and sometimes very funny, and sometimes not so very, but it's summer, and it's for the whole family, and what do you want? It beats heat rash and sunstroke."

Critic Gerald Nachman of the *Oakland Tribune* perhaps best summed up the movie. After describing its opening and closing, he remarked, "There are two very funny moments in *The Maltese Bippy* ... but the trouble is they're separated in the middle by a movie. Both moments are not only funny, they're completely un-movielike (which is much of what makes them so funny) ... So, while *The Maltese Bippy* is more amusing than a lot of other conventional comedies ... it is, finally, a motion picture, and it plays by Hollywood rules, so eventually it loses. Playing by the rules is what *Laugh-In* refuses to do, and if only *The Maltese Bippy* had let itself go in the madhouse manner of *Laugh-In*—as it does at the opening and close—it may well have been a 90-minute winner. What the boys have done, really, is settled for a sort of sophisticated Abbott and Costello movie ... It's not bad or corny or anything; it's just not them."

While *The Maltese Bippy* did have its few champions, the critics who hated it *really* hated it. It was considered one of year's biggest stinkers by some such as Joyce Haber who placed it on her Thirteen Worst Movies of 1969 list (it was such a big year for bad movies she could not keep it to ten films). The *Harvard Lampoon* also named the comedy spoof one of the Ten Worst Movies of the Year and bestowed on it the Dr. Christian Bernard Award for the movie, "which shows the worst job of cutting, this year's badly mangled aorta goes to Rowan and Martin's *The Maltese Bippy*."

As for the supporting cast, Mildred Natwick does well as the jabbering housekeeper and it is fun seeing Fritz Weaver do a Bela Lugosi imitation as Ravenswood. Julie Newmar makes a quite sexy femme fatale. Their valiant efforts keep the movie watchable, as does Lynley. The critic from *The Christian Science Monitor* felt similarly and remarked that "Carol Lynley…is both pretty and convincing as Robin."

Charles Champlin of the *Los Angeles Times* was one of the critics who found favor with *The Maltese Bippy*. In his lengthy review, he found it "fairly good fun. And even if it's not great fun, it's welcome enough, because amiable nonsense has not exactly been a staple of the movie diet lately." Like many critics, he praised the opening and closing scenes, but found that the plot "thins" during the midsection and is "all very, very dutiful." He wished the zaniness of the opening carried through the rest of the movie. Champlin never mentions Lynley until the last paragraph and perfectly described her contribution to the movie commenting, "Carol Lynley, by the way, is as near as we get to a love interest and looks fetching, but it's the wrong picture in which to have to be sincere."

Despite all the publicity the movie received, moviegoers did not fill the seats. Even undiscriminating younger audiences and the drive-in movie crowd were unimpressed and stayed away feeling that the movie was not hip or relevant enough to warrant the $3 admission. Most wanted something along the lines of the zippy *Laugh-In* and to see the TV cast members on the big screen. It was a disappointment to many that none were in the movie. As critic Gary Arnold remarked, "Does anyone watch *Laugh-In* because of Rowan and Martin? If so, I don't know him." Suffice it to say *The Maltese Bippy* was not a success at the box office nor did it recoup its budget with its less than $1 million gross.

MGM gets a lot of the blame for the film's failure. Instead of hiring young directing talent á la Bob Rafelson of *The Monkees* to give the movie a hip, zany approach, they went with pedestrian Norman Panama. When questioned if she thought he and producer/screenwriter Everett Freeman were part of the reason the movie failed, Carol replied,

> Of course, I knew them but they made no impression on me. I really have no memoires of either so I can't say. We shot it at MGM studios and I had a lovely dressing room with a big picture window. I spent a lot of time gazing out that window. I just wanted to get through making the film because I didn't like the material. As I said, I would do my scenes and then I was gone.

I didn't stick around to socialize much with anyone other than Dick Martin.[362]

The hype that Rowan and Martin were going to be the next big screen Abbott and Costello or Martin and Lewis turned out to be pure hyperbole. It was a lesson movie studios learned yet again - that a TV star's popularity does not automatically transfer to the big screen. Why pay when you can sit home and watch the performers for free? During the East Coast press tour, producer Robert Enders said, "I think people may find it difficult to accustom themselves to Dick and Dan as actors."[363] How right he was.

Dan Rowan said that he and Dick Martin "look hopefully for some sort of future in films."[364] Alas, disappointed with *The Maltese Bippy* both critically and financially, MGM then cancelled their contract. Plans for the already announced follow-up movies, *The Money Game* based on Adam Smith's bestselling novel about Wall Street and *The Servant Game* (a sort of *Some Like It Hot*) where Rowan and Martin were to play entertainers posing as a servant couple (one in drag, most likely Dick Martin) in the home of a TV executive to impress him, were shelved. Perhaps the studio realized that what attracted young viewers to *Laugh-In* were not Rowan and Martin, but its zaniness, and rapid-fire gags and vignettes. The duo never made a theatrical film together again. Instead of becoming the hottest TV stars turned movie stars, they followed in the steps of Liberace and George Gobel who also bombed on the silver screen at the height of their television fame with their tries at movie stardom. Luckily for Rowan and Martin, *Laugh-In* was still one of the most popular TV shows on the air and lasted another four years.

After her long absence from the big screen, Carol needed a big hit and *The Maltese Bippy* did not deliver, despite the promise it showed. The movie did not hurt Carol as much as it did Rowan and Martin (who co-opted all the pre-release publicity and took most of the blame when it bombed) and may even have helped her land more lady in peril roles to come. Nobody expects "the girl" in a horror movie spoof to be funny and steal the movie. With her short haircut enhancing her baby-face innocent look, Lynley is perfectly suited for the role because you are not actually sure what her motive is throughout the entire film and she keeps the audience guessing. Carol handled both the conventional haunted house scenes and the comedic moments quite well.

Years later, Carol's low opinion of the movie has not changed. She said laughing,

> Until this day, I cannot watch it. I don't make a habit sitting around seeing my movies. We all have egos but let's not go too far. That is the one if I notice it is airing, I try to catch it. I get about ten minutes into it and I am gone. I still cannot get through the entire movie![365]

As with *Shadow on the Land*, *The Maltese Bippy* did not get much TV air play in syndication during the seventies and eighties. It was also never released on VHS and only came out on burn-to-order DVD in 2015. Today, the comedy is a kitschy curio due to the only on-screen teaming of Rowan and Martin during their *Laugh-In* days and for seeing mini-skirted sixties icons Carol Lynley and Julie Newmar together in one movie.

8. On the Run with the Immortal

The possibility and ramifications of immortality are the focal points of *The Immortal* (1969), a well-received made-for-TV movie directed by Joseph Sargent and featuring a top-notch cast including Christopher George, Carol Lynley, Barry Sullivan, Jessica Walter, and Ralph Bellamy. This went into production almost days after *The Maltese Bippy* wrapped and featured one of Lynley's best roles.

The teleplay is by Robert Specht and based on the novel *The Immortals* by James Gunn. His book spanned 200 years' time and began with Marshall Cartwright, a bum who anonymously donates blood that miraculously rejuvenates a dying old man. Realizing that his blood contains "recuperative immunities" that can cheat death and maintain youth forever, the hunt is on for the Immortal as the effects are only temporary and continuous transfusions are needed to keep the recipient alive. The story stretches over two hundred years because the author wanted to show what the effects of immortality would have on a society. The science fiction aspect about living forever is a constant theme throughout, as are the sharp critical barbs against medical research and American society in terms of illness.

James Gunn was not thrilled when his agent notified him in 1966 that producer Everett Chambers who was producing TV's *Peyton Place* at the time and his story editor Robert Specht were interested in optioning his novel for a motion picture. Gunn told *Starlog* magazine years later, "I thought it was unfilmable because of its lengthy time span."[366]

The original treatment stuck close to Gunn's concept, though the Immortal was now the focus throughout, while in the book he appears only at the beginning and the end. The script was rejected by every studio in town though a reader at 20th Century-Fox thought it was "a novel idea for a chase story." Specht rewrote it with that angle in mind downplaying the fantastical elements and introduced a more interesting central character. He confessed years later in *Starlog*, "I didn't think there was any structure but *The Fugitive*, because this man was going to be pursued by *everybody*."[367] Though he thought it was an excellent idea for a series, he was instructed to write the teleplay erasing that from his mind and to deliver an entertaining script.

Publicity photo of Carol Lynley in *The Immortal* (Paramount Television, 1969).

This concession is not too surprising since *The Fugitive* was a phenomenal hit while sci-fi TV shows were not doing well in the ratings at the time. *Lost in Space* had just ended a three-year run and *The Invaders* had been cancelled mid-season after a year and a half on the air. *Star Trek* was in its third season and producer Irwin Allen had just launched his fourth sci-fi series *Land of the Giants*. Though popular with younger audiences, neither garnered big ratings.

Paramount Studios immediately bought the re-draft and green lighted a 90-minute tele-feature to be broadcast as part of the *ABC Movie of the Week*. With a respectable budget of $500,000 (quite high for a TV-movie back then) and a twenty day shooting schedule, Lou Morheim who worked on *The Outer Limits*, came onboard as producer (Everett Chambers had dropped out prior) and hired veteran director and future four time Emmy winner Joseph Sargent (whose then credits included episodes of TV's *The Fugitive*; *The Man from U.N.C.L.E.*; *Star Trek*; and *The Invaders*) to helm the film. Morheim also brought in favorite composer Dominic Frontiere from *The Outer Limits* to score the film.

Casting seemed to go smoothly for all but the lead role. Lee Majors came close to winning the part, but after a laborious search, Paramount and Morheim finally cast Christopher George as the Immortal. Explaining his decision, the producer told *Starlog*, "Chris was a conscientious actor and he liked the initial concept of his character, because it was all new to him. I was familiar with his work on *Rat Patrol*. He had that aggressive energy which helped him obtain the part."[368] Chris George was an excellent choice and made a worthy leading man for Carol who agreed to do the movie because "I thought Sylvia was a very good part and I wanted to work with Chris George. He was professional, easy going, and had a lovely sense of humor."[369]

Sylvia was indeed a good part. She was imperiled but also heroic wanting to stand by and protect her fiancé who was being sought after for his rare blood. She could have easily left him as he gently suggested, but Sylvia decides to stay, no matter the danger, and almost pays for it with her life.

The Immortal is the story of a racecar test driver named Ben Richards

(Christopher George) who donates his blood to help save his dying billionaire employer Jordan Braddock (Barry Sullivan) who has barely survived a plane crash. When Braddock makes a miraculous recovery to the chagrin of his greedy young wife Janet (Jessica Walter), his physician named Dr. Pierce (Ralph Bellamy) discovers that Ben's corpuscles contain antibodies which have healing powers and aging immunities.

At first Ben is elated with the news and shares it with his fiancée Sylvia Cartwright (Carol Lynley) who even makes a joke about how she will keep aging and he will not. Ben has ideas about donating his blood to help humankind despite Dr. Pierce's warnings about what could happen if he went public. Soon they realize that Ben's blood is only a temporary halt to the aging process as Braddock starts to grow old again. Realizing he will need regular transfusions; he offers Ben a life of luxury to become his and selected friends' own personal blood bank. Ben refuses to give up his freedom and Dr. Pierce advises him to take Sylvia and flee. He does not but agrees to meet with Braddock again who wants to discuss helping others with Ben's blood. Tricked, the racecar driver becomes imprisoned at Braddock's estate, after the world thinks he died in a car accident staged by the industrialist's men.

Itching to become a wealthy widow, Janet helps Ben escape. Knowing that he will be hunted by Braddock his whole life, Ben flees to Los Angeles with only Dr. Pierce and Sylvia knowing the truth. The months being separated from each other begin to take their toll and Ben lets Sylvia visit, knowing it could put their lives in danger. Sylvia takes extra precautions to make sure she is not followed. She and Ben are reunited and enjoy a romantic day together, but their idyllic reunion is ruined when Braddock's gun-toting henchmen arrive. Chasing the couple to the roof, Ben threatens to jump. Knowing they need him alive; they threaten to shoot Sylvia. She thinks they are bluffing and hearing police sirens, she makes a beeline to the ledge but is gunned down and rushed to the hospital.

Terrified of dying, Sylvia reveals Ben's secret to save her own life, but the doctor does not believe her. When he tells Ben her condition is grave, the Immortal offers his blood. Sylvia makes a miraculous recovery to the shock of the medical team, but the young woman is ashamed about what she did. With tears streaming down her face, she apologizes to Ben and says, "See. You can't trust anybody—not even me." Ben promises to come back for her but is once again pursued by Braddock's men and once again Janet, the Merry Widow wannabe, comes to his rescue. Eluding the goons, Ben writes a saddened Sylvia a Dear John letter wishing her well but realizing he must find his long-lost brother and that her life can only return to normal without him around.

Promotional print ad for *The Immortal* (Paramount Television, 1970) featuring Carol Lynley and Christopher George. *Billy Rose Theatre Division, The New York Public Library for the Performing Arts*

The Immortal aired on Sept. 30, 1969 and was the second made-for-TV movie to be broadcast as part of the new *ABC Movie of the Week*. It is also one of Lynley's best. The premise was original and the exciting film keeps the viewer fully enthralled. It also offered Carol a good role as the understanding Sylvia turned out to be an atypical lady in peril part for her. Though she is victimized and chased, Sylvia shows extreme back bone and courage standing up the thugs who have her and Ben at gunpoint. She diverts their attention from capturing Ben and in an act of bravery tries to signal the police despite their threats of shooting her. Carol is touching soon after as a contrite Sylvia begs Ben's forgiveness after she revealed his secret to save her own life. It was wonderful seeing Carol play a more determined, multi-dimensional heroine and she does an incredible job. Plus, she looked wonderful, especially in the funky purple sunglasses she wears while on the run from Braddock's goons. She and Chris George make a handsome couple and show great tenderness toward each other in their love scenes. The viewer can fully understand why Ben would take such a risk to see the lovely Sylvia once again.

The Immortal was extremely popular with the television viewing audience scoring a Nielsen rating of 20.3 rating. It was the second most watched TV show for the night and finished in 18th place for the week. The reviews were mostly positive. Percy Shain of the *Boston Globe* raved, "For a science fiction chiller—loaded with suspense and realism—you'd have to go far to beat *Movie of the Week*'s second world premiere presentation ... *The Immortal*." Kay Gardella of the *NY Daily News* found it to be "a better produced, better acted film than most."

Robert Specht said, "People were calling in asking, 'How did you do this on a TV budget?' And a couple of the actors had initially thought they were doing a feature."[370]

James Gunn however found fault with it. He was disappointed that the science fiction angle of immortality was downplayed and thought the hero "was not a thinking SF [science-fiction] man."[371] He specifically singled out the scene where the doctor tells Ben to take Sylvia and go on the run, but Ben refuses, thinking he can help sick children in the hospital. This was too sentimental and not rational enough for Gunn's tastes. He felt more sympathy for Braddock then Ben and Sylvia because "He wanted to make this blood widely available. That, to me, is a reasonable man, the only *real* SF character in the whole film."[372] Also, his book had the billionaire morphing from an elderly white-haired man to a virile dark-haired 30-year-old. In the film Braddock's revitalization is much less noticeable.

As for Carol she received positive notices. The reviewer in *Variety* found her character "sensibly enacted." Kay Gardella thought Carol to be "ingratiating" and remarked that Lynley and George's romantic scenes were "well played." However, Carol too was taken aback regarding *The Immortal*'s success. She opined, "I didn't think much of the movie when I started filming it. I just thought it was about a guy with this magical blood and thought well that's strange. And then Barry Sullivan was chasing after him and I thought it weird—and funny in a way. But to my shock it was a big hit."[373]

Sylvia Cartwright (Carol Lynley) is shot by thugs while trying to save Ben Richards (Christopher George) in *The Immortal* (Paramount Television, 1969).

The Immortal tied with *Bonanza* for an Emmy Award for Outstanding Achievement in Film Sound Editing and was also nominated for Outstanding Achievement in Cinematography for a Special or Featured Length Program Made for Television. It also was up for a Hugo Award for Best Dramatic Presentation along with *The Bed Sitting Room*, *The Illustrated Man*, and *Marooned*. Oddly, they all lost to the TV Coverage of Apollo XI.

*****

Impressed with the ratings and accolades, ABC-TV agreed there were more stories to tell for Ben Richards, so the network commissioned a weekly hour-long program for the 1970-71 television season. The highly promoted TV series *The Immortal* starring Christopher George premiered on September 24, 1970 almost one year after the TV-movie aired. Unfortunately, the successful team who brought the project to fruition—producer Lou Morheim, director Joseph Sargent, and writer Robert Specht—were all rejected by Paramount's executive VP Doug Cramer. Morheim was on his way out from Paramount anyway, but Specht was rightly disappointed not to be working on the series. Speculating why he was not hired, he said, "Cramer may have felt I was a slow writer because I didn't deliver the TV movie's script on time, but I couldn't deliver it until I felt it was right. Things got a little sticky. It's all money."[374] To add insult to injury, Paramount called Robert Specht's agent looking for a story editor to hire for *The Immortal*. He recommended Specht who created the show and never heard back.

Anthony Wilson was named Executive Producer and given a reported budget of $190,000 per episode. His last series as a producer was *Empire* in 1963 and then he worked as a story consultant on TV's *Lost in Space* and *Lancer*. His team of producers included Richard Caffey (*Garrison's Guerillas*, *The Survivors*); Gregg Peters (*Star Trek*, *Love, American Style*); William J. Hole, Jr. (*Peyton Place*); and Howie Horwitz (*Batman*). Following the network's orders, *The Immortal* became a clone of *The Fugitive* with Ben finding himself in a different town with a new prospective love interest each week, while still being pursued for his blood. Each episode would contain gun battles and screeching car chases galore. With that, Wilson ignored the advice to employ experienced science-fiction writers and opted for regular TV scenarists despite much input from James Gunn who knew the series would fail just by reading the few scripts sent to him as a courtesy.

Carol starred in the debut episode simply titled "Sylvia." At first, she was not interested in reprising the role and explained,

> The producers called me and said I had to appear in the first episode. I asked why. They said the network wanted Sylvia to be killed off in the first episode [she was not] so that Chris George's character could have a different girlfriend week after week. I first said no because my part, which wasn't big in the TV-movie, was even less here. They literally wouldn't accept no for an answer and cajoled me into appearing in that episode.[375]

Gene deRuelle worked as an Assistant Director on seven episodes including "Sylvia." He wrote, "I worked with Carol on *The Immortal*, which wasn't. The series premise was as stupid as it sounded with Chris George (God rest him) having blood which made him immortal. The bad guy [David Brian] was always trying to have Chris captured to get a transfusion. The series turned into one big car chase."[376] So much so that deRuelle revealed that "when producers realized that stunt man, Hal Needham, looked so much like Chris George there were days when Chris didn't even have to come to work. Again, one big car chase."[377]

When asked what he remembered about Carol Lynley, Gene deRuelle said, "There was nothing about Carol that made her stand out in my memory. I remember her as very professional (translation: she was on time and knew her lines) and pleasant."[378]

Narrator Paul Frees opened the debut episode "Sylvia" and each one that followed asking, "If you had million-dollar blood, *where* would you hide?" Ben is still seeking his brother while on the run from a callous tycoon named Arthur Maitland (David Brian) who calls him "the most valuable man in the world" and wants to "drain his blood." Ben then reads in the newspaper that his former girlfriend Sylvia Cartwright (Lynley) has agreed to marry wealthy David Hiller (Glenn Corbett). The proud groom-to-be is throwing an elaborate engagement party for her at his parents' estate and Ben travels there to see Sylvia one last time. Unfortunately, Maitland and his chief henchman Fletcher (Don Knight) are at the party knowing Ben would not be able to resist showing up.

Ben is helped by David's rebellious sister Sherry (Sherry Jackson) who introduces herself with the laughable lines, "My name is Sherry. I come sweet and dry. This is my best year." Sherry covers for Sylvia who gets to spend time alone with Ben where she reveals that the engagement to Hiller is a ruse to escape Maitland's thugs' constant hounding. As she professes her love for Ben, they are discovered by David and Fletcher. In the melee, Fletcher takes Sylvia hostage. David joins up with Ben and helps him flee the house to save Sylvia. After they do, a long arduous car chase begins. A heroic David surprises Sylvia by risking his life to divert the goons allowing her and Ben to escape. However, when one of the thugs gets the jump on Ben, Sylvia shoots him. A stunned Sylvia confesses to Ben that the second after pulling the trigger she realized that she cannot live her life on the run - despite her love for him. Ben understands and tells her to forget him, leaving her in the capable hands of David, as he journeys onward to find his brother.

"Sylvia" was disappointing and just a routine TV action-adventure episode with the science-fiction angle sucked out of it, but at least writer Robert M. Young allowed Lynley's character to remain feisty and brave. Sylvia tells off Maitland at the party, admits to only be using David, and then shows no hesitation as she shoots one of the thugs who attempts to capture Ben. Carol performs well and has an especially heartfelt moment at the end of the show where Sylvia tenderly breaks it off with Ben. She realizes her being with him has made her do terrible things that she normally would never have done, like expose a secret to selfishly save her own life and shoot a man. These are deeds she never wants to repeat and knows going on the run with Ben may force her to.

Former lovers Sylvia (Carol Lynley) and Ben (Christopher George) are reunited in "Sylvia" the debut episode on *The Immortal* (Paramount Television, 1970).

The costumers, though, really let Carol down here as Sylvia wears an unflattering white jumpsuit, a preview of the hideous fashions to come in the seventies - rather than the stylish, short dresses she wore in the telefilm.

Perhaps because an entire year had lapsed between the movie and the TV show's debut, *The Immortal* premiered with low ratings, mixed reviews, and almost constant comparisons to the superior series *The Fugitive*. Associated Press TV critic Lynn Sherr found "Sylvia" to be "farfetched but well mounted." Laurence Laurent of *The Washington Post* was not too impressed with the actors or the story, but was with the camera work and editing remarking, "They have provided the show with a lively, modern look." The critic in *The Baltimore Sun* couldn't contain himself with the blood puns calling the show "Run for Your Blood" and "a bloody bore." Percy Shain of the *Boston Globe* thought it "good 'escape television,'" and "the story had motion and suspense, but not much sense." Clarence Petersen of the *Chicago Tribune* found it "implausible," but added "the story is full of action … and despite its abysmal failings, it just might work."

Variety predicted that the show was "a fantasy far too unworldly to accept." They proved right. It was too absurd and dull for conventional TV action fans and not fantastical enough for the science-fiction lovers in the audience. Hence, the weekly ratings were disappointing. Its competition was *The Dean Martin Show* on NBC and the second half of *The CBS Thursday Night Movie*.

This should not have been too surprising for all involved since trouble behind-the-scenes started almost immediately due to the poor reception from the critics and audience. A hopeful Chris George revealed to the press, "It's such a unique type of show that we were groping for a while to find the right direction. We're not there yet, but with some luck we will be soon."[379] Unfortunately, they never did get the formula correct.

Gene deRuelle blames the lack of imagination and chase plot as the series downfall and why it could not get garner many viewers. He went to remark, "After fifteen episodes the network decided it was tired of paying for crashed cars and pulled the plug. Like I said, *The Immortal* wasn't. The reason for its demise was the producers. In TV, all writers are given producer credits.

There were six on *The Immortal*. You can't get six producers to agree on what time to go to lunch."[380]

Robert Specht and James Gunn agreed with deRuelle. Specht called the series, "a disaster,"[381] and Gunn remarked, "They never got beyond the chase. I was hoping they would explore the possibilities of Richards' immortalities."[382]

When asked if he thought the show could have been improved and saved, deRuelle responded, "The Line Producer was Howie Horwitz. If they had let him alone, he would have saved the series but no such luck. Howie was a meat and potatoes kind of producer. I believe he would have cut way down on the car chases and focused more on the sci-fi angle. I am just speculating here because I don't think the series could have been 'saved.' The premise was just too dumb, and the public really never seemed interested."[383]

Though Ben Richards could not die from disease, he could not escape the one thing that could kill him—low ratings. *The Immortal* was cancelled after only fifteen episodes.

Despite that most reference books list Carol as a series regular or a recurring character, "Sylvia" is her only appearance. Writer Robert M. Young was told that Paramount Studios did not have a contract with Carol and that the episode should end with Ben saying a final goodbye to Sylvia freeing him up for possible new romantic partners. Though it would have been to the show's advantage to keep Sylvia around to see how their relationship would survive with his being a hunted man and the fact that he was immortal, the decision was final. However, since they did not kill off Sylvia as originally told to Carol, perhaps they decided to let her live leaving the door open for a possible reappearance? Alas, it never came to be as *The Immortal* expired prematurely.

9. A Foulmouthed Hooker in a G-Rated Comedy!?!

Most moviegoers today do not remember the 1970 road comedy *Norwood*, the last of Carol Lynley's trifecta of features during this time. If they do know of it is usually because they are fans of its star, country singer Glen Campbell, or recall it being former NY Jets quarterback Joe Namath's first movie. Even for die-hard Lynley fans it does not rank high on their list due to her brief time on screen. This is thanks, or no thanks, to producer Hall Wallis who stupidly excised some of her more adult scenes in a mad obsession for a G-rating.

During the time of *Midnight Cowboy* and *Easy Rider*, the movie had a chance to be on the same adult level. The source material was the first novel by Charles Portis. It was an amiable tale of an easy-going country boy named Norwood Pratt just released from the marines whose goal is to sing on the Louisiana Hayride and his misadventures with a disparate group of people he encounters as he travels the road to get on the show. Though the book is set in the mid-fifties, the movie's screenplay moved it to 1969 while keeping all the adult situations. It was not until the editing process where the movie was shredded in a misguided quest by Wallis thinking a G-rating would increase its box office chances. This was a perfect example of greed winning out over substance with co-star Carol Lynley, as a foul-mouthed hooker, becoming the main casualty. However, she still stole the movie with a wonderfully comical performance.

In 1969, independent producer Hal Wallis was coming to the end of his tenure at Paramount Pictures. During the sixties he was mostly known for producing Elvis Presley movies such as *G.I. Blues*; *Blue Hawaii*; *Girls! Girls! Girls!*; *Roustabout*; *Paradise, Hawaiian Style*; and *Easy Come, Easy Go*. In between, he was able to slip in the Academy Award winning *Beckett* (1964). Wallis severed his connection with Elvis in 1966 because he felt that there was no longer an audience for the actor's brand of musical comedies. In 1969, Wallis scored a big hit with the western *True Grit* that won John Wayne an Oscar for his portrayal of Rooster Cogburn an ornery Marshall recruited by a teenage girl to avenge her father's murder. They are joined by a young Texas ranger looking for the same man. The young people were played by newcomers Kim Darby and country vocalist Glen Campbell.

True Grit was based on a novel by Charles Portis and Wallis also bought the rights to his *Norwood*. He thought *Norwood* would be the perfect follow-up for Glen Campbell who was now on television starring in his own variety series *The Glen Campbell Goodtime Hour* on CBS. The plot was reminiscent of the typical Elvis Presley movie with a handsome singing star, pretty scenery, and even prettier girls but much more adult in content.

After considering director James Frawley who had won an Emmy for directing TV's *The Monkees*, Wallis hired Jack Haley, Jr. to direct. He was the son of actor Jack Haley of *The Wizard of Oz* fame and had just won an Emmy for the Nancy Sinatra TV musical special *Movin' with Nancy*. This would be his first movie after working as producer and director on several highly acclaimed documentaries for David L. Wolper.

True Grit's screenwriter Marguerite Roberts was chosen to script *Norwood* and kept her screenplay quite adult following the tone of the novel. Norwood was still a handsome Southern country boy, but now a Vietnam vet who was not shy in trying to bed every gal he liked. The girls, all beautiful, were not your typical Elvis-girl movie characters: Yvonne was a cussin' hooker; Marie, an uptight New York City hippie coed; Kay, a fast-driving sexpot; and Rita Lee, a knocked up, unwed chatterbox. Add a midget, a dancing chicken, Joe William Reese as Norwood's football-loving GI buddy who wants to score a touchdown with Kay, and an Elvis movie this ain't.

One of the revised scripts beefed up the role of Rita Lee, so the producers decided (after giving up hope on getting Ali MacGraw) to cast Kim Darby reuniting her with Campbell. Football great Joe Namath, who was battling the NFL due to a nightclub he owned that was suspected of illegal gambling on the premises, was offered $60,000 for one week's work to play Joe Reese. Others cast were pretty Tisha Sterling who scored a hit opposite Clint Eastwood in *Coogan's Bluff* as Marie; character actor Pat Hingle as shady Grady Fring; Meredith MacRae from TV's *Petticoat Junction* as Kay; and comedy actors Leigh French and Dom DeLuise as Norwood's sister and shiftless brother-in-law.

One of the last roles cast was that of Yvonne Phillips who was described in the press releases as "a hillbilly hooker with a bit of Bonnie, as in Clyde." Paul Nathan wrote to Wallis that he thought Nita Talbot was right for Yvonne and commented, "She is not young, but she has a very hard, marvelous quality."[384] Carol got the role instead. Her casting was probably helped by her friendship with Jack Haley, Jr. who was engaged to Nancy Sinatra while Carol was dating her father, ol' Blue Eyes. For whatever reason she was considered for the part, it did not matter to Hal Wallis who gave his seal of approval via memo and wrote, "I did see Carol Lynley in a picture and she was excellent. I have no reservations about her at all and I am sure she could do it."[385] Carol was excited to play Yvonne because it was going to be an acting challenge and it was a type of character she rarely played. Shortly before filming began, Paul Nathan stated in a note to Wallis, "We had lunch with Carol Lynley Monday, and I was completely smitten. She is a lovely looking girl."[386]

Marguerite Roberts' script was submitted to the Motion Picture Association of America, Inc. who indicated that, as is, the movie would be rated M for mature audiences. It was indicated that the phrase "son of a bitch" was used too much; a potential nudity issue with Yvonne's seduction of Norwood

Publicity photo of Carol Lynley in *Norwood* (Paramount, 1970).

in the back of his car; and, most ridiculously, an objection to a character saying, "your ass." This letter did not seem to deter *Norwood*'s producers and director, and the screenplay remained unchanged. This is not surprising since Hal Wallis wanted a film with more adult substance than the Elvis Presley musicals he was pumping out during the decade.

Before filming began on *Norwood* in July, Wallis had jetted off to England to oversee his prestigious movie *Anne of the Thousand Days* starring Richard Burton and Genevieve Bujold. He left *Norwood* in the capable hands of Nathan who continually updated Wallis, outlining progress and problems. During filming, Wallis was on the phone every day to Hollywood and was sent dailies each week to review.

With casting complete, attention then turned to the film's star Glen Campbell who was worried about the adult nature of the story. Nathan made Campbell realize that it was not late sixties cool to gear his image to be the next Pat Boone and that it was quite acceptable for actors to have sex scenes on film. Nathan was so confident that he got through to his star that he wrote Hal Wallis and stated, "Glen is now perfectly willing to do scenes in the picture with his shirt off, and we will do this in Marie's apartment or wherever we can. He has trimmed down and really looks great. He has also agreed to go into the love scenes with a great deal of vigor with Marie and with Yvonne. He has also agreed that he will use occasional dirty language … but Glen now agrees the only word he will not use is 'son-of-a-bitch.'"[387] Nathan's optimism in his leading man was soon to be proved misplaced.

Campbell's discontent with the script resurfaced when he started to film his scenes with Lynley or shall we say refused to film his scenes even though he had already given assurances to Paul Nathan that he was OK with curse words as long as he didn't have to say them. Columnist Dorothy Manners reported from the set that a ruffled Glen Campbell stated, "I'm allergic to being called any of those names. It goes against my grain and I think the feeling of the scene can be obtained without those words."[388]

It was director Jack Haley, Jr. who stepped in with a compromise. Carol would say the words in the script as is but would mumble them a bit making them less audible. Campbell agreed and that is why for instance in their first scene you barely can make out the word "bitch" when she says it a second time.

Carol said, "I was aware of this but was not surprised because it is standard to try different approaches to a scene. That is not unusual in the least while making a movie."[389] The only minor problem with Glen Campbell that she copped to was at the motel where the cast was being put up during the location shoot. She commented,

> My room was right next to Glen's room, which was fine because he was a sweet guy, happily married, and he couldn't have been nicer. My only complaint was that he played his own records all the time. I always liked his singing very much but I got a little tired hearing 'By the Time I Get to Phoenix' over and over and over. I never said anything because he was so nice and figured that's what singers do.[390]

Most of Carol's scenes in the movie were verboten from the novel - from when Grady surprises Norwood with Yvonne as his passenger to New York, to their bantering and name calling as they drive east, to Yvonne pining for bartender Sammy Ortega, to Norwood learning from Yvonne that the cars they are driving on stolen and him abandoning them and her in Illinois after being chased by the police for running a stop sign. However, Marguerite Roberts added two more scenes that were shot but excised from the film. After escaping from the sheriff, Yvonne seduces Norwood in the automobile's back seat and tries to get him to give her one of the cars. A shot of her lounging seductively in the back seat turns up as her single card billing during the end credit roll.

After Kay and Joe Reese drive Rita Lee and Norwood (singing "Settlin' Down") to meet his sister, there was a scene where Norwood and Rita Lee meet up with Yvonne and Grady. Yvonne runs up to Norwood planting a big kiss on him to the consternation of Rita Lee. There was also a scene of a smitten Yvonne sitting in the passenger side of a car smiling at Norwood standing outside it.

Hal Wallis and Jack Haley, Jr. contradicted each other and themselves with the reasons why these scenes, particularly the lovemaking one with Lynley, were cut. Paul Nathan submitted the final revised script to the MPAA who wrote back on July 24, 1969 that if filmed, as is, the movie would receive a "M" rating for mature audiences. The ratings board had problems with Yvonne's double use of "son of a bitch"; unnecessary cursing; and using the phrases "peeing" and "your ass". If nudity made it into the final cut (if there was any, most likely it would have been from the Yvonne/Norwood love scene), the "M" rating was also in jeopardy. By this time, all these scenes were filmed and it looked as if the movie was not going to get a "G" rating, which at this time seemed not to bother Paul Nathan or Jack Haley, Jr. Not so Hal Wallis, who wrote that he wanted that lesser rating to increase the film's box office chances. Agreeing with some of what the MPAA suggested, he instructed Nathan to eliminate the curse words "by dubbing another word or making a wild track to go over someone else."[391]

Jack Haley, Jr. had right of first cut and Hal Wallis ordered Paul Nathan not to interfere. In a memo back to Wallis, Nathan expressed how he liked Haley personally, but found him professionally to be "a child."[392] Once Haley submitted his cut, Wallis would then screen the movie and make any edits he deemed fit. He also refused to watch the movie with Haley. The memos between Nathan and Wallis make it quite clear that they had no faith in Haley's edit and decided just to appease the director letting him deliver his final cut per the terms of his contract. Wallis already knew he was going to cut the film to shreds so he did not need to watch it with Haley.

This method of working via memo frustrated the first-time movie director who had to send his editing notes in writing to the producer. Prior to his final cut, it was Jack Haley, Jr. who suggested in a letter that cutting Lynley's final scenes because "the deletion would certainly save a great deal of time without hurting the story in any way."[393] Wallis seemed to agree since there was no protest from him and the scenes never made it into the final print.

Haley won some battles on minor points regarding Lynley's scenes. Wallis wanted to cut the Mann Act lines but agreed with Haley who wrote, "It's a strong joke and without it Yvonne suddenly turns on Norwood for no reason."[394] He also made Wallis realize that Norwood should be seen first singing "Rock of Ages" before seeing Yvonne dancing to rock music because the opposite way would wipe out the joke.

Though Wallis appeased his director, the lovemaking scene was another issue. Both Haley and Nathan fought to keep in the picture. Wallis was adamant that it had to go to assure his "G" rating. Nathan was the first to capitulate and wrote to Wallis, "I was wrong about trying to keep the cut of Yvonne and Glen in the morning in the back seat of the car. I now feel it should come out as you suggested."[395]

Reluctant passenger Yvonne Phillips (Carol Lynley) is not happy with her driver in *Norwood* (Paramount, 1970).

A determined Haley sent one last memo after the movie was previewed with agreed upon cuts (though Lynley's last scenes were run) on January 17, 1970. He began his letter with "I am terribly pleased with *Norwood*. The final editing and Al DeLory's scoring job are really superb efforts."[396] He then listed thirty-one changes he wanted made. Interestingly, the lovemaking scene was not mentioned. Either it was a done deal to cut it or the producers did it after this screening.

Co-stars Carol Lynley and Joe Namath behind the scenes while filming *Norwood* (Paramount, 1970).

Campbell was schizophrenic in the interviews he gave regarding *Norwood*. On one hand he feigned disappointment to hear about all the cuts being made in the editing room. He remarked that *Norwood* "turned out good, but it irks me because they wanted to get a 'G' rating, so they kept cutting a lot of the dialog from the picture after it was finished. You can't have more than one s.o.b. to get a 'G' rating."[397] He felt proud that he didn't curse in the movie, but added "Carol Lynley kept calling me 'you country s.o.b.' though."[398] Soon after, he boasted, "There was a scene where Carol Lynley was supposed to call me an SOB. I said I don't want that garbage in the show. I told them I wanted a movie my preacher could see."[399] The upshot from all this was that Glen Campbell vowed to study more closely future scripts offered him. This was moot because he never starred in a feature film again. His opinion of the movie changed too over time and he wrote in his 1994 memoir that *Norwood* was "a corny movie. It was a ridiculous story that set back the cause of country music and perpetuated every stereotype of country musicians as hicks."[400]

Just before the film was released, an over-confident Hal Wallis boasted, "*Norwood* should go over $20 million at the box office."[401] Despite his forcing cuts to get a G-rating, he then suggested *Norwood* was almost as "far out" as the comedy *Goodbye, Columbus* with Richard Benjamin and Ali MacGraw. "*Norwood* comes as close as anything. However, it isn't objectionable, isn't offensive."[402] It was not cool or hip enough to interest the young moviegoers who flocked to *Goodbye, Columbus* or *Easy Rider*. The only thing they had in common was that their leading players were relative newcomers.

Norwood also received a free boost in promotion from Continental Trailways whose bus terminals were prominently featured throughout the movie. The company displayed *Norwood* movie posters at most of its facilities and sponsored radio contests where winners received free bus trip and hotel accommodations at select cities.

In the movie, aspiring country music singer Norwood has just returned home from active duty with his pal Joe Reese (Joe Namath). Hitchhiking, they part ways with a promise from Joe to pay Norwood back the seventy dollars he borrowed. Norwood returns to his childhood home, now occupied by his flighty sister (Leigh French) and her opinionated, freeloading husband (Dom DeLuise) whom he does not get along with. Wanting out, Norwood agrees to drive a car owned by shady "talent manager" Grady Fring (Pat Hingle) from his hometown to New York City with promises that Grady will get him a spot on the Louisiana Hayride radio program.

When the ex-GI arrives the following morning, he is surprised to find another car hooked to the back of it via a tow bar and that he would have a pretty traveling companion named Yvonne Phillips. Carol amusingly brings to life the feisty, foul-mouthed, peach-eating Yvonne ("she is a dandy," exclaims Grady), who was spotted by one of Grady's talent scouts and is being sent to

New York. In both the novel and film, it is never made clear though just what "talent" Yvonne possesses. Screenwriter Marguerite Roberts retained from the novel the character's salty language and her continuous mentioning of Sammy Ortega a bartender who "can get me lined up real easy" and "we had a very good business association going." The type of business is unclear though savvy viewers know the tough-talking Yvonne is probably a hooker.

Yvonne is first seen exiting the car clad in a low-cut, backless, orange mini dress and heading over to where Norwood is standing with Grady. She does not even say hello and yells at Grady, "I hope you don't think that I am going to go to New York with this country son-of-a-bitch?" Trying to alleviate Norwood's trepidation, Grady says she is miffed because she "thought she was going up in a Delta jet." Furious, she tells Grady, "I wish Sammy Ortega was here. He'd break your arm." When Norwood interjects, she says, "I wasn't talking to you, peckerwood. But Sammy would get to you too if he felt like it you big mouthed country son of a bitch!" This second "bitch" was muffled by the sound dept., no doubt to get that "G" rating.

As they drive along, laid back Norwood tries to befriend Yvonne but blows it by calling her Laverne to her utter annoyance, "My name is not Laverne, it's *Yvonne*! But I don't want you calling me nuthin'!" Making matters worse, later he slams on his breaks when he spots a possum out in the fields. After Yvonne spills her canned peaches all over her dress, she yells, "Oh, son of a bitch! What the hell is wrong with you!?! You think I want to see some possum crawling through some fence!" After trying to clean off her dress, Yvonne slams the car door shut and calls Norwood, "the biggest peckerwood bastard in the whole world!" Crying, she wishes she was in Calumet City, Illinois with Sammy Ortega.

At one point as they are driving along, Yvonne hints that the cars are stolen when they enter Tennessee. She states smugly, "Well, you just crossed another state line. You know under these conditions they could put *you* in the federal penitentiary." Norwood replies, "I ain't afraid of the Mann Act." To which Yvonne retorts, "You are the peckerwood of all peckerwoods." After insulting each other back and forth, Norwood says, "I don't see how in the hell anyone from Belzoni, Mississippi can call anybody else a peckerwood anyway." To which Yvonne replies with a bit of haughtiness, "Look, for your information, I happened to have spent a lot of time in *New Orleans* and I count *that* as my home." Norwood snaps, "You could live in Hong Kong, Kalamazoo, or Podunk, Iowa for seventy-five years—Belzoni, Mississippi is still your home." She exclaims, "Don't you sit there and tell me where my home is!"

Demanding that Norwood stop the car, Yvonne storms out and sits in the passenger seat of the car being towed while the name calling continues. "Butt-headed peckerwood!" "Damn squirrel-headed dingbat!" As they drive along separately, Norwood is singing "Rock of Ages" while Yvonne is grooving to some funky jazz music. This is followed by a wonderfully shot and scored scene as the camera pans from right to left following horses running across a field and then the camera stops on Norwood's oncoming car and follows it - panning back right.

Yvonne is back in the car with Norwood. In the book there is a lengthy conversation the pair have about religion, which Roberts rightfully excised from her script. When Yvonne finally reveals that the cars that he has been hired to deliver are stolen ("They are about to burst into flames!") to try to get Norwood to give her one, he plows through a stop sign with the town's sheriff and deputy in hot pursuit. He decides to outrun them with Yvonne yelling in his ear, "Well Mr. High Pockets you just about got us nearly killed that time. What do you plan to do next!?!" A car chase ensues, and Norwood gets away when the car being towed breaks off and the cop car crashes into it.

At this point, day fades into night as Norwood drives to a secluded section of a park in Illinois. Yvonne being a hooker is hinted at again as she is about to drive off with the stolen car and Norwood begins wiping off his fingerprints. Taking a line from the book's narration, he says, "It's a proud day when the Marine Corps took them. Now they are up there in a drawer somewhere in Washington waiting to do me in." When he suggests that Yvonne do the same once she gets to Calumet City, she replies, "Why? I was never in the Marines—a couple of camps, maybe. You know I never did get to hear you on that guitar. Adios."

After parting ways with Yvonne, Norwood hitchhikes his way to the Big Apple to find Joe Reese. Instead of meeting up with his marine pal, he finds a hippie coed named Marie (Tisha Sterling) in his apartment. She informs him that Joe has returned to his hometown. She reluctantly agrees to let Norwood stay with her and they visit a local coffee bar where Norwood performs a song for the crowd. Back at her place, Marie tries to still act romantically disinterested in Norwood, but they tumble into a bathtub together.

Norwood then decides to take a bus to Joe Reese's hometown. During the trek, he befriends a little person named Edmund Ratner (Billy Curtis) with a dancing chicken and a pregnant, chatty, unwed girl named Rita Lee (Kim Darby) who is running from her beau, Wayne Walker (Sammy Jackson). Rita Lee and Edmund accompany Norwood to Joe Reese's home where they partake in a family cookout and spend the night. Norwood meets Joe's beautiful fast-driving girlfriend Kay (Meredith MacRae) who drives the trio to the bus depot the next day. Norwood realizes he has fallen for Rita Lee, but Wayne has followed them and wants her back. Thinking she has chosen the father of her baby, Norwood heads out to perform on the Louisiana Hayride radio show. There in the audience is a smitten Rita Lee in the front row.

Norwood opened throughout the South and in most major cities in late May and June 1970. In some cities, such as New York, it did not open until November after the release of Joe Namath's second movie, *C.C. and Company* co-starring Ann-Margret. Despite Carol's diminished role, she did promotion with co-star (and fellow victim of the obsession for a "G" rating) Tisha Sterling who recalled, "Carol is very sweet and I like her a lot. When we came off the plane (I think somewhere in South Texas), these people started speaking Spanish to us. I didn't speak a word of it and all of a sudden Carol was conversing with them in Spanish. I was so impressed! I didn't know she was bilingual."[403]

Reviews for the comedy were mixed. Charles Champlin of the *Los Angeles Times* called it "an amiable, easygoing often quite funny piece of entertainment." His major complaint about the movie was that "the pace is very slow without being leisurely. The jokes, always mild, tend to be hammered home and then lingered over." As for Lynley, he felt she and (Tisha Sterling and Meredith MacRae) "give excellent accounts of themselves." Gene Siskel of the *Chicago Tribune* found "the film's Southern humor hokey, but harmless." Robert Taylor of the *Oakland Tribune* amusingly called Carol's character "a prostitute with a heart of tin" but found the movie to be "all corn." Nadine Subetaik of *The Cedar Rapids Gazette* called the comedy "a relaxed little piece that seems made to order for the easy-going style of Glen Campbell." Some notices were nasty such as one anonymous reviewer who wrote, "You know a comedy is in trouble when Carol Lynley is the comedic highpoint."

Surprisingly, Carol received her most enthusiastic review from all places the U.S. Catholic Conference Film Division writing in the *Catholic Advance*. Its critic found *Norwood* to be "a corny entertaining movie" and added "Glen gets to sing a few songs, Joe passes the football around, Carol Lynley puts in a terrific stint as a Southern brassy blonde, and even the rooster gets to do his thing."

Corny, however, was not what Jack Haley, Jr. was aiming for when he began shooting *Norwood*. By watering down the script and cutting scenes and dialog at the last minute to get his "G" rating, Hal Wallis lost the young adult crowd who wanted something edgy. Some of the critics picked that up in their reviews such as Edgar Driscoll, Jr. in the *Boston Globe* who noted that "the kids will probably enjoy it. (We don't mean the college set.)." Howard Thompson of the *New York Times* wrote "the picture looks edited though a meat grinder." Commenting on Lynley, he said that she "looks and sounds as hard as nails. And such language—in a G-rated picture!"

Norwood also received backlash from people who felt that the G-rating and ad campaign touting the movie as family-friendly was misleading. One critic took to the pages of the *San Bernardino Sun-Telegram* and stated, "I must admit I did not watch the whole picture because after the first ten minutes in which Carol Lynley called Glen Campbell a bastard and an s.o.b. three times, along with other choice terms, my husband and I took our children and left. Nothing can justify that kind of language in a 'G' rated movie."[404] She raised some good points. With all those curse words, how did Wallis and Paramount obtain a G-rating? Were strings pulled? Was it worth the hassle in alienating the director to re-edit the movie? It again showed how misguided and stuck in the past Hal Wallis was with his decision to cut the film to shreds to get this rating when a true adult movie, which it began as, may have been better received.

Norwood is an easy laid-back pleasant diversion with hummable songs nicely sung by the star, but not much of a plot. It was a pleasant change of pace to see two Vietnam vets treated respectfully, which was not the case in many movies from this time. Carol Lynley looks terrific in her mini dress and short hair. By far, and even with the excising of some of her major scenes, she gives the liveliest performance and steals the movie with her comedic turn as the self-absorbed Yvonne who reluctantly drives cross country with "this country son of a bitch." She and Campbell play quite well opposite each other. Her feisty nastiness meshes well with his affable country boy who tries to stay the Southern gentleman but is pushed too far by his companion before he explodes. Yvonne is by far the most interesting character in the movie and one can see why Marguerite Roberts created more scenes with her than what were in the novel. It would have been wonderful if at least the lovemaking segment had not been cut extending Lynley's screen time.

At the box office, *Norwood* opened in forty-five theaters in four cities grossing $161,800 during its first week. It trailed behind other movies playing then including *Bob & Carol & Ted & Alice*; Hal Wallis' other production *Anne of the Thousand Days*; *The Grasshopper*, *M*A*S*H*; and *Let It Be*. The film's total gross was just under $2 million, what Elvis' late sixties films were earning and far short of Wallis' projection of $20 million, though it ranked a respectable thirtieth at the box office for the year. It was Carol's biggest box office grosser since *The Pleasure Seekers* in 1965. The movie did well in the South and at drive-ins, but more sophisticated moviegoers in the big cities ignored it.

With its G-rating and Glen Campbell in the lead singing several songs, they probably presumed it was going to be yet another Elvis Presley-type movie and ignored it. In the days of *Midnight Cowboy* and *Easy Rider*, the Elvis film was dead and younger people wanted something more substantial. They may have gotten that in *Norwood* if Wallis would have released the mature film Marguerite Roberts delivered with her script.

In October 1970 Jack Haley, Jr. began the war of words with Hal Wallis over his disappointment with *Norwood* when he contributed a piece to *Action* the magazine of the Directors Guild of America. Though he lavished praise on producer Hal Wallis ("the most decisive, best organized producer I ever worked with" and "an inherent genius for casting"[405]) and conceded that he learned a lot about producing from him, Haley then went on to label him in a negative way as an "auteur producer."[406] His complaint was that Wallis had to have control over the movie from beginning to end, which frustrated the new director. Haley remarked, "I had hopes of elevating Glen Campbell and *Norwood* above the usual Presley-type format. Hal was inclined to agree there was a chance to do just this."[407] However, once Wallis was determined to get that G-rating, Haley's input was no longer needed.

Haley goes on to report that after principal photography was completed, he began two weeks directing the second unit shooting something the director usually does not do ("I had willingly volunteered to do this because I felt this special photography was important to the picture"[408]) and that left him only thirteen days to deliver his cut to Wallis. He thought he would have a say with the editing, working in conjunction with Wallis, but the producer wouldn't even screen the movie with his director telling him, "It makes me nervous."[409] This is when those series of memos began circulating back and forth between them. Haley wrote, "How the hell you can discuss pace and performance or analyze the balance of individual scenes by way of memo-to-memo completely eludes me."[410] Describing his feelings at the time, he stated, "I've experienced the buzzing of gnats in one's ear, but I've never really felt like a gnat before."[411]

A Foulmouthed Hooker

Norwood (Glen Campbell) and Yvonne (Carol Lynley) are reunited in an excised scene from *Norwood* (Paramount, 1970).

Haley also complimented and apologized to Carol in the article and wrote, "In *Norwood*, she faced a challenge in playing a bitchy, foul-mouthed hooker … a vivid contrast to her usual virginal sweetheart roles. Carol was concerned about doing such a different character, but she pulled it off with great style. I'm sorry so many of her best scenes hit the cutting room floor. She was truly the worst victim in the last minute reach for a "G" rating."[412] To be fair, it was Haley, not Wallis, who suggested Lynley's later scenes be cut due to running time, not for content, so the producer was not fully responsible for her lack of screen time.

Of course, Hal Wallis did not take this lying down and rebutted him later to the press. The producer fired back, "It would seem to me that Haley's own statements point out where the fault lay. He was unable to get the performances he needed out of Glen Campbell, Joe Namath, or Carol Lynley. If he wasn't capable of doing a better job, why is he blaming everybody else…"[413] This is quite frankly hogwash and just an excuse to cover for his cowardice in releasing an adult movie. Campbell and Namath both were quite charming in their roles and Lynley was able to rise above the ingénues and damsels in distresses she was known for playing and truly deliver a lively amusing performance. Haley must get the credit in getting these commendable performances from them.

Wallis continued, "Considering the fact that this was his first film and I had made 250 before, I think I know a little more about editing and direction than he does. I've been in this business many years, you run into this, but not from neophytes. He has a lot to learn..."[414] Wallis totally ignores the fact that he was still in the Elvis-movie mind set of delivering a family picture despite the mature script in 1970. This was odd since he stated to the press that he ended his relationship with the King because his type of musical film was no longer in vogue. While shooting the movie, this desire for a G-rating was not relayed to Haley (or associate producer Paul Nathan) and he shot the screenplay thinking all were in agreement- desiring to rise above the typical, teenage musicals of the sixties. Haley even battled Glen Campbell to keep the salty language in while shooting. It was not until after the fact that Wallis had dollar signs in his eyes and felt the G-rating would attract a larger audience. As part of the old guard in Hollywood, Wallis was slow to grasp that younger audiences were craving more mature material not family-style hokum, which he delivered by cutting the movie to shreds. He did not own up to any of this and instead blamed his director.

Carol was unaware of any of this back and forth or why her scenes were cut. As for the criticism against Jack Haley, Carol said,

> I had known Jack forever. He was a happy guy and all smiles around his actors. He was more a friend than director to me. We remained close until his death. I always loved Jack very much. I am not a good person to judge his directing skill, but I thought he did an excellent job.
>
> I don't recall Hal Wallis ever being on the shoot. I had met him a few times when on the Paramount lot. We'd say hello but

that was about it. He was sort of a gruff type of guy but nice. Paul Nathan was there quite a lot though.[415]

Alas, *Norwood* goes down in Hollywood history as another one of those late sixties drive-in features that were too square to be hip. Movies such as *For Singles Only*; *The Cool* Ones; *The Impossible Years*; *Skidoo*; and *How to Commit Marriage* where studio heads thought they were capturing the hip attitudes of the time but failed miserably. In the case of *Norwood*, it is a real shame since there was strong potential there, in the novel and Marguerite Roberts' script, which was ably directed by Jack Haley, Jr. and beautifully photographed by Robert B. Hauser. All the performers do well even Kim Darby and Glen Campbell. Unfortunately, the misguided notion that a G-rating would bring in more business, and an uncomfortable leading man afraid that the movie would tarnish his good ol' country boy persona, damaged what could have been.

Jack Haley, Jr. rightly stated Lynley was the true victim in this sabotaged venture. Though she would go on to play murderesses and nutcases on TV and in film, she would never get the opportunity to play such an over-the-top funny character like *Norwood*'s Yvonne Phillips in a comedy ever again. Seeing how well she does in the scenes that remain, one wonders how the excised scenes played out with Yvonne now smitten with Norwood after only one roll in the hay. It is a testament to Lynley's talent that even with her short screen time she was able to deliver one of the film's best performances and leave the audience wanting more. Who knows if, perhaps, her scenes were left intact, she may even have generated buzz for a Best Supporting Actress Oscar nomination?

Hearing Haley's regret regarding Lynley's diminished role in *Norwood*, it is surprising that she was not cast in his next movie *The Love Machine* based on the Jacqueline Susann novel. There were four major female characters and the role of Amanda, a model and jilted girlfriend of ambitious newscaster Robin Stone, seemed perfect for her. Instead newcomer Jodi Wexler was cast. Most felt she was inadequate, and one critic specifically wrote that the part needed "a Carol Lynley or an Yvette Mimieux" to pull it off successfully.

10. Vampires and Druids and the Blob! Oh, My!

Norwood (which Carol called a "terrible movie"[416]) would be the actress' last theatrical feature until 1972. Reflecting on why she decided to do her latest trio of flicks, Carol explained at the time, "I have been supporting myself since I was ten years old ... so I was used to a certain lifestyle. I think it was insecurity on my behalf that made me accept roles in a lot of bad films."[417] At least her three latest movies gave her a range of characters to play from a murderous psychopath, to the lady in peril in a haunted house, to a foulmouthed hooker. And she performed quite well in all three.

Carol also admitted that she was having trouble fitting in with Hollywood's elite crowd - not that it bothered her much. She revealed to journalist Vernon Scott, "Socially, I'm a Hollywood dropout. I really don't understand the Hollywood social structure. There are A, B, and C guest lists ... I guess I's somewhere between Y and Z in the social lists. They've invited me to parties, but I am never invited back. I guess I don't do what is expected of A-list people."[418]

More concerned for her career than socializing, Carol shared her new game plan going forward. "I decided to change my lifestyle to something a little less extravagant. Then I started to work for television whenever I needed the money, instead of acting in bad films."[419] In January 1973, she reiterated this on *The Tonight Show Starring Johnny Carson* when Carson asked why he hadn't seen her much on the big screen prior to *The Poseidon Adventure*.

It is understandable after working with the likes of Kirk Douglas, Jack Lemmon, Otto Preminger, and Laurence Olivier, that Carol Lynley wanted to appear in important motion pictures and not work in B-movies or bad films. Producer Tony Tenser (commenting to biographer Tony Hamilton) said he was disappointed that he could not land Carol for AIP's *The Haunted House of Horror* and was surprised that she would not jump at the chance to co-star with Frankie Avalon.[420] Huh!?! Sue Lyon passed on this golden opportunity as well and Tenser settled for Jill Haworth, fresh off her successful Broadway run in *Cabaret*. Reportedly AIP also wanted to reunite Lynley with H.P. Lovecraft. She and Peter Fonda topped their list for the leads in *The Dunwich Horror* based on another of the author's stories. However, it did not come to pass. Sandra Dee and Dean Stockwell starred instead.

When asked about these movies, Carol does not recall turning them down. It is most likely that Lynley let her feelings known about not wanting to do B-movies with her agent, so perhaps he never even shared these AIP scripts with her? Carol remarked matter-of-factly,

> I always had to support my daughter and pay the rent and buy clothes and such to live. As I said, I never had the luxury of turning much of anything down. Of course, I didn't want to be a B-actress. I always considered myself a good actress and always striving to be a very good *actor*. Beginning with my first Broadway play with Dame Sybil Thorndike, I have always been fortunate to be surrounded by talented people 99% of the time.[421]

During this period, Carol did get offered a theatrical feature that turned out to be one of the best of the year, but she passed on the acclaimed *Five Easy Pieces*. The actress admits to rejecting the part of concert pianist-turned-rebel Jack Nicholson's almost sister-in-law (Susan Anspach stepped in). She explained, "I really wanted to play the waitress role [his trashy girlfriend], but it was already cast with Karen Black. Since the producers were only paying scale, I passed on the other role—big mistake!"[422] Indeed. The movie received almost unanimous critical acclaim and earned several Academy Award nominations, including Best Motion Picture.

To be fair, as Carol mentioned, she was a single mom supporting her daughter, so it is understandable why the money factor influenced her decision. Even so, perhaps if she had a savvy agent paying attention to what was going on in Hollywood, he could have encouraged her to take the role despite the lower salary. Up-and-comer Jack Nicholson had just scored big in *Easy Rider* and director Bob Rafelson was part of that new breed of hip independent filmmakers, who for the most part, were ignoring the typical Hollywood actresses when casting. Carol's early sixties contemporaries were also facing this situation. Opining on her experience, Diane McBain said, "We all received a backlash from the 'artsy' independent filmmakers. In their experimental filmmaking and acquiescing to the Hollywood standard, these filmmakers managed to break loose from established mores that maybe needed to be broken loose from—like the image of beauty—but were devasting to me personally. Everybody in Hollywood was so gorgeous and beautifully dressed in movies. Even when they woke up out of a dead sleep, they were beautifully made up. That was a bit silly. But at the same time, I was a part of this."[423]

The fact that Carol Lynley was offered any part from an independent filmmaker was an accomplishment, which she may not have realized. Someone, looking out for her career, should have cajoled her into taking the role as they did with *The Maltese Bippy*.

In between jobs, Carol traveled the world sometimes to visit her then boyfriend, the outspoken and rowdy Oliver Reed, while he was on location - even though he would not even think to visit her on set. She revealed in the book *What Fresh Lunacy Is This?*, "He was much too egotistical for that. So, I would sometimes go and see him when he was working. Mainly, it was just keeping him company, he liked to have company."[424] Reed seemed to be so self-absorbed, that according to Carol, he showed no interest in her career whatsoever. She remarked, "I don't think he really thought about it one way or the other. He was very centered on himself, as most actors are. The only thing that he ever asked me about was, did I really sing the song in *The Poseidon Adventure*? Other than that, he was never particularly interested in what I was doing or who I was filming with."[425]

In January of 1970, it was reported that Carol had been offered a recurring role on the hit espionage series *Mission: Impossible*.[426] The 1969-70 season was the first without its Emmy Award winning leading lady Barbara Bain. Several actresses (including Alexandra Hay, Lee Meriwether, Anne Francis, and BarBara Luna) were brought in as guest IMF agents (to abet series regulars Peter Graves, Leonard Nimoy, Greg Morris, and Peter Lupus), as producers were deciding who to make permanent. Carol said there was never any offer to appear on the show and exclaimed, "But I would have liked to!"[427]

Carol's TV work began during this time with her previously mentioned appearance on the debut episode of *The Immortal* followed by guest roles on *The Bold Ones: The New Doctors* and *The Most Deadly Game*. She then played a string of terrorized ladies whose lives were in jeopardy from desperate kidnappers and killers, to vampires, druids and the Blob. Carol really excelled in some of these roles that no doubt led to her most-remembered damsel in distress, Nonnie Parry, in the mega blockbuster *The Poseidon Adventure*.

When asked if this was a conscious decision to focus on playing the lady in peril, Carol replied, "That's where the work was. By the late sixties, women's roles were diminishing, but the thriller and suspense genres still offered many parts for actresses."[428]

As the seventies began, Lynley's fans probably also noticed the change in her appearance. In her movies released at the end of the sixties, Carol had a more glamorous look with her short flaxen hair and heavy eye makeup accentuated by false eyelashes. She then abandoned that guise and began wearing "her thin hair hanging straight to her shoulders, with only a dab of lip gloss, mascara, and blusher for makeup."[429] Carol added, "That's all the makeup I wear for films, too. I photograph better without much makeup on."[430] This was the start of her hippie-look period, which lasted well into 1974.

The Bold Ones: The Doctors starred Emmy Award winner E.G. Marshall as a brilliant neurosurgeon who has opened his own clinic, the Craig Institute, with David Hartman and John Saxon as his lead doctors. In the episode "Giants Never Kneel," from a teleplay by Sy Salkowitz and Nat Tanchuck (who co-wrote the unused script for *The Shuttered Room*), Carol played the loyal supportive daughter of an industrialist (Arthur Hill) who secretly enters the hospital for a physical and is diagnosed with an illness. When word leaks out, his company's stock falls and suspicions are aroused if he is truly sick or was it a ruse to manipulate the market. In an interesting footnote, Hill's character has an electroencephalograph and the prop did not work properly. A real machine was brought in and it is Hill's actual brain waves that are shown.

Syndicated television reviews found the episode to be "absorbing" and it is. Carol, however, really has nothing much to do other than to look worried throughout. Hence, it did not offer a memorable role.

Another forgettable part for Carol (where she was likely in it only for the paycheck) was on the short-lived TV detective series *The Most Deadly Game*. George Maharis and Yvette Mimieux (stepping in for Inger Stevens who died of a drug overdose after completing the pilot) play investigators who solve difficult murder cases under the tutelage of a master criminologist (Ralph Bellamy). Carol was a horse trainer and suspect in the death of a dude ranch owner (Robert J. Wilkie) in the episode, "Who Killed Kindness?" Other possible culprits included his son (Andrew Prine), his foreman (Paul Richards), and his bitter housekeeper (Sheree North).

Standard fare, though the reviewer for *The Evening Press, Binghamton, NY* commented, "Since the locale of this episode is a dude ranch, you might think there would be some lightness to the script. When there is, it's soon inundated by a wide variety of vicious emotions." He also found the episode was greatly helped by "an excellent guest cast."

For sixties cinema fans this is worth watching just to see Carol Lynley and Yvette Mimieux on screen together for the first and only time. Of the blonde baby dolls, these two were arguably the most similar in looks and screen persona.

Remembering Yvette, Carol remarked, "I liked her a lot. She is extremely intelligent and came from such a different background than me. She was very California. I liked her sister too who was a hairdresser and was a little more open than Yvette."[431] When told what Carol said of Yvette, her friend James Radford was rather surprised. Reportedly, from stories Carol told him and others, Mimieux allegedly commented that Lynley's daughter Jill was unattractive when she met the child.

Sister Meredith (Carol Lynley), Sister Ellen (Lois Nettleton), and Sister Frances (Jane Wyatt) await their fate in *Weekend of Terror* (Paramount Television, 1970).

The actress next returned to the suspense genre with the well-received TV-movie *Weekend of Terror* (1970) that aired on the *ABC Movie of the Week*. An interesting premise had three nuns with car trouble in the desert kidnapped by two thugs whose heiress that they snatched prior accidentally died while trying to escape. Carol of course was not cast as the enterprising, hip nun who tries to outmaneuver the kidnappers. Instead she was the naïve nun, first baffled because she cannot grasp why her friend would leave the order to live as a lay person, and then as to why these men have kidnapped them. When the latter becomes clear, she is petrified that they will be killed.

The money must have really been good for Carol to don full nun's habit in the blistering heat of the desert but that was not the only reason she accepted the role of Sister Meredith. "It wasn't uncomfortable at all," said Carol. "I am a Catholic school girl so for me to wear a nun's habit is a kind of a cheap thrill."[432]

A few actresses who worked with the film's leading man, Robert Conrad, found him to be full of himself. For instance, Diane McBain commented, "Robert Conrad was short. He also wore a huge ego so that no one would ever accuse him of being short. I had to stand in a hole, which the crew dug for me every time I had to be next to Conrad during our love scenes."[433] Statuesque Francine York concurred and said, "I walked in the holes and he walked on the hills."[434]

Carol had no trouble with Conrad or co-lead Lee Majors, but surprisingly the one person she did not relate to was Lois Nettleton. She remarked,

> I had worked prior with Lee Majors on *The Big Valley* and he was a sweetheart! I had no trouble at all working with Robert Conrad who was very professional. I found him to be sensitive and supportive. He was a bit of a gruff guy and not a mister milquetoast, but I liked him. We had nice chats and I had no problems with him.
>
> I liked Lois but she was on another planet. I never quite connected with that planet. She was very professional but like Shirley Booth she would burst out into song from time to time. As for who was the better singer, I would give it a toss-up.[435]

Weekend of Terror was briskly directed by the prolific and dependable Jud Taylor from a teleplay by Lionel E. Siegel that unfortunately contains a few plot contrivances though still holds the interest. Nicely filmed on location in the rolling desert of Apple Valley, California, brutal Eddie (Robert Conrad) and unstrung, nervous Larry (Lee Majors) are amateur kidnappers whose rich female hostage (Barbara Barnett) accidentally dies while fleeing from the horny Eddie. More upset that they blew the big ransom than the girl's death, they decide to pass someone else off as the victim and Eddie goes out to find her replacement. Lo and behold, he spots a pretty blonde with a broken radiator hose on the deserted highway and decides she would be a perfect replacement. However, when she closes the hood of her car there are two nuns sitting in the front seat. The babe in the go-go boots and miniskirt is the conflicted Sister Ellen (the always good Lois Nettleton), just returned from a leave of absence to experience civilian life. Her companions are Sister Frances (Jane Wyatt), an older resilient nun and Carol Lynley as Sister Meredith a younger wide-eyed, naïve nun who finds Ellen's doubts about the sisterhood confusing.

The men trick the nuns into thinking they are going to call them a tow truck from their home, but instead lock them in a cold basement as they continue negotiating the ransom with Louise's father (Tod Andrews). The nuns bicker on what to do next with Meredith puzzled by their kidnapping. Funniest line goes to Conrad's shirtless Eddie who entering the house yells down to the women, "Hey, nuns do you want a beer?" Things get tenser when Ellen overhears the guys talking about her playing the dead Louise and that they are going to kill the other two ("But we're nuns," one exclaims) so they cannot identify them. Nettleton's Sister Ellen gets the most screen time as she is paraded about town wearing a red wig and Louise's dress. Spending time with Larry, she begins to get through to his compassionate side. She keeps up a brave front and gives a clue to her mother superior that all is not right when she telephones to explain their absence.

Lynley's secondary character acts terrified throughout, especially when the sisters learn that the remaining two nuns will not be set free. The only explanation for Carol's saying yes to the role could be that Meredith does get two standout dramatic scenes at the end, when the kidnappers use her as the imposter (Ellen refuses even though she knows she will be killed) to grab the ransom. When it is discovered that Meredith is not the daughter, she is grilled at the police station but will not divulge any information for fear that her friends will be killed. The police are forced to trick her into revealing all she knows by producing a nun's habit covered in blood. Carol plays these scenes quite poignantly. After Eddie learned that his partner helped the two nuns hide, Larry, with Ellen as hostage, is trailed to an airfield where the unarmed kidnapper is shot by the police despite Ellen's pleas not to fire. A repentant Larry dies in Ellen's arms.

Though formulaic and knowing full well the nuns would survive, *Weekend of Terror* was still able to ratchet up the suspense (due to script and direction) and the cast was uniformly good though Lee Majors just wasn't able to fully arouse the audience's sympathy. A more sensitive actor should have been cast. Conrad though had no trouble acting like an ass. It received mostly positive notices when aired. The syndicated *TV Scout* column found the movie to have "plenty of suspense." "A good suspense drama" and "An excellent depiction of the terrors human beings can inflict on the spirit," wrote the TV critic in *The Hartford Courant*. The critic in *Variety* remarked, "Contrivance or not, the story hook led to a considerable amount of dramatic tension" and "Carol Lynley and Jane Wyatt had little more to do than to look frightened, and did that well." Percy Shain of the *Boston Globe* found the film to be "a taut, plausible suspense program ... convincingly enacted by an excellent cast."

Viewers responded favorably as well. *Weekend of Terror* earned a 23.1 rating with a 37 share. It finished the 1970-71 television season as the 22nd highest rated made-for-TV movie.

*****

1971 found Carol Lynley limited to only two television appearances playing the innocent but resilient lady in peril in the made-for-TV detective movie *The Cable Car Murder* and a paralyzed shut-in who may or may not be receiving threatening phone calls in the popular TV series *Mannix*. It also found her with new headshots by photographer Harry Langdon, Jr. (son of the popular silent film star Harry Langdon) that would become her most popular and used for acting submissions, in promotional ads, in magazine articles, the cover of *Playbill*, and even a few times in the annual *Screen World* by John Willis.

Recounting the story of the one beloved photograph by her and her fans, Carol's dear friend Marlin Dobbs wrote, "I lived in Los Angeles from 1996 through 2003. During those halcyon years, I was fortunate enough to spend quite a lot of time with Carol Lynley. She and I had met in 1995 and, simple as it may sound, we had just 'clicked' and almost instantly became great friends. I adored her candor and her great energy and of course her infectious laugh, all of which I got to experience when spending long afternoons and evenings with her at the Malibu beach bungalow she lived in during that time. Conversations were always spontaneous and thoroughly delightful, especially since Carol had the sharpest of memories when it came to anything related to her career.

"Once, the topic of her classic headshot came up," continued Dobbs. "I'd mentioned how unique her hairstyle was in that particular image and I asked how the look was achieved. With a hearty laugh, Carol simply responded, 'With a fan!' She then proceeded to retrieve the complete set of original contact sheets from that photo session with Harry Langdon; as we perused the many gorgeous and wonderfully varied images, she told me the story of working with Harry for the first time. She said that, at the time, he was an up-and-coming fashion photographer and that she really liked his work. Not long after their session began, she expressed concern about her very straight hair looking the same in every shot. When she glanced around the studio and noticed a big fan, she suggested that Harry bring it close and turn it on. He did, and in the ensuing images—including the well-known headshot—Carol's trademark straight hair seemed to take on a life of its own. She and Harry were both very proud of the result, especially in the image that was immediately chosen to be Carol's working headshot. The photo 'went everywhere!' according to Carol, and she even went on to say that 'it's the photo that put Harry on the map.'"[436]

Purportedly, Carol Lynley's favorite photo by Harry Langdon, Jr. that she used for publicity purposes during the early to mid-seventies.

Harry Langdon has equally fond memories of Carol. He recalled, "When I first started working with Carol, I had just finished enjoying the Woodstock generation period. As a photographer, you try to capture the era the session was being held in. My clients included Ann-Margret, Diana Ross, Dionne Warwick and others in the music industry. In between I would photograph actors or actresses from various levels of the Hollywood success ladder. Carol called and wanted to book a session. We were still in a time shooting in a more Earthy setting. Actors especially wanted to make sure they were not too glamorous because the casting people in Hollywood wanted actors who could portray more regular people. When Carol came in to meet me for the session, she was dressed very casually in blue jeans and a nondescript blouse. She looked like just any normal woman from that period. I didn't know too much about her but just took her for face value—her hair wasn't done perfect and she didn't have much makeup or even any makeup on. But Carol had a presence about her that quite often successful actors bring with them—they have a vitality or energy that comes from being in front of a camera. I thought, 'This is going to be good.' Carol was no aspiring actress or starlet—she had a stage presence about her. I wanted to retain that in front of the camera. In the pictures I took her hair is very natural, but her expression is one that is very captivating and I didn't have to necessarily tell her anything to arouse that. She just did her thing in front of the camera and I just started clicking away. One of the first pictures I took was with an old barrel we had grabbed out of an alley behind my studio in West Hollywood. She posed on it to try to retain a natural and organic essence. The photos surprisingly had so much impact and she apparently used them very successfully for casting and her fans.

"The photo with the fan blowing her hair up was the one she wanted the public to see," continued Harry. "A lot of actors come into the studio kind of guarded because they don't want you to see their inner selves. I try to crack through that sort of invisible armor. Carol allowed the camera to see her and apparently, she felt that shot was really her. I took many photos of her that day but that one just popped out. A real professional actor can objectively look at the pictures and not get too enmeshed in the details of how the hair looks or if there is a wrinkle in their clothes. They look beyond that and look for an energy in a picture that just jumps off the contact sheet. Carol was good at that. I would tell my clients we are dealing with your career. It is your livelihood and *you* will have to be the one to pick that perfect picture out—not your publicist or girlfriend or husband. Once published the fans can subliminally detect that energy that glows off the page. I tried to regenerate that feeling in the future shooting sessions with her."[437]

On television in 1971, Carol's *Mannix* was a change of pace episode for the series. Instead of a typical police procedural episode, it fell into the realm of suspense, with Carol's victimized, paralyzed, housebound character being terrorized by a threatening phone caller, or was she?

Mannix was one of the most popular TV detective shows on the air and garnered high ratings. Carol came on towards the end of season four. Mike Connors (whom Carol purportedly nicknamed Big Mike) starred as Joe Mannix a regular kind of guy who is a private investigator. His loyal secretary is Peggy Fair (Gail Fisher) a police officer's widow. The series was noted for its nonstop action and for the many fist fights and beatings Mannix endured. Lynley's episode "Voice in the Dark" was a departure. It was directed by Paul Krasny, a frequent contributor to the show, from a teleplay by Edward J. Lasko (his second for the series).

Carol played Dorothy Kinman, a once promising diver on the road to the Olympics now confined to a wheelchair due to a car accident that she caused killing her pregnant friend and the driver of the other car. His business partner Roger Stack (Paul Picerni) survived, as did her friend's bitter husband John Deemer (Jim Antonio), who still has not forgiven Dorothy. Now a recluse living in a hotel, the psychologically disturbed Dorothy begins receiving death threats over the phone though the police and her parents do not believe her. Carol is again in familiar territory. A terrified, frustrated Dorothy hires Mannix to help prove she is not making it all up. She tells him that the caller stays on the phone only for a few seconds to say, "I am going to kill you" before hanging up. Though Mannix believes her and takes the case, he intuitively surmises something is not right. He learns from his friend Lt. Tobias (Robert Reed) that Dorothy spent the last month of her recovery in a sanitarium before taking the apartment in the hotel and won't allow the police to tap her phone line.

After Joe convinces Tobias to believe Dorothy, they return to her apartment to find that she has overdosed on her medication. Dorothy comes to and tells Joe and Tobias that she received another call after Joe left. This time the man threatened that she would die in a gruesome way in the next couple of days. Shaken, she took some pills to help her fall asleep and forgot she had already taken a few earlier.

Mannix too begins to doubt Dorothy when a phone caller turns out to be a woman looking for a bookstore. A perplexed Dorothy insists there was a man on the line telling her that he was in her apartment and he can prove it if she looks under her wheelchair. Mannix discovers an ace of spades playing card taped to the bottom. Later, the same deck of cards falls out of the cabinet, arousing Mannix's suspicions of her even more. However, Mannix does speak with Deemer who admits he hates Dorothy but denies threatening her. As for Stack, Mannix cannot get to the elusive businessman.

Dorothy turns out to be telling the truth when the culprit masquerades as a cop and gets into her apartment. It is Stack, who strangled his business partner before the crash and used the accident to cover up his crime. He noticed an injured Dorothy watch him throw a match into the dripping gasoline. It all comes back to her when he reveals himself in the apartment and tries to throw her off the balcony to make it look like a suicide. Luckily, Joe and Tobias arrive in time to save Dorothy for the obligatory happy ending. The paralyzed diver chooses life and concludes with Mannix taking Dorothy outside for a stroll through the park.

Some critics felt this episode, buoyed by a good script centering on psychological suspense rather than typical fights and car chases, was refreshing. The *Toronto Star* reviewer wrote, "The simple plot (for a change) hinges on whether or not the harassed beauty is making up stories. Opening tease ought to hook fans, and Carol Lynley is able to convey the necessary cold, suspecting and resentful demeanor of the victim." Agreed, Carol's performance and manner keeps the viewers unsure if Dorothy is really being harassed or if she is just not in her right mind. Perhaps due to the distinct, slow delivery of her lines, angelic face, and faraway look in her eyes, this was the type of role that Carol seemed to be well suited for and always kept the audience guessing.

Publicity photo of Carol Lynley in "Voice in the Dark" on *Mannix* (Paramount Television, 1971).

Continuing in precarious situations, Lynley was once again in danger in the gritty made-for TV movie *The Cable Car Murder* aka *Crosscurrent* (1971) directed by future Emmy Award winner Jerry Thorpe from a teleplay by Herman Miller who wrote the screenplay to the hard hitting *Coogan's Bluff* with Clint Eastwood in 1968. The film also boasts a pulsating score by the acclaimed Jerry Goldsmith.

Warner Bros. Television produced *Crosscurrent* as a two-hour feature pilot film for CBS-TV starring the well-respected stage and film actor, Robert Hooks, who had a supporting role in the TV police series *N.Y.P.D.* from 1967 to 1969. Shooting began the second week of December 1970 on location in San Francisco. They were hoping it would get picked up as the first one-hour dramatic series to star an African American actor in a solo lead. Alas, it did not, and the pilot sat on the shelf despite a talented multi-cultural cast that included Jeremy Slate, Robert Wagner, Carol Lynley, Simon Oakland, Jose Ferrer, plus African American actors Don Pedro Colley, Ta-Tanisha, and James McEachin.

In November 1971, CBS finally aired the movie, retitled *The Cable Car Murder*, as part of *The New CBS Friday Movie*. The film opens with three black youths causing a disturbance on a San Francisco cable car as it approaches its last stop. When they flee and the passengers disembark, the conductor discovers a young white man dead. At first, detectives Lt. Lou Van Alsdale (Robert Hooks) and his amiable partner Sgt. Pat Cassady (Jeremy Slate) think the murder is drug-related that leads to crime czar Freddie Trench (Don Pedro Colley). However, the investigation turns in a different direction when the deceased is identified as Beau Cooper the son of ornery shipping magnate Frederick Cooper (John Randolph) whose other son Frederick Cooper, Jr. recently drowned under mysterious circumstances six months prior. Lynley (in the start of playing a string of hippie-types for the next two years culminating with her role as Nonnie in *The Poseidon Adventure*) is engaging and sympathetic as Cooper's free-spirited, maxi dress-clad daughter Kathy who has rejected her father's wealth and lifestyle. She teaches at a school for mentally disabled children. Worried for her safety, Cooper demands that Kathy move back home but she refuses wanting to keep her independence. When the police later arrive to question her, Kathy is in her classroom trying to get one of her students to say the word yes. Outside, she puts the boy on a swing while answering questions about her dead brother Beau and the last day they spent time together. The grilling upsets the girl and she asks the detectives to leave. Her grief turns to joy when the little boy says his first words.

Despite the pressure they are getting from their superior Capt. Goodlad (Simon Oakland) for their slow progress in solving the case, the detectives continue focusing on French, thinking he had his thug Don Cope (James McEachin) rub out Beau, especially when one of the boys Raphael (Mario Van Peebles) admits Cope paid them to cause the disruption on the cable car. However, Kathy gives Van Alsdale a new lead when she confesses that Junior had a heroin habit just before the bullets start to fly as they are walking toward the young woman's home. The detective is grazed but the hitman dies of his gunshot wound at the hospital. While there, Van Alsdale confronts Dr. Bedford (Jose Ferrer) about the heroin cover up and learns that Howard McBride (Robert Wagner), a trusted shipping executive working for Cooper, suggested it to save the family from scandal. Howard was once engaged to Kathy and was best friends with Junior who fell off his boat and died. After receiving a visit from the detectives who know of two large withdrawals from his bank account, an unnerved McBride reaches out to Kathy to meet. After jokingly taking her to task for revealing her brother's drug habit, she admits Junior told her about the missing money totaling over $130,000 from her father's company. Howard fingers Junior but Kathy begins to realize the person who had the most to gain with her brothers' deaths was Howard who could have easily stolen the money. After denying it at first, he confesses that he had no choice but to take it to pay off Junior's drug dealers. Kathy does not believe it and says so to his face. He makes a phone call and gets Kathy to accompany him to the docks where he says someone can prove his innocence. Instead, French and Cope, in cahoots with McBride, are there waiting to kill her. Luckily, Van Alsdale and Cassady have trailed them. While Cassady chases down French and Cope by car, Van Alsdale subdues McBride (who admits he stole the money because he felt it was owed to him) before he can strangle Kathy. The shaken girl then asks to see her father while Howard is

Kathy Cooper (Carol Lynley) puts her misguided trust in family friend Howard McBride (Robert Wagner) in *The Cable Car Murder/Crosscurrent* (Warner Bros. Television, 1971).

Reviews for *The Cable Car Murder* were mixed. *The Hartford Courant* found that "the production is smooth and direction brisk." The syndicated *TV Scout* called it "a good cops-and-robbers show ... spectacularly photographed, well-written and fast-paced." Percy Shain of the *Boston Globe*, on the other hand, remarked, "The San Francisco exteriors ... were a lot more real and vivid than the phony, murky story." In between was Cecil Smith of the *Los Angeles Times* who wrote, "For the first 45 minutes or so, it's very potent stuff [and] one of the year's most exciting films. Then it seems to fall a little too predictably into place. The bizarre becomes obvious, the puzzle becomes too workable."

The Cable Car Murder performed adequately with viewers earning an 18.3 rating and a 32 share. Placing 73rd amongst all TV-movies aired during the 1971-72 season; its middling ratings may have discouraged CBS from picking it up as a weekly series.

Arguably, *The Cable Car Murder* is one of Carol's best made-for TV movies and she performs extremely well as the counterculture Kathy sucked back into the world of her wealthy father. She had the perfect look and demeanor to play these types of fragile women, baffled by the unexpected predicaments in which they find themselves. The gritty film remained popular with fans of detective films even though the denouement was a bit too pat. They were happy for a time when the two-hour version under the original title *Crosscurrent* was released into syndication and ran for years before disappearing. The film to this day has a strong following who have clamored for it to be released on DVD or online streaming. As of 2020, it is still sitting in the studio's vaults as are many made-for-TV movies from the sixties and seventies.

*****

Carol next surprised her fans when she agreed to turn up as blob food in *Beware! The Blob* the sequel to the 1958 cult hit, *The Blob* starring Steve McQueen. The original was produced by Jack Harris who happened to live next door to *I Dream of Jeannie* actor Larry Hagman and his family. Reportedly, the idea came to Hagman to make a sequel while sitting in his bathtub and sipping champagne. He phoned Harris and convinced him to invest in a follow-up by promising, "We are all going to get rich from it."[438] Hagman had directed some episodes of his TV show, so he felt he had the experience to direct his first feature film.

Carol and Larry Hagman lived close by in Malibu during this time. He wrote in his memoir that he saw Carol on the beach one day and invited her to be in his movie about the Blob. She concurred,

> Yes, that was true. I lived about a quarter of a mile down the beach from him. Larry told me about the movie and I said great. He said, 'I am casting it up and down the beach.' I laughed and said, 'Okay.' He rounded up all his neighbors [Robert Walker, Godfrey Cambridge, Burgess Meredith, Shelley Berman] to be in the film.
>
> Larry was a great friend and so was his wife. He was a force of nature. It is difficult even to explain Larry. He was from Texas and just larger than life. His mother [Mary Martin] came around once and you couldn't believe he came out of her body. She was this tiny woman who was quite stylish and Larry was very loud and wore outrageous clothes. Who was I to say no to his offer? I did the film as a favor to Larry, but I have never seen it.[439]

Another reason Carol may have agreed so quickly was because she was going to work with Robert Walker. "I knew Bobby from New York where we took dance classes together. We were friends forever."[440] But even close friends can sometimes mistake you for another as Carol confessed laughing, "When I saw his father for the first time in a movie on TV, I thought it was Bobby Jr. They looked quite alike. I thought, 'Wow Bobby's doing a period piece good for him,' and then realized it wasn't him but his father!"[441]

Filming began in the spring of 1971 (though the film was not released until over a year later) on location in Diamond Bar and Pomona, California. The crazy birthday party scene, which Carol was a part of, was shot in a loft in Venice, California. It was reported that a fair amount of Anthony Harris' script was thrown out and a lot of scenes were improvised. Anthony was the son of producer Jack H. Harris. This may explain the awkward jumps from serious horror to slapstick comedy from scene to scene.

Unlike the other guest actors, who make no more than humorous cameo appearances, Carol has a significant role. Though played as a horror spoof, Lynley along with leads Robert Walker and Gwynne Gilford, deliver sincere performances and have the more intense scenes whereas the guest stars play it for laughs before becoming Blob snacks.

When asked how it was to be devoured by the Blob, Carol replied, "That was part of the deal. I could either live or die. I chose to be eaten by the Blob, so I was."[442] The audience doesn't actually see the Blob eat her character as the camera pulls away after a closeup of her terrified face. As Carol added, "That is as far as the scene went."[443]

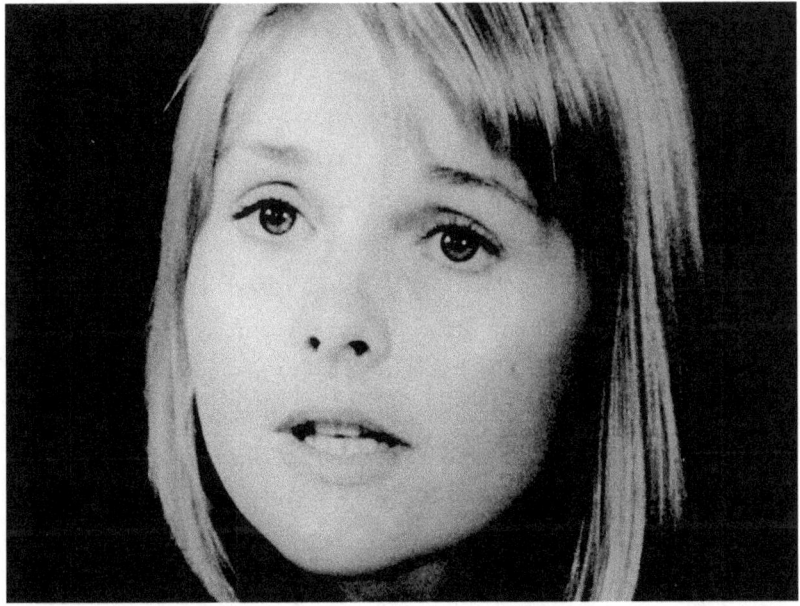

Carol Lynley as partygoer Leslie in *Beware! The Blob* (Harris Enterprises, 1972).

Carol also has fond memories of working with the then unknown actress, Cindy Williams. She recalled,

> When I agreed to do this movie, I was not sure what it would

be like. I was in a party scene with Cindy. We were sitting around waiting to shoot. Then it became dark and we were still sitting around. It was then about two or three in the morning, and Cindy and I are still sitting there. We spent the better portion of the evening into the morning hours just talking to each other. If I had to get stuck with someone for that amount of time, I am glad it was with Cindy. She was a lot of fun.[444]

As the movie opens, exhausted Alaska pipeline worker Chester (Godfrey Cambridge) sits watching TV after returning to his small town with a frozen sample of a blob-like material he stole. It accidentally defrosts and begins slithering on the ground eating an oblivious Chester's cat and his nagging wife (Marlene Clark). The movie then jumps to someone using a blowtorch on a sculpture. Removing the mask, the beautiful Carol Lynley is revealed as she shakes her hair into place. She is hippie-chick Leslie and, with her roommate Lisa Clark (Gwynne Gilford), is throwing a surprise birthday party for Lisa's boyfriend Bobby Hartford (Robert Walker). Two stoned hippies (Cindy Williams and Randy Stonehill) arrive bearing pot brownies. They split to smoke a joint and Lisa heads to Chester's house to pick up Bobby's present. There she finds him still in his lounge chair watching *The Blob* on TV screaming as he is being devoured by ... the Blob! She flees in hysterics and drives over to Bobby's house. Cutting back to Chester's home, the Blob has come and gone. The Blob next attacks a cop busting the two hippies smoking weed in a drainpipe. As the Blob devours them all, the camera pans to graffiti on the outside that says "Love" written in red dripping paint. The Blob strikes again, attacking a prissy barber (Shelley Berman) and his long-haired client; a fat man taking a bath; and three hoboes (Burgess Meredith, Larry Hagman, and Del Close).

Without proof, Bobby does not know what to think and Lisa begins to doubt what she saw. Arriving home, he wants to get her into the sack but opens the door to his surprise birthday party, which Lisa forgot all about. It is a loud, chaotic affair as his stoned friends put a crown on his head and carry him around the house. His pal Joe (Gerrit Graham) is clad in a gorilla suit jumping all around. A frantic Lisa yelling "Bobby" tries to follow her boyfriend, but her friends keep stopping her to talk. Leslie then appears carrying a birthday cake. She and their guests help the birthday boy blow out his candles. Asking where Lisa is, Leslie tells Bobby that she is not feeling well and is upstairs. Bobby finds Lisa whimpering in the bathroom and decides to take her back to his place to rest, but not before telling Joe he may return. On the way, they encounter the Blob that engulfs their car, but with the air conditioning on full blast, it retreats.

Leslie and her boyfriend Joe, still in his monkey suit, pull into a service station to gas up his dune buggy. As a frustrated Leslie sits in the passenger seat, Joe begins filling up the tank despite the station being deserted. He then starts putting oil cans into this back seat. A miffed Leslie says, "Joe, this time you are going to go too far. It's one thing to rip off gasoline, but it's another if you start *stealing* stuff. I won't put up with it."

Just then Bobby and Lisa pull up. As a frantic Lisa explains to Leslie about their encounter with the Blob, Bobby calls the sheriff. Meanwhile, Joe takes off in his dune buggy and Leslie remains behind with Lisa and Bobby. Joe encounters the Blob on the highway and skids right into it. His friends come upon his half-devoured car shortly after while heading to the bowling alley to find the sheriff. Leslie bolts from Bobby's pickup to help Joe, but she too is attacked and becomes the Blob's next meal. The movie climaxes in an ice rink next to a bowling alley where Bobby, with help from the authorities, freezes the creature. The final scene has the prideful sheriff standing on the frozen Blob being filmed for the nightly news, unaware that the klieg lights have melted it once again as it slowly makes its way to engulf him.

Some critics at the time were pleasantly surprised by this sci-fi parody (Hagman described it as "a pop horror film with no violence"[445]) played half-seriously and it garnered much better reviews than Lynley's last spoof *The Maltese Bippy*. Howell Raines of *The Atlanta Constitution* called it a "good-natured throwback to the monster-from-outer-space flicks of the 50s and early 60s." He praised Larry Hagman for his wise choice "to amuse more often than he tries to scare" and found the movie "more amusing and relaxing than a lot of more expensive and highly touted movies." Kevin Thomas of the *Los Angeles Times* called it a "cleverly devised science-fiction entertainment." He also praised the cast for giving "full-dimensioned … convincing" performances." Andrew Reschke found the performances from Lynley and the other guest stars to be "very entertaining."

Promotional poster art for *Beware! The Blob* (Harris Enterprises, 1972).

Tom Milne of the *Monthly Film Bulletin* had a different opinion of the movie and said this Blob "carries as much threat as a weight-watchers breakfast. It moves sluggishly, but is easily beaten at its own game by Larry Hagman's labored direction and by a script which takes an unconscionable time to dispose of guest stars…"

When filming was completed, Hagman boasted to the press, "I got all my friends in it for free and we shot it in 16 days for $110,000. I hope it makes $9 million like *Blob* did."[446] It didn't even come close. Most of that had to do with a scattered release and perhaps an audience not quite sure if the movie was a comedy or a straight horror/sci-fi flick. For the former it wasn't funny enough and for the latter is was not overtly scary. In some parts of the country it opened in the late summer/fall of 1972 (Atlanta, New York, Los Angeles, Baltimore, District of Columbia). In others it did not hit theaters until spring and summer of 1973 (Hartford, Boston, Chicago), usually as the bottom half of a double-bill. The producers also played with the title releasing the movie as *Son of Blob* in some cities.

The movie was re-released in the summer of 1981 with the tag line "The movie J.R. shot." This was in reference to the season cliffhanger on Hagman's TV series *Dallas* where it ended with a mystery person shooting his dastardly villain and leaving him for dead. It was a nice publicity stunt but did not bring in the masses. Needless to say, it was the one and only theatrical film Hagman directed.

As for Carol, she looks great and comes through this unscathed as she was well adept at playing bewildered characters during this period. Her Leslie is never quite sure what is going on. The actress basically disregarded the movie back then and credited the upcoming *The Poseidon Adventure* as her first theatrical feature since the release of *Norwood* in 1970. Since not many people saw *Beware! The Blob* she was able to get away with it.

*****

In November 1971 Carol received a television offer she could not refuse. She was enticed to star in two episodes of the suspense anthology series *The*

Evil Touch to be filmed in Australia. She remarked, "The money was good and I thought the scripts were excellent. Also, I had never been to Australia before."[447] She packed her bags and jetted off alone. Asked why she left her daughter behind by the Australian press, Carol stated at the time, "I have a housekeeper who takes good care of Jill while I'm away. I see more of her than most working mothers. I can go for months without working and I spend every day with her. When I do work … I like to take her to school myself."[448]

Carol was part of a lengthy list of American actors who made the journey including Darren McGavin, Vic Morrow, and Kim Hunter. Carol's episodes, however, did not air in the U.S. until early 1974.

Sometime upon her return from Sydney (with pit stops in Bangkok and London), Carol abandoned her country lifestyle in the canyons of Malibu and moved into the Chateau Marmont in West Hollywood, years before it became high-end fashionable. It was supposed to be short term, but she remained there for almost three years. As described by writer Victor S. Navasky, "In addition to holes in the rugs, some preposterous Hollywood feudal gothic architecture done up in lemonade pink, no restaurant, no room service to speak of, no cocktail lounge, no self-dial telephones, and a pool that's not heated, the Chateau Marmont generally has no rooms available."[449] At the time, besides Carol, residents included Tony Randall, Maximillian Schell, and Gram Parsons. Other celebrities who stayed there for brief intervals during this period included Francis Ford Coppola, Carly Simon, Graham Nash, Terry Southern and his companion Gail Gerber, and Ultra Violet. Some of the rooms were priced as low as $14 a night.

Carol settled into Suite 46 and disclosed to Marian Christy, "It's run by eccentrics for eccentrics. The apartment dwellers range from mafia types, to nice old ladies, to Filipinos. It's the kind of place where something gets broken and stays broken for forty years. The one nice thing about it is that you never have to worry about damaging anything."[450] It shouldn't be surprising that Carol took so well to the Chateau Marmont since she had a love for antiques and period pieces.

Remembering her mother during the early seventies, who could be found hanging out with likes of Phoebe Snow, Cass Elliott, the Eagles, or others at the hotel, her daughter Jill Selsman wrote, "My mom was always sporting a look. If it wasn't a Victorian granny dress, or hot pants and platforms, or my personal favourite - a long, baby-blue halter T-shirt dress with really expensive platform shoes in two colours (left was Easter blue, right was pale hospital-green) and an enormous jacket made from ostrich boa-feathers - it was elephant-bell trouser suits with floppy flowered hats. Whenever my mom went anywhere or did anything, she'd get stoned first, blow the smoke out the window (who was she kidding?) swathe herself in Joy perfume."[451]

Vanity Fair described Jill Selsman as the Chateau Marmont's resident Eloise. Now a writer and TV producer, Selsman reflected in 2019, "Back then people came to the Chateau to fall apart."[452] Her first adult friend was Gram Parsons who went to the desert for some musical inspiration and never returned. He died from a drug overdose at age twenty-six. This greatly affected Lynley's daughter who commented, "Gram was the first person I knew who died just because."[453]

In 2019, the Chateau Marmont celebrated its ninetieth anniversary and it no longer resembles in the least the hotel Carol called home all those years before. It is now the hip place to be seen and the prices reflect that. Gone are the days of shabby furniture, fraying carpets, and paying $14 a day for a room. Nowadays, a one-bedroom suite goes for $950 a night.

Now residing closer to Beverly Hills and Hollywood, Carol's social life seem to have perked up and she was seen at many Hollywood soirees, premieres (i.e. *Harold and Maude*), and the "in" places to be seen like P.J. Clarke's. She admitted at the time, now that she was pushing thirty, she was less reserved and enjoyed mingling and chatting with people at social functions. During this time, she was usually on the arm of her friends Bobby Darin or Jack Haley, Jr. or paramours David Frost or Oliver Reed. After attending the 5th anniversary party for the TV series *Mannix*, columnist Dick Kleiner remarked in his syndicated column that the "party was about the fourth time in a week that I had run into Carol Lynley who is nice to run into. Previously, she was seldom seen around town." Carol quipped, "I'm getting to be a gadabout."[454]

*****

In 1972, Lynley appeared three times on television and on the big screen cementing her reputation as one of the most effective actresses of this period to play the lady in peril. The fact that all were well-received with *The Night Stalker* breaking TV ratings records and *The Poseidon Adventure* becoming the highest grossing movie of 1973, only added to her popularity in playing this type of role though she did not take as big advantage of it as she should have.

A trio of TV roles (filmed before she trekked off to Australia for *The Evil Touch*) sent Carol into the world of the macabre. All were varying degrees of the terrorized leading lady and each was a bit different. In *The Night Stalker*, she was the supportive girlfriend of reporter Carl Kolchak (Darren McGavin) who suspects a series of Las Vegas murders were committed by a modern day vampire. On *Night Gallery*, she was the oblivious wife who brings home a statue that haunts her husband nightly. On *The Sixth Sense*, she was a fashion designer having visions of murders that took place at the house she is renting and determined to learn the truth.

The Night Stalker (working title: *The Kolchak Tapes*) turned out to be not your typical vampire horror film. It was a wise move by Carol to accept the important part of Gail Foster. It would become one of her best remembered roles due to the critical raves and huge ratings the TV-movie garnered.

In 1971, an unpublished novel titled *The Kolchak Papers* by Jeff Rice came to the attention of ABC-TV who optioned it as a made-for-TV movie to be produced by Everett Chambers who was the original producer on *The Immortal* and directed by John Llewellyn Moxey (*The House That Would Not Die*, *A Taste of Evil*). Rice was a newspaperman from Las Vegas and created this simple story of a reporter investigating a series of murders in his hometown that are being committed by a vampire and how he butts heads with his editor and local officials over it. However, Rice introduced a real quirkiness to it with his ornery smart-alecky down-on-his-luck reporter Carl Kolchak (always dressed in Hawaiian shirts, Bermuda shorts, and golf cap) and modernized his bloodsucker. His book was adapted into a teleplay by prolific horror writer Richard Matheson (chosen by Barry Diller, the head of ABC-TV at the time) whose films included *The Incredible Shrinking Man*, *House of Usher*, and *The Pit and the Pendulum*, plus episodes of such series as *The Twilight Zone*, *The Alfred Hitchcock Hour*, and *Star Trek*. Matheson praised Rice's manuscript and said, "The story was all there, the structure was there, and that's what got everybody excited. It was a sort of *cinéma verité* vampire story. It seemed so realistic."[455]

Due to running time, Matheson had to jettison many of the characters from the book and created a new one—Carol's Gail Foster. There was only one major female character in the novel named Sam who was a prostitute and Kolchak's street informant. ABC was nervous to have the female lead be a hooker, so Matheson changed her name and made her Carl's girlfriend. She still worked nights and would meet up with Carl at a casino, but they kept her profession vague. Matheson also made Gail be the one to bring the vampire idea to a doubting Kolchak. In Rice's story, Carl was of Romanian descent and believed in the vampire tales told to him by his grandfather.

There was no ambiguity in Carol's mind about Gail Foster. At the time she stated, "I play a Las Vegas showgirl. Not a hussy, but a girl who has been through the ringer and knows what life is all about. That's pretty far from the kind of role I've been associated with."[456]

Tired of playing the "sweet innocent who occasionally gets into trouble." Carol added,

> That kind of part is not for me anymore. Ann-Margret's performance in *Carnal Knowledge* has given actresses like me a phenomenal boost. She proved that an actress who has been typed for a certain kind of part can be brilliant in something else. Otto Preminger gave me a chance in *Bunny Lake Is Missing*, but the picture failed and I don't think I was really ready. *The Night Stalker* is another chance, and I'm hopeful I prove myself in it.[457]

Carol's comment comes off as a bit self-deprecating. *Bunny Lake* failed at the box office but not with most critics who lauded her exceptional performance. It helped her to grow into more mature roles playing the lady in peril or neurotic heroine, far removed from the virginal ingénue roles still played by some of her contemporaries. She also seemed to forget she just portrayed a psychotic killer in *Once You Kiss a Stranger* and a foul-mouthed hooker in *Norwoo* – both atypical roles for her. As an actor, of course she craved diverse types of roles, but even by 1972 she was still not embracing her skill in playing the imperiled heroine. Little did she know, her most popular hapless victim role was right around the corner.

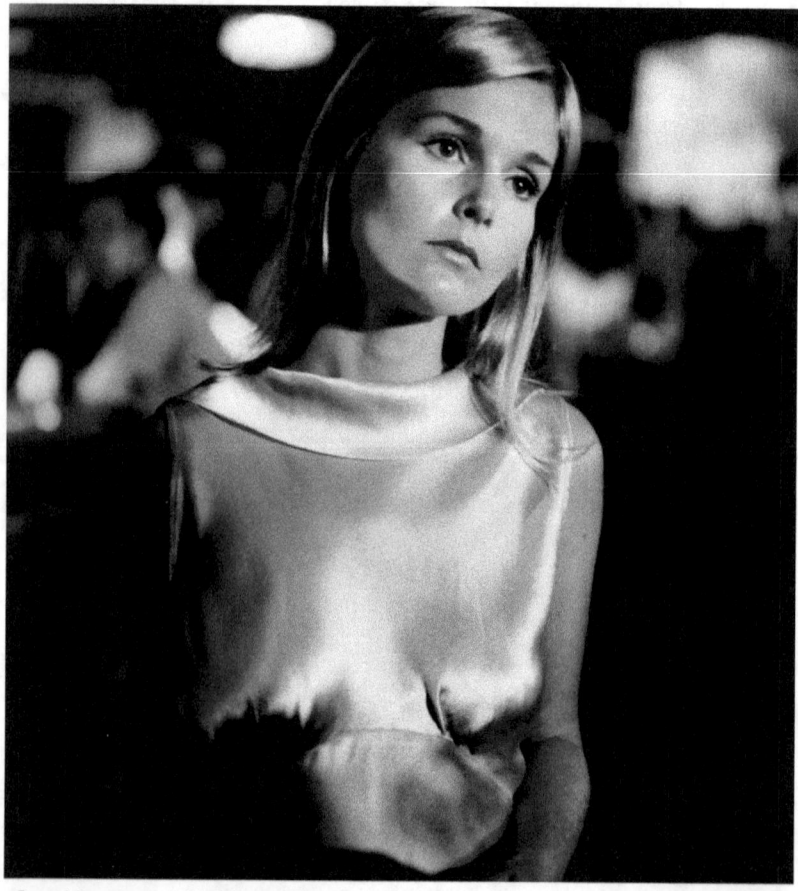

Carol Lynley as Gail Foster in *The Night Stalker* (ABC Circle Films, 1972).

Vampires and Druids

The movie, still titled *The Kolchak Tapes*, was allotted a budget of $450,000. While still in early pre-production, Chambers dropped out of the project (just as he did with *The Immortal*) to produce the TV series *Columbo* with Peter Falk and was replaced by Dan Curtis as producer. Up to this point in time, Curtis was best known for bringing the cult, gothic horror daytime series *Dark Shadows* to the public. The ABC-TV soap, which aired at 4 pm on the East and West coasts, was at the beginning quite slow moving and garnered dismal ratings until the producers went for broke and introduced actor Jonathan Frid as brooding vampire Barnabas Collins. The show shot up into the middle of the ratings pack and became must-see TV with an audience not known for soap watching—school children, teenagers, and men. Curtis branched out into movie production with *House of Dark Shadows* in 1970 and *Night of Dark Shadows* in 1971. He was excited to work on this project because he found it to be "a great story—so traditional yet so modern—and it had a sense of humor! It was a great premise waiting to be made into a great movie."[458] Despite his high praise for the story, Curtis almost turned down the opportunity because he knew Richard Matheson did not like him. Prior, the producer put forth a low-ball bid for the film rights of one of Matheson's novels and the author was insulted. Luckily for all, the two men put the past aside after a rocky first meeting and worked quite well together on this movie.

It was most likely producer Everett Chambers who hired Lynley after working with her on *The Immortal* before he left the production. Regarding his replacement, Carol found Dan Curtis to be "very gung-ho and terrific."[459] Curtis must have been happy with Carol's casting as he kept her as Gail Foster. Decades later, Lynley's enthusiasm for the role seems to have waned. She remarked,

> It was not a demanding part. All I had to do was look woeful and comfort Darren. But like I said, I had to work to support my daughter, so I didn't study every part with a magnifying glass. But I always liked Darren and he was fun to be around. He also was a generous actor. He would do things to help you look better and

beef up your part. If anything didn't make any sense, he would speak up to the director. He was always looking out for you.[460]

The film handled Gail and Carl's romance maturely considering that the couple is not wed and knowing a vampire tale would attract the kiddies. Their scenes in bed after implied lovemaking are glib and casual. Gail is not a nagging, marriage-minded gal because she knows Kolchak is not reliable or financially stable. She even lists all the newspapers and cities where he worked and was fired.

Exteriors for film were to be shot entirely on location in Las Vegas and interiors at the Goldwyn Studios in Hollywood from August 23 to September 10, 1971. Carol recalled,

> I spent most of the entire three weeks in Las Vegas. We filmed some of our scenes in a casino. I don't gamble. I have nothing against it but it does nothing for me. Whenever I get too close to someone, I know who is gambling, I cry—actually I sob. It is just the sight of people losing money that way that makes me sad.
>
> The first time it happened was when I was in London. My agent at the time invited me to dinner and then to do some gaming—that is what they call it there. I told him I don't gamble but he said I could sit there with him and will bring him good luck. After having an elegant dinner, we went to the gaming table with all these classy people playing. He sat me next to him and within the first half hour he lost about one thousand dollars and I started crying—not weeping but *crying*! Everybody who was playing you could tell were wealthy but just seeing people throwing money away into thin air—I just didn't get it. I was making everybody so uneasy they asked me to leave. They had to put me in a cab and send me home.[461]

Suffice it to say, Carol made sure to turn down any invitations to go to the casino when not filming.

Dan Curtis offered John Llewellyn Moxey the directing job. He had seen some of his British TV work and tapped him prior to helm a movie about Jekyll and Hyde with Jason Robards, Jr. that was never made. After reading the script, which Moxey loved and thought cleverly written, the director jumped at the offer. Looking back though he felt at times Curtis "hovered as producer" - wishing he directed. Curtis was not always 100% behind some of Moxey's creative choices, creating a slight problem per the director. However, not major enough to cause friction or distractions.[462]

Moxey was focused on juggling the horror and humor to make the picture exactly right. He revealed, "With *The Night Stalker*, the style was a mix of '40s newspaper drama and a gothic vampire story ... it's *The Front Page* blended with Bram Stoker. That was the challenge of *The Night Stalker*. Can you mix these two very different styles and make it work?"[463] He went on to credit Dan Curtis for helping him succeed in reaching that right balance and said, "Dan was a driving force in getting the script and casting right. Dan's casting ideas were excellent. He was a very good producer to work with, always open to discussion ... It was a very happy set."[464]

Darren McGavin liked Moxey and found him to be "terrific ... [with] a wonderful sense of enjoyment, which you hope to get in a director. He encouraged people."[465] Jeff Rice, who was involved with the filming (he did some location scouting and was even supposed to play the coroner until Dan Curtis came onboard as producer and had him replaced by Larry Linville), said that Moxey told him, "My actors are the *most* important people ... so are my crew, but my actors are the ones who get out there and *do* it."[466]

The film was also abetted by a truly original, mood-setting score by Robert Cobert who composed the eerie opening theme to *Dark Shadows*. Explaining his approach with *The Night Stalker*, he said, "It was spooky stuff, but it wasn't a *Dark Shadows* type of spooky. I mean, it was Las Vegas in 1971. That's the whole point. You need something that is spooky but contemporary—something with an edge to it."[467] According to Jeff Thompson, author of *The*

Television Horrors of Dan Curtis, Cobert delivered in spades. He remarked in his book, "This dichotomy of modern jazziness versus classic frightfulness perfectly captures the hybrid nature of *The Night Stalker*: realistic, scary, funny, shocking, irreverent, morbid, clinical, [and] supernatural."[468]

ABC meanwhile was not happy with the new title. After the theatrical feature *The Anderson Tapes* went into production, the network went back to *The Kolchak Papers*. Still not satisfied, they considered the ridiculous *Fee Fi Fo Fum, I Smell the Blood* before finally settling on the more appropriate *The Night Stalker*.

Gail (Carol Lynley) listens patiently as her boyfriend reporter Carl Kolchak (Darren McGavin) vents in *The Night Stalker* (ABC Circle Films, 1972).

According to Dan Curtis, a screening was held at 20th Century-Fox. The theatre was packed with every seat taken. He and ABC honcho Barry Diller had to stand in the back. The audience was enthusiastic throughout. They began clapping as the end credits rolled with a couple of quick cuts of each character and then a freeze frame with the actor's name. By the time they got to the last one, Barry Atwater, the moviegoers went nuts and were on their feet hooting and hollering. Per Curtis, "Diller turns and looks at me and says,

'We should have released this as a feature.' So, we knew we had a great movie on our hands."[469]

The Night Stalker opens with reporter Carl Kolchak (now a Polish-American who wears a seersucker suit, straw hat and white tennis shoes thanks to an inspiration from Darren McGavin himself), matter-of-factly narrating the story via a pre-recorded audio cassette tape. He recounts what transpired in Las Vegas for a book he is writing. "Chapter One. This is the story behind one of the greatest manhunts in history. Maybe you read about it, or rather what they let you read about it, probably in some minor item buried somewhere in a back page. However, what happened in that city between May 16 and May 28 of this year was so incredible that to this day the facts have been suppressed ... so when you have finished this bizarre account, judge for yourself its believability and then try to tell yourself, wherever you may be, 'It couldn't happen here.'"[470]

This narrative format would continue throughout the movie as he describes a series of strange murders of young women all during the middle of the night, beginning with twenty-three-year old Cheryl Ann Hughes, a swing-shift change girl at the Gold Dust Saloon. He continuously states the facts of the victim's name, age, occupation, employer, and cause of death. In this case, an added twist was that she was drained of blood.

Though Carol looks particularly beautiful here (the cinematographer was Michel Hugo who most notably shot Jacques Demy's *Model Shop* in 1969), she has nothing more to do than look concerned every time Kolchak informs her of another murder while she is working (their scenes were filmed at the Thunderbird Hotel's casino) or supportive when Kolchak laments the treatment he receives at the *Las Vegas Daily News* from his blustery editor Tony Vincenzo (Simon Oakland). She even irons his shirts after making love. Afraid for her safety working nights, Kolchak wants Gail to quit and she responds, "And you'll support me?" Knowing that he cannot, he lets the subject drop. However, in a nice twist, as the bodies begin to pile up, Gail is the one who first suspects the murderer may be a vampire. This is Carol's best scene as she literally drops a book on vampirism into the skeptical Kolchak's lap and makes him open his mind to the possibility. He does not want to believe it, but the victims' puncture wounds at the base of the neck and the severe loss of blood all point to a vampire. The suspect is finally identified as Janos Skorzeny (Barry Atwater), a supposed seventy-five-year-old man who looks and has the energy of a thirty-year old. Carl riles D.A. Paine (Kent Smith) and Sheriff Butcher (Clyde Atkins) with vampire wisecracks but they refuse to entertain that theory knowing it would be bad for city business. Carl's FBI friend Bernie Meeks (Ralph Meeker) and Vincenzo are a bit more open-minded about it. All come around when the police have the vampire trapped and riddle him with bullets only to see him get up and run away into the night.

One would suspect that Gail would be the last victim attacked and saved by her boyfriend, but she is not. This was a nice twist by Richard Matheson. Instead, with help from an informant, Kolchak learns where Skorzeny is living and armed with a stake, cross, and garlic ventures into his house backed by the police equally equipped. In an upstairs bedroom, he discovers the missing last victim tied to a bed post and used as a human blood bank. Skorzeny attacks Kolchak and they struggle. Bernie has accompanied the reporter and both have little success against his superhuman strength until Carl pulls open the heavy window drapes. The sunshine weakens the vampire just enough, so Kolchak can drive a wooden stake through his heart.

Gail is last seen when Kolchak finishes writing his fantastic story on Janos the vampire. So confident that his piece will get national attention, he proposes to an astonished Gail and suspects the New York City papers will want to hire him. He dashes out to turn in his article to Vincenzo leaving a beaming Gail to digest their good fortune. However, things go quickly sour when Vincenzo half-heartedly accepts the story and tells him Paine wants to see him. He then, uncharacteristically, throws Carl a compliment and says, "You're one hell of a reporter." At Paine's office, the local officials reveal they have killed his story and threaten if Carl does not leave town, they will issue a warrant charging him with the first-degree murder of Janos. Even Bernie

Jenks has been silenced. An infuriated Carl makes a grab for the phone to call Gail, but it is too late, and the officials have already sent her away. Slimy Paine sneers, "She's an undesirable element Kolchak and we don't want undesirable elements in Las Vegas." To make matters even worse, they will not reveal her whereabouts. As Kolchak drives out of Vegas, he narrates that he has put ads in newspaper personal columns from San Francisco to St. Louis but has had no success finding Gail Foster whom he thinks he will never see again.

Prior to its broadcast, ABC-TV peppered the screen with promos and print ads. One had text only and read:

A vampire killer loose in Las Vegas?
It's hard to believe, isn't it?
 But you will when you see
The Night Stalker
A real horror story.
Starring Darren McGavin and Carol Lynley.
A World Premiere
Movie of the Week ABC 8:30 pm

The Night Stalker aired on January 12, 1972 slotted in between two popular programs, *The Mod Squad* and *Marcus Welby, M.D.* It broke all ratings records scoring a 33.2 rating and a 48 share, making it the highest rated TV-movie up to that point. It was a record it held for years. An estimated 75 million viewers tuned in to watch Kolchak battle this new breed of vampire. ABC-TV's tantalizing promos that were broadcast prior did its job to attract the masses.

The commercial success of the movie took everyone by surprise including newspapers. Not many reviewed the movie prior to it being aired, most likely because they just dismissed it as a typical vampire horror movie. Of the critics who did review, almost all gave it praise. Paul Jones of *The Atlantic Constitution* found *The Night Stalker* to be "well done and certainly has some genuinely scary moments." Kevin Thomas of the *Los Angeles Times* raved, "It's an amusing but finally genuinely scary show ... making effective use of actual locales, director John Llewellyn Moxey and writer Richard Matheson stir up lots of old-fashioned thrills and chills with style and conviction." Months later when the movie was re-run, an uncredited reviewer found it to be an "unusual suspense drama" and quipped, "you'll get a fang out of it." Later syndicated print TV reviews remarked that it was "A near-brilliant mix of horror and comedy" with a "flawless cast."

A perceptive Gail Foster (Carol Lynley) is the first to suspect that the serial killer is a vampire in *The Night Stalker* (ABC Circle Films, 1972).

One of the people most dumbfounded by its popularity was Lynley who remarked, "To be honest, I didn't think much of it in terms of success. When it became such a hit I was as surprised as everybody else."[471]

Director John Llewellyn Moxey, on the other hand, was not surprised that the movie was so well-received and commented, "I always thought it was going to be a very special piece. The fun of it was the mixing of the humor and the horror. There was a lot of that in Jeff Rice's book ... Everybody understood that and elaborated on it—Richard Matheson's script, Darren's performance, the driving force of Dan Curtis as producer, my direction."[472] He also went on to compliment the actors and said that the movie had "a great cast. [Curtis] was the prime mover in bringing these first-rate people together, and everybody fit his particular role perfectly."[473]

Present throughout the filming, Jeff Rice expected *The Night Stalker* to be good due to his source material and what he witnessed, but even he was shocked on how many TV viewers tuned in. He credited fans loving a good horror story but then opined that it possibly was due to the changing times. Vietnam was still raging, and the public was becoming more cognizant of the lies being fed to them by the government. Rice mused, "Perhaps there was a general yearning for someone who would verbally fly in the face of authority; call a spade a spade; and put his ass on the line for his belief in the public's right to know what is really going on."[474]

Though *The Night Stalker* won Richard Matheson the Writers Guild Award for Best Written Television Adaptation and the Edgar Alan Poe Award for Best Written Television Feature or Mini-Series, he and the film were totally snubbed by the Emmy Award nominating committee. This was not surprising since horror and science-fiction were usually overlooked come awards time. This proved no different.

Of course, due to *The Night Stalker*'s surprisingly tremendous success ABC-TV wanted a sequel, and producer Dan Curtis, writer Richard Matheson, and actors Darren McGavin and Simon Oakland went on to do *The Night Strangler* (1974). This was followed by the Universal Television series *Kolchak: The Night Stalker* which debuted in September 1974 and lasted a single season. It was produced without the participation of Dan Curtis or Richard Matheson. Darren McGavin and Simon Oakland reprised their roles, but the show was now set in Chicago. Unfortunately, Lynley's Gail Foster was left out still unfound in the days before the Internet. It was a missed opportunity for fans of the original TV-movie and would have been great to learn what became of her.

Though Carol Lynley did not receive much individual praise for her performance in *The Night Stalker*, her second billing and being part of a first-rate ensemble cast still, no doubt, raised her profile in Hollywood. It would not be that surprising to learn if it brought her to the attention of her old studio 20th Century-Fox and got her the interview for her biggest hit, *The Poseidon Adventure*.

*****

Another memorable project came Carol's way with a guest star turn on *Rod Serling's Night Gallery*. This was a well-liked anthology show created and hosted by Serling as a follow up to his enormously popular *The Twilight Zone*. Each episode, of course, was in the vein of horror, fantasy, or suspense, and all began with Serling relating what was to come using a usually dark and disturbing painting hanging in a spooky gallery.

Lynley turned up in a second season episode after *Night Gallery* was removed from rotation as part of NBC's experimental *Four in One* series (which also included *McCloud*, *San Francisco International Airport*, and *The Psychiatrist*) during its first season on the air and given its own timeslot on Wednesday nights at 10:00 p.m. Her episode was entitled "Last Rites for a Dead Druid" (originally titled "Silent Partner"), which was directed by Jeannot Szwarc (who worked on approximately nineteen episodes of *Night Gallery* and later directed such feature films as *Jaws 2*, *Somewhere in Time*, *Supergirl*, and *Santa Claus: The Movie*) from a teleplay by Alvin Sapinsley (his fifth of six for *Night Gallery*). Carol was cast yet again as the perplexed heroine, who must react to the strange behavior of her husband, played by Bill Bixby (exuding sexiness in his seventies duds). Dominating the episode, Bixby is haunted with visions from a druid trapped in a statue recently purchased. Donna "Elly May" Douglas also appeared as Lynley's best friend.

"Billy Bixby and I had the same business manager and we knew each other through him," Carol revealed. "Working with Bill was a pleasure. He was very polite and gracious to the other actors. He was also a funny guy and I liked him a lot."[475]

"Last Rites for a Dead Druid" was paired with "The Waiting Room," written by Rod Serling, that aired during the first part of the hour. This is one of the series' most popular - where purgatory is a western saloon and some tough, bewildered gunslingers await their fate. Among the actors featured was Buddy Ebsen, so perhaps the coupling of his and Donna Douglas' episode was a ratings ploy since each co-starred on the recently cancelled *The Beverly Hillbillies*.

Commenting on his script, which he adapted from a 1935 short story called *Out of the Eons* by Hazel Heald and then changed profusely, Alvin Sapinsley said, "I tried to insert a little humor because ... there was not a great deal of humor in the people who ran the program—except Jack Laird [series' producer], who can be a very funny man."[476]

Jeannot Szwarc shared a story about the trouble they had with the network censor regarding a scene where Bixby's possessed character almost fries a cat. The director recalled, "We got in trouble because we wanted to show a cat being burned. I had to cheat on that. The way I originally shot it, you saw the cat being lowered into the barbeque, and then I cheated by cutting away."[477]

Standing in front of a creepy, reddish hue painting showing a silhouette of a man standing next to a hideous face of a demon, the episode begins with host Rod Serling's following introduction,

> "To those amongst you with a predilection toward antique collection or the occasional bargain hunting that takes place in out of the way nooks and stalls; this painting suggests a certain required wariness when it comes to your shopping. Because there are moments when behind some dusty book or in a cobwebbed corner of an ancient vestibule, you'll uncover a little objet d'art which can horrify the heck out of you—such being the case in this painting when a lady goes junking about and uncovers a mythological statue that has lived past its time ... and intrudes on hers. We call the painting *Last Rites for a Dead Druid*."

While antique shopping in Redondo Beach, Jenny Farraday (Lynley) and her friend Mildred McVane (Donna Douglas), a rich dippy divorcee who lives up to her name, stumble upon a life-size sculpture that they both think resembles Jenny's attorney husband Bruce (Bill Bixby). Jenny purchases it, but her husband is not happy. He chastises her for spending $75 "plus $5 for delivery" on it with an "I'm just the seventh junior partner of seven junior partners at work" speech - though we later learn he can afford a fulltime, German housekeeper.

Bruce immediately gets a weird vibe from the statue and while sleeping dreams that it is in his bedroom. The next day he visits the shopkeeper (Ned Glass) who sold it to Jenny. Bruce later shares with his wife what he learned—that the piece is pre-druid and is a sculpture of a man called Bruce the Black, a defrocked abbot who practiced sorcery and participated in human sacrifices, among other debauchery. Jenny is intrigued that Bruce may be a descendant of his. Bruce reiterates to her his disbelief in the story, but then the druid slowly begins to possess him. He passionately kisses a pleasantly surprised and willing Mildred and then apologizes profusely. As he lights the fire to the barbeque, a bearded sorcerer appears to him in the flames overtaking the young attorney's will. Not able to fend it off, Bruce gleefully grabs his neighbor's cat and holds it over the flames. The terrified cat's meows draws Jenny, Mildred, and their maid outside and Bruce drops the cat to the ground.

That night the druid appears again in his room and coaxes him to kill his wife so he could be with the willing Mildred. Trying to fight the urge as he is about to smother Jenny with a pillow, he finally breaks free from the druid's spell. He then goes to get a crowbar to destroy the statue. He raises his arm to strike it and yells, "This is where it ends." There is then an explosion that awakens Jenny. She comes running outside and is horrified to see that her husband and Bruce the Black have swapped places. Bruce has turned into a statue frozen in place with the raised crowbar while the sorcerer is now alive, as he glares at Jenny. The episode ends with the devilish Mildred trying to sell the new statue of Bruce to the same shopkeeper who sold the original one to Jenny.

"Last Rites for a Dead Druid," is engrossing right through to the end, which leaves the viewer wondering what happened to Jenny, last seen screaming in terror as her husband is turned into stone, and if that vixen Mildred was aligned all along with Bruce the Black or is now just under his influence? Credit goes to Szwarc, who keeps the suspense quotient high and the pace brisk. It is also helped by the creepy music score composed by Paul Glass, who brilliantly scored *Bunny Lake Is Missing*.

Bruce Farraday (Bill Bixby) examines the eerie statue his wife Jenny (Carol Lynley) purchased in "Last Rites for a Dead Druid" on *Night Gallery* (Universal Television, 1972).

Scott Skelton and Jim Benson, who authored *Rod Serling's Night Gallery: An After-Hours Tour*, thought "Last Rites" one of the series' most memorable and found Sapinsley's teleplay to be "a sharp-edged blend of humor and scares."[478] They added, "Jeannot Szwarc displays his usual deft hand at creating a uniquely suspenseful atmosphere using shadows, expressive color, visually startling camera work, and editing. His design of the dream sequence, with the statue appearing in the bedroom doorway (the background a vibrant, bloody orange hue) is masterful; the final transformation sequence is similarly well designed."[479]

Performance-wise, the episode is notable for the intense performance given by Bill Bixby and seeing corn fed Donna Douglas playing a sexy siren post-*The Beverly Hillbillies*. As the wife, Lynley looks beautiful and is puzzled throughout, not knowing what is causing her husband's erratic behavior. Even at the fade out, the look of terror on her face still has an aura of bewilderment as the druid makes his move on her. Most fans thought she performed with aplomb with Skelton and Benson remarking that Carol was "aptly vacant as Bixby's clueless wife."[480]

*****

The less remembered TV series *The Sixth Sense* offered Lynley a tour de force playing the main character—a woman terrorized by premonitions in a rented mansion. She delivers one of her best TV guest performances and arguably this episode is a highlight of the series. *The Sixth Sense* was a spin-off of the highly rated TV-movie *Sweet, Sweet Rachel* (1971) about a paranormal psychic investigator who researches a series of murders being committed by a psychic via telepathy. Creator Anthony Lawrence was recruited as executive story consultant on the new series however its original star Alex Dreier was replaced by the more TV handsome Gary Collins (whom Lynley described as being "a sweet, caring, soft-spoken guy"[481]) as new character Dr. Michael Rhodes. The first television show to tackle ESP since *One Step Beyond*, its episodes were framed as a typical detective series though filmed with a psychedelic touch apropos for the time and laced with "delirious visions, hallucinations, apparitions, delusions, nightmares, mind transfers, memories from strangers, premonitions." College professor Dr. Rhodes, specializing in parapsychology, would try to explain the paranormal happenings to the victims (and the audience) by using rational and scientific methods, however he would frequently encounter disbelief and skepticism in the characters (and the viewers as well).

Premiering on January 15, 1972 on ABC-TV, *The Sixth Sense* was a mid-season replacement during a particularly weak season on the network, which had already cancelled a fair number of its freshman shows. Promoting the new series, ABC-TV released the following press release to draw interest to it,

> You enter a strange room for the first time, yet you know you've been there before. You dream about an event that happens some days later. Someone begins to talk, and you already know what they're going to say. A coincidence? Maybe. But more than likely its extrasensory perception, a sixth sense that many scientists believe we all possess, but rarely use.

Up against CBS' ratings power house *Mission: Impossible* at 10 p.m. on Saturday night, the show held its own and began with a series of creepy, well-executed episodes including Carol's called "The House That Cried Murder." It was skillfully directed by Richard Donner (who would go on to direct such feature films as *The Omen, Superman, The Goonies, Lethal Weapon, Scrooged,* and *Assassins*) and written by Robert Hammer with an homage to Edgar Allan Poe. Commenting on Richard Donner's directing style, Margot Kidder, who worked with him on *Superman*, said, "Donner had acted, so he knew how it worked. Now, what he did which was amazing: he worked with each person's method. That is not easy to do, to know that much about acting that you can tell how different actors approach the work and then adapt to their skills."[482]

Carol concurred with Kidder and added, "What a great director. I had known Dick through Tom Mankiewicz and Jack Haley, Jr. so we were already acquainted. I always liked him. He was lively and quite funny. Just a pleasure to be around. Working with him was about the same way."[483]

With Donner at the helm, it is no wonder that the actress delivered a first-rate performance. When she was guided by topflight directors such as Robert Altman, Robert Aldrich, Otto Preminger, David Greene, Joseph Sargent, Ronald Neame, and Val Guest, she was able to give more than a competent performance and really get immersed into the role as exemplified here on *The Sixth Sense*.

Dressed in the colorful fashions of the day, Lynley gives an effective performance as the confused, sympathetic heroine. Here she portrays clothes designer Gail Summer who rents a country estate to get some peace and quiet while she begins work on a new line of clothes. While sketching a design one night, she has visions of a woman being drowned in a bathtub and of herself in a "50s model" automobile sinking in a nearby lake. Terrified and baffled at the same time, she goes to psychic investigator Dr. Michael Rhodes (Gary Collins) for help. Revealing that she has had psychic episodes all her life, Gail says that she was drawn to the house immediately and renting it became a weird obsession.

Dr. Rhodes' assistant discovers that the house belonged to a woman named Frances Dahlgren, who accidentally drowned in her bathtub years ago during a party at the house. Rhodes visits the delusional Anne Carver (Corinne Camacho), Frances' friend and one of the guests that night along with her husband Roger (Larry Linville). She is a fragile woman who believes Frances visits her and lets the doctor know about a card game played that night. Roger arrives home and is uncooperative asking Rhodes to leave.

Gail continues to experience psychic phenomenon and sketches a tree with the initials F.D. carved in it. While searching the grounds for it, Gail senses it is near the lake. They find it and Rhodes picks up an unusual metal object found near the tree. Back at the house, Rhodes and Gail, peering out the front window, see that same object is on the hood of a 1950 Sedan careening toward them. It crashes through the glass and Gail faints when she realizes it was just a vision that they had both oddly shared. This makes Rhodes believe there is a car submerged in the lake and he goes to Frank Orley (Robert Yuro), a mechanic and friend of the late Frances. When he recognizes the hood ornament, he agrees to drag the lake. He not only finds the car but his dead ex-girlfriend's body inside. Her name was Janet Lewis (Patricia Mickey) and she was one of the guests at Frances' ill-fated party along with Frank. He claims Janet broke up with him that night and she left in a huff to return east. He swears he did not kill her.

Gail meanwhile has a dream that she is being buried alive with a man shoveling dirt on her, while a gas leak slowly poisons her. Rhodes only comes to her rescue when her flailing causes a vase to crash to the floor. After she awakens, she identifies the man in her vision as the same one who murdered Frances in the bathtub. A reporter named Tom Walker (Jim Antonio) shows up. He was at Frances' house the night she died and threatens Rhodes to stop his investigation and leave it to the police. Soon after, the doctor is haunted by visions of being walled into a closet; trapped under a swinging pendulum as it descends lower and lower; and finally seeing his own body in a casket. He pieces together that all the visions are related to an Edgar Allan Poe card game the party guests were playing the night Frances died, and the cards must be hidden in the spots revealed in the visions. As he and Gail retrace their steps, they find four of the five Poe cards placed that night during the game. Anne is asked to help and as she sits in the drawing room reenacting the card game, Frances' spirit appears to Gail and Rhodes who follow her up to her bathroom. There they see Roger drown her and then kill Janet with a fireplace poker after she stumbled onto the murder.

The Sixth Sense was praised for its "distinct flair for creepiness and "The House That Cried Murder" was considered one of its finest episodes. The review in the syndicated column *TV Scout* read, "Combines elements of a classic ghost story and a classic whodunit into a compelling hour of viewing … You have to pay strict attention. It's complicated, but worth the effort and, as usual, visually quite stunning." Writing in *Terror Television*, its author called it "worthy of recognition … in which elements of *The Pit and the Pendulum*, *The Raven*, *The Tell-Tale Heart*, *The Premature Burial*, and other Edgar Allan Poe stories were projected as disturbing psychic visions."

Writing in *You're the Director, You Figure It Out: The Life and Films of Richard Donner*, author James Christie wrote, "Donner was known as an 'actors' director' who elicited strong performances from his cast, appreciated as well for his innate technical skill and artistic eye."[484] This was especially true for this episode from its meticulous production design and effects to the performances from the cast. Carol was a gaggle of nerves and on edge throughout as Gail, thanks to Donner's guidance. She is so vulnerable yet determined to find out the truth about Frances' death despite all the terrifying visions. It was wonderfully balanced against Gary Collins' more relaxed manner as Dr. Rhodes. There a few moments when you think Gail will flee the home in terror, but she keeps persevering to learn what really happened to the dead woman. This is one of the reasons the episode is so suspenseful. Carol's performance keeps the audience speculating if she will stay or run away.

Despite some other equally well-received episodes, *The Sixth Sense* could not draw viewers from *Mission: Impossible* and retain its initial ratings. ABC-TV still had faith in it and renewed the show for a second season, but it was axed after another twelve episodes. Wonder if Dr. Rhodes was able to see that coming?

Carol Lynley as Jenny Faraday in "Last Rites for a Dead Druid" on *Night Gallery* (Universal Television, 1972)

11. Hell, Upside Down

Undoubtedly, *The Poseidon Adventure* is Carol Lynley's most memorable movie and her biggest box office hit. Over the years *Poseidon* has built up a devoted cult following with legions of fans. One of their film favorites is Carol's hot pants, go-go booted, terrified hippie singer Nonnie Parry. This is surprising since the character isn't bellowing or combative like cop Mike Rogo; foul-mouthed like his wife Linda; wise cracking like overweight Belle Rosen; or bombastic like Reverend Scott. Credit goes to Lynley for giving a sympathetic, understated performance as the terrified Nonnie, who almost goes into a state of shock after the capsizing of the SS Poseidon making the audience feel empathy for her plight. It was not Lynley's most demanding role but remains her most beloved and remembered.

Considered the "Granddaddy of Disaster Movies," *The Poseidon Adventure* was produced by Irwin Allen, best known up to this point in time for his popular sixties science-fiction TV series *Voyage to the Bottom of the Sea*, *Lost in Space*, *Time Tunnel*, and *Land of the Giants*. Before he went into television, he won an Academy Award for the documentary *The Sea Around Us* and produced such feature films as *The Story of Mankind*; *The Big Circus*; *The Lost World*; *Voyage to the Bottom of the Sea*; and *Five Weeks in a Balloon*.

Thinking 20th Century-Fox would be interested in making the movie,

Allen bought the rights to Paul Gallico's novel *The Poseidon Adventure*. The adventure story's exciting plot, about the capsizing of an ocean liner and how a small band of disparate survivors try to make their way to the bottom (now top) of the ship, sounded like a sure thing. Fox then stunned Allen when they chose to pass on it. Avco-Embassy then struck a three-picture deal with the producer and Wendell Mayes was hired to deliver a script. The scale of *Poseidon* eventually scared off the studio heads who were used to making smaller films like *The Graduate* and *Easy Rider*. Luckily, Fox came under new management and decided to move ahead with the movie.

Academy Award-winning screenwriter Stirling Silliphant was hired to rework Mayes' screenplay, which included the rape of teenaged Susan Shelby, a homosexual character, and a few tawdry scenes. Acclaimed British cinematographer/screenwriter/director Ronald Neame was hired to direct after Fox decided that Allen's choice, veteran Gordon Douglas, was for some reason not a strong enough director to handle the massive production despite that his credits included such action movies as *Them!*, *Rio Conchos*, *In Like Flint*, *Tony Rome*, and *Barquero*. Ronald Neame received Academy Award nominations for his cinematography on *One of Our Aircraft Is Missing* and for co-writing *Brief Encounter* and *Great Expectations*. As a director, he was best known for *The Horse's Mouth*, *Tunes of Glory*, *The Chalk Garden*, and *The Prime of Miss Jean Brodie*. Neame admitted he was not an obvious choice to direct since most of his movies were dialogue driven and not action films. He was excited to accept the challenge.

After a few weeks of preproduction, Fox dealt Allen a second surprise blow when they once again passed on the movie due to the $5 million budget. When the studio head agreed to put up half, the wily Allen went out and literally hit up two wealthy friends to finance the difference.

With the funds secured, and an approved screenplay and director in place, casting began. Allen assembled an all-star cast to play the disparate group of characters. These included Gene Hackman, riding high from *The French Connection*, as Reverend Scott the leader of the band of survivors; Ernest Borgnine as New York detective Mike Rogo and Stella Stevens as his ex-prostitute wife Linda Rogo; Red Buttons as lonely haberdasher bachelor Mr. Martin; Jack Albertson as Manny Rosen and Shelley Winters as his wife Belle Rosen; Roddy McDowall (who, as a child, worked with then cinematographer Ronald Neame on *Murder in the Family* in 1938) as ship's steward Acres; newcomer Pamela Sue Martin as Susan and popular child actor Eric Shea as her brother Robin; Arthur O'Connell as the ship's resident clergyman; and Leslie Nielsen as the captain.

With her long blonde hair, vacant look in her eyes, and flower child persona, Lynley seemed to be the obvious choice for Nonnie. However, she was not, as Nonnie was one of the last roles cast. On the short-list when the film was still at Avco-Embassy were Judy Geeson, Judy Carne, and Lulu. Later, both Katherine Ross and vocalist Petula Clark purportedly passed on the role. Rumor had it, Cher was also considered. Another actress up for Nonnie was Celeste Yarnall. She impressed Irwin Allen when she guest starred on his TV series *Land of the Giants*. Her films up to that point included a co-starring role opposite Elvis Presley in *Live a Little, Love a Little* and the lead in *The Velvet Vampire*. Yarnall remarked, "Irwin Allen wanted me for the role … but the studio vetoed it because my name wasn't big enough."[485]

At the same time as this casting roundelay was going on, Carol was looking for the right film project having not appeared in a major studio theatrical feature in over two years. She felt now was the time to return to the big screen after working in television only. However, it could not just be any movie and had to have the potential to "be successful and … have a good part in it for me."[486]

Reportedly, Carol was sent the script for *Play It as Is Lays* and her agent wanted her to meet with director Frank Perry. Though she suspected the role of a faded actress would give whoever played it critical acclaim, she knew it was not for her and was too downbeat to attract a wide audience.[487] Lynley's instinct proved to be correct. Tuesday Weld took the part and received excellent notices while the audience stayed away making it a box office dud.

Carol was determined to find that commercial success. Her persistence paid off when out of the blue came *The Poseidon Adventure*. She almost missed the opportunity due to a previous appointment but when she could not reach her agent to postpone or cancel the interview, she had to take the meeting. She went on to explain,

> It was a Friday and I went in to meet with Ronnie Neame and Irwin Allen. We talked about the story and that was it. I went to the beach for the weekend. When I got back home on Monday, my agent was furiously trying to find me. I got the part—they cast me on the spot. I don't know why because they never even gave me a script to read.[488]

Obviously, Carol had the perfect look and quality that Neame and Allen wanted to bring Nonnie to life on the big screen. Commenting then what motivated her to do the movie, Carol said that its theme struck a chord in her and she felt it would with others as well. She described it as "a survival film. Everybody thinks at one time or another in life, 'Do I have it in me to survive?'"[489]

Carol had no time to second guess her decision and had to report to the studio the Monday she learned the part was hers. She recalled,

> We had to do costume fittings immediately. It was so hurried and rushed. Paul Zastupnevich already had Nonnie's look designed with the hot pants and the long vest. However, the one thing I brought to it were the boots. There was going to be a lot of water on that set. Having been a ballet dancer my entire life I knew that could get dicey. My boots were leather and rubberized underneath. I asked Ronnie and Irwin if I could use my boots because I felt comfortable wearing them. I was also confident that I wouldn't slip in them. They were fine with it.[490]

Pop singer Nonnie Parry (Carol Lynley) shrieks in terror as the SS Poseidon begins to capsize in *The Poseidon Adventure* (20th Century-Fox, 1972).

According to Irwin Allen, the movie was scheduled for "one of the longest shooting schedules in years. 70 days principal photography, 12 days of second unit work, 15 days miniature shooting and 10 days of special effects. That's more than 100 days of actual filming."[491] The first two weeks of filming were spent outside on the Queen Mary that was docked at Long Beach Harbor. The rest of the shoot was, for the most part, on upside-down sets at the Fox studio. "Stage 6 and stage 12," remarked Carol to Nelson Aspen on his online chat show. "Funny how I remember these things. And the water tank was on the back lot."[492] The cast was enclosed on these sets and with each other almost constantly. Where other movies have actors come in, do their thing, and then leave, the *Poseidon's* cast were tied to each other for the entire time.

After the capsizing scene, the movie was shot in sequence. This was a big advantage to cinematographer Harold Stine and his team. Stine explained, "The shooting in sequence really began at the point where the ship turned over. Up until then we shot out of sequence because the people playing the passengers were all clean and well-dressed. But from that point on, it became almost necessary to shoot in sequence, because quite a few of the people got scars on them; some got cuts and their clothes began to tear and get dirtier and dirtier as they tried to escape. Also, they got more and more tired as they struggled to get out and it was easier for the actors to play this progressively. It was easier for me and the special effects people, too, from the standpoint of lighting or how much fire to use, and so forth. It would have been very difficult in this kind of picture to jump around out of continuity."[493]

Stine also spoke of how they made the Grand Ballroom tilt during the start of the ship's capsizing. He revealed, "There was one corner of the set that was built on a platform measuring, perhaps, 20 by 30 feet and our principal characters were sitting with a group of other people at a table on that platform. The platform and part of the adjacent wall were attached to a hinge, so that we could raise the whole thing to an angle of 30 degrees. We used that for a number of shots to get the ship started over. We put in other tables with different people and changed the background a bit to get a number of cuts of the passengers starting to slide down and hanging onto the tables. What you will see on the screen in this sequence is real. Take Shelley Winters, for example - who can scream at the top of her lungs - she started hanging onto this table and screaming and calling for her husband, and we got the real thing. There was no pretense in that action."[494]

Not surprisingly based on what a technical shoot this was, Carol revealed that most of the cast had to put up with annoyances big and small. She remarked at the time, "I hated the heights. Red Buttons hated the water. Stella Stevens hated the dirt and so did Ernest Borgnine. Shelley Winters hated being fat, and Jack Albertson hated Shelley Winters, but even the people who hated each other loved each other."[495]

When Lynley accepted the role of Nonnie, the actress assumed that she would have a stunt double. They were on set ready to step in, but director Ronald Neame goaded his cast to overcome their fears and dislikes to make a better motion picture. His tactic worked for the most part. Carol was right there climbing the Christmas tree, standing on the ledge overlooking the ballroom, and climbing up the ship's stack. Regarding the later, Neame revealed in his memoir that he was able to get Carol and Red to climb up the six or seven stories by appealing to their egos. He was willing to use the stunt doubles but informed the pair that they would be forfeiting their close-ups. Knowing how vain actors are, up they went until the ship tilts and the stack blows up.

Despite her fear, Carol did most, but not all, of her scenes without a stunt double. She recalled, "After shooting scenes high up on the catwalks or ladders, Ronnie Neame would yell 'cut.' All the other actors would climb down except me. Gene Hackman's brother Bill was working on the film as a stunt coordinator and he would have to climb up and help me down!"[496]

The cast was continually drenched as the ocean kept pouring in and flooding the decks as the ship slowly sunk. Describing what it was like, Carol recalled, "In the scenes where water rushes in at us, which is quite frequently, the guys would say, 'don't worry, it would just come up to here,' pointing to the tip of my nose. But what they didn't say is it comes at you at 50 miles an hour!"[497]

Not all the scenes in the movie were as dangerous as they seemed. In a feat of movie magic, after the shaft blows up killing Acres, a frightened, drenched Nonnie is seen holding onto the ladder for dear life, as Martin and Mike Rogo try to prod her to start climbing. Here Neame acquiesced. This was not filmed high up on the ladder but shot in close-up with Carol standing on an apple box holding a mockup of the ladder to make it more comfortable for the actress. Red Buttons was on his knees.

Even though Neame (whom Carol praised as being "the ever-consummate gentleman"[498]) made a special accommodation for her here, Carol received her director's respect for being such a trooper overall. He commented before his passing, "When you see her when she got to the top of the [Christmas tree that was fear on her face. That was not acting there. She was absolutely petrified." Carol responded, "Ron was a wonderful director. He didn't get half the credit he deserved when the film became such an enormous hit."[499] Carol blames this on Irwin Allen whom she felt took most of the credit when the movie became a huge smash. This was in part Neame's fault as he admitted his biggest mistake was not asking for the credit "A Film by Ronald Neame," where he would be singled out.

Per Carol, Allen directed most of the second unit footage and with the cast for long shots with the extras. He would be on a big crane with a bullhorn barking direction. She described the producer as "the last of the old-fashioned mogul movie producers."[500] Neame was with the main cast every day and directed all their scenes. He was an extremely patient man according to Carol. When an actor would have an outburst, Carol recalls seeing Ronnie standing at the side of the camera taking a deep breath probably hoping it would blow over quickly, which is what usually happened.

Neame wrote about the many problems he had with Irwin Allen throughout the course of the movie. Issues started right from the get-go. "He was one of the most controlling producers ever, in both the positive and negative sense. In some respects, he was the worst type—a frustrated director. Though in my case he knew he had to be cautious since the president of the studio brought me in. One of our early disagreements occurred when he said he wanted the film shot based on storyboards prepared by his sketch artists. Or put another way, shoot the whole thing the way Irwin saw it."[501]

Neame refused and explained to Allen, "When I get actors on the set and begin to rehearse, all kinds of interesting things happen—the unexpected may develop into something exciting. It may be the same scene as written, but the emphasis could change for the better."[502] A compromise was reached, and Allen's storyboards were used only for the action scenes.

Opining on the director and producer's relationship, Carol remarked, "I know it was very difficult for Ronnie although he and Irwin were a good match. Irwin supplied the chutzpah and Ronnie supplied the technical know-how and the on-set dealing with actors."[503]

Another time Carol was impressed with Neame's professionalism was when Nonnie emerges from the air duct and must climb the ladder in one of the ship's stacks. Neame asked her how she wanted to shoot the scene. The way the camera was positioned; it was aimed straight up at her crotch. Carol told him she would angle her body. Even though there were many shots of her legs and behind, she thought that was sweet of him to bring to her attention.

Traumatized survivors Belle Rosen (Shelley Winters), Nonnie (Carol Lynley), Acres (Roddy McDowall), and Linda Rogo (Stella Stevens) await their next move to escape the sinking ocean liner in *The Poseidon Adventure* (20th Century-Fox, 1972).

Describing overall what it was like working on *Poseidon*, Carol revealed that it was, "hellish. I spent close to four months dripping wet wearing the same dirty clothes—it was physically exhausting. I started shivering at nine o'clock in the morning and I kept shivering all day."[504] Luckily, she nor any of her co-stars caught the flu. Carol continued,

> We'd go to hair and makeup, but they put the dirt in the hair

and dirt on the face. Just bang us with dirt. There was a point where you'd see them coming at you with a hose, that your whole body would say, 'No.' And I use to say, 'Please just put up a shower so I can get under and do it all at once.' Your hair person would wet you down, and then makeup would wet you down. And by the time makeup was finished, the hair would start to dry off. But, because of continuity it all had to match. So, you constantly had five or six people spritzing you.[505]

Things were not much better with her wardrobe. Carol added,

> As the shoot continued, the boots started to shrink due to being soaked all the time. They had to make cuts in them so I could still walk. At the end of filming the boots were wrecked and I had to toss them. Also, because the shorts I wore were wet all the time, they started shrinking as well. Irwin said, 'We can't have that.' I replied, 'I'm with you.' I was always going into wardrobe to have my shorts refitted or to get a new pair.[506]

One of Carol's most infamous scenes is when Nonnie, left with Red Button's Martin and Sella Stevens' Linda, screams hysterically when the water begins filling up the deck they remain on. James Radford reported, "Carol told me that she knew she'd be screaming all day to shoot the scene from different angles. As a Broadway trained actress, she wisely chose to use her diaphragm and project a low, animal-like scream of intense fear. By emoting and projecting, she was able to scream extensively and not lose her voice."[507]

During the many breaks in filming, to keep her mind off the heights, Carol sometimes kept busy crocheting, which she described then as "my security blanket"[508] or talking with the press. To drum up publicity for the movie, Irwin Allen hired director Andrew J. Kuehn to oversee a promotional, ten-minute short (actually an elongated trailer) about what went on behind-the-scenes in making *The Poseidon Adventure* with the entire cast featured as well as Neame and Allen. It was titled *The Return of the Movie Movie* and was screened to drum up interest in the film.

Allen was also constantly inviting journalists to visit the set and interview his stars. One was columnist Dick Kleiner who remarked, "I walked onto the set and it was topsy-turvy ... And the cast dirty and disheveled. On some of them, disheveling looks good—Carol Lynley, in shorts and smudged shirt and face, somehow looks exquisite despite it all."[509]

Another guest was journalist James Bacon. Hearing the rumors about Shelley Winters diva behavior—from her fighting with Jack Albertson to one day even trying to bar Ernest Borgnine from the set—he was disappointed that she was not in attendance during his visit. Interviewing Lynley for her take on Shelley, the actress said candidly in 1972, "Her tantrums throw us all into an uproar, but when she's not here, I miss the electricity."[510] Winters surely kept her costars on their toes and perhaps at the top of their game?

During other breaks in filming, Lynley would spend time with her ten-year-old daughter Jill who was a frequent visitor to the set, as were Gene Hackman's children and Stella Stevens's son. Sometimes the capsized ship's world remained with her even after leaving the studio for the night. Filming on upside-down sets were so disorienting that Carol revealed when returning to her apartment after a day's shoot, that her "bed seemed to be tilted."[511]

While filming, Carol also had to contend with receiving the sad news that her former co-star and friend Brandon deWilde had been tragically killed in a car accident. He was touring with the stage show *Butterflies Are Free* and the camper he was driving overturned near Denver, Colorado. When asked to comment, she replied, "As a child actor I was isolated. He was one of the few friends I had ... When he died, it killed off part of my childhood."[512]

Due to the disparate personalities filming in such close quarters for almost four months sometimes the cast just had to get away even for just a brief period. Tired of eating at the 20th Century-Fox studio commissary, one day Carol and Gene Hackman decided to lunch at a nearby Chinese restaurant that came highly recommended. He was an aficionado of the cuisine and she was learning how to cook Chinese food at the time. They arrived still in costume, with bathrobes wrapped around them, feeling a bit self-conscious. Per Carol at the time, "The waiter never raised an eyebrow. Makes you wonder how often shipwreck victims come in and order Peking duck."[513] It soon became the place to lunch on almost a daily basis for the entire cast except for Eric Shea who had to attend school. Coincidentally, his teacher was Frances Klemp who instructed an underage Lynley when she filmed *Blue Denim*.

For fans, the movie's biggest mystery is who sang "The Morning After"? The song, composed by Al Kasha and Joel Hirschhorn, is warbled by Nonnie during the movie first during a rehearsal scene that introduced the singer and her bandmates and later for a bit at the New Year's Eve gala. Before the movie opened, entertainment columnists were announcing that Carol would be making her big screen singing bow in the movie. In one of the most far-fetched reported stories, columnist Charles McHarry announced that scuttlebutt on Carol's singing was so positive that Lynley was "being eyed by talent agents for Vegas and the Catskills. The Concord's Phil Greenwald flew to the coast to offer Miss Lynley a five-figure sum to bring a song-and-dance act to his hotel for the Christmas season."[514] It is hard to believe that this was true.

Carol never boasted about her singing capabilities in any press she gave back then. In fact, she was quite matter of fact when asked point blank by journalist Barbara Wilson, a few months after the film wrapped, if her voice would be heard singing the song. Carol stated then,

> I worked for a week with a singer by the name of Renee [Armand]. She made the demo record of the song that I do … and I listened to it over and over again. She taught me how to hold the hand mike and how to work the cord. I ripped off her movements. Then we did a double track, my voice and her voice superimposed.[515]

For a long time, this scenario sounded the most plausible. The actress stuck to this theory, but in more recent years she has been called out for saying it was her voice only. During a Q&A at the 1999 Asheville Film Festival, an audience member asked her about the song. Carol replied that she did make a recording (which is true) but did not state it was used in the movie, only that Maureen McGovern re-recorded it for a single. However, Carol also never mentioned Renee Armand's version.[516]

In 2006, Lynley was asked point blank by John Clark of the *San Francisco Chronicle* on her supposed assertion, and Lynley replied,

> I've never claimed that. The thing with the song, I don't know. I worked with Renee Armand, a studio singer, who taught me the song. During the course of the movie Irwin had me record it. After that the Fox record people wanted me to do the record version of it. The guy showed me how he wanted me to do it, and I said no. So he got Maureen McGovern to do it, and it was an enormous success. Some people think I did it (in the film), some people think Renee did it, some people think Maureen did it. The only person who really knows is Irwin, and he's not with us anymore. Irwin was a secretive kind of guy.[517]

Carol was incorrect about the truth being unknown. Per *Poseidon Adventure* expert James Radford, "According to Joel Hirschhorn, Al Kasha, and Renee Armand, their previous working relationship is why Renee was chosen to sing the demo … and her voice was such a good match for Carol that Renee's audio was used. Other than the fact the Carol believed it was her voice, and may have been told at the time it was her voice, it was pretty much established in writing when the film came out that it was Renee's vocals used in the movie."[518]

The one thing that remained constant though was Carol's distaste for the ballad. She remarked, "I never really liked the song, so boy was I shocked when it became such a huge it!"[519] No matter what her opinion of the song or whose voice was actually used in the movie, Carol Lynley will forever go down in film history associated with "The Morning After."

During the shoot, Carol seemed to be in very good spirits and quipped in one interview, "Most women who start out as a star at 15 usually end up in the nuthouse by the time they're my age."[520] She went on to say how happy she was with her life at the moment. "I've had a checkered career. I've managed to come back at the age of 30, playing a 24-year-old pop singer, looking good and sounding good. I've done the whole transition from teenybopper, ingénue, young adult, to mature adult—which is where I am now. As actresses go, I'm pretty well-adjusted, even if I do say so myself, I'm mentally healthy."[521]

The only thing Carol admitted that was missing from her life was a love interest, but she mused, "I don't think it's necessary to be in love to be happy. That's kind of an outdated idea. God knows it's nice, but there are an awful lot of people who aren't in love and there is no reason why they should be called unhappy."[522]

Once *Poseidon* wrapped, a perhaps slightly depressed Carol Lynley emerged and she confessed to columnist Marilyn Beck, "I'm actually sad now that it's over. It's one of the best parts I ever had—very emotional, just like me."[523] To Dorothy Manners, she elaborated even further admitting that she always suffered a sense of melancholia after a film shoot comes to an end. Though a very private person, she admitted to becoming deeply involved in the filming process and with the people she is working with. The almost four months she spent on *Poseidon* had a more severe impact on her due to the longer shooting schedule. She missed "being cared for. The assistant directors always want to know where you are and where you'll be and there's always someone to talk to, to laugh with, or just be with."[524] She particularly missed Ernest Borgnine ("who always seems to be so strong"[525]) and director Ronald Neame, who she said would "pat her on the shoulder after a scene, and whisper, 'good.' I must need that kind of confidence building."[526]

Lynley's melancholia reportedly did not abate. Realizing she needed professional help, she allegedly began seeing a therapist whom she had not seen in several years. She revealed, "I have always been a bit solitary, and to be working closely every day with these people on the set—why, it was like being one of the family. The script had become my reality; I was only truly alive in front of that camera. You go into emotional decline when you finish the film."⁵²⁷ By August of 1972, Lynley was very cheerful and claimed to be feeling fine once again. Though she hoped her next screen assignment would not be as stressful as *Poseidon*.

Poster art for *The Poseidon Adventure* (20th Century-Fox, 1972).

Unfortunately, something may have still been off with Carol's psyche. In December of 1972 just before *The Poseidon Adventure* opened, the actress became more candid about working with the cast, particularly Red Buttons. It started with an article by Roger Ebert and then exploded with the infamous Earl Wilson interview. Carol was unhappy with Buttons mostly because he had the habit of stepping on her lines, intentionally or not. It throws actors off when another begins speaking their lines before they have finished saying their dialog and it diminishes their part. It is reasonable to resent an actor for this behavior. Carol began to vent to the press. With Ebert she remarked, "Red didn't like me very much. He made my life miserable because he thought I had a better part then he did. Of course, I did."[528] Carol next took it to extremes with Wilson. Publicist Bobby Zarem and Wilson were taken aback and tried to calm down the outspoken actress, but she was on a roll and exploded on the comedian. She raged, "I dislike him thoroughly. I had to put up with him in the picture, but I don't now. He steals scenes, he steps on lines." She went on to add that "He's a terrible human being."[529] That was the "G" rated version that was gleaned from the interview.

Of course, most of what Carol said was unprintable in a family newspaper due to the foul language (calling him a cunt, saying how shitty he acted towards her, and more). Wilson saved her outlandish tirade for an entire standalone chapter ("Carol Lynley Speaks Right Out") in his book, *Show Business Laid Bare*. Obviously, this was not typical Lynley behavior. She was not a Tuesday Weld or a Sue Lyon known for saying outrageous things to reporters. Carol never disparaged any of her costars in the past and this was shocking to say the least. When Carol let loose, she did not hold back.

Years later, Carol copped to saying all these horrible things and quickly regretted every word. She apologized to Red Buttons on three separate occasions (once even on a plane when they coincidentally wound up on the same flight) and he was gentlemanly enough to accept. Carol felt terribly and said,

I was wrong. I am not a person who admits to being wrong that often, but when I am, I own it. I was wrong to have said what I said. Not to make excuses, but I think I was very tired, but I don't know what came over me. The minute I said all those things I knew it was not right. I should never have done that. As I said before, I apologized to Red and he was nice about it.[530]

It was also reported in the news that a rift developed between Lynley and Shelley Winters who went on either *The Tonight Show* or *The Mike Douglas Show* and forgot Carol's name. The following day, Winters had her secretary call Lynley to say how funny it was. Carol did not get the humor in it, at her expense, and threatened to punch her in the nose. Some of this is true and Carol did feel disrespected by Winters because she "defended Shelley a lot to everyone who hated her."[531] That list included Gene Hackman, Jack Albertson, and Stella Stevens all of whom said so in the media. But that is how far as it went. According to Lynley the rest of the story was nonsense and she said laughing, "Anyone who even would attempt to punch Shelley Winters in the nose is a fool. I adored Shelley and for all her good-news and bad-news, she was one of a kind. She was an extremely talented actress."[532] The fact that Carol was invited to Winters' birthday parties over the years should also squash this rumor of the two disliking each other.

A few *Poseidon Adventure* sources seem to relish playing up that Carol Lynley did not get along with some of her co-stars and was difficult on the set. This is far from the truth. Other than her purported problems with Red Buttons, Carol got along with everybody. She had held out for at least two years for a good movie and when *Poseidon* came along, she was extremely grateful and knew it had the makings to become a huge hit. She had a solid reputation of being a consummate professional and she would have been quite foolish to all-of-a-sudden begin acting the diva with so much riding on this. Gossip columnists of the time loved to exaggerate reported trouble on movie sets. Carol seemed to have been a victim of this due to her bluntness with the press and exaggeration.

Martin (Red Buttons) and Linda (Stella Stevens) try to help a panicky Nonnie (Carol Lynley) as the deck floods in *The Poseidon Adventure* (20th Century-Fox, 1972).

Before *The Poseidon Adventure* was released, 20th Century-Fox planned a big promotional launch with television ads and the release of promotional lobby cards and stills. One of the most iconic images that came from this is of Lynley as Nonnie, with a shocked and terrified look on her face, reaching out as the ship begins to capsize. Fox also hired artist Mort Kűnstler to create painted poster and ad copy. His previous work could be seen in such disparate publications as *Classics Illustrated* and *Mad* magazine. Most movie assignments were for one painting, but Fox wanted two. Kűnstler recalled, "The agency gave me these almost cartoon-like sketches for both pictures of generally what they wanted. One was of Gene Hackman running right at you, with the ship upside down, the tables on the ceiling and people dropping off, and the big explosion of water breaking in the background ... it was used for the poster and all the ads. Now, the second one is in the engine room as the escape party is making their way across a catwalk, and Hackman is in the foreground hanging off a great big wheel valve. That was the other painting, and I only saw it on the double sheets, which had both images together on the same poster. Those were used on subways and buses."[533]

The Poseidon Adventure opens with a shot of the ocean liner battling rough seas as the title credits begin accompanied by John Williams' stirring brass-heavy bombastic opening theme that is used in various renditions throughout the adventure. The audience learns it is New Year's Eve and the SS Poseidon is making its final voyage traveling the Mediterranean Sea to Athens, Greece. On board is the owner's rep who forces the captain (a stoic Leslie Nielsen) to risk safety to get the ship to its destination on time. The passengers are introduced in some rather awkward moments filmed on the Queen Mary. Shortly after midnight, the ship is overturned by a 30-foot tidal wave setting the stage for the survival of a small ragtag group of passengers who must now climb/crawl/swim their way to the bottom (now top) of the ship. A hip minister named Reverend Scott (Gene Hackman), who preaches that people need to help themselves and stop relying on others, takes unofficial charge when lonely haberdasher bachelor Mr. Martin (Red Buttons) points out that any rescue needs to come from the bottom of the boat. An arrogant purser orders everyone to stay in the ballroom, assuring rescue is on the way. Scott and Martin round up only a few of the passengers to climb the Christmas tree to the next deck where injured ship's steward Acres (Roddy McDowall) is trapped. Agreeing to take the risk are tough-talking New York Detective Mike Rogo (Ernest Borgnine) and his equally pugnacious ex-hooker wife Linda (Stella Stevens); an old Jewish couple Manny (Jack Albertson) and his overweight wife Belle Rosen (Shelley Winters) on the way to see their grandson in Israel; and teenage Susan (Pamela Sue Martin) and her younger brother Robin (Eric Shea) whose parents are in Europe awaiting their arrival. The only other person Mr. Martin can wrangle to come is despondent hippie singer Nonnie (Carol Lynley) whose brother lays dead in her arms.

Just as the small group makes it up to the next deck, climbing an upside-down Christmas tree, the boat tilts and there is an explosion. Water then begins pouring into the ballroom. The remaining, terrified passengers make a go for the tree but due to their panic it breaks from its secured perch and falls backward into the rising waters, ensuring their deaths. The adventure then begins as Rev. Scott leads his shell-shocked band of survivors through the bowels of the ship with a goal to reach the bow. Brow beating his exhausted followers to not give up, he genuinely believes that God only helps those who help themselves. This theme of faith is a constant throughout the film. They make their way through the kitchen littered with burned dead bodies; crawl through an air shaft; climb the ladder in one of the ship's stacks; encounter more survivors heading in the wrong direction; swim through a flooded corridor to reach the engine room at the bow; and then navigate a catwalk that leads up to the part of the bow where the steel is thinnest. Not all survive the treacherous journey and only six make it out alive.

The Poseidon Adventure had its world premiere on December 12, 1972 at the grand opening of the National Theater in Times Square in New York City. First, there was much ado about turning on the theater's marquee lights, followed by a ribbon-cutting ceremony with Mayor John Lindsey doing the honors accompanied by cast members Carol Lynley, Shelley Winters, and Red Buttons. Based on all photos released from the event, everybody was all smiles and you would think Carol's infamous interview never happened.

The movie opened nationwide on December 25, 1972 with fantastic poster art and a tagline that read "20th Century-Fox presents an Irwin Allen production *The Poseidon Adventure*. Hell upside-down. Who will survive? Gene Hackman, Ernest Borgnine, Red Buttons, Carol Lynley, Roddy McDowall, Stella Stevens, Shelley Winters, Jack Albertson, Pamela Sue Martin, Arthur O'Connell, Eric Shea or Leslie Nielsen as the Captain." The artwork was much more impressive than the routine trailer where a dead-voiced announcer talks over the exciting film clips. So much more could have been done but thankfully it did not hinder moviegoers from buying tickets.

The movie received mostly positive reviews— "a fairly spellbinding adventure" (*The New York Times*); "pure escapist entertainment" (*Chicago*

Tribune); "a slick sea saga" (*Boston Globe*); and "strictly formula hokum, but reasonably diverting" (*The Washington Post*). Pans for the movie were along the lines of columnist Joyce Haber who called the movie "one of the biggest, most bloated, overstuffed films I've seen in years." Criticism was roundly received for the stereotyped characters and the banal script. Though almost all agreed the fantastic visual effects, the stunning cinematography, and remarkable production design overcame the screenplay's weaknesses as did Neame's slick direction that kept the action moving.

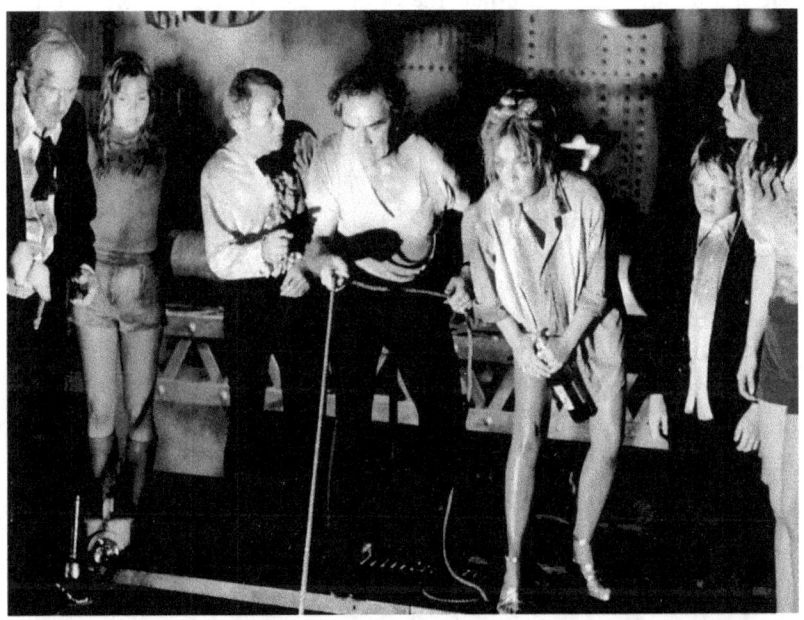

Manny (Jack Albertson), Nonnie (Carol Lynley), Martin (Red Buttons), Mike (Ernest Borgnine), Linda (Stella Stevens), Robin (Eric Shea) and Susan (Pamela Sue Martin) wait tensely to see if Rev. Scott and Belle made it to the engine room in *The Poseidon Adventure* (20th Century-Fox, 1972).

For her portrayal of Nonnie, Lynley received some fine notices such as "Her complete panic is especially effective" (Micheline Keating, *Tucson Daily Citizen*); "Carol Lynley is outstanding ... she expresses mixtures of terror, grief, and bewilderment convincingly at every turn." (Bill Rice, *The Times*

Record); "bouquets to Red Buttons, Stella Stevens, Carol Lynley, and, as always, Jack Albertson." (Beverly Duffy, *The Cedar Rapids Gazette*); "Carol Lynley ... performed with ease" (George McKinnon, *Boston Globe*); and "Carol Lynley is especially effective" (*Variety*).

To fans, one of the most endearing qualities about Nonnie (not discounting Lynley's shapely figure, clearly on display in white hot pants and an orange top with matching go-go boots, during the climbing-the-ladder close-ups) is her flower child innocence and vulnerability. You want to reach out and be the one to save her. The brother she loved so is gone and she feels she cannot go on either. She does not know how to exist without him. When Mr. Martin tells her that her sibling is dead and gently asks her to join the ragtag group of survivors, she follows like a frightened fawn after asking him, "Did you like his music?" as she strokes her brother's hair. Nonnie is perhaps the only character who shows true terror regarding their predicament - trapped in an upside-down sinking ocean liner trying to swim/climb/crawl to the now bottom of the ship. Martin throughout the movie encourages Nonnie that she must move on and offers a guiding hand. Though she is petrified and despondent due to her loss, she does not complain, as some of the other characters do, as they make their harrowing trek to safety.

Arguably, Carol's most remembered scene is when she and Martin venture into an upside-down barbershop. There, Nonnie brings up her brother ("My brother Teddy has lovely hair") and then stops, realizing he is dead as she huddles on the floor clutching a barber's cutting gown. She tearfully claims that she cannot go on without him. Martin touchingly tells her that she must, and we all go on as John Williams poignantly underscores the scene with an instrumental of "The Morning After."

Another memorable moment for Carol is when, needing to get to the engine room by way of a flooded corridor, Nonnie reveals, "I can't swim." A shocked Martin says, "You can't swim!?!" "No, not a stroke," she replies. Nonnie then tries to get Martin to stay back with her. Realizing that he would even though he thinks they will probably perish; she musters up the courage to hold her breath and hang on to his belt as he swims his way to the other side. He demands, "Don't let go," as they get into the water. She responds, with panic in her eyes, "Don't worry, *I won't.*" Nonnie survives due to Martin's encouragement to fight for her life. This was one of Carol's admittedly favorite scenes. Being a swimmer since she was four years old, she liked the challenge.

Carol also liked the scene when a petrified Nonnie is frozen in fear high up on the ladder in the air shaft with Martin and Ernest Borgnine's Rogo trying to get her to climb. Per Lynley, "People always say, 'Oh God, you look like you were really scared.' And I say, 'Well actually not really, you know. That was acting.'"[534]

Reportedly, Irwin Allen had a plan for Lynley's Nonnie to be the center of attention when finally rescued. He envisioned the camera on her in closeup as her head pops up into the daylight. Then as Nonnie fully emerges the camera would pull back to a long shot revealing several rescue boats nearby and helicopters flying overhead. Unfortunately, the producer had exhausted his budget and could not get additional financing. Alas he had to film the rescue in medium shot on the Fox backlot in a tank with the elated survivors hopping onto a single helicopter and flying away.

Another reason for Nonnie's popularity is that her character sang/lip-synched the film's Academy Award-winning song, "The Morning After." It is interesting to learn that the scene where she rehearses the number was longer with banter amongst the group members. As laid out in the Third Revised Final Shooting script dated March 24, 1972 the scene continued with Nonnie's brother Teddy criticizing her singing, claiming that she was half a beat behind. Nonnie disagrees and Teddy asks the drummer to back him up, but the poor fellow is suffering from sea sickness. Nonnie argues, "But, Teddy dear, does it matter if I'm sometimes behind or a little in front. Doesn't that sometimes give it a little more feeling?" Teddy remains obstinate in his view and after being told by him to "cool it," she finally demurs saying, "If you say so, Teddy."[535] They then begin rehearsing again. It is a shame that this wound up on the cutting room floor. This additional interaction would have helped the audience understand more of Nonnie's feeling of despair regarding the loss of her brother whom she clearly depends on.

It would be interesting to learn why it was cut. Some have speculated it was due to the ineptness of the guys hired to play her band mates. Carol does not know why it was cut but defends her co-stars,

> They were great guys and all of them were terrific. It is true they were musicians and not actors, which I liked. I was in a few scenes with them and they were very professional. I do not think they were why the scene was cut. Maybe they were just tightening up the film?[536]

Stuart Perry played Nonnie's brother Teddy (who had all his lines cut from the movie) and Carol shared a funny story. "In the scene where I am cradling my dead brother's body and Red is trying to get me to go with him, I look up and say, 'Did you like his music?' Stuart and I could not keep a straight face and kept laughing. Excuse me, somebody dies and you ask if you liked his music!?!"[537] Though the screenwriters could have come up with something better, Carol does deliver the line poignantly.

The excising of the rehearsal interplay between the band members did not bother Carol as much as another shortened scene. In the final cut, the upside-down barber shop scene ends with Martin's pep talk as a crying Nonnie lies on the floor. However, there was more dialogue between Nonnie and Martin in other drafts of the script. In the final script, it continued with Nonnie pulling herself together and getting up. She asks Martin, "Did you … ever lose someone you love?" He responds about his parents. In earlier drafts it goes even farther with Nonnie introducing herself to Martin and gives him a friendly kiss hello as the scene ends.[538]

Up to this point in the movie, Nonnie was the only survivor to have lost a loved one in the capsizing. Her character's feelings and frame of mind about the death of her brother would have been revealed. This would have given credence to her near catatonic state. Keeping at least more of this scene would have shown the audience that Nonnie had now found the will to live. With the scene ending as it did, Nonnie is just once again shown as the pathetic, frightened girl who needed to be pulled along. Carol was right to be disappointed on the edit and commented,

> They cut it pretty much in half. When I saw the final print, I was shocked because they cut the heart out of my character basically and made everything much more difficult. They don't ask the actors. You shoot it and then it's theirs. You don't know what's been cut until after it has been done. They do not come up to the actors and say, 'Oh by the way, on Friday we will be cutting this.' You don't find out until to maybe six months later. It's their decision but this was quite upsetting to me.[539]

Rev. Scott (Gene Hackman) leads Robin (Eric Shea), Susan (Pamela Sue Martin), Nonnie (Carol Lynley), Martin (Red Buttons), and the rest up a catwalk to the engine room in *The Poseidon Adventure* (20th Century-Fox, 1972).

Costume designer Paul Zastupnevich had worked with Irwin Allen for years and he too was outraged that the producer cut Carol and Red's scene. In Jeff Bond's book *The Fantastic Worlds of Irwin Allen* he is quoted as saying, "It was the most heartrending scene I ever sat through. In fact, the crew, when Carol and Red finished the scene, they applauded. When Irwin got it in the cutting room, he cut the scene in pieces. He would go back to Gene Hackman climbing the ladder with water coming down." Irwin's explanation was that he felt the audience would get impatient for more action. Zastupnevich said, "*He* got impatient. I was so upset at the time because I felt he destroyed an Oscar performance for both Red and Carol."[540]

Carol and Paul Zastupnevich remained close friends until his death in 1997. Gossip mavens had a field day touting their supposed "romance" in their columns due to their many appearances together at social functions in Hollywood and Beverly Hills. Paul even gifted Carol with clothes he designed over the years. The actress had many gay pals she liked to hang out with who would be erroneously be described as her newest love interest by the media.

During the first part of 1973, Carol was sent on a national promotional tour to support the movie. She did press interviews and made personal appearances. One of the more amusing was a newspaper ad touting her appearance at the Fashion Department at Woolworths Northwest Plaza in Missouri. Fans would not only get to meet the movie star but also receive a free autographed photo.

Carol was also all over the small screen promoting *The Poseidon Adventure*. She was a presenter, along with Gene Hackman, at the *30th Annual Golden Globe Awards* where *The Poseidon Adventure* received nominations for Best Motion Picture – Drama; Best Supporting Actress for Shelley Winters; Best Musical Score by John Williams; and Best Song. Winters was the only one who took home the Globe. Carol also made several TV talk show appearances including four times on *The Tonight Show Starring Johnny Carson*.

Carol was poised and in control during her first appearance on Johnny Carson's show. After telling Johnny why she had not made a feature film for close to three years, she thought *Poseidon* "would be a smash" based on her read of the script and hearing who was already cast. She was wary of the moviegoers' reactions and admitted, "I was nervous until I saw it with an audience—it was wonderful. You hear them laugh and cry." She then said that she never was in such a huge hit before (she shared that the movie already grossed $15 million in its first three weeks of release) and wasn't used to being constantly recognized, "On Monday's, about every third person stops you and says they saw the movie. That's dynamite!" Looking to the future, Carol said, she was determined to hold out for another good movie to come along "and that's scary too."[541]

When Johnny asked if it was a hard shoot, Carol replied yes being wet for almost four months straight on upside down sets was difficult. She revealed that she contracted a case of Impetigo (a bacterial skin infection more common in children) under her eye. They also discussed what it was like going on tour to promote a movie since Carol traveled to six major cities with *The Poseidon Adventure*. This is challenging work and not as glamorous as people think it is. Once she was back home in LA, Carol said she hit the jogging track to clear her mind.

Carol returned to Johnny's couch a month later in February and the host immediately brought up *The Poseidon Adventure* and mentioned that he did not realize that Carol had a fear of heights. She described how Gene Hackman's brother, who worked on the movie as a stunt coordinator, had to help her climb up and down the upside-down catwalks in the engine room towards the end of the film. Carson then joked about his phobias. Carol had nothing but praise for the TV talk show host,

> I liked Johnny Carson a lot. I found him to be quite humorous. He set you up to get a laugh and then leaned back to see how you handled it. I am not a comedienne or anything like that, so it was helpful. Obviously, he liked the way I handled it. He was always very good with me when I did his show. He was a generous man in that regard.[542]

The tremendous success of *The Poseidon Adventure* brought a new self-confidence to Carol Lynley. At first worried that if the movie was not a hit it was back to television for her; Carol was now thinking she had a chance in copping an Academy Award nomination. She remarked during 1973's awards season, "You see, this is one of Twentieth Century-Fox's biggest pictures this year; so they'll promote it a lot for awards by screening it to the academy members, which means I'll have a better chance for a nomination than actresses who are in movies that aren't big commercial successes."[543] In one or two interviews, she brought up Shelley Winters' previous two Oscar wins in hopes voters decided to share the wealth, so to speak, and nominate a new face (like hers) instead.

When the Academy Award nominations were announced *Poseidon* received eight—cinematography, art direction, sound, song, score, film editing, costume design, and, not surprisingly, one for Shelley Winters as Best Supporting Actress. Lynley and the rest of the cast were overlooked. This was not surprising as Carol did not have that one big moment in the movie. Perhaps if the barber shop scene had not been cut in half by Irwin Allen, it may have helped her chances.

Come Academy Awards night, the film took only two awards—Best Song for "The Morning After" and a Special Achievement Award for Outstanding Special Effects by L.B. Abbott and A.D. Flowers. Inexplicably, *Cabaret* swept all the creative arts categories except costume design only because it did not receive a nomination. *Poseidon* was robbed and arguably deserved recognition for at least cinematography and art direction over the musical. John Williams' exciting and tender score heightened the suspense and should have been recognized with an Oscar as well, but in a fluke lost to Charlie Chaplin for *Limelight*. Made in 1952, it was not released in Los Angeles until 1972.

Lynley and her castmates did receive one award for *Poseidon*. The *Harvard Lampoon* unjustly bestowed a Movie Worst Award for Worst Performance by a Cast in Toto. It was the third time the *Lampoon* recognized her.

Undoubtedly, the one thing *The Poseidon Adventure* brought Carol Lynley was newfound popularity. She explained back then, "A lot of people recognize me in public, which wasn't true before. When I was out on tour with the picture, strangers would come up and talk with me. One woman even patted me affectionately as though she believed I had actually gone through those terrifying experiences on the ship."[544]

The Poseidon Adventure was an immediate blockbuster and easily took *Boxoffice* magazine's Blue Ribbon Award for December 1972, given to the month's biggest movie. It would go on to become the highest grossing movie of 1973. Opening in late December 1972, the movie was still in theaters six months later. Its estimated total domestic gross was $42 million. In 2020 dollars that translates into approximately $252 million. It is credited with starting the disaster movie trend of the seventies. To milk even more dollars from the movie, in a shrewd move by Irwin Allen and 20th Century-Fox, *The Poseidon Adventure* was re-released to theaters for one week only in February 1974. The promotional ad proclaimed, "90,000,000 people have seen 'The Poseidon Adventure' ... If you've only seen it once, you haven't seen it all!" This was to get renewed interest in the film with Allen's preparations for a sequel and to help hype Allen's upcoming disaster movie *The Towering Inferno* (produced jointly by Fox and Warner Bros.) with Paul Newman, Steve McQueen, Faye Dunaway, and William Holden spearheading an all-star cast.

The movie's tremendous success took a lot of people by surprise especially some of the critics who trashed it. One was Bernard Drew who said the movie "aims to be the 'Grand Hotel' of the briny but it settles for being a flophouse." After being taken to task by his friends and readers for his snobbish review, he admitted to being quite tired when he watched the movie, among many, in a screening room during a two-week period in December. Drew then decided to give *Poseidon* another chance and see it this time in a theatre with the paying public. His dislike of the movie did not change but he was fascinated with the reactions of his fellow moviegoers and reported, "I did not find it fun, but I was amused observing the audience reaction. They talked to the actors, they screamed at them, they applauded. Watching this audience watch a screen full of stereotypes react to every trite situation in the most cliché fashion imaginable was wonderous to behold. It enabled me to endure the trash on the screen with far more equanimity than when I had seen in a private screening room filled with critics."⁵⁴⁵ His description sounds like what would become the norm, with future enthusiastic attendees watching the cult rock musical *The Rocky Horror Picture Show* and the teenage slasher films. It seems that even at this early stage, *Poseidon* was developing its own cult audience.

To this day, despite the put downs by some elitist film scholars and critics, *The Poseidon Adventure* remains one of the most popular disaster films of all-time and has a loyal, devoted following especially among men who came of age when it was released. The characters, though stereotypes, pull you right into the movie and you care what happens to all of them. After the eye-popping special effects and stunt work during the capsizing, the adventure begins as the small group of survivors need to climb/crawl/swim their way up to the bottom of the ship specifically the bow ("where the hull is thinnest") as it continues to sink. It is a tense exciting race against time and you root for all the characters to survive. However, in a surprise to audiences of the day and what set the standard for all future disaster movies, the all-star cast is picked off one-by-one sometimes in gruesome, sometimes in heroic fashion until there are only six remaining who climb out of the ship to safety.

The Poseidon Adventure remained so popular that a set from it was recreated at the Movieland Wax Museum located in Southern California. As you made your way through the exhibits, you turned a corner and found yourself in the upside down engine room of the SS Poseidon along with wax figures of Rev. Scott, Mike and Linda Rogo, and Martin and Nonnie. The set was quite realistic as were the replicas, especially Carol's. Reportedly, she was a bit creeped out about this, but it was quite a popular attraction. Unfortunately, the museum closed and all its props were auctioned off in 2006—and the answer is no, Carol did not bid on herself.

Wax figures of Carol Lynley as Nonnie and Red Buttons as Martin at the Hollywood Wax Museum, ca. 1985. *Photo by Tom Lisanti*

Gay men also have an extreme fascination with the movie. Jak Castro, president of the Poseidon Adventure Fan Club, stated that since many saw the movie while facing their sexual identity during puberty, "It was finding out that there were a lot of struggles at that age—about who we were and trying to live with this identity. It kind of made us realize that if they could survive, we could survive."[546] Of course, one of their favorite characters was Nonnie, so Carol was asked several times to make personal appearances at AIDS benefits where the movie would be screened.

The first was on November 19, 1995 when Mark Huestis of the Castro Theatre in San Francisco invited Lynley (and her other female costars) to speak at a screening of the movie to raise money for the San Francisco General Hospital's AIDS Ward. Stella Stevens said no, Pamela Sue Martin did not return any phone calls, and Huestis was not able to reach Shelley Winters. Only Carol agreed and she immediately hit it off with Huestis. Not only was the event sold out, but some audience members even came dressed as their favorite characters. This is where Marlin Dobbs first met his idol. She was radiant in a barely off-white sequin gown with bits of green sparkle and green leaves with squiggly stems throughout designed by her dear friend Paul Zastupnevich especially for the occasion.

Carol admitted at that time, "I didn't want anyone to think this was just a big ego stroke for me. The only reason I wanted to do this is because it seemed like a personal way for me to do something to help fight a very nasty disease."[547]

The Castro screening raised over $100,000. Carol was flabbergasted and confessed, "I was shocked at the frenzy I stirred. I never realized that I had such a gay following. I gave over twenty-five interviews in a span of three days—everything from local gay publications to morning talk shows and evening newscasts."[548]

Carol became friendly with Huestis who remarked in his memoir, "She taught me to always put your best foot forward, be honest, and *try* to be kind."[549] He invited her to participate in a number of events including a joint appearance with *Poseidon* co-star Stella Stevens for another screening, this time in Los Angeles. Carol remarked, "I adore Stella and loved spending time with her. She can be very funny."[550] The actresses even recreated the scene of Linda grabbing and yelling at a panicked Nonnie. The gays were in heaven. Asked why she thinks gay men love her so, Carol opined,

> I don't know what it is but I think it is just wonderful! I have been around gay people my entire life beginning with ballet classes and then attending professional schools. When I modeled a lot of the fashion photographers were gay. I never thought that gay people were particularly different or foreign to me. Gay people are just part of the world. Maybe gay fans picked that up? I really don't know.[551]

Carol Lynley with event organizer Mark Heustis and attendees at *The Poseidon Adventure* screening at the Castro Theatre in San Francisco, 1995.
Photo by Marlin Dobbs

Carol then graduated to making appearances at celebrity conventions where most fans want autographed photos of her from *The Poseidon Adventure*. She joked, "It's the disaster movie that refuses to die. If I even see a part of it, I feel wet all over again."[552]

Reflecting on the rest of some of her cast mates, Carol remarked thirty years later,

> Gene [Hackman] had just won the Oscar, and he was our champion. Stella and I got along great even though she and I are very different people. Jack Albertson taught me how to buck and swing. Jack use to be a tap dancer in vaudeville. Instead of doing hair and makeup, we'd do little vaudeville routines. He was a sweet guy.[553]

Lynley, though, had the most praise for Ernest Borgnine and Roddy McDowall. She said, "Roddy and I were ... kindred souls because we knew each other so well. Roddy was funny and witty and smart and just great. He was wonderful to work with when all hell would break loose ... you'd just look over to Roddy and he'd say, 'Oh well, children will be children. Let's get on with it.'"[554]

With such a bevy of stars trapped working together in such close quarters, it is not surprising that someone would have an off day, especially considering the conditions in which the cast had to film. When asked to give an example of 'all hell is breaking loose,' Carol explained,

> People get tired when you're with each other all the time. People lose their tempers or whatever. There were a few blowouts. It wasn't like a screaming, yelling, knock-down blowout. It was a very crowded situation and we were wet twelve to fifteen hours a day. That fire was real fire. Eventually somebody would get a little cranky, but it was like family.[555]

One family member who rarely talked about *The Poseidon Adventure* or attended any reunions was Gene Hackman. His on-set battles with Shelley Winters were infamous. When asked about her interaction with him, Carol replied,

> You could tell Gene Hackman didn't want to be making *Poseidon* but with me he was always pleasant, friendly, and professional. And yes, he didn't get along with Shelley Winters, but who did? I was on the set when they were filming their underwater scene. It was in a big glass tank. It looks like the camera was underwater but they were outside the tank. At one point, Gene comes out and right over to me. He said, 'Well, she finally did it.' I asked, 'Did what?' He replied, 'She finally tried to kill me!' I thought best not to ask how and just looked concern as he vented.[556]

During her appearance at the 1999 Asheville Film Festival, Carol was asked what she felt about her character Nonnie. She honestly admitted,

> I thought my character a bit of a wimp. I was always saying, '*No, I can't!*' And I'm not like that much as a person—number one. And number two, I'm a very good swimmer. And I just hated saying, '*But I can't swim!*' I hated being afraid all the time … I felt that the other characters were so strong … But it was such a pleasure to be part of the movie that is really crying over spilled milk truly.[557]

In 2005, both NBC-TV and Warner Bros. announced remakes of the classic movie. The cheaper TV-movie, titled *The Poseidon Adventure*, with Adam Baldwin (as Mike Rogo, the only holdover character), Rutger Hauer, and Steve Guttenberg screened first and was a dull time for most watching. In this version, the capsizing of the ship is caused by a terrorist's bomb rather than a tidal wave. Syndicated TV critic Robert Bianco remarked in the *Press & Sun Bulletin,* "Did there really have to be a movie after? What NBC may have forgotten is that our lingering fondness for this *Adventure* has less to do with its merits than with its contribution to the camp pantheon: Carol Lynley lip-synching "The Morning After" in her hot pants; Shelley Winters swimming to her death."

The following year, the highly anticipated theatrical remake of *The Poseidon Adventure,* simply titled *Poseidon,* opened. Reportedly, Carol and Stella Stevens were miffed, and rightly so, that they, and other surviving actors of the original, were not invited to at least make cameos in this updated version. Considering how popular *the Poseidon Adventure* still was, and that the cast was still beloved and big draws at celebrity autograph conventions, the producers should have included them in some capacity. Despite the snub, it did not deter Lynley from attending the premiere of *Poseidon,* along with Red Buttons, Pamela Sue Martin, and Sheila Allen. Although the movie contains eye-popping CGI effects, this is an inferior sequel. None of the actors including Josh Lucas, Kurt Russell, Jacinda Barrett, Richard Dreyfuss, and Emmy Rossum create any memorable characters nor leave a lasting impression unlike in the original. Once it ended, most moviegoers immediately forgot who survived if anyone really cared.

Regarding why the original is much more notable and has such a cult following to this day, Carol opined, "I can't quite explain it, but it just works. They call it campy, which is true, but there wasn't a bad actor there and it's very human ... the action is great. It's about survival which everybody understands, and you get drawn to the characters—even though I played the sappiest one!"[558]

A whole new generation of movie lovers have discovered *The Poseidon Adventure.* Reviewing the movie in 2019 for FilmSchoolRejects.com, Zoe Thomas perfectly summed up the movie and remarked, "Unlike modern disaster films, *The Poseidon Adventure* doesn't include huge moments of showing the actual disaster like the ship being turned upside down. Rather, the film only shows the audience the perspective of the characters being thrown around the ship. Even though this seems just to be the budget-friendly approach, withholding shots of the actual disaster puts more emphasis on the characters being the most important aspect of the story which is why this is one of the greatest disaster films ever made."[559]

This is not to say that the characters in *The Poseidon Adventure* do not have their detractors and not everyone is a fan of "sappy" Nonnie. Today's audiences, new to viewing the movie, can get a bit frustrated with her helplessness (and groan loudly at the screen when she reveals she cannot swim), as did feminists back in 1973. They bemoaned that all the women in the movie are dependent on men throughout. Aljean Harmetz spoke for many when she wrote in the *New York Times* back in 1973 that the movie "degrades its female characters" and save for Belle's heroic underwater swim, "almost nowhere in the film is a woman allowed to help or work together with a man."[560] Nonnie was called out for stereotyping women as feeble creatures who stumble about during a disaster and can only survive with aid from a man.

Though Harmetz raises valid points in her article, it still does not diminish the fans' love of Carol Lynley's touching portrayal of Nonnie and the movie itself. From Facebook fan pages, to web sites, to YouTube tributes, to screenings throughout the country, hearts still go out to Nonnie, who will always have a morning after.

12. Bad Girls, Harried Heroines, and Disaster Divas

1972 proved to be a banner year for Carol Lynley. She began it co-starring in *The Night Stalker* the highest rated made-for-TV movie at the time and ended it with her goal to appear in a big commercial success. She hit the bullseye with *The Poseidon Adventure*. Buoyed by its box office momentum, Carol even placed in the top forty-five actresses in *Boxoffice* magazine's All-American Screen Favorites Poll of 1973. Why then did she not appear in a feature film that year?

With these two hugely popular movies, Carol should have been in high demand and socially she seemed to be. "This is a company town," she stated at the time. "Life suddenly becomes so transformed, so exciting, if you are in a good movie. Everybody loves you. After each screening the phone doesn't stop ringing."[561]

The Poseidon Adventure, however, left Lynley physically and emotionally drained. She was worn out from such a strenuous shoot, being constantly wet and dirty and having to be on set most days. She explained, "Making *The Poseidon Adventure* was exhausting for the cast because we were in almost every scene and each other's scenes even if you had no lines to speak. If it was some other actor's moment, you had to be there even if just a portion of your body got on camera."562 It sounds as if it was both mentally and physically draining.

Things did not get much better after the movie wrapped. Carol admitted to the press in 1972 that she usually gets a bit depressed and melancholy after a shoot comes to an end. Here it was even more so since the cast and crew were together for four months in such close quarters and special bonds were formed. Then she injured herself when she tumbled down a flight of stairs at a friend's house in Topanga Canyon, severely bruising both her legs and her back. She knew she needed psychiatric help and soon was back to normal.563

Carol added, "That summer after we wrapped, I took my daughter and went to Ireland to relax. We spent a couple of months there at my aunt's."564 Ireland was chosen because the actress wanted to connect with her paternal side of the family. Her father, whom she did not have a relationship with, had a serious drinking problem and died almost ten years prior. Carol was intent on learning more about him because "I wanted to get back to my roots to see how I started."565 She continued, "I went to ... visit his family. I've come to know his sister quite well and I have become close to my cousins. But my father remains a mystery to me."566 Daniel also went to meet his relations and relayed that "they were all quite thrilled to have a movie star visiting. Carol became close to our cousin Una who was a stewardess for Aer Lingus. She would come out to LA and Carol would invite her to go to openings and things like that."567

Though Carol was getting closer to her father's relatives at that time, she was still estranged from her mother with no desire to resolve their issues. She confessed in 1973, "We have not spoken in years. I cannot tell you 'why' because that would be an unfair putdown to a woman who could not tell her side of it."568 Being a parent with her own daughter, when asked if she missed that bond with her mother, the actress replied, "You cannot miss something you didn't have. I'm not neurotic about presumed closeness missed. And I certainly don't fantasize and feel sorry for myself. It's simply that I am healthy enough to leave all my senses open and move towards something new without meaningless regrets."569

Carol added, "You might call her a stage mother but she wasn't as bad as the cliché characters you hear about. And she did save my money so I've … been financially independent."[570] Daniel backed this up and revealed that "they had an agreement that when my sister turned eighteen, they would split the money that Carol had in the bank."[571]

Commenting on his mother and sister's estrangement that lasted for their entire lives and how it affected his relationship with Carol, Daniel said. "There was never a falling out between Carol and me. She was still nice to me and I was somewhat in contact with her. When she was living in Malibu Canyon, she threw herself a birthday party and I attended with my first wife. I remember Bobby Darin was there. I think the strain of that relationship or lack of a relationship with our mother tainted her interaction with the rest of the family. She was friendly with our cousins back in Boston but she slowly estranged herself from all of us. I think we made her uncomfortable because she felt she would have to justify her decision to cut off our mother to the rest of us. Maybe in her mind she felt she wasn't doing the right thing—I don't know. I did see both sides of it and felt for Carol's point of view. The last time I talked to her was, I think, in the mid-seventies.

"I just went on with my life," continued Daniel. "I studied photography at Santa Monica City College and would up working at Jet Propulsion Laboratory for twenty-nine years. We did the pictures that would come back from the space craft such as Viking and Voyager. My mother passed away on August 6, 2002 in Redondo Beach. Until she died, if someone brought up Carol she would go on and on about her for hours. She was obsessed with Carol's career. It was the highlight of her life."[572]

With her family out of sight and out of mind, Carol's concentration was solely on *The Poseidon Adventure*. As previously mentioned, beginning in December 1972 and for the next few months, Carol did press interviews and appeared on TV/radio talk shows to promote the movie. When she finally focused back on acting, the Writers Guild strike of 1973 against filmed television programs was in progress and lasted until June 24th. She added at the time, "And by the time that was over, well, it's just taken awhile to get started again."⁵⁷³ Unlike how she took advantage of the buzz she generated with *The Night Stalker* that led to *The Poseidon Adventure*, Lynley did not benefit from the even bigger stir she received from the hit disaster movie. 1973 went by without the actress making a single feature film or made-for-TV movie. Perhaps her notorious interview with Earl Wilson where she lambasted co-star Red Buttons made producers wary of casting her thinking her leading men would feel uncomfortable?

Carol, however, felt the main reason her movie plate remained empty was because of the dearth of good parts for women. She quipped at the time, "Most pictures these days are being cast for ten guys and a whore."⁵⁷⁴ In another interview from this period, she again bemoaned about the lack of meaty roles available for actresses and seemed to be specifically characterizing her role in *The Night Stalker* when she said, "I think women should have equal opportunities to play interesting human beings. A woman is generally stuck in to show that a guy has a tender side."⁵⁷⁵ That described the character of Gail Foster to a tee.

The actress confessed to writer Valerie Clark that she pined for Hollywood's Golden Age when actresses like Katherine Hepburn and Claudette Colbert "played women who said what they thought and felt in snappy, if slightly competitive, dialogue."⁵⁷⁶ Carol added, "The Eisenhower Era killed all that. Donna Reed, June Allyson, and Jane Powell played plain back-in-the-kitchen women."⁵⁷⁷ Carol felt the earlier roles just weren't there in abundance during the sixties and seventies, and the parts offered her "get thinner and thinner."⁵⁷⁸

Holding firm for a strong role in a good dramatic movie, it was reported in the press that Carol was considered for the female leads in *The Man Who Loved Cat Dancing* with Burt Reynolds; *The Great Gatsby* with Robert Redford; and *Day of the Locust*. She claimed, "They were the only decent parts for girls."⁵⁷⁹ Carol failed to get cast. Perhaps out of frustration, she reverted to her strategy of holding out that had landed her *Poseidon*, but this time she did not accept any acting jobs in television as well. Unfortunately, her hopes for another *Poseidon* never materialized.

It is understandable that after appearing in such a massive hit as *The Poseidon Adventure*, Carol wanted to follow it up with a bigger role or a comparable movie. Perhaps she and her agent were aiming too high? When these offers did not come her way, instead of taking the rest of the year off to travel back to Ireland, her focus should have been on getting another genre film. Among 1973 and 1974 releases, one can see Carol essaying the roles played by Yvette Mimieux in *The Neptune Factor*; Pamela Franklin and Gayle Hunnicutt in *The Legend of Hell House*; Leigh Taylor-Young in *Soylent Green*; and, dare it be said, Ellen Burstyn in *The Exorcist* and Katherine Ross in *The Stepford Wives*. Lynley would have given effective performances in any of them and it would have helped keep up the push *The Night Stalker* and *Poseidon* brought her. In Hollywood, you need to strike while the iron is hot, and Carol did not. For all the good press and newfound fame that the movie brought her, Carol unfortunately squandered it all. Considering how she purposely kept herself off the movie screens until a good part surfaced for her in a movie with commercial appeal and then did not take advantage of it, is still mind boggling. Carol did not have the stature in the business to let all this time go by without a follow-up, especially since she touted *Poseidon* as her big comeback.

Explaining why she forsook television as well, she stated at the time, "In effect, this movie has made me a film star all over again. I cannot go back to television, although it paid my bills when there weren't any movies. I want to make a movie about love. Not like *Love Story*, but about a person's ability to love another human being."[580] To remain a film star you have to make *films* and unfortunately Carol didn't. The type of role she coveted on the big screen never surfaced. Television is where she wound up returning and to the suspense and thriller genres where she excelled.

But first with her hair now longer to the middle of her back, Carol booked another photo shoot with Harry Langdon, Jr. He recalled, "With this session we continued using that kind of organic presence but it with a bit more glamour to it, which was very easy for her to portray. This was after *The Poseidon Adventure* had come out and Carol was on a roll at that time. She again brought in her own clothes—nothing fancy. And she came without a publicist or agent or entourage. They really distract the subject from retaining that presence. Carol came solely on her own and that is the best way to shoot someone. We wanted to top ourselves and create something with even more impact and more intrigue than from the first session. It's very challenging. Her presence was worn kind of invisibly, but the camera was able to capture it. It is hard to describe but a lot of wonderful stage actors have that about them. They can just walk on a stage or in front of a camera and make a statement without having to be Hollywood glamorous. I was known for my glamour photos of Joan Collins and Cher but I had to be careful with Carol who didn't need to be flashy or use her hair to get the audience's attention. Carol just threw herself into the camera. In those days I was shooting half with black-and-white film and half with color. Most film actors didn't make much impact in black-and-white. With Carol it was the opposite. In her photos you don't notice there is no color because of the shape of her face and her hair and that special presence she embodied. Later, I started shooting her more in color but she was more powerful in black-and-white."[581]

Langdon then candidly admitted that it was around this time when "one thing led to another and I started dating Carol. We were both single and I had no idea what her personal life was or how complicated it was. She was just this beautiful, vivacious, feminine woman. We just went out to dinner or social events. We began to get very close romantically—or as close as one could get to Carol—because I found out later that she had a busy social schedule with a few different romances. I was just the Bohemian photographer in her life.

"I began to realize the closer I got to her that she threw herself into her roles," continued Harry. "That is what a good actor would do and just become that person they are portraying. I don't think I was ever able to get to know the real Carol Lynley because she was always playing one role or another. When I would take her out, I did not know if I was taking out Carol Lynley or the personality she was portraying at the time. I learned there were times after she finished playing a role she would go out to a retreat on the outskirts of Sherman Oaks. She said it helped her regain her identity again. Some wonderful actors to be convincing on the screen must transform themselves or be possessed by the person they are enacting. Carol would return and be Carol Lynley again for a brief time. I was totally able to relate to Carol's approach because I was consumed with my photography work. Each day I would try to get into my subject's world and try to understand where they are coming from and allow them to be the person they wanted to be in front of the camera. So being involved with Carol, I never really knew where I stood because she too was so involved with her craft. We worked together probably another three times or so into the eighties, but I gave up on a romance with her. It was kind of futile to continue having a relationship."[582]

Workwise, London came a-calling again with an offer of an excellent part that enticed Carol back to the small screen and the UK. She was top billed in "Death of an Old-Fashioned Girl" on the British TV anthology series *Orson Welles' Great Mysteries*, which aired in syndication in the U.S. As with *Journey to the Unknown* and *The Evil Touch*, *Great Mysteries* featured one American star in each episode. It was produced by John Jacobs for ITV and was distributed by 20th Century Fox Television. Each episode was shot on videotape rather than film and featured chilling theme music by John Barry and an introduction by Orson Welles. Carol's episode aired in the U.S. on November 24, 1973. Her delicate beauty was used against type as the true nature of the "old-fashioned girl" begins to emerge as the episode progresses.

Carol appeared on *The Tonight Show Starring Johnny Carson* just before she traveled abroad and told Johnny she was looking forward to meeting Orson Welles. When asked in 2019 if she did, Lynley responded disappointingly, "No, I didn't. The closest I ever came to Orson was seeing him across the room at a restaurant here in LA."[583]

Co-starring with Lynley was an esteemed British cast including Francesca Annis, John Le Mesurier, Jack Shepherd, and leading man Stephan Chase whose prior film credits included *Cry of the Banshee* and Roman Polanski's *Macbeth*. He stated via email that he took the job because the role had an "unusual name. [He was an] artist type—all cool, long hair, and of the times. Also, it was a good TV story."[584]

Carol Lynley as the manipulative Elizabeth Ann Zachary in "Death of an Old-Fashioned Girl" on *Orson Welles' Great Mysteries* (20th Century-Fox Television, 1973).

    Chase had nothing but high praise for his leading lady. He commented, "Carol Lynley does what she's paid for properly to the best of her ability within the constraints of the production—on time and sober. That's professional. She was easy, approachable, intelligent, and attractive, but like other actors has a job to do, particularly as the star of an episode, and was therefore somewhat withdrawn to keep her focus. Chit chat between takes and so on dissipates energy and self. Americans take it seriously. We kind of left Carol alone and I would see her after work walking the Kings Road happily alone. I don't think she needed any of us. Carol had a mix of sexy with a knowing innocence and a curvy little girl. [She was] a kind of Dolly Bird—an American version of it in those times. I certainly enjoyed the experience but didn't think for a second that she might 'consider' me!"[585] Carol was appreciative of the compliment, but sheepishly added, "Sorry I do not remember much about this program. Perhaps if I saw a photo?"[586]

The cast was led by director Alan Gibson who at only thirty-five years old had amassed several credits including the movies *Crescendo*; *Dracula A.D. 1972*; and *The Satanic Rights of Dracula*. He also had worked steadily in television including directing three episodes of *Journey to the Unknown*. Chase remembered, "He was a well-regarded director who worked a lot in the suspense and horror genres. He was easy going and fun. We all got along well. He was a big guy, so he was quietly authoritative and unobtrusive. I'm sure we tried to give Alan what he wanted—can't remember working with him again so maybe he didn't like me? I've gotten better the last few years for sure.""[587]

With regards to his other cast mates, Chase wrote, "Looking back, I liked being paid and rehearsing in Chelsea. With that cast—blessings galore, eh? John Le Mesurier was an old hand and he was effortlessly good. Jack Shepherd was always real and did well on TV. Francesca is a lovely woman. She was good and still works, but maybe she didn't go as far as she had hoped. She'd been at it since a child. I think she could have been bigger on TV, but it's timing and stuff offered and so on."[588]

"Death of an Old-Fashioned Girl" (story by Stanley Ellin and teleplay by Anthony Fowles) opens with an introduction by Orson Welles, looking mountainous wearing a sinister black hat and matching magician's cape with a big cigar in his mouth. He rambles on about how artists are like businessmen dealing with contracts and such as fog swirls around him. He also discusses how they use knives and other sharp objects to trim canvases ("knives, lots of knives … some razor-sharp weapons."). The viewer then sees a glimpse of a knife with what looks like red paint on it but Welles reveals that it is blood.

The story begins with a body lying in the studio of artist Paul Zachery (Stephen Chase). Downstairs he and his remaining party guests are being interviewed by Scotland Yard inspectors. In a flashback, it is revealed that ten years prior Paul was poor and unknown. It was due to his wife Nicole (Francesca Annis) that he was discovered by art dealer Sidney Goldsmith (John Le Mesurier) that took him and fellow artist David (Jack Shepherd) on as clients. A few years later at another successful gallery opening, guest Elizabeth Ann (Carol Lynley) mistakes Paul for David and apologizes claiming, "I'm just an old-fashioned girl. I know nothing about art." As she caresses his shoulder, Nicole spies the interaction. A year later at a party thrown by Nicole, Paul shows up with Elizabeth Ann and Nicole is rightfully furious. Spewing hatred at her husband and insulting Elizabeth Ann, she runs out and Paul is stopped from going after her by his sobbing girlfriend, who plays the wounded, but brave, "other woman." A month after their divorce, Nicole disappears and is found dead of a drug overdose in a hotel room. At the funeral, Elizabeth Ann grieves while Paul's friends glare at her with contempt.

Part two of the episode begins with David telling the inspector how he and his wife came to be at the fateful party. He reveals that Elizabeth Ann took over Paul's life and alienated him from his friends. She even mounted a campaign for Paul to win a prestigious art award by denigrating David. The party was in celebration of Paul's win though he was not in attendance. After all the guests have left except David, his wife, and Goldsmith, the artist confronts Elizabeth Ann about her scheming. She feigns disappointment in David's attitude, but when Goldsmith chides her as well, the claws come out. She confesses that she has convinced Paul to switch dealers saying spitefully, "They are the biggest you know. And some say the best." Goldsmith demands to see Paul, but Elizabeth Ann refuses as Paul won't allow anyone into his studio. They all barge in anyway and are stunned to see his new paintings and drawings of Nicole. All are impressed, except Elizabeth Ann who freaks out. She begins tearing up the drawings ranting, "Remember she's dead. And there is nothing you can do about it. So, stop thinking about her. Stop talking about her. Stop living with her." In a mad rage, she grabs a knife and goes to shred the main canvas, but she does not realize it is made of Masonite - "as smooth and resistant as polished steel" says Orson Welles in the epilogue. The knife bounces right off. She winds up stabbing herself in the gut instead and dies.

Promotional print ad for "Death of an Old-Fashioned Girl" on *Orson Welles' Great Mysteries* featuring Carol Lynley's headshot by Harry Langdon, Jr. Billy Rose Division, The New York Public Library for the Performing Arts

Back in the seventies, critic John McCarty of *Cinefantastique* magazine found most of the series' episodes to be "sluggish and uninteresting, sometimes even hopelessly amateurish in the production values" and found "Death of an Old-Fashioned Girl" to be one of its "low points." Critic Jackie Dyason of *The Stage and Television Today* also did not care for this episode disliking everything from John Barry's score ("an annoying James Bond-type jangle of rhythm"), to the production design ("clumsy colour dissolves in harsh greens and reds, from the men's faces to their memories"), to the story itself ("the undoubted talent of the cast was not exploited in this slight tale … the ending hardly justified this grandiose title.").

Regarding his feelings about the episode, Stephan Chase opined, "I think it was probably quite good for a TV thingy in those days and stylish—certainly watchable with that lot. I'd like to see it again!"[589]

For Lynley fans, this episode makes for a suspenseful half hour keeping the audience guessing who the killer was. Credit must go to director Alan Gibson for keeping the show moving at an entertainingly fast clip. Carol gives a finely tuned performance and wows during the finale. Based on the title and the character describing herself as "an old-fashioned girl," the viewer knows she will be offed and at first is sympathetic. However, Carol slowly reveals Elizabeth Ann's passive aggressive nature and the calculating viper she really is. Her emotional breakdown upon seeing the shrine that her husband has created for his dead first wife is excellent and perhaps one of Lynley's finest hours. Rarely has she played a character with such raw intensity. She also is well-paired with Stephan Chase who excels as the tormented artist. The supporting cast gives the pair strong backup. Though *Orson Welles' Great Mysteries* is forgotten by many, Carol's intense performance is truly a standout amongst her genre credits.

*****

At the end of 1973, Carol was hit hard again with the untimely death of a dear friend. This time it was Bobby Darin with whom she developed a close relationship. They were even Malibu neighbors for a time and author Al DiOrio recounted in his biography on the singer, "One afternoon, she [Carol Lynley] found him sitting on her porch playing the guitar. He was very depressed and seemed somehow preoccupied. He told her that he would be dying in two years, and that he was going away for a while."[590]

When Darin passed a few years later as he predicted, Carol was living at the Chateau Marmont and was devastated by his death. She said,

> He loved the ocean, and he loved Malibu, so I rented a hotel room there and I couldn't stop crying. I was laying out on the balcony. You know when you cry so much you get sleepy; at least I do. I was just lying there, and a seagull came down, very close, and I looked at it. Oh my God, it's Bobby's eyes. Bobby had these fantastic eyes. They weren't pretty, he wasn't a pretty guy, but they were lively. They took in everything.[591]

Beginning in 1974 and for the rest of the decade through the mid-eighties, Carol still played the terrorized lady in peril (*If It's a Man, Hang Up!*; *Flood*; *The Cat and the Canary*; various episodes of *Fantasy Island*; *In Possession*) in the thriller, fantasy, and suspense genres, but several of her other beleaguered heroines had more nuance. For instance, some had ulterior motives and were not as innocent as they seemed (*The Evil Touch*; *Tales of the Unexpected*). Others showed strength in times of danger by trying to take charge of the situation and fight back (*Death Stalk*; *The Beasts Are on the Streets*; *The Shape of Things to Come*). Also, Carol was not limited to these genres and was still landing diverse types of parts in movies and on television dramas and police shows.

The year started out for the actress with a high-profile guest role as the damsel in distress in a two-part episode of the adventure series *The Magician* starring Bill Bixby. Universal Television then offered two made-for TV movies the first being the suspenseful *The Elevator* about a disparate group of people (including *Poseidon* cast mate Roddy McDowall and screen legend Myrna Loy) trapped in a high-rise elevator with a claustrophobic, armed thief (James Farentino). Carol played his desperate girlfriend trying to free him with the help of an accomplice who inadvertently starts a fire, making matters even worse.

But first to air was one of her *Evil Touch* episodes she did back in 1971. *The Evil Touch* was like the British series, *Orson Welles Great Mysteries*. Instead of Welles introducing the story, here it was Anthony Quayle in a blueish fog-mist room. As with *Great Mysteries*, to attract an audience in the U.S., an American actor was usually the featured guest star in each episode. However, this series was filmed rather than videotaped and it was shot in Sydney, Australia and produced by prolific American radio pioneer Mende Brown, a.k.a. Himan Brown, who went into television during the fifties when he purchased Adolph Zukor's Famous Players Studio in New York City. Per Brown, *The Evil Touch* was an NBC production in conjunction with Amalgamated Pictures.[592] However, when the series finally made it to the U.S. it did not air on the Peacock network and instead went into syndication. It aired in the New York metropolitan area at 10:30 p.m. on Sunday nights on ABC-TV beginning in the fall of 1973. Carol's first of two episodes (shot back in 1971) did not air until January 1974 and then her second one in March.

A reporter, Gloria Braxton, from *The Australian Women's Weekly* visited the set during shooting of the second episode "Death by Dreaming." She described Mende Brown as being "tall, lithe, with snowy white hair and an affable yet dynamic manner."[593] They were shooting a scene in an old mansion and Brown remarked, "Wonderful old house …We saw this passing by one day, and came in and asked the owner if we could use it—at a price—and he said, yes, why not?"[594]

Seeing Carol Lynley sitting in a corner eating a piece of ham, Braxton wrote that she was wearing "an old-fashioned lace mobcap, a midi-length velvet skirt, and a thirties satin blouse."[595] Responding to her wardrobe, Carol stated,

> My cap? It's a dusting cap. In the old days, maids wore them to keep the dust out of their hair. I picked it out of a barrel full of old things in a San Francisco shop. They told me it was the late 1890s vintage. This skirt and blouse I got in some place in

London. I just love funky clothes. I gave up the ordinary kind two years ago. I buy clothes that go right back to the Victorian age. They had such beautiful materials in those days.[596]

In "Death by Dreaming," Carol played the dual role of a good sister and her ill-fated wild sister. The day of this shoot, Carol had scenes playing both parts. One sister had Carol's natural look while the other required a wig. When Braxton asked her if she found it difficult to play, the actress replied, "You've got to keep concentrating all the time. Especially when you do the end of one scene before the beginning. But you get used to it after a while."[597]

"Dear Cora, I'm Going to Kill You…" aired before "Death by Dreaming" and is the far better of the two episodes. It was directed by Mende Brown from a teleplay by Michael Fisher.

Carol Lynley, still in her long-haired hippie-look period, is perfectly cast as a popular but controversial print and radio advice columnist named Cora Blake. Is the angelic-looking Cora a fine upstanding lady as insisted by friends or "a gum-snapping, hard-nosed broad" as described by Lt. Brennan (Dennis Clinton), a police detective who is investigating the death of her husband? Carol always excelled as the bewildered, harangued lady-in-peril and here she is at her best, but is Cora as innocent as she pretends to be?

Cora's husband perished when somebody wired four sticks of dynamite to the ignition in his car right under the watchful eyes of the police department. Cora is terrified because she knows that the killer intended it for her, as she received three death threats in the mail. The first two letters she discarded, but when she received the third, she called the police who put the husband and wife into protective custody, but that did not stop the killer from booby-trapping the car.

After the burial, Cora is questioned once again by Brennan who becomes frustrated with the widow who cannot (or will not?) remember what the first two notes said. Then when he brings up her affair with family friend Harry Winston (Bruce Barry), her lady-like ways go out the window as she goes to slap him, but he catches her wrist. She calms down and explains that she was lonely because her husband traveled out of the country a lot, but the affair was short-lived and she realized that she genuinely loved her spouse.

Despite advice from the detective and her friends, Cora, wanting to "escape the nightmare," decides to disappear for a while. She retreats to her brother's rustic-looking house high up on the bluffs overlooking the sea. The bikini-clad columnist spends a quiet day just strolling on the beach and swimming in the ocean. At night, Cora settles down by a roaring fire with a pile of mail. As she reviews letters sent in by fervent readers, she nonchalantly pulls a revolver out from her purse and sets it on the table as she tapes her latest column. Her idyllic time is ruined when she receives a letter that states, "By the sea, by the sea, by the beautiful sea. You are going to die! Die! Die!" Shaken, she calls her former lover Harry. She tells him the letter was post marked two days before. He then convinces Cora that it is a coincidence since she only decided to go to the beach house that morning, but he promises to be there in an hour.

After Cora hangs up, she gets a phone call from a man who repeats what was in the letter. A terrified Cora tries to call the police, but the phone line goes dead. She then runs to her car, but it will not start. Back in the house, someone tries to break in with an ax as the lights go out. Cora runs screaming into the night and runs right into Harry. Escorting her back inside, Harry tries to calm Cora down. Rattled, she reveals that she sent the prior letters to herself and murdered her husband just to be with Harry, but now someone is really trying to kill her. Just then the lights go on and Lt. Brennan emerges. He had suspected Cora all along and now had the proof he needed thanks to Winston's help. Cora breaks down and says to Harry she did it all for him.

"Dear Cora, I'm Going to Kill You..." is nicely photographed at many picturesque locations including the beach scenes with Lynley fans getting a treat to see her in a bikini, which she rarely donned during the seventies. The episode itself is fast-paced and highly suspenseful keeping the viewer guessing to the end. Cora's paramour Harry is the prime suspect, so the twist ending is truly a surprise. Carol, looking so lovely, does a fantastic job in not giving away her character's true motives though the attempted slap of Brennan reveals that dear Cora is capable of violence. Anthony Quayle's epilogue is amusing as he informs the viewer that Cora is headed for prison and wraps up by asking, "Dear Cora, I wonder if there is someplace where *you* can write for advice?" before he ends with his weekly sign-off, "And so until next we meet, this is Anthony Quayle reminding you that there is a touch of evil in all of us. Good night."

Eydie (Carol Lynley) is comforted by Sgt. Parker (Owen Weingott) after discovering the truth of her sister's demise in "Death by Dreaming" on *The Evil Touch* (20th Century-Fox Television. 1974).

In "Death by Dreaming," Lynley once again played a character with psychic visions of murder. But unlike the first-rate "Dear Cora" episode, this one directed by Mende Brown and written by Mel Goldberg and Arthur H. Singer is disappointing and shoddily produced.

The episode opens with a montage of clips from Brooklyn's Coney Island and then scenes of young people dancing at a discothèque. An image of Carol Lynley wearing a white knit hat and white satin blouse and black skirt moving her arms back and forth awkwardly to the music is super imposed over the footage. Then it cuts to a white car pulling up to the curb. Lynley's character Eydie, newly arrived in town, is in the passenger seat and as she hugs her date good night, she has a vision of a young man with longish hair and a mustache standing over a woman dead on a bed. She jumps out of the car and bounds up the stairs to her home. Calling out the name "Norma," she runs into her bedroom, only to find the woman dead, just like in her premonition. As Eydie screams, the screen fades to host Anthony Quayle.

"A fascinating example of woman's intuition," Quayle states. "Or was it more than that? That frightening sixth sense that one can never quite prove—anyway I wish I had it. It would be quite pleasant to have advanced viewing of the demise of one's enemies. That way you can enjoy the experience twice. Don't you agree?" With that sinister suggestion the episode that fades to the opening credits.

Eydie is convinced her sister was murdered. Sergeant Parker (Owen Weingott) thinks Norma, who had a rap sheet of drug arrests, accidentally died of an overdose, which the autopsy supports. Eydie then gets close to her sister's sometime lover, rock star Hank (Sandy Harbutt), by pretending she is a reporter doing a story about groupies. She notices the medallion he is wearing was the same one Norma had. That night Hank breaks into her apartment and tries to strangle Eydie. She screams and he flees. Parker is skeptical of the story but says they will investigate. Convinced Hank is the killer; she dons a wig and pretends to be Norma. The singer is relieved that she is alive and confesses he did not mean to kill her when he administered the drug over her protestations. When Eydie removes her wig and accuses him of murder, he begins to strangle her. Luckily, Det. Parker arrives and throws him off. Hank stumbles and crashes through a window, falling to his death.

As he puts Eydie into a cab, the detective says he believes that she had some sort of premonition about Norma's death, but that Hank never broke into her apartment. They have proof he was on stage performing at that time. Obviously, Eydie had yet another premonition about her sister's fate.

While "Dear Cora" had twists and turns, "Death by Dreaming" is a standard, run-of-the-mill whodunit despite the addition of Eydie's sixth sense. The leading actors are dull and even the production values here are much inferior. The silliest scene is when Lynley as Eydie is shown walking and super imposed over stock footage of pedestrians on the streets in New York City. Obviously, it was the producer's attempt (unsuccessful as it was) to make the U.S. audience think the show was filmed here rather than Australia.

Carol looks lovely still in her hippie period (though dressed more demurely with simple blouse and skirts or a mini dress), but it was not an acting stretch for her in the least. The less-than-suspenseful script does not give her any meaty scenes to play and the dénouement is not surprising. Probably her best scene comes at the end where in flashback she plays a strung-out Norma. Not wanting to party anymore, she is forced to by Hank, who accidentally kills her when he shoots her up with heroin.

Perhaps due to it being a low-budget syndicated series, *The Evil Touch* was dumped into a late Sunday night timeslot. It was rarely reviewed by mainstream TV critics of the day and was cancelled after a single season.

Years after it had gone off the air, *The Evil Touch* found favor with horror aficionados. One of the first reference books to mention it was *Fantastic Television* by Gary Gerani and Paul H. Schulman. They described the series as being a "bizarre and unintentionally campy horror-fantasy-sci-fi anthology … on a shoestring budget. It featured well-known American actors … in decidedly morbid teleplays." Writing in the 2001 book *Terror Television*, author John Kenneth Muir commented, "For all its obvious cheapness, *The Evil Touch* is a strangely effective horror anthology. It is unabashedly low-budget, and it tends to go for gut-wrenching visceral horror rather than the more intellectual brand ... Nevertheless, *The Evil Touch* is a powerful and frightening entry in the Valhalla of modern horror television." Despite the renewed respect, *The Evil Touch* is still unavailable on DVD or Blu-Ray as of 2020.

*****

In between the airings of her *Evil Touch* episodes, Carol's appearances in the series *The Magician* and the TV-movie *The Elevator* were broadcast. *The Magician* was a well-received action-adventure TV series with a fantasy twist. Bill Bixby starred as Tony Blake, who was falsely accused of a crime and spent time in a South American jail. He escaped with another man who died and left his fortune to Tony, who became an illusionist. Blake's experience in prison haunts him, and he cannot refuse people in trouble who seek him out for help. A non-violent action-adventure series, Bixby had high hopes for it because his character "never carries a gun, a knife or any other weapon. He almost never uses physical force, but he can be completely intimidating with prestidigitation, sleight of hand and the sudden, unexplained appearance of fire."[598]

When Lynley guest starred, the series had undergone some revamping after a short hiatus. Her episode was the first to have Tony living in a grand apartment (his former home was a Boeing jetliner) atop a club called The Magic Castle run by his friend (Joe Sirola). This was a real-life club for magicians and was the first time it granted permission for a TV series to film there. It was a way to integrate more magic into the show and highlight other magicians in the process. The NBC show was also moved from its Tuesday 9:00 p.m. timeslot to Monday at 8:00 p.m. to try to attract younger viewers.

Magician Anthony Blake (Bill Bixby) helps his ex-girlfriend Janet Keegan (Carol Lynley) who is being threatened by the mob in "The Case of the Curious Counterfeit" on *The Magician* (Paramount Television, 1974).

The Magician was well-liked because of the way it incorporated magic into what was a typical seventies adventure series giving it an interesting edge. The always likable Bill Bixby, an amateur magician in real-life, performed his own illusions and was coached by Mark Wilson, one of the world's top magicians at that time. Bixby also promised never to reveal magicians' secrets—a vow he upheld. No trick photography was used for any of the magic tricks performed, and the producers touted that at the beginning of each episode with the announcement, "All of the magic you are about to see is performed, without trick photography of any kind, by Bill Bixby, the Magician."

In the two-part episode, "The Case of the Curious Counterfeit," Carol played Janet Keegan, the Magician's former flame. She escaped from some thugs, who broke into her studio and tried to kidnap her. Instead of going to the police, she runs to Blake, her old beau, whom she has not seen in years. Her dear ol' dad (Lloyd Nolan) used to be a big shot racketeer, and his rival Paul Gunther (John Colicos) wants his help to pull off a counterfeit bank note job, but he refuses to participate. Janet is the key to his cooperation.

Tony agrees to protect her when she will not stay at her estranged father's house. While he is performing his magic act on stage, Janet is followed up to his apartment and snatched. She is held at an abandoned prison where Tony attempts to free her but is thwarted. Injured, he flees, and a contract is put out on his life. With the help of his assistant (Jerry Watkins), he outsmarts the female assassin hired to snuff him out and with a grand illusion makes the gang's henchman (L.Q. Jones) think he is dead. Tony is then able to tail the gang, with Janet in tow, to the bank. Captured again, the idiotic thugs bind Tony's hands, but he escapes in a flash. He then foils their operation and rescues Janet in the process. Tony's final good deed is to reunite father and daughter.

"The Illusion of the Curious Counterfeit," directed by Sutton Roley, is fast-moving and action-filled—what you expect from this type of series. John Colicos is menacing, and Lloyd Nolan is equally good as the reformed mobster. As for Lynley, she basically has a role like the one she played in *Crosscurrent*—the estranged daughter, with daddy problems, who is victimized due to her parentage. Instead of a schoolteacher, here she is a sculptress. It was the type of role Carol always excelled at. Though the script does not provide any heavy emotional scenes, Carol gives a credible performance as the befuddled Janet not sure why she is being victimized. Working once again with Bill Bixby, they have a nice chemistry and make a handsome couple. It is too bad the episode ends with them toasting their friendship, killing any chance of a developing relationship. The series was cancelled after only one season.

Airing shortly after *The Magician* was *The Elevator* (1974) directed by Jerry Jameson from a teleplay by David Ketchum and Bruce Sheeley. The movie was filmed entirely on location at the Crocker Bank Plaza in downtown Los Angeles with an all-star cast including James Farentino, Myrna Loy, Roddy McDowall, and Teresa Wright. A claustrophobic thief is trapped in a stuck elevator on the thirty-second floor along with a disparate group of strangers with the car's cables slowly coming undone. This was one of many made-for-TV suspense movies made during the seventies that threatened a disaster that never happens due to the limited small screen budgets. Nevertheless, it is, surprisingly, an above average tale featuring a game cast and some witty dialog. And unlike others of its ilk from the time, the film does not get bogged down with boring flashbacks as the characters' fates hang in the balance.

During the making of the movie, Carol had one of the worst working experiences of her life due to co-star James Farentino. She explained,

> Jimmy Farentino didn't like me and I never knew why. Sometimes people have fantasies about you because of the work you've done or the people they know who know you. He was strange and I realized right away of his dislike for me, but I was okay with that and thought it would be no problem. He must have pushed a button with me. We were in a car and had a walkie-talkie connected to the AD who was monitoring the traffic. Jimmy and I got into an argument—what it was about I have absolutely no idea. I made sure the walkie-talkie was turned on so I had some proof of what was going on in the car. I am Irish

and I do have a temper. I think I lost my temper. He was Italian and he lost his temper. He then went to strike me and I ducked luckily because he is a strong guy. I come from New York City and not from the best of neighborhoods. Nobody takes a swing at me.

We finished shooting the scene and I got out. At this time, I am furious because I just was not used to people behaving badly and I don't take it very well. I am steaming mad and I walked over to where the other actors were. I see Roddy McDowall and Myrna Loy. I am frothing at the mouth as I went up to them. Roddy could tell something was wrong. I look over and Myrna looks like she wants to die. I thought, 'Oh, God this is terrible. I am behaving like an idiot in front of Myrna Loy!' I was so embarrassed and started to apologize to her."[599]

Every story has two sides, but is surprising to learn of Farentino's bizarre, inexplicable behavior. Perhaps he was good friends with Red Buttons? He was lucky that Carol did not report him to the director or the Screen Actors Guild. She reasoned, "Sometimes an actor's personal life can trigger things and that's the only reason I could think that caused Jimmy to go off. But after that happened, I kept my distance from him and always made sure there was somebody around. He was fine afterwards—it was weird. I just did what I had to do, the best that I could and didn't linger."[600] Farentino is quite lucky that his co-star was understanding and gave him the benefit of the doubt.

In *The Elevator*, Carol Lynley is Irene Turner, not one of the elevator passengers but the girlfriend and accomplice of jittery thief Eddie Holcomb (James Farentino). While driving towards a mixed-use office building still under construction, they lay out their robbery plan. He and his tough guy partner Pete (Don Stroud) go in and rob a company (that they have been staking out) after they receive their armed guard delivery of over $100,000. However, the theft goes awry, and the owner is shot and killed by Pete. Due to workers using the passenger elevator to deliver a 700-pound safe rather than the freight elevator, Eddie, with the briefcase of stolen money, gets on the elevator but Pete does not due to insufficient room. The added weight strains the elevator's bolts and they burst after the workers roll the safe off, sending the cab careening down a few floors It gets stuck in the section of the building that is still under construction. With the start of the Christmas holidays, the building is vacant except for the few security guards many floors below.

Promotional print ad for *The Elevator*. Billy Rose Theatre Division, The New York Public Library for the Performing Arts

Trapped with a panicky Eddie are a philandering Dr. Stuart Reynolds (Craig Stevens); his suspicious wife (Teresa Wright); his receptionist/girlfriend (Arlene Golonka); a slick real estate agent (Roddy McDowell); his wealthy chatterbox client (Myrna Loy); a greedy rich teenage boy (Barry Livingston); and his over protective mother (Jean Allison). Things go from bad to worse for the passengers when they discover that the alarm button is disconnected and that the emergency phone was never installed. A hyperventilating Eddie then loses it brandishing a gun and demanding to be set free. During a scuffle, his briefcase drops and the money scatters on the floor as the passengers realize it was stolen.

In typical Carol Lynley casting fashion, her thief is a clueless, puzzled one. Irene only agreed to drive the getaway car so she and Eddie could start a new life together. When Pete shows up without her boyfriend, he keeps her in the dark about the murdered man while she is in a panic to find Eddie. They are forced to leave the building by a security guard but break back in through the parking garage. When they establish that Eddie must be stuck in the elevator, Irene is determined to free him and cares less about the money unlike Pete. As they make their way up, a security guard has discovered the murdered man and calls it in to the police before being shot dead by Pete. Irene is a bit aghast of what Pete did, but quickly gets over it as rescuing her man from that elevator is her number one priority. They find Eddie and throw down a firehose to him so he can climb up. Pete then begins cutting the elevator's cables to finish off the passengers. Eddie tries to stop him but is thrown down the shaft landing on top of the elevator making it drop a few feet as bolts burst from the wall. Pete is killed by the police trying to escape while an injured Eddie climbs out again. He and Irene flee down a stairwell with the police in pursuit but come to a locked emergency door with a sign that ironically reads, "Closed use elevator." As for the passengers, they escape with help from the police seconds before the elevator plunges to the bottom.

ABC-TV promoted the hell out of the movie that was set to premiere on the *ABC Saturday Suspense Movie*. Full page ads ran in *TV Guide* and other magazines, but it was not enough to draw a big audience. The ratings were disappointing as it scored a 14.0 rating and a 22 share. For the 1974-75 made-for TV movie ratings rankings, it came in at a lowly 149th place.

Surprisingly, TV critics who usually dismissed the all-star, almost-disaster TV-movie, were kind to *The Elevator*. The *TV Scout* column, which was syndicated in many newspapers, found that "it grips you" and "the end is agonizing suspense." Percy Shain of the *Boston Globe* liked it even more and called it "a crackerjack crime yarn ... well-conceived and tautly played." Today, this TV-movie is long forgotten and rarely televised but worth a look for the actress' fans if found on DVD.

*****

Carol finally accepted her first movie role since *The Poseidon Adventure* when she was cast as thirties mobster Jack Palance's gun moll, who finds herself attracted to a reporter, in the slapdash misfire *The Four Deuces*. It was a belated re-entry into features for the actress and the publicity *Poseidon* brought her had long since waned. Explaining why she took this part, Carol said, "I play a heroine and that's nice. There aren't many parts for heroines anymore. I play the richest, most beautiful, most intelligent girl in the world."[601] Not sure how Carol came to this conclusion about her role considering what transpired on screen but on paper she must have considered it a worthy part. Per her definition at the time, "A good role is when a woman gets to do something! A bad role is playing the part of the main character's girlfriend or wife. He gets to do great things and comes home and tells her about it."[602]

Another reason Carol accepted the offer was because she got to design her own wardrobe. She stated, "They gave me a couple of thousand dollars and a woman who sews and really let me have a ball."[603] Her costumes ranged from a skintight, strapless, lowcut, silver lame evening gown, to a white pantsuit complete with matching fedora, to a typical thirties' high waisted skirt with matching jacket. All were beautifully tailored for her.

The Four Deuces began principal photography on March 18, 1974 at Culver

City Studios and various Los Angeles locations. The producers took out a full-page ad in *Variety* that same month hyping the movie thinking they had something special here. Lynley received a lot of press while making *The Four Deuces* due to a nude lovemaking scene. The hubbub was much-ado-about-nothing, as what appeared on screen was quite tame. Carol remarked, "I'm not really nude at all. When they shot it, I wore bikini pants and pasties—big pasties. I won't do a totally nude scene—at least, not in this picture. Maybe, if Zeffirelli asked me."[604]

After the shoot ended, Carol stated, "I really enjoyed this role because it gave me a chance to play a matured woman instead of the ingénue type."[605] Her character is no damsel in distress as she romances a mob boss, cheats on him with a reporter, stands up to her kidnappers, and then breaks up with the mobster even after he rescues her.

The Four Deuces was directed by novice William H. Bushnell, Jr. (only his second movie after the little-seen *Prisoners*) and produced by Menahem Golan and Yoram Goblus for AmeriEuro Pictures before they founded The Cannon Group later in the decade. It was a violent gangster yarn that tried to mix comic book humor with slam-bang action. It just did not work. Looking like she did in *Harlow* but with a less flattering wig and much less makeup, Carol's Wendy is the girlfriend of gangster Vic Morono (Jack Palance) owner of a speakeasy called The Four Deuces. She finds herself caught in the middle of her man's gangland feud with rival Chico Hamilton (an over-the-top Warren Berlinger trying to ape Cagney but missing by a mile). While Vic concentrates on his feud, Wendy falls for handsome reporter Russ Timmons (Adam Roarke), an F. Scott Fitzgerald wannabe, who is shadowing Morono for a story. He is astounded on seeing the gangland violence first-hand. In response to his disgust, Carol as Wendy gets to spout dialog like, "If you would bother to look beyond that stuffed shirt of yours, I think you would find things are not as sordid as you think." All-in-all, it is not worth the bother to find out especially since the film features an icky sex scene with the actress and Palance.

The Four Deuces received a limited release in the U.S. by distributor Avco

Embassy in the late summer and fall of 1975. Its tagline read, "The wicked wacky thirties ... Where Bonnie & Clyde, Dillinger and Capone left off ... The Four Deuces took over and the uproar started." In some areas it was put on the top of a double bill with another gangster movie *Lucky Luciano* starring Rod Steiger. The few newspaper notices mostly agreed the film was mediocre but were conflicted regarding Lynley. The reviewer in *Boxoffice* commented that the film "attempts to spoof gangster life ... the story contains no suspense and seems to rely on largely nonexistent humor." They did go on to praise Carol and said she "performs well in her role." Malcolm L. Johnson of *The Hartford Courant* remarked, "*The Four Deuces* tries to parody gangster movies, but after a promising start it sags into a routine and mostly unfunny reprise of the old clichés. It's a shoddy-looking piece of work." He did praise the comic book-style titles by David McMacken done in the manner of Chester Gould (creator of the *Dick Tracy* comic) that open the movie and carry throughout. Regarding Carol, he added, "Though she's now 33 and all grown up, she still blurts out her lines like a little girl."

Johnson also mentions the bad photography by Stephen Katz with many shots having a blue cast to them. Reportedly, the producers liked the effect first used in their movie *Lepke*, but here it just makes the poor production values look even sleazier.

It is head scratching to think this film was the best Carol could muster after appearing in the top grossing movie of 1973. As an actor it is understandable that she wanted to stretch and play something different, but this was a bad choice. One wonders what her agent was thinking to recommend this.

When speaking of agents, Carol mentioned she only had a few and remained overly loyal to them over the years. This was not a good strategy for an actress, especially if the agent is not delivering, or offering bad advice. They were probably part of the reason she did not hit super stardom.

Although she wanted to handle her affairs herself, Carol was resigned that she needed a male agent to negotiate on her behalf because of the studios' old boys' network. She stated at the time, "Talking money with a woman freaked them out. They could never quite work out what I was doing in their office.

Was I there to make an offer to them sexually? Did they have to proposition me? I was incapable of functioning."[606]

Carol reaffirmed that she said this and added, "It was all a man's world and a woman was not taken seriously. So, I had male agents and managers to work out the details for me."[607]

It was most likely due to *The Four Deuces* that Carol and Jack Palance began being credited as starring in *Godzilla vs. The Cosmic Monster* (a.k.a. *Godzilla vs. Mechagodzilla*) that came out the same year. It seems one publication, perhaps the *TV Guide*, mistakenly tied their names to it when it aired on television and other publications began to follow suit. Many Godzilla buffs have since stated after seeing many cuts of this movie that the duo is nowhere to be found.

*****

Carol next returned to the small screen with one of her best made-for-TV movies *Death Stalk*, based on the novel of the same name by Thomas Chastain, and in the vein of the hit movie *Deliverance*. A solid cast (Lynley, Vince Edwards, Vic Morrow, Anjanette Comer, Robert Webber, Norman Fell, Neville Brand, and Larry Wilcox pre-*CHiPs*), directed by Robert Day, braved the dangerous rapids of the Stanislaus and Tuolumne Rivers in the High Sierras near Sonora, California in this exciting saga. Ruthless escaped convicts take the wives of two vacationing San Francisco businessmen hostage in a desperate move to escape the authorities in hot pursuit.

Carol was excited to take this part and make this movie. Her character, though a lady in peril, has some backbone. She wants to fight back against the convicts who have kidnapped them, especially at the end of their journey knowing what their fate would be. Doing her own river rafting stunts did not deter her in the least and was the reason she eagerly wanted to do this. She enthusiastically revealed, "I am a water baby. My grandparents in Boston lived by the ocean and I would swim there every summer. I also like boating. I always loved being in and around water."[608]

VHS cover art for *Death Stalk* (1975) with pictured Carol Lynley, Robert Webber, Vince Edwards, Vic Morrow, and Neville Brand.

Carol's fervor for being on the water though caused a ripple and she explained,

> When we took the rapids for the first time, we really *took* rapids. The director yelled, 'Cut!' and we all piled out of the boats. We were then told we had to do it again. We got in the car and they drove us back up to where we had to start out from. As we climbed back into the rafts, Vic Morrow got angry with me and yelled, 'Don't ever do that again!' I said, 'Do what?' He said, 'You do know why we are doing the rapids again?' I replied, 'No, why?' He said, "You were smiling the whole time!' He wasn't happy about it. But I thought, 'Oh, my God!' When we started going over the rapids for my first time, I loved it but I didn't realize it was showing on camera. When we shot it the second time, I bit my tongue so I would look like I was in pain.[609]

Though Vic Morrow was upset with Carol, none of the others seemed to mind including director Robert Day whom Carol said, "Had a good sense of humor about it."[610] Among the other actors, Carol had the most praise for Anjanette Comer and exclaimed,

> Anjanette was great! The guys had a dressing room and they put us in the wardrobe trailer to change our clothes. I got to know her and found her to be very ethereal. I mean that in a wonderful way. It is not a quality you find in actors very much.[611]

Death Stalk opens with a jail break. It then intercuts shots of four convicts on the run with two couples on a river rafting camping trip. Pushed to climb the corporate ladder, mild-mannered Jack Trahey (Vince Edwards) agrees to ride the rapids with his obnoxious boss Hugh Webster (Robert Webber) despite the dangers of the rushing river he has selected. Accompanying them are Trahey's supportive wife Pat (Anjanette Comer) and Webster's younger trophy wife Cathy (Lynley). Their journey intersects with the prison escapees—the leader Brunner (Vic Morrow), older Cal Shepherd (Norman Fell), brutish Frank Cody (Neville Brand), and young naïve Roy Joad (Larry Wilcox). They surprise the couples while they are camped for the night. In the morning, they tie up the husbands and go off with their two rafts and wives. Cathy plays it aloof being stuck in a raft with creepy Cody, but Pat begins to develop a rapport with rugged, dangerous Brunner to stay alive. Meanwhile, their husbands free themselves and pursue the convicts in a third supply raft that was hidden. Their trek is full of quarreling resulting in egomaniac Webster firing Jack, who is grateful that he can now be free of this pompous ass.

While camped overnight, Joad lets it slip where the cons are headed in the earshot of Cathy who asks, "You're taking us to Canada?", sealing the ladies' fates. Knowing the cons are going to kill the wives to keep them quiet, Joad concocts a plot for them to escape. However, he is caught by Brunner trying to cut the rope holding one of the rafts. They scuffle and Joad hits his head on a rock and dies.

Pat realizes the only way they are going to stay alive is if they give themselves freely to the horny cons. She advises a reluctant Cathy to "just close your eyes and you'll think he's just another lush from the country club." Cathy is aghast at the thought of allowing Cody anywhere near her, let alone touch her. An indignant Pat then says it will be much easier for Cathy since she has had many a cheap affair, while Pat has been the dutiful wife whose only lover has been her husband.

Cody spots the husband's raft in pursuit and a rifle-toting Cal is sent to pick them off. He shoots Jack in the arm and the men paddle their way behind a rock. Jack hides behind the raft and under the water as it drifts. When a cautious Cal paddles over to it, Jack jumps out from the opposite side and pulls him into the raging river drowning him. When Webster is too cowardly to continue their trek, Jack shames him into the raft.

Pat again suggests that Cathy give in to Cody. The blonde then realizes that Pat is sexually drawn to Brunner and remarks, "Can't you face the truth even now? I know what men like Brunner are like. They're animals." This still does not deter Pat's attraction to the escaped convict. Reaching their destination, Pat gives herself willingly to Brunner while Cody takes Cathy into the woods. The scene builds with intensity as Brand perfectly plays the gross brute to Lynley's intended victim who still has some fight in her. With a look of anguish on her face, Cathy is slowly trailed by the brute. He pulls his knife and tells her to stop as he caresses her face. Disgusted, she pulls away and makes a run for it, unlike misguided Pat. Cody makes a game of it and gleefully chases after Cathy. He slaps her to the ground and she gives up. Thinking he can now have his way with her, he throws his knife on the ground. As Cody gets on top of her, Cathy reaches for the blade and stabs him violently in the back. He rolls off dead.

Meanwhile, Jack finally catches up to the group and sees his wife gently kissing Brunner under a tree. With the gun pointed at him, Brunner surrenders. Cathy emerges from the brush. Pat sidles up to her husband, but he displays no emotion toward her while Cathy goes to her weak husband's side. The movie ends on this note without a word spoken between the characters. It leaves the viewer to ponder the fates of these couples, especially Jack and Pat's, with her obvious attraction to her captor exposed.

Death Stalk was scheduled for airing during Thanksgiving week in 1974. However, NBC-TV received pushback for the adult nature of the program and, despite the money they put into advertising, re-scheduled it to air on January 21, 1975. Print ads proclaimed, "Suspense! It starts when four desperate convicts take two couples hostage. Builds when they carry off the women. Explodes when the women face their most secret feelings—and their men face the convicts' fury!" In a bit of creative billing, Carol Lynley was billed second behind Vince Edwards and before "Anjanette Comer as Pat Trahey." Vic Morrow was "Special Guest Star" with Neville Brand, Norman Fell, and Robert Webber listed as co-stars. Larry Wilcox did not receive top of the show billing.

Billing on the promo ads took a different turn. The original full-page ad in *TV Guide* had Vic Morrow, Vince Edwards, and Anjanette Comer's names in bold above the title with a still of the three actors in a scene from the film. Carol was reduced to below the line billing. Two years later when *Death Stalk* was aired on the *CBS Late Night Movie*, Carol was pictured and her name appeared alongside the two male leads. Comer was nowhere to be found. This is all not surprising based on the convoluted way they received credit in the film.

Due to the adult content, NBC prefaced its original presentation with the warning, "We suggest you consider whether the program should be viewed by young people or others in your home who might be disturbed by it." The threat of rape could be the only reason for this unnecessary warning. There is no sex or nudity and the violence is tame compared to others of its ilk.

The schedule change proved to be a bonanza for NBC. *Death Stalk* pulled in a huge 25.1 rating and 37 share. It was the sixth highest rated TV-movie for the entire 1974-75 season and was a vast improvement ratings-wise over *The Elevator*.

Critically, *Death Stalk* lives up to the hype. It is fast-moving, thrilling, and expertly acted. All were perfectly cast in their roles. The fact that the actors did much of the river rafting themselves also lends credibility to the film. Most critics of the day liked it. Olga R. Pannone of *The Hartford Courant* called it "a chilling drama of rape and revenge on a raging river." Kevin Thomas of the *Los Angeles Times* raved, "Lively and suspenseful. Steven Kandel and John W. Bloch's terse adaptation … progresses as rapidly as that river's treacherous current under Robert Day's vigorous direction. Although *Death Stalk* could almost make it entirely on its ruggedly beautiful scenery and its extensive riding-the-rapids sequences, it is developed with a steady sense of psychological validity as both criminals and their victims respond to pressures of their dangerous predicament. Performances are succinct and forthright all around."

Promotional print ad for *Death Stalk* featuring Neville Brand and Carol Lynley. *Billy Rose Theatre Division, The New York Public Library for the Performing Arts*

One of the reasons to watch is for the pairing of Lynley and her brunette counterpart Anjanette Comer as the main ladies in peril. Their careers followed a similar path, which led them to this moment. Both were hailed early on as being talented newcomers destined for stardom (Comer even earned an Emmy nomination for her guest appearance on *Arrest and Trial*). However, their more promising movies either failed either critically or at the box office, forcing them to turn to the small screen where they excelled as the terrorized heroine in made-for-TV movies and episodic television. Carol does an excellent job as Cathy. Despite the veiled insults thrown at her by Pat, she tries to warn her about men like Brunner. Cathy consistently refuses to let Cody have his way with her fighting off his advances to the end, even though she knows he will kill her. Carol convincingly takes Cathy from a frivolous country club wife, as she is presented at the beginning, to a woman of conviction who, despite her past, will not allow herself to be sexually assaulted just to save herself. She decides to fight back unlike her feckless friend.

The twist of Comer's Pat being drawn to Brunner also plays credibly due to her and Vic Morrow's performances. She is like a cat on a hot tin roof sexually desiring him but using her 'staying alive at any cost' as an excuse, while he plays it aloof knowing he can have her any time he wants. As Kevin Thomas opined rightly, "Morrow makes the convict ... a man oozing with the kind of self-confidence that makes the strong and unexpected sexual attraction he holds for the dismayed Miss Comer quite believable."

Death Stalk and Lynley have a surprising fan in director/screenwriter Quentin Tarentino. On the *Pure Cinema Podcast*, the Oscar winner mentioned *Death Stalk* as one of the best *Deliverance* rip-offs. Tarantino remarked, "I actually watched *Death Stalk* with my family when it aired on NBC. One of the things about it was it deals with this whole sexual aspect in the film and they made a big deal about that on NBC ... and kept warning you about it in between commercial breaks. Two couples going on a river rafting like in *Deliverance* going down the rapids. It is Vince Edwards and his wife Anjanette Comer and Vince Edwards' boss Robert Webber and his hot-to-trot wife Carol Lynley. Back then any movie with Carol Lynley I would watch. She was my go-to girl [and] that is why I watched it. From *The Poseidon Adventure* on I was a *big* Carol Lynley fan. And I was very mad when Maureen McGovern had a hit with 'The Morning After'. I wanted the Carol Lynley version."[612]

Focusing back on *Death Stalk*, Tarantino was fascinated with the plot point of the Anjanette Comer character's matter-of-fact realization that they must have sex with the convicts to keep themselves alive because once they reach their destination there is no reason for them to live. He continued, "That's her plan and it strikes the audience as pretty pragmatic. You get it. But the movie also suggests—and does more than hint, but it doesn't say—that Anjanette Comer is drawn to the masculinity of Vic Morrow as the leader. She's scared of him but drawn to his alpha male status ... That whole second half is when the movie gets really, really good. It was so intriguing I realized it was based on a book and so I got the book. I read the book and the movie is better than the book. The teleplay is better and richer and more rewarding than the book it is based on ... The best thing about the movie is the last scene. It is one of those scenes—it is almost frustrating because it stops just before whatever is going to happen happens. Because it does that it makes you talk about what happened. I watched it with two friends of mine and when the movie is over you talk about it for twenty minutes ... It is one of the most thought proving endings of any TV movie I ever seen because it demands a twenty-minute discussion."⁶¹³ Tarantino's assessment of *Death Stalk* is pitch perfect and why it deserves a full Blu-Ray or at least DVD release with him providing a commentary track

Death Stalk would be the last we see of Carol with her trademark long straight blonde hair. The Hippie and flower child look that was so popular on her was long over by late 1974, so it is not surprising Carol opted for a new hair style. Going forward, she now sported a shoulder-length bob parted on the left with the ends flipped under rather than out like she wore in the mid-sixties. Quite flattering, it emphasized her face and especially her high cheek bones though not quite as sexy compared to her look later in the decade. It also e her a more mature look, coupled with her wearing more makeup on screen again, which was reflected in the parts she would go on to play.

*****

Frustrated, perhaps, with the lack of acceptable film roles offered keeping her relegated to television, Carol returned to the stage despite her previous comments about her preference for movie work. Considering how she revered the theater early in her career, it is surprising to hear her opine,

> I like the intimacy of film. [On stage] you have to exaggerate for people to see and hear you. You can't see the audience because of the lights and you have to project outward. But in film you project inward—to the camera. And I don't like the formality of the theater and the breaks between acts. I like the montage things in film, where you do a little each day.⁶¹⁴

The stage role that was too good for Carol to pass up was the meaty part of Curley's wife—opposite James Earl Jones (with whom she had a brief romance) and Kevin Conway—in the revival *Of Mice and Men* by John Steinbeck at the John F. Kennedy Center in Washington DC. The

Studio portrait of Carol Lynley, James Earl Jones, and Kevin Conway in the Kennedy Center stage production *Of Mice and Men*, 1975. *Photo by Martha Swope ©Billy Rose Theatre Division, The New York Public Library for the Performing Arts*

play, keeping her in the thirties' milieu, had just closed on Broadway and the two leads continued in their roles. Lynley stepped in for Pamela Blair who originated the part in New York. Curley's wife is a vain beauty whose jealous husband does not like the attention she receives from the mentally disabled Lennie (Jones). It is understandable why Carol jumped at the chance to do this stage production since challenging parts like this in film were not coming her way. Describing her character during rehearsals, the actress remarked,

> If she had a name it would be something like Marlene. Steinbeck tells how she is all painted up, with hair hanging in little rolled clusters like sausages and how she says she could have gone places in show business, maybe even in Hollywood. In the '30s a lot of women went to the movies and believed ... they could be Jean Harlow. I'm playing Curly's wife like she is in heat. I'm not making an obvious play for sympathy; I think the pathos is there, it doesn't need underlining. I hope to be very good in the part. It's a funny thing, but here I am playing the kind of woman who would have delusions of being another Harlow, and once I played Jean Harlow herself.[615]

In the play, Carol's character wears "a pistachio green peplum dress with shouldered bows and sequined stripes."[616] This was not a costume but came from the closet of the actress who was into collecting vintage finery. Theater goers would never have guessed it cost Carol only five dollars and was found at a swap store in Hollywood. Carol quipped, "It's in great shape. I die in it every night ... and it has held up just fine."[617]

Opining on her favorite decade for fashion, Carol said, "The clothes women wore in the 1930s had a certain elegance and style. The fabrics were fabulous—the wool challis, the velvet, the silk. To buy these today I would have to spend the rest of my life doing cigarette commercials."[618]

Of Mice and Men had a limited run from March 12 to April 5, 1975. Overall, it received many positive notices with Richard L. Coe of *The Washington Post* raving, "This staging by Edwin Sherin is one to relish and remember." As for Carol, he remarked, "There is also an understanding portrait of Curley's wife by Carol Lynley, new to the part but aware that she's also playing a lonely sole."

During this time, Carol received some welcomed news. Producer Irwin

Allen was planning a sequel to *The Poseidon Adventure*. He had Stirling Silliphant working on a script titled *Beyond the Poseidon Adventure* and reportedly signed four of the movie's original actors whose characters survived the disaster—Carol, Ernest Borgnine, Red Buttons, and Jack Albertson. Per Lynley, she agreed to do the movie only if she didn't have to wear the hot pants from the original. She said, "Irwin promised me I'd have three nice changes of clothes."[619]

The screenplay had the survivors first being treated for shock at a hospital. They then board a train to testify against the Greek ship owners at a hearing in Switzerland. While passing through the Alps in a tunnel an earthquake hits, derailing the train and trapping the survivors. Per Carol, "That's the first 10 minutes of the movie. Irwin won't say what the great disaster is going to be, obviously the mere collapse of a tunnel on a train is just a warm-up for something really cataclysmic."[620] She added in another interview, "I'm just keeping my fingers crossed that the writers let me survive that disaster. Because it would be terribly nice to be able to look forward to the prospect of some income next year."[621]

Despite an exciting set-up, this movie never came to be because author Paul Gallico wanted a shot at writing a sequel to his original novel. Allen convinced him to author instead a follow-up book to the movie since there were so many differences between the two. Allen finally did produce a sequel using the same title *Beyond the Poseidon Adventure* in 1979 loosely based on Gallico's book.

Lucky for Carol and company, none of them were included in the movie even though a few are featured in the new novel. The misguided plot centered on two rival salvage teams looking to loot the vessel and encountering more survivors still roaming the upside-down decks of the capsized Poseidon in one of the worst sequels ever to hit the big screen. Most of the performances were atrocious, including those of Michael Caine, Sally Field, and especially Shirley Jones.

The big screen role Irwin Allen should have offered Carol Lynley was that of the secretary who was having an affair with Robert Wagner's businessman in *The Towering Inferno*. Carol could easily have played this ill-fated part and already proven she had a good screen rapport with Wagner having worked with him three times prior. Alas, Allen went with TV actress and movie novice, Susan Flannery (best known up to then as Dr. Laura Horton on *Days of Our Lives*). For some, Flannery (despite winning a Golden Globe for Most Promising Newcomer – Female) was not able to make her character sympathetic. Hence, when she takes that nosedive out of the window to escape the fierce flames, the audience's compassion is not all there whereas Carol would have brought more vulnerability and poignancy to the part arguably creating a bigger impact.

*****

Thankfully, London was calling again, offering Carol one of her best lady in peril roles of the decade. She delivered an excellent nerve-wracking performance in "If It's a Man, Hang Up!" on *Thriller*. This videotaped British television anthology series was created by Brian Clemens best remembered for producing and writing *The Avengers* TV series. Producer Lew Grade liked Clemens' idea and sold it to ABC-TV in America who agreed to pay $100,000 per episode to run as part of their rotating late-night *Wide World of Entertainment* umbrella. For American audiences, ABC dropped the *Thriller* title. Renamed *The Wide World of Mystery*, it aired Wednesday nights at 11:30 pm on the East and West coasts opposite *The CBS Late Movie* and NBC's *The Tonight Show Starring Johnny Carson*.

Per Clemens, the American network did not have any input into scripts or filming other than providing a list of American actors and actresses that they wanted in lead roles. They did accept British and foreign actors if they were known in the U.S. Associated Television, in partnership with Lew Grade, produced each episode. Many were written by Clemens, including Carol's episode based on his stage play *Lover*. Speaking in general about writing for *Thriller*, Clemens remarked, "I often do a script in a week, but I have the idea in my mind (for a long time). Thrillers are pretty easy to write

… I always write about things that scare me. What scares me is you're lying in bed and you hear the latch go on the back door and you know you've locked it. And of course the victims were often women because somehow they're more vulnerable and somehow people identify closely with them."[622]

Carol Lynley as fashion model Susie Martin in "If It's a Man, Hang Up!" on *Thriller/WIde World of Mystery* (ITC, 1975). *From Marlin Dobbs' Collection*

Lynley was cast in this episode during the time she was honing her dancing skills taking classes wherever she may be. She revealed to the *TV*

Times that one of her biggest regrets was "that she was born too late for the great era of Astaire-Rogers dancing films and it remains one of her greatest ambitions to use her skill in a film."[623] While shooting in London, Carol found time to take classes at an exclusive Covent Garden dancing school. Unfortunately, the big screen never took advantage of her dancing prowess, but an upcoming episode of TV's *Fantasy Island* put it front and center.

"If It's a Man, Hang Up!" took Carol back into "Voice in the Dark" territory, once again playing a woman being harassed by a threatening phone caller. Here though the suspense is cranked up and Carol has a better role as a vivacious fashion model with many male admirers who is at first indifferent to the calls but as they continue becomes more terrified realizing her life may be in danger. Per Marlin Dobbs, "Carol thoroughly enjoyed doing [this] one. She said they were all lovely to her and found Tom Conti fun to work with."[624] This was before Conti became known in the U.S. Carol described him as being "quiet but strong. I wasn't familiar with his work but I could see he was a talented actor."[625]

Susie (Carol Lynley) comforts her manager Greg Miles (Gerald Harper) who was beaten in the street by a mystery man in "If It's a Man, Hang Up!" on *Thriller/WIde World of Mystery* (ITC, 1975). *From Marlin Dobbs' Collection*

The episode opened with a teaser sequence as the tormentor is seen wearing black gloves dialing his rotary phone and peering through his binoculars without his identity revealed. He is eyeing a beautiful blonde who is undressing for the night. She dons a towel when she receives a phone call and goes to answer it only to hear heavy breathing at the end of the line. She hangs up ignoring it and returns to her bedroom.

The next day viewers learn the blonde is in-demand fashion model Susie Martin (Carol Lynley), who reports to work at a photo shoot modeling a long, caramel colored dress. Per Marlin Dobbs, she is wearing, "the Alice Faye gown she bought in the early seventies. She showed it to me once when I was at her place."[626] While away from home, her buildings' caretaker Murchison (John Cater) pays his daily visit to feed her small dog Toby, whom Susie has the unfortunate habit of keeping confined in the kitchen. Her place is oddly designed with closed doors to her bedroom, kitchen, and spare room situated in different corners of the apartment, all off the sunken living room.

The audience then meets some other men in Susie's life such as smitten photographer Terry Cleeves (Paul Angelis) who discovered Susie. He is jealous of her working with her married manager Greg Miles (Gerald Harper) whose interest in Susie is more than professional and the feeling is mutual. They are together when Cleeves pops over to Susie's unannounced with Bruno Varella (Tom Conti) a psychologist and huge fan of the model who wanted to meet her. They exit, and later Greg is attacked on the street by an unknown assailant.

That night the caller phones again and tells Susie he loves her and wants to be the only man in her life. Susie calls the police but feels foolish once constables Richard Lovell (Michael Byrne) and Henry Venner (David Gwillim) show up. She poo-poos the entire series of events but is frightened when a bloodied Greg breaks into her apartment through the back door. He does not want the police involved because of his wife.

While shooting an advertising campaign at Terry's studio, a glamorous Susie, with her hair pulled up into a knot and clad in a sexy, tight, silver lame evening gown with a bare back, gets another call from her mystery man who tells her how much he cherishes her. She does not tell anyone and then is surprised by her brother Peter (Colin Etherington) who is in town and too drunk to make it back to his university. The police stop by to check up on Susie and, standing in the doorway with Peter, does not tell them about the day's phone call nor introduces her brother. Henry's partner ribs him that he does not have a chance with the model. The caretaker is seen peering out of his unit where he has photos of Susie on the wall. Terry calls to set up a lunch with Susie, who declines, and he seethes when he hears a man's voice in the background. Demanding to know who it is, she tells him it is none of his business. Soon after, the mystery man is seen staring with his binoculars from across the street and watches Susie as she innocently kisses her brother good night.

The next morning Peter leaves a thank-you note and exists Susie's place where he is followed by a car that runs him down. Later, Terry shows up with flowers left by her doorstep. She assumes they are from Peter until the police arrive and inform of her his death. Susie collapses and does not believe it. She then realizes the flowers are "from him" as she stares at the phone. However, she still does not confide in the police. This entire time the caretaker has been eavesdropping from outside her apartment.

A contrite Terry returns home and confesses to Bruno that he was the one who beat up Greg Miles. The Italian already guessed that because he noticed some blood on his friend's hands and says, "I am a very observant man. I like to observe." He then advises Terry to stay away from Susie for a few days.

It is a night full of confessions as Murchison offers Susie his condolences and admits that he is such a major fan of hers that he clips photos and articles out of magazines. Having the honor to work for such a celebrity makes him feel important. Susie is too busy primping to pay much attention to the caretaker and when she goes to tip him, he declines as he lets his hand wrest on hers a bit too long. Soon after he leaves, the caller phones revealing that he can see Susie and wants her to take off her clingy dress. When she refuses and quickly pulls the drapes closed, he tells her that he has Toby. Terrified that he will harm her dog, a stunned Susie rips the dress as instructed and agrees not to go out at night with other men.

Constable Venner shows up with the missing Toby, who he claims he found at the caretaker's door. Susie is just so happy to see the dog that she does not at first question why the police officer stopped by. He insists that he will personally stay close by until they nab the caller but does not want his partner to know that he is going beyond the call of duty. Right after, Terry gets a phone call that takes him out of town without letting Bruno know.

A few days later Bruno shows up at Susie's, after trying to telephone several times, to see if this is normal behavior for the photographer. He then listens to her story and begins questioning the motives of Constable Venner. Susie freaks and thinks Bruno is the man harassing her and she locks herself in her bedroom. Bruno hides in the kitchen and listens when Venner shows up, convincing Susie to put Toby in a kennel for safety, and to stay at his cottage in Cambridge for a few days. It is obvious that Susie is beginning to develop feelings for the concerned police officer just as Bruno detected.

Giving up on Susie, Greg Miles assumes his affair with is assistant Betty (Sue Holderness) and they are interrupted at his studio by Bruno. He then immediately calls the model telling her he must speak with her, but she is on her way out with Venner. Just about to tell Greg where she is going, Venner hangs up the phone. Greg rushes out and an infuriated Betty screams that she will not be second best to anyone.

At Venner's cottage, he and Susie share a tender moment. The caller phones again wanting to meet her at a nearby inn. Venner runs out, leaving Susie alone, but Bruno is already in the house in an upstairs bedroom. He terrifies the model but admits that he placed the call to get Susie by herself. He explains why he thinks Venner is the stalker and then shows her Terry's dead body in another room. The constable returns and knocks out Bruno but cannot fathom why Susie fears him. Confused and terrified, she grabs a rifle off the wall and warns him to stay away. He approaches, and she surprisingly pulls the trigger killing him. A stunned Susie is glad to see constable Lovell who enters. As he locks the door behind him, he reveals that it is his house they are in, not Venner's. Susie slowly realizes that she killed an innocent man, as the threatening Lovell professes his love and wraps his hands around her neck. He is then stabbed in the back by Bruno, leaving him and Susie standing amongst the carnage.

Susie (Carol Lynley) poses during a fashion shoot in "If It's a Man, Hang Up!" on *Thriller/WIde World of Mystery* (ITC, 1975). *From Marlin Dobbs' Collection*

Most TV critics of the day ignored ABC's *Wide World of Mystery* and there are few reviews from when it aired. "It It's a Man, Hang Up!" was the series' opening episode during its fifth season. The *Thriller* fan site found this episode "quite enjoyable" and "despite the lack of originality, there are still some very frightening moments throughout as Suzy's stalker slowly closes in on her."[627] James O'Neill writing in *Terror on Tape* raved, "Here is a superior Brian Clemens-scripted TV horror with Lynley in top form ... It's genuinely suspenseful, with attention paid to detail and a wholly surprising surprise ending."

Aficionados of the series mostly agree "If It's a Man, Hang Up!" is one of the best due to Shaun O'Riordan's sharp direction, Brian Clemens' intriguing mystery plot that keeps the audience guessing, the shocking reveal, and Lynley's first-rate performance. Her Susie is at first a bit self-absorbed and oblivious taking all the male adoration for granted. When the phone calls first start, she tries to rationalize that it is just one of the annoyances of being a celebrity. But when her brother is run down and her dog taken, the danger she is in becomes a reality. Carol is then able to make a more frantic Susie vulnerable and sympathetic as she does not know whom to trust. Her scenes at the end, as a terrified, confused, rifle-toting Susie tries to grasp who is her actual stalker, are edge-of-your-seat riveting.

Reportedly, there were four alternate versions of "If It's a Man, Hang Up!" depending if seen on the original British TV broadcast as part of *Thriller* or the U.S. broadcast as part of *Wide World of Mystery*. The episode was so popular and well-received, that it was chosen along with a few others to be released as a stand-alone movie (it played in American syndication for years) and then in the eighties on VHS. The box cover art featured the eyeglass-wearing killer speaking into a phone's mouthpiece with the popular 1971 Harry Langdon headshot of Carol superimposed with her holding a telephone to her ear reflected on his glasses. The tagline proclaimed in dramatic fashion, "She's on the receiving end of terror!"

Both broadcasts differed from the UK and Australia ITC movie version and the American video release. Most of the changes involved the teaser opening, musical score, credit rolls, and in some cases scenes that were excised.

*****

Returning to the U.S., Carol was surprised to be invited to the White House by President Gerald Ford and the First Lady for a dinner honoring West German President Walter Scheel and his wife. Among the celebrities in attendance were Dick Cavett, Angela Lansbury, and Elke Sommer with after dinner entertainment provided by Tennessee Ernie Ford and his Opryland Singers. The Fords were known for throwing lavish entertaining parties so more invitees responded yes than anticipated. One hundred guests got to dine with the President and his special guests in the State Dining Room, while the others were hosted by Secretary of State Henry Kissinger in the Blue Room.

Carol wore a second-hand, clingy, flowered Chablis gown from the thirties that highlighted her shapely figure. She told *The Washington Post* that she bought it in London for fifteen dollars and quipped, "It's the first time I've worn it and I hope it holds together."[628] Her escort for the night was a White House aide who took her on a quick tour of the West Wing. A perplexed Carol remarked shortly after the gala affair,

> I don't know why I was invited. I figured they were casting blue-eyed blondes that week. Anyway, I got this gigantic engraved invitation and went to Washington. A state dinner is very formal, more formal than meeting the Queen of England. As you walk in a Marine guard yells, 'Miss Carol Lynley.'
>
> I sat next to Kissinger and we talked for an hour and a half. He's very funny, extremely antic. As I was leaving a reporter from *Women's Wear Daily* threw me against a wall and asked, 'What did he say?'

Career-wise, Carol opted for another theatre production, but this time on Broadway. Regarding the lack of good movie roles offered her and her return to the stage, Carol opined that the film industry is "male-dominated and where the ratio of male to female roles in the States is 18 to one. We have no alternative now than to look to men. Liv Ullman has her Bergman; Gena Rowlands has husband John Cassavetes; and Cybil Shepherd—Peter Bogdanovich. Most of the women who've got things together have had, and still have, to do it that way, which leaves actresses and single women like me trying to pull rabbits out of top hats."[629] This is a fair statement and Carol could have added to her list Jill Ireland and Charles Bronson, Sondra Locke and Clint Eastwood, and Mia Farrow and Woody Allen. Without these men in their corners, these ladies most likely would not have landed the lead roles they did.

With that said, Carol did land a standout role in a top show. She replaced Sandy Dennis in the hit Tony Award nominated Broadway comedy *Absurd Person Singular* by Alan Ayckbourn, which opened at the Music Box theatre on October 8, 1974. The play was in three acts and centered on the changing fortunes of a trio of couples at Christmas past, present, and future. Explaining why she accepted the part, Carol said, "I haven't been happy with most of the roles that have been offered to me in the past. This English play has an offbeat humor that appeals to me. I plan to do more and more theater in the future."[630]

When Lynley joined the cast in late June 1975, the only remaining original cast members were the esteemed Geraldine Page and Carole Shelley (who soon left and was replaced by Marilyn Clark). While in rehearsal, the cast learned the tragic news befallen former cast member Larry Blyden. Carol said at the time, "Larry died after an auto mobile accident in Morocco. There were a lot of sad people at the theater. Fritz deWilde, the stage manager, particularly. His son Brandon died from an automobile accident several years ago."[631]

New actors in the roles of the husbands were Fritz Weaver (*The Maltese Bippy*), Paul Shyre, and Curt Dawson who played Carol's ambitious controlling spouse Geoffrey who suffers a career disappointment. Carol's loopy Eva is first seen being addicted to anti-depressants and afraid of her husband. In the second act, she turns suicidal trying to off herself in hilarious fashion but thwarted by her friends. In the third act, she has turned a corner and is in control of her life and her husband.

Despite the cast changes, the critics were equally praiseworthy of the replacement actors. Lillian Africano of the *Ashbury Park Press* commented, "Even with the slight loss of glamour the changes involve, Alan Ayckbourn's laugh-filled script is still keeping audiences happy." In October, *New York Times* theater critic Clive Barnes revisited the play and raved, "The newcomers slide easily into the play ... and, perhaps best of all Carol Lynley, disenchanted to the point of catatonic withdrawal, matched by Curt Dawson as her repulsive yet boyishly charming Lothario of an architect husband."[632] It was a triumphant return to Broadway for the actress.

When asked what he was like to work in the theater with two acting giants such as James Earl Jones (prior in *Of Mice and Men*) and Geraldine Page, Carol raved,

> It was an honor to be on the stage with them. They were tremendously talented and such pros. When I did *Absurd Person Singular*, Geri had been doing the play for about a year. She would sometimes have these long pauses onstage and I would think, 'Ok, I can go with this. What is she going to do?' I would wait and then suddenly, she would be back spouting her lines wonderfully. The scene would go on.[633]

During the run of the play, Carol gave a few interviews announcing that she was signed for a new horror movie to be directed by Larry Cohen following up on his hit film *It's Alive*. She revealed, "I'll be shooting … in and around New York during the day. The film is titled *God Told Me To*, and the leading man is Robert Forster. I play his girlfriend, and Sandy Dennis plays his wife. I think it's funny that Miss Dennis and I both had the same role in *Absurd Person Singular*, and now we're doing our first film together. She's a fascinating actress, and I look forward to working with her."[634]

Carol added, "They got me a gown that Carole Lombard wore. They found it in a bin at the Fox lot. It's long and elegant like she'd have worn."[635] Despite this, Lynley did not appear in the film. When asked why, she replied, "I remember going for the costume fittings but cannot recall why I did not make the movie."[636]

Robert Forster, cast as a devout Catholic police detective, reportedly clashed with Cohen about his character chewing gum or not and departed after only two days filming. When Tony Lo Bianco was hired to replace him, Geraldine Fitzgerald was dropped as the detective's mother and replaced by Sylvia Sidney. Perhaps Cohen felt Lynley was also not a good fit with the new actor or perhaps they rewrote the part? Deborah Raffin stepped in as the detective's hippie-clad schoolteacher girlfriend with nary an evening gown in sight. Whatever the reason, it is disappointing that Carol lost out on appearing in this surprise cult horror film about people enacting heinous crimes and claiming, "God told me to."

Appearing back on Broadway brought Carol the most press she received since *The Poseidon Adventure*. She granted many interviews and, since this was during the height of the Women's Liberation Movement, a lot of the focus was on her being a single parent with no steady man in her life. Carol always came off quite confidently in her ability to care for and support her child as well as herself. She routinely stated that she did not need to be beholden to any man (though she never ruled out marrying again) and loved her independence. However, there is no doubt that her romantic relationships greatly affected her career. Instead of traveling the world to keep Oliver Reed company on his film sets, Carol should have been back in Hollywood following up *The Poseidon Adventure* with a big movie or television show. Worse was David Frost who would soon deliver the most fatal blow to Lynley's career.

Carol left *Absurd Person Singular* in early 1976 and returned to Hollywood where she settled into an apartment in Beverly Hills. She worked almost nonstop through 1984, alternating between features and television with some side trips to work in England and Canada. With her daughter almost an adult, Carol seemed to be extremely focused on her acting career. It is too bad she did not have this drive and determination post-*Bunny Lake Is Missing* and post-*The Poseidon Adventure* where her reviews for the former and the box office gross of the latter gave her career momentum that she did not take advantage of then. She may have propelled herself into a higher echelon in the Hollywood hierarchy and had an even better career.

Carol introduced a new hairdo with her return to the small screen in 1976. Unfortunately, it was the least flattering of her different looks over the years. She now sported longer shoulder length hair with short pageboy bangs that outlined her face, making it rounder that what it was. It was reminiscent of her hair style from *The Pleasure Seekers* but there the hair was shorter and the bangs longer and parted on the left. She kept this hair style for upcoming film roles in *Flood*, *Bad Georgia Road*, and *Fantasy Island*.

Carol's first TV guest appearance in 1976 was as one of many red herrings in the solid mystery laden "Who's Who in Neverland" on *Quincy, M.E.* starring Jack Klugman as a medical examiner solving crime mysteries with his scientific knowledge. This ninety-minute episode was the series' second broadcast and was an excellent whodunit about a woman (Joanna Barnes) found dead under an assumed name in a seedy motel. Presumed to be a prostitute, she is cremated before the autopsy is completed. Soon after Quincy learns that she was a socialite who had just authored a steamy, fictional account of her life and the people in it. When her literary agent on the East Coast is learned to have died mysteriously as well, Quincy suspects they were murdered. His medical office uncovers that both victims were killed using some type of germ warfare once used by the military. Anyone who had knowledge of the manuscript's contents seem to be marked for death.

This episode is intriguing, however, this is not one of Carol's finest moments. She seems a bit ill-at-ease throughout as a literary agent named Lynn Dressler who masquerades as a real estate property manager in search of the missing manuscript. The motives of her character keep the audience guessing though. She tells Quincy she never saw a page of the book, but makes it known to the London publisher (Monte Markham) that she read it all. Carol seems to just shout her lines in a confrontational scene with Klugman's Quincy. Her most real moment, where she seems most at ease, occurs when Lynn and Quincy are held at gunpoint by the killer at an airstrip. The scene is tense and well-played by all. Carol is also not helped by some unflattering mid-seventies dresses and skirts she is forced to wear.

A footnote about this episode is that Carol is first seen clad in a blue dress descending a staircase with gun in hand. This clip, stopped just before you see the actress' face, was used in the opening montage for the entire eight seasons the program aired.

Carol was next seen in "Trial by Prejudice" on the extremely popular series *Police Woman*. She convincingly played a despicable robbery suspect named

Nina who, when caught by the police, falsely accuses Angie Dickinson's Sgt. Pepper Anderson of sexual molestation when left alone with her in the back of a squad car. Nina jumps on Pepper and then with her hair messed cries for help. Due to lack of evidence, charges against Nina are dropped but Pepper is still subjugated to a departmental investigation based on the accusations brought by Nina and two other inmates. When Pepper's supervisors ask about a past relationship with her Police Academy roommate Marlena Simpson (Patricia Crowley), Pepper remains mum and turns in her badge. Pepper is protecting Marlena's secret - that she is a Lesbian. Things get worse for Pepper, when she follows Nina to where her cohorts in crime are gathering. During a melee, Pepper shoots and kills her accuser. Marlena is ready to jeopardize her career to save Pepper at her hearing, but one of Nina's accomplices comes forth with the truth. All of course is resolved at the end and Pepper returns to the force.

Reportedly, this episode was loosely based on an actual case that happened in Los Angeles. However, the outcome was different, as the policewoman resigned before the police board could review. The writers also wisely conferred with the Gay Media Task Force to evaluate the script and make sure it did not demean the homosexual community. This was quite a mature subject matter for a standard police procedural TV series. Nina is probably one of the vilest characters Carol ever played and she successfully gets the audience to despise her. The syndicated reviewer for *TV Scout* remarked, "The show takes itself seriously and is interesting drama but gets lost in its predictable formula."

Carol then returned to the lady in peril roles when Irwin Allen came a-calling again. Perhaps trying to make up for not going ahead with *The Poseidon Adventure* sequel, he cast her in his first made-for-television disaster movie, *Flood*. With an estimated budget of $2.25 to $2.4 million, it was the most expensive TV-movie up to that point in time. As you would expect from Irwin Allen, just like with his theatrical pictures this too featured an all-star cast albeit on a lesser scale—Martin Milner, Robert Culp, Barbara Hershey, Richard Basehart, Teresa Wright, Cameron Mitchell, Eric Olson, Francine York, and in a guest cameo *Poseidon Adventure* veteran Roddy McDowall.

When asked if Irwin Allen had changed any since *The Poseidon Adventure*, Carol replied laughing,

> No, he was pretty much the same. He was a character and I liked him very much. He directed some scenes like he did on *Poseidon*. Irwin directed the same way he produced. He was *the* guy in charge.[637]

Flood was financed by Warner Bros. International and NBC-TV. Knowing that the movie studio was lacking product for its foreign markets and that the network could not afford a $2 million movie, the shrewd Allen brought them all together. He explained, "I created a marriage between Warne Bros. International and the network—to the profit of both and to myself, of course. The studio and NBC put up the money for *Flood*. It is a bargain for both. After it is shown on TV it is released abroad in theaters. The beauty is that Warner International needs films that don't translate the American idiom. They can almost be seen without dialogue. They are action films with basic human appeal. All they really need are sound effects and music."[638]

Pregnant Abbie Adams (Carol Lynley) makes a frantic phone call to the hospital after going into labor in *Flood* (Warner Bros. Television, 1976).

Based on his boasting, it seems Allen did not have much regard for his actors. *Flood* was shot on location in the Oregon town of Brownsville (with a then population of 682) and at the Fall Creek dam and reservoir. Allen remarked that they chose Oregon because he claimed, "it has more dams than any other area in the country" and selected Fall Creek because "the area is spectacular. I hired the entire town of Brownsville for extras and bit players."[639] He then went on to exclaim that "the special effects are terrific. You actually see the dam collapsing and the town disappearing."[640]

Actress Francine York had a long history working for Irwin Allen, making guest appearances on some of his TV shows such as *Lost in Space* and *Land of the Giants*. Recalling the producer and her cast mates, she remarked, "Irwin could be wonderful, and he could be a tyrant. He was the last of the Mike Todd showman producers. Truthfully, I was always afraid of him. You never knew what he was going to come up with next. One time he came down … and he said, 'I don't like your skin. It looks too pale. You need more make-up. Are you well?'" Martin Milner was nice. Barbara Hershey and Carol Lynley were wonderful. And of course, I adored Richard Basehart."[641]

Carol concurred about Barbara Hershey and added,

> We spent a lot of time together. I was always curious about Barbara because she was such a wonderful actress. I was so fixated on her that I do not remember much about the other actors I worked with. And Irwin Allen was such a larger than life figure he blotted everybody else out. Not purposely, but he was just that kind of a guy.[642]

Costume designer Paul Zastupnevich, who created the Oscar-nominated frocks in *The Poseidon Adventure*, also worked on *Flood* and many other Irwin Allen productions. Paul jokingly quipped in the press with Carol by his side that he made her "pregnant in just five hours."[643] Unfortunately, his costumes designed for her here are not nearly as memorable as her hot pants and go-go boots from the previous movie.

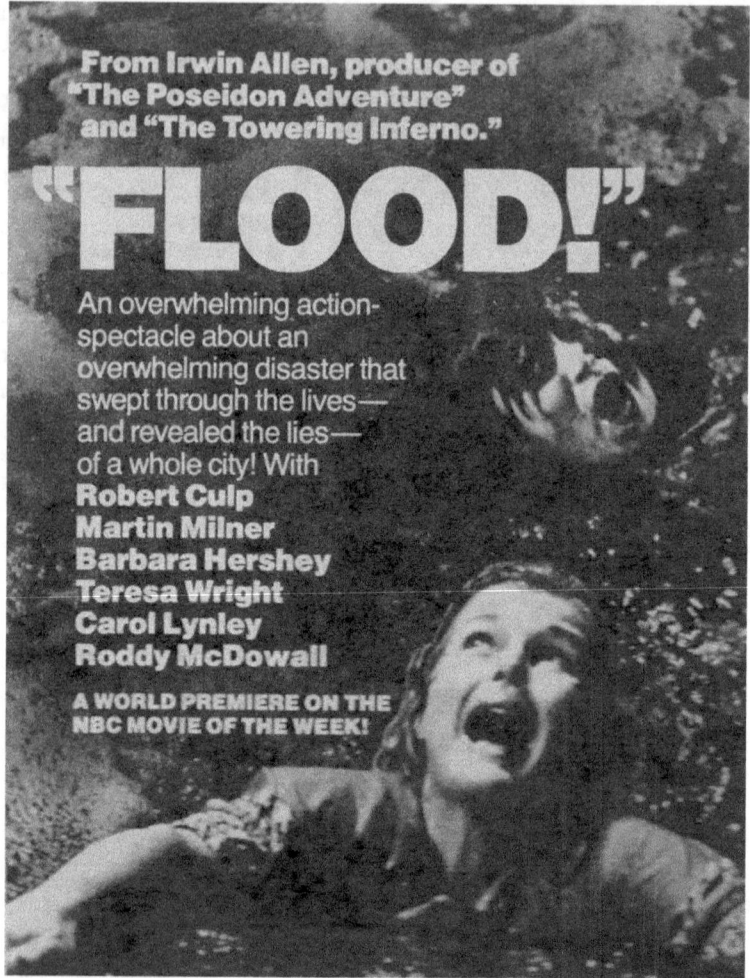

Promotional print ad for *Flood* featuring Carol Lynley.

Flood begins with ace helicopter pilot Steve Brannigan (Robert Culp) coming to the rescue of the mayor's son Andy Cutler (Eric Olson) who lays injured at the earthen part of the town's dam where a stream of water has burst through. After flying his passenger (Roddy McDowall) to his fishing lodge, Steve notifies Paul Burke (Martin Milner) a schoolteacher and Councilman. Burke pleads with Mayor Cutler (Richard Basehart) and the town board to act. Excessive rains have caused the dam to leak. Fishing season is about to begin, and it is the resort town's biggest source of revenue, so Cutler will not allow the opening of the flood gates to drain the lake so the dam can be repaired. Instead, he orders his harried dam supervisor Sam Adams (Cameron Mitchell) to keep plugging the sprouting leaks. Of course, the dam eventually bursts killing Sam instantly and flooding the town. This sets up the remainder of the movie with the rescue of the citizens including Lynley as Sam's nine-month pregnant wife Abbie who is trapped in her flooded home and hapless Andy who holds onto a fallen tree as it is pushed by the raging waters. They are the fortunate ones who are saved unlike Teresa Wright as Andy's mother who perishes as she tries to rescue a young boy that she thinks is her son, and Ann Doran as Cutler's loyal secretary who is washed away when the flood waters destroys the office where she is trapped inside.

Lynley's image was used prominently in the print ads and promotional photos since she appears in perhaps the movie's most elaborate set piece. Before the flood hits, she assures her fretting husband that she will make her doctor's appointment at the hospital. She does and is instructed by her doctor (Whit Bissell, who had played Lynley's doctor in *Once You Kiss a Stranger*) and his nurse (Francine York) to return by 3 p.m. to check herself in. However, she never gets a chance to go back as severe labor pains render her unconscious just before the disaster happens. Realizing that Abbie may be trapped in her flooded home, Burke and his girlfriend nurse Mary Carver (Barbara Hershey), the mayor's daughter, make a harrowing rescue jumping from Brannigan's helicopter to the roof of the Adams' house. As they climb down the staircase to the flooded first floor, they call out for Abbie but cannot find her. Eventually they hear the groans from the terrified woman as she clings to floating furniture with her foot caught between two crossbeams. As the river's water keeps rising, Milner must dive under the water to free her. When her foot is set free, they get the pregnant woman on to a waiting rowboat outside.

Considering Irwin Allen gave the world *The Poseidon Adventure* and *The Towering Inferno*, *Flood* did not live up to expectations. The first half consists of beautiful aerial shots of Oregon and of Martin Milner and Robert Culp warning all who will listen that the dam is going to burst. When it does, the effects are disappointing and cheesy, despite the movie's big budget for the time. The dam looks like a model made of packed dirt with toy trucks and cars on top. As water (from hoses no doubt) spurt through, the sand turns to mud before it collapses. The raging flood in the town seems to be running water in a tank put in front of a screen with previously filmed scenes of panicked extras running through the town. Too much stock footage of real floods filmed from above is used that do not match the new footage. The rescuing of Lynley's Abbie is the film's most exciting and well-produced scene.

Reviews for *Flood* were mixed. Earl Bellamy was roundly criticized for his routine direction. The *Los Angeles Times* said, "*Flood* fails to offer much fun or excitement." Geoff Brown of the *Monthly Film Bulletin* found it to be "comfortably packaged and perfectly acceptable" and amusingly described the dam bursting as resembling "some monstrous culinary catastrophe (a torrent of gravy demolishing a wall of flaky pastry)." Warner Bros. International and NBC were happy with the final product and that is what counted most. They made a deal with Irwin Allen for nine more pictures in the next 2 ½ years.

Nurse Mary Cutler (Barbara Hershey) and her boyfriend Paul Burke (Martin Milner) attempt to rescue Abbie (Carol Lynley) from her water ravaged home in *Flood* (Warner Bros. Television, 1976).

Newsday called Carol Lynley "a water disaster movie pro" and she lives up to the description during the flood scenes where she is shown dripping wet à la *The Poseidon Adventure*. Playing the lady in peril once again, she easily projects fear and terror regarding her predicament after her home floods. Later she is touching when she learns her husband perished when the dam burst. Overall though the role was not much of stretch for the actress, but she handled it effectively.

As per the studios' pact, *Flood* was released theatrically overseas to decent reviews. For instance, Marjorie Bilbow of *Screen International* commented, "It is easy to smile patronizingly as we mentally tick off each stock character, every cliché of conflict and suspense. But the formula has been well tried out and, in its own pretentious way, the film is a good workmanlike production that does its job involving and entertaining."

Although the image of Carol drenched. clutching furniture in her flooded home was used as the central selling point to exploit the movie in print ads and posters, the actress did not promote *Flood* like she did with *The Poseidon Adventure*. There are no known press interviews or talk show appearances with her touting the movie. She probably realized that compared to *Poseidon* that stayed afloat, *Flood* was a sinker.

*****

Lynley found herself in front of the movie cameras again in her first theatrical movie since *The Four Deuces*. *Bad Georgia Road* (working titles *Thunder Mountain* and *Out of Control*) was a straight-forward rollicking B-movie along the lines of *Macon County Line* and *White Lightning* with a touch of Lina Wertmuller's *Swept Away* and aimed directly at drive-in moviegoers. With this film, Carol now joined some of her contemporaries such as Yvette Mimieux who had a big hit with the low-budget, drive-in smash *Jackson County Jail*.

Carol is no shrinking violet in *Bad Georgia Road*. As a big city sophisticated snob, she leaves the Big Apple to live on her inherited southern estate only to learn that it is a rundown house with a profitable illegal still manned by a drunken caretaker and a brutish moonshine runner who she locks horns with. This character was by far more interesting than the gun moll she played in *The Four Deuces*. Asked why she took the role, Carol replied at the time, "Because there is conflict and humor in the character. As an actress it gives me dramatic latitude. This is what so many superficial roles don't have."[644] This is true as this part required Carol to enact a gamut of emotions—from funny lightweight scenes when the city slicker tries to adapt to living in her ramshackle abode with a moonshine operation, to powerfully dramatic moments when she is assaulted by the brutish driver who she finds herself inexplicably attracted to.

New York fashion editor Molly Golden (Carol Lynley) decides to keep her rundown Southern estate complete with a profitable but illegal still in *Bad Georgia Road* (Dimension, 1977). *From Marlin Dobbs Collection*

Co-star Gary Lockwood liked his character too and described him as "a streetwise gorilla … He's a knowledgeable ape."[645]

Also, in the movie was John Goff, a writer and actor who was making a name for himself in exploitation movies at this time with his appearances in *Lady Cocoa*, *C.B. Hustlers*, and *The Witch Who Came from the Sea*, among others. On *Bad Georgia Road* he did double duty as actor and assistant director. When asked how he got the jobs, he wrote, "It was through George "Buck" Flower. He was involved in casting some of the smaller roles and had me in for the role I ultimately performed. We were writing partners also at that time, saw one another or at least talked daily. He was the original AD on it but was having some problems with Terri Schwartz, the production manager. The two of them weren't seeing eye to eye on some things. Not sure what but he asked if I wanted to take the gig over because he wanted out. I needed the money at the time—three kids, a wife, rent, and food—so I said 'sure.' Terri was rough to work around. I shut my mouth, did my job and took the checks."[646]

The movie was a Producers Group production and was set to be distributed by Golden Films International. It was produced, directed, and co-written by John C. Broderick. He attended the London School of Film Technique before returning to Hollywood. Starting out as assistant director (including working for Terrence Malick on *Badlands*) and production manager led him to producing a few low-budget movies such as *Big Bad Mama* and *Sixpack Annie*. This was the first movie he directed. He accepted the assignment because "I liked the electricity that crackled when the main characters clashed. From the moment Carol Lynley meets Gary Lockwood, the clash begins, and it doesn't let up until the movie ends. This is an 'upper' picture. It's an entertaining film with Lynley and Lockwood turning in some powerful performances."[647]

Asked what he thought of novice director John C. Broderick, Goff commented, "I wasn't expecting much because of what I'd heard from Buck. My observation was that John liked the title [of director] but lacked the knowledge. He was a nice enough guy and had some people around him he was used to working with like Terri, Tak Fujimoto, and some others.

They had good relationships, close and closed. I had the feeling I was an outsider walking into a hornet's nest and there wasn't much that made me feel otherwise through the shoot. A friendly face was Michael Riva [the film's art director], who I'd met prior to this shoot. I appreciated that."[648]

Sharing his experience making the movie, which was not shot in the South but in the area around Lake Piru, California, Gary Lockwood said, "I loved doing that film. I became really, really good friends with the director John Broderick. He was a really nice guy. I also worked with Carol Lynley … and she was a lot of fun and very nice. We shot the whole thing in about a month. The budget … was probably the lowest I ever worked on."[649]

John Goff too only had praise for Carol's professionalism working on this film. He wrote, "I thought she was a trouper. The budget for the film certainly wasn't what she was used to. When I was involved the title of it was *Molly*. Maybe they did that to entice her to it. Conditions were 'rugged' to say the least. I didn't have much interaction with her other than to call her to the set when needed but I remember her as friendly and professional but not personal. She was a seasoned pro. If she had any problems with anything, I wasn't aware of them."[650]

As for Gary Lockwood, Carol did not offer much praise and replied, "I knew Gary for years. [Long pause.] All I will say is that is he a talented actor."[651] When told of Carol's hesitation, John Goff does not know why based on what he observed and shared, "I just remember them both being very professional. They knew their lines, hit their marks, and didn't mess around on set. I was never aware of anything going on between them. Never saw any fireworks regarding each other's performances or personal time. They worked together as professionals; didn't see a lot of chemistry there. But, again, being something of an outsider I wasn't privy to getting together off set with any of them.

"Gary was perhaps more accustomed to working rugged conditions than Carol Lynley," continued John. "He came on set very friendly, down-to-earth, ready to do what was needed. Never would have pegged him for the astronaut from *2001: A Space Odyssey*. I had the feeling he was treating John Broderick the same as he'd treated Stanley Kubrick. Here he was what he was in the film—a good ol' boy."652

Based on this description, it is not surprising to learn that Broderick did not have much work to do with his lead players and Goff confirmed, "He seemed happy with what he got and was pretty content with letting his actors mold their own [performances]. As I said he liked the title of director."653

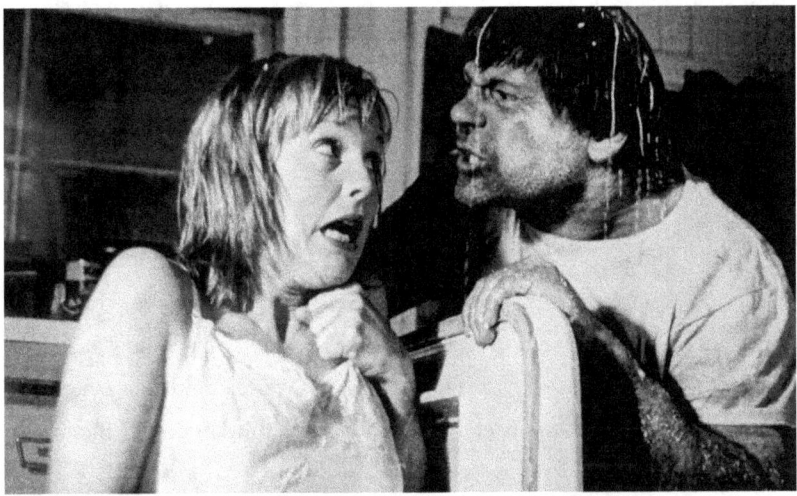

Fed up with the condescending way he has been treated, moonshine runner Leroy Hastings (Gary Lockwood) decides to teach haughty Molly (Carol Lynley) a lesson in *Bad Georgia Road* (Dimension, 1977). *From Marlin Dobbs Collection*

The movie is impressively shot by cinematographer Tak Fujimoto (whom Broderick felt did "an excellent job"654). Just prior to working on *Bad Georgia Road*, he shot second unit footage for *Star Wars*. After toiling in B-movies, the talented cameraman jumped to A-list features in the eighties such as *Pretty in Pink; Married to the Mob; Silence of the Lambs; Philadelphia;* etc. Despite his talent, Fugimoto did not make a good impression on John Goff, who wrote that he was "very aloof and chilly. He had his crew, as did most cinematographers at that time and they worked like a well-oiled machine. They all had their 'inside gags' but outsiders weren't allowed in. I don't recall

John Broderick even having a lot of input for camera work. I've worked with some very talented cinematographers (Don Burgess, Dean Cundey, and Eddy Van Der Enden) and all have been very open, warm, and friendly to everyone around. I didn't find Fujimoto to be that at all."[655]

Tom Kibbe who played Darryl, Molly's city slicker boyfriend who accompanies her, summed up the production and said, "I do remember it was a fast shoot over a few weeks' time, a small crew and very much an ensemble family-like atmosphere."[656]

For John Goff, the "family" froze him out and he felt that "It wasn't particularly enjoyable for me. I was a stranger, I guess you could call it, coming into the project as I did. After the first week I was just trying to get along, do the job, and take home a payday."[657]

After filming wrapped and post-production was completed, John Broderick was extremely satisfied and had high praise for his film. He gushed, "Frankly, I feel we have an engrossing movie with Lynley and Lockwood performing in the tradition of famous movie love teams that clashed. *Out of Control* hits with the impact of Cagney's grapefruit landing in the face of Mae Bush!!!"[658]

In the movie Lynley played Molly Golden, a brash, haughty New York City magazine fashion editor, who is informed that she is the sole heir to her uncle's estate in Alabama. With dollars in her eyes, she quits her job, packs up the car, and with her prissy "boyfriend" Darryl (Tom Kibbe), heads south with talk of sitting on her plantation's veranda and being served mint juleps by her servants. When she arrives, she gets a rude awakening and finds she was left a rundown dilapidated house complete with a bible-quoting handyman Arthur Pennyrich (Royal Dano) with a love for hooch, a refrigerator on the porch, and lots of unpaid bills.

She spies Arthur going into a back garage with a handsome burly redneck named Leroy Hastings (Gary Lockwood) who lives on the property. It is hatred at first sight between Molly and Leroy. She learns that her uncle was making his living from distributing moonshine and Leroy is his fast driving runner who is skilled at avoiding the police and a rival syndicate led by Mr. Shields (John Goff). Headstrong and pushy, Molly wants her cut and more say in the business causing lots of friction between the two as they continuously bicker and insult each other. Their squabbling is fun, with Lynley and Lockwood giving it their best, and a nice contrast to the fast-paced car chases and fist fights. It is never made clear if Darryl is gay or straight, but he sees what is going on underneath the name calling between Molly and Leroy and, hating the shabby living conditions, hightails it back to New York.

Molly's condescending attitude, parading around the grounds in a bikini and then skinny dipping, finally takes its toll on Leroy. When Arthur goes missing, she demands Leroy do all the work at the still himself to make their next scheduled run. Fed up with the New Yorker, Leroy bursts into her house and promises to give her a poking that she has been craving. Molly puts up a fight but the brute overpowers her and takes her on the kitchen floor. He then goes back to the garage where he lives. An infuriated Molly grabs a shotgun he left behind and follows him. While he is lying on the bed, she pulls the trigger to kill the SOB, but he removed the bullets. She then goes to clobber him with it. Instead, she gives in to her sexual attraction and this time make consensual love. Afterwards, she does state that what he did to her prior was illegal, but the egotistical lout knows she will not say a word. With today's #MeToo movement, this scenario most likely would have been altered for today's moviegoers. The two then team up to keep the moonshine flowing and their customers happy as they outsmart the cops and out race the syndicate. Though Molly tries to change, Leroy remains a brute, physically abusing her (when she sits to rest after loading the car, he yanks her up by the arm and gives her a kick to the rear to continue working) in his attempts to tame the shrew. Charming, isn't he?

Throughout the film Leroy is constantly demanding more money due to the risks he takes running Molly's moonshine. At the end, with a gun-toting Molly by his side in his car, he asks for a sixty/forty split in his favor. Molly counters with fifty/fifty. He replies, "Okay, but I get to lay you any time I get the craving." She says, "Same for me—deal?" "Deal," he answers in perhaps a way to show despite the assault they are now on equal footing, as the film freezes on them driving down a bad Georgia road with a reprise of the title tune playing.

Golden Film's executives were satisfied with the final edit of *Out of Control*, as it was then called, that John Broderick delivered. Its president, Don Reynolds, raved, "Lynley and Lockwood ignite each other in this film. They come on with overpowering impact that is bound to fascinate moviegoers who are looking for a good movie."[659] His publicist, Joe Mass, predicted that the movie "doesn't need a big publicity campaign. It's a fascinating film and the word-of-mouth will get around that this is a top-notch film."[660]

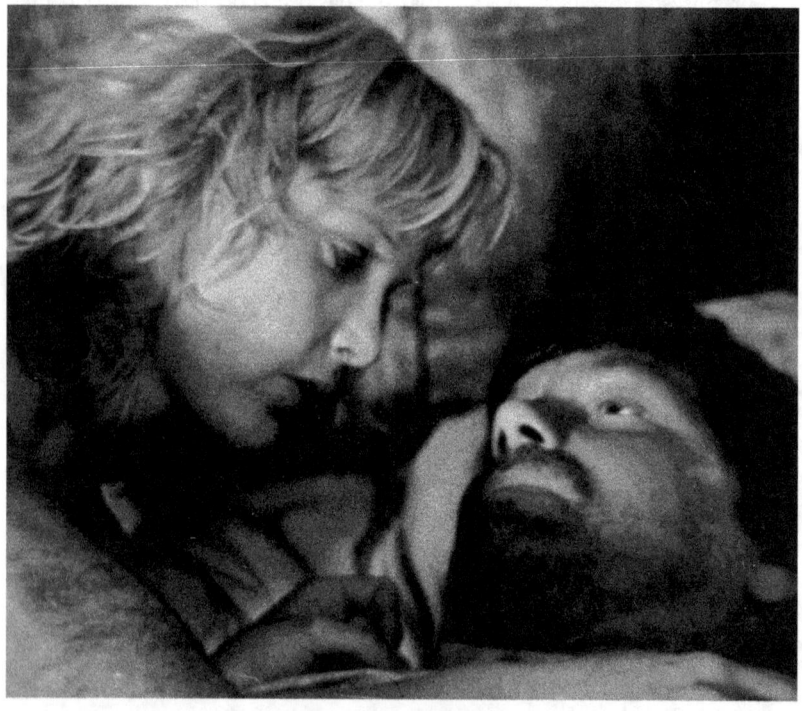

After being sexually assaulted by Leroy (Gary Lockwood), Molly (Carol Lynley) threatens to kill him before succumbing to his animal magnetism in *Bad Georgia Road* (Dimension, 1977).

Despite their intentions and praise, and their registering the movie with the Motion Picture Association of America where it received a PG-rating, Golden Films did not release the movie. It was acquired by Dimension Pictures (founded by exhibitor Lawrence Woolner and not to be confused with Dimension Films) in April 1977. The company changed the title to *Bad Georgia Road* (even though it takes place in Alabama) and added a catchy upbeat song called "Runnin' Moonshine" sung by Ron Wiggins over the opening credits. The film's wonderful poster art included an artist's rendering of a scantily clad Carol Lynley with enhanced big boobs, a head shot of Gary Lockwood, souped up cars, and a tag line that read "They're makin' time to the county line!" It was an obvious attempt to lure indiscriminate movie fans that enjoyed such Southern-fried drive-in films as *Macon County Line*, *White Lightning*, and *Gator* back into the theater.

Dimension first released the movie in the Atlanta, Georgia area where it raked in an impressive $102,000 during its initial week in theaters. However, the movie never got a wide national release and just popped up at regional theaters scattered about the southern U.S. during 1977 when *Star Wars* dominated the box office and the nation's attention. Dimension then unloaded the movie to another company that took over distribution. In July, *Bad Georgia Road* traveled north and trailed *Star Wars* with the second biggest take in the Minneapolis area. It also played Austin and Pittsburg. The movie finally petered out by November where it played two drive-ins in the San Francisco area taking in a "bumpy" $4,300 over its first weekend, per *Variety*. In the summer of 1978, it was back in the theaters but this time as the bottom of a double bill with either *The Great Smokey Roadblock* starring Henry Fonda or *Hi-Riders* starring Mel Ferrer.

Lynley received no praise for this hillbilly moonshine opus. Most newspaper reviewers ignored it including the trades such as *Variety* and *Boxoffice*. About eight years later, Jimmy McDonough and Bill Landis writing in *Film Comment*, remarked that movie was "an inert but unusual moonshiner … attractively shot by Tak Fujimoto."

Carol was not happy with the final product. She commented, "I didn't like this movie and it didn't do well. Back then it was a boys' club and they could get away with this type of ending. I don't think they could now."[661] John Goff agreed and opined, "I'll have to go along with Carol on that point. 'It was the times.' It was brutal, especially watching it in current times. But it never became an issue at the time. Looking back, yes, it could have been finessed better, but it wasn't so it is what it is."[662] This is true and the director could have possibly toned down the assault into more of a seduction with Molly at first resisting but then submitting to Leroy's animal magnetism.

Overall, *Bad Georgia Road* is entertaining, and it is quite a treat to see Carol do well in this type of role and film. Though she over does the haughtiness a bit to the point of shrillness in the earlier scenes, Carol really put her heart and soul into the character. She is so engaging in this different type of role and gets the audience to come around to liking Molly. This is due to the more down-to-Earth moments such as when her exasperated Molly confesses to Darryl that she cannot go back to New York because she quit her job and gave up her apartment. She ponders starting over in a new city before deciding to stay and make a go of the predicament she is in. It is the first time the audience feels some sympathy for her. Carol is also funny in the scenes where Molly finds herself in the middle of bar room brawl or tipsy after having her first swig of moonshine. And of course, she handles her dramatic moments with strong conviction. She is well-paired with Gary Lockwood who is perfect as her sexy redneck agitator (and fills his tight jeans quite nicely) and he helps elevate the movie. There is a believable heat between the duo that finally draws these opposites together. Despite the misguided rape-turned-lovemaking scene, *Bad Georgia Road* remains a rollicking fun time for Lynley fans. If given a national release, moviegoers with a love of action movies may have enjoyed it as well.

Though it was not a blockbuster by any means, *Bad Georgia Road* was a popular booking on the drive-in film circuit and this was not a surprise to movie salesman Jimmy Murphy. He remarked to *Chicago Tribune* journalist Tim McNulty at the time, "I hate to use the word 'redneck,' but we try to appeal to, well, rednecks. Every picture ever made with a moonshine theme has made money."⁶⁶³ McNulty went on to describe the audience at one drive-in screening of *Bad Georgia Road* arriving in their Chevy pickups carrying "married women in curlers, gum-chewing teen-age vixens, macho men wearing suspenders but no shirts."⁶⁶⁴ What a sight this must have been but hey they were paying customers.

In late 1978, the film was sold to the pay and cable TV market. It then became a staple of late-night broadcast television and eventually received a video release in the eighties.

*****

Back on the small screen, Lynley appeared in another crime drama and it was one of her best. In the gritty detective series *Kojak*, starring Emmy Award winner Telly Savalas as the lollipop-sucking, no-bullshit New York detective Lt. Theo Kojak, Lynley guest-starred with Christopher Walken in "Kiss It All Goodbye." This episode was noted for being one of a handful directed by its star though it was not planned. Earl Wilson reported, "Telly Savalas told Carol Lynley emoting in *Kojak*, he'd like to direct her some time, next day director Ed Abrams went to a hospital with kidney stones, and Telly took over as director."⁶⁶⁵

Remembering working with Savalas, the actor and director, and with the then unknown Christopher Walken, Carol commented with a laugh,

> Telly was very good and just like *Telly Savalas*! He had the same mannerisms but only he was on the other side of the camera. He was also a flirt and a bit of a ladies' man. He would look at me and say, 'No! No, the eyes I can tell.' I asked, 'Tell what?' And he replied, 'You don't fancy me. I can tell.' I exclaimed, 'No, of course I do Telly.' But he didn't believe me. Of course, he was right. I certainly didn't fancy him but I would never want him to know that. Actors have egos. And I didn't mind that he knew it was a no because it made my life even easier.

I loved working with Chris Walken. I used to go to the Children's Professional School in New York with Chris when I was about twelve years old. That is where we first met. In person, he is not intense or scary at all. When his face relaxes, he can look quite menacing and he is not at all. He loves to laugh and laughs quite a lot. When he does, he looks like a little boy. I remember I called my agent when we finished shooting. I told him that I just worked with Chris Walken and that he is going to become a big star. And he did.[666]

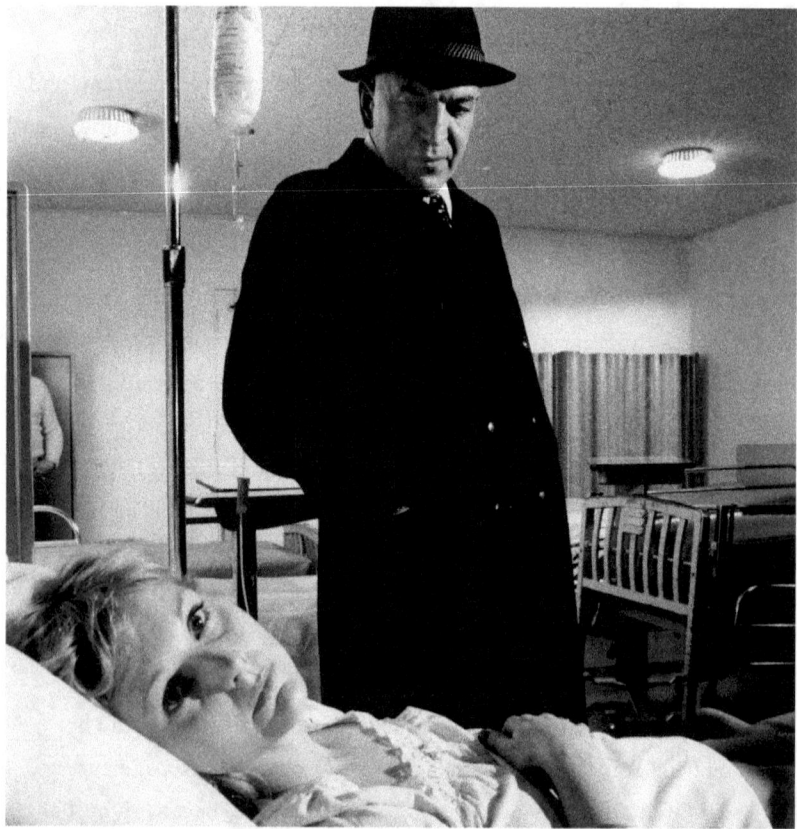

Kojak (Telly Savalas) visits paralyzed model Polly Ames (Carol Lynley) who was accidentally shot by Det. Crocker in "Kiss It All Goodbye" on *Kojak* (Universal Television, 1977).

Considered one of the series' finest, "Kiss It All Goodbye" featured Carol as a high fashion model who is accidentally shot by Det. Crocker (Kevin Dobson) during a botched fur heist and becomes paralyzed. You can tell right from Carol's first scene that Savalas spent time cultivating a performance from her. Polly, lying in her hospital bed, tells Kojak that she is a model and that to keep healthy and her legs shapely she goes for long walks, which led her in front of the building where the robbery occurred. As he goes to leave, she throws off the bed sheet and asks him if he thinks her legs are pretty. She then cries out that she cannot feel them. The next day Crocker learns that the doctors are reluctant to remove the bullet lodged in Polly's back, leaving her a paraplegic for now. When he shows up to her room, the look on his face reveals all and Polly asks him to leave as she contemplates her future in a wheelchair. Kiss all the modeling goodbye. Carol, prodded by her director no doubt, projects a nice range of emotions in these scenes from confusion, to despair, to anger arousing audience sympathy.

Crocker is devastated about what he did to Polly and begins seeing the wheelchair bound young woman determined to help her walk again. They grow closer and Polly develops feelings for him. Then Polly gets a visitor. It is Ben the thief from the burglary (played by a young sexy, yes sexy, Christopher Walken) who kisses her hello. It turns out that Polly was the lookout and not an innocent bystander as believed. He admits he tipped off the cops to get their third partner Jaime, who was killed in the gun battle, out of the way because he could not trust him. Not wanting to jeopardize her relationship with Crocker, Polly gives Ben written permission to enter her safety deposit box to retrieve his share of the money.

Meanwhile Kojak and crew are closing in on the thieves as they place Jaime and Polly in Cleveland at the same time of a similar fur heist. When they discover Polly visited her bank three days after each burglary, they realize she was part of the robberies.

Ben gets spooked at the bank rightly thinking the cops are watching and Polly set him up. In tears, Polly tells him to take all the money and she will not rat him out to the cops. She is desperate to keep Crocker from finding out the truth. Ben won't back off and insists they go together to the bank and then run off. Carol is appealing as Polly comes to terms that her idyllic time with Crocker must come to an end. He calls just then with good news from another doctor who thinks she can operate, but Polly is harsh with him not wanting anymore false hope about walking and never wanting to see him again. Crocker is shaken and then learns from Kojak that Polly was the lookout. He refuses to believe it and rushes over to her apartment just as Ben and Polly are exiting. Ben tries to make a break for it, but it collared by Kojak.

At the station house, Crocker and Polly have one last moment together. As he says goodbye, Polly sadly tells him that she wished they met before she got involved with the robberies. When Crocker says she would have looked right past him to the good-looking guys, Polly says no she would not have. He then gives her a kiss goodbye. Kojak tells Polly that Crocker still has faith in her and Polly poignantly replies that she just wanted her time with him to last a bit longer knowing it would not be forever.

When rerun on the cable channel MeTV in 2016, the staff called it "a standout episode." Telly Savalas deserves a lot of credit for that and for Carol's extremely convincing and sympathetic performance. It also helped that Carol worked with three superior actors—Savalas, Christopher Walken just before winning his Oscar for *The Deer Hunter*, and Kevin Dobson keeping her on her A-game. Though the audience learns she is not an innocent, Carol's touching performance and sweet chemistry with Dobson's remorseful Crocker have us hoping they can stay together, even though the odds are slim. Too bad Carol never got to work with director Telly Savalas ever again.

Of Lynley's later TV work, this performance was truly worthy of an Emmy nomination. Carol goes through a litany of feelings from anger and despair to sympathy and confusion as Polly must face the reality of her situation regarding the loss of her ability to walk and that the mutual feeling developing between her and Crocker is based on a lie. She also had to keep the audience on her side even though the viewer knows she was not an innocent bystander. Unfortunately, Carol's episode aired during the same period as the mini-series *Roots* and *Rich Man, Poor Man, Book II*. And although there were separate acting categories for Limited Series that year, actresses from these heralded series dominated the Best Actress for a Single Performance in a Drama or Comedy Series what is now called Best Performance by a Guest Star. Why these actresses were not restricted to the Limited Series categories is just another mystery of the Primetime Emmy Awards and how they do things.

It was shortly after this that the New York Health & Racquet Club began using Carol Lynley as the celebrity face of the club. Per a friend, it was done without her permission. Some type of agreement must have been reached as Carol continued appearing in ads extolling the virtues of joining a fitness center, before it became the norm. Photos of her working out or in the pool were included in the advertisements, which lasted to about 1981.

13. Welcome to Fantasy Island!

The bad girl roles continued for Carol Lynley with the made-for-television movie *Fantasy Island* and Carol excelled as a vile woman with murder on her mind. This was the pilot for the long running series created and produced by Aaron Spelling and Leonard Goldberg. Three people pay $50,000 to live out their wildest fantasies executed by the island's mysterious host Mr. Roarke and his sidekick Tattoo. There is a dark undertone to the movie and was quite sinister with a horrific ending for two of the story arcs. Mr. Roarke comes off more menacing than mysterious and there were several hints that he may not have been mortal. The ominous tenor of the show was downplayed and Mr. Roarke water-downed when it became a weekly series, which was too bad as the pilot put it in the realm of superior fantasy.

Explaining how the idea for *Fantasy Island* came to him, Aaron Spelling said that he and his partner were at a pitch meeting with the head of ABC-TV, Brandon Stoddard. The producers were pushing some ideas for TV-movies and Stoddard rejected all six pitches. He wanted something more exciting. In frustration Spelling jokingly asked if he wanted to have people go to this great island where all their sexual fantasies come true. Stoddard loved the idea and from this *Fantasy Island* the movie (less the carnal antics) was born from a teleplay by Gene Levitt forever listed as series creator.

Reportedly John Huston was considered for Mr. Roarke, but Spelling wanted Ricardo Montalbán. The network asked why? Spelling sensed that his nationality was the unspoken reason for their trepidation, so he made the point that not only was Montalbán a brilliant actor but the Roarke character is never clearly from heaven or hell, his accent would enhance the mystery. ABC then pushed for Orson Welles but knowing how difficult he could be to work with, the producer held strong and his choice won the part. For the role of Tattoo, Spelling's casting director saw Hervé Villechaize in the James Bond movie *The Man with the Golden Gun* and knew he would be perfect.

Spelling assembled an all-star cast to live out the fantasies. Hired, and billed alphabetically, were Bill Bixby, Sandra Dee, Peter Lawford, Carol Lynley, Hugh O'Brian, Eleanor Parker, Victoria Principal, Dick Sargent, and Tina Sinatra.

Sinatra had appeared in a few TV shows such as *It Takes a Thief*, *Adam-12*, and *McCloud* earlier in the decade, but had not acted in almost five years. She recalled, "I got the part because my mother called Aaron Spelling and Leonard Goldberg. She asked them to please give me a job and they did. Aaron was darling and we had known him for several years through mutual friends."[667]

Spelling cast Tina as a secretary attending the wake of her supposedly dead boss. Commenting on her co-star, Tina said, "I would watch Carol Lynley at Jax, a privately-owned clothing store in Beverly Hills, where we all used to shop. I met her prior to [*Fantasy Island*] through Jack Haley, Jr. who was a close friend of hers. I think it was at a charity event. Whenever I was in her company, I was envious. I wanted to look like that. Young brunette women want what they don't have."[668]

"I didn't know who else was cast until I arrived on the set," continued Sinatra. "I had known Ricardo Montalbán throughout my youth and always adored him. I was delighted to see Peter Lawford because I hadn't seen him in so many years. There was an estrangement between him and my dad for some time. That was an experience for me emotionally and I even thought I could get them back together. I could not. Eleanor Parker was a goddess to me. She was very private, but she was fond of my dad. They had done *The Man with the Golden Arm*. She had nothing but time for me. I was a green eighteen-year-old and she was almost mothering to me because she knew I was petrified."[669]

Fantasy Island and Lynley received a lot of press during the filming, all due to a broken goblet. In a scene being filmed on October 21, 1976, some of the cast was gathered around a dining room table. Carol's character, in a fit of despair, threw her wine glass across the room at a wall behind Peter Lawford. Per Carol,

> I was given a real heavy glass by the director [Richard Lang]. I asked for a breakaway one but was told I had to use this. I thought if this glass broke large shards of glass would scatter. They set up a blanket away from Peter who was beside the camera and told me to aim for it. I was not comfortable doing this even though they assured me it would not break, so I threw it as instructed. It hit the top of a chair and shattered. I heard the director call cut. Peter then yelled out. When he pulled up his pants leg there was a huge gash and he was bleeding. I became hysterical. I was never hurt on set and never wanted to hurt anybody while working. They rushed him off to the hospital and the director said we had to reshoot. I was too upset to continue. Tina Sinatra whom I knew for years helped calm me down. She was great. I was able to pull myself together to redo it.[670]

Peter Lawford was taken to UCLA Medical Center. He was hospitalized for a few days and required stitches before being released. About a month later, Lawford was readmitted to the hospital suffering from severe pains in that same left leg. A few weeks after on Christmas Eve, the actor filed a lawsuit seeking $2.5 million in damages against defendants 20th Century-Fox, producer Aaron Spelling, and Carol Lynley. In the suit, Lawford claimed, "the cut required 22 stitches, hospitalized him for nine days and caused prolong limping which aggravated a spinal disc condition."[671] He contended the injury has affected his career with loss of contracted work. His lawyer added that a doctor warned that "a permanent disability seems to be developing."[672]

The lawsuit was a not a publicity ploy and was real. Carol, still upset with the director to this day, revealed,

> I had to get an attorney. I really liked Peter. When he came back to work, he wasn't mad with me and said, 'Don't worry love, I had to include you for insurance purposes.' They settled out of court. I think he got workman's comp for all the time missed.[673]

The two-hour *Fantasy Island* movie had three story arcs. In arguably the weakest one, an older military GI (Bill Bixby) travels back in time to relive a cherished romance with a beautiful woman (an emaciated Sandra Dee) he met in England during WWII. More exciting was a big game hunter (Hugh O'Brian) wanting to experience the ultimate thrill of being the hunted but is thrown for a loop when he awakens to find an innocent woman (Victoria Principal) handcuffed to him. Lynley was featured in the third and most engrossing segment that has a wealthy woman named Eunice Hollander Baines (Eleanor Parker) fake her own death (she supposedly died in a boating accident) so she could attend her funeral and see what relatives and friends really thought about her. Eunice runs the mill in the town named after her grandfather. Attendees to her service are Eunice's sophisticated husband Grant Baines (Peter Lawford), her meek brother Charles Hollander (Dick Sargent), her trusted secretary Connie Raymond (Tina Sinatra), and Carol Lynley as Eunice's estranged sister, Liz Hollande (in *Return to Peyton Place*, Carol was Parker's daughter). A lush with a foul mouth, Liz was run out of town by Eunice due to the embarrassment she had caused the family.

Eunice disguises herself as a maid (poor Parker is saddled with a most unattractive wig, glasses, and fake nose) and listens in as her family insult each other and reveal what they really thought about the dearly departed. Liz keeps lapping up the booze and wants to party while the others look at her with disdain. At dinner, Charles admits that he loved and admired Eunice and could never have made the mill as successful as she did. Connie reveals that she thought her boss was a dreadful person ("she had a sharp tongue and short temper") and purposely led her to believe that she was having an affair with her husband just to get under her skin. The biggest surprise though is Liz who throws that infamous wine glass across the room after breaking down and admitting that she loved her sister who raised her after their parents died. Touched, Eunice informs Roarke that she is going to reveal herself to her sister who is in so much pain. She goes to Liz's bedroom and the two have a joyous reunion. Once Eunice exits, Liz opens her closet door and out pops two-timing Grant with whom she has been having an affair. He cannot believe that Liz's suspicions that something funny was going on about the way and where Eunice died were right. The steely-eyed tramp (Carol at her best here) now wants to grant Eunice's fantasy and make her a real corpse at her funeral. At first reluctant, Grant agrees to go along with her scheme to rid themselves of Eunice for good.

Liz tells Eunice that Grant is so despondent over her death that she thinks he is suicidal. She leads her sister up to the cliffs overlooking the rocky shore. Peering over the edge, Liz lets out an "oh, no!" As Eunice goes to see below, Liz (Carol looking especially terrific with the wind blowing back her hair) takes a step backwards and hisses, "Eunice everything I said last night was a lie. I don't love you, I *detest* you and Grant detests you too. We just wanted you to know that before you die." Liz rushes forward to push Eunice and the next shot is of someone falling to their death. There is a funeral the next day, but it is not for Eunice, but for Liz. Somehow, perhaps due to "the grace of God" or Mr. Roarke's magic, Liz slipped and took the plunge instead of her sister. Eunice then fires Connie (who retorts with the best line in the film, "I look forward to your next funeral") and decides to stay married to Grant if he remains a faithful husband. If he falters, she will immediately press charges for attempted murder. Grant willingly accepts his punishment.

ABC-TV advertised the movie with trailers and print ads with copy that read, "If you had $50,000 and a weekend to live out your wildest fantasies, what would they be? See it all come true on ... *Fantasy Island*." Carol was prominently pictured along with Ricardo Montalbán, Hugh O'Brian, Bill Bixby, and Peter Lawford.

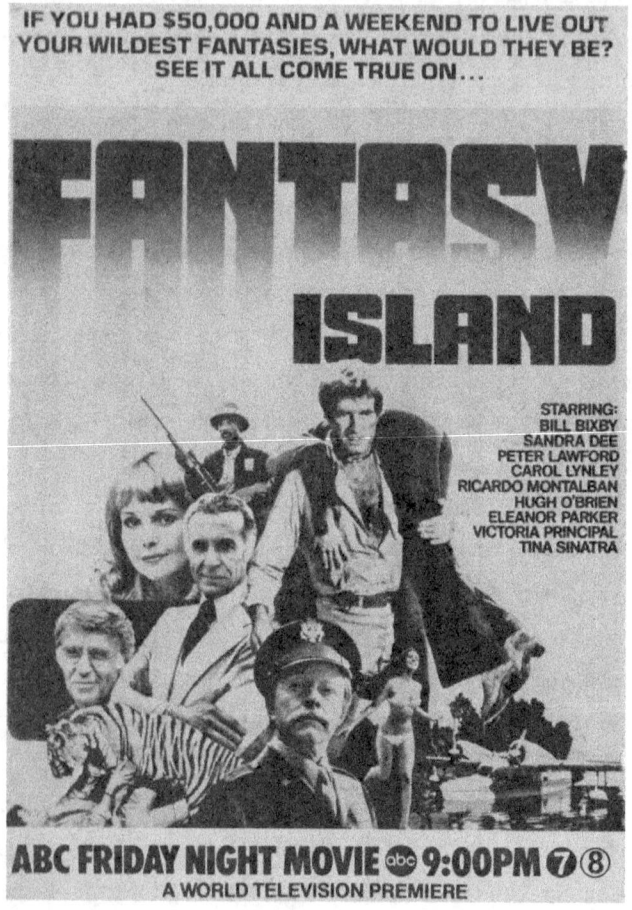

Promotional print ad for the TV-movie *Fantasy Island* (1977).

The critics did not take kindly to *Fantasy Island*. Even Kevin Thomas of the *Los Angeles Times*, who usually had something complimentary to say, described it as being, "relentlessly tedious and unconvincing" and found "the largely veteran cast tries hard against impossible odds."

Reviewers though are not the final say and despite the critical barbs, the audience loved what they saw. Airing on January 14, 1977, it received a 26.4 rating and a 42 share. It was the seventh most watched TV show the week it was televised. This took Carol by surprise. "I thought the plot was strange. Then to my amazement it became a big hit. I thought, well, Aaron knows what he is doing so obviously I am going to go along with it."

Asking for her concluding thoughts on *Fantasy Island*, Tina Sinatra remarked, "It was a high point in my career. I don't have many standout moments as an actor, but this was one of them for sure because of the cast I worked with. I remember reading a review that said I was the meanest secretary since Eve Harrington. It wasn't surprising to me that it was successful because in those days everything Aaron Spelling and Leonard Goldberg did became a hit."[674]

ABC then commissioned a sequel (without Lynley) that was entitled *Return to Fantasy Island*. Spelling was about to go to work on a third film when the network decided they wanted a weekly series, however they wanted Hervé Villechaize replaced with a beautiful girl. Spelling refused because Hervé and Ricardo worked excellently as a team. Seeing that Spelling was not going to budge, the network acquiesced. The sequel aired on January 20, 1978 and the series started the week after.

Little did Carol know that she would return to *Fantasy Island* - a lot. Once it became a series, she appeared in an additional ten episodes, the most of any guest actor or actress. Her roles ranged from a ballerina, to a high-class call girl, to a woman who sold her soul to the devil. Carol loved being able to play different characters and when asked if she had a favorite, the actress responded, "In the one I like best I play a Philadelphia bus conductor who longs to go back to the days of chivalry and romance."[675] She felt this was one of the better scripts.

Besides the money ("It got my daughter through college and every time they sent me a script I said yes."[676]), Carol really enjoyed doing *Fantasy Island* because of its star Ricardo Montalbán. She fondly remarked at the time, "Ricardo is such a sweet, lovely guy. I don't think there is anyone in the business who has a bad word to say about him. It's just the happiest set. He treats everybody beautifully and everybody then treats everybody else beautifully."[677]

Regarding Hervé Villechaize, Carol commented, "Hervé was always interesting. He was a troubled soul and being that small didn't help."[678]

In an on-camera interview with the Manhattan cable-access TV show *Media Funhouse*, Carol shared a story of sitting with Hervé one day on the set. He had a gun that he kept twirling in his fingers. When she asked if it was loaded, he replied, per Carol, "I wouldn't have it any other way." Because of his size, he was afraid of being kidnapped and carried the gun for protection. When Carol asked if he really needed to have it on the set, which was a safe location, Hervé said someone could easily grab him and put him into their car. Carol joked, "Before they could pick him up, he'd shoot'em."[679]

Fantasy Island reunited Carol with many of her male costars over the past years including Stuart Whitman (*Hound-Dog Man, Shock Treatment*), John Saxon (*The Cardinal*), Doug McClure (*The Virginian*), Roddy McDowall (*Shock Treatment, The Poseidon Adventure*, etc.), Lloyd Bochner (*Harlow*), Paul Burke (*Once You Kiss a Stranger*), Gary Collins (*The Sixth Sense*), and Dale Robinette (*The Beasts Are on the Streets*). Reportedly, Carol enjoyed working again with Burke, Whitman, and of course McDowall the most. She added, "I believe Roddy and I have the most episodes We joked that we came and went off that island so much that we didn't know where we were—or who we were!"[680]

Carol's earlier episodes were best. She looked fantastic in all and the scripts were more interesting. The series was showing its age in the early eighties' episodes, though the second to last one with the Angel of Death was a highlight.

In half of Carol's episodes, she was the guest wanting to live out her wildest fantasy. After hearing the comforting and familiar words of Tattoo shouting "Ze plane! Ze Plane!", he and Mr. Roarke would get in their electric cart and be driven down to the dock to meet it. Carol would disembark as Mr. Roarke would share with Tattoo and the audience the fantasy of choice. Most of Carol's episodes were in the supernatural realm though a few were just about searching for love.

Carol Lynley's happy hooker toasts to her upcoming paradise stay in "Lady of the Evening" on *Fantasy Island*. (Columbia Pictures Television, 1980).
Collection of Marlin Dobbs

"Lady of the Evening," directed by Don Weis (*The Gene Krupa Story*, *Pajama Party*, and many TV shows), was Lynley's first guest appearance on *Fantasy Island* after it was picked up as a weekly series. It aired on February 25, 1978. This episode, "Carnival," and "The Devil and Mandy Breem" were arguably her most memorable due to well-written scripts and fine turns by the actress. The show shot quickly, so viewers should not expect any Emmy Award winning performances, but Carol and her co-stars approached each episode respectfully and professionally. If she had not and behaved like a diva, the producers would not have invited her back so often.

In this episode, Carol gets her turn to play a prostitute à la her co-star Stella Stevens did as Linda Rogo in *The Poseidon Adventure*. Though her character, Renee Lansing, is worried about running into former johns like Linda was, Renee is neither as feisty nor retired, but cautious and on vacation. Renee is an in-demand New York City high class call girl whose fantasy is to spend a relaxing week where nobody would recognize her. Even a hooker needs a break. At the hotel pool she literally runs into debonair Bill Fredricks (Paul Burke), who knocks her drink out of her hand and offers to replace it. A nervous Renee declines and runs off. Later, Bill spots her at the hotel's lounge and brings a drink over. They begin chatting about the Ralph Waldo Emerson book she was reading, and he reveals that he teaches high school. Renee is attracted to him, but when he puts his hand on top of hers, she recoils. Pretending a friend is meeting her, she politely asks him to leave.

The next day, Bill runs into Renee sitting cliff-side gazing at the scenery. Again, when he gets too personal, she becomes paranoid and goes to depart. While trying to maneuver her golf cart out, it gets caught in reverse and flips over, dangling over the cliff. Bill pulls the terrified Renee to safety. When he makes a joke about taking her back to his "Spiderman's web" to claim his reward, she immediately thinks he wants to have sex and insults him. She just cannot get her mind off work. Claiming he was joking, Elaine replies, "The hell you were." Miffed, Bill tells her a simple thank you was all he wanted, but even that was too hard for her.

Renee apologizes to Bill and treats him to dinner where she has a fabulous time. They make plans to spend the entire next day together. Returning to her room for the evening, she is startled when she receives a phone call from Roy Burke (Peter Mark Richman) a former john who recognized her in the dining room. She lies and says he has the wrong person. Later they run into each other on the tennis courts and Roy goes along with her ruse as she explains to Bill that they met at a fashion convention.

Shortly after, Renee confronts Mr. Roarke and demands a refund as she specifically stipulated that she was not to run into any former clients. Roarke tells her that he suspects her deeper motive for her fantasy was to leave her former life behind and move forward with a nice guy like Bill. The only way she could do that is to confront her past. Furious with Roarke, she insists on being put on the next flight out. Storming back to her room, Roy turns up and agrees to keep her secret in exchange for a roll in the hay. She refuses and he belittles her for thinking that she is the white picket fence-type of girl and would become bored within weeks. At dinner, Renee rebuffs Bill when he asks to visit her in New York. When he questions why, she tearfully says, "Because I'm a hooker." To her surprise, he admits that he was one of her johns about four years prior. He fell in love with her and came to Fantasy Island to hopefully begin a romance. After he professes his love, she tells him never to stop as they embrace.

Carol is sweetly vulnerable as the call girl so worried about her past. She is perfectly reunited with her *Once You Kiss a Stranger* co-star Paul Burke, who gives a much more animated performance here than he did in that movie. The ending is truly a surprise, even though it is a stretch that Lynley's character did not remember him at all. She must have been some busy call girl. Even so, due to Carol's performance, you cannot but help to root for Renee to find happiness.

"Carnival," which aired on December 2, 1978, was Carol's second guest star trip to *Fantasy Island* and it was directed by former actor Georg Stanford Brown of *The Rookies* fame. She looks absolutely stunning here with her long, wavy blonde hair style, and clad in blue and peach blouses and dresses which highlighted her blue eyes.

Here she played Dorothy Weller, a young secretary who wishes to return to Guadalupe. Two years prior after a three-day love affair with Tom (Stuart Whitman), "the man of her dreams", she went into a coma after a car accident. When she awoke, everybody denied that he existed. Her fantasy is to determine once and for all if he was real or just a figment of her imagination.

After being dropped off in a village bearing an incredible resemblance to the one in Guadalupe, Dorothy hears a familiar tune blaring from a local cantina. She rushes in only to be informed by the bartender that the gentleman who requested the song has departed, but she recognizes the wine he was drinking and the Turkish cigarettes he was smoking. She is positive it is her former lover and later, after receiving an anonymous note, heads to the beach boat house where Tom makes his presence known to her. He reveals that the car crash was no accident and that they were both meant to be killed because of his work as a spy. By dropping out of sight afterwards, he kept her out of danger.

Reunited, the lovers' idyll is ruined by a hired assassin (Luke Askew) sent to execute Tom. After almost becoming roadkill, Tom meets up with Dorothy at the village carnival and tells her that they need to leave immediately. While fleeing, the assassin catches up to them and shoots Tom fatally. After watching the funeral from afar, he leaves the island satisfied his mission was accomplished. Mr. Roarke brings a heartbroken Dorothy back to the cantina where she met Tom, only to be shocked to find out that he is still alive. At first angry with Mr. Roarke, he explains to her that he helped Tom fake his death so "he could die and you both could have a chance to live." The reunited lovers embrace and decide to remain on the island to start a new life together.

This episode is intriguing. Brown keeps the action moving and Carol looks spectacular. He gets a truly superior performance from her and arguably it is her best trip to the island for her fans.

Publicity photo of Roddy McDowall, Ricardo Montalban, and Carol Lynley in "The Devil and Mandy Breem" on *Fantasy Island* (Columbia Pictures Television, 1980).

In one of her most popular appearances, Carol starred in season four's debut episode "The Devil and Mandy Breem," which aired October 25, 1980. Eerie and dark, this above average episode, directed by actor Vince Edwards (who had acted with Carol twice previously), comes closest to the original TV-movie in that sense.

Carol is quite effective and is on edge throughout as a selfless, caring wife who has sold her soul to the devil (Roddy McDowall) the year before to save the life of her husband Philip (a stoic Adam West) fatally injured in a car accident. A year later, Mephistopheles is back (McDowall dressed in all black and lit with a red filter giving him a hellish glow) to collect. Mandy wants Roarke to help save her life, but she neglects to tell him from whom. A frustrated Roarke goes along with the fantasy and even obtains a rare blooming potted orchid for her that Mephistopheles requested be handed to him in return for her soul. However, the demon dupes her knowing nothing can live in his grasp, and the terrified Mandy finally confesses all to an irked Roarke and her disbelieving husband. Seeing how strong their love and adoration is for each other, Roarke agrees to help them beat the devil and even considers that Mephistopheles may have used them to get to him.

It is here where the episode goes a bit awry though there is a surprising twist. Instead of a raging battle between good and evil in a fog-shrouded garden where the characters meet, we get talk of loopholes in the written contract. The Breem's try to sneak off but are beaten back by some tacky special effects of goblins and such. Agreeing that he is contractually bound to take three souls—no more or less—Mephistopheles is stunned when Roarke reveals that Mrs. Breem is pregnant voiding the pact since there are now four souls. Montalbán plays it cool and sincerely while McDowall hams it up. Knowing he is defeated; the enraged devil bares his horns and vows to be back since he and Roarke have all of eternity to settle their score. This is another instance where the question of Roarke's mortality is revealed.

The Breem's are elated that they are free, but Mandy feels badly that Roarke had to lie. He suggests she see her family doctor once she returns home. Later, as the glowing couple board the airplane to leave, Tattoo says to Roarke, "I knew you wouldn't lie about the baby. But how did you know? You are not a doctor." Roarke smiles and simply replies, "Indeed."

In Carol's favorite episode "Cyrano" directed by the prolific Brit, Don Chaffey (*One Million BC*, *Pete's Dragon*) and airing on October 24, 1981, the too-pretty actress is oddly cast as Marjorie Denton a Philadelphia bus driver. She is just 'one of the guys' during her working days and wants to visit a place where men were chivalrous and passionately romantic. Carol is given three strong leading men in this episode—John Saxon, Simon MacCorkindale, and Lloyd Bochner, elevating this easily above the episode's other story arc featuring Bart Braverman and Judy Landers. Also noticeable is the strongly missed absence of Tattoo and the presence of the prickly sweet Wendy Schaal as Julie, Roarke's assistant.

In the episode, Roarke sends Marjorie back in time to the days of Cyrano de Bergerac. Arriving at a pub, Marjorie (Carol looking fantastic all glammed up in her period attire and resembling Marie Antoinette) is immediately noticed by dueling Gaston du Brielle (Simon MacCorkindale in a horrid long brown wig) who asks his friend Cyrano (John Saxon) to help win her heart since the sight of her beauty paralyzes him. Buying a sonnet from his friend, Gaston introduces himself to Marjorie and after reading his love poem to her ("It's beautiful," she gushes) ends it with a kiss of her hand. She agrees to meet him in the courtyard in an hour and then catches the cad with another woman reciting the same poem. Furious, she literally runs into Cyrano who apologizes for Gaston's behavior but, still mourning his love Roxanne, declines to get to know the infatuated Marjorie better. Unbeknownst to her, she catches the eye of the Marquis de Sade (Lloyd Bochner) who fantasizes aloud to his friend how enticing Marjorie would look stretched on the rack or whipped.

Gaston tries to win back Marjorie, but she tells him to "get lost." The Marquis comes to her rescue with Gaston backing off and, without asking his name, impetuously agrees to accompany him to his chateau. Disguised as a friar, Roarke tries to warn Marjorie away from the evil de Sade, but she is caught up in the excitement of having two men fighting over her. Hearing that Marjorie went off with de Sade, Gaston and his two pals race off to save her, as does Cyrano who rationalizes that he owes her for the kind words she said about his writings.

Finally realizing she is dining with the Marquis de Sade when he promises to demonstrate the pleasure of pain, Marjorie panics. Cyrano arrives to take her to safety but winds up in a duel with de Sade. Friar Roarke reappears and makes Marjorie feel guilty about her desire for chivalry. He tells her that he cannot control the outcome. After a vigorous duel, Cyrano emerges the victor but Roarke whisks Marjorie away before she can express her love to him. As Marjorie is saying her goodbyes to Roarke and Julie, she learns to her surprise that a college professor was enacting his fantasy as Cyrano and they go off together.

Publicity photo of Carol Lynley as a bus driver wanting to relive the days of chivalry in "Cyrano" on *Fantasy Island*. (Columbia Pictures Television, 1981). *Collection of Marlin Dobbs*

The blonde beauty's final appearance on *Fantasy Island*, as a sole fantasy-seeking guest, was in the episode entitled "Lost and Found" airing on April 7, 1984. Once again, she was playing the wife of Adam West. Both Hervé Villechaize and Wendy Schaal were gone from the series by this time. Roarke's latest sidekick was the future Mr. Belvedere, Christopher Hewett, as Lawrence. He and Montalbán had no chemistry whatsoever and put the final nail in the coffin as the ratings had been declining since Hervé departed due to a salary dispute.

In "Lost and Found," Carol is directed by Bob Sweeney, her second time working with him. Here she is Sheila McKenna a successful interior designer who comes to Fantasy Island to find a new man—not an exciting premise. The twist is that Sheila is still legally married to her husband Frank (Adam West) who cheated on her while away on business in Aspen. He shows up all contrite to win her back and is followed by his business partner Ronald (Dale Robinette) who has the hots for Sheila and her deceitful best friend Margot (*The Young and the Restless*' Jaime Lyn Bauer) who we discover pursued and bedded Frank. The show gave Carol the full star treatment with many costume changes and hair styles to rival anything seen on *Dynasty*. They even throw in a fully clothed catfight with her rival in a swimming pool. Carol's beauty alone however cannot overcome the weak story with the predictable happy ending.

In Lynley's remaining episodes, she turns up on the island as part of others' fantasies. For example, in "The Dancer," Lynley finally gets an opportunity to demonstrate her dancing prowess as "a broken-down ballerina."[681] It was directed by former dancer Gene Nelson and aired on November 17, 1979. Big Jake Farley (Max Baer, Jr.), who Tattoo describes as "a king-sized cowboy" is a wealthy businessman who made his money in uranium. He credits his success to a beautiful prima ballerina named Valeska Demarco (Lynley) who vanished from the world of ballet eight years prior. At the time, Jake was down on his luck and snuck into the theater to watch her perform. Falling madly in love, he vowed to make something of himself so he would be her equal when they finally meet. His fantasy is to make that happen and finance a comeback performance for her, inviting the world's six top dance critics. Though appreciative, Valeska only sees Big Jake as her patron and does not notice his feelings of love. He also does not know that there is a rich, debonair rival for her affections named Todd Sinclair (Frank Aletter) who has been pursuing the dancer for years.

Carol Lynley gets to show off her ballet moves as an aging prima ballerina in "The Dancer" on *Fantasy Island*. (Columbia Pictures Television, 1979).
Collection of Marlin Dobbs

During rehearsal, a frustrated Valeska collapse. She admits to her teacher Selena (Lilyan Chauvin) that her legs are shot and she cannot dance. Selena gives her encouragement and reminds her that she has exhausted her savings. This comeback is her last chance. The ballerina gets back to work. The big day comes and Valeska gives it her best. Carol does own actual dancing, which is quite impressive. That is her even in the long shots. Just as her performance is coming to an end, the dancer's leg gives out and she tumbles to the ground. As Roarke comes to help her, Valeska sobs, "I can't do it anymore. I can't." As the saying goes, "those who can, do; those who can't, teach." Seeing a young ballerina dance to a ballet specially choreographed just as she is about to leave with Sinclair (a set up courtesy of Mr. Roarke), Valeska cannot help but to shout out instructions to her. Encouraged by Big Jake to teach, he convinces her to come back to Dallas with him to open a ballet school providing the requisite happy ending.

In "The Power," directed by George McCowan (*The Shape of Things to Come*) and airing on May 10, 1980, Larry Linville is a mild-mannered man who is given (by Mr. Roarke) the power of telekinesis because he wants control in his life. Carol has fun with her bad girl role as a sexy vixen named Stephanie who wants to use his newfound skill to cheat at a high-roller craps tournament. When he refuses, she has his girlfriend (Julie Sommars) kidnapped and blackmails him to participate. He at first aids Stephanie but then double crosses her. When her thugs go to kill his girlfriend, Fred uses his power to defeat them. Lynley makes one stunning crime boss. In the craps game scene, she dons the same aqua gown with the low bodice and deep slit up the center that she had worn as a presenter on the Academy Awards seven months prior. Not only did the actress get another use from this fabulous frock, but (per the Screen Actors Guild) members would receive an extra wardrobe payment if wearing their own clothes. This would not be the last time crafty Carol would don something from her closet on the screen.

Lynley's remaining episodes were in the supernatural realm again. "Man-Beast," was directed by George W. Brooks (film editor turned TV director) and aired on May 16, 1981. It has the silliest plot of all her appearances and, as with "The Devil and Mandy Breem" an orchid is involved. The cast played it straight and rises above the material. Carol is Elizabeth Tabori the wife of accountant David Tabori (David Hedison) who accompanies him to Fantasy Island because he wants to rid himself of his horrible, recurring nightmares. Describing them to Roarke, he finds himself in a dark cave and hears heavy, labored animal breathing when his wife appears. She is repulsed by something, and he knows she is in danger, but he cannot find his voice to warn her when a hairy claw reaches out and grabs her. The nightmare ends there, but when he awakens, he is out of bed and in their attic. His only clue is a flower, a rare African orchid, that is in every dream. Roarke realizes that it is not his imagination and that Tabori is a werewolf based on connection to the flower (that cures werewolf-itis?). Tabori finds that unbelievable, as does the viewing audience no doubt, but that night under a full moon, he transforms into a wolfman and faces the truth. The always reliable David Hedison (who turned into a half-man, half-fly in 1958's feature film, *The Fly*) gives an intense portrayal, more so than the episode deserved. Carol is given silly lines to say like "that will give me time to touch up my makeup" when asked to leave the room by Roarke, and must act concerned and scared, which she does with aplomb especially at the end when she risks her life to give her husband the lifesaving orchid.

In the "Angel's Triangle," directed by Bob Sweeney and airing on November 6, 1982, Lynley once again is the catalyst sparking trouble in the supernatural world. Here she is Catherine Harris enjoying a second honeymoon on Fantasy Island. Unbeknownst to her, she is trailed by Michael, the Angel of Death (Gary Collins cast against type to very good effect), who is in love with her and needs Roarke's advice on how to deal with this strange human emotion. Seven years prior, Michael let Catherine survive a car crash on her first honeymoon in which she should have perished. Catherine and her husband Brent (Doug McClure) are finally getting a do-over but he is supposed to die after a horse-riding accident and Michael is there to take his soul after it happens. Michael's love for Catherine is so intense that he once more goes against fate and lets the intended live giving her a happy ending. Is there any other on *Fantasy Island?* Arguably, this is Carol's weakest episode. Besides being saddled with a less than flattering hairdo, she does not have much to do but fret throughout and has absolutely no chemistry with a stoic, bloated Doug McClure. Her scenes with Collins have more of a spark and you wind up rooting for him to win Catherine. As a footnote, the other segment "Natchez Bound" featured Carol's frequent co-star Roddy McDowall, once again putting them on the same set during shooting.

Fantasy Island kept Carol gainfully employed and kept her face well known to the public since the show was extremely popular. She could always count on an episode or two per year. She has become so identified with the show that as recently as 2017, when film critic John Podhoretz of *The Weekly Standard* was reviewing the remake of *Murder on the Orient Express*, he stated that he just re-watched the 1974 original and jokingly quipped, "And when we finally get to the Istanbul train station from which the Orient Express is departing, it plays like a version of the opening three minutes of *Fantasy Island*, during which Mr. Roarke introduces all the guests and we get to see Carol Lynley as a stewardess who wants to go back to high school and Bert Convy as a stationery salesman who wants to find Bigfoot."[682]

Promotional print ad for 1982 guest star appearance in "The Angel's Triangle" on *Fantasy Island* starring Ricardo Montalbán and Hervé Villechaize.

14. Remake It Again, Sam

Shortly after making the original *Fantasy Island* TV-movie, Carol Lynley landed an iconic genre role and, not surprisingly, the offer came from England. She was perfectly cast as the ultimate lady in peril, Annabelle West, in yet another remake of the classic haunted house story *The Cat and the Canary*. Carol followed in the illustrious footsteps of, among others, Laura La Plante in the 1927 silent version and Paulette Goddard in the 1939 remake, co-starring Bob Hope.

This was Carol's most promising theatrical film since *The Poseidon Adventure* with a meaty part for her as well. Alas, once again major distribution problems vexed the production and this entertaining remake unjustly did not get a national release in the U.S.

The Cat and the Canary by John Willard began as a one-act play and then was expanded into a full-length stage thriller premiering on February 7, 1922 at the National Theatre in New York City. It was a straightforward mystery of heiress Annabelle West (Florence Eldridge) who has just inherited a fortune from the deceased Cyrus West, because she is the sole heir with the West surname, but must survive the night in his creepy mansion to prove she is legally sane. If not, there is a second will with the name of the alternate heir. Accompanying her is the rest of Cyrus' greedy irate family members, including a mentally deranged one, who received nothing.

The play was a huge hit and in 1927 a silent film version directed by Paul Leni was released from Universal Pictures with Laura La Plante as Annabelle. A talkie retitled *The Cat Creeps* followed in 1930 directed by Rupert Julian with the heroine now played by Helen Twelvetrees. This was produced by Carl Laemmle who also did a Spanish language version that same year called *La Voluntad del Muerto* starring Lupita Tovar. *The Cat and the Canary* came back to the big screen for the fourth time in 1939 as a star vehicle for comedian Bob Hope and lovely Paulette Goddard with more emphasis on comedy than scares. Carol jumped at the chance to bring her interpretation of Annabelle West to the big screen and said. "It was an excellent part and I liked the character a lot. I had done English accents before and I am quite good at it if I do say so. I enjoyed playing British roles especially working with a British cast."[683]

It was almost thirty-five years before producer Richard Gordon decided to dust off the play and bring it back to the big screen. When asked why, Gordon replied, "The subject offers pure entertainment in the classic movie sense, with all the modern ingredients of action, romance and horror. Paul Leni's silent version had, of necessity, to make certain changes in the story to accentuate the director's expressionist visual style. The immensely popular Bob Hope version was adapted entirely to Hope's comedy style. Our screenplay, written by Radley Metzger, has gone back to the original play. We believe we have more closely preserved the spirit of Willard's play than any of the previous films."[684]

Partnering with Radley Metzger was odd since he was well-known for his artsy soft-core porn movies. A graduate of City College in New York, he began directing English-dubbed versions of many foreign movies including one German film acquired by Gordon. This is how they met and became friends. By the late sixties, Metzger was directing such sexy hits as *Camille 2000* and *The Lickerish Quartet* before moving into more hardcore features using the name Henry Paris. When asked how he settled on Metzger as his director, Gordon replied, "I used to talk to him often about the possibility that one day we might do something together. When I decided that I would like to make *The Cat and the Canary*, I mentioned it to him and he reacted very enthusiastically, and so we came to the conclusion that this was a good time to do something together, especially as he was interested in writing the screenplay as well as directing."[685]

With a director and screenplay in place, Gordon now had to cast the key roles. Since the movie was going to be filmed in England, the producer wanted a mixture of American and British actors. Though he never stated otherwise, it seems that Carol Lynley was the first choice to play British fashion designer Annabelle West. Gordon knew she had made a fair number of films and TV shows in Great Britain. He added, "She was popular in England and she liked working there, and she enjoyed the idea of going back to London to do this film."[686]

Attorney Allison Crosby (Wendy Hiller) is snatched unbeknownst to a distracted Annabelle West (Carol Lynley) in *The Cat and the Canary* (Grenadier Films, 1978). *Billy Rose Theatre Division, The New York Public Library for the Performing Arts*

The lone American relative was the character of Paul Jones, a songwriter. This was the role beefed up for Bob Hope in the 1939 version though the character was renamed Wally Campbell. Here he is played by the personable Michael Callan. Unfortunately, the budget did not allow the producers to reach out to a more bankable leading man at the time, but Gordon was satisfied with his choice.

In the play and the previous film version the lawyer named Crosby was played by a man. The producers tried to cast one but hit several snags. The closest to getting the part was James Mason but then he wanted to rewrite the screenplay. Casting director Rose Tobias Shaw then suggested that since they were trying to modernize the story by changing the period from the twenties to the thirties, and including a filmed will reading with Cyrus West badgering his heirs, perhaps Crosby should be played by a woman. Gordon and Metzger liked that idea and her first suggestion, Academy Award winner Wendy Hiller (*Separate Tables*, *A Man for All Seasons*), took the role of Allison Crosby.

The role of Cyrus West was taken by Wilfred Hyde-White (*The Third Man, My Fair Lady*) after Robert Morley and Alastair Sim passed on it. Also signed were Honor Blackman (*The Avengers, Goldfinger*) as big game hunter Susan Sillsby; Olivia Hussey (*Romeo and Juliet, Black Christmas*) as her cousin and "roommate" Cicily Young; Edward Fox (*The Go-Between, Day of the Jackal*) as Hendricks a psychologist from the nearby asylum for the criminally deranged; and stage actress Beatrix Lehmann (after Flora Robson, Cathleen Nesbitt, and Elisabeth Bergner all declined) as the housekeeper Mrs. Pleasant.

Causing the biggest headache for the production was Horst Buchholz (*The Magnificent Seven, One, Two, Three*). Though German, he was hired to play dashing pilot Charlie Wilder. The company was in pre-production with the cast ready to begin shooting when the actor personally called Richard Gordon to relay that he was dropping out of the movie because he had forgotten he had an option to do a play in Germany. Gordon admitted that he practically hung up on the actor not believing his excuse. He opted not to sue him for breach of contract but now had to scramble to fill his role. Afterwards, the producer followed up and found no evidence of Buchholz doing a German play during this time.[687]

British actor Peter McEnery (*The Moon-Spinners*, *Entertaining Mr. Sloane*) had been cast as surgeon-turned-pharmacist Harry Blythe. He replaced Buchholz as Wilder and casting director Rose Shaw brought in Academy Award nominee Daniel Massey (*Star!*) to play Blythe. However, Gordon and Metzger had no idea the trouble these two would cause during production.

Filming began in December 1976. Carol reportedly stayed at London's five-star Blakes Hotel, which was popular for celebrities though the movie was shot elsewhere. The creative team decided that they did not want to shoot on sets in a studio. Associate producer Ray Corbett recommended Pyrford Court in Surrey outside of London. It was the ancestral home of Lord Iveagh of the Guinness Trust, which was founded to help find affordable housing for low-income families. *The Omen* also shot sequences at Pyrford Court. Both exteriors and interiors were shot at this location.

The house was empty, so set decoration was needed and as might be expected from an unlived English manor, the working conditions were not the greatest. Per Gordon, "We were shooting in the winter, and it was very cold. Everybody was sort of huddling around space heaters in the library and trying to keep warm in between shooting. [The house] was not properly heated. Of course, the lights from the filming helped to warm it up, but it was not the most comfortable location in the world."[688]

Carol was not impressed with Radley Metzger and commented,

> He didn't do much directing. Only thing he would say is 'Print it.' Considering he had a cast that included Dame Wendy Hiller, Wilfrid Hyde-White and all these well-known and well-respected actors, he didn't do much with us. I was told before we started filming that his background was in softcore porn. I had never met anybody who had worked in that industry on either

side of the camera. We had lunch prior and he seemed alright to me.[689]

Per Gordon, most of the cast, including Lynley, behaved as seasoned professionals and went with the flow. "Carol was very cooperative and had had experience in making low-budget movies as well as major studio pictures. She'd had experience working in England and she enjoyed the whole thing. We had no problems with her whatsoever."[690] Carol returned the compliment and said Richard Gordon "was delightful and professional. When on the set, he never interfered with anything."[691]

Olivia Hussey found Carol to be "very professional and sweet. But we really did not spend much time together so we didn't get to know each other at all. I loved talking to Honor Blackman and to Michael Callan—really fun people. Also, Daniel Massey whose sister Anna (I worked with her on stage in *The Prime of Miss Jean Brodie*) sent me much love."[692]

Regarding her co-stars, Carol recalled,

> The actors, or artistes as they called us, would have lunch every day around this long table in what they called the artiste's dining room. It was only actors—no crew. Dame Wendy would always sit at the head of the table because the English are very formal with stuff like that. She was a sweetheart. One day we were talking about Radley and some of the cast had nicknamed him Rattles. I never called him that. Dame Wendy asked me why they called him Rattles. I replied, 'Don't you know about his former career?' She replied, 'No, what was it?' I said, 'Pornography.' She literally spit her food out across the table in surprise. She calmed down and said, 'Oh, but I had dinner with him last night!' Then it became Rattles' former career whenever it was brought up.
>
> I knew Michael Callan from New York. He's an excellent, excellent actor but got sidetracked by being pleasant and nice.

Overall, I was so fascinated and honored to be working with Dame Wendy, Olivia Hussey, Honor Blackman, and the entire cast.[693]

Would-be heirs Dr. Harry Blythe (Daniel Massey), Paul Jones (Michael Callan), Annabelle West (Carol Lynley), Susan Sillsby (Honor Blackman), and Cicily Young (Olivia Hussey) follow housekeeper Mrs. Pleasant (Beatrix Lehmann) to their rooms in *The Cat and the Canary* (Grenadier Films, 1978). *Billy Rose Theatre Division, The New York Public Library for the Performing Arts*

When asked if she knew why some called Radley Metzger, Rattles, Carol replied, "I think it was because he was quiet and a bit nervous. But when you are working with actors of this caliber you don't have to worry about a lot."[694]

Not all went smoothly with the cast though. Daniel Massey and Peter McEnery both behaved badly. According to Gordon, they "thought they were doing us a favor by appearing in this film."[695] Massey did not take it all seriously and was drinking at the time. Rather than bonding with the other cast members, he hitched his wagon to bad boy McEnery. During the filming of a scene where most of the cast is assembled around the dining room table for supper, Metzger needed a few more minutes to get an important shot. McEnery announced it was lunchtime, got up, and walked off the set shocking the crew and his costars. Most offended, per Richard Gordon, was Wendy Hiller who yelled after him in a bellowing voice, "I think that is one of the most obscene gestures I've ever encountered in my career."[696]

Describing her opinions of the two actors, Carol said,

> I remember that Peter McEnery was there but that's it. I liked Daniel Massey but he could be grumpy. He was always complaining about Radley. We would stick up for him and say, 'Come on, he's doing a decent job.' Daniel was not happy about working with him and let it be known.[697]

While in production, Gordon ran a full-page ad in *Variety* touting the movie. It read: "It's 1934 (and appearing in suspiciously alphabetical order) are Honor Blackman, Michael Callan, Edward Fox, Wendy Hiller, Olivia Hussey, Beatrix Lehmann, Carol Lynley, Daniel Massey, Peter McEnery, Wilfrid Hyde-White in *The Cat and the Canary*. Produced by Richard Gordon. Directed by Radley Metzger."

The Cat and the Canary opens in 1904 at Glencliff Manor with a scene of a cat eyeing a caged canary while the voice of a small boy is heard calling for the feline. As the boy runs out of the forest to join a wheelchair-bound old man, Cyril West (Wilfrid Hyde-White), calling out for "Miou Miou," the camera pans to the murdered cat hanging from a tree. Explaining the opening, Richard Gordon revealed, "I felt that we needed something to grab the audience in the beginning because by the nature of the story, once you get underway, there has to be quite a lot of dialogue and exposition before you come to any action. In order to sort of 'reassure' audiences that they were going to see something that would be in nature of a thriller, we wanted an opening sequence that would grab everybody's attention and make them wonder, 'What's all this about?' They would keep that thought in the back of their minds, and eventually it would all tie up together."[698]

The film then jumps to 1934 and the twentieth anniversary of West's death. It is a dark and stormy night. The deceased's attorney Allison Crosby (Wendy Hiller) and trusted housekeeper Mrs. Pleasant (Beatrix Lehmann) unchain a crate containing Cyrus' will as cars begin to pull up outside the home. In a novel twist from the original, the will is read on film, with synchronized sound, by the deceased. As they remove the reel, they notice a live moth, which raises suspicions, since the crate should have remained sealed since 1914.

The invited West heirs begin to enter. Harry Blythe (Daniel Massey) is a former surgeon involved in a scandalous mishap that cost him his license and is now a pharmacist. His nemesis is his cousin Charlie Wilder (Peter McEnery), a WWI flying ace who worked as a stunt man in Hollywood and now endorses toothpaste. Susan Sillsby (Honor Blackman) is a world-famous big game hunter accompanied by her cousin and "roommate" Cicily Young (Olivia Hussey). Jokey Paul Jones (Michael Callan) is an American songwriter.

The last guest to arrive is Lynley as aspiring fashion designer Annabelle West. Carol projects an instant charm and nimbleness with her lilting British accent as she apologizes for her tardiness. This is the ultimate damsel in distress role that Carol was born to play. She is visually perfect for the part. Kudos go to hair stylist Sarah Monzani who makes the less-than flattering hair style Carol was sporting in 1976 quite fashionable for the thirties period.

After the cousins get reacquainted, Mrs. Crosby calls them to dinner and they are joined by Cyrus West on film. He berates his heirs unmercifully and entertainingly calling them "leeches," "a bunch of bastards," and "parasites" in the movie's most amusing moments. The dinner served by Mrs. Pleasant is the exact one Cyrus is eating right down to the wine. In one great moment, Mrs. Pleasant walks from right to left behind the screen placed at the head of the table just as she did back in 1914. This was filmed with perfect timing and symmetry. As the heirs banter back and forth and make side deals, Cyrus finally reveals that his heir is anyone with the surname of West. A gleeful Annabelle is the sole living West, so she inherits his entire estate including the fabulous West diamond necklace. There is one stipulation. She must spend the night in the manor and if by morning she survives or is not declared insane, the fortune is hers. If not, there is a second film with the next in line for the inheritance.

After the will is revealed, the guests mingle about the hallways and rooms of the manor. The walls are painted white and it is sparsely furnished except for the library and bedrooms that were reopened for the occasion. Of the few pieces of furniture left, most are covered with white sheets making the house quite bright. Richard Gordon commented, "That was Radley's concept and I think it worked well. We didn't want it to be yet another 'spooky old country house horror film' where everything takes place in the middle of the night. That was too old-fashioned, I think that idea had sort of rather gone out of style by then."[699]

Edward Fox as Dr. Hendricks makes a crashing entrance through the window. Claiming nobody heard his knocking, he apologizes, but explains that he runs the insane asylum down the road and that one of their patients has escaped. He is highly dangerous and likes to sneak into houses where he waits until all are asleep and then pounces like a cat with his claw-like fingernails. All are there except Annabelle and Cicily. He then compares the traits of Charlie, Harry, and Susan to his killer-on-the-loose but also claims that songwriters can cut with their words and that all lawyers are man-eating sharks. When Cicily wanders in, he immediately recognizes her as the girl who was dancing at a London club when she was drugged and almost raped by its manager and who she then killed in self-defense. She readily admits this is true. However, Hendricks adds the part she omitted, that she shot him six times in the head and the body was mutilated.

Meanwhile an oblivious Annabelle is unpacking in her room. All agree not to tell her about the roving maniac, but Susan purposely spills the beans. After it is revealed that Annabelle has had love affairs with her kissing cousins Charlie and Harry, both still madly in love with her though the feelings aren't mutual, the heiress is then summoned to the library to meet with Mrs. Crosby. As the attorney begins to reveal that she is privy to family secrets due to her access to family diaries and photo books, the clock begins to chime and a black cat wanders in. Distracted, Annabelle picks up the cat with her back to Mrs. Crosby who is grabbed by an unseen stranger emerging from a secret passage behind the bookcase and dragged away. When the clock stops, Annabelle turns and finds she is alone in the room and has been talking to herself. Nobody believes Annabelle that the lawyer just vanished, and Susan insinuates that Annabelle may be hallucinating.

Confident that she is sane, Annabelle turns her attention to finding the West necklace. With the word "ice" on the cork of the wine served at dinner ("something that has been waiting to take a breath in twenty years" was Cyrus' clue to finding the jewels) and Paul's help they find it frozen in the crate that housed the film. A vain Annabelle dons the necklace before retiring to bed. She is awakened when the Cat sneaks into her room through a secret passage and rips it off her neck. Her screams draw the house guests who come rushing in. Most doubt her story but only snide Susan is brash enough to suggest that Annabelle is losing her mind. That is, until Paul accidentally discovers the secret passage entrance and the mutilated body of Mrs. Crosby falls out, in one of the film's most startling moments. When Susan reminds Annabelle of her warning about this madman, the heiress retorts that perhaps Susan's spot-on description was no coincidence. Shortly after, Susan sneaks back downstairs to the dining room, where Mrs. Crosby's body is laying, to snatch the key that unlocks the second film. Unbeknownst to her, the Cat is in the room hiding under a sheet. He pounces on her and she breaks free only to be grabbed by him. Always the big game hunter and now the prey, Susan proves more frightened kitty than tiger and just screams in fear before she meets a grisly death.

Paul gets the same idea as Susan and leaves Annabelle in another locked room. She discovers a hidden passageway and holding the gun Susan had given her, goes to look for Paul. Instead, she runs into the Cat who drags her to a secret room full of scalpels and knives. Clawing at his face, Annabelle realizes it is a mask. The Cat is Charlie Wilder, angry that he was not the heir despite being his uncle's favorite. He admits to killing Cyrus' cat long ago, Mrs. Crosby, and Susan. When Hendricks bursts into the room, Annabelle runs to him for protection but then quickly learns he is in on the murderous plot. A war buddy, Charlie promised him lots of pretty faces to carve up and a portion of the money.

Charlie leaves the two when he realizes he dropped his medal in the dining room. Going over to Mrs. Crosby's body, he removes the sheet only to find Paul who punches him in the face. The songwriter figured out who the next in line was and a fight ensues. It ends when Mrs. Pleasant enters the room and shoots Charlie dead. She then tells Paul that Annabelle is in mortal danger. While all this commotion is going on there is no sign of Cicily or Harry who is never on screen again probably due to Daniel Massey's hiring for a brief period.

Susan (Honor Blackman) and Annabelle (Carol Lynley) after the reading of the will in *The Cat and the Canary* (Grenadier Films, 1978). *From Marlin Dobbs' Collection*

With Mrs. Pleasant's gun in hand, Paul bursts into the room where Annabelle is being held and shoots Hendricks as he is about to carve up the pretty blonde's face. Despite all the carnage and bloodshed, the next morning Annabelle and Paul are all smiles and in a chipper mood, as bodies are being carried out of the house. It is an odd tone to take and a bit bizarre. They say goodbye to Cicily and then sit down to watch the second filmed will. After greeting good morning to his "bunch of leeches and bastards," Cyrus West reveals that since this film is being watched the West heir was insane or did not live through the night. He then names Charlie Wilder as next in line for the fortune because of how nice the boy was to West after his beloved cat disappeared. The movie ends with a beaming Annabelle and Paul in a kiss that makes you wonder why Annabelle seems to like keeping it in the family so to speak.

A seasoned distribution deal maker, Richard Gordon had several of them in place. He first wanted *The Cat and the Canary* to open in England, but the distributor in Italy beat him to the punch. However, the distributor advertised the movie as "Agatha Christie's *The Cat and the Canary.*" A letter from her estate threatening a lawsuit quickly brought it to light. Marketing materials supplied by the production company quoting the review in *Films in Review* that read "infinitely superior to *Death on the Nile*" confused the distributor, thinking *Cat* was also by Christie, and blamed it all on Richard Gordon. It is unclear if that really helped the movie in Italy where it was a moderate hit finishing as the 85th highest grossing movie for the period 1978-79.[700]

The Cat and the Canary was then released in England (via Gala Film Distributors), France, Germany, and eventually all over the world except in the United States.

Reviews from various countries were from fair to good with Wilfred Hyde-Whyte and Wendy Hiller receiving the most kudos. Terry Boyce of the *South China Morning Post* thought the film "attracted a brilliant cast with just about everyone you could wish to have for a tale of mystery and suspense." While Liam Lacey of *The Globe and Mail* unfairly compared it to the superior

Murder on the Orient Express and called *The Cat and the Canary* "a spoof within a thriller within a star vehicle." As for the cast, he quipped, "Carol Lynley ... providing much of the suspense by spending most of the movie in a diaphanous slip and threatening to bare her bosom to fate or temptation." He disliked Michael Callan and remarked that he gave "the only directly offensive performance."

In August 1978, it was reported that Radley Metzger's company Audubon signed a deal with Cinema Shares International (CSI) to release *The Cat and the Canary* in the U.S. When asked why Audubon did not just distribute it in the U.S., Metzger replied, "It wasn't really our kind of film, we couldn't have done it justice ... even one as elaborate as that. Richard Gordon sold it in almost every country in the world. Quartet Films had it. They were a substantial art distributor. They had *Breaker Morant*. So, it did well worldwide for us."[701]

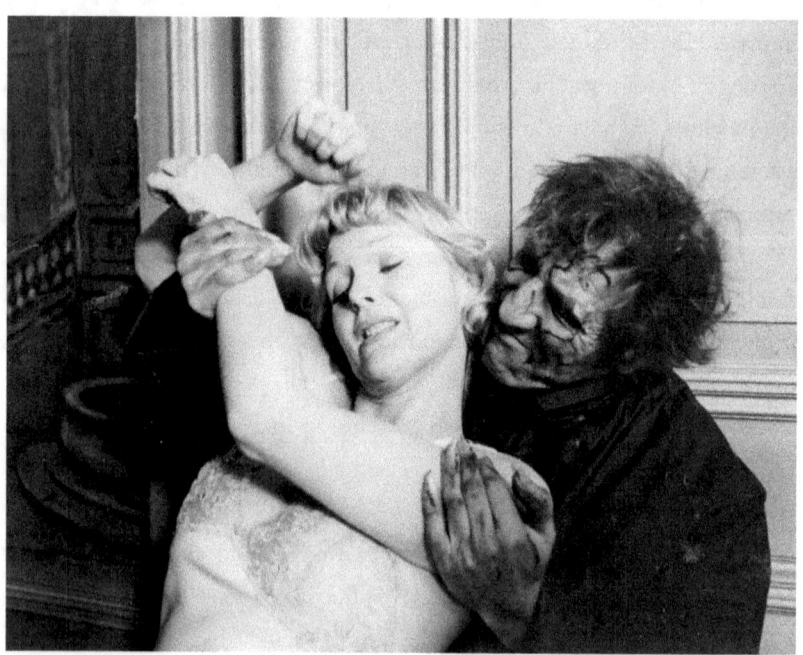

Annabelle (Carol Lynley) struggles to break free from her maniacal abductor in *The Cat and the Canary* (Grenadier Films, 1978).

CSI had until the end of 1978 to get the movie in theaters. To help with the promotion, Audubon delivered to CSI "a trailer (produced by the film's London-based producer Richard Gordon), artwork, and assorted promo materials."[702] CSI submitted the thriller to the New York Film Festival, but it was rejected. Believing that it needed that venue to launch a proper theatrical release, CSI gave up on the film and booked it for one day into the Coral Ridge Theatre in Fort Lauderdale, Florida during the last week of December 1978 to meet its contractual obligations. CSI then struck a deal to sell the pay TV rights to Home Box Office. However, Audubon filed a lawsuit in February 1979 blocking that sale and claimed that CSI breached its agreement.

In August 1979, the N.Y. State Supreme Court agreed with Audubon, which won back theatrical, pay TV, and television rights. This case was closely followed because it was "a rare instance of attempting to legally define what constitutes a best-efforts 'theatrical release' as the term is used in standard distribution contracts."[703] Judge Frank J. Blangiardo found in favor of Audubon after a three-day trial due, in part, to the fact that the one-day showing did not include any print promotion, TV and radio spots, or trailers. Testimony from defense witnesses from CSI was also used against the company where staff admitted CSI felt the movie had "little theatrical value."[704]

Sadly, for the movie and Lynley, it was a hollow victory. No other distributors were interested in releasing *The Cat and the Canary*, which may have been considered outdated compared to the popular slasher movies of the time such as *Halloween* and *Friday the 13th*. In 1981 and 1982, it played in a few art houses in the major cities and notices were better than expected. This is frustrating to hear because if it had gotten a full fledge distribution back in 1978, following the release of such popular movies as *Murder on the Orient Express* and *Death on the Nile*, it may have done well. And it would have been great to see Carol in another box office hit after *Poseidon*.

According to Radley Metzger, "Castle Hill Productions had ancillary rights and they did a tremendous job selling to pay TV and cable ... it actually supported me the last ten years on the ancillary rights."[705]

The reviews, for the most part, were positive and the critics liked Carol as Annabelle. Richard L. Shepard of *The New York Times* called it a "breezy pleasant enough diversion" and he found Lynley to be a "lusciously designed heroine." Susan King of the *Los Angeles Times* remarked that "Carol Lynley and Daniel Massey seem to be having a good time mugging away in this 'dark and stormy night' horror story." While most reviewers loved the Hyde-White scenes best, Scott Cain of the *Atlanta Constitution* raved, "The best scene involves Carol Lynley … and Wendy Hiller … Miss Lynley is babbling merrily and turns her back on Dame Wendy for a few moments. Miss Lynley does not see—but the audience does—a bookcase swing open, a cloaked figure reach out, grab Dame Wendy and abduct her. That's the last time she's seen—alive, that is."

James O'Neill writing in *Terror on Tape* found *The Cat and the Canary* to be an "enjoyable remake with Lynley ideally cast. Spirited acting from the veteran cast … and sharp direction … keep this constantly on the mark."

Carol gave an excellent, nuanced performance as Annabelle complete with a very convincing British accent. She makes Annabelle not just a goody-goody harried heroine. Visually perfect, her character starts out joking and gleeful, but like her relatives, a bit anxious to know who the sole heir is. Once it is disclosed that it is Annabelle, Carol plays up some of her character's flaws. She seems self-absorbed and quite ambivalent to her former lovers and cousins who are still fighting over her. And her greediness is revealed as she is determined to find the diamond necklace that was willed to her. When she does, she vainly wears it to bed. Later, when abducted by her cousin and his accomplice, a fierce Annabelle emerges desperate to stay alive.

Carol was proud of this movie and opined that it was "a stylish murder mystery … very much like *Death on the Nile*."[706] She added, "Working on this film was a wonderful experience for me. I never knew why the film wasn't released in the U.S. When it turned up on cable television, a lot of friends told me how much they enjoyed it."[707]

In 2014, *The Cat and the Canary* and Radley Metzger received their just due when it played at The Film Society of Lincoln Center as part of a retrospective movie tribute to the director and his career.

15. Imperiled from the Earth to the Moon

From 1977 to 1979, Carol Lynley's film and TV roles ranged from a big zoo veterinarian, to an adulterous wife, to an undercover policewoman, to a pregnant mother, to a moon maiden in a variety of genres. Though not all these projects were successful, her career was on the upswing and coupled with her appearances on *Fantasy Island* and other Aaron Spelling shows, one of the busiest working periods of her career.

Even in a domestic drama like *Having Babies II* (1977), Carol winds up as the lady in peril whose young foster son holds extreme resentment towards the unborn baby his mother is carrying. Carol gave arguably her most natural seventies small screen performance in this TV-movie that was well-directed by Richard Michaels (*Bewitched*, *Love, American Style*, and many other TV shows). This was a sequel to the popular *Having Babies* (1976) that starred Susan Sullivan as Dr. Julia Farr, an obstetrician involved with her pregnant patients. In the follow up, Carol stepped in at the last-minute for actress Loretta Swit who had to drop out of the project due to an injury from a minor accident.

Giving up on the bangs and now again with long hair albeit wavy just below her shoulder in one of her most flattering looks; Lynley plays Sally Magee and is well-paired with Cliff Gorman as her husband Arthur, a hot-headed, working-class guy. Thinking they could never have children they take in a troubled young boy Danny (an equally good Robbie Rist, most remembered as Cousin Oliver on *The Brady Bunch*) whose last family beat him so badly he was hospitalized. When Sally surprisingly becomes pregnant, Danny's insecurities about the baby get the best of him and he begins acting out (stealing items from his father, ripping out pages of newborn babies with the mother in magazines, etc.), frustrating and alarming his parents. Sally takes a loving, understanding approach trying to reason with Danny and assure him the baby will not change his parents' feelings for him. Lynley is quite effective trying to reach the boy and frustrated that she cannot. However, her less understanding husband wants to punish his son with a hard whack on the behind for his behavior.

Housewife Sally McGee (Carol Lynley) and fashion model Trish Canfield (Paula Prentiss) are in precarious states due to their pregnancies in *Having Babies II* (Paramount Television, 1977).

Hating the baby-to-be, Danny plans an accident, loosening the rungs to his treehouse to deliberately hurt his mother who he asks to come up and help him with something. Sally carefully climbs up rung by rung, while praising Danny for being so creative and handy. The nervous boy has a change of heart and tries to stop her from taking another step, but she does anyway and falls to the ground. When Arthur yells at his son for being so foolish to have his mother climb up, Danny confesses to what he did and his hatred of the baby. At the hospital Dr. Farr assures Arthur that mother and baby are fine, but that does not stop him from returning Danny to the adoption home where he was living prior. Driving Sally back to their house, Arthur reveals what he did and Carol plays Sally's anger and frustration with much conviction, telling Arthur that he had no right to do that without her consent and she vows to get her son back. Arthur and Sally pay a visit to Danny, but the counselor sees there are problems in their marriage and will not allow Danny to return yet. After Sally gives birth, Arthur surprises his wife by bringing Danny to the hospital and the boy is genuinely happy to have a baby brother as the Magee family is reunited.

The other major story arcs that were less interesting in *Having Babies II* involved an aging pill-popping fashion model (Paula Prentiss giving a standout performance and having a terrific scene with Rist in the doctor's waiting room as they both share their dislike for babies) who endangers her unborn child due to neglect by her husband (Tony Bill); a childless couple (Cassie Yates and Wayne Rogers) who are having trouble conceiving and go through some comical methods to get pregnant; and two vapid teenagers (Tracy Marshak and Michael LeClair) experiencing first love and the risks involved in going all the way.

Print ads for this *ABC Friday Night Movie* read, "An all-new sequel to last year's hit! Behind the birth of a child…" All four story arcs are pictured, with Carol lying on the ground with Cliff Gorman looking up at Robbie Rist in his treehouse with the tag line, "Threatened by the new baby, an adopted child strikes out at his parents."

This was another popular hit for Lynley, as it did quite well with the indiscriminate TV audience pulling in a 19.2 rating and 33 share of the viewing audience. Critically, reviews were mixed. Judy Flanders of *The Washington Star* found it better than the original and raved, "Carol Lynley and Cliff Gorman do a terrific job ... Good dialogue, interesting characters, excellent direction ... Light, funny, sometimes a little sad. But delightful." The reviewer for the *Pittsburgh Post-Gazette* remarked, "There should be a ready audience for this sequel ... the plot device is repeated here to fairly good advantage." Other critics found there were too many unrelated stories going on and all were treated in a superficial manner. Limiting to one or two for more character development was what the TV-movie needed instead of going, as *Los Angeles Times* critic Kevin Thomas said, "the Pregnancy, American Style" route. Despite how well Carol does, for some reason she rarely played the benevolent mother again on screen.

An interesting side note was that producer Richard Briggs was able to get the Adoption Guild of Valencia to allow the production to shoot the scenes with Lynley, Gorman, and Rist on its premises. Members rounded up about twenty children who arrived with their mothers. So excited to be in a movie, they all donated their salaries to the Adoption Guild.[708]

Carol next played the glamorous, adulterous wife of a wealthy industrialist (Barry Sullivan) trying to land a big government contract, in the low budget feature *The Washington Affair*, produced and directed by Victor Stoloff. He sets up a blackmail scheme to film a handsome, married engineer (Tom Selleck) in bed with a high-class hooker only to discover he is having an affair with his wife.

Sullivan previously played Carol's stepfather in *Harlow* and now he was portraying her husband. The pair also appeared together in the TV-movie *The Immortal* and an episode of *It Takes a Thief*. Commenting on her frequent cast mate, Carol said fondly, "He was a journeyman actor with an enormous amount of experience. He was extremely articulate and a gentleman ... it was always a joy to come to a set and to see Barry."[709]

Proving she had an eye for talent, Carol revealed that it was thanks to her that Tom Selleck got cast though he may not think that was such a good thing after all. She explained,

Tom was drop dead gorgeous! I had the job and went to a meeting with the director. Afterwards, he walked me out and we went through the waiting room area where a bunch of actors were lined up waiting to read to play my boyfriend. I chatted briefly with each one and they all seemed nice. When we got to my car, the director asked me, "so, which one did you like best?' I immediately said without hesitation, 'Tom!' He looked like a movie star and he dwarfed the other guys. He had something special about him.[710]

Post-*Magnum P.I.* promotional ad for *The Washington Affair* with a now top-billed Tom Selleck, Carol Lynley, and Barry Sullivan. *From Marlin Dobbs' Collection*

The Washington Affair made headlines because it was financed by the Walter G. O'Conner Company in Hershey, Pennsylvania where ninety percent of it was filmed in new studio facilities. The company was well-known for producing radio and television commercials, training films, and promotional materials. Most of the action in the movie takes place on sets built for Sullivan's office and Selleck's hotel room.

Budgeted at a little more than $1 million, exteriors were also shot in Washington DC and New York City. Pennsylvania was so excited to be hosting a movie shoot that Carol and Barry Sullivan were invited to present the winner's trophy to the first-place horse and owner at the Penn National Racecourse.

The Washington Affair was an almost scene-by-scene redo of Victor Stoloff's 1966 melodrama *Intimacy* with Barry Sullivan playing the same exact role. The film takes place in literally just a few rooms, mostly Sullivan's office and Selleck's hotel suite. There are just a few exterior shots, making it not much of a contender for a theatrical release. As Carol stated a few times, she had a child to support so sometimes you take what is offered. "You make some decisions not necessarily waiting for the heavens to open up."[711]

Commenting on his first film project despite the distribution hurdles it no doubt would face, O'Conner boasted, "What we are making here is a good middle of the road film. It will be entertaining and exciting but will not get involved with the kind of language and violence in many films today. The film will leave something to the imagination."[712] It sure did because audiences had to imagine what was on screen since the film was never released. During the days of *Star Wars*, this claustrophobic remake could not find a distributor and was shelved. It materialized on VHS in 1983 after Selleck (now top billed) had become a household name due to the success of his TV series *Magnum P.I.*

The film is not that bad and was a bit ahead of its time with all the spying which goes on today incessantly with cell phones and public cameras recording the public's every move. Plus, the movie has a surprising surprise ending and Carol looks gorgeous throughout. She and the virile Selleck made one sexy couple.

Carol began a succession of television appearances in March of 1978 beginning with a guest turn as a policewoman in "Angel in Blue" on *Hawaii Five-0* starring Jack Lord and James MacArthur. This aired on March 9th and was directed by the prolific Allen Reisner who just had a huge hit with the miniseries *Captains and the Kings*. When it was announced that Lynley was going to guest star on the hit CBS detective series, fans thought they were going to be treated to a reunion of the actress with her first motion picture leading man, James MacArthur from *The Light in the Forest*. So did Carol who took the part to reunite with him on screen again and for the paid trip to Hawaii. Alas, the former co-stars only appear in two scenes together.

The episode featured Carol as an undercover police officer recruited from another island who infiltrates a drug gang. However, she is perhaps one of the most ineffectual cops in the history of seventies television. She plants a bug, allowing Five-0 to track the gang, but she is sent undercover without a gun or any way to get in touch with her contacts. She then falls for one of the gang members, jeopardizing her mission. After he discovers her ruse, he agrees to help her and hatches his own plan to keep them alive, which she follows. However, in an act of bravery he takes a bullet meant for her and dies.

This was an atypical role for Lynley, as she was rarely cast as a policewoman. At first her character starts off authoritative when she stands up to Jack Lord's Steve McGarrett, who admits he does not want to send her undercover because she is a woman. However, the character soon turns into the hapless damsel-in-distress, who needs a man to rescue her. Carol, looking stunning especially in her beach attire, has nice chemistry with Mexican film star Enrique Novi in his U.S. TV debut, as the conflicted drug dealer, and their love scenes are tender and sweet. However, you just cannot quite accept Lynley as an experienced policewoman due to the turn the teleplay takes. Her character should have taken charge of the situation when her cover is blown, but instead the bewildered detective is led around by the drug smuggler she has fallen for.

Lynley was back in the hands of director Allen Reisner for NBC TV's fantasy movie *Cops and Robin* airing on March 28. She also was reunited with one of her favorite *Poseidon Adventure* co-stars, Ernest Borgnine. This was a reboot of the short-lived ABC-TV series *Future Cop*. In it, Borgnine and John Amos played veteran police officers Joe Cleaver and Bill Bundy, assigned to train a rookie named Officer Haven (Michael Shannon), who has no interests in sports, women, or anything else other than police work. The officers find it odd, until Cleaver accidentally stumbles upon the truth that Haven is a robot and is sworn to keep it a secret even from Bundy. Produced by Paramount, this was a limited run series and although better than it sounded, the network cancelled it after airing five episodes.

Unfortunately, *Future Cop* is not remembered for being underrated sci-fi but for the landmark plagiarism lawsuit that vexed it. Writers Harlan Ellison and Ben Bova shopped a pilot based on their 1970 short story "Brillo" about a robotic police officer in the future to Paramount Pictures and ABC, both of whom passed on it. Paramount then went ahead with *Future Cop* with the only difference being it was set in the present and that the robot was humanoid and had a mentor. The writers sued and in 1980 were awarded by a jury $337,000 in damages. Ellison used part of his settlement to rent a billboard across the street from studio that read "Writers—Don't Let Them Steal from You!"

Despite the cancellation of *Future Cop*, Paramount still had faith in the premise and NBC agreed to air the TV-movie *Cops and Robin* featuring the same lead actors but with some minor plot changes. Per executive producer Gary Damsker, "We now have a kind of family type police show with an android." He went on to explain that they "eased up on the science-fiction aspects by trying to make the android more humanistic. He doesn't have to be regenerated as often."[713]

In the story, Cleaver's former partner before Bundy was murdered five years earlier and his wife who was a witness went into hiding. With her whereabouts exposed and her life in danger, she agrees to testify but only if her five-year-old daughter Robin can be protected. Enter Cleaver and Haven to the rescue.

Carol received guest star billing and appears in only a handful of scenes that do not affect the main plot. She played the perky Dr. Alice Alcott (a replacement for Irene Tsu as Dr. Tingley from *Future Cop*). Wearing oversize round glasses and her hair in a ponytail to give Alcott the sexy intellectual look, Alice is first seen increasing Haven's creativity by programming him to absorb all knowledge of cooking. Cleaver is perplexed since the robot does not need those skills in the line of duty. Wanting him to adopt more human traits, Alcott suggests that Haven move in with Cleaver since they have been working so well together. The cop objects but when the scientist says he is a carpenter, plumber and master chef, Cleaver welcomes his new roommate with open arms. Shortly after, Carol's Alcott pops in to check on Haven and to see if his actions are becoming less robotic and more humanistic. Alice is not on screen until the wrap-up as the scientist tries to repair the damaged Haven, which she does to the relief of his concerned partner.

Though Borgnine and Shannon are well-teamed, the audience still did not take to this premise. The movie was padded out with longer than usual establishing shots and almost a full tour of Knotts Berry Farm to fit its two-hour timeslot. Also, it aired opposite ABC's powerhouse Tuesday night lineup of *Happy Days*, *Laverne and Shirley*, *Three's Company*, and *Soap*. Not surprisingly, its ratings were mediocre and it did not get picked up as a series. Too bad, because Lynley's Dr. Alcott, no doubt, would have been (at least) a recurring cast member.

Cops and Robin may have been one of the TV movies Carol was referring to later when she stated that not all her television forays were top grade. She explained, "That's when an actress really has to work the hardest. I have an expression I use when we're on the set and about to film a scene that's somewhat below par. I say, 'it's silk purse time,' you know the expression about turning a sow's ear into one."[714]

Carol's third and final primetime television appearance in March was on the 31st in "A Title on the Door and a Carpet on the Floor" an episode of *Richie Brockelman, Private Eye*. Another limited series, this was a spinoff from the extremely popular *Rockford Files* and starred Dennis Dugan as twenty-two-year-old private investigator Richie Brockelman who drove a cool Mustang. Carol played Jean Hollister who hires him to follow her husband Stan (Charles Siebert) who she suspects is cheating on her. Stan suddenly turns up dead, just as Richie receives a generous buyout offer from a large security firm. His new bosses try to distract him from his original case that has developed into much more including industrial espionage and murder. The disappointing episode, written by creators Stephen J. Cannell and Steven Bochco, was as confusing as its title and was not a memorable role for Carol.

Though boyishly charming and personable, Dugan could not save the routine private detective show and it was not renewed. Its title song "School's Out," by Mike Post and others, was the series' most lasting feature, although Dugan made two additional guest appearances on *The Rockford Files*.

Shortly after came the more adventure-related *Sword of Justice* starring the handsome Dack Rambo as Jack Cole, a wealthy playboy framed for embezzlement. While doing time in prison, he picked up a few new tricks such as lock picking, safe cracking, electronic surveillance, etc. He now uses his new-found skills to help those in need. In "The Skywayman," Jack, who can also fly a plane, rents a WWI biplane to join Carol's aerial circus being used as a front for drug trafficker Robert Alda and his pilot Edd Byrnes who does the smuggling. The show's gimmick was that after uncovering the bad guys, Jack would leave his calling card "a sword of justice" at the scene.

*****

After playing a litany of terrified imperiled women, most of whom had to be rescued or saved by a man, Carol finally landed two heroic roles. In the made-for-television disaster movie *The Beasts Are on the Streets* (1978), she is a resourceful veterinarian working at a zoo when a truck barrels down a good portion of the fencing allowing the animals to run free. And in the Canadian science-fiction feature *The Shape of Things to Come* she is the governor of the moon who tries to lead her people to safety when attacked by enemy forces.

In *The Beasts Are on the Streets*, it is head park ranger Dale Robinette and Dr. Carol Lynley to the rescue when an accident frees many animals from a wild animal park. She tends to the injured beasts while the park rangers must round up the missing animals before trigger-happy local hunters kill some of the more dangerous. This action-filled made-for-TV disaster movie was directed by former film editor Peter R. Hunt (who helmed one of the best James Bond movies, *On Her Majesty's Secret Service*) and produced by Joseph Barbera. The teleplay was by Laurence Heath (who also wrote Carol's episode "The Case of the Curious Counterfeit" on *The Magician*) based on a story by

Frederic Louis Fox. It was the first live-action production from animation kings Hanna-Barbera Productions, Inc.

The movie was shot on location at the Lion Country Safari in Grand Prairie, Texas. When asked what she thought of the overall making of *The Beast Are on the Streets*, where her co-stars included lions and tigers and bears, oh my, the actress replied,

> I loved making this movie because I am an animal lover. I enjoyed working with them. We had a professional animal trainer [Ralph Helfer] who was always with me. He showed me how to handle the animals some of which I have never interacted before in my life. It was interesting and fun.[715]

Publicity photo of Carol Lynley in *The Beasts Are on the Streets* (Hanna-Barbera Productions, 1978).

Carol had to work with several unusual species of animal during the movie and hide any fear she may have had. In one scene, her character had to give artificial resuscitation to a camel. Joking that she is probably the first actress that ever had to do that on screen, she said at the time, "During my career I've kissed Robert Wagner, Oliver Reed and Kirk Douglas but this is ridiculous."[716] Carol had to pry open its jaw, blow down a tube and thump his heart at the same time. She recalled,

> The animal trainer was glued to my hip. He was an expert and knew what he was doing. He would say what was good for each animal and I would follow his instructions. With the camel scene, he came over and said, 'Okay Carol now this is how you are going to handle the camel. But I must tell you they spit. You do not want to get near that when it happens.' I then asked, 'How do I know when it is getting ready to spit?' He told me and I said okay. We did the resuscitation with the camel and I got out of the way very quickly.
>
> There was another scene with a hippo. My animal trainer said, 'I have to tell you Carol, hippos are bad news. I am going to give him a shot to tranquilize him a bit because you cannot control a hippo. They go nuts for no reason whatsoever. We can't have that.' When it came time to shoot the scene, the hippo was looking a bit groggy. That was okay by me! After we got the shot and the director yelled cut, the trainer and I just ran to get away from the hippo because they aren't smart and could charge at anything that might set them off.[717]

Regarding the humans she worked with, Carol opined, "Peter Hunt was friendly but my closest relationship, other than with the trainer and the animals, was with Dale Robinette. He was easy to get along with and such a great guy. I couldn't have asked for a nicer partner."[718]

The Beasts Are on the Streets begins with a narrator thanking the American Humane Society for their help in backing the movie. As with most disaster movies, the audience is introduced to the main characters within the first fifteen minutes or so. Dale Robinette is handsome park ranger Kevin Johnson who finds one of the camels lying on the ground about to give birth. He calls for the park's resident vet Dr. Claire McCauley (Carol Lynley) who he is romantically involved, to the pleasure of her young daughter Sandy (Michelle Walling sporting a distracting Farrah Fawcett haircut not quite becoming for a pre-teen). Johnson has accepted a job in Nairobi and wants Claire and Sandy to accompany him. Claire is more concerned with the camel who is going through a painful breach birth. She turns the baby for a normal delivery and then gives it artificial resuscitation by blowing air into a tube positioned in its mouth to start it breathing again. Also working at the park are junior rangers Eddie (Philip Michael Thomas pre-*Miami Vice*) and ladies' man Rick (Casey Biggs) who host tours of the park and feed the big cats.

These introductions are intercut with Billy Green Bush as Jim Scudder a rifle-toting, redneck hunter driving with his pal, and get into a road rage situation with a fatigued truck driver hauling a huge tanker of flammable liquids. After having a shotgun aimed at his head, the driver exits the highway. As he approaches the wildlife park, he suffers a heart attack and crashes through a long stretch of fence where numerous animals are feeding. As the tanker explodes into flames, the panicked animals flee the park causing a ten-car pileup on the road outside.

This leads to all sorts of harrowing situations for the residents of the nearby town which is overrun by the marauding animals. A tiger and a bear engage in a fierce struggle at a large amusement park, sending hundreds of patrons fleeing. Johnson and his rangers tranquilize them before a police officer almost shoots the tiger. Two thrill-seeking teenagers in a hot rod, after harassing some ostriches, barely escape as rhinos destroy their car, and two lions prowl the countryside as terrified residents are trapped in their homes. It is up to Claire to take charge at the zoo to tend to any wounded animals and Kevin to direct the safe round up of the beasts with the help and, in some case hindrance, of the police and the public, before trigger-happy hunters like Scudder kill them. He and some of his cohorts are portrayed so recklessly that the audience cannot help but root for the animals to best them. While hunting down some lions on his property at night, Scudder accidentally shoots his own son.

Carol does well in her role of Dr. McCauley playing her with compassion and sincerity. Despite her admitted uneasiness working with some dangerous animals, you would never know it due to the way she naturally interacts with them throughout the course of the movie. She and Dale Robinette make an effective team and have real chemistry. They bicker over his relocating to Nairobi and her decision to go to the Serengeti without asking each other. Unfortunately, Carol is then regulated to the park and off the screen much too long especially since she received top billing.

The last portion of the movie is the weakest and is just a series of incidents as it focuses on the three escaped lions, beginning with the lost, wandering lion cub Zeke with his mama on his trail. He makes its way to Claire's house where her daughter lets him in only to have the mother lion burst in afterwards. Trapped in her bedroom with the cub, Sandy, after phoning her mother, climbs out the two-story window, but the dim bulb does not close it behind her. Guess all that hair blinded her judgement. Zeke follows her as does the upset mama. Kevin and Claire arrive just in time to save Sandy as both lions run off. The cub then makes it over to the local hospital followed by his mother. After being shot with a tranquiller gun by Kevin, the mother wanders into the operating room where they are trying to save the life of Scudder's son. As she begins to fall asleep, mother and cub are reunited.

The last animal to be recaptured is Rinaldo, the park's star attraction. The lion is spotted in the woods and hunted down by more hotrodders who inadvertently start a brush fire trapping the beast. After Kevin tells a beaming Claire that he has postponed his move to Africa until the park is functioning normally again, the pair agree to discuss their future together. Kevin is then off to save Rinaldo after a helicopter pilot informs him of the lion's predicament. They chopper into the middle of the flames and tranquilize him. Kevin with help from Eddie and Rick, then carry and pull him into a net and fly out of harm's way.

DVD cover art for *The Beasts Are on the Streets* with pictured Philip Michael Thomas, Dale Robinette, and Carol Lynley.

You just knew that reviewers had their knives sharpened ready to slice this movie apart when it aired on May 18, 1978, but almost begrudgingly they had positive things to say amongst the criticisms. Kevin Thomas of the *Los Angeles Times* remarked that the "opening sequences are spectacularly staged" and that it "maintains momentum nicely." This should have come as no surprise since the experienced Peter Hunt directed one of the most exciting action-packed Bond movies and went on to direct such adventure features as *Gold* and *Shout at the Devil*.

William A. Henry of the *Boston Globe* offered a more philosophical review. He called it "a work of junk genius" and went on to add, "As in the old series *Emergency*, from which this film takes its structure, there is scarcely any continuing plot, just disconnected episodes, and little real tension, because everything is quickly resolved. Yet it is compelling, because it plays on our species' arrogance, our human fear of being burned or drowned by the nature we have tamed, or worse, eaten by the animals we have mastered and enclosed."

A few weeks after the fast moving and entertaining TV-movie aired (earning a fair 15.6 rating and 29 share, not enough to warrant a TV series, if that was the thinking of Hanna-Barbera), a person from West Chester, Pennsylvania wrote into the "Viewers' View" column in the *Philadelphia Inquirer* and remarked, "*Beasts Are in the Streets* was excellent. Carol Lynley was especially marvelous. Why didn't NBC advertise it more?" That viewer turned out to be none other than a teenaged Nelson Aspen (who wrote this book's foreword) and remarked, "I was such a little Carol Lynley nerd, I'd write into the papers and mags, just hoping to get something printed with her name on it! [Sound familiar!?!] Not even my own name!"[719] Seems Lynley had more than one junior PR man adept at getting her mentioned in print. Despite the promotional efforts, this would turn out to be Carol's final made-for-TV movie.

*****

Carol's frequent visibility on the small screen during the late seventies even extended to daytime. She popped up on such TV chat shows as *Dinah!*

and *The Mike Douglas Show*, and game shows such as *All Star Secrets* and *The Hollywood Squares*. Of the later, where she appeared numerous times usually in the bottom middle square or in the middle row to the left or right of Paul Lynde in the center square, Carol commented, "You can do thirty movies and eight Broadway plays but there are a lot of people who don't consider you a star till they see you in that box. Lots of people don't go to movies and know nothing about the theater."[720]

Carol sat next to Lynde frequently and she revealed that she was in attendance during one of his infamous, drunken, belligerent tirades. She recalled, "He got so sloshed during the taping that he walked over to the contestants and started screaming obscenities at them. Then he tried to strangle one of them!"[721] Not surprisingly, Lynde was not long for the show and was fired that same year.

Commenting on this period of her career, Carol said at the time, "I like working and TV afforded me some good roles so I go from TV to films to TV and back again for the better part of my career. It's funny, even though I do a lot of TV, I think of myself as a film actress rather than a television star."[722] At this juncture, Carol seemed more receptive to TV roles based on how they were written rather than just accepting them for a paycheck as she had done in the past.

Sometimes timing is a factor too when TV parts are offered. Carol was handed a guest role of a lifetime by Lorimar Productions. However, due to a scheduling conflict, she was unavailable to play beleaguered Valene Ewing, wife of Gary Ewing and sister-in-law of nasty oilman J.R. Ewing, in the season two opener "Reunion" on the CBS series *Dallas*. It had just come off a five-episode run in the spring of 1978 to decent ratings but was not yet the phenomenon it became. Ne'er-do-well alcoholic brother Gary (David Ackroyd) and his estranged wife Valene were the parents of teenage Lucy Ewing (Charlene Tilton) who lived with her grandparents on their sprawling Southfork Ranch. Gary's return and Lucy's finding her mother working as a waitress upsets dastardly, greedy older brother JR (Larry Hagman). Carol and

Charlene resembled each other so much it is easy to see why she was the first choice, though her talent and professionalism must also have been a factor.

Carol's unavailability had to do with her off-again, now on-again boyfriend David Frost. Purportedly, she received the offer but filming commenced just at the start of her planned three-week holiday in India with Frost. Because of her prearranged trip and her feeling that it was just another guest star part, she passed on it. With Carol honoring her commitment to Frost, Joan Van Ark took her place on *Dallas* and then went on to star in the long running spinoff, *Knots Landing*.

To say this was the mistake of Lynley's career is an understatement. Although *Dallas* had yet to become a phenomenon, Valene was a meaty lead role in a straight drama with a first-rate cast including her friend Larry Hagman, Barbara Bel Geddes, Patrick Duffy, and Jim Davis. The fact that it was not an Aaron Spelling production or a cop/detective series, where she guest starred mostly at the time, should have been enough for her to say yes. It is a shame her agent did not have the foresight to cajole her into taking the part and to postpone the vacation.

On the *Dallas* DVD commentary, producer David Jacobs mentioned that they originally wanted Carol Lynley for Valene and it took Larry Hagman by surprise. Being friends, she should have at least contacted him to get the scoop on the series before turning the role down. She did not and was probably too embarrassed to have ever admitted to Hagman such a colossal mistake. Though Carol boasted in many interviews that she never felt the pressure to remarry because she didn't need a man to take care of her and valued her independence, she seemed to let the men in her life come before her career at times. A huge role literally fell into her lap and she let Valene slip away, to the forever disappointment of her fans and, no doubt, her pocketbook.

How serious was the single actress really with David Frost at that time? Who knows? But during their reconnection, Lynley made headlines across the country when she and CBS critic David Sheehan were caught making out during the stage performance of *Sly Fox* at LA's Shubert Theatre. According to columnist Harry Haun, it was the show's miffed playwright Larry Gelbart squirming behind the amorous couple who ratted them out to the press.[723] Carol didn't deny the report and seemed to relish that they "acted absolutely outrageously. We went bananas. And I couldn't have enjoyed it more. I mean, I've never necked in a movie house, and there I was doing it in a theater –while George C. Scott was performing on stage."[724] This was not one of Lynley's finest hours and soon after she and Frost called it quits for good. Years later, after his death, Carol was asked to describe him and she opined, "He was an extraordinary person, and that kind of sums him up."[725]

Perhaps Carol should have spent the time away from David Frost socializing with her pal Fred Astaire instead. They had known each other for years and were close. Astaire called her one of his dearest friends in interviews he gave at the time. Per Carol, her relationship with Astaire remained strictly platonic. She fondly reminisced,

> He had this ability to turn every twenty-four hours into a joyful experience ... He was a father figure to me. Fred would call me up and say, 'Let's go out and get drunk.' And I'd say, 'Oh, all right.' Not that Fred would ever get drunk—he enjoyed cocktails. Then he'd say, 'Let's make it two weeks from Thursday,' and we'd go to the Bistro. I would have white wine and he'd have an old-fashioned. He loved those very thirties cocktails .... and he was not a fancy eater. When we went to Chasen's, he'd have chicken potpie; when we went to the Bistro, he also had chicken potpie.[726]

Carol remained friends with Fred Astaire until his death at age eighty-eight. She wanted to refute a story that he was sickly for a lengthy period and commented,

> Fred was active to about two months prior to his passing. When he was seventy-six, he had a grandson who was a skateboarder. Fred decided to try it out. One day he fell off it and broke his wrist. When I went to see him, he told me his doctor

said, 'I don't think it is a good idea to take up skateboarding at your age.' Fred never let his age stop him from doing things and he continued right on skateboarding."[727]

In late 1978, Carol was available to travel to Canada for the sci-fi feature *The Shape of Things to Come* but in retrospect maybe she wished she had other plans. Reportedly, the promising movie was to be produced by Sylvia Anderson, most famous for the cult sci-fi TV series *Space: 1999*. However, she left the project and the notoriously cheap producer of many an exploitation movie, Harry Alan Towers, came on board as executive producer. He remarked, "Around the first *Star Wars* success, when Science-Fiction was very popular, I felt that it was a good time to turn to the master ... H.G. Wells."[728]

Towers originally envisioned this as a $6 million combined CTV television series and theatrical release. Not surprisingly, considering Towers track record, he could not raise the funding and the television option was dropped. The film was financed in part by CFI Investments, Inc. and SOTTC Film Production Limited. CFI was formed in 1976 to develop and fund Canadian film productions. To qualify, a motion picture needed a certain percent of cast and crew to be Canadians and to shoot in the country. The movie was given a $3.2 million budget and filming began on October 23, 1978.

H.G. Wells wrote the original novel *The Shape of Things to Come* in 1933, which was made into the 1936 movie *Things to Come* and his name was used to exploit this new movie. However, Towers admitted that "it is not based upon the H.G. Wells novel. Nor is it a remake of the 1936 movie ... in some respects, the new *Shape* will more closely resemble *Star Wars* than the Wells' original."[729] Other than two characters being descendants of the character portrayed by Raymond Massey in Wells' *Things to Come*, there are no other similarities.

Towers was quite a character with a horrible reputation for shortchanging and not paying his cast and crew in a timely matter. However, they continued to work with him. Describing her experience playing a female Tarzan in *Eve*,

Celeste Yarnall recounted that Towers "was absolutely wild! My husband didn't take kindly to me not getting paid and showed up at Towers' office with a water pistol pretending it was a gun. Shelley said, 'If you don't pay Celeste, she's not going to show up.' I'm missing from the film for a long stretch ... They re-wrote the whole middle of the script so that they could keep shooting."[730]

Yarnall's story was just one of many about the penny-pinching Towers. Nicholas Campbell was aware of the complaints about the producer regarding paying his actors but felt a starring role in a major motion picture would help his career. He wisely took an offensive approach in dealing with the notorious Towers. Campbell remarked, "He was a ridiculous man, but I had an affection for him though he was pretty sleazy. You had to get your money upfront. There was no point relying on a union or a lawyer or anything like that. You had to get a big piece of it upfront. It was kind of obvious just meeting him. He was always sweating ... He'd ask you a question and he wasn't paying attention for the answer—that kind of thing."[731]

Towers brought in producer William Davidson and script writer Martin Lager who both worked on the Canadian sci-fi series *Starlost*. Campbell commented that Lager "was a great guy and takes himself really seriously. He was a really good writer and wrote some very edgy stuff [*The Shape of Things to Come* excluded]."[732]

Also assembled by Towers was an impressive veteran cast: Jack Palance, Barry Morse, John Ireland, and Lynley along with fresh faces in their first starring film roles Campbell (a Mark Hamill look-a-like) and Eddie Benton (replacing the infamous Koo Stark, former girlfriend of Prince Charles). Benton would later change her name to Anne Marie Martin and marry novelist/screenwriter/director Michael Crichton.

Palance played a tyrannical scientist on a planet called Delta III who has overthrown its governor (Carol Lynley) and has declared war on New Washington the Earth's outpost on the moon. Asked to comment on her role, Carol replied, "In the press release I'm described as the noble Niki, but I took it even further—I'm wonderful, terrific, a know-all, a leader of armies—I was telling 80 people [actually no more than a dozen tops] who were marching behind me what to do, which is a great joke, because I usually get lost going around the block."733

A vivacious Carol Lynley during a break in filming *The Shape of Things to Come* (Film Ventures, 1979). *From Marlin Dobbs' Collection*

Recalling his co-stars, Nicholas Campbell said, "Carol Lynley...was one of the most charming people ever. Carol knew Jack Palance well. Jack came in after we were shooting for a while …He was the craziest, kookiest guy ever."[734] Campbell went on to share that the studio where they were shooting was north of Toronto. One day, Palance got upset with something [director] George McCowan said or did. Jack walked off the set and decided to hitchhike back to Toronto.[735]

Carol called Palance, "Big Jack" and added,

> He was a tall guy with a deep voice and did all those movies where he beat up and shot many people. Surprisingly, he was polite and soft-spoken but he was a handful. With Jack you never knew what could happen. My focus was dealing with Jack on a day to day level. Keeping him happy and *quiet*. My attention was more on him [than the director or other actors] and think that was the way he wanted it.[736]

Toronto Star reporter Bruce Kirkland spent a day on the set and corroborated that Jack Palance was the diva on this movie. He wrote, "Everyone's a bit worried about Palance, the prima donna. He has made it clear he doesn't like still photographers; he doesn't like the click of the camera; he doesn't even want to catch sight of one out of the corner of his eye. Palance also won't give interviews … A source with the film says Palance's acting has really impressed them, though: 'He's worth the aggravation.'"[737]

When told of Palance's distaste for still photography while shooting, Carol said, "With Jack you never knew. He may have felt that way but if he really wanted that I doubt it. I personally never heard him say anything like that."[738]

The same journalist found Lynley a joy to be around. He proclaimed, "She is the lifeblood of this movie, at least behind the scenes, the warmest and most approachable of all. She also has a pride that dictates she'll do her best in front of the cameras."[739]

He then shared a humorous story of how only Carol could get Jack Palance to loosen up. When scampering across the set she caught her foot on a loose board. "Jack Palance booms out from the sidelines in his sonorous voice 'you're as graceful as ever Carol – stumble, stumble, stumble.' The fleet-footed Lynley, an accomplished amateur ballet dancer and figure skater, flies over to Palance and playfully punches him in his stomach for revenge, patting his slight paunch. He towers over her, grimacing."[740]

Of course, since this movie was basically a rip-off of *Star Wars*, with less than stellar visual effects, there are a lot of cute and not-so-cute robots rolling about. Special effects director Wally Gentleman (who previously worked on *2001: A Space Odyssey*, among other projects) did the best he could with the miniature and matte work considering the budget restraints.

Carol gave several press interviews to promote the movie and talked about the making of her first and last "big" outer space sci-fi adventure. She remarked, "I never saw the original *Things to Come*, but when I was in Canada, I was told that the part I play—Niki the governor of [the moon]—is based on the part Raymond Massey played in the original. It's wonderful to play a perfect person commanding vast armies and a whole citadel of faithful followers in outer space. There are no humans left on Earth in the movie [there are actually], we're all on [the moon], but you can be sure we just don't sit around eating hamburgers. In a way the movie will be a little like *Star Wars*. There's lots of action because my lieutenant Jack Palance tries to take my planet away from me, and Barry Morse helps me get it back."[741]

Columnist Roderick Mann was happy to hear that Carol was coming back to the big screen and agreed with her dislike of her costume. He bemoaned, "It seems an awful waste to put someone as shapely as Carol Lynley into a movie and then make her wear one of those dreary Mao-type outfits."[742]

Also disappointing for the actress was the lack of romance. Lynley said, "There's no nudity or sex on my planet … I was talking to Charlton Heston about that. When you are a leader like governor, president, Moses, they never write you a sex scene because you're too busy leading your people. No time for sex!"[743]

Sharing some more stories on what went on behind-the-scenes, Nicholas Campbell added, "It was nothing like we can change the lines and make it better. There was nothing you can do. By this time George McCowan had been picked clean by ex-wives ... He was one step from an iron young. He used to smoke six packs of Parliaments every day and had them all lined up in his little chair. And he had an oxygen [tank]. George was a real talented guy who just got soured by life. One day we were shooting a scene ... and it was freezing. George McCowan was sitting in a car facing the other way watching through the rearview [mirror]. There were no monitors in those days. You actually had to get out and go look through the eyepiece to see what the shot was going to be. Everybody relied on camera operators ... He just didn't really care about stupid stuff."[744]

George McCowan also didn't consider *The Shape of Things to Come* a serious subject matter. He admitted, "This material doesn't call for a philosophical approach. This is different than *Star Wars* and *Close Encounters*. It's simpler, so that dictates the flavor, in a sense."[745] Perhaps if McCowan would have tried something innovative to elevate the material rather than just accept it as is, he would have delivered a much better film and not have received such scathing reviews.

Considering what Lynley had to go through to film *The Shape of Things to Come*, it is surprising that she never complained. A Yoga enthusiast, she remarked, "It is true that I avoid getting involved in the tensions and stresses around me. It goes back a long way—I'm determined to hold onto my own center of peace."[746]

Carol pinned her hopes on this movie after none of her previous four movies made much of an impact on the big screen. She did not think it was because they were bad but "because of poor distribution." She was correct about that but nothing could have helped the wonky *The Four Deuces* or the claustrophobic *The Washington Affair*. *Bad Georgia Road* and especially *The Cat and the Canary* could have been hits if given a full national release.

Kim (Eddie Benton), Jason (Nicholas Campbell), Dr. Caball (Barry Morse), Niki (Carol Lynley), and Merrick (Ardon Bess) listen intently as Omus issues his threat in *The Shape of Things to Come* (Film Ventures, 1979).

Pre-release, the magazine and newspaper interviews Carol gave about making the movie rarely included a photo of her in it. Instead, she provided some very sexy photos of herself in frilly lingerie shot of Harry Langdon. Commenting on her departure from the more earthy photos taken earlier in the decade, Harry opined, "Life changes and Carol was a beautiful woman. She didn't have to try to be sexy and sensual, she just was. It really didn't matter what she was wearing. Her lingerie shots were very fetching."[747]

This photo found its way into *Time* magazine, among others, where Carol was asked about her costumes in *Shape of Things to Come*. She replied, referring to the sexy frock she was wearing, "I hope that in the year 2000 women still wear clothes like this."[748] Not so in *Shape* where her outfit was, as described by Carol, was "a unisex Mao outfit."[749] She added, "And if that's the shape of things to come then I'd say it's rather depressing."[750]

The *Shape of Things to Come* opens with a prologue à la *Star Wars* to set up the story,

> The time is the tomorrow after tomorrow. Earth has been polluted and devastated by the great robot wars and is all but deserted. Man has moved onto the moon, colonized its surface and erected vast cities in what was once wasteland. Ranging further out into deep space he has embarked on an even greater era of adventure and discovery. But the survival of mankind is dependent on a continuing supply of the miracle drug RADIC-Q-2. And RADIC-Q-2 is produced only on the distant planet Delta III.

Earth's domed lunar colony is called New Washington (filmed at the Cinesphere Dome in the Ontario Place Amusement Park in Toronto) and has turned into a community of pacifists who listen to a robot named Lomax for guidance. The peaceful planet is attacked by the renegade Omus (Jack Palance who is seen only in his control room), a one-time protégé of New Washington's Dr. John Caball (Barry Morse), who has forcefully seized rule of Delta III from its leader Niki (Carol Lynley) who has gone underground with some of her loyal followers. His planet supplies the moon colony with RADIC-Q-2, which is needed to combat radiation poisoning. Omus has sent a cargo ship manned by one of his robots on a suicide mission to crash into New Washington as a warning and then via video threatens to stop the supply of RADIC-Q-2. His robot survives the crash and is rebuilt by Kim Smedley (Eddie Benton). Renamed Sparks, it is now part of the resistance.

Dr. Caball, a descendant of Raymond Massey's Oswald Caball from *Things to Come*, and his son, pilot Jason (Nicholas Campbell), want to mount an offensive attack against Omus but they are hampered by Lomax and New Washington's Senator Smedley (John Ireland) who do not believe in warfare. Dr. Caball prepares the new spaceship Star Streak, built for space exploration only, to fly but he is exposed to radiation in the process and keeps it a secret.

Kim disagrees with her father and accompanies the Caball's and Sparks as they steal the Star Streak and head to Delta III to battle Omus and restore order.

Lynley as Niki appears on screen for the first time around the thirty-minute mark. She is outside the city proper with a loyal band of followers, armed with only spears and shields, and is organizing them to enter the citadel to fight to take control of Delta III. She sneaks into the citadel and makes it to the control room where she calls New Washington begging for help. Omus and one of his robots enter and she flees before hearing their reply. Omus does and puts out a red alert. Niki makes it back to her followers where they are attacked by Omus' robots (roughly six to eight men in ridiculously designed robot suits). With two warriors killed, the band is down to less than ten fighters as they flee once again into the outside wasteland. Meanwhile, the Star Streak malfunctions and they are forced to make a pitstop on Earth where they encounter a gaggle of children wearing bad blonde wigs in desperate need of RADIC-Q-2, which the space travelers promise to bring back. Omus' robot army discovers where Niki and the others are hiding out and attacks.

The Star Streak gets caught in a magnetic field surrounding Delta III and goes through what Sparks determines is "time dilation," which is never explained. Arguably, since there are many silly scenes, this is the most ridiculous as poor Campbell and Benton roll around the ship's control room trying to enact weightlessness, but it comes off more as a bad modern dance piece with them desperately reaching out to each other. The Star Streak receives Niki's distress beacon and they land close by. As they meet up, they are attacked by Omus' robots. The battle ceases when Omus appears in holograph form (a rotating image of Palance's head and shoulders) and invites Dr. Caball to meet to discuss a truce, but Niki warns that it is trap. Caball decides to take the risk.

Omus explains his plan to be the emperor of New Washington and Cabal calls him a madman, only to die from a severe radiation burn delivered by Omus. Caball's body is found by his son, Kim, and Niki while Omus's robots take out the last of Niki's army. Omus reveals to Jason his plot to destroy Delta III and all who remain. Sparks, meanwhile, reprograms Omus' cadre of robots that turn on him and keep him trapped in his control room as the planet disintegrates around him. Jason, Kim, Niki and Sparks are able to escape, along with a copious supply of RADIC-Q-2 before the planet explodes, due to Omus' plan to obliterate any evidence before taking control of the moon. The movie ends with the voice of the departed Cabal reassuringly espousing, "Out there is the vastness of space, the unknown where all possibilities exist, and man's future is limited only by his imagination and his vision of the stars."

Carol described, in detail, her unconventional approach to tackling the last scenes of the movie where the actors must react to the destruction of Delta III, which was done separately with special effects. She said,

> When we shot it things were very tricky, because you're not dealing with human relationships, it's total fantasy. Near the end of the movie, the planet we came from just blows up before our very eyes. I asked if it was going to be a big explosion and was told that it would be like a series of explosions. See, it's all special effects and none of us had seen them ... So, when they did my closeup, they came in really tight, and I'm looking out, supposedly seeing all that, and with no dialogue. All I could think of, if I may be so bold, was a series of orgasms. Rhythmic—I just experienced that inside my head, which might not come over on film as something sexual, but it will come over as a serious consideration.[751]

The Shape of Things to Come was distributed by International Film Distributors and opened in Canada, the United Kingdom, and several other foreign countries in May of 1979 with the tag line, "Beyond the Earth...Beyond the moon...Beyond your wildest dreams! H.G. Wells' *The Shape of Things to Come*." It also was scheduled for a national U.S. release via Film Ventures

International (Allied Artists was originally announced) that same month, but bad luck struck again for Lynley and this film too was hampered by major distribution problems. It only played in a limited number of U.S. markets and in some parts of the country it did not show up on the big screen until November. Considering the sci-fi competition that year (including *Alien*, *The Black Hole*, and *Star Trek: The Motion Picture*), it does not come as a complete surprise.

Carol Lynley as Niki, Governor of the Moon in *The Shape of Things to Come* (Film Ventures, 1979).

As expected, the movie received limited reviews and most of them were mediocre at best. Kevin Thomas in the *Los Angeles Times* called it a "standard sci-fi adventure" and found the writing and direction to be "uninspired." He ended the review with "*The Shape of Things to Come* is decent in both its special effects and its humanist sentiments but pretty lackluster in this post-*Star Wars* era. Morse is staunch, Ireland and Lynley are adequate, and Palance predictably comes on like Ming the Merciless."

Variety liked it less and declared the film to be an "Unexciting, skimpy remake ... with minimal box office prospects ... Muddily thought out, photographed, and acted." Tim Pulleine of the *Monthly Film Bulletin* despised the movie and commented, "Whatever reservations one might have about the windy portentousness of his original, H. G. Wells must be spinning in his grave at the appropriation of not merely his title but his name by this risibly inept and remorselessly trivial space-opera ... this one displays not a shred of the ambition with which (at least) its predecessor must be credited."

As for Carol, she is not that bad and takes her role quite seriously. She just does not have the resonant of voice to play a leader totally convincingly. However, you can tell she enjoyed playing this atypical role for her of leader Niki.

Yvette Mimieux was also starring in a sci-fi epic *The Black Hole* at the same time and she too did not make a thoroughly believable authoritative figure for the critics and some of the audience. In an interview with Mimieux, journalist Joe Baltake opined that despite giving credible performances, "Yvette and friends [Sandra Dee, Tuesday Weld, and Carol Lynley] have all had trouble sustaining the public's belief in their maturity."[752] Yvette responded, "Looking back on it, I guess we were all conspired against in a negative way. The roles weren't there—at least, not good ones—and there wasn't much interest in general. But I wasn't much interested either."[753] Carol shared Yvette's frustrations in the dearth of good roles for women in many an interview she gave back in the day. And she found it hard for producers and casting directors to not keep thinking of her as the teenage ingénue.

When asked what he thought of *The Shape of Things to Come*, Nicholas Campbell admitted, "I never bothered to see it ... There are people who like cheesy movies, but this doesn't even qualify in that score."[754]

Campbell was spot on with his assessment. Several low-budget *Star Wars* rip-offs were produced between 1977 and 1980 including *Starship Invasions*; *Battle Upon the Stars*; *Message from Space*; *Galaxina*, and *Starcrash*. The latter (starring David Hasselhoff, Christopher Plummer, and Caroline Munro) has a cult following because as filmmaker/author Ernie Magnotta noted in *Scary Monsters* magazine, it had a "plethora of wonderfully fun images, loveable characters, quirky dialogue, etc."[755] Everything the deadly serious and lifeless *The Shape of Things to Come* lacked.

While *The Cat and the Canary* was an entertaining remake that the actress could be proud of, *The Shape of Things to Come* was just a Harry Alan Towers quickie production trying to exploit the *Star Wars* formula and the H.G. Wells name. Fans saw right through it and, to this day, still vent online about how they were ripped off when they paid to see it in the theater. However good the miniature effects were, the cheap, unimaginative looking robots and interior sets of New Washington, Delta III, and the Star Streak look straight out of Saturday morning TV fare like *Jason of Star Command*. It remains one of the most hated sci-fi films of that period. In 2018, ALotLiving.com named it one of 30 Films That Ruined the Seventies. At least it is still remembered for something to this day.

*****

Carol closed out the seventies with a special guest star turn opposite Julio Iglesias in the Spanish musical romance *Todos los días, un día* (*Every Day, One Day*) from Columbia Pictures Spanish Theatrical Film Division. Iglesias was one of the most popular singers in the world at the time and basically played himself. A full-age ad in *Variety* proclaimed, "With a sensational soundtrack… spectacular settings in three continents…big-budget production values…and an absorbing intimate story about the isolation and loneliness of the glittering life at the top…this is the surefire Latin blockbuster of the year."

Though the *Variety* ad touted his leading lady, Isa Lorenz, as "a top Latin actress", she was a half Cuban, half-German New York City born Elite model making her first and only movie. Iglesias' scenes with a glamorous Carol Lynley (who was fluent in Spanish, but it is unclear what language she spoke on screen) were set at a disco in New York. She and singer Tony Martin received guest star billing. Carol admitted to being surprised about one term in her contract. She had to agree to "do nothing to embarrass the government of Spain during the duration of filming ... Apparently it's a standard clause in all Spanish film contracts."[756]

This sexy photo by Harry Langdon, Jr. was used by Carol Lynley for publicity purposes in 1978 during and after making *The Shape of Things to Come*. From Marlin Dobbs' Collection

Todos los días, un día played in some major U.S. cities, opening in late spring in New York and Los Angeles, but was virtually ignored by the English-language press.

During this time Carol was receiving reams of publicity. Photos of her out on the town were turning up in newspapers and magazines across the country. Her social life seemed to be in full swing for the public to read about. When asked by columnist Dick Kleiner, why all of a sudden the change when prior Carol was a bit more discreet, the actress replied, "First, I was always shy and it's only recently I realized I actually enjoy going to parties. The second and most important reason is that when I was just a single parent, with a daughter to raise, that was my prime responsibility. Now I have more time to myself."[757]

This new attitude seemed to affect her professional life as well. For the next few years, Carol continued keeping extremely busy on television plus one feature film that received a wide release. When asked why she was getting so much work, the actress (who had not looked this stunningly beautiful since the mid-sixties, now that she was back to wearing makeup and keeping longer hair again) replied at the time,

> I just turned 37 and I think things are just beginning to open up for me. For a long time, I looked ten years younger than I was. That meant that there were many actors I could not play opposite because I looked like their daughters, and nobody would believe I could play their wives. But now I look like I'm in … my mid to late-20s, and I'm beginning to play better roles.[758]

Though the actress was busy, she was not getting roles in the highly touted popular mini-series of the day and her appearances in made-for-TV movies ceased with *The Beasts Are on the Streets*. Though she was regularly guest starring on dramatic series, most were produced by Aaron Spelling, and had a bit of a stigma to them. Spelling was known to employ actors whose careers had declined or faded. His entertaining, smartly crafted series such as *Fantasy Island*, *The Love Boat*, *Charlie's Angels*, *Hart to Hart*, etc., though extremely popular with viewers, were considered by the critics and others in Hollywood as being frivolous with less than stellar scripts. They were not known to jump start a career unless you were cast as a series lead, which Carol never was.

It is undeniable though that Carol looked fantastic at this point and was in perhaps the best shape of her life. A lot of this had to do with her discovery of yoga years prior. Per her daughter Jill, Carol was a practitioner, "when everyone still made fun of it."[759] Carol then became a student of Bikram Choudhury who had founded a hot yoga studio in Beverly Hills. The Indian yoga instructor developed a 26-posture series of positions and kept his studio's temperature at over 100 degrees. He would wear only a Speedo while leading his sweaty class, which attracted many celebrities. Besides Carol, attendees included Raquel Welch, Shirley MacLaine, Quincy Jones, Candice Bergen, Yvette Mimieux, Juliet Prowse, Keir Dullea, Susan Strasberg, Irene Tsu, and Marianna Hill. The actress was such a devout follower that Choudhury selected her as a model for his instructional book on Bikram yoga released in the early eighties.

Carol's age seemed to be a hot topic in the late seventies and in another interview from that time she stated that "I don't want to look 18 when I'm 45. I'd love to look like a hot 35 when I'm 45. There's something spooky about people whose faces remain children forever."[760]

Carol then added that she could not wait until she turned fifty because she'd look a decade younger. She said, "And the best parts for women are written for 40-year-olds."[761] Lynley would soon face a rude awakening. There were a lot more actresses over forty than there were good roles so the competition was fiercer than she may have expected.

Perhaps Carol was just putting up a front for the public and really did know the score. Years later she admitted to a friend that she dreaded her fortieth birthday because she knew it was the death knell for actresses in Hollywood and that her career would slow down immensely. Unfortunately, she was correct.

16. Soaps to Suspense

The Me-Decade began for Carol Lynley in a couple of sudsy dramas two of which were proposed series. Due to the success of CBS' *Dallas* and then *Knots Landing*, Lorimar decided to produce another serialized drama for television called *Willow B: Women in Prison* and brought it to ABC instead. This was before *Dynasty* launched on that network. Undoubtedly, when Lorimar came a-calling again, Carol probably jumped at the chance when asked to do a primetime soap pilot for the production company, co-starring with Elizabeth Hartman, Susan Tyrell, Sally Kirkland, and Ruth Roman.

The Australian serial *Prisoner* was the first to air in primetime in the U.S. on KTLA in Los Angeles. Set in a fictional women's detention center, it told the story of the female inmates and the people who worked there. The one-hour, violent and rather adult show for the time quickly developed a dedicated cult following. In 1980 it was broken into two half-hour segments and sold into syndication as *Prisoner: Cell Block H* where it became a surprise late night hit.

Though they knew there were going to be comparisons, Lorimar went ahead with their pilot *Willow B: Women in Prison*. Rather than being filmed, it was shot on videotape to give it the same feel as *Prisoner* and other daytime serials. Tape was also less expensive than shooting film. The executive producers were Michael Filerman (*Knots Landing*, *Falcon Crest*) and Lee Rich (*Eight Is Enough*, *Flamingo Road*). It was directed by future Emmy winner Jeff Bleckner (*Hill Street Blues*) and written by Gerry Day after much research and prison officials' approval.

Filerman immediately dismissed the similarities to *Prisoner* and stated, "We worked very hard to not be exploitative. We want viewers to understand what people really go through under these circumstances. If anything, we thought more of that old movie, *Caged*, with Eleanor Parker, and how it changed her life."[762]

With this enthusiastic and talented production team behind it, there were high hopes for this pilot. Carol recalled,

> I played an ex-debutante turned hooker! I remember we shot this at a real women's prison. Each day we would drive to the studio and then get on a bus to the location. We each had to have a background check to get into the prison. I was in my dressing area and heard one of the actresses crying. She was rejected because her husband was an ex-convict and she had no idea. What a way to find out. They had to escort her off the premises and she was sent back to the studio. There were real inmates around and I was on edge. When I wasn't in a scene, I would stand off near one of the actors Jared Martin who was quite tall. I felt safe being next to him.
>
> I had known Sally Kirkland for years. Her mother was a fashion editor and used to hire me when I was a child model. Sally is great and I adore her. I was most excited to work with Ruth Roman but I really didn't get to know her unfortunately.[763]

The pilot focused on two inmates at Willow B, a minimum-security prison. Socialite Debra Clinger is the new kid on the cellblock, sentenced to 28 months for a felony manslaughter charge. Trisha Noble is a veteran inmate who takes Clinger under her wing and wants to be just more than friends.

Besides Lynley, whose prisoner receives a conjugal visit from her husband that goes wrong, other prisoners included the previously mentioned Hartman who misleads her mother into thinking she is traveling the world, a frazzled Tyrell, and Kirkland as a helpful junkie, plus Liz Torres, Lynne Moody, and Virginia Capers. Ruth Roman is the stereotypically corrupt, hardnosed guard, handsome Jared Martin (the only male eye candy in sight) is a sympathetic prison guard, and John P. Ryan is one of Roman's shady flunkies.

Producer Michael Filerman was deeply disappointed that ABC did not pick up the pilot and felt it did not get a fair shake. He remarked, "I think they (ABC) were a bit nervous about the subject matter. They're not used to the serialized drama we have with *Dallas*. They were not sure just how tough we'd be in what is a sensitive story area—lesbianism, dehumanizing, harassment." He thought they would have had a better shot if ABC would have greenlit a short order of six episodes. "That is one of the major problems of our pilot. We had 13 running characters, but with only one hour we had to cut down in probing the lives of other characters and just show the two girls. The key to a drama of this kind is that the situation is resolved but the problem continues."[764] He had hoped to expand outside the prison to show the home lives of the guards and how it affected their jobs. Also shown would have been the lives the prisoners left behind and perhaps conjugal visits. It sounds like a precursor to Netflix's hit streaming series *Orange Is the New Black*, without the nudity and foul language

The critic from the *Pittsburgh Post-Gazette* called *Willow B*, "Grimsville, a prison drama that piles on one indignity after another on the pretty young socialite who lands in the slammer." A more positive review came from *People* magazine that commented, "For lack of other lurid topics, the networks fall back on the females-in-cages gambit. But this TV movie ... is superior to most of the genre. Debra Clinger, Elizabeth Hartman, Carol Lynley and Sarah Kennedy are ... sympathetic inmates." In between was Tom Shales of *The Washington Post* who remarked that *Willow B* made "*Dallas* look like *Little House on the Prairie*" and that it was "a disposable but enjoyable wallow." Shales did criticize the pilot for being on the sleazy side compared to others of its ilk, so perhaps that may have factored into the network's decision to pass on it. It is too bad because the premise sounds interesting backed up by the excellent cast. It would have been a treat to see Carol as a series regular even if for a short season.

*****

During this period Carol was constantly traveling from the East Coast to the West Coast and back. She was asked once why it was cheaper living in two apartments rather than one as she stated once on a talk show. The actress explained, "I split my time between New York, my base, and Los Angeles. I'm always flying back and forth because of my work. And since I don't believe in long stays with friends, I'd have to live in a hotel during all my commutes. Hotel living is awfully expensive, and my yearly rent is much less than a year's hotel tab."[765]

Carol never stopped considering herself a true New Yorker and remarked on the way of life in the Big Apple, "I love the pace of New York, and even though most film-making still goes on in Los Angeles, I've always maintained an apartment here, to recover from the slow way of life there.

"I have never been mugged, robbed, or burgled," she continued musing about New York. "You have to have some street sense, of course, and be aware of potential danger. New Yorkers are generally born with it and instinctively use body language to protect themselves. You just don't walk around looking lost and gawking at the sights."[766]

When staying in town, Carol was continually active in New York City's social scene. Photos of her were published in various newspapers attending movie premieres, theater openings, and art exhibitions. She could be found in the winter ice skating at Wollman Rink in Central Park and yearly taking dance classes at Luigi's Jazz Centre. Founded by dancer Eugene Louis Faccuito (while working in Hollywood musicals he was nicknamed Luigi by Gene Kelly), who was famously known for teaching dancers how to use their bodies properly, decreasing the risk of injuries. His studio attracted novices,

Broadway chorines, and celebrities including Lynley, John Travolta, Liza Minnelli, Robert Morse, BarBara Luna, and Gail Gerber.

A recipient of the Theatre World Award in 1957, Carol was also active with the Theatre World Award organization during this time where she was a presenter at a few of their ceremonies honoring debut performances on the New York stage.

Acting, though, was still Carol's number one priority. Where the work was is where she could be found. It was announced around this time that Lynley would be appearing with Frankie Avalon in the slasher movie *Premonitions* to be shot in Oregon and directed by Alan J. Levi. The former teen idol was cast against type, as a hatchet wielding psycho who escapes from an asylum and goes on a killing spree. Lynley was mentioned as playing the neurotic mother of a handicapped, teenage Donna Wilkes who had once received a blood transfusion from the killer. For whatever reasons, Lynley did not appear. The part was taken by Antoinette Bower and the movie retitled *Blood Song*.[767]

When asked if he knew anything about why Carol did not make the movie, Levi replied with a laugh, "No, but she dodged a bullet. The producers were allegedly connected to the Mafia out here. That's how they raised the money for it. My assistant director held all the money in escrow but under the control of the two producers. They ran away with my entire salary. I had to take them to court."[768]

In 1981, Carol briefly traded the dirty streets of New York for the beauty of the Colorado River in the Grand Canyon for *The Best of Friends*, a promising one hour dramatic special sponsored by Liberty Mutual. It was directed by Emmy nominee Ron Satlof (*McCloud*) and was adapted from Ernest Hemingway's short story *The Three-Day Blow* by Venable Herndon who co-wrote *Alice's Restaurant*. Hemingway's tale dealt with two teenage boys who spend time in a Michigan cottage getting drunk and discussing their fathers and one of the boy's recent romantic breakup. *The Best of Friends* was about an adult love triangle set on the Colorado River. Huh? When asked why the name change, Carol opined, "They must have thought *Best of*

Friends would attract a wider audience. Maybe they thought nobody would understand *Three-Day Blow*."⁷⁶⁹

Carol liked the role offered to her and exclaimed, "I jumped at the chance to play the part because I love the outdoors. I really like to exercise, and to breathe the clean fresh air of the country. And it invigorates me."⁷⁷⁰ She later added, "I had never been to the Grand Canyon. I was intrigued and the script was okay, not great, but okay. I liked Peter Graves' work and I knew Alex Cord. It was only a three week shoot so I thought it would be good so off I went."⁷⁷¹

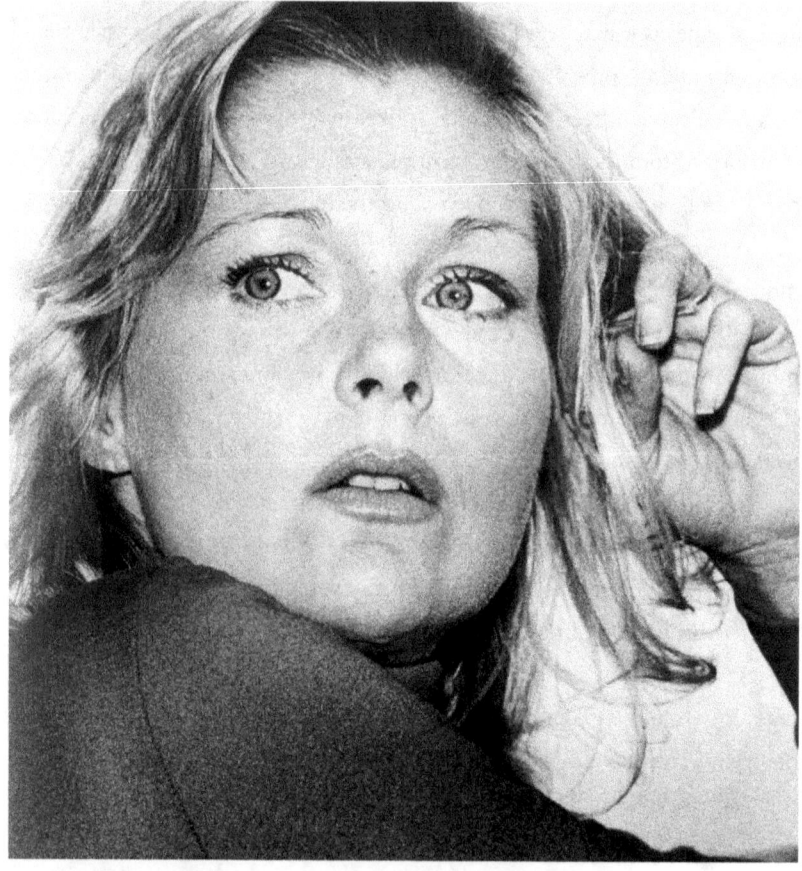

Publicity photo of Carol Lynley as an adulterous wife in the syndicated TV special *The Best of Friends* (Robert Halmi Productions, 1981).

The shoot was a true adventure for the actress, who gave a few interviews about making the show. Despite the hardships, it was one of her most exhilarating experiences. She spent two weeks in the wilds of the Grand Canyon and shooting rapids on the Colorado River. Carol remarked, "I loved the location shooting in the Grand Canyon—amazing for a girl from New York City ... I never even went camping as a child."[772] Recounting her time away, she shared in 1981,

> We started filming in Boulder City, Colorado. Then we went across the desert where wild burros roam—they're beautiful. Then we went to Lake Mead for more shooting. Then we flew in a Cesena to a bluff on an Indian reservation, where vans met us to take us down to the bottom of the Grand Canyon. Then we sailed for 2 ½ hours down the Colorado River to where our houseboats were moored. It was terrific!
>
> We lived in the houseboats for three weeks. There was no TV, of course, no telephone, no electricity except when they ran our generators a short time at night and in the early morning. The only thing I really missed was the *New York Times*. Although the Cesena flew the exposed film out every night, it never brought in any papers. Just after the election and no news for three weeks.[773]

Although Carol was always the consummate professional, there was a minor incident that set her off. She revealed,

> *The Best of Friends* called for me to be in the water a lot. I've played many parts in which I spent time in the water. But ... I had to don a wet suit for the first time. The water was so cold that we needed the suit under our clothes to keep warm. Nobody told me that you have to be perfectly dry and powdered down before getting into a wet suit. I got the suit on halfway when it became stuck. I couldn't get it on or off. It took three people half

an hour to get me out of the suit. It was the only time that my Irish temper flared up during filming."[774]

Describing the plot, Carol said, "I am in love with my husband's best friend, and the friend is a river rat who takes people through the white water. It was filmed at the bottom of the Grand Canyon—in November. I hop on and off boats and jump in and out of the river. It was very, very cold."[775] Peter Graves played the jilted banker husband and Alex Cord was his best friend and his wife's lover. An interesting side note is that the movie was produced by Robert Halmi, Sr. and his son Robert Halmi, Jr. who founded the Hallmark Channel.

When asked what he recalled about making *The Best of Friends*, Alex Cord wrote, "Carol Lynley was sweet, drop-dead beautiful, and a dream to work with. She was the brightest part of the day despite an undercurrent of inherent sadness. I think 'lady in peril' is an apt phrase. It seems a good fit for too many Hollywood beauties. My heart goes out to all who love Carol. She deserved every bit of it."[776]

"The biggest challenge for me was getting in that bloody frigid river and keeping my teeth from chattering," continued Cord. "Not fun."[777]

Despite Carol's enjoyable experience making *The Best of Friends*, it was unfortunately not well-received. Most critics found fault with the script's bastardization of the original Hemingway story, though almost all agreed the scenery was spectacular. Tony Schwarts of the *New York Times* especially hated it and quipped that is was "Hemingway lobotomized for dopes." Carol did get a nice mention from Harriet Van Horne in *Newsday* who wrote, "There is a nice potential—given a fair script and a gifted director—in the beautiful, childlike actress, Carol Lynley." But she went on to expound this was not it.

*****

You know you are in a world of fantasy when a thirty-eight-year-old Carol Lynley ages from sixteen to fifty. That is just what she does in the

TV pilot *Judgement Day* directed by Alan J. Levi. It was right out of Aaron Spelling's *Fantasy Island* playbook, down to the cast of players that included Carol and frequent co-star and friend Roddy McDowall, but produced jointly by Ed Friendly Productions and NBC. Also appearing were Barry Sullivan, Victor Buono, Robert Webber, John Larch, and in minor roles Beverly Garland. Priscilla Pointer, Hari Rhodes, Terry Kiser, and Maxwell Caulfield in one of his earliest TV appearances.

Levi was under contract to Universal Television (he directed many episodes of their fantasy series *The Invisible Man*, *The Six Million Dollar Man*, *The Bionic Woman*, and *Gemini Man*) and had worked previously with Ed Friendly. He recounted, "In 1969, I was an associate producer on *Laugh-In* and I worked for Schlatter-Friendly Productions for about two years. Ed was partners with George Schlatter. I also was a producer on a couple of their TV specials and then I directed a show for them called *Arnold's Closet Revue* with Arte Johnson. That is how I became friendly with Ed and then later he wanted me to direct this pilot."[778]

When asked to describe the pilot, Levi opined, "It was a program where people got a second chance. There were a couple of other shows like this on the air then. One was called *Time Express* with Vincent Price and his wife Coral Browne. It only lasted four weeks. I directed the pilot and one of the episodes. *Judgement Day* was kind of like that as both went back into time."[779] [In *Time Express*, the train passenger could relive a special moment in their past and had to make the decision to keep their then choice or to change it; and in *Judgement Day* the jury would see both the good and bad sides from the newly deceased's past to decide either heaven or hell.]

Parts of making this pilot were a blur to Levi because "I had a 102 fever for most of the shoot, and even missed one day of filming, which was the only time in my entire career. If I recall, my doctor ordered me to stay home and Ed Friendly directed on that day. I think for the entire filming I was sort of 'out of it' to be frank."[780]

Per Carol, when she walked into the makeup room the first day, there was Roddy who joked almost on cue, "Oh God, not you again!"[781] When Carol confessed to Roddy that she had a crush on the makeup supervisor, he advised that she was probably not his "type" and she listened to her observant friend.

Regarding the lead actors, Levi remarked, "It was a marvelous cast. I worked with Barry Sullivan a couple of times including on the mini-series *The Immigrants*. I loved Barry. He was a total, total pro. I brought Roddy McDowall and Victor Buono into the project because I thought both fitted the roles of Mr. Heller and Mr. Heavener. I worked with Roddy several times. He was the best you could ever wish for—such a pro and a wonderful guy. He was fun and a helpful actor to everybody else. Roddy was also a lover and expert on old films which I am. We just didn't stop talking in between takes—just a marvelous guy. Victor Buono was very quiet with a wonderful sense of humor. He was a big man!"[782]

As for Lynley, when told that she was almost thirty-eight years old when she did this, Alan Levi exclaimed, "You're kidding! She looked like she was in her late teens and looked damn good. Carol Lynley was adorably sweet and professional. I didn't have to give her too much direction. I do remember asking her in one scene how she felt in this situation and she said, 'a little awkward.' I said, 'Okay. Let's see that awkwardness.' That's the way I direct. I don't tell actors to do something but ask them what they are feeling. If they feel a certain way or have an emotion of some sort, and I don't quite see that feeling or emotion, they go away and examine how they can bring it outward to the screen. Carol had the most interaction with Roddy. His character approached her more and was in her face more. I could tell Roddy and Carol enjoyed working with each other. They spent a lot of time together off the set.[783]

"Women have an ego that is sometimes difficult to breach, "continued Levi. "But Carol was very receptive when we had to make her look much older. She accepted it very well. We put a silver wig on her and lines on her face. She still looked great."[784]

Playing Lynley's husband was veteran actor Robert Webber. They had worked together previously in the feature *The Stripper* and the TV-movie

Death Stalk where they portrayed a married couple. However, this time Webber caused a bit of a stir on-set, per Carol.

> Bob Webber's a sweetie and a wonderful actor but a character. [There is a scene where] we've supposedly just made love. We're under the covers so you can see nothing. He's shirtless and has two pairs of shorts on, you know. I've got something on; we're covered and had the sheets on top of us. I said, 'Bob nobody's asking you to take your clothes off. We don't even have to kiss we have to look like we just had sex.' He calmed down, but he'd been storming around the set in his bathrobe. Both the director and I were just like, huh? I had to keep talking to him and talking to him. It took us about half a day to get him back into bed.[785]

When hearing this story, Levi quipped with a laugh, "At least she didn't have to lay in bed with Victor Buono!"[786] He then added, "Seeing how great Carol looked, Bob probably was afraid he was going to get excited. Usually if an actor or actress doesn't want to do something like that, I try to find a compromise position literally and figuratively to get it done."[787]

In this proposed series, set in purgatory, the deceased's life would be judged in a courtroom where Mr. Heavener (Victor Buono, looking mountainous dressed in all white) and Mr. Heller (Roddy McDowall, looking dapper in a black tuxedo) would battle for their soul. The Judge (Barry Sullivan) presided over the court with a jury of peers set to render a verdict. Despite the cutesy names and plot, this was played as a serious courtroom drama.

Carol Lynley was the dearly departed, a state governor named Harriet Egan who succumbed to Leukemia and whose soul hung in the balance. Looking much too matronly for a fifty-year-old in today's eyes, she sits in the middle of the courtroom between Heavener and Heller (who each have a ledger containing details of her life) and opposite the Judge. Above him was the jury, hidden behind a scrim where they were lit from behind so they looked like silhouettes. Heller is there to reveal all of Harriet's sins. He calls her a "whore" and a "slut" before exposing her past as an unwed, teenage mother, giving up her baby for $2,000 cash and working as a prostitute in a Reno bordello to save money for college in Los Angeles.

Though Carol looked stunning for her age, even she could not realistically pass for sixteen. Scenes of her arguing with her boyfriend (Maxwell Caulfield) over her pregnancy or being called a tramp by her drunken mother (Priscilla Pointer) before getting slapped across the face or with her hair in pig tails, beginning her time working in a whorehouse are a stretch even though Carol gives it her all. Alan J. Levi felt she pulled it off with gusto. He opined, "I thought Carol looked good enough (a Gidget-type look) to play all ages. It was never discussed to have a 'younger' cast member. Especially since we saw her age along the way and making a transition from one actress to another might have proven confusing. I thought she did a wonderful job as both the younger and older."[788] True, Carol quickly grows into the part as the character matures and grabs the viewers' attention.

The audience then learns from the lawyers that she became a high-class call girl to pay her way through law school. Heavener countered with the reasons why Harriet made some of these decisions and the good that came out of them. (i.e some of that hooker cash went to pay her sick mother's medical bills). After graduating top of her class, she was fired from her law firm secretarial job when they learned of her extracurricular activity. She then changed her name to Harriet Miller and moved to another state.

The viewers see her meet Charlie Egan (Robert Webber), a shady real estate developer who she helps cement a deal between him and the homeowners who rallied against his planned shopping center. Wanting to do more for the community, Harriet decides to become a politician. After a night of lovemaking where she reveals her past as a hooker and that she is not interested in Charlie's big bucks, Harriet pressures Egan to get her a meeting with Burton Randolph (John Larch), the most politically powerful man in the state. She refuses to be bought but agrees to offer him her savvy advice.

As Heller accuses Harriet of taking advantage of the voters, Heavener claims she is a "selfless public servant." Harriet's political success was due to "Burton Randolph calling the shots all the way" infers Heller. The rest of the episode goes back and forth with Heller accusing Harriet of being a crooked politician (selling out her principals to win elections and even marrying Charlie Egan for political gain) and Heavener showing how she bucked the manipulating men around her to remain honest and give the voters one of the most successful administrations in her state. The case is finally sent to the jury who vote nine thumbs up to three thumbs down. Shen then walks down a corridor with Mr. Heavener and into the heavenly ether.

Despite the cast and crew's commitment to the program, NBC did not pick up *Judgement Day* as a series but did air the pilot in the dog days of August 1981. Alan Levi was surprised it did not become a weekly series and explained, "It came off as a serious drama but Roddy and Victor brought some comedic verbal sparring to it. It wasn't the laugh out loud type of comedy but more light banter. Even when Roddy would explain about something Carol did in her past to prove she was a bad person, he did it with tongue-in-cheek and a lot of attitude. Ed Friendly seemed to be happy with it at the end. It was unbelievable to me though that NBC would be in collaboration and then not buy it. Most pilots back then were not done by the networks but by individual producers. Ed had big ties to NBC and I thought he would have been able to get it on the air but it didn't go. After recently watching it, I can understand why. It was fun but there was too much courtroom and not quite enough flashbacks. The courtroom became fairly repetitive even though I love Roddy McDowall, who was terrific. Having more flashbacks would have made it a more interesting story."[789]

Levi is correct in his assessment of the pilot. It was a bit too talky with Heavener and Heller recounting much of Harriet's past before the audience got to see a flashback. If these scenes were just kept to their witty banter back and forth it would not have slowed down the action. McDowall is too entertaining as Heller and should have been a bit more sinister and hellish—

someone you do not want to spend eternity with. Sullivan is too sullen as the judge and the part needed an actor with more personality.

Another minor quibble with *Judgement Day* was it seems not enough attention was paid to detail regarding period hairstyles or costumes to indicate the change of decades from the forties through the seventies, which makes it a bit confusing. Budget limitations may have been a factor. Alan Levi commented, "If I remember correctly, the main 'jury' set cost a lot of our budget—but that's no excuse. I usually leave the makeup and hair expertise up to the folks who know more about that than I, so I have no explanation. Don't think it was money—I think it was due to a bit of sloppy research by those responsible. For me - I have no excuse. I may have goofed!"[790]

The pilot was a tour de force for Lynley, giving her one of her best TV roles. She goes from a knocked-up, desperate, bobbysoxer who sells her baby, to a call girl, to an aspiring lawyer, to a dedicated politician. She does it with such aplomb while looking fantastic throughout. Watching Carol emote with much conviction while sparring with Robert Webber or John Larch, you could see she would have been a good match to go up against Larry Hagman's JR Ewing on *Dallas* or any villain from the other primetime soaps of the period. It is a shame that she never got the opportunity because she had the glamour and talent to enhance any of them.

The only flaw with Lynley's performance, and it may not have been of her choosing, is that Harriet's fiery personality that the viewer sees in the flashbacks, is nowhere to be found in the courtroom. Harriet sits there, blank-faced for most of the trial, and only rarely reacts to Heller's outrageous accusations. Perhaps the show was trying to present the newly, dearly departed in a state of shock from her recent passing and her soul's predicament - leaving Mr. Heavener to defend her?

When asked if *Judgement Day* had been picked up as a series would he have continued directing episodes, Alan replied, "Would I have stayed with it? Probably so, [because] I enjoyed working with Victor Buono and of course Barry and Roddy."[791]

Soaps to Suspense

*****

During 1980 and 1981, Carol continued working for Aaron Spelling. She guest starred on *The Love Boat* (unbelievably cast as the best friend of Donna Pescow from TV's *Angie*, who is engaged to Ben Murphy), *Charlie's Angels* (looking fabulous as an assassin pretending to be a Hawaiian tourist on a singles trip who romances David Doyle's Bosley to keep her true identity hidden), and *Hart to Hart* (her fourth time working with Robert Wagner and playing a government witness on a cross country train trailed by assassins including Florence Henderson, from TV's *The Brady Bunch*, hired to stop her from testifying).

Regarding her feelings toward the super successful producer who was always there with an acting job for her, Carol exclaimed,

Promotional print ad for the episode "Hartland Express" on *Hart to Hart* with Carol Lynley, among the guest stars.

Aaron Spelling was great! I met him when he was married to Carolyn Jones. I used to go over to their house with my daughter when she was little. He was well-spoken and extremely well-read. As a producer, he knew what he was doing and handled a whole bunch of things on a set extremely well. He was the best.⁷⁹²

In between Spelling shows were guest stints on other series such as the short-lived police/detective comedy *Baker's Dozen* starring Ron Silver (her first appearance on a sitcom—a long time coming) and the Canadian-produced *The Littlest Hobo* starring London the German Shephard. This sent Carol back to the zoo as an investigative TV reporter covering a story on missing animals. It was filmed during the 1980 Actor's Strike, which lasted three months, postponing Carol's scheduled guest appearance on *Charlie's Angels*. To keep working she headed north and to her furry co-star. She remarked, "I love working with the animals—although you always have to stay a little behind a large cat. If they are going to attack, they'll always go for the person in front of them."⁷⁹³

Carol finally landed a glitzy primetime soap, but the proposed made-for-cable TV series *Balboa* turned out to be no *Dynasty* or *Dallas*. Her character is part of a romantic triangle with two disparately diverse types of men played by Tony Curtis and Steve Kanaly of *Dallas* fame. It was produced, directed, and written by James Polakof previously known for his low-budget exploitation movies such as *Swim Team, Sunburst, Love and the Midnight Auto Supply*, and *Satan's Mistress*. Here he was working with a $1.5 million budget, via production company Entertainment Artists.

It was shot entirely on location in Balboa and Newport Beach. When asked why he chose these locations to set the film, Polakof, who moved his production company to Newport Beach four years prior, responded, "It's a slice of life as we see it down here. The real thing we are after is the visualization of the lives of some of the people who live in the community. Newport is the quietest kept secret of the jet set. It's a racy place, it's not the old-fashioned fishing village it used to be."⁷⁹⁴ Polakof filmed parts of his show (originally titled *Lust for Love*) on the beaches of Newport Beach and Corona del Mar, the John Wayne Tennis Club, City Council chambers, and yachts and homes of private citizens. He wisely employed many residents as extras and frequented many local businesses for props and costumes.

It was reported that during pre-production, "outside interests"[795] felt that they had a chance to sell the production as a television series or mini-series and the title was changed to the more generic *Balboa*. Since it was peppered with semi-nudity and strong language, the idea was to pitch it to HBO or Showtime, who had just gotten into the original, scripted TV series game, and where censorship was not a factor.

Tony Curtis, who was living in Spain at the time, enjoyed making this movie immensely. He described his character, Ernie Stoddard, as being "a 600-pound gorilla. He sleeps where he wants to and dresses the way he wants to."[796] That day, Curtis' over-the-top costume consisted of a black velvet suit with matching hat and a walking stick. Seems all that was missing was the handlebar moustache he could villainously twirl. Curtis then gushed that although working in Newport Beach was wonderful, it was the camaraderie between the cast and crew that made the shoot even better for him. He added, "We appreciate the fact that we are working in a business that's decimated. The fact that we're working is a privilege for all of us."[797]

Despite Tony Curtis' pronouncements to the press, what went on behind-the-scenes was another story according to James Polakof. Commenting on working with Lynley and Curtis, he wrote, "It was a pleasure to direct Carol Lynley. At all times, she was a true professional and could be counted on for consistent performances."

Providing an example to prove his point, Polakof recounted, "One instance, I recall quite well, is when I was directing a scene with Carol and Tony Curtis. Unfortunately, during the film, Tony was often erratic due to his drug use. In this scene, we had just completed Tony's close-up, when he pivoted and ran upstairs in the house we rented for the production. We still had Carol's close-up to film and I promptly sent my A.D. to fetch Curtis. We patiently waited, but after about ten minutes the A.D. returned to relate that Tony refused to conclude the scene. Apparently, he quickly had resumed his drug use, conveying Miss Lynley is a professional and we should use a stand-in in his place for her close-up. I became infuriated, and so would most actresses. But in a calming voice, Carol said, 'Let it be. I can handle this without Tony.' Of course, I considered this behavior to be unacceptable and threatened to withhold Tony's pay if he did not complete his part. He needed the money and reluctantly returned. This is but one example of Carol's professionalism and dedication to doing what it takes to make a movie the best it could be."[798] Despite his unprofessional behavior, Carol reportedly liked working with Tony Curtis. It was burly Chuck Connors that she particularly did not care for.

Though Polakof thought he was bringing much needed attention to the Newport Beach area, there was a small but vocal contingent of residents who were up in arms. They felt his production was showing their community in a fictitious and negative light. After an article ran in the *Los Angeles Times* highlighting the making of the film, one Newport inhabitant named Stephen G. Freeman wrote into the newspaper and remarked, "I've lived here for 37 years. Several high-budget films by well-known directors were done here. They may have added nothing to our lore, but neither did they denigrate."[799] He jokingly ended his letter with "Shouldn't we do something to ward off such communal threats? Like maybe have the police helicopter spray the area occasionally with funky movie-maker/anti-jet setter solution?"[800]

In *Balboa,* Carol delivers a sincere performance as strong-willed and independent Erin Blakely, a widow with an eight-year-old daughter. Erin is romantically pursued by greedy, though charming, financier Ernie Stoddard (Curtis) who wants to bring gambling to exclusive Balboa Island and good guy architect Sam Cole (Kanaly) who is trying to stop him. He and others think Stoddard had a hand in the death of Erin's late husband. The cast also included Jennifer Chase as a gold digger with a conscience; Chuck Connors as a self-made tycoon and Stoddard's rival; Sonny Bono as a playboy tennis instructor (is there no other kind?); Henry Jones as a vengeful resident who lost his fishing fleet due to Stoddard; and Cassandra "Elvira" Peterson, Lupita

Ferrer, and Catherine Campbell as lovely, conniving lasses who all have a score to settle with Stoddard. With these barracudas circling him, it is no wonder Stoddard doggedly pursues Lynley's disinterested Erin since she seems to be the only worthy catch in the bunch.

Asked to describe the finished *Balboa*, James Polakof responded that "it's a cross between *Dallas* and *Dynasty*. Really, the idea behind this movie is these people in this community have everything money can buy. The only thing they can't buy is happiness."[801] Unfortunately, *Balboa* was rejected by the major cable channels of the time. Showtime opted for another soap *A New Day in Eden* from executive producer Michael Jaffe instead. It was another missed series opportunity for Lynley.

DVD cover art for *Balboa* featuring Carol Lynley, Steve Kanaly, Jennifer Chase, and Tony Curtis. *From Marlin Dobbs' Collection*

Polakof then decided to revert *Balboa* back into a theatrical feature. However, it was too lengthy and had to be edited down. Chunks of story were dropped to bring it down to ninety minutes and new footage had to be shot with Martine Beswicke as the on-screen narrator to bridge many omitted scenes. Jensen Farley Pictures was going to distribute it in 1983, but the company went bankrupt.

Balboa then sat on the shelf until it was unceremoniously released on VHS by Vestron Video in 1986. This truncated version was unsurprisingly not well-received. The reviewer in *Variety* called it a "poor man's ... *Dallas* and *Dynasty* ... suffering from extremely clichéd dialog. Feature is short on action, concentrating on lots of chatty talk ... Filmmaker James Polakof directs in perfunctory fashion, with an underwhelming cast." Particularly awful are Jennifer Chase and Lupita Ferrer as a married cougar on the prowl, but even they cannot spoil the gorgeous Newport Beach scenery. Despite its short comings, there is enough good here that makes you curious for the complete edit to see how it might have played as a prospective series.

Carol had another shot for a soap opera courtesy of Lorimar. She was on a list of actresses considered for the role of Susan Sullivan's devious gold-digging sister on the hit soap *Falcon Crest*. However, the producers decided to go younger (Carol had just turned forty years old) and Laura Johnson won the role of Terry Hartford in 1983.

It is interesting that it was Lorimar that offered work to Carol in primetime soaps rather than Aaron Spelling. She guest starred on many of his series except his soaps - never landing a role on his biggie *Dynasty*, or even the short-lived *Glitter* and *The Colby's*. On the latter, Carol arguably would have made a far more interesting Francesca Colby opposite Charlton Heston than the lifeless Katherine Ross.

*****

Leaving glitzy Newport Beach behind, it was back to gritty New York City for Carol and her biggest movie hit since *The Poseidon Adventure*. She was cast (after Caroline Munro reportedly dropped out) as ineffectual assistant district attorney Mary Fletcher in the violent, "R" rated revenge thriller *Vigilante* (1983) starring Robert Forster and Fred Williamson. It was co-produced and directed by William Lustig, who had just scored with the hit horror film *Maniac* (1980) starring Joe Spinell and Caroline Munro, and scripted by New York writer Richard Vetere. Lustig's producing partner at Magnum Motion Pictures was Andrew V. Garroni.

Tony Musante was the first choice for the lead role. However, he and his screenwriter wife Jane Sparkes had problems with the script and asked for a meeting with the producers to go over their suggested revisions. Per Lustig, Musante acted oddly, and he and Garroni both felt uncomfortable working with him. Frank Pesce, who was cast as a gang banger, suggested Robert Forster whom the director had just seen in *Alligator*. He was offered the role and accepted. Lustig remarked that Forster did an amazing job and was cooperative throughout. He and Lustig have remained friends ever since.[802]

A couple of weeks prior to principal photography, the producers were able to get Fred Williamson for one day's work to shoot a promo reel for a then very important film sales market (MIFED) in Milan, Italy to generate interest from foreign markets. These distribution pacts could be leveraged for goods and services that the production could not currently afford to pay. The intense promo reel, some of which was incorporated into the opening of the movie, with Williamson schooling his neighbors on crime in New York City and the ineffectual police force and courts, screened hourly at the convention. It resulted in lots of curiosity, but reportedly no pre-sales.[803]

Regarding her role, Carol shared, "This role was written for a man, but because there weren't enough women in the cast, the character's name was changed to Mary. I didn't know this, but SAG has rules that a certain number of minorities are to be cast in every film and women are still considered a minority."[804]

Carol worked for one full week on the movie. According to William Lustig, when they began shooting the courtroom scene, Joe Spinell who was cast as the defense attorney could not be found. The director who had worked with him previously was aware of his substance abuse issues but it had never interfered with work. Now it did and he was a no show. Lustig sent Andrew Garroni to find the actor while he shot scenes around him. In some, with Lynley facing the judge, a stand-in was used when only a portion of the defense attorney's body had to be on camera. With help from Spinell's friend Frank Pesce and the bartender from the pub Spinell was last seen the night prior, Garroni was able to track him down to the home of an actress he left the bar with. He was sound asleep and Garroni had to get him showered and dressed before taking him to the set. Spinell was very apologetic and the producer assured him that no one was mad at him. Well, not exactly no one. Per Lustig, Spinell's mother was one of the courtroom extras and she gave him a dressing down once he finally arrived.[805]

Once Spinell began shooting, he shared an idea he had for his and Lynley's characters with William Lustig. Per the director, "He came to me and he was dead serious. He wanted to add a back story with him and Carol Lynley. He said 'Bill, what if Carol Lynley and I were former lovers. And now we are at the opposite ends—I am a defense attorney and she's a DA. What if we have a flashback of us making love on this beach?' He wanted me to go and shoot this."[806] Lustig appreciated Spinell's attempt to beef up his role but ultimately rejected the idea.

Robert Forster is Eddie Marino, an average, blue-collar, factory worker who rejects his co-worker Nick's (Fred Williamson) offer to join their neighborhood vigilante group because he believes the police and the law should administer justice. He holds this belief even after his wife disrespects a bunch of rowdy gang bangers while pumping gas. They follow her home where they beat her to a pulp and kill their eight-year-old son. When the gang leader Rico (Willie Colon) is captured, a shell-shocked Eddie goes to meet with assistant district attorney Mary Fletcher (Carol Lynley) who Frank Pesce jokingly dubbed "the Marsha Clark of *Vigilante*"[807] in one of the Blu-ray's commentaries. She motions out her window, high above New York City, and rattles off crime statistics to Forster's Marino to convince him to press charges. Her fervor and promise to have the thug locked away for a long time persuades Eddie to sign the complaint. This scene is more powerful than it sounds with an effective Lynley playing Mary quite persuasively.

At the hearing, Rico's buddies have his attorney (Joe Spinell) pay off the crooked judge (Vincent Beck). As Mary's objections are overruled, defense attorney and judge (played too broadly by Beck to be believable) bargain down to probation as a frustrated and shocked Mary looks on helplessly. Seeing Rico walking out with his gang of thugs, Eddie loses it and goes to attack the judge. In an ironic twist, he is charged with contempt of court and sent to a short stint in prison. This is the last of Carol's scenes, which is a pity. The rest of the exciting movie has a revenge-minded Eddie hooking up with Nick's vigilante group to wipe out Rico and his crew, including his girlfriend and the judge, all in violent fashion.

Asst. DA Mary Fletcher (Carol Lynley) and Eddie Marino (Robert Forster) at the courtroom bail hearing for the gangbanger who allegedly murdered his son and assaulted his wife in *Vigilante* (Magnum Motion Pictures, 1983).

After post-production was completed, William Lustig took *Vigilante* to the Cannes Film Festival in May of 1982. It screened to a packed house and he easily found distributors for national and foreign markets. When released, not surprisingly, the film did not endear itself to the critics of the day. However, the reviewer from *Variety* was spot on with his assessment, "*Vigilante* is an extremely violent, hard-edged action picture in the familiar genre popularized by *Death Wish*. Literally a case of 'overkill,' film's plotting and violent effects are quite unpleasant, meaning while it stands to clean up in action houses, *Vigilante* will likely prove a turnoff for wider audiences."

As the *Variety* critic predicted, adventurous moviegoers flocked to the theaters and made this low-budget exploitation indie one of the top 50 box office hits of 1983. *Vigilante* would turn out to be Lynley's last theatrical feature to get a national distribution in the U.S. It is also notable because Carol got to work with director William Lustig, who like Radley Metzger, developed a cult following. Both were under-appreciated back then but today have been honored for their bodies of work with film festivals and such keeping the films Carol made with them alive with many historians and cult movie buffs.

*****

During this time Carol spent more of her time on the stage, especially as the decade progressed. For many actors doing regional theater was an effective way to earn a living and continue plying their craft. And, as Lynley once remarked, the stage afforded roles that she normally was not offered in film and on TV.

Carol appeared in revivals and original works throughout the U.S. and Canada. Among her stage credits were *Bus Stop* (playing the lead role of Cherie the talentless performer yearning to become a Hollywood star created by playwright William Inge) at the La Marida Civic Theatre in Los Angeles. It was a brave of Carol to take a chance on it since it was one of Marilyn Monroe's most iconic movie roles. However, the stage seemed to be providing her the diverse and challenging parts that actors crave. Regarding her decision to play Cherie, Carol said,

> It was an interesting part. I had known Bill Inge from New York because he was always around the theater district. I approached doing this as a play different than the film. I never met Marilyn Monroe. I wish I had because I have always been a huge fan of hers. She was such a fascinating actor.[808]

She also appeared in *The Rainmaker* as spinster Lizzie Curry opposite Joe Namath as con man Bill Starbuck at Granny's Playhouse in Dallas. The city was so excited to have Broadway Joe in town that reportedly country singer Charlie Pride threw a big welcome bash. Among the guests were Carol, Kris Kristofferson, Mickey Mantle, and almost the entire Dallas Cowboys football team.

Carol's other stage credits included the acclaimed Lesbian drama *Last Summer at Bluefish Cove*; *A Dash of Spirits* with William Lithgow; and *Steel Magnolias* as M'Lynn at Stage West in Edmonton, Canada. When asked how she approached acting on stage while doing *Magnolias*, Lynley responded, "I like to work positively, in a relaxed, enjoyable way ... But the end result is all that matters. Some actors approach everything as an obstacle to overcome. That's not my style."[809]

Among those stage appearances, Carol won the most kudos for her performance in *Romantic Comedy* by Bernard Slade in 1982. She portrayed playwright Phoebe Craddock opposite Rex Harrison's son Noel Harrison (*The Girl from U.N.C.L.E.*) as her first-time collaborator who happens to be newly engaged. Of course, romantic sparks ignite that they try to ignore over a nine-year period. On Broadway, the roles were originated by Mia Farrow and Anthony Perkins. Seeing the touring production at the Birmingham Theatre, *Philadelphia Daily News* critic Shirley Eder raved, "This new production is wonderfully directed by Tom Troupe and deliciously performed by Carol Lynley, Noel Harrison, Carol Bruce ... [it] comes to life as it never did on Broadway."

Carol was still a wanted commodity on television. During 1983 and 1984, producer Aaron Spelling provided work keeping her jumping from New York to LA. Her most memorable guest stint was the year prior on Spelling's soapy drama series *Hotel* (featuring some of the worst young actors of the decade as regulars playing various hotel employees), which was in the vein of his prior hit shows *Fantasy Island* and *The Love Boat*. In playwright Thom Thomas' first script for the TV show, "Hope, Faith, & Charity," Carol played Zan Elliot a Lesbian playwright who reunites with her college friend, recent divorcee Eileen Weston (Barbara Parkins), after not seeing each other in twelve years. Carol had no qualms playing a Lesbian but wished they would had given her a different love interest, though the professional she is, Carol plowed through it. She confessed,

> Aaron Spelling called to offer this part to me. I don't' know why he thought of me for it. After thinking about it, I decided I could do it no problem. However, I wasn't crazy about Barbara Parkins who I found to be a bit of a princess. I am not into that kind of behavior at all. As I said previously when I am uncomfortable around somebody I am not there. I am nice and professional, but I do not sit around and shoot the shit. I go off to do something else. I don't get involved. It worked quite well for me since they then pass it off to somebody else.
>
> What helped me a great deal to act opposite Barbara was her beautiful head of dark hair. Whenever I had to look longingly at her, I would shift my gaze to her pretty mane instead.[810]

Before the episode aired, an optimistic Thom Thomas remarked, "A lot of character motivation went with some cuts which were made when scenes ran too long, and a director was fired. But I'm hoping for the best. I understand about 80 percent of my script is still there."[811]

The reunion between college friends Zan and Eileen is a happy one until Zan comes out as a Lesbian to her friend and admits she has always been in love with her. This makes Eileen extremely uncomfortable and begins to question her own sexuality. Though she has seen Zan nude many times before, she freaks when her friend drops her towel after showering to get dressed. Eileen hops into bed with the first man that makes a pass at her just to prove that she is straight. Zan hooks up with the hotel's pretty young fitness trainer who leaves the room in the morning as Eileen returns. Zan confesses that she needed to be with somebody too. Eileen refuses to attend the opening of Zan's play because it is a disguised look at their relationship but at the last moment has a change of heart. Meeting up in the hotel's bar, the two toast, not to the past, but to their lives in the present.

Though Carol emotes well and makes a believable gay woman, she sports another misguided hairdo with curly bangs that makes her look like a French poodle (although she looks gorgeous in scenes with her hair up when exercising or wet after she emerges from the shower). That aside, this episode is important because the frank dialog about being gay is quite surprising and daring for the time. It confronts, head on, the issue of coming out later in life and the effects it has on loved ones without religious or moral judgements. The characters' reactions are quite believable and nothing here is sensationalized, though the story is truncated, having to share airtime with two other forgettable subplots. This episode is worth a look and *Hotel* would go on to feature two more episodes dealing with homosexuality.

*****

During the early eighties, horror movies were in vogue again thanks to the popularity of such films as *Halloween* and *Friday the 13th* that ushered in the teenage slasher movies. Usually it was the vulnerable virginal young heroine left alive at the end who must battle the maniac one-on-one after her friends have been slaughtered in gruesome ways. Back in the day, Carol would have been the perfect lady in peril for these types of movies but now in her forties she had aged out and was not even considered to play any of the mother roles that turned up in these movie franchises.

Carol was more akin to suspense than horror and the small screen came through for her. The actress once remarked during an interview, "I always get movies in England—in January or February…brrr, it's cold."[812] That continued into the first half of the eighties, but instead it was British television that offered two of her best genre parts from this time in her career. In *Tales of the Unexpected*, she is an aging, adulterous husband killer who gets her comeuppance due to her vanity and in *Hammer House of Mystery and Suspense*, she and her spouse are haunted by a series of unexplainable visions.

The anthology series *Tales of the Unexpected* was filmed in New York and in its seventh season before Carol Lynley guest starred. It had begun in 1979 as *Roald Dahl's Tales of the Unexpected*, but the acclaimed writer disassociated himself from the series after two years.

"The Gift of Beauty" was directed by Bert Salzman who worked on several episodes during this season. He was best known for his Academy Award winning short film *Angel and Big Joe* in 1975. He also wrote the teleplay based on a story by Joseph Dougherty. The part he created, played by Carol, was of an older married woman who falls for a younger man. Together they successfully plot the demise of her rich husband. Insecure with her relationship and her looks, she tries a variety of health and beauty treatments to look younger. It was a meaty role for Carol and she made the most of it

Carol co-starred in this episode with two ex-cast members from the acclaimed and popular TV soap opera *Ryan's Hope*. Randall Edwards played the scheming, ditzy but highly loveable Delia Coleridge from 1979 to 1982 and Mackenzie Allen was the handsome, good guy police detective Sgt. Jim Speed from 1981 to 1982. After departing the soap ("It was a mutual decision. They really had nothing more for me to do."[813]), Allen had a few small roles in film and television but this was his first lead.

Asked about co-starring with Carol Lynley, the actor remarked, "She was not unfriendly, but she was a bit reserved and aloof when she shouldn't be. I never discussed this with her, but I think she may have resented working with an unknown. I remember we had to do a bed scene after our lunch break one day. As we were lying there waiting for the crew to set up, she told me that she had the most wonderful roast beef sandwich with raw onions for lunch. I think she may have done this deliberately or at least didn't care. She had a production assistant assigned to her. I called over to the girl and said, 'Carol, would like to have some gum or mints. *Have you got any?*'"[814]

Despite this incident, Allen enjoyed the experience making this in New York City and added, "The shoot went relatively easily. We filmed this in a brownstone on Fifth or Madison Avenue in the Seventies. Bert Salzman was an extremely nice man and a wonderful director who was easy to work for. He was very encouraging to me and made me comfortable. He wasn't harsh or demanding but a regular down-to-Earth New York kind of guy. I remember writing him a letter thanking him for the opportunity."[815]

Carol Lynley, wearing an unflattering brunette wig draped with gray streaks, played one-time high fashion model Elizabeth Kendrake Farrow seen holding court at the wake for her wealthy chemist husband Claude who had just perished in an automobile accident. She discreetly hands a key to a handsome young mourner who later rendezvous with the widow at her posh townhouse. There it is revealed that he is her young lover named Ray (MacKenzie Allen) whom she plotted with to tamper with the breaks of her husband's car. The murderous lovers can now be together in Switzerland, where Elizabeth has transferred her entire inherited fortune. However, the older woman is insecure with her looks and their age difference. Prodded by Ray, she begins an intense exercise and beauty treatment program to keep the young stud interested.

After going on a shopping spree to purchase more youth-oriented clothes, she goes the last step and becomes a gorgeous blonde. Ray takes her to a photographer to get a new passport photo to match her fake age of twenty-nine that she puts on the application. Despite Ray's pleasure with the fresh look, Elizabeth is still insecure. While jogging together around the Central Park Reservoir, she lags gasping behind and watches him flirting with a pretty, young flight attendant. He denies it and says she was only a kid. Deflated, she tells Ray, "Exactly—and I'm not just a kid. I'm just someone who is breaking her back to look like a kid so her young stud lover won't leave her for somebody who is just a *kid*."

Desperate to hold onto her looks and remain young, Elizabeth contacts the rep of The Gift of Beauty Company, which coincidentally has mailed her a brochure. A dark-haired saleswoman named Rebecca (Randall Edwards) arrives with anti-aging creams and lotions guaranteed to deliver eternal youthfulness. After Elizabeth takes a bath with herbal salts, Rebecca applies some lotions that smell like ether to a relaxed Elizabeth's face. Rebecca then begins to question Elizabeth about her husband. When the widow admits she knew nothing of his work, Rebecca reveals that she was his assistant and mistress. She discovered what Elizabeth and Ray did and was exacting her revenge. The lethal lead concoction on Elizabeth's face is poisonous and is slowly entering her blood stream through her open pores. Already, a horrified Elizabeth is partially paralyzed and cannot move her toes. Applying more of the poison to Elizabeth's face, the terrified woman asks, "What are you doing to me?" Rebecca menacingly replies, "I promised you eternal beauty and *I plan to deliver*."

As Rebecca puts on a blonde wig, Ray comments that she is now the spitting image of Elizabeth. They can now go to Switzerland to claim the money she hid in a Swiss bank account. The prone Elizabeth is still alive laid out in a long silver gown and cries out to Ray. He apologizes to her, but since Rebecca found out the truth, he had to help her or she would have turned him in to the police. Elizabeth suffocates from her gift of beauty, as the two murderous schemers go off to claim her money.

"The Gift of Beauty" is engrossing and nicely filmed on location throughout New York City. It reaches the expected conclusion, but with a bit of a surprise twist. The viewer is expected to believe that Ray would be the one to kill Elizabeth as that is the undertone of the entire episode. The fact that he really did love her but chooses his freedom over her is not surprising since he did help her kill her husband. The last scene of Rebecca, now the spitting image of Elizabeth, and Ray discussing their plans in Europe while a terrified Elizabeth, still barely alive, listening is quite macabre.

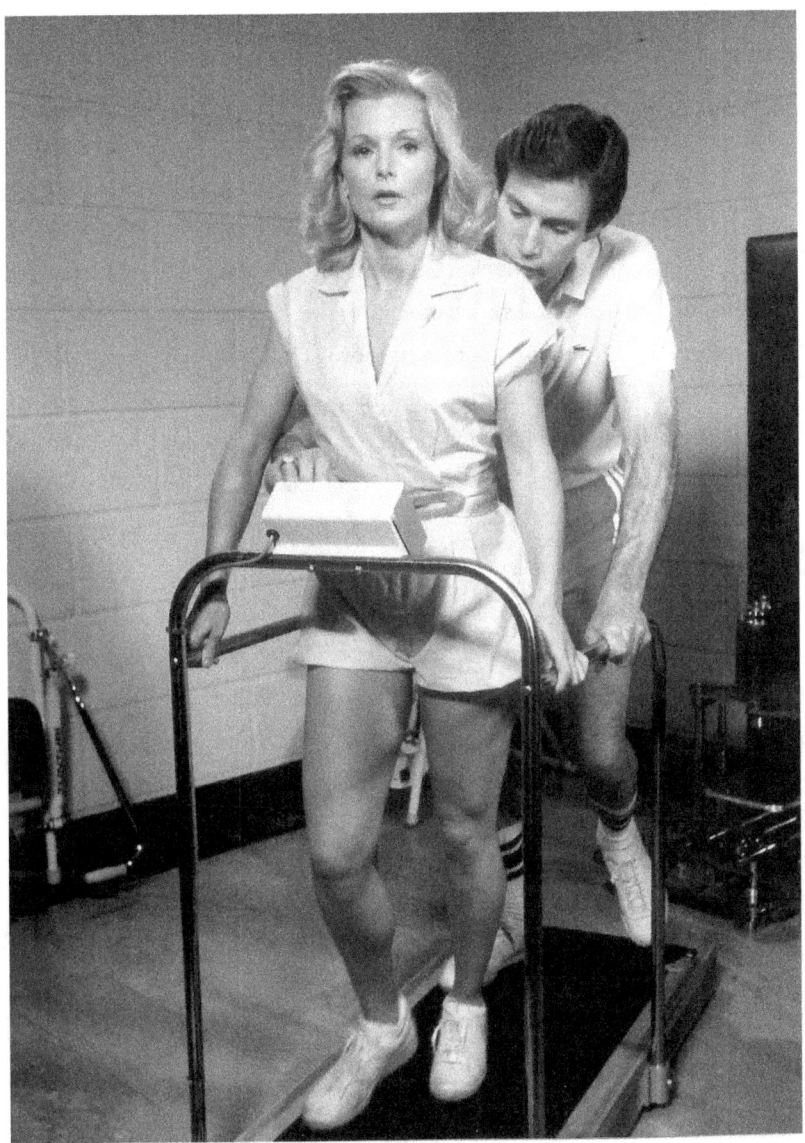

Vain husband killer Elizabeth (Carol Lynley) tries to stay in shape for her young lover Ray (MacKenzie Allen) in "The Gift of Beauty" on *Tales of the Unexpected* (ITV, 1984).

Carol is excellent in this part and has nice chemistry with MacKenzie Allen, who is quite convincing as a callous cad prodding his older paramour to regain her beauty. Lynley has one standout moment when she confronts her boy toy on the jogging path in Central Park. She really conveys the frustration of the older woman pushing herself physically to the brink to stay youthful, but whose body is just exhausted. Despite her efforts, the age difference between them will always be there as she is reminded when catching him eyeing a younger woman. Even though Elizabeth is a vain, adulterous murderer and you want to hate her, Carol still makes the viewer feel some empathy towards this insecure, aging woman desperate for love.

What is ironic about this episode is that Carol and Randall Edwards are natural blondes who were playing brunettes. When they each are supposed to have donned the same blonde wig, it was their own golden locks that are seen. There is an uncanny resemblance between the two actresses, who could easily have passed as sisters.

Lynley was forty-two years old when she essayed this role and was a trooper in taking the part. Her career had slowed by 1984, as it did for many of her contemporaries such as Sue Lyon, Diane Baker, Anjanette Comer, Yvette Mimieux, Susan Strasberg, Alexandra Hay, and others. Hollywood was, and is, quite cruel to actresses of a certain age despite their talent and looks. Keeping their age secret or trying to look younger at all costs became the norm for many. Carol though always stated that she believed in the natural aging process. For her to play such a vain beauty desperate to look decades younger must have been an ironic thrill for her.

*****

Carol had to journey to London to do her next British TV production that was jointly produced by 20th Century-Fox and Hammer Productions - and it was well worth the trip. She was cast as Sylvia Daly, the upscale American wife of businessman Frank Daly (Christopher Cazenove), in the debut episode "In Possession" on *Hammer House of Mystery & Suspense,* its

U.K. title. In the U.S., the series was syndicated as *Fox Mystery Theater*. This was to be Lynley's last lady in peril role in the thriller/fantasy/suspense genres. Carol admitted when she first got the script, "I didn't understand it. They had to explain it to me. I didn't get it at first. It was about a couple experiencing paranormal visions and hallucinations."[816]

Directed by the esteemed Val Guest (*The Day the Earth Caught Fire, Casino Royale, When Dinosaurs Ruled the Earth*), it is no surprise it is one of the series' most well-received. Carol revealed,

> Val always sat in this big 1930's type chair on the set. It looked to me as he had this chair since he started directing back in the forties. It was leather and had pockets to put things. He was quite tall, so I think it was customed-built for him since he obviously spent a lot of his time in it and he loved it. The rest of us had these portable chairs that you can drag around.[817]

Regarding her leading man, Carol said with a sigh,

> I was besotted by Christopher Cazenove. I liked working with him because he was an excellent actor but I also was crazy about him. We shot this on location in an old house, so Chris and I shared the same dressing room. When one of us had to change into our costume, the other would leave. When I wasn't in front of the camera, I was sitting in the dressing room talking with Chris who was just wonderful. I would get up in the morning, go to the location, go into our dressing room to change, and then go onto the set which was a bed many times, and I would lay down next to Chris for the rest of the day. I did that almost every day for three weeks. I was in heaven! I was *so* in love with him—*he was not in love with me*—but it was wonderful. He was madly

in love with Greta Scacchi. He felt for her like I did for him. He knew of my feelings and was nice about it. Our relationship

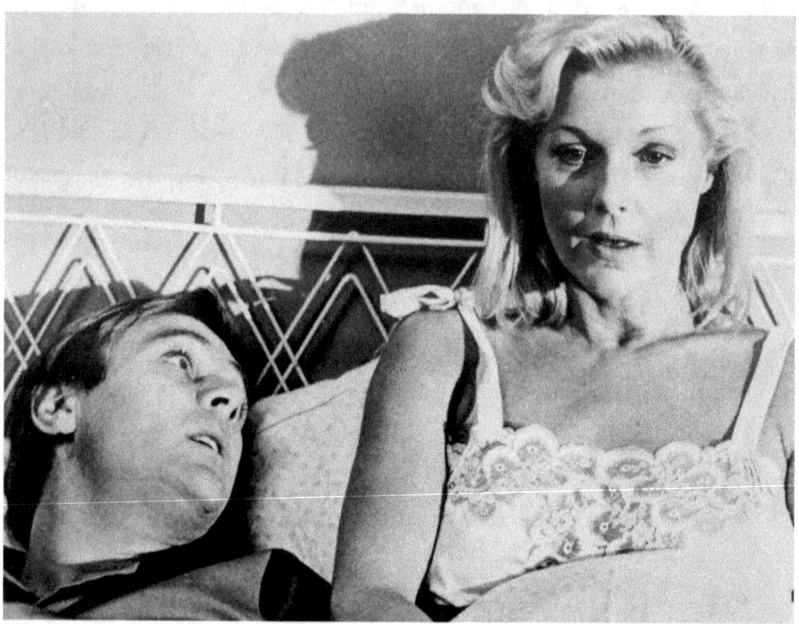

Frank Daly (Christopher Cazenove) and his wife Sylvia (Carol Lynley) try to rationalize the visions they experienced in *In Possession* (20th Century Fox Television/Hammer Films, 1985). *From Marlin Dobbs' Collection*

This episode begins with vacationing Sam and Sylvia Daly (Christopher Cazenove and Carol Lynley) returning to their hotel room after a night of drinking, only to find a young woman caring for her elderly mother. Confused, they contact the front desk. When the manager accompanies them back into the room, the women are gone. The couple thinks they may have inadvertently gone into the wrong room until Sam notices the old woman's cane leaning against the window. Jumping ahead two years, Sylvia meets her husband for lunch at a local Italian restaurant where he informs his wife that he is being transferred to Africa, but omits telling her that on his way to meet her that he saw the same two women in the park. Sylvia is excited about relocating though she amusingly mixes up Africa with the Middle East.

As their possessions are loaded onto a truck for storage, one of the movers ask what the couple wants to do with a white birdcage that he found in one of the closets. Neither has ever seen it before and dismiss it as a practical joke played by one of Sam's friends. Later, as the couple's neighbors Jack Mervyn (David Healy) and his wife Betty (Judy Loe) come down to the Daly's empty apartment for a champagne farewell toast, Sam sees the birdcage and a whole furnished room in the reflection from the mirror over the fireplace. Soon after, visions begin haunting Sylvia as she sees the same woman (Jessica Prentice) from the earlier incident drowned in the bathtub and later stuffed into a trunk in a closet. Both she and Sam then see the woman's husband Mr. Prentice (Bernard Kay) creepily berating her and then turning on them thinking they are his wife's sister and her husband. After fleeing the flat, they run up to Jack and Betty's only to find a woman living there who recognizes them as relatives of the Prentice's. Baffled and scared, they run outside and flag down a patrol officer who searches the apartment and finds nothing out of the ordinary. Sam is then accidentally locked out of their home while a hysterical Sylvia is menaced by the increasingly agitated husband who thinks she is his wife Jessica and she hides in the closet where Sam finds her after breaking in. The couple is on the verge of a hysteria not knowing what is happening to them as they seem to be trapped in "a time warp."

The nightmare continues as they discover Prentice forced his wife to sign over her power of attorney to him and then drowned her in the bathtub before stuffing the body in a trunk and dumping it at the bottom of a nearby canal. The more the Daly's try to run from their visions the more they can't escape. Finally, morning arrives and the couple agrees that they experienced the same nightmare and nothing was real, though Sylvia finds the broken glass she dropped that night on the bathroom floor and Sam later runs into the police officer on the street. While breakfasting with their neighbors, a still skeptical Sylvia asks about the prior residents of her apartment thinking that she and Sam may have relived an earlier murder. When that theory does not pan out, Sam and Sylvia stick to their "it was all a dream" pact. As they are about to depart for Africa, they run into the real estate agent who has arrived with the flat's new tenants—Mr. and Mrs. Prentice.

A truly chilling ghost story, "In Possession" is considered one of the *Hammer House of Mystery & Suspense's* best episodes. Writing in *The Women in Hammer Horror: A Biographical Dictionary and Filmography*, author Robert Michael 'Bobb' Cotter, raved, "It is one of the scariest installments in the series."

In Possession was released as a standalone movie on VHS and played on cable TV. Credit goes to Val Guest who creates an atmosphere of creepiness. The original script by Michael J. Bird keeps the audience intrigued, trying to guess what is happening to the Daly's. The obvious denouement is that they are seeing visions of a murder from the flat's past but the ending where they realize they were seeing into the future is shocking and clever. Carol opined, "At the end, we are supposed to go off to Botswana in Africa, which I found odd. I wasn't sure if this was going to work."[818] But work it did. Carol's effective performance of bewilderment and near hysteria coupled with Christopher Cazenove's character trying to remain macho calm, but underneath just as baffled and scared as his wife, helps the proceedings making it one hell of a ride. Unfortunately, it just did not get Carol much notice back in the U.S.

Returning to Hollywood, Lynley guest starred on Aaron Spelling's newest series *Finder of Lost Loves*. Anthony Franciosa starred as Cary Maxwell, a private eye who helps reunite people with someone they long to see again from their past. In "Forgotten Melodies," Bo Hopkins is a man with amnesia who asks Maxwell to find out who he is. Carol played his wife living in Arizona who has not seen him in four years. After they are reunited, Maxwell is contacted by a new client looking for her husband and it is the same man the private eye just left in Arizona.

At the time, it is most probable that Carol did not expect this to be her last network primetime TV appearance, but it unfairly was. It was as if someone just turned off a switch. Primetime work for her just disappeared in a flash. It was simultaneously surprising and ludicrous. It just shows how cruel

Hollywood could be to aging actresses. Aided by a good script and skilled director, Carol could deliver a first-rate performance as she just proved most recently with *In Possession*. Though she was now in her mid-forties, she still looked fabulous and did not deserve to be cast aside.

Carol was quite aware of this. Appearing on the local Los Angeles TV chat show *Joan Quinn Etc.* a few years later, she rightfully bemoaned her lack of small screen work and exclaimed, "I never even have done a *Murder, She Wrote*! I'm the only actor in Los Angeles who hasn't and I am beginning to take this very personally. They have been through the *Player's Directory* fifteen times using every actor. I told my agent that I am going to haunt them in the middle of the night. I'm beginning to feel a little left out." Joan Quinn assured Carol that they would get to her and that the show's frequent director, Walter Grauman, even watched her program. They never did. It remains mind-boggling why the TV roles came to a screeching halt after working so steadily in the medium for almost thirty years.

Prior to going to London to work with Christopher Cazenove, Carol appeared in the first stage reading of a new one-woman play called *Lombard* by Michael B. Druxman. Carol was excited to play the legendary Carole Lombard, especially since she was named after her. She filled a 99-seat theater on Melrose Avenue, but it was her only performance because it took several years before the show was fully produced.

17. High Rise Horror

Like some of her sixties contemporaries who didn't become superstars or land a hit TV series and who were still in the business, Carol Lynley was able to obtain roles in independent feature productions that received a limited theatrical release or went straight to video. Aisles of video stores contained exploitative, low-budget titles in the action/adventure/horror/thriller genres starring a familiar name or two and usually displayed on the bottom shelves below the more popular titles. However, Carol did not become a Stella Stevens or a Karen Black who did not have the will to turn down any Grade-Z drivel no matter how sub-par the script. For example, Stevens' films from this period included *Monster in the Closet*; *Little Devils: Plan 10 from Outer Space; The Birth*; *Dinosaur Valley Girls*; and *The Granny*, among others. She stated her strategy and explained in 1994, "Taking whatever I can get and making the most of it is all I can do in order to stay alive in this business. You keep trying to be in good movies, but some of them are just so horrendous. It's very frustrating to be so much better than the pitiful, shitty little things you're offered all the time and not be able to get the best agent with the most clout, 'cause they don't care, you know."[819] Though Carol probably also wished to be steadily working in good movies, she seemed to be more selective. She did appear in two direct-to-video horror movies in the early nineties but did not appear in any thereafter. Perhaps she had forsaken the video work for stage roles because she did not want to tarnish an already commendable movie career?

Carol next landed a feature film titled *Dark Tower*. Unfortunately, what seemed promising on paper did not always translate into a first-class production and wound up going the direct-to-video route in the U.S. The movie's back story is probably more interesting than the film itself.

Dark Tower was produced by the prolific Sandy Howard. Arguably, his most respected film was *A Man Called Horse*. During the rest of the seventies he produced some popular adventure and horror movies such as *The Neptune Factor, The Devil's Rain, Skyriders, The Island of Dr. Moreau*, and *Meteor*. In the eighties he had a few surprise low-budget hits such as *Angel, Vice Squad*, and *Hollywood Vice Squad*. *Dark Tower* would be one of his last movies and seeing what the production went through it is no wonder. Howard was in the vein of notorious producer Harry Alan Towers. Michael Masciarelli who received an associate producer credit on the movie described Howard, whom he worked with many times, as having "a unique personality. He was quite the character in Hollywood and looked the part of a big time Hollywood producer. There was a joke that he owed money to nine out of ten people in town. He loved the process of making films and traveling the world making them."[820]

With a respectable $5.2 million budget, *Dark Tower* was a rip-off of the popular series of *Poltergeist* films. A mysterious spirit or ghost is haunting a half-constructed office tower in Barcelona, Spain. It attacks the people surrounding the building's resident architect, Carolyn Page. Security consultant Dennis Randall, who has some psychic abilities, is brought in to investigate. The movie went into pre-production in December 1986 with plans to shoot on location. Howard had a three-picture distribution deal with the New York-based company Spectrafilm, which varied by movie. Per VP of Distribution Nick Perrott, Spectrafilm had world releasing rights for *Dark Tower*.[821] Then in January of 1987, Howard sued three production companies (based in Texas, Spain, and Australia, respectively) that breached their agreement to put up financing. He was seeking $250,000 in damages and $1 million in punitive damages.[822] Whatever the outcome, financing materialized.

It was originally announced that Roger Daltrey (lead singer of The Who) was signed to play the security chief and Lucy Gutteridge (*Little Gloria... Happy at Last, Top Secret!*) would star as Carolyn. The supporting cast included genre vets Carol Lynley, Kevin McCarthy (*Invasion of the Body Snatchers, Piranha*), Anne Lockhart (*Battlestar Galactica, Serpent Warriors*), and Oscar nominee Theodore Bikel (*The Defiant Ones*).

Tapped to direct was Ken Wiederhorn who co-wrote the screenplay with Ken Blackwell and Robert J. Avrech from the latter's story. Wiederhorn was the first to win the Student Academy Award for his short film *Manhattan Melody*, an honor he shared with Columbia University classmate Reuben Trane. Wiederhorn's professional career was not as prestigious and among the films he directed were *Meatballs Part II* and *Return of the Living Dead II*.

Wiederhorn had not work long on the movie before he was replaced by Academy Award-winning cinematographer and master horror film director Freddie Francis. He began directing during the early sixties forming a long association with Hammer Films and later Amicus Productions. His previous movies of the macabre included *The Evil of Frankenstein* (1963), *Nightmare* (1964), *Torture Garden* (1968), *Dracula Has Risen from the Grave* (1968), *Tales from the Crypt* (1972), and *Son of Dracula* (1974). Wiederhorn remained on the movie as co-executive producer with Tom Fox.

Explaining in his memoir how he became involved with *Dark Tower*, Freddie Francis shared, "Sandy Howard ... wanted me to direct a film for him for years. He called me up to say that his director had had family problems and couldn't continue, and would I do it? Looking back at it I wonder if that director had personal problems, or was it a problem with the film? Anyway, filming had already begun in Spain, and I told Sandy to send me the script. To my surprise it wasn't at all bad, and, although I was aware of its shortcomings, I thought, 'Well, it's Spain and I can do with a bit of sun. Besides, the story might just work. "[823]

The film's two leads were also a factor in Francis saying yes since he thought they would be good in their roles. However, things quickly took a downturn once he arrived on location. The "tower" selected to shoot interiors was only six stories high and Howard rented out the fifth floor, even though the script has the story set on the thirteenth floor. When Francis brought this to Howard's attention, the response was basically just deal with it and that the director "could keep the camera away from the windows or shoot around it keeping the camera low."[824] Speaking of which, Francis then learned that Howard had not yet hired a cinematographer. He suspected that the producers wanted him to double as both to save money but Francis was not having that. He recruited camera operator Gordon Hayman who he had worked with several times prior. This would be his lone Director of Photography credit.

With everything now in place, the shooting schedule had one week for preparation and then six weeks to shoot in and around the "tower" with time off for the Christmas holidays. Problems continued, per Francis, who remarked, "Roger Daltrey was simply not up to the task. Not to put too fine a point on it, he was not the greatest actor. Lucy Gutteridge was much better but she wasn't working well either, perhaps because of Roger."[825] To make matters worse, prior to filming Gutteridge sent her measurements to the film's costume designer but they were almost all incorrect. Her outfits were too small and all had to be let out. This led to a disastrous first week of shooting before the Christmas break.

While at home in England, Francis called Howard and told him both leads needed to be sacked and the producer readily agreed. Per Francis, "They were replaced on my approval by Michael Moriarty and Jenny Agutter, both of whom are actors of the highest quality. All the footage that had been shot with Daltrey and Gutteridge was scrapped, and shooting commenced once again."[826]

It was about this time that Carol came aboard. Explaining why she accepted the offer to play the secretary, she revealed,

> I said yes to do this small part because they were shooting in Spain. I had a fiancé at the time and things weren't working out.

This allowed me to get away from him for at least a week and a half and to figure out how to break away from him when I got back. I flew to Barcelona. When I did my first scene, I was jet-lagged out of my mind. It was with Jenny Agutter whom I adored—such a wonderful actress. She was just so easy to get along with. We filmed my scenes, which weren't many, and Freddie called cut. Everybody looked at me because there wasn't much for me to do. They were in shock when I was released so soon. I came back later to shoot one more scene with Theodore Bikel.

Asked what she thought of her director, Carol replied, "Freddie Francis was a bit like Val Guest—very polite and sweet. They had that old school quality about them—just so courtly and lovely to work with."[827]

Although filming with the new leads was going smoothly, another issue arose. Francis knew the special effects were going to make or break the movie, but he described the six members of the effects team as "useless. Certainly, none of the mechanical effects (explosions) ever worked."[828] He and Howard agreed that a new effects team would be hired once back in LA for post-production and that Francis would fly over to supervise them and the final edit.

Francis was not the only one having a challenging time with the movie. In a 2017 interview, Jenny Agutter chose *Dark Tower* as her worst film. She remarked that it "was beset with problems. It was a gothic horror set in a modern tower block in Spain, which got pulled down while we were filming. The continuity person would have long Spanish lunches with wine and continuity went out of the window for the afternoon."[829]

Actor Doug Jones, however, has much affection for the movie due to Ms. Agutter. He was hired to play her dead husband early in his career and could not believe he was working with one of the stars of *An American Werewolf in London*. He commented, "I was so star struck by her … I was still a newbie in Hollywood and here I was chasing her around in hallways, manhandling her – It was grand!"[830]

Filming came to an end and Freddie Francis returned to England where he waited for Howard's call to come to LA. He waited and waited but the phone never rang. He revealed, "Eventually I heard that Sandy had completed the effects and edit without me, and I was devastated. I had been foolishly hoping to give the film some energy by making sure both these final stages were executed properly. Sometime later I saw the completed product and I was so shocked and appalled, especially by the effects (I remember that one explosion had been cut in backward) that I insisted that my name be taken off the picture, which is why the director's name appears as Ken Barnett, a name that Sandy chose."[831]

VHS cover art for *Dark Tower* (1987).

Though third-billed, *Dark Tower* gives Carol Lynley little to do. As Tilly Ambrose, the overprotective secretary to the career-driven and talented architect Carolyn Page (Agutter), she spends the movie retrieving files or holding calls for her on-edge boss. Nervous Carolyn should be, as she is witness to a window washer seemingly pushed to his death by some invisible force and a possessed security agent who goes on a shooting spree in the lobby. As he is about to kill Carolyn, cornered in the elevator, he is shot dead. Security investigator Dennis Randall (Michael Moriarty) is brought in and immediately begins to experience psychic visions, including a man with no eyes who turns out to be Carolyn's dead husband. Lynley does have one nice scene with Theodore Bikel as a parapsychologist, hired by Randall, who questions Tilly about Carolyn and the mysterious goings-on at the office tower. Nervously sipping a glass of wine, a jittery Tilly makes an excuse to leave. After that, Lynley's Tilly appears only briefly and does not even get a good death scene. Her character is nowhere to be found during the climactic battle with the tower's vengeful spirit, who turns out to be Carolyn's deceased husband. Seems the overly ambitious architect killed her loathsome hubby by burying him alive in one of the building's main supports. In the comic-bookish ending, he materializes as a demon to avenge his murder and succeeds, dragging his wife back to his resting spot where she joins him for eternity.

Dark Tower was released theatrically abroad in 1987. Creative poster art had a group of people looking at the tower where, towards the top, it morphs into a coffin. The tagline read, "It reaches Heaven…and touches Hell!" Spectrafilm though passed on distributing it in the U.S. Perhaps if Francis would have stuck it out with Roger Daltrey, his name may have given the movie a little boost at the box office. Michael Moriarty did not have the clout to draw an audience, so it is no surprise *Dark Tower* sat on the shelf for two years before going directly to VHS. It unceremoniously slipped into video stores in 1989 with new box cover art and a witty tagline that read, "In a city that never sleeps, this building is a nightmare."

Dark Tower was ignored by most publications, but the always reliable

Variety provided a review. Their critic called it "perfunctory" and "plays like a bloated segment (usually 1-reel long) from one of Francis' horror anthologies." As for the special effects-laden finale, *Variety* found them to be "decidedly chintzy." Other problems plaguing the movie are underdeveloped supporting characters not giving the actors much to do performance-wise; badly dubbed Spanish actors; and, other than during the opening credits, not taking full advantage of the beauty of Barcelona. On the positive side, the music by Stacy Widelitz is eerie and heightens the suspense, and the over-the-top ending is so bad it is fun—cheesy special effects and all.

Freddie Francis shared his final thoughts about *Dark Tower* and said, "I am by no means proud of the fact that I directed it, but in fairness it honestly might at least have been a reasonable picture if the obvious problems had been avoided and two of the most important elements, the effects and the edit, had been carried out to a better standard. *Dark Tower* was the ignominious end to my feature directing career, and though I was offered other projects (mostly horror subjects), I had long last learned not to be seduced by the opportunity of directing again."[832]

18. Some Memories Are Better Left Buried

Carol Lynley left the lady in peril far behind with her next film, the suspenseful *Blackout* (1988). It was produced and directed by Doug Adams (his first and only movie) and scripted by Joseph Stefano most remembered for his screenplay *Psycho* adapted from Robert Bloch's novel. In the film's opening credits his screenplay is based on an original screenplay by Doug Adams, Laura Ferguson, and Cynthia Williams. Stefano was brought in to rewrite and punch up the suspense. According to Adams, the story was "inspired … by his own experience when his father disappeared for a year when he was a teenager."[833]

Blackout is a sort of warped *Bunny Lake Is Missing* meets *The Shuttered Room*. A young woman named Caroline Boyle returns to her childhood farm in a small California town after four years away looking for her missing father who deserted the family when she was four years old—or did he? She received a cryptic letter from him and is convinced that he is alive. While her Uncle Alan greets her with open arms, her unwelcoming mother Esther keeps trying to run her off. Has daddy returned home? Why does her cold-hearted mother keep trying to get rid of her? What is her uncle not telling her? Did her father have a secret love affair with her friend's mother? And who or what is in the attic?

Back in the day, Lynley would have played the befuddled heroine, but now at age forty-five she is the hard-as-nails, shotgun toting mother from hell who wants nothing to do with her offspring (Gail O'Grady later of *NYPLD Blue* fame) who has trespassed on her twisted domestic life with her brother (Michael Keys Hall). It was a challenging role for Carol to sink her teeth into and totally against type to play such a tough broad. Esther Boyle was eons away from the hapless Nonnie Parry.

Arledge Armenaki was hired to be the cinematographer. His prior films included such low-budget fare as the cult film *Disco Godfather*, *Grad Night*, and *Off the Mark*. Explaining how he got involved with *Blackout*, he said, "Doug Adams went to the American Film Institute and I also went there but he was a few years behind me. He had seen some of the work that I had shot while he was putting together the script with Joe Stefano. He contacted me to see if I would be interested in working on the film so he sent me a copy of the script. I took a meeting with Doug and Joe whose deal made him one of the producers. We met and it all went well. Things proceeded and we were trying to raise money for the film because Doug was just out of AFI. He was also from the [San Francisco] Bay area and had a lot of contacts with people who might be able to assist him. We shot a showcase short that took us about four or five days to a week. It highlighted the essence of the film with different actors and was basically what the film was supposed to be. I loved this short and thought it was a very good piece. Doug used it with his business prospectus and showed it to prospective investors. He was able to put together an investment portfolio. I was hoping that if he liked my work on the showcase he would invite me to come along and shoot the feature. I didn't have that many credits at that point in time either. The investors and Joe Stefano were okay that was I invited on board."[834]

As the hired cinematographer, Arledge Armenaki's first assignment was to scout locations throughout Southern California with Doug Adams. Exteriors for the main house in the orange grove were shot in Santa Paula. All the interiors of the house were shot in four different homes in Pasadena and Altadena. Armenaki said, "One of things I am most proud about this film is that we used all these houses that were about forty miles apart for different scenes. Orange groves outside one house, the attic in another, the kitchen in another and I think it looks seamless and nobody noticed."[835]

With a budget estimated to be under $2 million, *Blackout* began production in the spring of 1987 without an actress to play the mother. Armenaki explained, "There was another actress (whose name I cannot remember) that was cast for the part. I never met her, nor did she work on the film but I think at one point she came to a rehearsal. She had some cockamamie psychiatrist excuse letter basically to get released from the film because she needed rest to recuperate. In my opinion it was just a way for her to get out of her signed contract. We were under the gun and had to start production. This was the difficult part because we began filming for two and half weeks and were hoping that were going to get a new actress to play the mother. Our original schedule went out the window by day three. We were just scrambling and shuffling the schedule around every which way just to shoot because of the location and actor availability. During this time, I know the casting director was presenting actresses to Doug Adams every day. Different people's names came and went. Lynley talked with Doug and she agreed to do the film. Everybody was so happy that we now had an actress to play the mom and Carol was happy to be there. It was like your long-lost mother had returned home."[836]

Since Joe Stefano was also listed as producer, he was on the set frequently and was reportedly hands off. However, it was as screenwriter that he caused some disturbances per Armenaki who revealed, "He wrote the script and the actors were supposed to follow word for word. That was the only movie I have ever been on where the writer had that clause in the contract. Joe insisted that the director stick to the script as written. I got along great with him and so did Carol Lynley."[837]

Though his hands were tied by the screenplay, Doug Adams seemed to take it in stride and he too had a good relationship with Stefano. When asked to describe how Adams was as a director, Armenaki replied, "He worked well with the actors and they were comfortable with him. He walked them through the scenes and knew what he wanted. He did what any director at that stage in his career could do at a high level. Looking at it now in retrospect, could he have done something different? I think he may have been able to pull more out of the actors particularly Gail O'Grady whose character could have had more of an arc."[838]

In a coincidence, Carol's first scene filmed was her actual initial scene in the movie and they had a minor issue with it. Per Arledge, "Carol insisted about doing her own makeup and that was part of her contract. As the Director of Photography, her makeup was really overdone and very theatrical. Here she was playing a farmer living on an orange grove and she is wearing bright red lipstick, eye shadow, and all this other stuff. It was bizarre for the character. Doug told me not to say anything because he was just so thankful to have her. I said okay, and we shot all the scenes. After the second day he talked to Carol for quite a bit and told her that we don't need that much makeup. I wasn't a part of those conversations and they spoke off set. On the third day she arrived on set with much less and more appropriate makeup. She still did it herself but let the makeup artists assist her. About three quarters of the way through the schedule we went back to the location where we shot Carol's first scene to film her close-ups. Though she now had less makeup on you couldn't tell the difference between the shots done previously.

"Carol was easy to work with," added Armenaki. "She was friendly and personable. Gail was more difficult in that she was a little aloof. She kept going off set when her agent called, things like that. She would say, 'I just got a commercial.' We'd be like good for you honey we are all happy for you. Gail has been married six times and divorced six times—I think that says quite a bit."[839]

Regarding her feelings about working with Gail O'Grady, Carol commented,

> I liked her and she looked liked me. It was one of her first

movies and I noticed she was finding her way around. I thought she had a lot of talent. What happens though sometimes—I saw it here with Gail and have seen it before with some other actors—is that when you cast people who are new to acting and new to film acting, with no theater background whatsoever, and they have a big part in a movie they think they are *movie stars*. They know they're not. I think the reason they misbehave sometimes is they feel if they act like a star then they are a star, although they know they are not because they just started. I am very understanding of this. They start out humble but two days later they are ordering people around. It's not that they want to be mean, but they are frightened and they figure they are going to act like a star but that is not what stars do.

The best-behaved people are generally the most talented. The bigger they are almost 99% the nicer they are. When I worked with Laurence Olivier you couldn't find a nicer, kinder, more considerate actor around—the same with Noël Coward and Gene Hackman. When you run into someone who is a total shit, it usually means they are bad actors and they are afraid somebody is going to find out. It is a distraction.[840]

Another creative design problem arose on *Blackout*, during Joanna Miles' scene, due to the outfit she was given to wear. Arledge explained, "Joanna Miles wore a dress that absolutely matched the wallpaper. When she stood up for a medium shot, she literally blended right into the wall because the pattern on her dress and the wallpaper were almost identical. It was a Sunday and I remember saying, 'We can't shoot this. It just won't work.' Doug was begging me to make it work. I said we could shoot it but there is no magic in the camera that is going to change things. It's a rare event for something like that to happen. We then shot the porch scene where Caroline arrives and then Macy's opened. Someone ran over to get Joanna a new dress for the scene."[841]

Carol Lynley as Esther Boyle, a mother from hell, in *Blackout* (Ambient Light Enterprises, 1988). *From Marlin Dobbs' Collection*

Arguably, Carol's best moment in the movie is her confrontation with her daughter in the tool shed. She is all steely-eyed and unfeeling as she matter-of-factly relays a lie about her missing husband to Caroline. Armenaki was impressed with Carol and remarked, "It was probably Carol Lynley's biggest scene in the movie in terms of performance and having a big monologue she had to pull off. She was amazing just being there working with the crew and the director. We all worked hard on the art direction. I think it was particularly good here. We had these gruesome outlines of rough-looking tools hanging up and the earth moving piece of equipment there so she would have a place to rest on. I am proud of this scene because we really worked with Carol to help be expressive with her character while using interesting camera movement that also emphasized the dialog while giving Gail a big shot at the end where she is left empty trying to reflect the same thing with just the image of her."[842]

Never had Lynley appeared semi-nude on screen, but she does here—her bare breasts are glimpsed while making love to a mystery man. Despite her *Playboy* spread, the most she had revealed prior was a bare back or a side view of her uncovered bosom. According to Armenaki, Carol was a true professional. He said, "I don't think Carol Lynley had any problem with her nude scene at all. It was done matter of fact and she didn't have any issues. Obviously, when you shoot scenes like that you get the set lit with a stand-in. Then everybody who was not essential clears the set [before] Carol came on to shoot the scene."[843]

Regarding her decision to do this, Carol opined,

> Perhaps because of the time I was working and from where I am from, I never have had a lot of no-no's that other people have. Nudity seemed normal to me. I didn't have a suburban upbringing or anything like that. If you'd been a model where everybody is running around without their clothes on all the time or a dancer where people don't really wear a lot of clothes, you grow up not having shame for your body. It never occurred to me that anybody else would think otherwise. Of course, now I know they do.[844]

Carol did have a lovemaking scene with Michael Keys Hall where she was clothed and he was not. She did have her own requirement for this scene. Per Arledge, "She didn't want the little girl to see all the nudity. We filmed with hand-held cameras except for the reveal shot, which was with the Steadicam. Carol was fine with it. We painted the room all white and just had the wooden bed there. We worked hard to get a quick dissolve cut when the little girl is pulling back with the screwdriver. That was a separate shot and she actually never saw anything else that was going on in this scene."[845]

Blackout opens with a close-up of an idle car's front grill. That car and others in a parking lot are revealed as the camera pulls back and pans to a busy road. The camera then focuses on a white automobile driven by a young blonde woman. There is an open letter on the passenger seat and it is read by a man in a voice over, "My dearest daughter—what they told you about me isn't true. I didn't desert you by choice. Please believe me because I need your help now. Please come home—your dad."

The woman is Caroline Boyle and she has not been home since she left over four years prior. Entering her house with a suitcase in hand, she calls out to her mother and Uncle Alan but neither respond. She then goes upstairs thinking her father, Richard Seymour, may be there. Someone wearing a plaid shirt, blue jeans, and work boots then grabs a shotgun. It is Caroline's mother, Esther, who thinks there is a prowler in the house. When her daughter reveals her identify, Esther is not amused, especially since emotionless Caroline thinks daddy has come home.

Despite her mother's chilly reception, Caroline is determined to stick around and find her father though she neglects to tell mommy dearest about the letter. Driving into town she runs into her high school sweetheart pretty boy, tight jean-clad Luke Erikson (Joseph Gian). His writing aspirations on hold, he now works as a mechanic for Eleanor Carpenter (Joanna Miles), the mother of Caroline's former best friend Angela (Deena Freeman) who owns a service station. When Luke mentions that he heard from Eleanor that Caroline's father was dead, she decides to pay them a visit. After a happy reunion with Angela, Eleanor takes Caroline up to her room for a private chat. Eleanor informs the girl that her father hated everything about Esther except her beauty, which was his obsession. Deep down though, he loved

Eleanor who has many poems that he wrote to her to prove it. Holding a framed photo of Richard and Caroline as a child, she tells Caroline that her father loved her dearly and that he would never have left that house without a goodbye unless he did not leave it alive. She has always suspected foul play.

Back at the family ranch, Uncle Alan has prepared a homecoming meal for his niece. Caroline shows Alan the letter she received, and her Uncle is furious with her father for being so cryptic. He calls him a gambler and a cheat. When his niece suggests he may be in the house, Alan says she is free to search but she will not find him there. She then reveals what Eleanor told her, including the supposed love poems. When Caroline asks if her mother will give him a hard time if she stays the night, Alan replies that now that Esther has aged she has mellowed and that they live like an old married couple without the passion. While preparing for bed, Caroline hears noises in the attic and gets a feeling that she is being watched. When she goes to investigate, thinking it may be dear old daddy, a black cat jumps from the attic knocking her backwards down the stairs.

The next morning a fearful Caroline faces her angered mother after quarrelling with Alan who storms out of the house. Asking why her mother hates her so, Esther cruelly states that she wanted a child by the man she loved and not a man she despised like her father. The mean-spirited bitch then adds that she walked in on daddy dearest molesting Caroline when she was seven years old. She warns her daughter to stop her foolish search and inexplicably offers to recommend a good gynecologist in Oxnard. Caroline however refuses to believe what her mother is shoveling. Later, Alan confirms the sordid tale.

Caroline returns to the Carpenter home to speak again with Eleanor only to find the woman on the floor unconscious and her bedroom in shambles. With her mother in a coma, Angela coaxes Caroline to go for "a nice dinner" with Luke rather than mope around the hospital. At the restaurant, Caroline sees flashes of a bloody bed and while in the bathroom she thinks someone is watching her from the window, which keeps moving. When the screwdriver that was lodged in it falls to the ground, Caroline is relieved and puts it into her handbag. After dining and slow dancing, Caroline feels like she is "suffocating" and Luke drives her home, but makes a pit stop at the local, secluded make-out point overlooking a lake. Caroline admits she has never been and confesses that she has had only one relationship in Chicago that did not work out due to her being "shut down" from life. When she admits that she is still a virgin, horn dog Luke makes his move, only to have Caroline flashback to her stabbing someone as a child. She reaches for the screwdriver and begins stabbing Luke who fights her off. The nut job goes screaming into the night. When she comes to her senses, she goes back for the injured Luke and drives him home. The sheepish Caroline tends to his wounds and then sneaks back into the Carpenter home to look for that photo. However, she only finds the empty frame.

Arriving home in the early morning hours, Caroline sees a shadowy figure on the front porch. Spooked, she flees into the orange groves where she once again is knocked unconscious. Later that morning she awakens and finds that someone draped a blanket over her. She finds her mother primping in front of the bathroom mirror. After Caroline admits that the blood on her clothes is Luke's and that she had to stop him using a screwdriver, Esther exclaims, "Dear God, not again" and rushes out of the room. Caroline decides to leave for good but when packing her suitcase in her bedroom she notices dust coming down from a hole in the ceiling. She ventures up into the attic only to find a barren mattress, an armchair, a television set with a VCR hooked up to it, a few porno tapes, and that missing photograph of her as a child with her father. From the window, she sees over the orange groves to a wind tower on the property.

Caroline then confronts her mother in the farm's workshop regarding the bombshell she dropped about the screwdriver stabbing happening again. Esther admits that that not a day goes by when she sees bits of that terrible night flash before her eyes. She tells Caroline that she had already caught her father in bed with her once when Alan was home. They threatened to call the police if it ever happened again. Then six months later when Caroline had the flu and Alan was away on business, she found Richard buck naked on top of Caroline. She scuffled with him. Then suddenly Caroline began stabbing her father over and over with something in her hand. Esther tells her devastated daughter that she nearly had to break her wrist to get her to drop the screwdriver. To protect Caroline, she claims she dragged her husband's body out to the grove and buried him there. She told everyone, including Alan, that Richard had run off and deserted the family. They all believed her, including Caroline, who never once asked about him. As she exits the workshop, Esther advises her daughter to "go pack a bag Caroline and go back where you came from."

Esther gives Caroline a sleeping pill to rest after hearing such earth-shattering news. Luke stops by to see her, but Esther tells him to forget about her and sends him away, but adds that she will tell Caroline to say goodbye to him this time before skipping town. At the hospital, Eleanor awakens and tells her daughter that somebody tried to kill her. She thinks Esther hit her over the head and instructs Angela to tell Caroline to leave the Boyle ranch quickly. Angela phones Caroline instead and then there is a quick cut to a topless Esther, with her hair disheveled, sitting in the attic. She says to a mystery man, "That was good." Caroline sleeps through the ringing but Alan picks up the phone. He lets Angela know that Caroline was given a sedative and cannot be awakened. Proving she is perhaps one of the dumbest characters to ever grace a suspense movie, Angela tells Alan that her mother suspects that Caroline is in danger. At that moment Eleanor goes into cardiac arrest and Angela drops the phone.

Caroline is awakened from her sleep by muffled noises coming from the attic. Listening closely, it sounds like two people having sex. Running out of the house, while seeing flashes of the night she supposedly killed her father, she peers up at the attic to see her topless mother in the window being boned from behind doggie-style.

After losing her mother, a bereaved Angela goes wandering around town at night and finds herself in front the Boyle home. She enters and calls for Caroline, who ran out earlier. Hearing crying, Angela hesitantly makes her way up into the attic. Someone slams her head with a two-by-four. Trying to flee, she is grabbed by neck and shoved headfirst into the attic's window where she dies instantly.

The next morning, the camera pans from Angela's dead body, still in the window, to the ranch hands below who are turning off the grove's heaters. Still clad in her robe, Caroline enters the house to her mother and uncle having breakfast and lets them know she slept in the office next to the barn. As Caroline rushes to her room to pack, Alan quickly follows. Hearing the tale Esther told, Alan suggests to his niece that her mother may have been the one that killed Richard. He promises Caroline not to tell her and then wonders aloud that if her father is dead who wrote the letter—surely not Esther who did not want to see her daughter ever again. Caroline thinks her father is still alive and hiding from her. They then notice dust falling again from the ceiling. Alan goes to investigate and makes his niece stay behind in her room. She peers out the window to see that Esther has climbed up to the top of the wind tower to try to restart it. Regarding this last shot, Arledge revealed some movie magic and said, "When Caroline is looking out the window at her mother that water tower is in a whole different city. We built a faux set which was just a window on scaffolding and had her stand there. There was no point of view of the tower from the actual window."[846]

Caroline panics and runs to the attic stairs calling out for her uncle. When he does not reply, she tries to get her mother's attention but Esther ignores her. With trepidation, Caroline climbs the stairwell to the attic and finds her uncle passed out on the floor. As she goes to reach down and see if he is alive, the television pops on playing a porno film. Knowing someone is sitting in the chair, Caroline slowly makes her way over and is horrified to find the slashed Angela. She screams and trips. As she gets her bearings, she flashes back to what happened so many years ago. Her father (Scott Lincoln) returned early from a business trip to catch his wife and her brother having sex. Irate, as he goes to pull his naked brother-in-law off his wife, Alan reaches for a screwdriver and stabs him to death as Caroline watches in horror screaming for her daddy. As Esther tries to wrench the weapon out of Alan's hands, Caroline comes over and takes it from them.

Finally recalling what really happened, Caroline finds her grinning uncle standing over her. He admits to sending that letter and almost getting caught by Esther. If he had, "there would be no sex for a week." He pulls his niece up to him and plants a kiss on her lips only to receive a knee to the balls in return. Alan reveals why he had to kill the Carpenter women and how Caroline will learn to love and want him like he does her. Pulling her down the stairs so they can shower together, Caroline is able to break free and heads towards her mother on the wind tower with her uncle in pursuit. He chases her through the groves and picks up a fallen screwdriver at one point. Esther is watching all from above on the wind tower, but again it is movie trickery as Armenaki recounted.

VHS cover art for *Blackout* (1988).

Esther finally does a loving thing for her daughter and pushes off the engine which falls onto Alan, killing him instantly. She then jumps. Before expiring, she tells her daughter, "Don't waste your tears on me," as she reaches out to hold the hand of her dead brother. The movie wraps with Luke escorting Caroline holding a suitcase out of her home and into her car as they drive away.

All-in-all, *Blackout* was a relatively smooth shoot for Arledge Armenaki. He was able to be creative with several scenes freely and even had to be resourceful to accommodate the actress for one of her scenes. He said, "Carol has a fear of heights and did not want to go to the top of the tower which was about thirty-five feet tall or basically about two and a half stories up. We used a stunt person for the big wide shots and point-of-view shot. The art department then built a second tower that was about ten feet off the ground. It was done in pieces and assembled when we needed it. Carol did go up on this and we shot all her medium shots and close-ups. These just have sky behind them, which makes sense since we were shooting up at her, so you would see the sky and not any trees or anything. That is the way we got Carol to play those scenes. Actually, we would have to build scaffolding to get the camera up there if Carol did climb the high tower, so it was probably a smart move the way we did it anyway."[847]

With filming complete, *Blackout* moved into post-production where Armenaki had a chance to watch them orchestrate the movie at 20th Century-Fox. He said, "Don Davis did the score. Being part of this as a cameraman to see your images with a full orchestra working on the film was truly a high. I think it took three or four days. They had the full orchestra for some parts and just strings for other parts. They broke it down and showed different sections. Don and the film editor Zach Staenberg later worked on the *Matrix* movies. Zach and I were good friends at that time. He was a remarkable editor [and won the Academy Award for *The Matrix*]."[848]

Per Arledge, after post-production was completed there was a premiere party, which Carol Lynley attended. *Blackout* played several film festivals and markets, such as Cinetex '88, organized by the American Film Institute in Hollywood and MIFED held in Milan, Italy, but Doug Adams was never able to get a national theatrical distribution deal. "You must be very tough to go through all that," opined Arledge. "I think that was one of the issues why he never directed again."[849]

Without a distributor, the movie played in Los Angeles, and a few other places, for a week in 1989, before going direct-to-video later that year. This was unfortunate and a recurring problem that seemed to have vexed Lynley's post-*Poseidon* feature film career. The movie was reviewed in the *Los Angeles Times*, but critic Michael Wilmington was not a fan and called it a "sub-*Psycho*, sub-*Marnie* lady-in-peril pastiche" and that "Doug Adams doesn't handle it any more notable than dozens of other copycats who have preceded him." As for Carol, he described her character as "a mean-tempered mom, which comes at you like a bad memory."

When asked his opinion of the movie, Arledge reflected and then responded, "The mother and brother have a sick relationship, but it doesn't play out well near the end. I don't know how it could have been worked out better in as far as the script. The film also had other peculiar moments like when Caroline stabs Luke. Where did that come from? I think Carol and Gail O'Grady were well cast together and played opposite each other nicely. Michael Keys Hall was a little stiff. If he and Gail would have elevated the depth of their performances, I think the film would have been more dramatic than melodramatic and connected better with an audience. Still I think it holds its own and some people gave it decent reviews."[850]

This is true. The audience never really learns what drove Caroline away. Did she subconsciously suspect her mother and uncle were having an incestuous relationship? Caroline is an enigma made even more so by the somber performance given by O'Grady. And the scene where she goes nuts and attacks Luke with the screwdriver just comes out of left field with no explanation. However, even with these plot holes, Adams keeps the suspense building to what really happened to Caroline's father.

Carol Lynley gives a truly intense performance playing this mother from hell. The hatred of her daughter is evident from their first encounter and never lets up. When Carol's Esther hisses that she wanted a baby with a man she loved and not her despised husband, it all makes sense then that the other man was her own brother and that an offspring between them could never be. In the scene where Esther tries to be motherly, bringing her daughter a cup of tea and a sedative, Carol projects how hard it is for Esther to show Caroline any love. After heroically saving the life of her daughter, Esther still chooses her brother over her child - even facing her own death.

Unfortunately, Carol's performance in *Blackout* was not appreciated by as many people as it should have been. The one exception was syndicated film critic and drive-in movie lover, Joe Bob Briggs. Writing in the *Orlando Sentinel*, he remarked that *Blackout* was "'Psycho from a Woman's Perspective'" and "one of the nastiest movies I have seen in a long time." He added that the cast deserved Drive-In Academy Award nominations singling out Lynley, "as the meanest mother in film history, for saying, 'If you want, I'll give you the name of a good gynecologist in Oxnard' and making it sound like 'You scum!' and, in her most sensitive moment, 'Go back where you came from.'"

According to Arledge, *Blackout* also received a warm reception at a Las Vegas film festival honoring cinematography that took place almost a year later when the movie had already gone to video. "Doug and I went," recalled Arledge. "They loved our work in the film and they had a screening in one of the casino's theaters. The place was packed, and the audience gave us a roaring applause. It was the best screening we ever had for the film. People really got it and responded to it. You just felt like the film was going to go somewhere. It's the life of a cameraman. If you get hooked up with some big hit when you are young your career can go somewhere. I didn't, but I shot several films that I am fairly proud of. They never quite took off, so you just keep working and do your thing."[851]

19. From Rampaging Rats to Hideous Demons

In between *Dark Tower* and *Blackout*, Carol Lynley returned to playing the lady in peril guest starring on the popular, award-winning, Canadian TV detective series *Night Heat*, which aired as part of *CBS Late Night* in the summer of 1987. Though filmed in Toronto, it was set in a fictitious American city. What set it apart from other series was that it was shot entirely after dark. It followed the exploits of reporter Tom Kirkwood (Allan Royal) who writes the "Night Beat" column for a local newspaper and police detectives Kevin O'Brien (Scott Hylands) and Frank Giambone (Jeff Wincott) assigned to the overnight shift.

Carol guest starred as Grace Barnett in the episode entitled "Grace," directed by George Mendeluck and written by Robert Forsyth. A battered wife, Grace approaches Kirkwood at the scene of a hit-and-run and asks if he would like to witness another crime. She matter-of-factly states, "I'm going to kill my husband." The pretty blonde is an upper middle-class housewife whose stressed spouse Roy (Tony Musante) likes to use her as a punching bag with sharp jabs to the stomach. The latest lands her in the hospital emergency room. Grace tries to break free with the help of Kirkwood, however, her privileged background and upbringing makes her think she is not like those other abused women and refuses to go to a shelter. Even with support from

Kirkwood and her fear of being alone, she returns home despite having to sleep with a knife in her nightstand for protection. Taunted by an angry Roy, Grace finally has had enough and slashes her attacking husband, but he plunges the knife into her stomach. In an ironic twist, the parallel story has a prostitute arrested and jailed for killing her violent, hated pimp with her car while Roy walks away free for the murder of his wife. He only gets a few months in jail for assaulting a cop afterwards.

Night Heat was Lynley's second to last TV guest star appearance. What happens to Grace is disturbing but true to what women go through in real life. Carol has just the right voice and manner to play this high-minded woman who, though brutalized by her spouse thinks, she is atypical based on her class and position in society. Taken care of by men all her life (first her father and then husband), she is terrified to walk away from her abusive husband and thinks killing him is the only way to be free. Even when she lands in a safe space away from him, her insecurities get the best of her. She foolishly returns home, even though she needs to sleep with protection. Unfortunately, it is not enough to save her. It was a heavily dramatic part, and Carol makes an impressive impact though frustratingly still not enough to land her more network TV gigs.

Carol then got some publicity when she was cast in Bernard Slade's mystery/suspense play *Fatal Attraction* that was set to open in Kansas City, Missouri. It was during the time of the hit movie of the same name starring Glenn Close and confused many people. Carol explained, "I hear we got there first with the title, because Slade's work has already been presented on the London stage starring Susannah York [1984]. Oddly enough, the character I portray does have similarities to Glenn's film role, but that's just happenstance."[852] It was another lady in peril role (or was it?) for the talented blonde. Her character was a beautiful but fading actress still popular with the Hollywood crowd. Spending time at her beach house, her ex-husband, who has come to claim his belongings, is murdered and a photographer who has stalked her for years shows up as well. Throw in a smitten police detective and a Lesbian agent and the mystery deepens. Despite Salde's hopes, the play never made it to Broadway.

After failing to be cast as the new Iris Wheeler on the daytime drama series *Another World*, its producers offered her a short-term role as a judge in consolation in 1988. The following year, the *Philadelphia Daily News* reported that Lynley was in town filming a reported two-hour TV pilot for CBS called *Travelin'*, directed by Corey Allen and starring Lee Majors. He played a country wanderer who befriends a newspaper journalist (Ellen Greene) after rescuing her from a mugging in Philadelphia. Fascinated with his way of life, she decides to join him on his journeys and document them for her column. It was not picked up as a series, but the network aired a truncated hour-long version in August. However, the title was changed to *Road Show* and Carol was nowhere to be found.

She then returned to the thriller realm with her final television episodic guest appearance on the syndicated half-hour anthology series *Monsters* in 1990. Her episode "Stressed Environment" was the third season opener. It was directed by Jeffrey Wolf. As a film editor, he worked for Laurel Entertainment that produced *Tales of the Darkside* and then *Monsters*. Recalling how he came to direct "Stressed Environment," he said, "I had directed two previous episodes. This episode was supposed to be directed by the series' producer Michael Gornick. I think he picked this episode as something that he really wanted to do but couldn't for some reason. They called me to ask if I would do it. The role of the female scientist had not yet been cast. They gave me a choice of a few actresses [including Barbara Bouchet and Yvette Mimieux]. I had remembered Carol Lynley from a movie she did where she is on the beach somewhere [possibly *Once You Kiss a Stranger*] and as a kid I kind of fell in love with her. Growing up Jewish I had a thing for blonde girls. The show was filmed in Brooklyn and Carol was living in an apartment in Manhattan. I went to meet her there and didn't have to cajole her to take the part, which surprised me."[853]

"Stressed Environment," written by Neal Marshall Stevens the series' creative consultant/story editor, is a creepy episode, especially for people who truly have a fear of rats, but the cartoony effects mar the suspense. Lynley played Dr. Elizabeth Porter, a brilliant scientist who has spent almost twelve years of her career in the basement of a laboratory experimenting with the effects that several types of pesticides have on rats. At least that is what she was supposed to have been doing. Instead, she created a stressed environment to learn about the evolution of intelligence using rats as her subjects. They live behind the walls of a mock kitchen set up with cupboards and appliances. For the last three months none of the rats have been heard or seen. When a lab technician goes in to unclog a pipe, she is attacked and killed by a rat carrying a makeshift spear. Stop motion effects are used for the rats and they are laughable. Porter then tries to defend her experiment to her superior Dr. Robert Winston (Victor Raider-Wexler) with scenes of a solo Lynley in medium shot giving a long, serious diatribe about why she should be allowed to continue.

Porter is ordered to gas the rats but they are immune and survive. After the lights go out, her assistant Keith (Scott J. Weir) discovers the rats have entered the electrical grid and have sabotaged it, trapping the trio in the lab when the power goes out. Winston and Keith devise a plot to exterminate this new species of killer rats, but Porter desperately pleads the rodents' case to let them live because they were taught violence. She wants to try to communicate with them. Here, Carol excels as Porter slowly starts to unravel and the audience discovers she is determined to save her experiment at all costs.

Winston overrules her and goes in but the rats are prepared for combat. Using mouse traps as launch pads, they shoot spears at their target killing him. Porter goes in to try to save the doctor, but it is too late. Instead she finds an injured rat. She gently picks it up and attempts to comfort it. Back outside, she stumbles over the dead Keith who perished when the roof caved in courtesy of the rat patrol. Then to Porter's astonishment, a leader of the rats speaks to her. He threatens her and she responds that she can kill too while holding the canister of poisonous gas. Then in one of the most startling scenes of Carol's entire career, the now totally mad scientist loosens her hair, opens her arms in a loving embrace, and tries to seduce the rat instead! He freaks out, naturally, and orders his minions (in a guinea pig type of squeal) to attack her and the spears fly again. Lying there dying, she gasps, "How human you are" and tries to grab the canister but it rolls away as she expires.

Carol Lynley, ca. late 1980's. *From Marlin Dobbs' Collection*

Lynley convincingly plays the character as a serious and dedicated scientist with no traces of madness. However, as the situation with the rats becomes more and more precarious, Lynley lets her lunacy emerge. Recalling the shoot and working with Carol, Jeffrey Wolf remarked, "This was shot quickly in four days for about $100,000. It was an intense gig. Carol never had any complaints. She was a pro and I let her do her thing. I was so involved with making the rats work and trying to make the episode as odd and quirky as I could. When she succumbs to the rats at the end, I let her go with what she felt most comfortable [as she unsuccessfully tries to sexually entice them]. The producer liked to have a sexy feel to every episode. Carol being someone who could do that now as an older woman made it kind of interesting and sick."[854]

This could have been a standout episode as Jeffrey Wolf keeps the plot moving and suspenseful. He said, "Yes, I tended to gear my episodes toward the suspense over the horror."[855] However, it is the effects team that makes it sillier than expected but that did not seem to bother Wolf who liked the added element of humor. Viewing it again, the director opined, "I think Carol was great. I was happy with the show. It was quite funny as well."[856]

Shortly after filming this episode, columnist Liz Smith reported that Carol Lynley was expected to join the cast of *Twin Peaks* during its third season, playing the up-to-now unseen FBI employee Diane whom Agent Cooper (Kyle MacLachlan) records messages to.[857] However, ABC-TV surprisingly did not renew the series. Years later, creator Mark Frost refuted this claim in the book *The Complete Lynch* and thought some PR guy planted the story. According to him, they had not settled on anyone for the part.[858] Carol, however, said she was offered and agreed to play Diane but ABC cancelled it. There was no reason for Carol to make this story up. When the character finally appeared on screen in the 2017 Showtime revival, the role was played by long-haired, blonde Laura Dern, who was similar in type to Lynley.

Though *Twin Peaks* did not come to be, Carol's return to the New York stage did. She co-starred in the Off-Broadway production *The Sea Gull: The*

Hamptons: 1990 adapted and directed by R. Jeffrey Cohen. It was an updating of Chekhov's classic drama, from 19th Century Russia to present day America, and was staged at the RAPP Arts Center. Lynley had the lead role of the aging, vain actress Arkidina, but unfortunately the play received widely mixed reviews by the New York critics. An extremely positive one came from *Backstage* whose reviewer Sy Syna remarked that "Carol Lynley—with 41 films behind her—is ideally suited to Arkadina" and "Cohen's achievement is stunning: a fresh vision of a great play, most of it realized by a fine cast and technical support." Though Carol performed well, this revival is best remembered for the first-rate performances given by newcomers Laura Linney as Nina and D.B. Sweeney as Constantine before they were famous.

Lynley then made fleeting appearances in two horror movies. Producer Fred Olen Rey became infamous during the eighties and nineties for making low-budget, direct-to-video exploitation movies using younger actors and actresses and surrounding them with veteran actors. Reportedly, Carol was paid $15,000 for one day's work.

Spirits (1990) is one of the few from the time that he only directed and did not produce. It also received a limited theatrical release in a few cities including Los Angeles before going direct-to-video. Some horror fans liked Rey's effort to make a serious scare fest combining plot points from *The Legend of Hell House*, *The Exorcist*, and *The Evil Dead*. Erik Estrada is Father Anthony Vicci, a tormented priest who ten years earlier had a one-night stand with a parishioner who went on to butcher her family. Now that they are tearing down her home, he is being taunted by a demon who takes different forms, including that of a horny, busty nun. He confesses his past indiscretion to Sister Gillian (Lynley) who tries to talk the priest into praying away his sins and not to revisit the house. Meanwhile, a team of paranormal types led by Dr. Richard Wicks (Robert Quarry) decide to spend the weekend in the home to investigate the creepy goings on. He brings with him a psychic (Brinke Stevens), a historian (Oliver Darrow), and a scientist (Kathrin Lautner). The three almost immediately become possessed by the murderous wife or the original owner, a defrocked priest whose soul is also trapped in the home.

Father Vicci comes to the team's rescue when all hell breaks loose and helps exorcise the demon, but other spirits remain to his horror at the fade out.

The movie is a bit too talky for this type of fare and is hindered by the cheap effects. Regarding this production, shot in a reported nine days in a modern, not so creepy, abode, Michael J. Weldon writing in the *The Psychotronic Video Guide* joked, "Here are some other signs of a haunted house: a plywood door breaks, a hole in the basement changes dimensions, and a microphone shadow 'mysteriously' appears."[859]

Carol is back in nun's garb for the third time and luckily for her, she remains fully clothed, unlike Michelle Bauer playing a succubus in a habit out to seduce the priest. Typical of videos from the time, she is completely nude while Estrada remains fully clothed. The former *CHiPs* star does emote with conviction and Carol plays her part sincerely. At first, she is sympathetic to the guilt-ridden priest, but then becomes gently forceful trying to get him to remain in the church instead of returning to the house. When she realizes that he cannot be stopped, she morphs into a foul-mouthed demon. Their scenes, all filmed at a church, are by far the best acted in the movie with Carol adding a touch of class to the proceedings.

Next, the actress has nothing more than a walk-on cameo in the surprisingly well-crafted, atmospheric, direct-to-video *Howling VI: The Freaks* (1991) directed by Hope Perello and co-produced by John C. Broderick who directed *Bad Georgia Road*. An in-name only sequel without having anything to do with the original *The Howling* and its follow-ups, this was about a circus carnival owned by vampire R.B. Harker (Bruce Martyn Payne) that puts down stakes in a small town. Harker has been on the trail of a drifter/werewolf (Brendan Hughes) and wants to add him to his collection of freaks.

Carol is Miss Eddington, the town's rich matriarch who visits the carnival one night. She is first revealed when Harker pulls back the curtains on his trailer as she is standing outside fanning herself. Later she is wooed by Harker and, fascinated with the freaks, accepts his offer for a tour where she reveals that she owns the local bank. That is the last we see of Miss Edgington until her mutilated body is discovered later. Carol's screen time is so brief that if you blinked, you would miss her. Also, if you listen carefully while she and Harker are walking toward his trailer, Carol's voice sounds different, as if someone else looped the three or four lines of dialogue she had in post-production.

Regarding *Spirits* and *Howling VI*, Carol said,

> I wish to apologize for making these films. I've never seen either film and don't ever intend on seeing them. I ... appeared in one [*Howling VI*] as a favor [to a friend]. I made sure I didn't have much screen time ... I did my scenes and then flew home.[860]

Carol next had a role in the never completed movie *Heartfelt* in 1992. It was directed by Paul S. Parco (*Deadly Alliance*; *Pucker Up and Bark Like a Dog*) for Heartfelt Productions and Flora Films. It had an impressive cast that also included Joe Dallesandro, Priscilla Barnes, Lesley-Anne Down, and Meg Foster. Dallesandro and Barnes played parents of a young girl (Megan Hughes) whose traumatic home life wreaks havoc on her professional career as a dancer. Joe Dallesandro recalled, "She's involved with something nasty. I don't really remember much of the plot. What I do remember is that they had a whole bunch of people—cast and crew—to whom they kept saying, 'We'll pay you next week, we'll pay you next week.' And I wasn't going to allow that."[861] Mired in legalities, the film remained unfinished. Paul S. Parco went on to produce and direct a few more movies through 2001.

For the next two years or so, Carol was inactive in film and on television though she did appear in her first infomercial. It was for a face cleanser made from sugar cane. Purportedly, she looked fabulous in it. Also, during this period, Lynley was interviewed in *People* magazine where she revealed that various publishers had shown interest in her autobiography. However, she remarked, "But the trouble is, sooner or later they want you to dish up the dirt. Then I have to say, 'Guys, what can I tell you? I haven't committed a murder. I haven't done porno. I haven't been married 18 times. I don't make threatening calls. I have my vices—but they're all awfully normal.'"[862]

Not acting much did not depress her since her "real passion of late"[863] was painting and traveling. However, she went on to say, "I'm in transition; I'm playing middle-aged parts, which is a good idea! Eventually I want to make the next transition, to where I'm playing snowy-haired old ladies, my Helen Hayes period."[864] Though she was keeping up a good front for the press, Carol must have been frustrated with the lack of acting work. She still looked great and believed in her talent. The fact that she could not even land that guest role on *Murder, She Wrote* was mind boggling. Perhaps she did not have an aggressive agent working on her behalf?

An opportunity for Lynley that almost came her way was revealed by the producers of the drag queen comedy *To Wong Foo, Thanks for Everything, Julie Newmar* starring Patrick Swayze in 1995. As negotiations with the former Catwoman dragged on regarding the use of her name in the title, it was revealed that they were going to replace Julie with Carol Lynley. This was probably the impetus for Newmar to finally sign off.

20. Three Cons and a Kid

The following year saw Carol before the movie cameras in *Neon Signs* (1996). This would be her last movie lead, but at least she went out on a high note, giving one of the most entertaining performances of her career. Unfortunately, as her luck would have it, not many people got the chance to see it. Carol did make fleeting appearances in a few films afterwards, but all were inconsequential as compared to her co-starring role in this morality tale, dressed up as a violent and stylish road movie. Carol and Barbara McNair are two Thelma and Louise type, smalltime crooks (ironically named Grace and Faith) on a robbery spree across the desert. Heading to Las Vegas, they first rendezvous with William Smith's con man who is planning to rip off a high stakes' poker game. Along the way the ladies pick up a hitchhiking, naïve young loner who ingratiates himself with this trio of thieves. As expected, things go awry when the double-crossing begins and the bullets fly.

Neon Signs was distributed by Tri Vision Entertainment, an independent Los Angeles-based company with ties to Japan and Korea. Lazar Saric provided the original screenplay and it was directed by Marc Kolbe. A first-time director, Kolbe had experience working on music videos and had a company that specialized in producing them. He came from a show business background. His father was prolific Hugo-award winning TV director

Winrich 'Rick' Kolbe (*Magnum P.I., Star Trek: The Next Generation, Star Trek: Voyager, 24*) and he was the godson of actor Dennis Weaver (*Gunsmoke, McCloud*).

William Smith was the first actor cast. When asked how Carol Lynley came to be Grace, Kolbe replied, "Our casting person brought Carol along with Barbara McNair. We felt they would be a great team together with William Smith. We could totally see that they could have had a relationship at some time in their lives."[865]

Carol called making *Neon Signs* one of the most pleasant working experiences she ever had due to the cast and crew. Recalling her co-leads, Carol commented, "Matt Dotson was a sweet kid and Barbara was terrific. I didn't get to know William Smith that well. But Barbara and I were together a lot. We just laughed our heads off the entire time."[866]

Young lead Matt Dotson began as a stunt player, which led to TV commercial work. Moving to Hollywood from Oregon, he studied acting with Joe Palese of The Actor Space. After appearing in a Walt Disney pilot titled *Family Values*, he was cast as Otis in *Neon Signs*. The actor revealed that it was blind luck that got him the audition. A friend came to town "to chase the dream" and contacted him desperate for a place to stay because all her stuff, including her purse, was stolen from the hotel where she was residing. He was in Oregon, and told her if she could get to his apartment in Studio City, there was a key under the mat (per Matt, she said, "You seriously keep a key under the mat!?!"[867]) and he would return shortly. Matt came home to a spanking clean apartment and a movie script on his coffee table. His friend had met a man who happened to be one of the producers of *Neon Signs* and he gave her a lift. Inside Dotson's home, he saw the actor's headshots and thought he could be the one to play Otis, so an audition was to be arranged. Matt was in disbelief. He was getting commercials and usually brought in to read for guest roles on TV but not film leads. Matt hit it off with the producer but was told he had to go through the normal audition process."[868]

"There was another producer who didn't have as much faith in me," revealed Dotson. "My producer friend told me that it was down to two of us and he said, 'If you go with this guy you are going to get *90210*. If you go with this guy over here, you are going to get somebody who really is going to act.' Method acting though is not acting and you try to portray life as it happens."[869]

Dotson had a gentle sweetness about him and an innocent looking face that made the perfect combination to play the teenager who befriends the trio of grizzled thieves. Dotson remarked, "In my mind, the choice I made was that everything Otis knew he learned from Lulu, television, or the people that came through the motel. They were in the middle of nowhere. I had to be quite simple with the role and just break it down that this kid had been abandoned. All he has is right in front of his face so that is all he knows. Every experience he is going to have outside of the motel is entirely new for the first time. During the auditions, I was the only one who played it this way."[870]

An outstanding feature of *Neon Signs* is the sun-drenched desert locale, beautifully captured by cinematographer Howard Wexler. He attended USC Cinema and then began an internship with cinematographer Mario Tosi (*The Marcus Nelson Murders, Buster and Billie, Carrie, MacArthur, The Stunt Man,* etc.). Wexler's first feature as Director of Photography was *Trading Partners* in 1984 and he has worked consistently ever since. Two films that feature standout work from Wexler are the Andy Sidaris-directed actioners, *Hard Ticket to Hawaii* (1987) with Ronn Moss and *Picasso Trigger* (1988) with Steve Bond.

Recalling the shoot on location in the desert, Marc Kolbe wrote, "We shot for thirty-one days, if I remember. We took over the whole town of Boron, in the Mojave Desert. It was a crazy shoot. We didn't have a lot of money, but somehow, we had full rein of this little town. And during the day, as we were shooting, we would have constant sonic booms coming from the Stealth Fighter Planes going into Edwards Air Force Base, as they hit the sound barrier. We were shooting a scene in a gas station where Carol pistol whips the attendant. Just then a plane hit the sound barrier and the sonic boom made the windows almost blow out in this old gas station. I thought the place was going to blow up. The attendant that gets pistol whipped is

Lazar Saric, the writer of the film. Everyone pitched in to make this film happen. I feel that Carol saw that and worked extra with us, to make the project happen. She also helped Matt Dotson, who was new and took him through the scenes. It was great to have such a veteran cast, that could really help out and work with such a tight budgeted film."[871]

Howard Wexler concurred with Kolbe that filming went quite smoothly and said, "There were no real problems shooting in the desert, except for a fierce wind that came up one night in California City and blew over a 5k lamp. We shot at a photogenic location that still exists today near Edwards Air Force Base. Most of my work over the years has always looked more expensive than the budget. *Neon Signs* had some good production values and the project seemed to have serendipity of luck."[872]

When asked about Lynley and her costars, Wexler had nothing but praise for them and wrote, "I only have fond memories of the cast and crew from *Neon Signs*, especially the old lady [Vivienne Maloy] in the motel at the opening of the film. Carol was pleasant to work with, on time as far as I can remember, with a great attitude. She was into the part and enjoyed the character—and didn't mind the cheap motel accommodations. She got along well with Barbara McNair, as well as Bill Smith and the rest of the cast and crew. We were like a little entourage with a ten-person crew at the most—guerilla-style filmmaking."[873]

Marc Kolbe concurred and added, "Carol Lynley was wonderful. They all were—so easy to work with. Being a low budget film, we didn't have all the perks, but they worked with us and made it easy for us to take care of them."[874]

Recalling the scene where Carol and Barbara's characters rob a high stakes poker game, Lynley said,

We have guns and burst into this hotel room where these guys are sitting around playing cards. I am not a gun person, so they had to show me how to handle it like I mean it. As we filmed it, we shoot the guys and say our lines. When Barbara said something like that we must go now, I just ad-libbed a response. Barbara and I ran out of the scene and laughed our heads off.[875]

DVD cover art for *Neon Signs* (1996).

This being Kolbe's first movie, the novice followed a preconceived plan on how he would approach directing the movie and getting a performance from his cast. Luckily for him, the actors hired were such pros that they made his job a bit easier. Describing, he wrote, "Growing up with a father who was a director and godfather who was an actor, I learned to work closely with the actor. I am not one to stand at the monitor all day. I like standing next to the camera as much as possible and work with the actor. I do like to get a performance that they are happy with as well, so it was a team effort. Being that this was my first, I really had a great crew behind me. Most of them, I had worked with before."[876]

He continued, "The energy that Carol had with Barbara was great, as well as Bill Smith. They seemed to have fun with the characters and the project. Which made it easy on me, so I got to watch how they reacted to each other in the scene, which was great. They worked well together like they had been friends for ages. They really got along and on set, they snapped into the characters, quickly. I mean the characters were really them except for the killing part."[877]

Newcomer Matt Dotson confirmed that he too was taken with the trio of actors and exclaimed, "Working on that film was an incredible experience. It was an honor to just be on set with those veterans let alone play around every day for a month. *Red Dawn* is one of my favorite movies and I couldn't believe I was working with Bill Smith who played the Russian leader. Of course, I knew Carol Lynley and Barbara McNair from my parents watching their films when I was a kid. It was neat to know that I was going to work with veterans that put some serious time into the business and earned their licks.

"Acting came natural to me," continued Matt. "I really didn't take any classes until I was in LA when I studied with Joe Palese who comes from a Stanislavski/Method type background. However, it was like a switch that you turn on and turn off. It really depends on the director you are working with and the set you are working on in terms of how long you are there to stay in character. Marc Kolbe was so awesome with the environment at the motel being the way that it was—it was perfectly conducive to that style of acting. I was able to immerse myself 110% into my part. I was able to stay in character the entire time I was on set. Some directors don't quite understand that mentality but I have a lot of respect for it. This was a great environment for me to just dive in. Will, Carol and Barbara are old-school too. Of course, we would joke around, but that doesn't mean you are not in character. They treated me on set in character and they were in character. Between takes, the way they were treating Otis in the scene, is the way they treated me at lunch. They would joke and rib me the way they did with Otis. They would just keep going and I would just be in that side of Matt Dotson that is Otis. This was my first experience to be the lead in a film and it was probably the best learning experience I could ever had."[878]

When told of the complimentary things said about her by Marc Kolbe and Matt Dotson, Carol replied quite humbly, "I have always made a point of being professional and treating people respectfully. I have been lucky and about 99% of the time I have been treated professionally by the people I have worked with. As I said, the more talented they are, the nicer they are."[879]

As the title credits roll for *Neon Signs* they are accompanied by a haunting, country-tinged theme from composer Tim May (his only credited film score). The movie opens in black-and-white, giving it a nourish feel, as a young mother professes her love for her young son, Otis, before abandoning him at the run-down Desert Lake Motel & Casino (with "Coming Soon" taped over Casino) in the middle of the California desert. The chain-smoking muumuu wearing proprietress Lulu (Vivienne Maloy), a former Vegas showgirl, finds the boy and is about to dial child services but decides to keep the pleasant kid around. The movie then flashes forward in color to the present where the quiet, amiable Otis (Matt Dotson) is still living and working at the motel. Guessing it is his eighteenth birthday; Lulu gives him a compass and says, "It helps you find direction." When the old woman dies in her sleep that night, Otis decides to head to Las Vegas - over two hundred miles away.

While trying to hitch a ride, he comes across two abandoned cars on the side of the road. Two women come out of the dunes arguing over 'why they had to shoot'. Fans of Carol Lynley and Barbara McNair will be pleasantly surprised and thrilled as they come on like a tornado, playing Faith and Grace, sniping at each other. Carol gives arguably her most forceful performance and has some of the film's best lines. When seeing Otis near her automobile, she barks, "Hey! Get away from that car!" To some Lynley fans, this scene may be reminiscent of *Once You Kiss a Stranger* when she emerged from the surf aiming a harpoon gun and told a little girl to "get off my beach!". When Otis explains he is walking to Las Vegas, the duo is flabbergasted as it is over 200 miles away. As he calculates how many miles he can walk per hour and per day, the exasperated ladies offer him a ride though Faith asks first, "Are you a good boy?" As he prepares to get in, Faith says to Grace, "Next town we ditch the kid." As they drive off, the camera pans to a dead body lying in the sand.

McNair and Lynley are so much fun bickering as they drive the open desert roads with Otis in the back seat. When Grace takes the wheel, Faith pulls out a bottle of whiskey and offers a swig to Otis. When he says he does not drink, Faith asks, "And why not? What else is there to do at your age?" They then stop at a diner to eat and the ladies notice Otis looking all around in wonder. When Faith asks if he has ever been in a diner before, he responds no. She laughs and quips, "What rock did you crawl out from under?" Heading to the restroom, sneaky Grace swipes the tips left for the waitress and then they skip out on the bill but only after getting ten dollars from naïve Otis for his share. The duo drives off leaving Otis outside the diner.

The ladies head directly to a gas station. As Grace fills up the tank, Faith enters and goes right up to the cashier reading a gun magazine. She pulls out her gun and sticks in right in his face. Grace trails in and begins helping herself to a drink while Faith clears out the cash register when Otis wanders in. Grace instructs him to take what he wants and tells him to get in the car. Faith then points her gun at the forehead of the attendant and asks menacingly, "Do you believe in God?" Taking Otis with them so he does not rat them out to the cops, the duo plot to lose him when they meet up with a guy named Clyde.

Tired from all her thieving and robbing, Faith asks Otis if he wants to drive and he agrees, but the ladies quickly notice he does not know how. When chastised for not saying that he has not learned, he responds matter-of-factly, "How do you know if you can't do something unless you try to do it?" Grace responds, "Good point" and off they go with a shaky Otis behind the wheel. Arriving safely at the Del Mar Motel, Grace and Faith argue about getting separate rooms due to Grace's snoring, leaving Otis in the parking lot to fend for himself. Trying to sleep in the front seat of the car, Otis spies a burly man exiting Faith's room and then heading over to Grace's where she greets him in the doorway with a kiss and a hug.

The next morning, the man Otis noticed room hopping is Clyde (William Smith), a grizzled guy who has been around and takes an immediate liking to the boy. He makes him promise not to tell the ladies that he spent time with each. In exchange, Clyde offers Otis a ride, much to the chagrin of Grace and Faith. He drops the pair of lovelies off at a local beauty parlor and goes for ice cream with Otis to kill some time.

With their overly made up faces and new 'dos, the ladies primp in the mirror over where they tied up the beauticians. Faith threatens in a haughty voice, "Oh, and ladies, if I hear a peep out of you, I am not going to recommend this place to *any* of my friends." They then hop into Clyde's big red convertible, after he plies them with exaggerated compliments on their new looks, and they drive away. Discovering that Otis only has thirty dollars to his name, Clyde takes it and promises to make it more. Arriving at another motel, Faith hisses, "If I have to spend any more time with the Hardy Boys I am going to puke. Clyde, when are we going to discuss business?" In their room, Clyde then reveals to Otis that he and the ladies are planning to steal from some bad characters and wants the boy to make his own decision if he wants in or not.

He does not and leaves when Grace and Faith come over. Clyde explains the score - that these high rollers, with $50,000 each, have a high stakes poker game once a month at the motel where they are staying. They only allow the mother of the guy who owns the motel in to make drinks and serve food. Plan is to take her out and replace her with Grace or Faith. Clyde chooses Grace and an irate Faith demands to know why. He says, "Because she has a sunnier disposition," to which Faith responds, "Fuck you!" Clyde then admits he will not be participating and will let the ladies handle it because he feels the men will be too embarrassed to admit that they were robbed by women. Clyde's plan works like a charm and the "old ladies" pull off the heist to the amazement of their victims. At a hangar where they are to divide the money evenly, Faith announces that there is "a change in plans" and aims her gun at Clyde and Otis while Grace announces that "two is a nice even number." Clyde then tricks them to thinking each has double-crossed the other. Grace and Faith then turn on each other with insults and threats. Clyde shoots off his gun and Grace shoots Faith who fires back at her. Both ladies lay dead on the floor as Clyde grabs the stolen loot and rushes an upset Otis out.

The rest of the movie moves quickly and Lynley and McNair are sorely missed. Clyde offers to give Otis some money to go it alone, but the boy decides to continue to Vegas with Clyde who reveals he has one last job to pull. However, he is double-crossed by his vengeful, estranged daughter Jody (Alisa Christensen) and her counterfeiting husband (one of the poker players). With a hail of bullets, Otis gets an injured Clyde out of the girl's house with the $250,000 he came with. As they drive away, Clyde succumbs to his injury, and the movie ends with the virtuous Otis walking towards Vegas again, but this time with a satchel of money on his back, proving the innocent shall inherit the Earth.

Unfortunately, there are no trade reviews for *Neon Signs* because the movie was never released theatrically. The producers opted to bring the movie to the American Film Market. Held annually in Santa Monica, it is a marketplace where films are bought and sold. Though there are screenings, it is not a film festival. Matt Dotson attended and here is where, he stated, he got to know the real Carol Lynley. Seems on and off set during filming the actress kept in character a lot. Dotson said, "Those comments her character would make on camera ribbing Otis continued off. She was the most solid giving me crap the way she did Otis. She acted irritated around me the entire time. At certain moments, I thought 'Does she really hate people?' But no, she was playing this out. For instance, at lunch she would give me crap as we were in the food line. She'd turn and say, 'Are you going to eat *that*!?!' I would literally sit at the end of the table almost shunned by her and the others at certain times. So that is what I mean when I said I really didn't meet Carol Lynley until the American Film Market. That was great because we talked outside of character and talked about the business, which did not come up while we were shooting."[880]

Explaining why *Neon Signs* never played a film festival or received even a limited theatrical release, Marc Kolbe stated, "We looked at getting into a few festivals, but the other investors wanted to sell, and by selling for a DVD release, it disqualifies you to run in many of the festivals. So, a big learning experience for me. I wish we could have done a bit more on that front."[881] It is a shame considering all the hard work that went into making this film and how wonderful it turned out that the producers threw it all away.

It is disappointing that the public never got the chance to see Carol in *Neon Signs* on the big screen. She and Barbara McNair are quite good as pistol-packin' mamas in Marc Kolbe's surprisingly interesting, gritty little movie. They are backed up by the sun-drenched desert locations beautifully captured by Howard Wexler; the sweet naivete that Matt Dotson brings to the boy caught up in their hi-jinks; and burly conman William Smith pulling all the strings. The film may have given Carol that much needed boost to get her back on the radar of casting directors.

Kolbe was not the only one disappointed about this outcome. So was Matt Dotson who was hoping *Neon Signs* would lead to more acting gigs. He commented, "Whoever was in control did not do a good job. This should have been an indie feature and entered into film festivals right away. The producers were only after making money instead of making art. It was frustrating for me and Marc because it was a heartfelt project for him."[882]

Asked for his concluding thoughts on *Neon Signs*, Matt Dotson replied, "Ironically, I just showed my daughters the film … [they] got a kick out of ribbing me as Otis. For the most part I am the opposite, yet they see those Otis qualities in me, and they have been quoting lines daily, "There are no do-overs in life Otis." I gave my best at the time we filmed *Neon Signs*, worked with champion veteran actors and actresses, had the utter pleasure of working with Marc Kolbe while learning a ton about my craft and myself. I would not change the experience for the world. Good times!"[883]

21. Final Act

The late nineties began with a nice cameo role for Carol Lynley in the short film *Vic* directed by the late Sage Stallone, son of Sylvester Stallone. The script was by actor/writer/producer/director Will Huston based on a story by Sage. It is a powerful and tragic look at the cutthroat world of the Hollywood casting process. Unfortunately, Stallone ran out of money and the short was not completed until 2006 when it popped up at a few film festivals. Remembering Sage Stallone, whom Carol adored, she said,

> I had never done a short film before. I went to meet with Sage and thought, 'This guy has got something—he's good.' Not because he was Sly Stallone's son, but Sage really had a feeling for film and acting and actors. I was there filming for about four or five days. I was very impressed by him. He would come close and tell you what he wanted you to do. I tried not to look at him because he was *so* gorgeous. He looked like his father but without the unusual characteristics of Sly's face. Sage was much more handsome. On top of that he was just very nice. He was nice to everyone—not just nice but thoughtful and made sure everybody knew what they had to do. He never pushed anybody around. He was just a sweet guy.

I remember also suddenly that all these teenage girls would show up. I think Sage was in his late twenties at the time. I'd see one girl hanging around make-up and another by the camera. Everybody who worked on the film and had a female relative or friend around that age brought them on the set to meet Sage who took the time to talk with them. He would listen to what they had to say and then thank them. He would excuse himself to go back to directing and the girls would be walking on air. I felt so badly when he died. It still hurts.[884]

In *Vic*, Lynley's former co-star from *The Alfred Hitchcock Hour*, Clu Gulager, delivers a truly heartfelt and moving performance as a down-on-his-luck character actor struggling for work and reduced to playing bit roles in low budget horror movies. Along comes the part of a lifetime, offered by an enthusiastic young director (Clu's son Tom Gulager) who is a fan, but the fear of auditioning rattles Vic. Desperate for the part, the misguided actor thinks dyeing his gray hair black and using tanning bronzer will make him look younger and seal the deal. It is truly painful to then watch his audition go so awry. Carol performs with class, playing an opinionated, outspoken casting director who is not sympathetic to Vic in the least. The impressive cast also included Gregory Sierra, John Philip Law, Peter Mark Richman, Richard Herd, Robert F. Lyons, and Gary Frank.

Next for Lynley was *Flypaper* (1999), a quirky, violent tale set in LA directed by Klaus Hoch (his first and only motion picture) and featuring an off-beat cast including Craig Sheffer, Robert Loggia, Illeana Douglas, Lucy Liu, and James Wilder. Carol played an upper-class housewife cooking in her kitchen when two of the characters crash into it. As they argue, she continues silently preparing her meal while listening in, coming off as a bewildered bystander in her own home. Surprisingly, Carol has no lines to recite.

Per a tweet from Illeana Douglas, "To my shock Carol Lynley was a nonspeaking day player in my scene. Painfully, no one knew who she was. She told me that she was doing the movie so she could make her insurance. She was kind, and humble, and I'll always treasure acting with her."[885] This may explain why Carol accepted such minor parts in her next few films. It was a sad situation that someone of Carol's stature, with over forty years of working as an actress, had to be reduced to this to maintain health insurance.

Carol had another nothing role (but at least this time she had lines) in the promising indie film *Drowning on Dry Land* (1999) starring Barbara Hershey and Naveen Andrews (of *Lost* fame). It was scripted by Julie Jacobs and directed by Carl Colpaert. Eileen Brennan was scheduled to play Carol's part but she became ill days before the shoot. Hershey had remained friendly with Carol over the years since they worked together on *Flood* and called her to see if she was available. Carol was and of course said yes.

In the movie, Manhattanite and abused wife (Hershey) offers to pay a NYC taxi driver (Andrews) $300 a day to take her to the desert to start a new life. The focal point is the relationship between the pair as they make the drive west. Carol does not come on screen until the end and is seen briefly as the owner of a rundown desert motel where the couple beds for a night. She even plays one scene behind a screen door where you can barely make out her appearance.

Though buoyed by the strong performances by the two leads, the weak screenplay bogs them down. *Drowning on Dry Land* too never received a theatrical release and went direct-to-video. Hershey and Andrews fared better. They became romantically involved and their on-and-off again relationship lasted until 2009.

Carol was thrilled when she finally got to play a grandmother in the surprisingly well-received family, fantasy film *A Light in the Forest: The Legend of Holly Boy* (2003) directed by special effects wizard John Carl Buechler (*From Beyond, Re-Animator*) who had a hand in writing the screenplay along with Frank Latino and Gary LoConti. This would be Carol's last feature film and how appropriate that it has almost the same title as her first *The Light in the Forest* (1958). Teenage Britta (Danielle Nicolet of *The Flash* fame) comes to Hollywood to live with her grandmother, who shares the tales of mystical Christmas spirit Holly Boy (Christian Oliver) and his nemesis King Otto (Edward Albert) who turned him into stone in the land of the Hollywoods.

Feeling lonely and out of place at her new high school, Britta inadvertently brings Holly Boy back to life with her sadness, but the curse also resurrects his enemies putting Hollywood in danger. Top-billed Lindsay Wagner plays Britta's supportive teacher and the Queen of the Hollywoods.

Carol acquitted herself well as the story telling octogenarian, but the movie is disjointed with cheesy effects and characters that seem out of place in sunny modern-day Los Angeles. Unfortunately for Carol it did not lead to any more similar type roles.

It was around this time when the actress began making regular appearances at celebrity autograph conventions in California and around the country. She was hesitant at first to participate, but quickly loved it. Normally, the invited guests had to pay their own way to the event though some organizers do cover air fare and hotel accommodations for conventions outside of the Los Angeles area. The celebrities are usually given a table to lay out their photos for purchase—autographed of course. Attendees stroll up and down the aisles gawking at the celebrities and sometime engaging them in conversation. For the most part it is truly an enjoyable time for all but could sometimes make for awkward moments between some rude fans and the celebrities. Carol remarked,

> I didn't want to do it originally, and I thought, well if I don't like it, I'll never do it again. It's as simple as that. I found I loved it. It is very ego affirming. Sometimes you think maybe you've been forgotten or you haven't worked in a while, I mean, actors are very insecure people. When you see these people coming at you with love and adoration in their eyes, you say, 'Oh, I could do this next weekend.' I like the attention and the whole process. I'm good with people.[886]

Besides interacting with her fans, Carol was able to reconnect with many former co-stars. She also got to meet, for the first time and became chummy with, rival *Harlow* actress Carroll Baker. She shared,

> I run into Carroll Baker from time to time, and we do look [like] we could be sisters easily. When we see each other it's like, 'Carol,' 'Carroll.' We jump up and down, and hug and kiss. People sort of back away because they think we're going to get into some sort of cat fight or whatever. I had dinner with her one night in San Francisco. You know I'm still a fan of hers. I said, 'Oh Carroll, you worked with James Dean and George Stevens, such critical people you've worked with. What a great career you've had and *Babydoll*. You look so beautiful Carroll to this day.' And she says, 'Oh Carol shut up!' 'No, no Carroll I really mean it.' We had fun. She's great.[887]

The warm relationship between Lynley and Baker almost progressed to working together. Per Jak Castro,

> Carol wanted something which would exploit their names and history. One project they both wanted to do was a remake of *Whatever Happened to Baby Jane?* although it had already been remade by the Redgrave sisters. Lynley wanted the Jane role with Baker taking the Blanche role. They were also looking at theatrical plays they could do together and that's where I came in. I had a production company at that time and I wanted to produce the show. One of the shows we were looking at was a play called *A Couple of White Chicks Sitting Around Talking*. I had also spoken to Stella Stevens about doing this show with Carol with the idea of selling it as a *Poseidon Adventure* reunion for the two of them. Carol was game as she loved the attention of theater audiences, but Stella didn't like to do theatrical shows, she preferred film. Nothing got farther than meetings unfortunately, so I moved on.[888]

*****

Although Carol Lynley was on the radar of directors Quentin Tarantino and John Waters during this time, neither ever hired her for any of their movies. Considering the violent subject of his films, Tarantino had more opportunities to use actors from the past (i.e. Robert Forster, Michael Parks, Nicholas Hammond, etc.) in supporting or cameo roles in his projects than actresses. Pam Grier is probably the only female star of the seventies he provided a comeback vehicle for in *Jackie Brown* proving that even with retro casting older actresses in Hollywood still have an exceedingly challenging time. Carol did not even rate being a character or a co-star of fictitious actor Rick Dalton on a movie poster in *Once Upon a Time in … Hollywood*. John Waters, who was friendly with Carol, could have easily cast her in any of his quirky mainstream movies as he did with Pia Zadora, Joey Heatherton, Polly Bergen, and others, but for whatever reasons never did.

Looking at it from another point of view, writer/blogger Shaun Chang opined. "I think it's better to be overlooked, yet still be respected and appreciated by Tarantino and Waters in terms of not being hired by them, then to be subjected to the self-aggrandizing condescension that Ryan Murphy expresses towards veteran actresses. Murphy purports to pay them tribute by acting as a 'white knight' who thinks he is restoring their honor by dramatizing a version of their lives. But what I think he's doing is misguidedly forcing his own agenda onto these actresses. He's unable to see them as anything other than victims of Hollywood and the so-called 'patriarchy.'"[889]

"I met Carol several times and had good, fun conversations with her," continued Chang. "She struck me as someone too proud and smart to want that for herself. I admit I wasn't a close confidant but what I'm trying to say is that there's not one self-respecting actress I know, Carol Lynley included, who I think would appreciate or welcome that sort of Ryan Murphy condescension. They can handle not being hired, that's par for the course in that industry, what they can't handle is someone feeling sorry for them."[890]

With a lack of acting offers, perhaps Carol decided to "avoid the stresses around her," as she once said, and enjoy life outside of performing. She had given up her New York apartment in the mid-nineties and had returned to Malibu, taking a place right on the ocean. According to her friends, she had a very peaceful life there.

Carol Lynley on the deck of her Malibu beach home with friend Marlin Dobbs, 1999. *Courtesy of Marlin Dobbs*

Back in 1978, Lynley stated she did not believe in old age and remarked, "I have Dame Sybil Thorndyke to thank for this. A long time ago, I was chosen to play her granddaughter. Then she was well in her 80s and her husband was over 90, but they had great energy. And neither one of them gave their age a thought. Her attitude was to make your own standards and not be influenced by mass opinions. She never stopped learning or expanding her interests, and she never relaxed her standards."[891]

Lynley appeared to be following this advice, keeping busy traveling, painting, and swimming. Though she had not had any job offers since the early 2000's, per Marlin Dobbs, "She would still go out on auditions from time to time, up to about 2013. I remember her telling me about an audition she went on around 2010 where she ran into Angie Dickinson. They were up for the same role. Carol said it was great seeing Angie and they talked and laughed for a long while even after their auditions were over."[892] It is quite amazing considering the long resume and sterling reputation each actress had, that they would still be called in to read for a part.

Marlin added, "The last audition Carol told me about was for a guest spot on the TV show *Supernatural*. She said the director or the producer had asked for her specifically. Shame it didn't work out."[893] Upon speculation, Carol may not have gotten the part because time had taken its toll on her looks, coupled, perhaps, with getting too much sun living on the beach in Malibu. Carol was also hindered by a hip operation that slowed her down. She looked the way a woman should in her seventies and this may have taken producers and casting directors by surprise. Gone was her flawless porcelain skin and distinct high cheekbones, which is expected with growing older.

It is sad to say, but fans want their ingénues and young leading ladies to never age—perhaps it stops them from facing their own mortality? This desire to remain forever young is the reason actresses like Raquel Welch and Jane Fonda are today plastic clones of their younger selves. Unlike dozens of her peers, Lynley did not believe in plastic surgery or Botox injections. Many of her fellow Baby Doll blondes (Sandra Dee, Tuesday Weld, Yvette Mimieux, Diane McBain, and Sue Lyon) seemed to have this same outlook. They were not desperate to maintain their youthful beauty and instead aged naturally. Since most were former models whose livelihood depended on their looks, this may surprise some. Dee and Lyon gave up acting in their late thirties and none of the rest worked steadily in film past the age of sixty. Tuesday Weld came closest, acting until the age of fifty-eight.

Carol was also battling another obstacle to getting acting roles. She successfully fought typecasting early on in her career and shook off the ingénue image. Later, however, she became so adept at playing the beleaguered heroine and lady in peril well into her early forties, producers and casting directors never gave her the opportunity to transition to the benevolent mother or character parts that she desired. It seems they just did not consider her for these types of roles. Hence, as she entered her sixties and seventies, it became even harder for her to be cast in the white-haired grandmother parts. Sadly, Carol's "Helen Hayes period" never materialized.

After not going out on auditions in a few years, perhaps Carol was thinking of making a comeback when she contacted Harry Langdon, Jr. out of the blue. He revealed, "I think it was in 2017 or 2018 when Carol called me. I thought 'Wow, Carol Lynley!' It brought back many fond memories. She said, 'Hi, Harry, how are you? Are you still shooting?' She asked if I would be interested in doing a new photo session and how much do I charge nowadays and if I could do it for a certain amount. I told her, 'I'd love to Carol!' That was the last I heard from her and guess she changed her mind."[894] Or perhaps she did not feel physically fit enough to go ahead with the session?

There is no telling if Carol Lynley would have ever had that fourth comeback with grandmother roles as she suddenly and unexpectedly died in her sleep on September 3, 2019. All were shocked by her passing. Most of the major U.S. newspapers ran an obituary as did many international sources including *The Guardian*; *The Independent*; *Fotogramas*; *The Dominion Post*; *Daily Express*; *The Timaru Herald*; and even Cuba's *Vanguardia*.

Fan tributes were posted on Facebook and tweeted on Twitter. As she expected, Lynley was most associated with *The Poseidon Adventure* in obituaries that ran online in *The New York Times*, *The Hollywood Reporter*, *Vanity Fair*, *People*, *SyFy Channel*, and many more.

A few people who knew and worked with her released remembrances on social media as well. Her long-time friend Sally Kirkland tweeted, "My sister & close friend since our teens when my mother put her on the cover of *Life* magazine. Her talent, grace, and beauty will be missed but never 4gotten."[895] Actress BarBara Luna posted on Facebook, "Remembering the first time we met, I labeled Carol Lynley sweetness."[896]

Her *Neon Signs* costar Matt Dotson left a heartfelt post on Facebook, "She was such a pleasure to just to be around and to work with—so sweet and funny, tough as nails, and faithfully sincere with a touch of grace. I learned so much technically and personally from her in the moments we shared on and off set. She was such a pro. I am truly lucky to have had those times and it was a real honor to have just shared space with her. My heart breaks right now but remembering her smile warms my heart and reminds me I should smile more. She really lit up a room with that smile."[897]

Carol's daughter Jill Selsman released an official statement to *People*, "She loved working in film as much as she loved going to the movies. I saw everything as a child with her. She was curious about the world around her, loved to spend time with interesting people, of all stripes and was generally a very peaceful person. Very live and let live. She had an easy approach to life and always took the good with the bad. She was a bon vivant. There really was no situation that couldn't be improved or ignored because there really was so much fun to be had, why dwell on things you can't change, which is what I think she's doing now. Clearly, you can't change death, but if there is a world beyond, she's dancing with her great friend Fred Astaire and enjoying her new life as much as she enjoyed her previous one."[898] Here's hoping.

Reportedly found in Carol's wallet at the time of her death were her Screen Actors Guild card and her gym membership. She remained physically active and ready for work to the end. After being cremated, her ashes were spread in the surf at her beloved Malibu.

In conclusion, over a fifty-year period, Carol Lynley achieved a highly commendable body of movie and TV work especially in the thriller/fantasy/suspense genres. She should be remembered (and hope this book proves it) as one of the most memorable actresses who essayed the lady in peril in film and television during the sixties and seventies. She delivered exceptional performances in the stylish thrillers, *The Shuttered Room* and *The Cat and the Canary*; and the extremely popular made-for-TV movies, *The Immortal*; *Fantasy Island*; and the horror classic, *The Night Stalker*—all of which spun off TV series. She even appeared in two TV British anthology shows' ninety-minute episodes—*If It's a Man, Hang Up!* and *In Possession*—that were so popular and well-received that they were released as standalone syndicated movies. Most impressively, whereas other actresses of her generation may, if lucky, have one truly iconic movie role, Carol has two. For cinéastes, she will always be remembered as the desperate mother searching for her daughter in the cult mystery thriller *Bunny Lake Is Missing*, while the general movie going public instantly remembers her as terrified pop singer Nonnie in the granddaddy of seventies disaster movies, *The Poseidon Adventure*. To her legions of fans, Carol Lynley will always have a morning after.

22. Film & TV Credits Listing

Theatrical and Direct-to-Video Feature Films
The Light in the Forest (Buena Vista, 1958) d. Hershel Dougherty
Holiday for Lovers (20th Century-Fox, 1959) d. Henry Levin
Blue Denim (20th Century-Fox, 1959) d. Phillip Dunne
Hound-Dog Man (20th Century-Fox, 1959) d. Don Siegel
Return to Peyton Place (20th Century-Fox, 1961) d. Jose Ferrer
The Last Sunset (Universal, 1961) d. Robert Aldrich
The Stripper (20th Century-Fox, 1963) d. Franklin J. Schaffner
Under the Yum Yum Tree (Columbia, 1963) d. David Swift
The Cardinal (Columbia, 1963) d. Otto Preminger
Shock Treatment (20th Century-Fox, 1964) d. Denis Sanders
The Pleasure Seekers (20th Century-Fox, 1964) d. Jean Negulesco
Harlow (Magna Pictures, 1965) d. Alex Segal
Bunny Lake Is Missing (Columbia, 1965) d. Otto Preminger
The Shuttered Room (Great Britain; Warner Bros.-Seven Arts, 1967) d. David Greene
Danger Route (Great Britain; United Artists, 1968) d. Seth Holt
Cotter (unreleased, 1968) d. Paul Stanley

The Maltese Bippy (MGM, 1969) d. Norman Panama
Once You Kiss a Stranger (Warner Bros.-Seven Arts, 1969) d. Robert Sparr
Norwood (Paramount, 1970) d. Jack Haley, Jr.
Beware! The Blob/Son of Blob (Jack H. Harris Enterprises, 1972) d. Larry Hagman
The Poseidon Adventure (20th Century-Fox, 1972) d. Ronald Neame
The Four Deuces (Embassy Pictures, 1975) d. William H. Bushnell
Bad Georgia Road (Dimension Pictures, 1977) d. John C. Broderick
The Washington Affair (unreleased, 1977) d. Victor Stoloff
The Cat and the Canary (Great Britain; Quartet Films, 1978) d. Radley Metzger
The Shape of Things to Come (Canada; Film Ventures International, 1979) d. George McCowan
Todos Los Dias, Una Dia (Argentina/Spain; 1980) d. Orlando Jimenez-Leal
Vigilante (Artists Releasing Corporation, 1983) d. William Lustig
Balboa (Direct-to-Video, 1986) d. James Polakof
Dark Tower (Spain; Fries Distribution Company, 1987) d. Ken Barnett (Freddie Francis & Ken Wiederhorn refused credit)
Blackout (Ambient Light Enterprises, 1988) d. Doug Adams
Spirits (American Independent Productions, 1990) d. Fred Olen Rey
Howling VI: The Freaks (Direct-to-Video, 1991) d. Hope Perello
Heartfelt (Unfinished, 1992) d. Paul S. Parco
Neon Signs (Direct-to-Video, 1996) d. Marc Kolbe
Flypaper (Trimark Pictures, 1997) [name removed from credits] d. Klaus Hoch
Drowning on Dry Land (Cargo Films, 1999) d. Carl Colpaert
A Light in the Forest (RGH/Lion Shares Pictures, 2003) d. John Carl Buechler
Vic (Short, 2006) [filmed in 1998] d. Sage Stallone

Made-for-TV Films & Episodic Guest Appearances

General Electric Theater "A Hat with Roses" d. Don Medford. May 20, 1956. CBS

Goodyear Television Playhouse "Grow Up" August 26, 1956. NBC

The Alcoa Hour "The Big Wave" d. Norman Felton. September 30, 1956. NBC

Alfred Hitchcock Presents "The Young One" d. Robert Altman. December 1, 1957. CBS

The DuPont Show of the Month "Junior Miss" d. Ralph Nelson. December 20, 1957. CBS

General Electric Theater "The Young and Scared" d. Jack Smight. May 18, 1958. CBS

Pursuit "The Vengeance" d. Herbert Hirschman. October 22, 1958. CBS

Shirley Temple's Storybook "Rapunzel" d. James Neilson. October 27, 1958. NBC

General Electric Theater "Deed of Mercy" d. James Neilson. March 1, 1959. CBS

General Electric Theater "The Last Dance" d. David Greene. November 22, 1959. CBS

Henry Fonda and the Family (special) d. Bud Yorkin. February 6, 1962. CBS

The Alfred Hitchcock Hour "Final Vow" d. Norman Lloyd. October 25, 1962. CBS

Alcoa Premiere "Whatever Happened to Miss Illinois?" November 22, 1962. ABC

The Virginian "The Man from the Sea" d. Hershel Daugherty. December 26, 1962. NBC

The Dick Powell Theatre "The Rage of Silence" d. Don Taylor. January 29, 1963. NBC

Bob Hope Presents the Chrysler Theatre "The Fliers" d. Sydney Pollack. February 5, 1965. NBC

Run for Your Life "In Search of April" d. Stuart Rosenberg. February 14, 1966. NBC

Bob Hope Presents the Chrysler Theatre "Runaway Bay" d. Stuart Rosenberg. May 25, 1966. NBC

The Man from U.N.C.L.E. "The Prince of Darkness Affair" d. Boris Sagal. October 2 & 9, 1967. NBC

The Invaders "The Believers" d. Paul Wendkos. December 5, 1967. ABC

The FBI "False Witness" d. Jesse Hibbs. December 10, 1967. ABC

Journey to the Unknown "Eve" d. Robert Stevens. September 26, 1968. ABC

The Big Valley "Hell Hath No Fury" d. Virgil W. Vogel. November 18, 1968. ABC

Shadow on the Land (TV-movie) d. Richard C. Sarafian. December 4, 1968. ABC

The Smugglers (TV-movie) d. Norman Lloyd. December 24, 1968. NBC

It Takes a Thief "Boom at the Top" d. Paul Stanley. February 25, 1969. ABC

The Immortal (TV-movie) d. Joseph Sargent. September 30, 1969. ABC

The Immortal "Sylvia" d. Don McDougall. September 24, 1970. ABC

The Bold Ones: The New Doctors "Giants Never Kneel" d. Daryl Duke. October 25, 1970. NBC

The Most Deadly Game "Who Killed Kindness?" November 7, 1970. ABC

Weekend of Terror (TV-movie) d. Jud Taylor. December 8, 1970. ABC

Mannix "Voice in the Dark" d. Paul Krasny. February 20, 1971. CBS

Crosscurrent aka *The Cable Car Murder* (TV-movie) d. Jerry Thorpe. November 19, 1971. CBS

The Night Stalker (TV-movie) d. John Llewellyn Moxey. January 11, 1972. ABC

Night Gallery "Last Rites for a Dead Druid" d. Jeannot Szwarc. January 26, 1972. NBC

The Sixth Sense "The House That Cried Murder" d. Richard Donner. February 5, 1972. ABC

Orson Welles' Great Mysteries "Death of an Old-Fashioned Girl" d. Alan Gibson. November 24, 1973. Synd.

The Magician "The Illusion of the Curious Counterfeit" d. Sutton Roley. January 14 & 21, 1974. NBC

The Evil Touch "Dear Cora, I'm Going to Kill You" d. Mende Brown. January 27, 1974. Synd.

The Elevator (TV-movie) d. Jerry Jameson. February 9, 1974. ABC

The Evil Touch "Death By Dreaming" d. Mende Brown. March 24, 1974. Synd.

Death Stalk (TV-movie) d. Robert Day. January 21, 1975. NBC

Wide World of Mystery "If It's a Man, Hang Up!" d. Shaun O'Riordan. May 5, 1975. ABC

Quincy, M.E. "Who's Who in Neverland?" d. Steven H. Stern. October 10, 1976. NBC

Police Woman "Trial By Prejudice" d. Barry Shear. October 12, 1976. NBC

Flood (TV-movie) d. Earl Bellamy. November 24, 1976. NBC

Fantasy Island (TV-movie) d. Richard Lang. January 14, 1977. ABC

Kojak "Kiss It All Goodbye" d. Telly Savalas. February 22, 1977. CBS

Fantasy Island "Lady of the Evening/The Racer" d. Don Weis. February 25, 1978. ABC

Hawaii Five-O "Angel in Blue" d. Allen Reisner. March 9, 1978. CBS

Cops and Robin (TV-movie) d. Allen Reisner. March 28, 1978. NBC

Richie Brockelman, Private Eye "A Title on the Door and a Carpet on the Floor" d. Arnold Laven. March 31, 1978. NBC

The Beasts Are on the Streets (TV-movie) d. Peter R. Hunt. May 18, 1978. NBC

Sword of Justice "The Skywayman" d. Ray Austin. October 19, 1978. NBC

Fantasy Island "Carnival/The Vaudevillians" d. Georg Stanford Brown. December 2, 1978. ABC

The Love Boat "Dream Ship/Best of Friends/Aftermath" d. George Tyne. February 10, 1979. ABC

Fantasy Island "Nobody's There/The Dancer" d. Gene Nelson. November 17, 1979. ABC

Fantasy Island "My Fair Pharaoh/The Power" d. George McCowan. May 10, 1980. ABC

Willow B: Women in Prison (pilot) d. Jeff Bleckner. June 29, 1980 ABC

Fantasy Island "The Devil and Mandy Breem/The Millionaire" d. Vince Edwards. October 25, 1980. ABC

The Littlest Hobo "Mystery at the Zoo" d. George McCowan. November 6, 1980. Synd.

Charlie's Angels "Island Angels" d. Don Chaffey. December 14, 1980. ABC

Fantasy Island "Man-Beast/Ole Island Oprey" d. George W. Brooks. May 16, 1981. ABC

The Best of Friends (special) d. Ron Satlof. August 30, 1981. Synd.

Fantasy Island "Cyrano/The Magician" d. Don Chaffey. October 24, 1981. ABC

Hart to Hart "Hartland Express" d. Dennis Donnelly. November 3, 1981. ABC

Judgement Day (pilot) d. Alan J. Levi. December 6, 1981. NBC

Fantasy Island "King Arthur in Mr. Roarke's Court/Shadow Games" d. Philip Leacock. January 23, 1982. ABC

Baker's Dozen "I Was Told You Were a Racetrack" d. Tony Mordente. April 21, 1982. CBS

Fantasy Island "The Angel's Triangle/Natchez Bound" d. Bob Sweeney. November 6, 1982. ABC

The Fall Guy "Pleasure Isle" d. Daniel Haller. October 5, 1983. ABC

Hotel "Faith, Hope & Charity" d. Alf Kjellin. November 23, 1983. ABC

Fantasy Island "Lost and Found/Dick Turpin's Last Ride" d. Bob Sweeney. April 7, 1984. ABC

Tales of the Unexpected "The Gift of Beauty" d. Bert Salzman. June 30, 1984. Synd.

Finder of Lost Loves "Forgotten Melodies" d. Bob Sweeney. December 22, 1984. ABC

Hammer House of Mystery & Suspense "In Possession" d. Val Guest. January 12, 1985. Synd.

Night Heat "Grace" d. George Mendeluk. August 11, 1987. CBS

Film & TV Credits

Another World (short-term role as Judge Martha Dunlay) August 1989. NBC
Road Show (unsold pilot) [Carol's scenes deleted] August 15, 1989. CBS.
Monsters "Stressed Environment" d. Jeffrey Wolf. September 30, 1990. Synd.

23. "Carol Lynley for the Block": Select Game Shows, Talk Shows and Other Appearances as Herself

(Broadcast dates listed are for the New York City metropolitan area)

Prize Performance
Summer 1950

A TV talent show for CBS-TV that was first hosted by Arlene Francis and then Cedric Adams. This was eight-year-old Carol Lynley's first television appearance. Her talent was dancing but she did not win the night's competition.

The Mickey Mouse Club
February 26, 1958

Carol Lynley made a brief appearance to promote her first movie *The Light in the Forest* produced by Walt Disney. She spoke about modeling and on-screen kissing with the Mouseketeers. Annette Funicello then took over introducing preview scenes shown from the movie.

I've Got a Secret
March 26, 1958

This was a special edition of the popular game show featuring only teenagers as contestants and celebrity guests. Chain-smoking Garry Moore was the host and panelists this night were Bill Cullen, Jayne Meadows, Dick Clark, and Betsy Palmer.

Poor Carol Lynley had to come on wearing a horrible pointy-nosed black mask to conceal her identity. Called "Miss X," she held up a newspaper whose headline read "Teen-Ager Wins Raves in Broadway Hit!" Moore then added that she was the star of the play *Blue Denim* easily giving away who she was making no sense for the disguise. Her secret was a connection to Jayne Meadows who thought it was the fact that Carol played the daughter of her husband Steve Allen in a TV show. However, it was that Carol's *Blue Denim* co-star Burt Brinkerhoff had worked with Jayne the previous year in *Tea and Sympathy*. Though looking adorably cute, Carol was in between performances of her play and did not get to say much before rushing off the stage to make the start of her show.

The 31ˢᵗ Academy Awards
April 6, 1959

This year the Oscar special was co-hosted by Bob Hope, David Niven, Tony Randall, Mort Sahl, Laurence Olivier, and Jerry Lewis at the RKO Pantages Theatre. Carol Lynley appeared not as a presenter, but as a model (along with other young aspiring actresses including Sandra Dee and Janet Leigh) wearing original gowns designed by Cecil Beaton who would win an Oscar that night for his costume designs for *Gigi*. She participated in a production number featuring Maurice Chevalier (who was receiving an honorary Academy Award) singing "Thank Heavens for Little Girls" to the elegantly clad Lynley and others.

The Arthur Murray Party
September 29, 1959

Dancers Arthur and Kathryn Murray, who owned a chain of dance studios, hosted this popular variety show that began in 1950. Carol Lynley was a guest during its last season on the air with her *Blue Denim* co-star Brandon deWilde, Jackie Cooper, and Carol Channing—all of whom competed in a celebrity dance contest. Merv Griffin was the guest vocalist and composer Richard Adler made an appearance.

Hostess Helen O'Connell interviews Carol Lynley on *Here's Hollywood* (NBC-TV, 1961). *From Marlin Dobbs' Collection*

Here's Hollywood
July 19, 1961

Co-host Helen O'Connell interviewed Carol Lynley about progressing from adolescent to adult. The other guest was Gene Kelly.

Stump the Stars
January 14, 1963

The retitled revival of the fifties hit game show *Pantomime Quiz* was still produced and hosted by Mike Stokey. Carol Lynley and Vincent Price were the celebrity guests who joined regulars Sebastian Cabot, Hans Conreid, Diana Dors, Beverly Garland, Richard Long, and Tommy Noonan as two teams competed in a game of charades.

The 35th Academy Awards
April 8, 1963

Carol Lynley accepted the Best Cinematography – Color Academy Award for the absent Freddie Young who won for *Lawrence of Arabia*.

Hollywood and the Stars
"Sirens, Symbols, and Glamour Girls II"
October 13, 1963

Carol Lynley is mentioned as one of the up and coming new glamour girls and a clip of her in *Under the Yum Yum Tree* is shown. Joseph Cotten narrated.

The Tonight Show Starring Johnny Carson
December 10, 1963

Carol Lynley's first noted guest appearance on this iconic late-night talk show. At this time, it was still broadcast from New York. Also guesting on this night were Larry Blyden and British comedian Dave King. Ed McMahon was the announcer and Skitch Henderson the bandleader.

Hollywood and the Stars
"Anatomy of a Movie"
February 3, 1964

A behind the scenes look at the making of the epic motion picture *The Cardinal*. Carol Lynley is seen during the shoot and in narration talking about her experience working for Otto Preminger. Narrator Joseph Cotten first states why Otto Preminger wanted the actress to not be a blonde in the movie and how her character transgressed from a sensitive young woman torn between her strict Catholic family and her love for a

Jewish boy, and how she later becomes an embittered taxi dancer with a Spanish lover.

Carol remarked that she found it easier playing scenes in a real church or home rather than on a sound stage because of its authenticity despite the crew running around and limited time at a location. She added, "Otto insisted I concentrate no matter what. That I think of my part and nothing else. This is perhaps the most important thing I learned to do on a picture."

Password
April 30, 1964

Carol Lynley, with her *Pleasure Seekers* bouffant hair style, and Jack Jones were the celebrity guests on the primetime game show hosted by Allen Ludden. Carol came out strong and got her partner to guess the first password "chief" with the clue "Indian." However, they lost the match. She also lost the second match despite her use of illegal hand gestures that got her playfully scolded by Ludden. Carol came back to win the final match and then played the Lightning Round. With her partner guessing four of the five words from her clues, she helped him win two hundred dollars.

You Don't Say!
June 29 - July 3, 1964

Hosted by Tom Kennedy, this popular daytime game show featured two teams of two (a celebrity and a contestant) who would give each other no more than three clues to help their partner sound out the name of a famous person or fictional character. It was similar to *Password*. Carol Lynley and Sal Mineo were the guests this week.

The Celebrity Game
July 26, 1964

Carl Reiner hosted this primetime quiz show, a retool of the popular fifties program *People Will Talk* and a sort of precursor to *The Hollywood Squares*. Three contestants "try to read the minds of the stars" and guess how the celebrity panel would answer morality-type questions. One player at a time would pick a celebrity and guess if they answered yes or no to the question. For the first two rounds if they all guess correctly, they win $25 each, if two guessed correctly they win $50 apiece, and if only one reads the mind of the star they take the entire $100. The final round was worth $300. Playing on this night along with Carol Lynley were Paul Ford, George Hamilton, Hedda Hopper, Oscar Levant, Della Reese, Allan Sherman, Dana Wynter, and Alan Young.

Hopper wrote about her experience in her column and remarked, "Being on 'Celebrity Game' is not only fun, but you get to know the celebrities … Allan Sherman boasted that he put Carol Lynley in show business. 'She was a fat little girl then,' said he. Well, she certainly has slimmed down to a beautiful size 6.' The quips flew so fast, Carol said it was like taking a trip to outer space."[899]

The Celebrity Game
August? 1964

Carol Lynley was back for a second go-around alongside Nick Adams, Jacques Bergerac, Paul Ford, Celeste Holm, Hedda Hopper, Oscar Levant, June Lockhart, and Allan Sherman. This episode was sponsored by the American Tobacco Company and featured ads for Tareyton and Pall Mall cigarettes. Hence, it was no surprise that Levant puffed away on cigarette and after cigarette throughout the show.

The first question was if the panel agreed with a foreign actress who claimed that American men had bad manners. Carol said no to that and no to the following question, if it was a mistake just to marry for romantic love. She added, "I think you can get into terrible trouble for marrying for romantic love, but you have a great amount of fun getting into terrible trouble." The actress received a big laugh from the audience and the panel. The last question posed to the celebrities was if a woman was more attractive if she was a little plump. The one male contestant chose no while both his female opponents said yes. Surprisingly, all the women on the panel and two of the men voted no—so much for sisterhood in 1964.

Hollywood Goes to a World Premiere
August 1964

A news featurette highlighting the world premiere of the feature film *Mary Poppins* at Grauman's Chinese Theatre. Producer Walt Disney and the musical's leads Julie Andrews and Dick Van Dyke were interviewed. Carol Lynley was one of many celebrities shown in attendance including Angie Dickinson, James Franciscus, Annette Funicello, Celeste Holm, Brian Keith, Roddy McDowall, Mary Tyler Moore, Connie Stevens, Tom Tryon, and Efrem Zimbalist, Jr.

Girl Talk
November 27, 1964

Carol Lynley was a guest on this syndicated chat show hosted by the loud, and sometimes overbearing but always entertaining, Virginia Graham. The show featured three female celebrities and Graham revealed that they do not know who they are appearing with until they arrive at the studio. The reason? "If the guests knew with whom they would be on, 60 percent of them wouldn't take part," said Graham.[900] Also, on this episode were actresses Joan Alexander and Barbara Feldon.

Hollywood '65
May 11, 1965

A local Los Angeles program hosted by John Willis eight years before he became the long-running host of the New England morning news/variety program, *Good Day!* This episode was a salute to the recently released motion picture *Harlow* from Electronovision. Producer Bill Sargent and co-stars Carol Lynley and Ginger Rogers were the guests along with Robert Goulet.

The Celebrity Game
May 15, 1965

Carol Lynley was a celebrity panelist along with Dana Andrews, Eve Arden, Phyllis Diller, Merv Griffin, Elsa Martinelli, Lee Marvin, Jan Murray, and Alan Young. One of the questions under discussion was whether if it was "unladylike for two women to fight over the same man."[901]

Reflets de Cannes
May 16, 1965

During the filming *Bunny Lake Is Missing* in London, Carol Lynley accompanied Otto Preminger to the Cannes Film Festival to promote his latest movie *In Harm's Way*. While there, they appeared on this recurring French documentary series that was "the first show of the French television about movies, and the only one dedicated to the Cannes Film Festival, by interviewing stars, and showing backstage footage devoted to the event, the gala evenings, the competing films, and everyday life in Cannes."[902] Also appearing in this episode were two of the film's leading players, Kirk Douglas and Patricia Neal, plus Olivia de Havilland, Gina Lollobrigida, and Rita Tushingham, among others.

The Celebrity Game
May 20, 1965

Carol Lynley was a celebrity panelist along with Morey Amsterdam, Angie Dickinson, Phyllis Diller, Dan Duryea, Art Linkletter, Della Reese, Charles Ruggles, and Efrem Zimbalist, Jr.

ABC's Nightlife
October 8, 1965

Hosted by Les Crane, with comedian Nipsey Russell as his Ed McMahon, this was ABC's bid to try to oust Johnny Carson as King of late-night television in this irreverent take on talk shows. Guests on this night were Carol Lynley and producer/director Otto Preminger (promoting their upcoming mystery/thriller *Bunny Lake Is Missing*), actress Lilia Skala, and actor/jazz musician Tiger Haynes.

The Mike Douglas Show
October 6, 1965

Affable Mike Douglas hosted one of the most popular and longest running variety/talk shows in daytime history. Comedienne Phyllis Diller was the co-host for this week when Carol Lynley guested to promote her new movie *Bunny Lake Is Missing*. Also appearing were the American folk band The Womenfolk.

The Young Set
October 11, 1965

As proclaimed each day in the introduction, *The Young Set* was "Today's ideas, today's stars, today's minds." A not-so-young Phyllis Kirk was the moderator, though it was reported that network executive Leonard

Goldberg really wanted Carol Lynley or Pamela Tiffin for the job. They got Carol as a guest though and on this episode she, Brandon deWilde, and Johnny Desmond revealed what it was like being child stars.

Promotional print ad for Carol Lynley's guest appearance on *The Gourmet Show* with David Wade in 1966.

Girl Talk
October 18, 1965

Carol Lynley was a guest again on Virginia Graham's chat fest joining this time Arlene Francis and Vivian Vance. The topic was "lovers."

1966 Hollywood Deb Star Ball
January 7, 1966

Originating from the Hollywood Palladium, Steve Allen and his wife Jayne

Meadows, hosted the 13th Annual Deb Star Ball showcasing the twelve most promising female newcomers (including Phyllis Davis, Sally Field, Peggy Lipton, Cheryl Miller, Melody Patterson, and Edy Williams) chosen by Hollywood's top makeup and hair stylists. Presenters included Vic Morrow, Troy Donahue, Ryan O'Neal, Ben Gazzara, Dean Jones, and Robert Reed.

Carol Lynley, a Deb Star in 1957, was presented a special award "as the former Deb Star to most fully realize the potential she showed when presented at the Ball." She likely received this recognition because she had most recently co-starred opposite acting giant Laurence Olivier in *Bunny Lake Is Missing* and more than held her own.

The Gourmet Show
October 23, 1966

David Wade was a local Dallas TV personality who found his niche in 1957 doing food demonstrations. He became popular enough to host his own weekly, local cooking show. Eventually, his show went national in syndication. He was recognized by the American Culinary Arts Society as America's leading food demonstrator and he would go on to write numerous cookbooks, beginning with *Dining with David Wade*. Carol Lynley was just one of the many celebrities (including Charlton Heston, Gregory Peck, and Robert Taylor) who stopped by to cook with Wade and share some of their favorite recipes.

ABC Stage'67
"David Frost's Night Out in London"
February 2, 1967

Producer, writer, talk show host David Frost took viewers on a "dawn-to-dusk" tour of swinging London in a convertible with on-again, off-again girlfriend Carol Lynley by his side as the sun was setting and the wind blowing. They introduced pre-taped segments with Laurence Olivier, Peter Sellers, Albert Finney, singer Libby Morris, and female impersonator Danny La Rue, among others. The special was conceived and written by *Get Smart* creator Buck Henry, John Cleese (soon of *Monty Python's Flying Circus*), and Frost.

Barbara Delatiner, reviewing the special for *Newsday*, hated it. She found LaRue to have made "the biggest impression" and facetiously remarked that Lynley "made what may have been the most profound and wittiest contribution to the evening. After an elaborate introduction from Frost, she said, 'Thank you David.' And then she giggled loud and strong. It was the giggle that was witty. Not the line of dialog."[903]

Everybody's Talking
July 17 to 21, 1967

Reported to be the last network TV show to broadcast in black-and-white, this short-lived game show was hosted by Lloyd Thaxton (*The Lloyd Thaxton Show* and founder of *Tiger Beat* magazine) with Wink Martindale and Charlie O'Donnell as the announcers. The show began with three in-house contestants trying to guess what random people on the street were describing - be it a person, place, or thing. The quicker they guessed correctly, the more money they won. In the summer, celebrities took the place of the contestants with each playing for a random viewer selected by postcard.

During this week, Tammy Grimes, Dwayne Hickman, and Pat Paulsen were the on-set guests while Carol Lynley and Frank Fontaine were on tape with the people on the street.

Host David Frost and Carol Lynley cruise the streets in "David Frost's Night Out in London" on *ABC Stage 67* (ABC-TV, 1967).

Project '68
November 11, 1967

Tony Thomas produced this series for the CBC Radio in Canada. He hosted this episode entitled "How to Be a Movie Star." One of themes discussed was how hard it was for female actors to maintain a lengthy career as compared to their male counterparts. Carol Lynley was a guest on this star-studded broadcast along with Tony Curtis, Bette Davis, Olivia de Havilland, Mia Farrow, Charlton Heston, Burt Lancaster, Maureen O'Sullivan, Barbara Stanwyck, Robert Taylor, Loretta Young, and many more.

Tony Thomas asked Lynley if "a giddy social life was a necessary part of movie success?" She replied, "I don't think so. There are a lot of people who do and it is a popular thing here to go out and be seen and maybe you'll meet that director who thinks you're absolutely right for the film he is doing next. I think it is a lot of hot air myself. I think there is a great tendency to say all Hollywood people drink too much and do other things too much and get divorced. I don't think that's true. I think you'll find perhaps a great percentage of slightly more neurotic people here." He then asked if she thought her social standing in Beverly Hills had anything to do with the parts she gets in pictures and any bearing on her career. Carol emphatically stated, "No, none whatsoever. My social standing in Beverly Hills I think is about nil. If you are going to judge that on the fact that I ever worked, I would say I was lucky that I ever worked." Carol then went on to admit that she was jaded to a degree but it was more defensive and a form of self-protection especially when a lot of people disagree with you.

The Hollywood Squares
November 13 to 17, 1967

Hosted by former actor Peter Marshall, this was one of the most popular daytime game shows of all-time and spawned a syndicated nighttime version. Nine celebrities' occupied squares in a three-story platform shaped like that of a tic-tac-toe board. Two contestants had to decide if the panelists answered various questions correctly to get the "X" or "O." Whoever obtained tic-tac-toe either vertically, horizontally, or diagonally was the winner.

Carol played the Hollywood Squares this week along with Marty Allen and Steve Rossi, Morey Amsterdam, Cliff "Charley Weaver" Arquette, Wally Cox, Abby Dalton, Monty Hall, Eartha Kitt, and Rose Marie.

The Hollywood Squares
November 20 to 24, 1967

Carol Lynley returned for a second week in a row playing along with Marty Allen and Steve Rossi, Morey Amsterdam, Cliff "Charley Weaver"

Arquette, Wally Cox, Abby Dalton, Janis Paige, Rose Marie, and William Shatner.

The Joey Bishop Show
February 1, 1968

Joey Bishop had his own late-night talk show for three seasons on ABC up against NBC's powerhouse *The Tonight Show Starring Johnny Carson*. Carol appeared on this night along with Bishop's sidekick Regis Philbin, George Burns, Frankie Valli, and jazz pianist Erroll Garner.

Dee Time
June 22, 1968

Carol Lynley was a guest on this live BBC talk show hosted by former radio disc jockey Simon Dee.

The Tonight Show Starring Johnny Carson
November 13, 1968

Johnny Carson did a week of shows in Los Angeles. Carol Lynley took a seat on the couch along with future co-stars Dan Rowan and Dick Martin (prior to making *The Maltese Bippy*), Robert Wagner, Dinah Shore, and the 1968 Olympic decathlon champion Bill Toomey.

KCET Auction
April 22-26, 1969

Local public television station KCET in Los Angeles hosted its first ever on-air auction to raise money to support the network. Airing Tuesday through Saturday from 6 p.m. to midnight, items up for purchase included "everything from a mink coat to a house in Mexico to a rib roast." Even a thoroughbred horse was on the list. Carol Lynley was one of the celebrity auctioneers along with Steve Allen, Anne Baxter, Dick Clark, Buddy Ebsen, Henry Fonda, Henry Gibson, Tippi Hedren, Marty Ingels, Michael Jackson, and others.

The Movie Game
November 17 thru 21, 1969

Sonny Fox originally hosted this syndicated celebrity panel show pitting two teams of three celebrities against each other testing their knowledge of movie history. Playing along with Carol Lynley were Louis Nye, Agnes Moorehead, Rudy Vallee, and series' regular Army Archerd, among others.

Promotional photo for *The Movie Game* (Henry Jaffe Enterprises, 1969) with (seated) Rudy Vallee, Carol Lynley, Louis Nye, and Agnes Moorehead. Standing: Host Sonny Fox and Army Archerd. *From Marlin Dobbs' Collection*

The David Frost Show
December 15, 1969

The popular British talk show host had his own American syndicated series that lasted from 1969 to 1972. His on-again, off-again paramour Carol Lynley sat down for a chat along with Muhammed Ali, Molly Picon, Myrna Loy, and novelist John Updike.

The Merv Griffin Show
July 16, 1971

Carol Lynley was a guest on Merv Griffin's late-night talk show on CBS opposite NBC's *The Tonight Show Starring Johnny Carson*. Also appearing were Teresa Graves, Ron Ely, Jack Jones, and Desi Arnaz, Jr.

The Merv Griffin Show
September 10, 1971

Carol Lynley guested along with Trini Lopez, Laurence Harvey, and Joe Flynn.

The 4th Annual NAACP Image Awards
November 21, 1971

Not fully televised, this year's ceremony honoring achievements by African Americans in film, television, and music was hosted by Bobby Darin and Denise Nicholas of TV's *Room 222*. The impressive roster of presenters included Jim Brown, Diana Ross, Isaac Hayes, Gail Fisher, Cicely Tyson, Marvin Gaye, Clarence Williams III, Richard Roundtree, and Judy Pace. Why Carol Lynley was a presenter is a mystery, but she announced the award for Television Show of the Year. The winner was *Mannix* and producer Ivan Goff was on hand to accept.

The Tonight Show Starring Johnny Carson
December 13, 1971

Carol Lynley returned to the show, now broadcast from the NBC studios in Burbank, California. Ed McMahon was still the announcer but Doc Severinsen had taken over as bandleader. David Steinberg was this night's substitute host and other guests were advice-columnist Amy Vanderbilt, *Fiddler on the Roof* actor Leonard Frey, basketball player Earl "the Pearl" Monroe, and impressionist David Frye.

The Merv Griffin Show
April 3, 1972

Carol Lynley was a guest during the first season of Merv Griffin's show that moved from CBS late night to syndication. Other guests included Joe Flynn, hair stylist George Masters, and Anne Marie Bennstrom, the cofounder of the spiritual retreat Ashram.

The Democratic National Telethon
July 8-9, 1972

This was a nineteen-hour nationwide telethon organized by John Y. Brown, Jr., chairman of Kentucky Fried Chicken, after President Nixon blocked a proposed dollar checkoff by taxpayers to finance presidential campaigns.[904] It was a fundraiser for the Democratic Party. Carol Lynley was part of the star-studded event along with Paul Anka, Burt Bacharach, Carol Burnett, James Caan, James Darren, Angie Dickinson, Henry Fonda, Charlton Heston, Dean Jones, Jack Lemmon, June Lockhart, Gregory Peck, Debbie Reynolds, Roger Staubach, Connie Stevens, Leslie Uggams, Dionne Warwick, Shelley Winters, and more.

The Other Side of the Stars
July 22, 1972

This syndicated special featured informal interviews with celebrities Carol Lynley, Jackie Cooper, Johnny Mathis, and Jo Anne Worley.

The Tonight Show Starring Johnny Carson
August 29, 1972

Joey Bishop filled in as host with this evening's guests Carol Lynley, Dr. Joyce Brothers, comedian Rip Taylor, and vocalist Lou Rawls.

Return of the Movie Movie
Fall 1972

Promotional documentary on the making of *The Poseidon Adventure* directed and written by Andrew J. Kuehn. Carol Lynley and her co-stars appeared as did producer Irwin Allen, director Ronald Neame, and others.

The Santa Claus Lane Parade
November 21, 1972

Broadcast live in Hollywood, but syndicated throughout the rest of the country, the annual star-studded parade's theme this year was the "Toys and Joys of Christmas." Down a one mile stretch of Hollywood Boulevard, bands, floats, animals, and celebrities came forth to celebrate the holiday season. The Grand Marshall this year was Gen. Robert E. Cushman, Jr. of the Marine Corps. Celebrities participating along with Carol Lynley were her *Poseidon Adventure* co-star Gene Hackman, Elizabeth Ashley, Pat Boone, Zsa Zsa Gabor, Cesar Romero, the Supremes, Yul Brynner, and Samantha Eggar, among others.

The Earle Doud Radio Show
December 1972

Earle Doud was a comedy writer/producer and sometime actor who had his own radio show broadcast on WOR in New York. Carol Lynley guested before the premiere of *The Poseidon Adventure* to promote her new movie.

The Lilian Reynolds Show
December 12, 1972

Out there promoting *The Poseidon Adventure*, Carol appeared on this radio talk show broadcast live on WHBI from Lilian Reynolds' apartment.

The Mike Douglas Show
December 21, 1972

Singer Eddy Arnold was the co-host for this week when Carol Lynley guested to promote her new movie *The Poseidon Adventure*. Also appearing were humorist Leo Rosten, 11-year-old banjo player Scotty Plummer, and comedian Jerry Clower.

The Poseidon Adventure Premiere
December 21, 1972

This taped TV special covered the live New York premiere of *The Poseidon Adventure* at the brand-new National Theater in Times Square on December 13 for syndication. Carol Lynley (accompanied by publicist Bobby Zarem) was in attendance along with co-stars Red Buttons, Shelley Winters, producer Irwin Allen and many other celebrities including Joan Fontaine.

The Dick Richards Show
January 15, 1973

Continuing stumping for *The Poseidon Adventure*, Carol appeared on this radio talk show broadcast on WHBI.

The Tonight Show Starring Johnny Carson
January 18, 1973

Carol Lynley and Ernest Borgnine appeared together to promote their new, smash hit movie *The Poseidon Adventure*. Bandleader Artie Shaw, Eubie Blake, and Pfc. John Williams also guested on this night. Unlike her two previous appearances, Johnny Carson was hosting.

Ed McMahon was off, so Doc Severinsen filled in for him as announcer and on the couch, while Tommy Newsom took over for Doc as band leader. Surprisingly, Williams, a champion archer, was the first guest and demonstrated his archery skills before trying to teach Carson how to handle a bow and arrow.

Lynley, clad in a white lacey maxi dress, was the second guest and was interviewed through two commercial breaks. Here, and with her future appearances, she seemed to ignore Doc and later Ed McMahon, and did not greet them. She immediately had the audience laughing when Johnny mentioned that he was offered to do a touring production of a play with her. The only play Carol had toured with up to this point in time was *Anniversary Waltz* when she was twelve. She assumed he meant that and he was offered the part of her father. Johnny feigned indignation and the audience howled. Carol sheepishly said, "I think I made a terrible mistake." The play was *Under the Yum Yum Tree*, which Carol recalled she turned down more recently but could not remember why. To counter her blunder, Carol apologetically replied, "I'm not young enough to play your daughter. How is that?" At the time Carol was approaching her thirty-first birthday and Carson was forty-seven years old.

Besides talking about *The Poseidon Adventure*, which monopolized most of the interview, they also talked about aging. Carol confessed that she liked growing older because "I find myself much more relaxed. I find myself liking people much more and having a better time." Hunching her shoulders, she added, "When I was younger, I was much more afraid of everything."

Johnny also asked Carol if she studied acting. Carol said that she had never taken classes but since working from the age of ten, acting opposite the likes of Laurence Olivier, Noël Coward, Ernest Borgnine, Gene Hackman, and others was her acting class. She never retreated to her dressing room when not in a scene and would remain on set to watch and learn from them. She then remarked, "I want to have a career at 82." To achieve her goal she continued, "You have to be good at what you do. You have to grow and develop."

You could tell that Johnny Carson was really taken with the vivacious beauty. He told the audience that during the commercial break, Carol apologized again for thinking he was old enough to play her father. He thought it was funny and was not insulted in the least. And he paid her a most flattering compliment when he said, "You are such a refreshing guest and seem to speak your mind" to which she replied, "I do—sometimes to a fault." No doubt that was regarding her notorious Earl Wilson interview about Red Buttons. The favorable impression Carol made on Carson (she was not an egotistical self-promoter unlike other actors) possibly explains why she was invited back on the show another three times in 1973.

Ernest Borgnine followed Lynley to Johnny's couch and he told Carol that in the morning he was watching her on TV in the movie she made with Clifton Webb. He thought she was "radiant." Carol was a bit embarrassed and said seeing that film (*Holiday for Lovers*) for her was like looking at "baby pictures."

When bandleader Artie Shaw came out after Borgnine, he referenced Johnny's discussion with Carol that her studio bio claimed that she was "a compulsive self-improver." Carol was not happy about that because she felt it made her sound like someone who was not happy with herself and always changing. Shaw disagreed with Carol's assessment and they got into a spirited discussion with poor Ernie Borgnine sitting between them in silence. Both agreed they were driven and needed to be working.

The 30th Annual Golden Globe Awards
January 28, 1973

Golden Globe Awards were rewarded for the best in film and television for 1972. Carol Lynley (riding high with *The Poseidon Adventure*) was a presenter along with Desi Arnaz, Jr., Charles Bronson, Carol Burnett, James Caan, Dyan Cannon, Richard Chamberlain, Chad Everett, Eva Gabor, Gene Hackman, Florence Henderson, Jill Ireland, Walter Matthau, Diana Ross, Marlo Thomas, Trish Van Devere, and Robert Young.

Per Joyce Haber, actor Bud Cort was Carol's escort to the awards ceremony and the actress was clad "in gray satin á la Harlow with nothing under it; on her it looked good."[905]

The Tonight Show Starring Johnny Carson
February 23, 1973

Carol Lynley made a return appearance a little more than a month after her previous time on the couch. She guested along with McLean Stevenson, singer Harry Chapin, and novelist Joseph Wambaugh. Ed McMahon was back and Doc Severinson was leading the band.

Coming out after Stevenson, she wore what looked like a navy-blue velour skirt with a light blue blouse. Johnny immediately brought up *The Poseidon Adventure*. The conversation then veered all over the map from suitors (Carol revealed that one unnamed guy [Oliver Reed] gave her a crate of apples and they stayed together for two years), to the recent LA earthquake, where Carol was alone in bed when it struck, to Johnny saying he read that Carol never wanted to remarry because of the paper work. She copped to it and explained that people were forever getting certificates to prove their existence from birth through death. She had no qualms living with a man but was not going to make it legal due to the hassle.

However, the most outrageous comments Carol made were about the author (Esther Vilar whose name was never mentioned) who wrote the book *The Manipulated Male*. Carson brought her up since she was a recent guest. An indignant Lynley said if she was on his show that night, she'd "punch her in the nose. She was so insulting towards women." One point that angered Carol so was that Vilar felt that women had it easy staying home while their husbands went off to work every day.

Dinah's Place
May 4, 1973

Carol Lynley was the main guest on Dinah Shore's daytime talk show on NBC.

The Tonight Show Starring Johnny Carson
August 10, 1973

Carol Lynley was a guest along with Joey Bishop, country singer/songwriter Mac Davis, and actor/comedian Marty Brill. Clad in a stunning, casual, flowing, light blue gown holding an ivory cigarette holder, Carol came on second after Bishop.

There was a brief mention that *The Poseidon Adventure* was amazingly still playing in theaters eight months after it opened in December of 1972, but that was it. Carson asked Carol about the gardenia pinned to her dress and she told him it was not real. He then made a joke about girls on prom night racing home to get their gardenias in the refrigerator before they turned brown.

Carol talked about a road trip she took with seven friends who all piled into a big camper and traveled to Colorado and New Mexico. She thought they would be camping under the stars, but they stayed at motels along the way. Trying to act sophisticated, though looking like a little girl, Lynley asked for a light to smoke her cigarette and immediately started gagging. Carson snatched it away and jokingly scolded her, as the audience and Carol laughed.

Carol also brought along a painting she had created. It was a point-of-view scene from the eyes of a child on one side of a fence, looking at a tall sunflower on the other side growing near the beach. Carson thought it was an oil painting, but Carol revealed it was acrylic with real sand mixed in for the beach section. At first glance it looked simplistic, but after Carol explained her process it took on a new perspective in the eye of the beholder. Her time with Johnny was limited to just the one commercial break.

The Tonight Show Starring Johnny Carson
September 20, 1973

Carol Lynley returned to the show making her second guest appearance with Harry Chapin. It was also her fourth and last time on the show in 1973. Other guests were Orson Bean, child actor Ricky Segall, and musical performer Monti Rock.

Carol came on fourth after Segall, Bean and Chapin and once again only spoke with Carson between one commercial break. She wore a lovely silver satin gown ("It's like wearing butter," she quipped) with the same gardenia pinned to it from her previous time on the show. And Carson made the exact same comment about girls wearing them to the prom.

Carol really had nothing to say professionally other than she was headed to London to do an episode of *Orson Welles' Great Mysteries* and then traveling to Ireland to spend time with her family. She shared her love of going to flea markets and swap meets (where she found her gown) and another great find—a jeweled necklace she paid $40 for that was worth thousands. They also talked men's fashions such as Zoot suits, platform shoes, and clogs. It was a laid-back unexciting interview and the least enthralling of her appearances.

The Hollywood Squares
December 24 to 28, 1973

For this holiday week Carol joined Marty Allen, Cliff "Charley Weaver" Arquette, James Brolin, James Coco, John Davidson, Paul Lynde, Joan Rivers, and Karen Valentine.

The Hollywood Squares
February 11 to 15, 1974

Carol Lynley appeared this week with Marty Allen, Cliff "Charley Weaver" Arquette, James Brolin, John Davidson, George Gobel, Paul Lynde, Rose Marie, and Lily Tomlin.

The Hollywood Squares
May 4, 1974

Carol Lynley made an appearance on the nighttime version of the popular game show along with Edward Asner, Pearl Bailey, Ernest Borgnine, Mike Connors, Buddy Hackett, Paul Lynde, Suzanne Pleshette, and Karen Valentine.

The Hollywood Squares
November 25 to 29, 1974

Carol Lynley guested this week along with Jack Albertson, John Davidson, George Gobel, George Hamilton, Florence Henderson, Paul Lynde, Joan

Rivers, and Karen Valentine.

The Hollywood Squares
December 12, 1974

Carol Lynley returned to the nighttime version of the game show this time with John Davidson, Dom DeLuise, Sally Field, George Gobel, George Kennedy, Paul Lynde, Roddy McDowall, and Joan Rivers

Empathy
March 19, 1975

Carol Lynley and James Earl Jones guested on this WWDC radio talk show from Washington DC to discuss working on stage in *Of Mice and Men*.

Movie Talk
August 3, 1975

Carol Lynley and Anthony Perkins were guests on this WMCA radio talk program hosted by Julian Schlossberg.

Back Stage with Carol Lynley
August 17, 1975

This WNYC radio special program featured Carol Lynley backstage at the Music Box Théâtre as she prepared for a performance of the hit Broadway comedy *Absurd Person Singular*.

Casper Citron Viewpoint
August 21, 1975

Carol Lynley spoke with Casper Citron on his nationally syndicated radio talk show broadcast from the Algonquin Hotel on WQXR in New York. His other guest this day was Polish pianist, composer, and conductor Ignace Strasfogel.

The Steve and Judy Show
August 23 & 30, 1975

Carol Lynley was the lone guest on this fifteen-minute radio chat show that broadcast on WHBI during the early evening drive time. Her interview was split into two parts.

The Joey Adams Show
September 8, 1975

Carol Lynley of *Absurd Person Singular*, and Donna Theodore and John Cullum of *Shenandoah* were guests on the comedian's daily radio program broadcast on WEVD.

The Toppers
September 23, 1975

Carol Lynley was the sole guest on the premiere of this new morning radio interview and talk show on WHBI.

The Critic's Circle
October 20, 1975

Entertainment journalist Jack O'Brian hosted this daily radio interview show for WOR-AM. Carol Lynley was a guest on this day along with actress Dorothy Stickney and Paul Myers, Chief of the Billy Rose Theatre Collection at the New York Public Library.

Not for Women Only
October 22, 1975

This was a topical, syndicated talk show hosted by Barbara Walters. Hugh Downs originally joined as co-host. He hosted solo on this day with guests Carol Lynley and Julius Fast, author of *Body Language* discussing self-assertion.

Hollywood Profiles
Fall 1975

Carol Lynley was a guest on Dick Strout's syndicated radio show taped at KTLA studios in Los Angeles.

The Tonight Show Starring Johnny Carson
November 28, 1975

Carol Lynley's last known appearance on *The Tonight Show* was sans Johnny Carson. McLean Stevenson was the fill-in host and other guests were Marvin Hamlisch, Steve Allen, country singer Larry Gatlin, and Jim Moran.

Almost Anything Goes!
January or February 1976

This was the American version of the popular British series *It's a Knockout*. Three teams consisting of residents of the same town from the south, east, and west regions of the country competed against each other in a series of outrageous events. The winning team would move on to the next round of competition until a tournament champion team was crowned. Each event was titled such as "Spring Cleaning" (housewives race to complete exaggerated chores) and "Easy Riders" (players shoot balls at baskets mounted on moving bicycles).[906]

Sportscasters Charlie Jones and Lynn Shackleford called the play-by-play, with producer Sam Riddle and Regis Philbin reporting from the field. A different celebrity coach was assigned to each team every week. Reportedly, a very energetic Carol Lynley was coach of the blue team when she appeared. Unfortunately, there was no other information uncovered about her appearance.

Gourmet Gala Cook-Off
October 6, 1976

Celebrities came out to demonstrate their cooking expertise in this fundraiser for the March of Dimes held in the Grand Ballroom at the Waldorf Astoria. Carol Lynley whipped up a braised berry dessert. Other participants included Betsy Bloomingdale, baseball player Rusty Staub, and theater producer Lee Guber. Highlights were aired on local New York City newscasts.

Hostess Dinah Shore with guests Joshua Logan, William Holden, Lee Marvin, and Carol Lynley on *Dinah!* (CBS Television, 1976).

Dinah!
December 17, 1976

Dinah Shore hosted this popular, syndicated daytime talk show the year after NBC cancelled *Dinah's Place* in 1973. This episode was a celebration of director Joshua Logan. Guests paying tribute were Carol Lynley (whom he directed on Broadway in *Blue Denim*), William Holden, Lee Marvin, Mary Martin, and Ray Walston.

Junior Almost Anything Goes!
March 6, 1977

Hosted by Soupy Sales, this was a Saturday morning kids' version of the primetime adult game show *Almost Anything Goes!* airing on ABC. Children competed each week in some bizarre competitions using a variety of food, grease, paint, etc. This week's coaches were Carol Lynley, Louis Nye, and Sugar Ray Robinson.

The Hollywood Squares
October 24, 1977

Carol Lynley appeared on the primetime *Hollywood Squares* along with Wayland Flowers and Madame, Paul Lynde, McLean Stevenson, Leslie Uggams, Dick Van Patten, Abe Vigoda, Paul Williams, and Jonathan Winters.

The Hollywood Squares
December 5 to 9, 1977

Carol Lynley returned to play the daytime *Hollywood Squares* along with Diana Canova, David Doyle, Wayland Flowers and Madame, George Gobel, Paul Lynde, Martin Mull, Joan Rivers, and Dick Van Patten.

Commenting on why she was such a frequent guest on the game show, Carol remarked during the seventies, "It's a nice way to make money. You're paid $1,000 for about two hours work. You're briefed on areas but nobody is given the foolish questions. Paul Lynde's answers are usually spontaneous. He always had a quick wit."[907]

The Hollywood Squares
January 2, 1978

Carol Lynley was back on the primetime *Hollywood Squares* along with John Byner, Wayland Flowers and Madame, Lorne Greene, Paul Lynde, McLean Stevenson, Leslie Uggams, Paul Williams, and Jonathan Winters.

The Paul Ryan Show
1978

Carol Lynley was the sole guest on Paul Ryan's Los Angeles cable access program one night in 1978.

Celebrity Challenge of the Sexes
March 7, 1978

Needing a show to compete with the hugely popular *Happy Days* on ABC, CBS decided to make the recurring specials, *Celebrity Challenge of the Sexes*, a weekly series beginning in late January. Each week, male and female celebrities would compete against each other in various solo sporting events. The program was hosted by former sports director Tom Brookshier and featured McLean Stevenson as coach of the men and Barbara Rhoades as coach of the women. It was filmed at Saddleback College in Mission Viejo over a series of weekends.

Carol Lynley hit the bowling lanes matched against Carl Reiner. A ratings disaster, this was the last episode televised.

The Hollywood Squares
April 10 to 14, 1978

Carol Lynley appeared this week with Gary Burghoff, Norman Fell, Melissa Gilbert, George Gobel, Florence Henderson, David L. Lander, Paul Lynde, and Joan Rivers.

The Mike Douglas Show
July 6, 1978

Actress Sandy Duncan was Mike Douglas' co-host for the week and the guests on this day included Carol Lynley (demonstrating some of her ballet dance movements with Sandy and Mike), Elliot Gould, Ronnie Schell, Samantha Song, and Marilyn French.

Good Morning America
January 15, 1979

This ABC morning news/entertainment program was co-anchored by David Hartman and Sandy Hill at the time. Carol Lynley was the lite celebrity guest this morning since also appearing were Andrew Young, the U.S. ambassador to the United Nations and Governor George Wallace of Alabama.

The 21st Annual Grammy Awards
February 15, 1979

Hosted by John Denver, it is a mystery why Carol Lynley was asked to be a presenter since she had nothing to do with the music industry. Perhaps it had to do with on-again boyfriend David Frost who also presented? Other performers and presenters on this night included Frankie Avalon, the Bee Gees, Debby Boone, Natalie Cole, Neil Diamond, Quincy Jones, Kris Kristofferson, Chuck Mangione, Barry Manilow, Lou Rawls, Kenny Rogers, Barbra Streisand, Donna Summer, Frankie Valli, Dionne Warwick, and Paul Williams.

All Star Secrets
March 5 to 9, 1979

Hosted by Bob Eubanks, five celebrities would share confidences with the producers, and it was up to three contestants to guess which secret belong to which celebrity. The contestant who garnered the most money would win a special prize. The show aired from January through August 1979. Carol Lynley appeared this week along with Kaye Ballard, Ken Berry, Rex Reed, and Wolfman Jack.

The Hollywood Squares
March 12 to 16, 1979

Carol Lynley's last reported appearance on the game show was with Foster Brooks, Mike Connors, Mary Crosby, Antonio Fargas, Jayne Kennedy, Paul Lynde, John McCook, and Jerry Stiller & Anne Meara.

Carol, wearing a coral blouse and sitting in the left middle square, was the secret square on March 12 and was called on four times. One of the questions asked her was 'when do most couples make love?'. She chose at 10:35 p.m. and was correct. The rest she got wrong, including if Jack Palance and Shelley Winters had the record for loudest screen kiss (she said false but it was true) and what type of man makes the most faithful mate (Carol went with the leg man but it was ones who admires derrieres, per a University of Illinois study).

Easter Seal Telethon
March 24-25, 1979

The Easter Seals is a nonprofit corporation founded to help children and adults with disabilities through a variety of assorted services. They organized a televised fundraiser every year. This telethon originated from KTLA in Los Angeles and was hosted by Jack Klugman, Vic Tayback, and Don Kirshner with LeVar Burton as co-host. Carol Lynley pitched in to raise money for the cause on this night along with Peter Allen, Joyce DeWitt, Kevin Dobson, Glenn Ford, Wolfman Jack, Bruce Jenner, Peter Marshall, Robert Mulligan, Tony Orlando, Connie Stevens, Donna Summer, and Jon Voight, among many others. On April 14, 1979, the Easter Seals announced that they had raised $12.6 million - up 64% from 1978. It ran for twenty hours beginning Saturday night into Sunday afternoon.

The 51st Annual Academy Awards
April 9, 1979

This year's ceremony, which would go on to win the Emmy Award for Best Variety Special, was executive produced by Jack Haley, Jr. and directed by Marty Pasetta. Johnny Carson hosted, and the presenters were literally a Who's Who of Hollywood's past and present. Besides Carol Lynley, other celebrities handing out the golden Oscar included Lauren Bacall, Warren Beatty, Robby Benson, Ray Bolger, Yul Brynner, George Burns, James Coburn, Francis Ford Coppola, Dom DeLuise, Richard Dreyfuss, Mia Farrow, Cary Grant, Jack Haley, Audrey Hepburn, Shirley Jones, Margot Kidder, Kris Kristofferson, Ali MacGraw, Shirley MacLaine, Dean Martin, Steve Martin, Kim Novak, Gregory Peck, Valerie Perrine, Christopher Reeves, Ginger Rogers, Diana Ross, Telly Savalas, Ricky Schroder, Brooke Shields, John Wayne, Raquel Welch, Robin Williams, David L. Wolper, and Natalie Wood.

Lynley was escorted to the ceremony by David Frost during their on-again romantic period. Always a knockout, Carol looked smashing on this night clad in an aqua blue, "satin bustier-styled" gown with a slit up the middle and carrying "an embroidered Oriental jacket." Carol flashed a lot of skin with her bosom and legs on display. However, her dress was elegant and not trashy in the least. The color brought out her blue eyes and beautifully contrasted with her shoulder length blonde hair. Not surprisingly, she wound up on many of the Best Dressed lists for this night. Writing in the book *The Complete Book of Oscar Fashion*, author Reeve Chace said that Carol, "rachets up the fashion meter in this brilliant aqua gown, which features a high slit and gathered bodice."

Carol, alongside Robby Benson, presented the awards for Best Short Film – Animated and Best Short Film – Live Action. Johnny Carson introduced the pair remarking, "Now to present the awards for Best Short Subjects, two stars that began acting at the ages of five and ten and between them they have thirty-seven years' experience. You figure it out. Here they are Carol Lynley and Bobby Benson." After Carson's obvious mistake with Benson's name, you can then hear someone saying, "Robby." After the duo read the nominees for the first award, Carol says, as she ripped open the envelope, "And the winner is—I love doing this—the winner is *Special Delivery*."

3rd Annual Circus of the Stars
June 20, 1979

This edition featured ringmasters Lauren Bacall, Sammy Davis, Jr., Jerry Lewis, Anthony Newley, and Bernadette Peters. Carol wore a lovely, bright blue sequined leotard as she led a group of horses through their paces. Other celebrities under the big top this night were Charo, Gary Collins, Jaime Lee Curtis, Tony La Bianco, Lee Meriwether, Mary Ann Mobley, Valerie Perrine, Martin Sheen, and Betty White, among others.

Quest of Quests
September 19, 1979

In 1979, the press reported that Carol Lynley was going to be a judge at the Miss Universe pageant in Australia but that never came to be. However, she was invited Down Under to judge their Country's popular pageant, Quest of Quests, which was sponsored by the department store chain Waltons. Carol remarked at the time, "This may sound odd but, do you know, I've never seen a beauty contest?" Twelve finalists from various local pageants vied to become Australia's entry into the Miss World competition held in London that year. The event was televised from Albert Hall in Canberra and reportedly watched by three million viewers. Women's organizations protested outside, due to the Miss World's decision to promote the bikini during the swimsuit competition. Nevertheless, the pageant went on and seventeen-year-old Jodie Day of Brisbane was crowned the winner.

The Greatest Show on Earth
February 1, 1980

Actor Michael Landon and his family hosted this NBC primetime special highlighting the best of Ringling Bros. and Barnum & Bailey Circus. The show featured cameo appearances from such celebrities as Carol Lynley, Arlene Dahl, Alice Ghostley, Donny Osmond, Ann Reinking, Joan Rivers, Joe Torre, and Henny Youngman.

The American Movie Awards
February 11, 1980

This was the first televised awards show from the National Association of Theater Owners. The ceremony (produced by Jack Haley, Jr. and David Frost) was co-hosted by Angie Dickinson, Dudley Moore, and Frost with Susan Anton the lone musical entertainer. Favorite movies and performers were selected by moviegoers from across the country. Considering who the producers were, it should be no surprise that Carol Lynley would make an appearance. Presenters included Peter Falk, Tony Franciosa, William Holden, Christopher Lee, Jack Lemmon, Rita Moreno, Ricky Schroder, Suzanne Somers, Donna Summer, and Donald Sutherland. Burt Reynolds and Jane Fonda were named Favorite Actor and Actress and Clint Eastwood received a special award for career achievement.

"Carol Lynley for the Block"

Carol Lynley modeling the gown Grace Kelly wore in the film *To Catch a Thief* on the TV special *Omnibus* (Marble Arch Productions, 1980).

Omnibus
June 15, 1980

This ABC-TV special was producer Bob Shanks' attempt at reviving the once popular series that aired on CBS and NBC in the fifties. It was known for being a classy informational entertainment/arts program covering all forms of stage, dance, music, etc. This special was hosted by Hal Holbrook and followed that format with performances from the New York City Ballet and Sandy Duncan in *Peter Pan*, among others.

One of the segments was a tribute to Academy Award fashion designer Edith Head with actresses (including Carol Lynley, Valerie Perrine, Yvette Mimieux, Jill St. John, Cindy Williams, and Linda Gray) clad in some of her iconic movie costumes. Carol modeled the Marie Antoinette gown worn by Grace Kelly in *To Catch a Thief*. The network decided not to pick up *Omnibus* as a weekly series.

Dance Fever
November 15, 1980

Choreographer Deney Terrio, best known for teaching John Travolta his dance moves in the hit movie *Saturday Night Fever*, hosted this weekly dance competition. Carol was one of the celebrity judges, along with Avery Schreiber and Ronnie Schell, this night. Guest musical performers were Two Tons o'Fun before they became The Weather Girls.

A dancer herself, Carol was stoked to be appearing on the program per journalist David Alexander who wrote. "Carol Lynley sits in a Beverly Hills restaurant looking self-assured and … ecstatic. In fact, she seems to be glowing as if she were a 20-year-old actress who had just landed her first starring role. What is exciting this veteran of Broadway, television, and … feature films is her scheduled appearance that night on the syndicated dance show *Dance Fever*. After being idled by the then four-week-old actors' strike, Carol is going back to work."[908]

Richard Thomas American Dance Foundation Benefit
May 18, 1981

Actor Richard Thomas, of *The Waltons* fame, headlined this fundraiser at the Beacon Theatre in New York City for the organization founded and operated by his father. Carol Lynley performed a dance number as did James Coco and cast members from *Sophisticated Ladies* and *Barnum*. Not televised in full, portions turned up on local newscasts.

The Third New York Big Laff Off
September 12, 1982

Robert Klein hosted this Showtime comedy special featuring five relatively unknown standup comics vying for a $5,000 prize and a talk show appearance. The program was taped live at the Copacabana in May. The finalists were Rob Bartlett, Joe Bolster, Ron Darian, Carol Siskind, and Steve Sweeney. The celebrity judges' panel consisted of Carol Lynley, Phyllis Newman, Tony Roberts, and Lee Salomon of the William Morris Agency.

March of Dimes National Telethon
July 3-4, 1983

The March of Dimes annual two-day telethon to raise money to prevent birth defects was co-hosted this year by Hal Linden, Mary Ann Mobley, Sarah Purcell, Gary Collins, and Carol Lynley, among others.

The Joan Fontaine Show
ca. 1986-1989

The acclaimed, Academy Award winning actress hosted her own half-hour chat show on public cable access in New York from the late seventies until the mid-eighties. Carol Lynley was a sometime substitute hostess and when Fontaine left New York, she took over for a brief time before the show ended. Carol recalled, "John Springer [a publicist and then founder of John Springer Associates] called me and asked if I could fill in for Joan who couldn't do her show one day. I said yes because I liked John a lot. I did a couple of them and found I liked interviewing people. It was fun. I got B.D. Wong the day after he won the Tony Award. The director got sick and they discontinued it."[909]

Star's Table
September 5, 1986

Originating from the Roosevelt Hotel in Hollywood, former *Entertainment Tonight* reporter Dixie Whatley hosted this CBN Cable Network talk show with a different weekly co-host. Carol Lynley and Allen Fawcett were the guests on this day with co-host Monty Hall, former game show host of *Let's Make a Deal*.

The Dr. Ruth Show
May 15, 1987

Noted sex therapist Dr. Ruth Westheimer hosted this advice show on the Lifetime cable channel. Each episode featured a sole celebrity guest. Among the topics discussed with Carol Lynley were how dishing the sexual dirt helps sell celebrity memoirs and why the actress would not go there with hers if she decided to write one.

The Joe Franklin Show
1988

Carol Lynley guested on the long-running, syndicated talk fest alongside good friend and actress Sally Kirkland and Los Angeles Century Cable Public Access host Mr. Pete.

The Joe Franklin Show
December 31, 1989

This rollicking New Year's Eve episode saw the return of Sally Kirkland (whom Joe called his "co-host") and Carol Lynley joined by George Maharis. In her introduction of Carol, Sally revealed that they had been friends since modeling together as children and just gushed over Lynley. You could tell they really had a loving friendship.

With Sally holding up to the camera stills from Carol's various movies, Lynley discussed a variety of topics including some of the icons she worked with such as Dame Sybil Thorndike, Noël Coward, Geraldine Page, and Laurence Olivier. When Franklin asked if Olivier was a stiff Brit, Lynley exclaimed, "He wasn't stiff at all—quite the opposite. He insisted we call him Larry." The tragic death of Gig Young was brought up and, being a huge Jean Harlow fan, Franklin asked about making the movie *Harlow* and if she ever met Carroll Baker. Coincidentally, she had just the night before. "We laughed. We cried. And I told her I have been signing autographs for her for years."

Joe asked her if she liked working in film or on stage more. Keeping to her past preference, Carol replied, "I prefer the camera. I really get off on the camera. I really do. It's an ego thing, I feel the heat and I like it." When Franklin questioned if she had lost out on any roles she really wanted, she said, "About fifteen to twenty. A couple I turned down. Shouldn't have." He then asked if it was a mistake and she shrieked, "*Mistake*!?! Mistake is not the word!" Obviously, the role of Valene on *Dallas* must have been going through her mind.

Carol promoted her new movie *Blackout* that was now available in video stores and said she played a real baddie. She then went on to say how lucky she was to play a variety of roles from nuns to killers and was glad she was never typecast. Sally said today she looked like a Botticelli angel. Carol also mentioned her talk show and said she would love to interview Joe on it. He agreed. Sally interjected and said she just appeared on it ("I think I wore black leather").

George Maharis came out next and when speaking of Inger Stevens mentioned that he worked with Carol on an episode of his TV series *The Most Deadly Game*. Carol remembered this clearly because "George and I were caught in a fire."

Arguably, this is one of Joe Franklin's best latter shows and is entertaining from beginning to end. The celebrities are really enjoying themselves as they take a trip down memory lane and have a great rapport with each other.

Preminger: Anatomy of a Filmmaker
October 28, 1991

An Austrian documentary in English, produced in tandem with Otto Preminger Films and narrated by Burgess Meredith examining the career of the larger-than-life producer/director. Carol Lynley, one of many who worked with Preminger, is interviewed. Others included Saul Bass, Michael Caine, Ossie Davis, Ken Howard, Deborah Kerr, Wendell Mayes, Don Murray, Patricia Neal, Vincent Price, George C. Scott, Frank Sinatra, James Stewart, and Tom Tryon.

Joan Quinn Etc...
February 5, 1992

This local Los Angeles talk show was hosted by Joan Quinn, a member of the California Arts Committee, the former West Coast editor of Andy Warhol's *Interview* magazine, and the society editor of the *Herald Examiner*. Her guests on this program were hotel manager Erhard Hotter and Carol Lynley.

Carol looked fetching in an oversize, canary yellow blouse and short tan skirt. She was simply vivacious the entire time, talking and laughing about her decision to relocate back to Los Angeles from New York; her friendships with Tuesday Weld and Carroll Baker; how she progressed from child model to actress and her mother's role in it; her new movie *Heartfelt*; her desire to do a *Murder, She Wrote*; and the infomercial she was about to shoot back East. Carol also revealed her desire to land a long-running hit TV series which she felt "she deserved" and to become "part of Americana."

Interestingly, she also discussed her local New York talk show and how she had to adjust to being a host rather than the guest. She relayed laughing, "When I first started doing it having been interviewed all my life, it was very difficult for me not to talk. I would ask a question. I would answer it. I would tell a funny story. My producer would give me lessons on asking the question and then shutting up."

Bikram Choudhury, Yoga Master
1994

A promotional video for yoga master Bikram Choudbury's classes held at the Yoga College of India in Beverly Hills. Carol appears briefly (and it looks like it may have been filmed a few years prior) and states that actors are used to being pampered and catered to but Bikram "kicks ass if you pardon my language." Other celebrities offering testimonials include Shirley MacLaine, Quincy Jones, and Richard Benjamin.

On the Town with Mike Farah
October 9, 1997

This was a weekly local talk show from Toluca Lake, California hosted by Mike Farah. He normally interviewed celebrities at charity events but for this edition he attended an autograph show. Carol Lynley, of course, talked about making *The Poseidon Adventure* and how she was so looking forward to seeing *Titanic*. She also had to correct Farah several times for his erroneous statements about *Poseidon*.

Off the Menu: The Last Days of Chasen's
October 1997

This feature documentary was given a limited theatrical release. It celebrated the famed Chasen's restaurant that closed its doors in April 1995 and was filmed during its final weeks. Located in West Hollywood, comedian David Chasen opened it in December 1936 and quickly became known for its chili. For some years the Academy hosted its Oscar after-party there and it became a magnet for Hollywood's A-list.

Carol Lynley is among the celebrities (including Maureen Arthur, David Brown, Sally Kellerman, Jack Lemmon, Ed McMahon, Suzanne Pleshette, Don Rickles, Rod Steiger, Sharon Stone, Donna Summer, and Jane Wyman) who reminisced about the restaurant. She was a frequent diner there during the sixties and seventies, usually accompanied by David Frost (who appears here as well) or her dear friend Fred Astaire.

Carol comes off well, but unfortunately her name is misspelled in the credits as "Linley." This was a sloppy and insulting mistake by the producers.

On Stage: Nelson's World
December 12, 1997

This live online computer chat show was launched during the early days of the World Wide Web on the Microsoft Network. Produced, written, and hosted by entertainment reporter Nelson Aspen, his good friend Carol Lynley was a guest this night discussing her career. Audience members had to go online to nelsonsworld.msn.com where they could just follow the written conversation or type in a question for Carol. If it sounds prehistoric, it was compared to the present, but at the time it was revolutionary.

"Carol Lynley for the Block"

Carol Lynley and Nelson Aspen during her appearance in *On Stage: Nelson's World* in 1997. *Courtesy of Nelson Aspen*

E! True Hollywood Story
"Natalie Wood"
December 14, 1997

This popular long-running series, narrated by Phil Crowley, focused on celebrities' lives before and after they became famous. Carol was one of many sharing stories about Natalie Wood.

New with Nelson
1999

Per host Nelson Aspen, "*New with Nelson* were little spots that aired on screens in the Ralphs supermarket chain and gas stations. A precursor to today's little webisodes! As I recall, Carol did two with me, one at Arnie Morton's Steakhouse and one at the Beverly Hills Hotel."[910]

TV Guide Television
1999

On this half-hour lifestyle series Carol Lynley discussed her long acting career in film and on stage with entertainment reporter and friend Nelson Aspen.

E! True Hollywood Story
"Death of a Dream Girl: Karyn Kupcinet"
September 29, 1999

The short life and unsolved death of starlet Karyn Kupcinet, the daughter of columnist and TV host, Irv Kupcinet, is explored. Carol became friendly with Karyn Kupcinet when she appeared in the Chicago stage production *Anniversary Waltz* in the early fifties. Lynley recalled, "My understudy was Karyn Kupcinet … who everyone called 'Cookie.' We used to hang out together, she took me to her school and I used to go to her parents Irv and Essie's place for dinner. They were really nice to me. Kup was at the height of his media power at the time, there was nothing to be gained by hanging out with a twelve-year-old."[911]

E! Mysteries and Scandals
"Gene Tierney"
December 13, 1999

Hosted by A.J. Benza, a former gossip writer for the *New York Daily News*, this popular series showcased notorious scandals and wicked lives of departed celebrities using interviews and reenactments. Actress Gene Tierney was the subject of her own episode due to her psychological problems that resulted in shock treatment and cut short her acting career.
Former co-star Carol Lynley is interviewed and remarked that Tierney, "was gloriously beautiful and just an understated actress. In scenes where she

could have gone over the top, she went under and just held you." Later in the program, Carol detected from working with Tierney in *The Pleasure Seekers* that "she seemed to inspire a great deal of loyalty from these people in a business that doesn't really inspire loyalty."

Cult Culture: The Poseidon Adventure
December 31, 2003

This documentary for the Fox Movie Channel celebrated the 30th anniversary screening and reunion of the iconic disaster movie hosted by *The Poseidon Adventure* Fan Club in 2002. Stella Stevens narrated, and Carol appeared, talking about her experience making the movie and why she felt it is so beloved. Also featured are Joel Hirschhorn, Ronald Neame, and Ernie F. Orsatti, among others,

Media Funhouse
2005

Carol Lynley was a guest on cineaste Ed Grant's public access talk show that aired in New York City on the Manhattan Neighborhood Network. Carol talked about working on *Fantasy Island*, her friendship with Roddy McDowall, and other aspects of her lengthy career.

Inside Edition
November 16, 2005

On this entertainment news program, the host caught up with Carol Lynley, one of the stars of *The Poseidon Adventure*, regarding the NBC TV-movie remake that was to air the following weekend. The cameras came into Carol's modest rented bungalow in Malibu with its million-dollar view of the Pacific Ocean.

Jenseits von Hollywood - Das Kino des Otto Preminger
2006

Documentary on Otto Preminger made for German television. Carol Lynley is featured along with Peter Bogdanovich, Geoffrey Horne, Don Murray, Kim Novak, Victoria Preminger, and Eva Marie Saint.

The Poseidon Adventure – The Cast Looks Back
2006

A video short featuring Carol Lynley with co-stars Sheila Allen, Red Buttons, Pamela Sue Martin, Roddy McDowall, and Stella Stevens sharing anecdotes about making the classic disaster movie.

Sunrise
June 23, 2011

This is one of Australia's most popular morning shows, featuring a mix of news, entertainment, sports, and current affairs à la *Good Morning America* and *The Today Show*. Carol Lynley was interviewed by its entertainment reporter and friend Nelson Aspen.

Bibliography

"12 Young Actresses on Deb Star Ball." *The Hartford Courant*, January 2, 1966.

Adams, Marjory. "The Misfortunes of Gig Young: A Girl (and Blood) in His Soup." *Boston Globe*, October 1, 1967.

___. "Star of 'The Collector' Samantha's Hard Work Won Prize." *Boston Globe*, July 30, 1965.

Adams, Millicent. "Young Star Shines in Dramatic Roles on Stage and Screen." *The Washington Post and Times Herald*, July 12, 1959.

Adler, Dick. "A New Partner for Dan Rowan—The Werewolf." *Life*, May 23, 1969: 54-60.

Alexander, David. "Carol Lynley: At 38, She Keeps Her Great Looks with a Steady Diet of Work." *Season Pass Entertainment Guide*, October 1980: 34, 35.

Alpert, Hollis. "The Big Star Derby." *Woman's Day*, February 1964: 16, 19, 105.

___. "Movies: Now After Five Years and Three Names, She's on Top." *Woman's Day*, November 1960: 8, 10, 12, 14.

Ames, Walter. "Costly Lunch Brings Results for Director; Hayes Stricken on Set." *Los Angeles Times*, November 2, 1957.

Amory, Cleveland. "Model to Actress, Carol Lynley Made It." *Pittsburgh Press.* July 5, 1978: 25.

"'Answered the Flute,' at Finch. Begins Studio Three's Project." *New York Times,* March 10, 1960.

Archer, Eugene. "France Will Lift Film's Export Ban." *New York Times,* August 2, 1961.

"Ask Them Yourself." *Burlington Free Press.* September 24, 1978: 93.

Aspen, Nelson. *Hollywood Insider Exposed! Secrets, Stars & Show Biz.* New Holland Publishers: Australia, 2008.

"At First They Thought This Young Lady Wasn't Pretty, but Now—Wow!" *Chicago Daily Tribune,* March 31, 1959.

"Audubon Wins Back Rights; 'Best Theatrical Efforts' Hit on 'The Cat and the Canary.'" *Variety,* August 15, 1979: 7, 44.

Bacon, James. "Set Isn't Same without Shelley." *The Evening Press, Binghampton, New York.* July 12, 1972: 8-B

Baltake, Joe. "Mimieux: Look Who Grew Up." *Philadelphia Daily News,* December 12, 1979: 32.

____. "This Critic Likes Fashion." *The Austin American Statesman,* November 4, 1979.

Barnes, Clive. "The Stage: Quality 'Takeover' Trend." *New York Times,* October 9, 1975.

Bass, Jennifer and Pat Kirkham *Saul Bass: A Life in Film and Design.* London: Laurence King, 2011.

Beck, Marilyn. "Carol Lynley in 'Poseidon' Sequel." *The Atlanta Constitution,* May 15, 1974.

___. "Carol Lynley Likes Her Free Lifestyle." *Pacific Stars and Stripes,* August 15, 1978: 17.

___. "Ex-Mrs. Carson Is Willing." *The Atlanta Constitution,* July 21, 1972.

___. "Marilyn Beck's Hollywood Hotline." *Pasadena Star-News,* December 10, 1972: A-10.

___. "Marilyn Beck's Hollywood Hotline: Bickering Blondes Continue to Battle." *The Salt Lake Tribune,* 1973.

___. "That's Showbiz." *The Hartford Courant*, June 9, 1969.

___. "That's Show Biz: Gene Hackman's Back Home." *The Hartford Courant*, June 30, 1970.

Bettinson, Gary. "Tales from the Kryptonians: *Superman* at 40." *Cinema Retro*, Vol. 14, Issue 42, 2018: 32-43.

"Bill Bixby Keeps Promise Not to Reveal Magic Tricks." *The Hartford Courant*, January 6, 1974.

"'Bippy' Premiere to Be Televised." *The Hartford Courant*, June 1, 1969.

Black Saint, The. "Interview Doug Jones [*Hellboy 1 & 2, Pan's Labyrinth*]." *Horror News Net*, August 25, 2014, http://horrornews.net/87301/interview-doug-jones-hellboy-1-2-pans-labyrinth/.

Blanco, John. "60s Starlet Carol Lynley on a Checkered Past: From Broadway to Fantasy Island." *Bay Area Reporter*, November 9, 1995: 35, 43.

Bond, Jeff. *The Fantastic Worlds of Irwin Allen*. Santa Monica, CA: Creature Features, 2019.

Boon, Joseph P. "Carol Lynley Recalls Brandon de Wilde." *Bucks County Courier Times*, December 1, 1972.

Borseti, Francesco. *It Came from the 80s! Interviews with 124 Cult Filmmakers*. Jefferson, NC: McFarland & Company, Inc., 2016.

Bowie, Stephen. "*The Invaders*: The Nightmare Has Already Begun." *The Classic TV History Blog*, http://classictvhistory.com/EpisodeGuides/invaders.html, 2007.

Bozung, Justin. "The Last Hollywood Cowboy: An Interview with Gary Lockwood." *Shock Cinema*, No. 42, 2012: 13

Brown, Royal S. Liner notes to *The Cardinal Original Motion Picture Soundtrack*. Preamble, PRCD 1778, CD, 2010.

Browning, Norma Lee. "Hollywood Today." *Chicago Tribune*, May 1, 1969.

___. "Hollywood Today: Connie's Big Scene," *Chicago Tribune*, January 19, 1970.

___. "Hollywood Today: Sixty-Grand Debut." *Chicago Tribune*, July 31, 1969.

___. "Hollywood Today: Tom's on His Way!" *Chicago Tribune*, June 10, 1970.

___."Rowan and Martin Shun TV Format in Their First Movie." *Chicago Tribune*, September 7, 1969.

Bryce, Allan, ed. *The Dark Side, the Magazine of the Macabre and Fantastic Presents Amicus the Studio That Dripped Blood*. Liskeard, Cornwall: Stray Cat, 2000.

Butler, Ivan. *Horror in the Cinema*. New York: Paperback Library Edition, 1971.

Byrne, Julie. "Luis Estevez, Fashion 'Doer,' Can Do It All—and in a Hurry." *Los Angeles Times*, February 4, 1969.

Callahan, Michael. "Peyton Place's Real Victim." *Vanity Fair*. March 2006.

Campbell, Glen and Tom Carter. *Rhinestone Cowboy: An Autobiography*. New York: Villard Books, 1994.

Campbell, John. "The Upside-Down Filming of *The Poseidon Adventure*." *American Cinematographer*, September 1972.

"Can Rowan, Martin Win in Films?" *The Atlanta Constitution*, May 10, 1969.

Canote, Terrence Towles. "Plagiarism—the Sincerest Form of Flattery." *A Shroud of Thoughts*, October 7, 2007, http://mercurie.blogspot.com/2007/10/plagiarism-sincerest-form-of-flattery.html

Capalbo, Carmen. "'Deal with Me as You Would Any Novice.'" *New York Times*. April 14, 1991.

Carmody, Jay. "Dull Year It Was for Girls." *The Evening Star*, January 26, 1964: E-4.

"Carol Lynley." *People*, November 28, 1994. https://people.com/archive/carol-lynley-vol-42-no-22/

"Carol Lynley, a beauty with soft blue eyes…" No source, n.d.

"Carol Lynley, David Frost Plan Australia Idyll." *The Austin American Statesman*, August 6, 1978.

"Carol Lynley [in] World Premiere Movie." *Austin (Minn.) Herald*, May 12, 1978: 5A.

"Carol Lynley Is 'The Best of Friends.'" *San Bernardino Sun*, August 23, 1981.

"Carol Lynley Loves Latest Role." *The Daily Herald (Provo, Utah)*, January 10, 1972: 19.

"Carol Lynley: Poseidon's Happy Survivor." *Anderson Daily Bulletin*, February 26, 1973.

"Carol Lynley Stars in 'Fliers.'" *The Atlanta Constitution*, February 1, 1965.

"Carol Lynley: Sweet—And Not So Sweet." *Show*, March 1964: 62.

"Carol Lynley to Tour Six Cities for 'Bunny.'" *Box Office*, September 27, 1965: 9.

"Carol's Football Date." *Variety*, October 6, 1965: 22.

"Carolina Schedules 'The Shuttered Room.'" *Florence Morning News*, January 21, 1968.

Carroll, Gretchen. "Research for Carol." *Pittsburgh Press*. December 10, 1967: TV-4.

Carroll, Harrison. "Behind the Scenes in Hollywood: Scene Explodes into Melodrama." *Kokomo Morning Times*, June 18, 1966, 11.

Carter, Graydon, ed. *Vanity Fair's Tales of Hollywood*. New York: Penguin Books, 2008.

"Celeb Spotting," *Philadelphia Daily News*, February 15, 1989: 43.

"'Celebrity Game' Panel." *Ithaca Journal*, May 8, 1965.

Chace, Reeve. *The Complete Book of Oscar Fashion: Variety's 75 Years of Glamour on the Red Carpet*. New York, NY: Reed Press, 2003.

"Children Are Generous." *The Robesonian*, October 30, 1977: 3.

Christie, James. *"You're the Director, You Figure It Out: The Life and Films of Richard Donner*. Duncan, Oklahoma: 2010.

Christy, Marian. "Carol Lynley—A Free Spirit." *Boston Globe*, January 7, 1973.

Clark, John. "Speaking of DVDs: Carol Lynley." *San Francisco Chronicle*, May 21, 2006.

Clark, Natalie. "They All Fell for Frost." *Daily Mail*, September 5, 2013, https://www.dailymail.co.uk/femail/article-2413108/David-Frost-From-singer-wooed-egg-sized-diamond-model.html

Clark, Valerie. "I'm No Threat to Men Says Feminist Carol Lynley." *TV Times*, April 12-18, 1975.

Clinton, Franz Anthony. "An Interview with Brian Clemens." *Thriller*, http://www.markmcm.co.uk/blacknun/thriller/interviews.html

Cloud, Barbara. "Pitt Prof's 'Brother of Dragons' Focus on Teen Drug Problem." *Pittsburgh Press*. November 6, 1983: H2.

Connolly, Mike. "Business Is Bad." *Desert Sun*. December 8, 1959: 4.

___. "Notes from Hollywood." *Pasadena Independent*, November 16, 1966: 51.

___. "Wendy Not Kidding." *Desert Sun*. November 11, 1959: 4B.

Connor, Floyd. *Pretty Poison: The Tuesday Weld Story*. New York: Barricade Books, 1995.

"Conversation with Carol Lynley, A." *Fox Movie Channel Backlot Pass*, July 8, 2001. www.thefoxmoviechannel.com/backlot/ lynley/part2c.html,

"'Cops and Robin Airs Thursday," *Burlington Free Press*, March 26, 1978.

Cotter, Robert Michael "Bobb." *The Women of Hammer Horror: A Biographical Dictionary and Filmography*. Jefferson, NC: McFarland and Company, 2013.

Cowie, Susan D. and Tom Johnson. *The Films of Oliver Reed*. Jefferson, NC: McFarland and Company, Inc., 2011.

"Crash Kills Pilot, Injures 2 Film Men," *Los Angeles Times*, July 12, 1969.

Crist, Judith. *Judith Crist's TV Guide to the Movies*. Toronto: Popular Library, 1974.

Crosby, John. "The Little People." *New York Herald Tribune* [European Edition], May 12, 1965: 16.

Dahl, Arlene. "Arlene Dahl Selects Tomorrow's Leading Lovelies." *Chicago Tribune*, October 13, 1963.

___. "Carol Finds It Takes Time to Style Hair." *Chicago Tribune*, September 2, 1963.

Davis, Victor. "Carol Lynley Has a Lust for Success," *The Sunday Gleaner Magazine*, February 25, 1973.

Dawidziak, Mark. *The Night Stalker Companion: A 25th Anniversary Tribute*. Los Angeles: Pomegranate Press, 1997.

De Castro, J. "The Star of Reflets de Cannes: The Public Image of the Cannes Film Festival." January 2015.

DeLatiner, Barbara. "On Television: 'Night in London Is Morning After.'" *Newsday*, February 3, 1967.

"Dimension Pictures Adds 'Georgia Road' to Slate." *Boxoffice*, April 18, 1977: 4.

DiOrio, Al. *Borrowed Time: The 37 Years of Bobby Darin*. Philadelphia, Pennsylvania: Running Press, 1981.

Dixon, Wheeler W. *The Films of Freddie Francis*. Metuchen, NJ: The Scarecrow Press, 1991.

Donnelly, Tom. "'Mice and Men' and Carol Lynley with Homage to Harlow." *The Washington Post*, March 12, 1975.

Dougherty, Eugene G. Letter from Motion Picture Association of America, Inc. to Hal Wallis. Apr. 24, 1969. Hal Wallis Papers, Margaret Herrick Library, Academy of Motion Pictures Arts and Sciences.

Drew, Bernard. "*The Poseidon Adventure*: Box Office Smash ... But Why?" *The Journal-News, Nyack, New York*. February 4, 1973: 9E.

"Dummy Delay." *San Antonio Express and News*. November 3, 1968, 145.

Dunne, Philip. *Take Two: A Life in Movies and Politics*. New York: McGraw-Hill, 1980.

Ebert, Roger. "Interview with Carol Lynley." *Chicago Sun-Times*, December 4, 1972.

Ellis, David A. *Conversations with Cinematographers*. Lanham: Scarecrow Press, 2011.

Engels, J.A. "Carol Lynley: Growing Up at 30." *San Bernardino Sun*, May 20, 1972, A-12, A-14.

Evanier, David. *Roman Candle: The Life of Bobby Darin*. [S.I.]; Rodale, 2004.

Fanning, Win. "Carol Lynley Enjoys Outdoor Film Stint." *Pittsburgh Post-Gazette*, August 21, 1981.

___. "On Hope Show, in Documentary Pioneer Fliers Get Their Due on TV." *Pittsburgh Post-Gazette*, February 9, 196: 35.

___. "Previn Debut Exciting on TV." *Pittsburgh Post-Gazette*, September 13, 1976: 25.

"Faye Dunaway: Star, Symbol, Style." *Newsweek*, March 4, 1968: 42 – 50.

Ferguson, Michael. *Joe Dallesandro: Warhol Superstar, Underground Film Icon, Actor.* New York: Open Road Integrated Media: 2015.

Fernandez, Alexia. "Star of *The Poseidon Adventure* and Former Girlfriend to David Frost, Dies at 77." *People*, September 5, 2019. https://people.com/movies/carol-lynley-star-the-poseidon-adventure-dies/

Fine, Linda. "Carol Lynley: The Face That Doesn't Change." *Model's Circle*, December 1975:38-41.

Finnigan, Joseph. "Who'll Be Top Stars in 1964?" *The Hartford Courant*, January 3, 1964.

Francis, Freddie with Tony Dalton. *Freddie Francis: The Straight Story from Moby Dick to Glory, a Memoir.* London: The Scarecrow Press: 2015.

Freedland, Nathaniel. "Getting a Real-Life Look at Dickie Martin's Gums." *Toronto Daily Star*, June 7, 1969.

Freedman, Richard. "Carol Lynley Is Flying High." *Pittsburgh Press.* January 21, 1979: H-4.

Freeman, Alex. "That's Show Biz: Burt Lancaster Seeks New Leading Lady." *The Hartford Courant*, July 8, 1966.

___. "That's Show Biz: Carol Lynley Says She'll Stay in England." *The Hartford Courant*, January 10, 1970.

Freeman, Stephen G. "Jet Set Hoopla in Newport Beach." *Los Angeles Times*, June 20, 1982.

Frost, David. *An Autobiography: David Frost*. London: HarperCollins, 1993.

George, Jim. "The Stellar Stella Stevens." *Cinema Retro*, Vol. 14, Issue 42, 2018.

Gerani, Gary. "Episode Guide to *The Invaders*." *Starlog*, September 1978.

Gerani, Gary and Paul H. Schulman. *Fantastic Television*. New York: Harmony Books, 1977.

"Golden Films New 'Out of Control.'" *Hollywood Studio Magazine*, Vol. 11, No.1, November 1976: 13.

"Goodbye, Age of Innocence." *Life*. May 3, 1963: 41, 42, 44, 47.

Gordon, Alex. "The Pit and the Pen of Alex Gordon: *The Cat and the Canary*." *Fangoria*, No. 11, 1978: 40.

Goudas, John N. "Carol Lynley's All Over Screen." *Pittsburgh Post-Gazette*. July 19, 1978: 43.

Gough-Yates, Kevin. "Seth Holt." *Screen*, V. 10, no. 6, Nov/Dec 1969.

Graham, Sheila. "Inside Hollywood with Sheila Graham." *Independent Star-News*, July 24, 1966: 52.

Grams, Martin. *The Alfred Hitchcock Presents Companion*. Churchville, MD; ORT Publishing, 2001.

Green, Earl. "A Review of the Nearly Forgotten TV Show, 'Future Cop' on DVD." *Retroist*, April 13, 2016, https://www.retroist.com/2016/04/13/future-cop-tv-show-dvd-review/

Green, Paul. *A History of Television's The Virginian, 1962-1971*. Jefferson, NC: McFarland & Company, 2006.

Haber, Joyce. "'Bippy' Opening on the Outskirts." *Los Angeles Times*, June 9, 1969.

___. "Campbell Finds Success by 'Going Against the Grain.'" *Los Angeles Times*, April 12, 1970.

___. "Larry Hagman—Wild Man of Malibu Beach." *Los Angeles Times*, September 26, 1971.

___. "Lerner Seeking Answers to 'Coco.'" *Los Angeles Times*, February 24, 1969.

___. "McCarthy – the Subject Is Rumors." *Los Angeles Times*, August 25, 1971.

Haley, Jack, Jr. Memo to Hal Wallis. October 9, 1969. Hal Wallis Papers, Margaret Herrick Library, Academy of Motion Pictures Arts and Sciences.

___. Memo to Hal Wallis. November 3, 1969. Hal Wallis Papers, Margaret Herrick Library, Academy of Motion Pictures Arts and Sciences.

___. Memo to Hal Wallis. January 20, 1970. Hal Wallis Papers, Margaret Herrick Library, Academy of Motion Pictures Arts and Sciences.

___. "Years from Now, When You Talk About This..." *Action*, Vol. 5, No. 5 September-October 1970:14, 15.

Hamilton, John. *Beasts in the Cellar: The Exploitation Film Career of Tony Tenser*. Godalming, England: Fab Press, 2005.

Harmetz, Aljean. "'The Poseidon Adventure's' Treatment of Women Is All Wet." *New York Times*, January 21, 1973.

Harrington, Curtis. *Nice Guys Don't Work in Hollywood: The Adventures of an Aesthete in the Movie Business.* Chicago, IL: Drag City Inc., 2013.

Haun, Harry. "She Kisses & Tells & Regrets." *New York Daily News*. July 30, 1978: 6.

Heffernan, Harold. "She's Blonde but Not Dumb." *The Atlanta Journal and Atlanta Constitution*, March 1, 1957.

Hegarty, Neil. *Frost: That Was the Life That Was: The Authorized Biography*. London: WH Allen, 2015.

Heitland, Jon. *The Man from U.N.C.L.E. Book: The Behind-the-Scenes Story of a Television Classic*. New York: St. Martin's Press, 1987.

Henniger, Paul. "Prison Tale Worries ABC." *The Evening Press, Binghamton, NY*, June 29, 1980: 1, 8.

Hilburn, Robert. "Campbell Reaches Superstar Status." *Los Angeles Times*, Jul. 11, 1970.

Hirsch, Foster. *Otto Preminger: The Man Who Would Be King*. New York: Alfred A. Knopf, 2007.

Hirschl, Bee Pail. "Jayne Mansfield: The Friend Is Gone But the Friendship Endures" *Pittsburgh Post-Gazette*, June 24, 1987: 11.

Hoberman, J. "Video: Deciding to Trust Your Sense. Or Not," Arts and Leisure. *New York Times*, January 25, 2015: 17.

"Hollywood: Carol's Comeback." *New York Daily News*, July 10, 1972: 53.

Hopper, Hedda. "Carol Lynley: An Appealing Talented 16." *San Antonio Express*, September 14, 1958 77.

___. "Carroll Baker to Star on Broadway." *Los Angeles Times*, May 22, 1961.

___. "Looking at Hollywood: Ann Sothern's Daughter to Be Starred." *Chicago Tribune*, December 15, 1964.

___. "Looking at Hollywood: Disney Film of Sea Chase to Start Soon." *Chicago Daily Tribune*, April 29, 1961.

___. "Looking at Hollywood: Hedda Exchanges Quips on TV's Celebrity Game." *Chicago Tribune*, June 30, 1964.

___. "Looking at Hollywood: Ice Skater Carol Heiss Signed for First Movie,' *Chicago Daily Tribune*, July 28, 1960.

___. "Teen-Age Carol Lynley No 'Blue Denim' Girl. *The Sun*, February 1, 1959.

___. "What a Difference a Few Years Make!" *The Hartford Courant*, June 23, 1963.

Houser, Bob. "Demo Brigade's Light Charge." *Independent Press-Telegram (Long Beach, California)*, June 25, 1972: 34.

"Howard Sues Re: 'Tower.'" *Variety*, January 28, 1987, 7.

Huestis, Mark. *Impresario of Castro Street: An Intimate Memoir*. San Francisco, CA: Outsider Productions, 2019.

Hughes, David. *The Complete Lynch*. London: Virgin, 2001.

Humphrey, Hal. "Jackie Cooper's Movie to Be Shown on NBC." *The Derrick*, November 27, 1968: 20.

Hyde, Nina S. "Carol Lynley, a Star in Second-Hand Robes." *The Washington Post*, March 29, 1975.

"Is the Movie Rating System G for Good? Mother Says Only Disney Really Safe." *San Bernardino Sun-Telegram*, August 9, 1970, D-1.

Jancovich, Mark. "Beyond Hammer: The First Run Market and the Prestige Horror Film in the Early 1960s." *Palgrave Communications*. Vol.3, Issue 1. December 2017: 1-14.

"Joan Harrison: Fright-Minded Series Maker." *Los Angeles Times*, September 2, 1968.

"Joe's Barbershop." *TV Guide*. July, 11, 1970: 9-11.

Johnson, Erskine. "Showbeat: Miss Blue Denim Now in Silk and Satin." *Santa Cruz Sentinel*. April 14, 1963: 19.

Jones, Paul. "David Aided with Goliath 'Invaders.'" *The Atlanta Constitution*, December 5, 1967.

Julian, Robert and Orland Outland. "OutLand: The Annals of Queerdom." *Bay Area Reporter*, December 17, 1992, 30.

"Junior Miss of 'Junior Miss,' The." *TV Guide*, December 15, 1957: 15.

Kaufman, Dave. "'Overnight' Success of 15 Years: Glen Campbell, Vet Performer at 31, Earning Over $2,000,000 Yearly from Disks, Pix, TV, Concerts." *Variety*, August 13, 1969:2, 43.

Kaufman, Michael T. "Broadway Greets New Movie Theater." *New York Times*, December 13, 1972.

Kelleher, Ed. "Indy Distrib Spectrafilm Widens Its Spectrum." *The Film Journal*, Vol. 90, Issue 2, February 1, 1987.

Kendall, Bob. "Lynley and Lockwood Are in Love in Golden Films New 'Out of Control.'" *Hollywood Studio Magazine*, Vol. 11, No.1, November 1976: 12, 13.

Kirgo, Julie. Liner notes to the *Blue Denim* Blu-ray. Twilight Time, 2018.

Kilner, Lara. "Call the Midwife Star Jenny Agutter on How It's Harder to Swear When You're Wearing a Habit and Wimple." *Mirror*, March 12, 2017, https://www.mirror.co.uk/tv/tv-news/call-midwife-star-jenny-agutter-10002509.

Kirkland, Bruce. "It's Not a Star War on Kleinburg Set: Cameras Carve the Shape of Things to Come in Canadian Sci-Fi Film." *Toronto Star*. November 19, 1978: B1.

Kleiner, Dick. "Beauty Looking Forward to Life at 50." *Pittsburgh Press*. April 22, 1979: J-1

___. "Dick Kleiner's Showbeat: Carol Lynley Dull? Well, Not Exactly," *Santa Cruz Sentinel*, September 27, 1964, 31.

___. "England Changed Carol Lynley." *Santa Cruz Sentinel*, May 19, 1967: 17.

___, "'Poseidon Adventure, The': A Big Film with a Big Cast." *Burlington (N.C.) Times-News*, June 14, 1972: 7A.

___. "Showbeat: At Last, Carol Lynley Plays the Heroine." *The Bee*, May 29, 1974: 6-A.

___. "TV Scout Reports." *The Odessa American*. March 20, 1972: 17.

Korman, Seymour. "Statistics Show…" *Chicago Daily Tribune*, February 3, 1962.

Krebs, Albin. "Notes on People." *New York Times*, December 25, 1976.

Kubasik, Ben, Anthony Scaduto and Michael Fleming. "Behind the Scenes." *Newsday*, July 1, 1986.

___. "Teen Star Says Innocence Can Bring Trouble." *Newsday*, July 30, 1959.

Lane, Christina. *Phantom Lady: Hollywood Producer Joan Harrison, the Forgotten Woman Behind Hitchcock*. Chicago, IL: Chicago Review Press, 2020.

Lane, Lydia. "Beauty: Lynley Avoids the Tensions." *Los Angeles Times*, November 19, 1978.

Larsen, John. "Teens-Ville U.S.A. Carol Too Serious to Date Bores." *Boston Globe*, November 13, 1960.

Lattanzio, Rick. "Stream of the Day: *Bunny Lake Is Missing* Was Ahead of Its Time as a Tale of Gaslighting and Abduction." *IndiWire.com*, April 24, 2020, https://www.indiewire.com/2020/04/watch-bunny-lake-is-missing-criterion-channel-stream-of-the-day-1202226013/?fbclid=IwAR20OAWi9jGXJMoMfHG-9iO5fRXBsSG4BBq7fH1q9Oy-y1ulfuR4YMTKyl8

Laurent, Lawrence. "Bixby Tries Non-Violent, Action-Adventure." *The Washington Post*, September 2, 1973.

___. "NBC Holds Its Lead in Ratings," *The Washington Post, Times Herald*, October 14, 1969.

___. "'The Immortal' May Not Be," *The Washington Post, Times Herald*, August 23, 1970.

"Lawford Back in Hospital." *Los Angeles Times*, November 29, 1976.

"Lawford Sues Over Injury on Movie Set." *Los Angeles Times*, December 25, 1976.

Leslie, Ann. "Carol Starts Movie with Olivier, Coward." *El Paso Herald Post*, May 8, 1965.

Levinson, Peter. *Puttin' on the Ritz: Fred Astaire and the Fine Art of Panache, A Biography*. New York: St. Martin's Press, 2009.

Lewis, Emory. "Lynley's Back on Broadway—Belatedly." *Jersey Record*, July 27, 1975: B-19, B-22.

Lisanti, Tom. *Drive-In Dream Girls: A Galaxy of B-Movie Starlets of the Sixties.* Jefferson, NC: McFarland and Company, Inc., 2003.

___. *Dueling Harlows: Race to the Silver Screen.* CreateSpace, 2011.

___. *Fantasy Femmes of Sixties Cinema: Interviews with Twenty Actresses from Biker, Beach, and Elvis Movies.* Jefferson, NC: McFarland and Company, Inc., 2001.

___. "Francine York: Out of This World!" *Filmfax*, October 2000/January 2001: 68-73.

___. "From Teen Queen to Scream Queen: The Many Faces of Carol Lynley." *Filmfax*, February/March 1997: 56-60, 70.

___. *Glamour Girls of Sixties Hollywood,* Jefferson, NC: McFarland and Company, Inc., 2008.

___. "Nod to Nonnie, A." *Cinema Retro.* Vol. 8, Issue 24, 2012: 14, 15.

Lisanti, Tom and Louis Paul. *Film Fatales: Women in Espionage Film and Television, 1962-1973.* Jefferson, NC, McFarland and Company, Inc., 2002.

Lloyd, Norman. *Stages: Norman Lloyd. Interviewed by Francine Parker.* Hollywood, CA: Directors Guild of America and Scarecrow Press, 1990.

Loynd, Ray. "14 ½ Weeks Old: 'Bippy' Premieres Tonight." *Los Angeles Times*, June 5, 1969.

___. "Rowan, Martin in Movie? You Bet Your Sweet Bippy." *Los Angeles Times*, April 9, 1969.

___. "Rowan, Martin to Do Two Comedies at MGM." *Los Angeles Times*, April 5, 1969.

Lynley, Carol. "Arlene Dahl: Carol Lynley Is Guilty of Being Convivial." *Philadelphia Daily News.* March 18, 1965: 38.

"Lynley in Garb for the Year 2020." *Time*, December 11, 1978: 107.

"Lynley Replaces Swit," *The Robesonian*, September 18, 1977: 2.

Maays, Stan. "Meet Carol Lynley: A Living Doll." *The Abilene Reporter News*, September 26, 1968.

"Magician to Film from Magic Castle." *Los Angeles Times*, January 3, 1974.

Magnotta, Ernie. "'Bad Movies' That Hurt So Good: *Starcrash*." *Scary Monsters.* January 2019: 36-46.

"'Maltese Bippy, The: Rowan and Martin Make Movie Comedy." *Kokomo (Ind.) Tribune*, June 1, 1969.

Maltin, Leonard, ed. *Leonard Maltin's 2015 Movie Guide*. Penguin Group US, 2014.

Mann, Dave. *Harry Alan Towers: The Transnational Career of a Cinematic Contrarian*. Jefferson, NC: McFarland and Company, Inc., 2014.

Mann, Roderick. "From Playmate to Governor." *Los Angeles Times*, February 22, 1979.

Manners, Dorothy. "Actress Unhappy Because Dirty Words Cancelled." *Anderson Daily Bulletin*, August 14, 1969.

___. "In Hollywood: Carol Lynley Has Slow Recovery After New Film." *Anderson Daily Bulletin*, August 4, 1972: 6.

Martin, Betty. "Movie Call Sheet: Color Film Corp. Formed." *Los Angeles Times*, August 17, 1965.

Masters, George. "The Masters Touch." *New York Daily News*, March 2, 1969.

McBain, Diane. *Famous Enough: A Hollywood Memoir*, Albany, GA: BearManor Media, 2014.

McCarthy, Dan. "1st Feature Film: Hershey: Hollywood East." *Lebanon Daily News*, July 22, 1977: 17.

McHarry, Charles. "On the Town: Numbers Game." *New York Daily News*. October 19, 1972: 17C.

McKenna, Michael. *The ABC Movie of the Week: Big Movies for the Small Screen*. Lanham: The Scarecrow Press, 2013.

McLean, Patricia. *All Fall Down: The Brandon deWilde Story*, Rockland, Maine: Maine Authors Publishing, 2015.

McLellan, Dennis. "It's Intrigue 'Balboa' Style: TV Drama Filmed in Newport." *Los Angeles Times*, June 10, 1982.

McManus, Margaret. "At 15, Television Star Carol Linley[sic] Not Anxious to Grow Up." *Daily Boston Globe*, December 15, 1957.

McNulty, Tim. "Southern Moonshine Films Big Business in Drive-Ins." *Colorado Springs Gazette-Telegraph*, July 10, 1977: 46.

Miller, Edwin. "Carol Lynley: Read Her Thoughts." *Seventeen*. May 1958: 132-133, 186, 188-189, 191.

Mitchell, Charles P. *The Complete H.P. Lovecraft Filmography*. Westport, CT: Greenwood Press, 2001.

Morehouse, Rebecca. "Hot Lights, Clinches Often Have an Effect." *The Home News*, August 4, 1975: 6.

Morehouse, Ward. "Carol Lynley 'In Love with All the Critics.'" *The Sun*, June 22, 1958.

Moss, Ruth. "Carol Lynley Finds 13 Is Lucky in Her Stage Career." *Chicago Daily Tribune*, November 17, 1955.

Muir, Florence. "Noel's 'Pretty Polly' to Be Carol Lynley." *The Washington Post*, September 13, 1966.

Muir, John Kenneth. *Terror Television*. Jefferson, NC: McFarland and Company, Inc., 2001.

Nathan, Paul. Memo to Hal Wallis. Jan. 7, 1969. Hal Wallis Papers, Margaret Herrick Library, Academy of Motion Pictures Arts and Sciences.

___. Memo to Hal Wallis. January 17, 1969. Hal Wallis Papers, Margaret Herrick Library, Academy of Motion Pictures Arts and Sciences.

___. Memo to Hal Wallis. February 26, 1969. Hal Wallis Papers, Margaret Herrick Library, Academy of Motion Pictures Arts and Sciences.

___. Memo to Hal Wallis. March 5, 1969. Hal Wallis Papers, Margaret Herrick Library, Academy of Motion Pictures Arts and Sciences.

___. Memo to Hal Wallis. March 6, 1969. Hal Wallis Papers, Margaret Herrick Library, Academy of Motion Pictures Arts and Sciences.

___. Memo to Hal Wallis. March 10, 1969. Hal Wallis Papers, Margaret Herrick Library, Academy of Motion Pictures Arts and Sciences.

___. Memo to Hal Wallis. March 28, 1969. Hal Wallis Papers, Margaret Herrick Library, Academy of Motion Pictures Arts and Sciences.

___. Memo to Hal Wallis. June 25, 1969. Hal Wallis Papers, Margaret Herrick Library, Academy of Motion Pictures Arts and Sciences.

___. Memo to Hal Wallis. September 24, 1969. Hal Wallis Papers, Margaret Herrick Library, Academy of Motion Pictures Arts and Sciences.

___. Memo to Hal Wallis. October 24, 1969. Hal Wallis Papers, Margaret Herrick Library, Academy of Motion Pictures Arts and Sciences.

Navasky, Victor S. "It's Shabby-Genteel but the Stars Love It." *New York Times*, May 5, 1974.

Neame, Ronald and Barbara Roisman Cooper. *Straight from the Horse's Mouth: Ronald Neame, an Autobiography*. Lanham, Md.: Scarecrow Press, 2003.

"Need Teenagers with 30 Years' Experience for TV Storybook." *Daily Boston Globe*, October 26, 1958.

"Newsgram." *The International Film Journal*, Vol. 79, Issue 13, June 24, 1977: 8.

Newton, Gloria. "The Two Faces of Carol Lynley." *The Australian Women's Weekly*. December 1, 1971: 17.

Nicholls, Liz. "VCR Foul-Up Like Cold Turkey to Oscar Addict." *Edmonton Journal*, April 2, 1989: C1.

O'Neill, James. *Terror on Tape*. New York, NY: Billboard Books, 1994).

Oppenheimer, Peer J. "Carol Lynley: She's Learning How to Cry." *Family Weekly*, January 3, 1965: 12.

___, "The Teen-Ager Who Grew Up Too Fast," *The High Point Enterprise*, June 13, 1965, 71.

Parrott, Jennings. "Newsmakers: Justice Sees More Free Speech Disputes." *Los Angeles Times*, October 21, 1976.

Parsons, Louella. Editorial. *Los Angeles Herald-Examiner*, September 9, 1963.

___. "'Reluctant Debutante' to Be Disney Find, 15." *The Washington Post and Times Herald*, June 18, 1957.

Peary, Gerald. "Highsmith." *Sight and Sound*, (Spring, 1988), 104.

Pelswick, Rose. Article in the *New York Journal-American*, 1961.

"Penn National Will Honor Carol Lynley and Barry Sullivan." *Lebanon Daily News*, June 7, 1977: 11.

"People." *Maclean's*. September 1, 1980: 30.

Pfeiffer, Lee. "Making Baddies Cry 'U.N.C.L.E.': An Interview with Stefanie Powers." *Cinema Retro*. Vol. 15, Issue, 44, 2019: 26-29.

Phillips, Mark & Alain Bourassa. "Deaths of the Immortal: Part Two." *Starlog*, January 1993: 67-69.

___. "Lives of the Immortal: Part One." *Starlog*, December 1992: 58-62.

Pierson, Jim. *Produced and Directed by Dan Curtis*. Los Angeles: Pomegranate Press, 2004.

Podhoretz, John. "Evil on the Rails." *The Weekly Standard*, December 4, 2017: 43.

Poggiali, Chris. "Interview with Mort Künstler." *Cinema Retro*, Vol 8: Issue 24, 2012: 18.

"Problems in Making a Series in Britain—By an American." *The Stage and Television Today*, October 10, 1968: 10.

Purcelli, Marion. "A Swinging Look Ahead: A Shorn Carol Arrived in London." *Chicago Tribune*, September 1, 1968.

Radcliffe, Donnie and Jacqueline Trescott. "A Meister-Dinner for a Meistersinger." *The Washington Post*, June 17, 1975: B1 – C2, column 3.

Radford, James. "Poseidon: Behind the Scenes." *Cinema Retro*. Vol 8: Issue 24, 2012: 16.

"Radley Metzger's 'Cat and Canary' to Cinema Shares." *Variety*, August 16, 1978: 7.

Reisfeld, Bert. "Preminger Filming 'Bunny' in Former London Stables." *Los Angeles Times*, June 16, 1965.

"Return to Peyton Place: Destined to Be One of the Most Widely-Discussed Screenplays of 1960." *20th Century-Fox Dynamo*, February 1960: 66, 67.

Reynolds, Jim. "Forever Lovely Carol Lynley." *Interview*, May 1979.

Rice, Charles D. "How Old Is Carol?" *Los Angeles Times*, August 25, 1957.

Richey, Jeremy R. "Screaming Skin and a Shattered Life. Back to the Shuttered Room." *Soledad*, No. 3, October 2019.

"Robert Hooks Will Star in 'Crosscurrent.'" *New York Amsterdam News*, December 5, 1970.

Robin, Marcy. "Dan Curtis News." *Shadowgram*. No. 81, November 1997: 11.

Roegger, Berthe. "Preview: SF Films of '79: The Shape of Things to Come. *Starlog*, May 1979: 52, 53.

Rohrbach, Edward. "New TV Series Puts Emphasis on Subtle Evil." *Chicago Tribune*, September 22, 1968.

Rozzo, Mark. "Secrets of the Chateau Marmont." *Vanity Fair*, February 2019.

Sauer, Georgia. "Personality Profile: Carol in Focus...From 'Denim' to Liberation." *Chicago Tribune*, December 17, 1972.

Scheuer, Philip K. "Hal Wallis: Mr. Durable of Independent Film-Makers." *Los Angeles Times*, December 28, 1969.

___. "Otto's Midas Touch Pays Off." *Los Angeles Times*, March 30, 1965.

___. "'Poseidon Adventure' Filming on Queen Mary." *Los Angeles Times*, April 21, 1972.

Scheuer, Steven H. "Gifted Starlet Not Ready to Study Acting." *The Hartford Courant*, March 1, 1959.

___, ed. *Movies on TV, 9th edition*. New York: Bantam Books, 1981.

Schudel, Matt. "Actress in 1972 Blockbuster *The Poseidon Adventure*, Dies at 77." *The Washington Post*, September 6, 2019. https://www.washingtonpost.com/local/obituaries/carol-lynley-actress-in-cult-classic-the-poseidon-adventure-dies-at-77/2019/09/06/89c8715a-d0bc-11e9-b29b-a528dc82154a_story.html?arc404=true

Schumach, Murray. "Hollywood 'Shock:' Mental Illness Drama Gets Some Footnotes." *New York Times*, September 8, 1963.

Scott, John L. "'Charlemagne' Role for Eleanor Parker." *Los Angeles Times*, June 5, 1963.

Scott, Vernon. "How Does Anyone Explain a Girl Like Carol Lynley?" *Leader Times, Kitanning, PA*, June 25, 1969.

___. "'Poseidon Adventure' Turns into Expensive Venture for Producer." *El Paso Herald-Post*, August 26, 1972: 4.

___. "Scott's World: 'Flood' the Most Expensive TV Film." *Columbus Telegraph*, November 22, 1976.

Segaloff, Nat. *Final Cuts: The Last Films of 50 Great Directors*. Albany, GA: BearManor Media, 2013.

Sellers, Robert. *What Fresh Lunacy Is This?: The Authorized Biography of Oliver Reed*. London: Constable & Robinson, 2013.

Selsman, Jill. "Hollywood 90046." in *Hollywood Handbook*. ed. André Balazs. New York; Universe Pub., 1996.

Selsman, Michael. *All Is Vanity: Memoirs of a Hollywood Operative*. New World Digital Publishing, 2009.

Shain, Percy. "Not Even TV People Proud of These Emmys." *Boston Globe*, May 26, 1963.

Shearer, Lloyd. "Otto Preminger: Hollywood's Most Controversial Character." *Boston Globe*, June 27, 1965.

Sheppard, Eugenia. "Inside Fashion: A Nice Quiet Movie." *New York Post Magazine*, December 14, 1972: 7.

Shull, Richard K. "TV's All-American Boy." *Express and News San Antonio, Texas*, Mar. 1, 1970: 23.

Silliphant, Stirling. *The Poseidon Adventure*: typescript. March 24, 1972.

"Sixties Star Lynley Joins AIDS Movie Benefit." 1996.

Skelton, Scott and Jim Benson. *Rod Serling's Night Gallery: An After-Hours Tour*. Syracuse, NY: Syracuse University Press: 1998.

Sloan, Robin Adams. "Gossip Column." *Asbury Park Press*, November 1, 1987, G18.

Smith, Cecil. "Critic Turns Actor; Already He's Type-Casting Victim." *Los Angeles Times*, March 1, 1959.

___. "The World of Polly Bergen." *Los Angeles Times*, May 7, 1961

Smith, Don G. *H.P. Lovecraft in Popular Culture: The Works and Their Adaptations in Film, Television, Comics, Music and Games*. Jefferson, NC: McFarland & Company, Inc., 2006.

Smith, Liz. "Carol Lynley Latest to Scale a 'Twin Peaks' Comeback." *Los Angeles Times*, August 30, 1990.

"Stagione 1978-79: i 100 film di maggior incasso," *Hit Parade Italia*, http://www.hitparadeitalia.it/bof/boi/boi1978-79.htm

"Starlets Out to Shine: Eight of Hollywood's Brightest Newcomers Start Their Long Climb Up the Ladder to Movie Stardom." *Pageant*, June 1958: 46-53.

"Success Story at Fifteen." *Life*. April 22, 1957: 128-133.

Taraborrelli, J. Randy. *Sinatra: Behind the Legend*. New York, NY: Grand Central Publishing, 2015.

Tarantino, Quentin. "Tarantino's Reviews!" Interview with Elric Kane and Brian Saur. *Pure Cinema Podcast*. Podcast audio, April 1, 2020. https://purecinemapodcast.libsyn.com/tarantinos-reviews-with-quentin-tarantino.

Taylor, Nora E. "'Laugh-In' Stars: 'Some Sort of Future in Films.'" *Christian Science Monitor*, June 14, 1969.

Terry, Carol Burton. "Off Camera." *Newsday*, August 23, 1981.

Terry, Clifford. "The Movies: Allan Carr, Counselor to the Stars." *Chicago Tribune*, October 13, 1974.

Thomas, Bob. "Carol Lynley Has Short Retirement." *Los Angeles Times*, July 3, 1962.

Thomas, Kevin. "Gig Young: It's Harder to be No. 2." *Los Angeles Times*, September 6, 1966.

Thomas, Zoe. "'The Poseidon Adventure' Is the Quintessential Disaster Movie." FilmSchoolRejects.com, May 14, 2019. https://filmschoolrejects.com/the-poseidon-adventure/

Thompson, Jeff. *The Television Horrors of Dan Curtis: Dark Shadows, The Night Stalker and Other Productions, 1966-2006*. Jefferson, NC: McFarland and Company, Inc., 2009.

Towers, Harry Alan. *Mr. Towers of London: A Life in Show Business*. Duncan, OK: BearManor Media: 2013.

"Trailways Depots Plugging *Norwood*." *Variety*, Apr. 18, 1970:6.

Tranberg, Charles. *I Love the Illusion: The Life and Career of Agnes Moorehead*. Albany, GA: BearManor Media, 2007.

UPI. "Girl Talk." *Great Bend Tribune*, November 15, 1964: 26.

___. "Glamour Girl Group Gets Carol Lynley." *Desert Sun*. June 13, 1963: 4.

Vadeboncoeur, Joan E. "Carol Lynley Is Young at 30." *Syracuse Herald-Journal*, February 7, 1972: 20.

Vinciguerra, Thomas. "Underwater, and Over the Top in 1972." *New York Times*, May 2, 2006: 1ST, 16ST.

Wallis, Hal. Memo to Paul Nathan. June 14, 1969. Hal Wallis Papers, Margaret Herrick Library, Academy of Motion Pictures Arts and Sciences.

___. Memo to Paul Nathan. September 29, 1969. Hal Wallis Papers, Margaret Herrick Library, Academy of Motion Pictures Arts and Sciences.

"Wallis Prefers 'Then' to 'Now' Pix." *Variety*, June 18, 1969: 1, 70.

Warga, Wayne. "'Ronald Neame Tries Hand at Action Film." *Los Angeles Times*, June 18, 1972.

Watts, Stephen. "Whatever Became of 'Bunny Lake?'" *New York Times*, May 23, 1965.

"WB-7A Film Retitled 4th Time." *The Hollywood Reporter*, October 24, 1968.

Weaver, Tom. *The Horror Hits of Richard Gordon*. Duncan, OK: BearManor Media, 2011.

Weinraub, Judith. "An American G.I. in London Finds Success as a Designer." *New York Times*, January 2, 1973.

Weldon, Michael J. *The Psychotronic Video Guide*. London: Titan Books, 1996.

Wells, Ross. *EXploZion!* iUniverse, 2002.

"'What's Going On,' Not a Question, But a Winner." *Los Angeles Sentinel*, November 25, 1971.

"Where Are They Now? Carol Lynley." *Biography Magazine*, January 2001: 36.

"Where Are They Now? Carol Lynley: From *Yum-Yum Tree* to *Fantasy Island*." *Rona Barrett's Hollywood*, [ca. 1980]: 32, 61.

White, Brynn. "Encore: Forbidden Fruit." *Film Comment*, May 2008: 22, 23.

White, Diane. "At Large: Still Haunted by the Sixties." *Boston Globe*, March 3, 1977.

Wilson, Barbara. "Will 'Adventure' Mean End to Oblivion for Carol Lynley?" *The Philadelphia Inquirer*, December 15, 1972.

Wilson, Earl. "Buttons Makes Carol See Red." *Independent*, December 29, 1972.

___. "It Happened Last Night." *Courier-Post Cherry Hill, NJ*, December 10, 1966: 28.

___. "It Happened Last Night." *Newsday*, October 6, 1965.

___. "It Happened Last Night: Carol Bares Talent Only…" *New York Post*, October 4, 1965.

___. "Last Night with Earl Wilson: Carol's Sexless Planet." *New York Post*, November 29, 1978: 54.

___. "Lynley Wants Children." *The Lima News*, July 21, 1975: 23.

___. "Oscar-Winning Actress Loves Paunchy Comedian," *Reno Evening Gazette*, January 21, 1977.

___. *Show Business Laid Bare*. New York: Putnam, 1974.

___. "Westbury Music Fair Slates Judy Garland." *Independent-Press Telegram*, May 12, 1967.

Wolters, Larry. "Miss of 15 Wins Big TV Role." *Chicago Daily Tribune*, December 12, 1957.

Wood, Tom. "International Yum Yum." *New York Morning Herald Tribune*. May 5, 1963.

___. "Story of Disintegrated People." *New York Morning Herald Tribune*. September 22, 1963.

"'World Premiere' of Old Movie." *Corpus Christi Caller-Times*, December 29, 1968: 9G.

Yakir, Dan. "Carol Lynley: The Shape of Things to Come." *New York Post*, May 16, 1979: 39.

"Young Hollywood through the Decades." *People*. November 18, 1996.

"Your Letters: More Carols for Carol." *Seventeen*, July 1958: 17.

Zimmerman, Jill S. "An Image to Heal." *The Humanist*. Vol. 57, Iss. 1. Jan./Feb. 1997: 20-25.

Zunser, Jesse. "Star? Don't Be Silly! Carol Lynley, at 17, Makes the Hop from Stage to Screen—and Stardom—Seem Easy." *Cue*, 1959: 18.

End Notes

1 Preface
Mark Jancovich, "Beyond Hammer: The First Run Market and the Prestige Horror Film in the Early 1960s," *Palgrave Communications*, Vol.3, Iss. 1, (Dec. 2017), 11.
2 Carol Lynley, Telephone interview with author, 2019.
3 Ibid.
4 Matt Schudel, "Actress in 1972 Blockbuster *The Poseidon Adventure*, Dies at 77," *The Washington Post*, September 6, 2019, https://www.washingtonpost.com/local/obituaries/carol-lynley-actress-in-cult-classic-the-poseidon-adventure-dies-at-77/2019/09/06/89c8715a-d0bc-11e9-b29b-a528dc82154a_story.html?arc404=true

Introduction
5 Diane White, "At Large: Still Haunted by the Sixties," *Boston Globe,* March 3, 1977.
6 Carol Lynley, Telephone interview with author.
7 Ibid.
8 Sharon Day, "Carol Lynley & Jamie Lee Curtis: The Princesses of 70s Horror," *Ghost Hunting Theories*, September 3, 2009, www.ghosthuntingtheories.com.
9 Jeremy R Richey, "Screaming Skin and a Shattered Life. Back to the Shuttered Room," *Soledad*, No. 3, October 2019.
10 Carol Lynley, Interview with Jak Castro, 2003.
11 James O'Neill, *Terror on Tape*, (New York, NY: Billboard Books, 1994), 6.

The Early Years: Child Model to Teen Idol
12 Lynley, Telephone interview with author.
13 Ibid.
14 Daniel Jones Lee, Telephone interview with author, September 19, 2019.
15 Ibid.

16 Margaret Kenney, Email interview with author, April 18, 2019.
17 Lynley, Telephone interview with author.
18 Millicent Adams, "Young Star Shines in Dramatic Roles on Stage and Screen," *The Washington Post and Times Herald,* July 12, 1959.
19 Jones Lee, Telephone interview with author.
20 Ibid.
21 Lynley, Telephone interview with author.
22 Jones Lee, Telephone interview with author.
23 Ibid.
24 Cleveland Amory, "Model to Actress, Carol Lynley Made It," *Pittsburgh Press,* July 5, 1978, 25.
25 Jesse Zunser, "Star? Don't Be Silly! Carol Lynley, at 17, Makes the Hop from Stage to Screen—and Stardom—Seem Easy," *Cue,* 1959: 18.
26 Jim Reynolds, "Forever Lovely Carol Lynley," *Interview,* May 1979.
27 Emory Lewis, "Lynley's Back on Broadway—Belatedly," *Jersey Record,* July 27, 1975, B-19.
28 Charles D. Rice, "How Old Is Carol?" *Los Angeles Times,* August 25, 1957.
29 Linda Fine, "Carol Lynley: The Face That Doesn't Change," *Model's Circle,* December 1975, 38.
30 Diane McBain, *Famous Enough: A Hollywood Memoir,* (Albany, GA: BearManor Media, 2014), 232.
31 Tom Lisanti, *Drive-In Dream Girls" A Galaxy of B-Movie Starlets of the Sixties,* (Jefferson, NC, McFarland and Company, Inc., 2003), 34.
32 Jill S. Zimmerman, "An Image to Heal," *The Humanist,* Vol. 57, Iss. 1, (Jan./Feb. 1997).
33 Jones Lee, Telephone interview with author.
34 Amory, "Model to Actress, Carol Lynley Made It."
35 Jones Lee, Telephone interview with author.
36 Tom Donnelly, "'Mice and Men' and Carol Lynley with Homage to Harlow," *The Washington Post,* March 12, 1975.
37 Reynolds, "Forever Lovely Carol Lynley."
38 Lewis, "Lynley's Back on Broadway—Belatedly," B-19.
39 Edwin Miller, "Carol Lynley: Read Her Thoughts," *Seventeen,* May 1958, 186.
40 Ibid, 186, 188.
41 Ibid, 189.
42 Jones Lee, Telephone interview with author.
43 Zunser, "Star? Don't Be Silly!"
44 Oppenheimer, "Carol Lynley: She's Learning to Cry," 12.
45 Jones Lee, Telephone interview with author.
46 Miller, "Carol Lynley: Read Her Thoughts," 188.
47 Lynley, Telephone interview with author.
48 Christina Lane, *Phantom Lady: Hollywood Producer Joan Harrison, the Forgotten Woman Behind Hitchcock,* (Chicago, IL. Chicago Review Press, 2020), 253.
49 Miller, "Carol Lynley: Read Her Thoughts," 186.
50 Ibid.
51 Zunser, "Star? Don't Be Silly!"
52 Ward Morehouse, "Carol Lynley 'In Love with All the Critics," *The Sun,* June 22,

1958.
53 Dan Yakir, "Carol Lynley: The Shape of Things to Come," *New York Post*, May 16, 1979, 39.
54 Jones Lee, Telephone interview with author.
55 "Being Quiet Made Her a Star," *Daily Boston Globe*, May 4, 1958.
56 Edwin Miller, "Carol Lynley: Read Her Thoughts," *Seventeen*. May 1958.
57 "Your Letters: More Carols for Carol," *Seventeen*, July 1958, 17.
58 "Need Teenagers with 30 Years' Experience for TV Storybook," *Daily Boston Globe*, October 26, 1958.
59 Ibid.
60 Charles Tranberg, *I Love the Illusion: The Life and Career of Agnes Moorehead*, (Albany, GA, BearManor Media, 2007), 188.
61 Lewis, "Lynley's Back on Broadway—Belatedly," B-22.
62 Monika Henreid, "A Little More on Carol Lynley," *Instagram*, September 8, 2019.
63 Ibid.
64 Lynley, Telephone interview with author.
65 Hedda Hopper, "Carol Lynley: An Appealing Talented 16," *San Antonio Express*, September 14, 1958. 77.
66 Philip Dunne, *Take Two: A Life in Movies and Politics*, (New York: McGraw-Hill, 1980), 289.
67 Patricia McLean, *All Fall Down: The Brandon deWilde Story*, (Rockland, Maine, Maine Authors Publishing, 2015), 98.
68 Jones Lee, Telephone interview with author.
69 Julie Kirgo, Liner notes to the *Blue Denim* Blu-ray, Twilight Time, 2018.
70 "Hound-Dog Man," BAMPFA, December 5, 1980, https://bampfa.org/event/hound-dog-man.
71 Mike Connolly, "Business Is Bad," *Desert Sun*," December 8, 1959, 4.
72 Cecil Smith, "Critic Turns Actor; Already He's Type-Casting Victim," *Los Angeles Times*, March 1, 1959.
73 Ibid.
74 Steven H. Scheuer, "Gifted Starlet Not Ready to Study Acting," *The Hartford Courant*, March 1, 1959.
75 Lynley, Telephone interview with author.
76 Rose Pelswick, Article in the *New York Journal-American*, 1961.
77 Ibid.
78 Mike Connolly, "Wendy Not Kidding," *Desert Sun*, November 11, 1959, 4B.
79 Jones Lee, Telephone interview with author.
80 Hollis Alpert, "Movies: Now After Five Years and Three Names, She's on Top," *Woman's Day*, November 1960, 12.
81 Lynley, Telephone interview with author.
82 Carol Lynley, On-camera interview, Asheville Film Festival, 1999, https://www.youtube.com/watch?v=t2o3NZZZUb0&t=3s.
83 Lynley, Telephone interview with author.
84 John Larsen, "Teens-Ville U.S.A. Carol Too Serious to Date Bores," *Boston Globe*, November 13, 1960.
85 Lynley, Telephone interview with author.
86 Lynley, Asheville Film Festival, 1999,

87 Lynley, Telephone interview with author.
88 Jones Lee, Telephone interview with author.
89 Brynn White, "Encore: Forbidden Fruit," *Film Comment*, May 2008, 23.
90 Lynley, Telephone interview with author.
91 "Return to Peyton Place: Destined to Be One of the Most Widely-Discussed Screenplays of 1960," *20th Century-Fox Dynamo*, February 1960, 66.
92 Lynley, Telephone interview with author.
93 Ibid.
94 Ibid.
95 Jones Lee, Telephone interview with author.
96 Ibid.
97 Michael Callahan, "Peyton Place's Real Victim," *Vanity Fair*, March 2006.
98 Ibid.
99 Lynley, Telephone interview with author.

A Sex Kitten Purrs…Briefly
100 Bob Thomas, "Carol Lynley Has Short Retirement," *Los Angeles Times*, July 3, 1962.
101 Lynley, Telephone interview with author.
102 Ibid.
103 Dan Jenkins, "The Single-Minded Quest of Carol Lynley," *TV Guide*, August 3, 1963, 27.
104 Percy Shain, "Not Even TV People Proud of These Emmys," *Boston Globe*, May 26, 1963.
105 Curtis Harrington, *Nice Guys Don't Work in Hollywood: The Adventures of an Aesthete in the Movie Business,* (Chicago, IL: Drag City Inc., 2013),
106 Ibid.
107 Ibid.
108 Lynley, Telephone interview with author.
109 Ibid.
110 Lee Pfeiffer, "Making Baddies Cry 'U.N.C.L.E.': An Interview with Stefanie Powers," *Cinema Retro*, Vol. 15, Issue, 44, 2019, 27.
111 Carol Lynley, On-camera interview with Eckhart Schmidt, "Carol Lynley Remembers", *Bunny Lake Is Missing Blu-ray,* Indicator, 2006.
112 "Goodbye, Age of Innocence," *Life*, May 3, 1963, 42.
113 Tom Wood, "International Yum Yum," *New York Morning Telegraph*. May 5, 1963.
114 Hedda Hopper, "What a Difference a Few Years Make!" *The Hartford Courant*, June 23, 1963.
115 Tina Sinatra. Telephone interview with author, March 3, 2018.
116 Wood, "International Yum Yum."
117 Georgia Sauer, "Personality Profile: Carol in Focus…From 'Denim' to Liberation," *Chicago Tribune*, December 17, 1972.
118 Erskine Johnson, "Showbeat: Miss Blue Denim Now in Silk and Satin," *Santa Cruz Sentinel*, April 14, 1963, 19.
119 Arlene Dahl, "Arlene Dahl Selects Tomorrow's Leading Lovelies," *Chicago Tribune*, October 13, 1963.
120 Lynley, Telephone interview with author.

121 Carol Lynley, On-camera interview, *Preminger: Anatomy of a Filmaker*, Otto Preminger Films, 1991.
122 Lynley, Telephone interview with author.
123 Lynley, On-camera interview, *Preminger: Anatomy of a Filmaker*.
124 UPI, "Glamour Girl Group Gets Carol Lynley," *Desert Sun*, June 13, 1963, 4.
125 Royal S. Brown, Liner notes to *The Cardinal Original Motion Picture Soundtrack*, Preamble, PRCD 1778, CD, 2010.
126 Jenkins, "The Single-Minded Quest of Carol Lynley," 28.
127 Jenkins, "The Single-Minded Quest of Carol Lynley," 27.
128 Jones Lee, Telephone interview with author.
129 Ibid.
130 Tom Lisanti, *Fantasy Femmes of Sixties Cinema: Interviews with Twenty Actresses from Biker, Beach, and Elvis Movies*, (Jefferson, NC, McFarland and Company, Inc., 2001), 71.
131 Oppenheimer, "Carol Lynley: She's Learning to Cry," 12.
132 Hollis Alpert, "The Big Star Derby," *Woman's Day*, February 1964, 19.
133 Ibid, 105.
134 Ibid.
135 Lynley, Telephone interview with author.
136 Murray Schumach, "Hollywood 'Shock:' Mental Illness Drama Gets Some Footnotes," *New York Times*, September 8, 1963.
137 Ibid.
138 Ibid.
139 Lynley, Telephone interview with author.
140 Louella Parsons, Editorial, *Los Angeles Herald-Examiner*, September 9, 1963.
141 Lisanti, *Fantasy Femmes of Sixties Cinema*, 85.
142 Lynley, Telephone interview with author.
143 Ibid.
144 Ibid.
145 "On the Foreign Screen: Bleak and Brilliant," *The Times of India*, June 23, 1966, 11.
146 Lynley, Telephone interview with author.
147 Dick Kleiner, "Dick Kleiner's Showbeat: Carol Lynley Dull? Well, Not Exactly," *Santa Cruz Sentinel*, September 27, 1964, 31.
148 Ibid.
149 "Young Hollywood through the Decades," *People*, November 18, 1996.
150 "Carol Lynley Stars in 'Fliers,'" *The Atlanta Constitution*, February 1, 1965.
151 Ibid.
152 Louella Parsons, "Carol Lynley: Still Young and Foolish," *New York Journal-American*, June 6, 1965.
153 Earl Wilson, "It Happened Last Night," *Newsday*, October 6, 1965.
154 Jones Lee, Telephone interview with author.
155 McBain, *Famous Enough: A Hollywood Memoir*, 232.
156 Ibid, 233.
157 Lynley, Telephone interview with author.
158 Carol Lynley, "Arlene Dahl: Carol Lynley Is Guilty of Being Convivial," *Philadelphia Daily News*, March 18, 1965, 38.

159 Ibid.
160 Bee Paul Hirschl, "Jayne Mansfield: The Friend Is Gone But the Friendship Endures," *Pittsburgh Post-Gazette,* June 24, 1987, 11.
161 Paul Nathan, Memo to Paramount Legal Dept., June 25, 1965.
162 Lynley, Telephone interview with author.
163

She's Not There
Stephen Watts, "Whatever Became of 'Bunny Lake?'" *New York Times*, May 23, 1965.
164 Ibid.
165 Hedda Hopper, "Looking at Hollywood: Ice Skater Carol Heiss Signed for First Movie," *Chicago Daily Tribune*, July 28, 1960.
166 Hedda Hopper, "Looking at Hollywood: Disney Film of Sea Chase to Start Soon," *Chicago Daily Tribune*, April 29, 1961.
167 Cecil Smith, "The World of Polly Bergen," *Los Angeles Times*, May 7, 1961.
168 Hedda Hopper, "Carroll Baker to Star on Broadway," *Los Angeles Times*, May 22, 1961.
169 Eugene Archer, "France Will Lift Film's Export Ban," *New York Times*, August 2, 1961.
170 John L. Scott, "'Charlemagne' Role for Eleanor Parker," *Los Angeles Times*, June 5, 1963.
171 Hedda Hopper, "Looking at Hollywood: Ann Sothern's Daughter to Be Starred," *Chicago Tribune*, December 15, 1964.
172 Ibid.
173 Lynley, On-camera interview with Eckhart Schmidt.
174 Joe Baltake, "This Critic Likes Fashion," *The Austin American Statesman*, November 4, 1979.
175 Lynley, On-camera interview with Eckhart Schmidt.
176 Lynley, Telephone interview with author.
177 Watts, "Whatever Became of 'Bunny Lake?'"
178 Ibid.
179 Bert Reisfeld, "Preminger Filming 'Bunny' in Former London Stables," *Los Angeles Times*, June 16, 1965.
180 Philip K. Scheuer, "Otto's Midas Touch Pays Off," *Los Angeles Times,* March 30, 1965.
181 Margi Rountree, Email exchange with author, September 10, 2018.
182 Lynley, Telephone interview with author.
183 Ibid.
184 Ibid.
185 Tom Donnelly, "'Mice and Men' and Carol Lynley with Homage to Harlow," *The Washington Post*, March 12, 1975.
186 David Frost, *An Autobiography: David Frost*, (London, HarperCollins, 1993), quoted in Neil Hegarty, *Frost: That Was the Life That Was: The Authorized Biography*, (London, WH Allen, 2015).
187 Ibid.
188 John Crosby, "The Little People," *New York Herald Tribune* [European Edition], May 12, 1965, 16.
189 Lynley, Telephone interview with author.

190 Lynley, On-camera interview with Eckhart Schmidt.
191 Lloyd Shearer, "Otto Preminger: Hollywood's Most Controversial Character," *Boston Globe*, June 27, 1965.
192 Lynley, On-camera interview with Eckhart Schmidt.
193 Ibid.
194 Ibid.
195 Ibid.
196 Lynley, Telephone interview with author.
197 Earl Wilson, "It Happened Last Night: Carol Bares Talent Only…" *New York Post*, October 4, 1965.
198 Jennifer Bass and Pat Kirkham, *Saul Bass: A Life in Film and Design*, (London: Laurence King, 2011).
199 Lynley, Telephone interview with author.
200 Foster Hirsch, *Otto Preminger: The Man Who Would Be King,* (New York, Alfred A. Knopf, 2007), 404.
201 Lynley, Telephone interview with author.
202 "12 Young Actresses on Deb Star Ball," *The Hartford Courant*, January 2, 1966.
203 Sarah Khan, "Feminist Flashback Friday: Ann Lake ('Bunny Lake Is Missing'), *Cinefilles: Real Girls. Reel Talk*, http://www.cinefilles.ca/2015/09/04/feminist-flashback-friday-ann-lake-bunny-lake-is-missing/, September 4, 2015.
204 J. Hoberman, "Video: Deciding to Trust Your Sense. Or Not.," *New York Times*, January 25, 2015, Arts and Leisure, 17.
205 Ibid.
206 Rick Lattanzio, "Stream of the Day: *Bunny Lake Is Missing* Was Ahead of Its Time as a Tale of Gaslighting and Abduction," *IndiWire.com*, April 24, 2020, https://www.indiewire.com/2020/04/watch-bunny-lake-is-missing-criterion-channel-stream-of-the-day-1202226013/?fbclid=IwAR20OAWi9jGXJMoMf HG-9iO5fRXBsSG4BBq7fH1q9Oy-y1ulfuR4YMTKyl8
207 Ibid.
208 Lynley, On-camera interview with Eckhart Schmidt.
209 Lynley, Telephone interview with author.
210 Lynley, On-camera interview with Eckhart Schmidt.

Terror in Dunwich
211 Hedda Hopper, "Everyone Wants Sonny and Cher," *Los Angeles Times*, September 30, 1965.
212 Nat Segaloff, *Final Cuts: The Last Films of 50 Great Directors,* (Albany, GA, BearManor Media, 2013).
213 Peer J. Oppenheimer, "The Teen-Ager Who Grew Up Too Fast," *The High Point Enterprise,* June 13, 1965, 71.
214 Betty Martin, "Movie Call Sheet: Color Film Corp. Formed," *Los Angeles Times*, August 17, 1965.
215 Lynley, Telephone interview with author.
216 Ibid.
217 "Carol Lynley in Hard Roles," *Winnipeg Free Press*, March 5-12, 1966, 14.
218 Lynley, Telephone interview with author.
219 Ibid.

220 Charles P. Mitchell, *The Complete H.P. Lovecraft Filmography*, (Westport, CT: Greenwood Press, 2001), 185.
221 Robert Sellers, *What Fresh Lunacy Is This?: The Authorized Biography of Oliver Reed*, (London: Constable & Robinson, 2013), 121.
222 Susan D. Cowie and Tom Johnson, *The Films of Oliver Reed*, (Jefferson, NC: McFarland and Company, Inc., 2011), 85.
223 Lynley, Telephone interview with author.
224 Ibid.
225 Ibid.
226 Ibid.
227 Ibid.
228 Joshua Cohen, "Australia and the Theatre Made Judth Arthy Tough," *The Globe and Mail*, May 9, 1973.
229 William Hall, "Oliver Reed: Last of the Hell-Raisers," *Los Angeles Times*, February 24, 1974.
230 Lynley, Telephone interview with author.
231 Kevin Thomas, "Gig Young: It's Harder to be No. 2," *Los Angeles Times*, September 6, 1966.
232 Ibid.
233 Harrison Carroll, "Behind the Scenes in Hollywood: Scene Explodes into Melodrama," *Kokomo Morning Times*, June 18, 1966, 11.
234 Ibid.
235 Rebecca Morehouse, "Hot Lights, Clinches Often Have an Effect," *The Home News*, August 4, 1975, 6.
236 Karl E. Meyer, "American Dollars and British Pride," *The Washington Post*, June 26, 1966.
237 Marjory Adams, "The Misfortunes of Gig Young: A Girl (and Blood) in His Soup," *Boston Globe,* October 1, 1967.
238 Lynley, Telephone interview with author.
239 Ibid.
240 "Carolina Schedules 'The Shuttered Room,'" *Florence Morning News,* January 21, 1968.
241 Ibid.
242 Mike Connolly, "Notes from Hollywood," *Pasadena Independent*, November 16, 1966, 51.
243 Adams, "The Misfortunes of Gig Young."
244 Rex Reed, "'My Kind of Face Has a Bigger Future Than Ever,'" *New York Times*, October 29, 1967.
245 Lynley, Telephone interview with author.
246 Mitchell, *The Complete H.P. Lovecraft Filmography*, 182.
247 Ibid, 184.
248 Don G. Smith, *H.P. Lovecraft in Popular Culture: The Works and Their Adaptations in Film, Television, Comics, Music and Games*, (Jefferson, NC, McFarland & Company, Inc., 2006), 55.
249 Richey, "Screaming Skin and a Shattered Life."

Suave Spies to Invading Aliens

250 Sheila Graham, "Inside Hollywood with Sheila Graham," *Independent Star-News*, July 24, 1966, 52.
251 Ibid.
252 Lynley, Telephone interview with author.
253 Lynley, Telephone interview with author.
254 "Carol Lynley Talks about Herself." *Screen Stars*, August 1964: 29.
255 Florence Muir, "Noel's 'Pretty Polly' to Be Carol Lynley," *The Washington Post*, September 13, 1966.
256 Earl Wilson, "It Happened Last Night," *Courier-Post Cherry Hill, NJ*, December 10, 1966, 28.
257 Lynley, Telephone interview with author.
258 Allan Bryce, ed., *The Dark Side, the Magazine of the Macabre and Fantastic Presents Amicus, the Studio That Dripped Blood,* (Liskeard, Cornwall, Stray Cat, 2000), 47.
259 Ibid, 48.
260 Ibid.
261 Kevin Gough-Yates, "Seth Holt," *Screen*, V. 10, no. 6, Nov/Dec 1969, 17.
262 Lynley, Telephone interview with author.
263 Lynley, Telephone interview with author.
264 Graydon Carter, ed., *Vanity Fair's Tales of Hollywood,* (New York: Penguin Books, 2008), 173.
265 Victor Davis, "Under the Hollywood Sign: Carol Lynley Has a Lust for Success," *The Sunday Gleaner Magazine*, February 25, 1973,
266 Alex Freeman, "That's Show Biz: Carol Lynley Says She'll Stay in England," *The Hartford Courant*, January 10, 1967.
267 Earl Wilson, "Westbury Music Fair Slates Judy Garland," *Independent Press Telegram*, May 15, 1967, A-10.
268 Dick Kleiner, "England Changed Carol Lynley," *Santa Cruz Sentinel*, May 19, 1967, 17.
269 Vernon Scott, "How Does Anyone Explain a Girl Like Carol Lynley?" *Leader Times, Kitanning, PA*, June 25, 1969.
270 Ibid.
271 Alex Freeman, "That's Show Biz: Burt Lancaster Seeks New Leading Lady," *The Hartford Courant*, July 8, 1966.
272 "Faye Dunaway: Star, Symbol, Style," *Newsweek*, March 4, 1968, 44.
273 Ibid.
274 Lynley, Telephone interview with author.
275 Valerie Clark, "I'm No Threat to Men Says Feminist Carol Lynley," *TV Times*, April 12-18, 1975.
276 Lynley, Telephone interview with author.
277 Ibid.
278 Tom Lisanti and Louis Paul, *Film Fatales: Women in Espionage Film and Television, 1962-1973,* (Jefferson, NC, McFarland and Company, Inc., 2002), 197.
279 Ibid, 158.
280 Ibid, 152.
281 Tom Lisanti, *Glamour Girls of Sixties Hollywood,* (Jefferson, NC, McFarland and Company, Inc., 2008), 19.

282 Lynley, Telephone interview with author.
283 Gary Gerani, "Episode Guide to *The Invaders*," *Starlog*, September 1978, 47.
284 Paul Jones, "David Aided with Goliath 'Invaders,'" *The Atlanta Constitution*, December 5, 1967.
285 Ibid.
286 Lynley, Telephone interview with author.
287 Ibid.
288 Stephen Bowie, "*The Invaders*: The Nightmare Has Already Begun," *The Classic TV History Blog*, http://classictvhistory.com/EpisodeGuides/invaders.html, 2007.
289 Marion Purcelli, "A Swinging Look Ahead: A Shorn Carol Arrived in London," *Chicago Tribune*, September 1, 1968.
290 Lynley, Telephone interview with author.
291 Gretchen Carroll, "Research for Carol," *Pittsburgh Press*, December 10, 1967, TV-4.
292 "Joan Harrison: Fright-Minded Series Maker," *Los Angeles Times*, September 2, 1968.
293 Ibid.
294 Edward Rohrbach, "New TV Series Puts Emphasis on Subtle Evil," *Chicago Tribune*, September 22, 1968.
295 Norman Lloyd, *Stages: Norman Lloyd. Interviewed by Francine Parker*, (Hollywood, CA: Directors Guild of America and Scarecrow Press, 1990), 196.
296 Lynley, Telephone interview with author.
297 "Problems in Making a Series in Britain—By an American," *The Stage and Television Today*, October 10, 1968, 10.
298 Lynley, Telephone interview with author.
299 Ibid.
300 "Dummy Delay," *San Antonio Express and News*, November 3, 1968, 145.
301 Lynley, Telephone interview with author.
302 Stan Maays, "Meet Carol Lynley: A Living Doll," *The Abilene Reporter News*, September 26, 1968.
303 Ibid.
304 Lane, *Phantom Lady*, 272.
305 Vernon Scott, "Carol Lynley Decides TV Is Not for Women," *New Castle News*, December 13, 1967, 43.
306 Lynley, Telephone interview with author.
307 Ibid.
308 Hal Humphrey, "Jackie Cooper's Movie to Be Shown on NBC," *The Derrick*, November 27, 1968, 20.
309 Ibid.
310 Ibid.
311 Ibid.
312 Lynley, Telephone interview with author.
313 "Joe's Barbershop," *TV Guide*, July, 11, 1970, 11.
314 Ibid.
315 Julie Byrne, "Luis Estevez, Fashion 'Doer,' Can Do It All—and in a Hurry," *Los Angeles Times*, February 4, 1969.

316 Lynley, Telephone interview with author.
317
Murder in the Rough
Lynley, Telephone interview with author.
318 Howard Kazanjian, Email interview with author.
319 Ibid.
320 Gerald Peary, "Highsmith," *Sight and Sound*, Spring, 1988, 104.
321 Kazanjian, Email interview with author.
322 Lynley, Telephone interview with author.
323 Kazanjian, Email interview with author.
324 Lynley, Telephone interview with author.
325 Kazanjian, Email interview with author.
326 Ibid.
327 Ibid.
328 Ibid.
329 Ibid.
330 Ibid.
331 Lynley, Telephone interview with author.
332 Kazanjian, Email interview with author.
333 J. Randy Taraborrelli, *Sinatra: Behind the Legend*, (New York, NY: Grand Central Publishing, 2015).
334 Richard Freedman, "Carol Lynley Is Flying High," *Pittsburgh Press*, January 21, 1979, H-4.
335 Judith Crist, *Judith Crist's TV Guide to the Movies*, (Toronto: Popular Library, 1974).
336 Lynley, Telephone interview with author.
337 Ibid.
338 Kazanjian, Email interview with author.
339 Ibid.
340 Ibid.

What's a Bippy?
341 Ray Loynd, "Rowan, Martin to Do Two Comedies at MGM," *Los Angeles Times*, April 5, 1969.
342 Ray Loynd, "Rowan, Martin in Movie? You Bet Your Sweet Bippy," *Los Angeles Times*, April 9, 1969.
343 "Can Rowan, Martin Win in Films?" *The Atlanta Constitution*, May 10, 1969.
344 Ibid.
345 "'The Maltese Bippy:' Rowan and Martin Make Movie Comedy," *Kokomo (Ind.) Tribune*, June 1, 1969.
346 Clifford Terry, "The Movies: Allan Carr, Counselor to the Stars," *Chicago Tribune*, October 13, 1974.
347 Lynley, Telephone interview with author.
348 Loynd, "Rowan, Martin in Movie?"
349 Nora E. Taylor, "'Laugh-In' Stars: 'Some Sort of Future in Films,'" *Christian Science Monitor*, June 14, 1969.
350 Dick Adler, "A New Partner for Dan Rowan—The Werewolf," *Life*, May 23, 1969,

55, 57.
351 Lynley, Telephone interview with author.
352 Ibid.
353 Ibid.
354 Ray Loynd, "14 ½ Weeks Old: 'Bippy' Premieres Tonight," *Los Angeles Times*, June 5, 1969.
355 Joyce Haber, "Even Col. Parker Has His Film Price," *Los Angeles Times*, April 2, 1969.
356 Loynd, "Rowan, Martin in Movie?"
357 Norma Lee Browning, "Rowan and Martin Shun TV Format in Their First Movie," *Chicago Tribune*, September 7, 1969.
358 Norma Lee Browning, "Hollywood Today," *Chicago Tribune*, May 1, 1969.
359 Nathaniel Freedland, "Getting a Real-Life Look at Dickie Martin's Gums," *Toronto Daily Star*, June 7, 1969.
360 "Can Rowan, Martin Win in Films?"
361 "'The Maltese Bippy:' Rowan and Martin Make Movie Comedy."
362 Lynley, Telephone interview with author.
363 Taylor, "'Laugh-In' Stars: 'Some Sort of Future in Films.'"
364 Ibid.
365 Lynley, Telephone interview with author.

On the Run with the Immortal
366 Mark Phillips and Alain Bourassa, "Lives of the Immortal: Part One," *Starlog*, December 1992, 59.
367 Ibid, 60.
368 Ibid, 61.
369 Lynley, Telephone interview with author.
370 Phillips and Bourassa, "Lives of the Immortal: Part One."
371 Ibid.
372 Ibid.
373 Lynley, Telephone interview with author.
374 Mark Phillips and Alain Bourassa, "Deaths of the Immortal: Part Two," *Starlog*, January 1993, 67.
375 Lynley, Telephone interview with author.
376 Gene deRuelle, Email interview with author.
377 Ibid.
378 Ibid.
379 Marilyn Beck, "That's Show Biz: Gene Hackman's Back Home," *The Hartford Courant*, June 30, 1970.
380 deRuelle, Email interview with author.
381 Phillips and Bourassa, "Lives of the Immortal: Part One," 59.
382 Ibid.
383 deRuelle, Email interview with author.

A Foulmouthed Hooker in a G-Rated Comedy
384 Paul Nathan, Memo to Hal Wallis, March 6, 1969.
385 Hal Wallis, Memo to Paul Nathan, June 14, 1969.

386 Paul Nathan, Memo to Hal Wallis, June 25, 1969.
387 Paul Nathan, Memo to Hal Wallis, July 23, 1969.
388 Dorothy Manners, "Actress Unhappy Because Dirty Words Cancelled," *Anderson Daily Bulletin*, August 14, 1969.
389 Lynley, Telephone interview with author.
390 Ibid.
391 Hal Wallis, Memo to Paul Nathan, July 29, 1969.
392 Paul Nathan, Memo to Hal Wallis, September 24, 1969.
393 Jack Haley, Jr., Memo to Hal Wallis. October 9, 1969.
394 Jack Haley, Jr., Memo to Hal Wallis. November 3, 1969.
395 Paul Nathan, Memo to Hal Wallis, October 24, 1969.
396 Jack Haley, Jr., Memo to Hal Wallis, January 20, 1970.
397 Joyce Haber, "Campbell Finds Success by 'Going Against the Grain,'" *Los Angeles Times*, April 12, 1970.
398 Ibid.
399 Richard K. Shull, "TV's All-American Boy," *Express and News San Antonio, Texas*, Mar. 1, 1970: 23.
400 Glen Campbell and Tom Carter, *Rhinestone Cowboy: An Autobiography*, (New York: Villard Books, 1994).
401 Philip K. Scheuer, "Hal Wallis: Mr. Durable of Independent Film-Makers," *Los Angeles Times*, December 28, 1969.
402 Ibid.
403 Lisanti, *Fantasy Femmes of Sixties Cinema*, 278.
404 "Is the Movie Rating System G for Good? Mother Says Only Disney Really Safe," *San Bernardino Sun-Telegram*, August 9, 1970, D-1.
405 Jack Haley, Jr., "Years from Now, When You Talk About This...,'" *Action*, Vol. 5, No. 5 September-October 1970, 14.
406 Ibid.
407 Ibid.
408 Ibid.
409 Ibid.
410 Ibid.
411 Ibid.
412 Ibid.
413 Haber, "Jack Haley, Jr.—Less Tact Than Talent.'"
414 Ibid.
415 Lynley, Telephone interview with author.

Vampires and Druids and the Blob! Oh, My!
416 Barbara Bladen, "The Marquee," *The Times San Mateo*, December 8, 1972.
417 Sauer, "Personality Profile: Carol in Focus...From 'Denim' to Liberation."
418 Scott, "How Does Anyone Explain a Girl Like Carol Lynley?"
419 Bladen, "The Marquee."
420 John Hamilton, *Beasts in the Cellar: The Exploitation Film Career of Tony Tenser*, (Godalming, England: Fab Press, 2005).
421 Lynley, Telephone interview with author.
422 Ibid.

423 Lisanti, *Fantasy Femmes of Sixties Cinema*, 13, 14.
424 Sellers, *What Fresh Lunacy Is This?*
425 Ibid.
426 Norma Lee Browning, "Hollywood Today: Connie's Big Scene," *Chicago Tribune*, January 19, 1970.
427 Lynley, Telephone interview with author.
428 Ibid.
429 Sauer, "Personality Profile: Carol in Focus…From 'Denim' to Liberation."
430 Ibid.
431 Lynley, Telephone interview with author.
432 Ibid.
433 Lisanti and Louis Paul, *Film Fatales*, 210.
434 Ibid, 315.
435 Lynley, Telephone interview with author.
436 Marlin Dobbs, Email with author, January 21, 2020.
437 Harry Langdon, Jr., Telephone interview with author, January 26, 2020.
438 Norma Lee Browning, "Hollywood Today: The Good Life, Hagman Style: Bathtub for Six," *Chicago Tribune*, September 19, 1971.
439 Lynley, Telephone interview with author.
440 Ibid.
441 Ibid.
442 Ibid.
443 Ibid.
444 Ibid.
445 Joyce Haber, "Larry Hagman—Wild Man of Malibu Beach," *Los Angeles Times*, September 26, 1971.
446 Percy Shain, "Leading the Good Life," *Boston Globe*, November 14, 1971.
447 Lynley, Telephone interview with author.
448 Gloria Newton, "The Two Faces of Carol Lynley," *The Australian Women's Weekly*, December 1, 1971, 17.
449 Victor S. Navasky, "It's Shabby-Genteel but the Stars Love It," *New York Times*, May 5, 1974.
450 Marian Christy, "Carol Lynley—A Free Spirit," *Boston Globe*, January 7, 1973.
451 Jill Selsman, "Hollywood 90046," in *Hollywood Handbook*, ed. André Balazs (New York; Universe Pub., 1996), 180.
452 Ibid, 176.
453 Mark Rozzo, "Secrets of the Chateau Marmont," *Vanity Fair*, February 2019.
454 Dick Kleiner, "TV Scout Reports," *The Odessa American*, March 20, 1972, 17.
455 Mark Dawidziak, *The Night Stalker Companion: A 25th Anniversary Tribute* (Los Angeles: Pomegranate Press, 1997), 31-32.
456 "Carol Lynley Loves Latest Role," *The Daily Herald (Provo, Utah)*, January 10, 1972, 19.
457 Ibid.
458 Jim Pierson, *Produced and Directed by Dan Curtis*, (Los Angeles: Pomegranate Press, 2004), 17.
459 Lynley, Telephone interview with author.
460 Ibid.

461 Ibid.
462 John Llewellyn Moxey, "Interview with Director John Llewellyn Moxey," *The Night Stalker* [Blu-ray], Kino Lorber, 2018.
463 Dawidziak, *The Night Stalker Companion*, 60.
464 Ibid.
465 Ibid, 59.
466 Ibid, 55.
467 Ibid, 63.
468 Jeff Thompson, *The Television Horrors of Dan Curtis: Dark Shadows, The Night Stalker and Other Productions, 1966-2006,* (Jefferson, NC, McFarland and Company, Inc., 2009), 120.
469 Dan Curtis, "The Night Stalker: Dan Curtis Interview," *The Night Stalker* [Blu-ray], Kino Lorber, 2018.
470 Dawidziak, *The Night Stalker Companion*, 48.
471 Lynley, Telephone interview with author.
472 Dawidziak, *The Night Stalker Companion*, 55.
473 Marcy Robin, "Dan Curtis News," *Shadowgram*, No. 81, November 1997, 11.
474 Dawidziak, *The Night Stalker Companion*, 64.
475 Lynley, Telephone interview with author.
476 Scott Skelton and Jim Benson, *Rod Serling's Night Gallery: An After-Hours Tour*, (Syracuse, NY: Syracuse University Press, 1998), 268.
477 Ibid, 269.
478 Ibid, 268.
479 Ibid, 269.
480 Ibid.
481 Lynley, Telephone interview with author.
482 Gary Bettinson, "Tales from the Kryptonians: *Superman* at 40," *Cinema Retro*, Vol. 14, Issue 42, 2018, 36.
483 Lynley, Telephone interview with author.
484 James Christie, *You're the Director, You Figure It Out: The Life and Films of Richard Donner*, (Duncan, Oklahoma, 2010).

Hell, Upside Down
485 Lisanti, *Fantasy Femmes of Sixties Cinema*, 207.
486 Barbara Wilson, "Will 'Adventure' Mean End to Oblivion for Carol Lynley?" *The Philadelphia Inquirer*, December 15, 1972.
487 Ibid.
488 Lynley, Telephone interview with author.
489 Joseph P. Boon, "Carol Lynley Recalls Brandon de Wilde," *Bucks County Courier Times*, December 1, 1972.
490 Lynley, Telephone interview with author.
491 Vernon Scott, "'Poseidon Adventure' Turns into Expensive Venture for Producer," *El Paso Herald-Post*, August 26, 1972, 4.
492 Carol Lynley, Online interview with Nelson Aspen, *Nelson's World Report*, May 16, 1997.
493 John Campbell, "The Upside-Down Filming of *The Poseidon Adventure*," *American Cinematographer*, September 1972.

494 Ibid.
495 Eugenia Sheppard, "Inside Fashion: A Nice Quiet Movie," *New York Post Magazine*, December 14, 1972, 7.
496 Lynley, Telephone interview with author.
497 "Sixties Star Lynley Joins AIDS Movie Benefit." 1996.
498 "A Conversation with Carol Lynley," *Fox Movie Channel Backlot Pass*, July 8, 2001, www.thefoxmoviechannel.com/backlot/ lynley/part2c.html.
499 Lynley, Telephone interview with author.
500 Ibid.
501 Ronald Neame and Barbara Roisman Cooper, *Straight from the Horse's Mouth: Ronald Neame, an Autobiography*, (Lanham, Md.: Scarecrow Press, 2003), 239.
502 Ibid.
503 Ibid, 240.
504 Lynley, Telephone interview with author.
505 "Conversation with Carol Lynley," *Fox Movie Channel Backlot Pass*.
506 Lynley, Telephone interview with author.
507 James Radford, "Poseidon: Behind the Scenes," *Cinema Retro*, Vol 8: Issue 24, 2012, 16.
508 Joan E. Vadeboncoeur, "Carol Lynley Is Young at 30," *Syracuse Herald-Journal*, February 7, 1972, 20.
509 Dick Kleiner, "'The Poseidon Adventure': A Big Film with a Big Cast," *Burlington (N.C.) Times-News*, June 14, 1972, 7A.*
510 James Bacon, "Set Isn't Same without Shelley," *The Evening Press, Binghampton, New York.*, July 12, 1972, 8-B.
511 Boon, "Carol Lynley Recalls Brandon de Wilde."
512 Ibid.
513 "Hollywood: Carol's Comeback," *New York Daily News,* July 10, 1972.
514 Charles McHarry, "On the Town: Numbers Game," *New York Daily News*, October 19, 1972, 17C.
515 Wilson, "Will 'Adventure' Mean End to Oblivion for Carol Lynley?"
516 Lynley, Asheville Film Festival, 1999,
517 John Clark, "Speaking of DVDs: Carol Lynley," *San Francisco Chronicle*, May 21, 2006.
518 James Radford, Email exchange with author, September 20, 2019.
519 Lynley, Telephone interview with author.
520 "Hollywood: Carol's Comeback."
521 Ibid.
522 Ibid.
523 Marilyn Beck, "Ex-Mrs. Carson Is Willing," *The Atlanta Constitution*, July 21, 1972.
524 Dorothy Manners, "In Hollywood: Carol Lynley Has Slow Recovery After New Film," *Anderson Daily Bulletin*, August 4, 1972.
525 Ibid.
526 Ibid.
527 Davis, "Carol Lynley Has a Lust for Success."
528 Roger Ebert, "Interview with Carol Lynley," *Chicago Sun-Times*, December 4, 1972.

529 Earl Wilson, "Buttons Makes Carol See Red," *The Independent, Long Beach, CA*, December 29, 1972.
530 Lynley, Telephone interview with author.
531 Ebert, "Interview with Carol Lynley."
532 Lynley, Telephone interview with author.
533 Chris Poggiali, "Interview with Mort Künstler," *Cinema Retro*, Vol 8: Issue 24, 2012, 18.
534 "Conversation with Carol Lynley," *Fox Movie Channel Backlot Pass*.
535 Stirling Silliphant, *The Poseidon Adventure*: typescript, March 24, 1972, 39.
536 Lynley, Telephone interview with author.
537 Ibid.
538 Silliphant, *The Poseidon Adventure*: typescript, 277.
539 Lynley, Telephone interview with author.
540 Jeff Bond, *The Fantastic Worlds of Irwin Allen*, (Santa Monica, CA: Creature Features, 2019), 406.
541 Carol Lynley, On-camera interview with Johnny Carson, *The Tonight Show Starring Johnny Carson*, January 18, 1973.
542 Lynley, Telephone interview with author.
543 Sauer, "Personality Profile: Carol in Focus…From 'Denim' to Liberation."
544 "Carol Lynley: Poseidon's Happy Survivor," *Anderson Daily Bulletin*, February 26, 1973.
545 Bernard Drew, "*The Poseidon Adventure*: Box Office Smash … But Why?" *The Journal-News, Nyack, New York*, February 4, 1973, 9E.
546 Thomas Vinciguerra, "Underwater, and Over the Top in 1972," *New York Times*, May 2, 2006, 16ST.
547 Blanco, "60s Starlet Carol Lynley on a Checkered Past."
548 Lynley, Telephone interview with author.
549 Mark Huestis, *Impresario of Castro Street: An Intimate Memoir*, (San Francisco, CA: Outsider Productions, 2019), 190.
550 Lynley, Telephone interview with author.
551 Ibid.
552 "Where Are They Now? Carol Lynley," *Biography Magazine*, January 2001, 36.
553 "Conversation with Carol Lynley," *Fox Movie Channel Backlot Pass*.
554 Ibid.
555 Ibid.
556 Lynley, Telephone interview with author.
557 Lynley, Asheville Film Festival, 1999,
558 Nelson Aspen, *Hollywood Insider Exposed! Secrets, Stars & Show Biz*, (New Holland Publishers, Australia, 2008), 127.
559 Zoe Thomas, "'The Poseidon Adventure' Is the Quintessential Disaster Movie," FilmSchoolRejects.com, May 14, 2019, https://filmschoolrejects.com/the-poseidon-adventure/
560 Aljean Harmetz, "'The Poseidon Adventure's' Treatment of Women Is All Wet," *New York Times*, January 21, 1973.

Bad Girls, Harried Heroines, and Disaster Divas
561 Davis, "Under the Hollywood Sign: Carol Lynley Has a Lust for Success."

562 Lynley, Telephone interview with author
563 Dorothy Manners, "In Hollywood: Carol Lynley Has Slow Recovery After Film," *Anderson Daily Bulletin (Anderson, Indiana)*, August 4, 1972, 6.
564 Lynley, Telephone interview with author.
565 Christy, "Carol Lynley—A Free Spirit."
566 Lewis, "Lynley's Back on Broadway—Belatedly, B-19."
567 Jones Lee, Telephone interview with author.
568 Christy, "Carol Lynley—A Free Spirit."
569 Ibid.
570 Barbara Bladen, "The Marquee," *The Times San Mateo*, December 8, 1972.
571 Jones Lee, Telephone interview with author.
572 Ibid.
573 Marilyn Beck, "Carol Lynley in 'Poseidon' Sequel," *The Atlanta Constitution*, May 15, 1974.
574 Marilyn Beck, "Marilyn Beck's Hollywood Hotline," *Pasadena Star-News,* December 10, 1972, A-10.
575 J.A. Engels, "Carol Lynley: Growing Up at 30." *San Bernardino Sun*, May 20, 1972, A-12, A-14.
576 Clark, "I'm No Threat to Men Says Feminist Carol Lynley."
577 Ibid.
578 Ibid.-
579 Dick Kleiner, "Showbeat: At Last, Carol Lynley Plays the Heroine," *The Bee*, May 29, 1974, 6-A.
580 Wilson, "Will 'Adventure' Mean End to Oblivion for Carol Lynley?"
581 Langdon, Jr., Telephone interview with author.
582 Ibid.
583 Lynley, Telephone interview with author.
584 Stephan Chase, Email interview with author.
585 Ibid.
586 Lynley, Telephone interview with author.
587 Chase, Email interview with author.
588 Ibid.
589 Ibid.
590 Al DiOrio, *Borrowed Time: The 37 Years of Bobby Darin,* (Philadelphia, Pennsylvania: Running Press, 1981), 178.
591 David Evanier, *Roman Candle: The Life of Bobby Darin*, ([S.I.]; Rodale, 2004), 245.
592 Newton, "The Two Faces of Carol Lynley."
593 Ibid.
594 Ibid.
595 Ibid.
596 Ibid.
597 Ibid.
598 Lawrence Laurent, "Bixby Tries Non-Violent, Action-Adventure," *The Washington Post*, September 2, 1973.
599 Lynley, Telephone interview with author.
600 Ibid.

601 Kleiner, "Showbeat: At Last, Carol Lynley Plays the Heroine."
602 Fine, "Carol Lynley: The Face That Doesn't Change," 39.
603 Ibid.
604 Kleiner, "Showbeat: At Last, Carol Lynley Plays the Heroine."
605 Ibid.
606 Clark, "I'm No Threat to Men Says Feminist Carol Lynley."
607 Lynley, Telephone interview with author.
608 Ibid.
609 Ibid.
610 Ibid.
611 Ibid.
612 Quentin Tarantino, "Tarantino's Reviews!", Interview with Elric Kane and Brian Saur, *Pure Cinema Podcast*, podcast audio, April 1, 2020, https://purecinemapodcast.libsyn.com/tarantinos-reviews-with-quentin-tarantino.
613 Ibid.
614 Boon, "Carol Lynley Recalls Brandon de Wilde."
615 Donnelly, "'Mice and Men' and Carol Lynley with Homage to Harlow."
616 Nina S. Hyde, "Carol Lynley, a Star in Second-Hand Robes," *The Washington Post*, March 29, 1975.
617 Ibid.
618 Ibid.
619 Kleiner, "Showbeat: At Last, Carol Lynley Plays the Heroine."
620 Donnelly, "'Mice and Men' and Carol Lynley with Homage to Harlow."
621 Beck, "Carol Lynley in 'Poseidon' Sequel."
622 Franz Anthony Clinton, "An Interview with Brian Clemens," *Thriller*, http://www.markmcm.co.uk/blacknun/thriller/interviews.html
623 Clark, "I'm No Threat to Men Says Feminist Carol Lynley."
624 Marlin Dobbs, Email exchange, September 19, 2019.
625 Lynley, Telephone interview with author.
626 Marlin Dobbs, Text message with author, November 9, 2019.
627 "*If It's a Man – Hang Up!*" Thriller, http://www.markmcm.co.uk/blacknun/thriller/5a.html
628 Donnie Radcliffe and Jacqueline Trescott, "A Meister-Dinner for a Meistersinger," *The Washington Post*, June 17, 1975, C2, column 3.
629 Clark, "I'm No Threat to Men Says Feminist Carol Lynley."
630 "Carol Lynley, a beauty with soft blue eyes…", no source, n.d.
631 Morehouse, "Hot Lights, Clinches Often Have an Effect."
632 Clive Barnes, "The Stage: Quality 'Takeover' Trend," *New York Times*, October 9, 1975.
633 Lynley, Telephone interview with author.
634 Lewis, "Lynley's Back on Broadway—Belatedly," B-19.
635 Earl Wilson, "Lynley Wants Children," *The Lima News*, July 21, 1975, 23.
636 Lynley, Telephone interview with author.
637 Ibid.
638 Vernon Scott, "Scott's World: 'Flood' the Most Expensive TV Film," *Columbus Telegraph*, November 22, 1976.
639 Ibid.

640 Ibid.
641 Tom Lisanti, "Francine York: Out of This World!" *Filmfax*, October 2000/January 2001, 71.
642 Lynley, Telephone interview with author.
643 Win Fanning, "Previn Debut Exciting on TV," *Pittsburgh Post-Gazette*, September 13, 1976, 25.
644 Bob Kendall, "Lynley and Lockwood Are in Love in Golden Films New 'Out of Control,'" *Hollywood Studio Magazine*, Vol. 11, No.1, November 1976, 12.
645 Ibid, 12, 13.
646 John Goff, Email interview with author, October 27, 2019.
647 Kendall, "Lynley and Lockwood Are in Love …,'" 13.
648 Goff, Email interview with author.
649 Justin Bozung, "The Last Hollywood Cowboy: An Interview with Gary Lockwood," *Shock Cinema*, No. 42, 2012, 13.
650 Goff, Email interview with author.
651 Lynley, Telephone interview with author.
652 Goff, Email interview with author.
653 Ibid.
654 Kendall, "Lynley and Lockwood Are in Love …," 13.
655 Goff, Email interview with author.
656 Tom Kibbe. Email interview with author, March 3, 2018.
657 Goff, Email interview with author.
658 Kendall, "Lynley and Lockwood Are in Love …," 13.
659 "Golden Films New 'Out of Control,'" *Hollywood Studio Magazine*, Vol. 11, No.1, November 1976, 13.
660 Ibid.
661 Lynley, Telephone interview with author.
662 Goff, Email interview with author.
663 Tim McNulty, "Southern Moonshine Films Big Business in Drive-Ins," *Colorado Springs Gazette-Telegraph*, July 10, 1977, 46.
664 Ibid.
665 Earl Wilson, "Oscar-Winning Actress Loves Paunchy Comedian," *Reno Evening Gazette*, January 21, 1977.
666 Lynley, Telephone interview with author.

Welcome to Fantasy Island!
667 Tina Sinatra. Telephone interview with author, March 3, 2018.
668 Ibid.
669 Ibid.
670 Lynley, Telephone interview with author.
671 "Lawford Sues Over Injury on Movie Set," *Los Angeles Times*, December 25, 1976.
672 Albin Krebs, "Notes on People." *New York Times*, December 25, 1976.
673 Lynley, Telephone interview with author.
674 Sinatra. Telephone interview with author.
675 Win Fanning, "Carol Lynley Enjoys Outdoor Film Stint," *Pittsburgh Post-Gazette*, August 21, 1981.

676 Lynley, Telephone interview with author.
677 Fanning, "Carol Lynley Enjoys Outdoor Film Stint."
678 Lynley, Online interview with Nelson Aspen.
679 Carol Lynley, On-camera interview with Ed Grant, *Media Funhouse*, February 20, 2009, http://mediafunhouse.blogspot.com/2009/02/carol-lynley-on-her-stays-on-fantasy.html
680 Lynley, Telephone interview with author.
681 Lynley, On-camera interview with Ed Grant, *Media Funhouse*.
682 John Podhoretz, "Evil on the Rails," *The Weekly Standard*, December 4, 2017, 43.

Remake It Again, Sam
683 Lynley, Telephone interview with author.
684 Alex Gordon, "The Pit and the Pen of Alex Gordon: *The Cat and the Canary*," *Fangoria*, No. 11, 1978, 40.
685 Tom Weaver, *The Horror Hits of Richard Gordon*, (Duncan, OK: BearManor Media, 2011), 197.
686 Ibid, 199.
687 Ibid, 200.
688 Ibid, 204.
689 Lynley, Telephone interview with author.
690 Weaver, *The Horror Hits of Richard Gordon* 206.
691 Lynley, Telephone interview with author.
692 Olivia Hussey, Online interview with author.
693 Lynley, Telephone interview with author.
694 Ibid.
695 Weaver, *The Horror Hits of Richard Gordon*, 207.
696 Ibid, 206.
697 Lynley, Telephone interview with author.
698 Weaver, *The Horror Hits of Richard Gordon*, 208.
699 Ibid, 204.
700 "Stagione 1978-79: i 100 film di maggior incasso," *Hit Parade Italia*, http://www.hitparadeitalia.it/bof/boi/boi1978-79.htm
701 Stephen Gallagher, "The Libertine," *Filmmaker*, Summer 1997, https://filmmakermagazine.com/archives/issues/summer1997/metzger.php
702 "Audubon Wins Back Rights; 'Best Theatrical Efforts' Hit on 'The Cat and the Canary,'" *Variety*, August 15, 1979, 44.
703 Ibid, 7.
704 Ibid.
705 Gallagher, "The Libertine."
706 Yakir, "Carol Lynley: The Shape of Things to Come," 39.
707 Lynley, Telephone interview with author.

708 Imperiled from the Earth to the Moon
"Children Are Generous," *The Robesonian*, October 30, 1977, 3.
709 Lisanti, *Dueling Harlows: Race to the Silver Screen*, 111.
710 Lynley, Telephone interview with author.
711 Ibid.

712 Dan McCarthy, "1st Feature Film: Hershey: Hollywood East," *Lebanon Daily News*, July 22, 1977, 17.
713 "'Cops and Robin Airs Thursday," *Burlington Free Press*, March 26, 1978.
714 John Goudas, "Carol Lynley's All Over Screen," *Pittsburgh Post-Gazette,* July 19, 1978, 43.
715 Lynley, Telephone interview with author.
716 "Carol Lynley [in] World Premiere Movie," *Austin (Minn.) Herald*, May 12, 1978, 5A.
717 Lynley, Telephone interview with author.
718 Ibid.
719 Nelson Aspen. Email with author, July 19, 2018.
720 "Where Are They Now? Carol Lynley: From *Yum-Yum Tree* to *Fantasy Island*," *Rona Barrett's Hollywood*, [ca. 1980], 32.
721 Hollywood Kids, The, "Q&A: Carol Lynley," *Movieline*, 1992, quoted in Robert Julian and Orland Outland, "OutLand: The Annals of Queerdom," *Bay Area Reporter*, December 17, 1992, 30.
722 Goudas, "Carol Lynley's All Over Screen."
723 Harry Haun, "She Kisses & Tells & Regrets," *New York Daily News*, July 30, 1978, 6.
724 Marilyn Beck, "Carol Lynley Likes Her Free Lifestyle," *Pacific Stars and Stripes*, August 15, 1978, 17.
725 Natalie Clark, "They All Fell for Frost," *Daily Mail*, September 5, 2013, https://www.dailymail.co.uk/femail/article-2413108/David-Frost-From-singer-wooed-egg-sized-diamond-model.html
726 Peter Levinson, *Puttin' on the Ritz: Fred Astaire and the Fine Art of Panache, A Biography*, (New York: St. Martin's Press, 2009), 359.
727 Lynley, Telephone interview with author.
728 Harry Alan Towers, *Mr. Towers of London: A Life in Show Business*, (Duncan, OK: BearManor Media, 2013), 100.
729 Berthe Roegger, "Preview: SF Films of '79: *The Shape of Things to Come*, *Starlog*, May 1979, 52.
730 Lisanti, *Fantasy Femmes of Sixties Cinema*, 201.
731 Nicholas Campbell, On-camera interview, *Jason's Journey, The Shape of Things to Come* Blu-ray, Underground Studio, 2016.
732 Ibid.
733 Yakir, "Carol Lynley: The Shape of Things to Come," 39.
734 Campbell, On-camera interview, *Jason's Journey*.
735 Ibid.
736 Lynley, Telephone interview with author.
737 Bruce Kirkland, "It's Not a Star War on Kleinburg Set: Cameras Carve the Shape of Things to Come in Canadian Sci-Fi Film," *Toronto Star,* November 19, 1978, B1.
738 Lynley, Telephone interview with author.
739 Kirkland, "It's Not a Star War on Kleinburg Set."
740 Ibid.
741 Freedman, "Carol Lynley Is Flying High."
742 Ibid.

743 Earl Wilson, "Last Night with Earl Wilson: Carol's Sexless Planet," *New York Post*, November 29, 1978, 54.
744 Campbell, On-camera interview, *Jason's Journey*.
745 Kirkland, "It's Not a Star War on Kleinburg Set."
746 Lydia Lane, "Beauty: Lynley Avoids the Tensions," *Los Angeles Times*, November 19, 1978.
747 Langdon, Jr. Telephone interview with author.
748 "Lynley in Garb for the Year 2020," *Time*, December 11, 1978, 107.
749 Ibid.
750 Roderick Mann, "From Playmate to Governor," *Los Angeles Times*, February 22, 1979.
751 Reynolds, "Forever Lovely Carol Lynley."
752 Joe Baltake, "Mimieux: Look Who Grew Up," *Philadelphia Daily News*, December 12, 1979, 32.
753 Ibid.
754 Campbell, On-camera interview, *Jason's Journey*.
755 Ernie Magnotta, "'Bad Movies' That Hurt So Good: *Starcrash*," *Scary Monsters*, January 2019, 36.
756 Mann, "From Playmate to Governor."
757 Dick Kleiner, "Beauty Looking Forward to Life at 50," *Pittsburgh Press*, April 22, 1979, J-1.
758 Ibid.
759 Alexia Fernandez, "Star of *The Poseidon Adventure* and Former Girlfriend to David Frost, Dies at 77," *People*, September 5, 2019, https://people.com/movies/carol-lynley-star-the-poseidon-adventure-dies/
760 David Alexander, "Carol Lynley: At 38, She Keeps Her Great Looks with a Steady Diet of Work," *Season Pass Entertainment Guide*, October 1980, 35.

Soaps to Suspense
761 Kleiner, "Still Looking Young: Lynley's Beauty Seems 'Unreal.'"
762 Paul Henniger, "Prison Tale Worries ABC," *The Evening Press, Binghamton, NY*, June 29, 1980, 8.
763 Lynley, Telephone interview with author.
764 Henniger, "Prison Tale Worries ABC, 1."
765 "Ask Them Yourself," *Burlington Free Press*, September 24, 1978, 93.
766 Freedman, "Carol Lynley Is Flying High."
767 Gerald Ettner, "Warmth, Diversity from Frankie Avalon," *Philadelphia Inquirer*, October 11, 1980, 4-A.
768 Alan J. Levi, Telephone interview with author, November 25, 2019.
769 Fanning, "Carol Lynley Enjoys Outdoor Film Stint."
770 "Carol Lynley Is 'The Best of Friends,'" *San Bernardino Sun*, August 23, 1981.
771 Lynley, Telephone interview with author.
772 "Carol Lynley Is 'The Best of Friends.'"
773 Fanning, "Carol Lynley Enjoys Outdoor Film Stint."
774 "Carol Lynley Is 'The Best of Friends.'"
775 Carol Burton Terry, "Off Camera," *Newsday*, August 23, 1981.
776 Alex Cord, Email interview with author, November 19, 2019.

777 Ibid.
778 Levi, Telephone interview with author.
779 Ibid.
780 Ibid.
781 Lynley, On-camera interview with Ed Grant
782 Levi, Telephone interview with author.
783 Ibid.
784 Ibid.
785 Lynley, Interview with Jak Castro.
786 Levi, Telephone interview with author.
787 Ibid.
788 Alan J. Levi, Email interview with author, December 16, 2019.
789 Levi, Telephone interview with author.
790 Levi, Email interview with author.
791 Levi, Telephone interview with author.
792 Lynley, Telephone interview with author.
793 "People," *Maclean's*, September 1, 1980, 30.
794 Dennis McLellan, "It's Intrigue 'Balboa' Style: TV Drama Filmed in Newport." *Los Angeles Times*, June 10, 1982.
795 Ibid.
796 Ibid.
797 Ibid.
798 James Polakof. Email interview with author.
799 Stephen G. Freedman, "Jet Set Hoopla in Newport Beach," *Los Angeles Times*, June 20, 1982.
800 Ibid.
801 Ibid.
802 William Lustig, "Audio Commentary #1 with Co-Producer/Director William Lustig and Co-Producer Andrew V. Garroni," *Vigilante* [Blu-ray], Blue Underground, 2016.
803 "Promotional Reel," *Vigilante* [Blu-ray], Blue Underground, 2016.
804 Lynley, Telephone interview with author.
805 Lustig, "Audio Commentary #1."
806 William Lustig, "Audio Commentary #2 with Co-Producer/Director William Lustig and Stars Robert Forster, Fred Williamson and Frank Pesce," *Vigilante* [Blu-ray], Blue Underground, 2016.
807 Frank Pesce, "Audio Commentary #2 with Co-Producer/Director William Lustig and Stars Robert Forster, Fred Williamson and Frank Pesce," *Vigilante* [Blu-ray], Blue Underground, 2016.
808 Lynley, Telephone interview with author.
809 Liz Nicholls, "VCR Foul-Up Like Cold Turkey to Oscar Addict." *Edmonton Journal*, April 2, 1989: C1.
810 Ibid.
811 Barbara Cloud, "Pitt Prof's 'Brother of Dragons' Focuses on Teen Drug Problem," *Pittsburgh Press*, November 6, 1983, H2.
812 "Where Are They Now?"
813 MacKenzie Allen, Telephone interview with author.

814 Ibid.
815 Ibid.
816 Lynley, Telephone interview with author.
817 Ibid.
818 Ibid.

High Rise Horror
819 Jim George, "The Stellar Stella Stevens," *Cinema Retro*, Vol. 14, Issue 42, 2018, 51.
820 Franceso Borseti, *It Came from the 80s! Interviews with 124 Cult Filmmakers*, (Jefferson, NC: McFarland & Company, Inc., 2016), 23.
821 Ed Kelleher, "Indy Distrib Spectrafilm Widens Its Spectrum," *The Film Journal*, Vol. 90, Issue 2, February 1, 1987, 8.
822 "Howard Sues Re: 'Tower,'" *Variety*, January 28, 1987, 7.
823 Freddie Francis with Tony Dalton, *Freddie Francis: The Straight Story from Moby Dick to Glory, a Memoir*, (London: The Scarecrow Press, 2015), 209.
824 Ibid, 210.
825 Ibid.
826 Ibid.
827 Lynley, Telephone interview with author.
828 Francis with Tony Dalton, *Freddie Francis*, 210.
829 Lara Kilner, "Call the Midwife Star Jenny Agutter on How It's Harder to Swear When You're Wearing a Habit and Wimple," *Mirror*, March 12, 2017, https://www.mirror.co.uk/tv/tv-news/call-midwife-star-jenny-agutter-10002509.
830 The Black Saint, "Interview Doug Jones [*Hellboy 1* & *2*, *Pan's Labyrinth*]," *Horror News Net*, August 25, 2014, http://horrornews.net/87301/interview-doug-jones-hellboy-1-2-pans-labyrinth/.
831 Francis, *Freddie Francis: The Straight Story*, 211.
832 Ibid.

Some Memories Are Better Left Buried
833 "'Psycho' Screenwriter Pens 'Blackout' to Screen at MIFED," *Screen International*, October 22, 1988, 2.
834 Arledge Armenaki, Telephone interview with author.
835 Ibid.
836 Ibid.
837 Ibid.
838 Ibid.
839 Ibid.
840 Lynley, Telephone interview with author.
841 Armenaki, Telephone interview with author.
842 Ibid.
843 Ibid.
844 Lynley, Telephone interview with author.
845 Armenaki, Telephone interview with author.
846 Ibid.
847 Ibid.
848 Ibid.

849 Ibid.
850 Ibid.
851 Ibid.

From Rampaging Rats to Hideous Demons
852 Robin Adams Sloan, "Gossip Column," *Asbury Park Press*, November 1, 1987, G18.
853 Jeffrey Wolf, Telephone interview with author.
854 Ibid.
855 Ibid.
856 Ibid.
857 Liz Smith, "Carol Lynley Latest to Scale a 'Twin Peaks' Comeback," *Los Angeles Times*, August 30, 1990.
858 David Hughes, *The Complete Lynch*, (London, Virgin, 2001).
859 Michael J. Weldon, *The Psychotronic Video Guide*, (London, Titan Books, 1996), 526.
860 Lynley, Telephone interview with author.
861 Michael Ferguson, *Joe Dallesandro: Warhol Superstar, Underground Film Icon, Actor,* (New York: Open Road Integrated Media, 2015).
862 "Carol Lynley," *People*, November 28, 1994, https://people.com/archive/carol-lynley-vol-42-no-22/.
863 Ibid.
864 Ibid.

Three Cons and a Kid
865 Marc Kolbe, Email interview with author.
866 Lynley, Telephone interview with author.
867 Matt Dotson, Telephone interview with author,
868 Ibid.
869 Ibid.
870 Ibid.
871 Kolbe, Email interview with author.
872 Howard Wexler, Email interview with author.
873 Ibid.
874 Kolbe, Email interview with author.
875 Lynley, Telephone interview with author.
876 Kolbe, Email interview with author.
877 Ibid.
878 Dotson, Telephone interview with author.
879 Lynley, Telephone interview with author.
880 Dotson, Telephone interview with author.
881 Kolbe, Email interview with author.
882 Dotson, Telephone interview with author.
883 Ibid.

Final Act
884 Lynley, Telephone interview with author.

885 Illeana Douglas, Twitter post, September 9, 2019, 12:21 AM, https://twitter.com/Illeanarama/status/1170915039588446208
886 Lynley, Interivew with Jak Castro.
887 Ibid.
888 Jak Castro, Email exchange with author, 2019.
889 Shaun Chang, Email exchange with author, April 11, 2020.
890 Ibid.
891 Lane, "Beauty: Lynley Avoids the Tensions."
892 Marlin Dobbs, Text message exchange with author, December 22, 2019.
893 Ibid.
894 Langdon, Jr. Telephone interview with author.
895 Sally Kirkland, Twitter post, September 6, 2019, 11:53 AM, https://twitter.com/sally_kirkland/status/1170002135368421376
896 BarBara Luna, Facebook post, September 6, 2019, 7:57 AM.
897 Matt Dotson, Facebook post, September 10, 2019, 8:13, AM.
898 Fernandez, "Star of *The Poseidon Adventure* and Former Girlfriend to David Frost, Dies at 77."

"Carol Lynley for the Block" Game Show, Talk Show, and Other Appearances as Herself

899 Hedda Hopper, "Looking at Hollywood: Hedda Exchanges Quips on TV's Celebrity Game," *Chicago Tribune,* June 30, 1964.
900 UPI, "Girl Talk," *Great Bend Tribune,* November 15, 1964, 26.
901 "'Celebrity Game' Panel," *Ithaca Journal*, May 8, 1965.
902 J. De Castro. "The Star of Reflets de Cannes: The Public Image of the Cannes Film Festival," January 2015.
903 Barbara DeLatiner, "On Television: 'Night in London Is Morning After," *Newsday*, February 3, 1967.
904 Bob Houser, "Demo Brigade's Light Charge," *Independent Press-Telegram (Long Beach, California)*, June 25, 1972, 34.
905 Joyce Haber, "Wit On, Off Camera at Golden Globes," *Los Angeles Times*, January 30, 1973.
906 "Almost Anything Goes," *TV Guide*, March 6 – 12, 1976, A-24.
907 Morehouse, "Hot Lights, Clinches Often Have an Effect."
908 Alexander, "Carol Lynley: At 38…"
909 Lynley, Telephone interview with author.
910 Nelson Aspen, Email, October 30, 2019.
911 McDonald, "Carol Lynley of *Bunny Lake Is Missing* and *The Poseidon Adventure*."

Select Index

3rd Annual Circus of the Stars 643
4th Annual NAACP Image Awards, The 623
7 Women 127
21st Annual Grammy Awards, The 640
30th Annual Golden Globe Awards 340, 629
31st Academy Awards, The 608
35th Academy Awards, The 610
51st Annual Academy Awards, The 642, 643
1966 Hollywood Deb Star Ball 616, 617

ABC 4:30 Movie, The xx, 150
ABC Friday Night Movie 469
ABC Movie of the Week 153, 235, 237, 238, 272
ABC Saturday Suspense Movie 378
ABC Stage '67 617, 618, 619
ABC Wednesday Night Movie 192
ABC's Nightlife 615
Absurd Person Singular xiv, xxi, 403-405, 633, 634
Academy Awards 62, 72, 87, 119, 120, 342
Adams, Doug 549-552, 563, 564
Adams, Marjory 24, 35, 47, 67, 71, 119, 146
Africano, Lillian 403
Agutter, Jenny 544-547
Albertson, Jack 317, 320, 325, 331, 333-336, 348, 393, 632
Alcoa Hour, The 9
Alcoa Premiere 59
Aldrich, Robert 43, 44, 48, 311
Alfred Hitchcock Hour, The 56-58, 154, 180, 588

Alfred Hitchcock Presents xxiii, xxx, 14-16, 56, 57, 180
All Star Secrets 483, 640
Allen, Irwin 235, 315-319, 322, 324, 325, 327, 337, 340, 342, 343, 393, 394, 407-409, 411, 412, 623, 626
Allen, MacKenzie ix, 530, 531, 533, 534
Allen, Steve 608, 616, 622, 635
Almost Anything Goes! 636
Alpert, Hollis 42, 74, 75
Altman, Robert 14, 311
American Movie Awards, The 644
Anderson, Donna 41
Ann-Margret xxxv, 63, 74, 81, 82, 84, 87, 88. 90, 95, 99, 101, 161, 219, 259, 295
Annis, Francesca 359, 361, 362
Anniversary Waltz 6,7, 627, 654
Another World 567
Anspach, Susan 268
Answered the Flute 41
Archerd, Army 622
Armand, Renee 326, 327
Armenaki, Arledge ix, 550-555, 560, 562-564
Arthur Murray Party, The 609
Arthy, Judith 136, 142
Aspen, Nelson ix, xiii-xv, 31, 319, 482, 652-654, 656
Astaire, Fred xx, 396, 485, 486, 596, 652
Atkinson, Brooks 18
Avalon, Frankie 268, 507
Ayckbourn, Alan xxi, 403

Bacall, Lauren 76, 78, 642, 643
Back Stage with Carol Lynley 633
Bacon, James 325
Bad Georgia Road 406, 413-423, 491, 572
Baker, Carroll xxvii, xxviii, 90, 161, 590, 591, 649, 650
Baker, Diane 25, 30, 35, 49, 50, 128, 173, 534
Bakers' Dozen 518
Balboa 518-522
Balenciaga, Cristóbal 84
Balin, Ina 53
Ballard, Lucien 204
Baltake, Joe 99, 497
Barnes, Clive 403
Barnes, Joanna 24, 406
Basehart, Richard 407, 409, 410
Bass, Saul 111, 112, 650
Beasts Are in the Streets, The 365, 476-482, 500
Beaton, Cecil 608
Beatty, Warren 54, 161, 642

Beauchamp, Emerson 119
Beck, Marilyn 328
Bee, Molly 24, 25
Bellamy, Earl 412
Benson, Jim, 309, 310
Benson, Robby 642, 643
Benton, Eddie 487, 492, 493
Berman, Shelley 286, 288, 290
Bess, Ardon 492
Best of Friends, The 507-510
Beware! The Blob xxiii, 285-291
Beymer, Richard 62, 63, 128
Beyond the Poseidon Adventure 393
Big Valley, The 187
Bikel, Theodore 543, 547
Bikram Choudhury, Yoga Master 651
Bird, Michael J. 538
Birds, The 57
Bixby, Bill 198, 306-310, 365, 372-374, 430, 432, 434
Black, Karen 269, 541
Blackman, Honor 454, 456-459, 462
Blackout ix, xxxviii, 549-565, 649
Blood Song 507
Blue Denim (film) xxiv, xxviii, xxx, 32-36, 48, 53, 326, 609
Blue Denim (play) 14, 16, 18, 19, 26, 42, 89, 608, 637
Blyden, Larry 403
Bob Hope Presents the Chrysler Theatre 89, 131, 196
Boehm, Sydney 76
Bold Ones, The: The Doctors 270, 271
Bonnie and Clyde 147, 154, 161, 163
Booth, Shirley 153, 154, 193-196
Borgnine, Ernest xiv, 316, 320, 325, 328, 333-335, 337, 348, 393, 473, 475, 627-629, 632
Bouchet, Barbara 63, 108, 157, 158, 160, 567
Bower, Antoinette 507
Bowie, Stephen x, 177
Brand, Neville 45, 382, 383, 385, 386, 388
Brandt, Thordis 167
Briggs, Joe Bob 564
Brinkerhoff, Burt 16, 18, 42, 608
Brisson, Frederick 63, 65, 68
Broderick, John C. 415-418, 420, 572
Brown, Mende 366, 367, 370
Bruce, Carol 527
Buchholz, Horst 54, 454, 455
Buechler, John Carl 589

Bunny Lake Is Missing xix, xxiii, xxiv, xxxii, xxxv, xxxvii, 96-125, 132, 148, 150, 155, 201, 222, 295, 296, 309, 405, 549, 596, 614, 615, 617
Buono, Victor 511-513, 515, 516
Burke, Paul 201, 206-208, 210, 213, 215, 436, 438, 439
Bus Stop 526
Bushnell, William H., Jr. 380
Butler, Ivan 123, 148
Buttons, Red 317, 320, 321, 324, 330-336, 339, 340, 345, 350, 356, 376, 393, 626, 628, 656

Cable Car Murder, The 200, 275, 281-285, 374
Callan, Michael 454, 456-459, 464
Cambridge, Godfrey 286, 288, 290
Campbell, Glen 247, 248, 251, 252, 255, 260-265
Campbell, Nicholas 487, 489, 491-493, 497, 498
Capalbo, Carmen 10, 11
Cardinal, The xxx, 63, 64, 68-72, 74, 75, 91, 98, 103, 111, 610
Carey, Phil 206, 208-210, 213
Carroll, Harrison 138
Carroll, Kathleen 94, 215
Carson, Johnny 268, 340, 341, 615, 621, 627-631, 642, 643
Casper Citron Viewpoint 634
Castro, Jak x, 345, 591
Cat and the Canary, The xxii, xxiii, xxxiii, 125, 365, 451-466, 491, 596
Cazenove, Christopher 534-536, 538, 539
CBS Late Movie, The 387, 388, 394
CBS Late Night 565
CBS Thursday Night Movie, The 186, 225, 244
Celebrity Challenge of the Sexes 639
Celebrity Game, The 89, 612, 614, 615
Chace, Reeve 642
Chambers, Everett 233, 235, 294, 297
Chambers, John 182
Champlin, Charles 229, 260
Chandler, Jeff 50, 52, 53
Chang, Shaun x, 592
Charlie's Angels 501, 517
Chase, Jennifer 520-522
Chase, Stephan ix, 359-361, 364
Chateau Marmont 12, 131, 292, 293
Chevalier, Maurice 608
Choudhury, Bikram 501, 651
Clark, Valerie 356
Clemens, Brian 394, 400
Coe, Richard L. 119, 392
Cohen, Larry 172, 173, 404

SELECT INDEX

Cohen, R. Jeffrey 571
Colby's The 522
Collins, Gary 310, 312, 314, 436, 448, 449, 643, 647
Comer, Anjanette 382, 384, 386-389, 534
Connolly, Mike 155
Connors, Chuck 520
Connors, Mike 279, 632, 641
Conrad, Robert 273, 275
Conti, Tom 396, 397
Coop, Denys 110, 120
Cooper, Jackie 191-193, 609, 625
Cops and Robin 473-475
Cord, Alex ix, 508, 510
Corey, Wendall 20, 23
Cort, Bud 629
Cotter xxii, 188-190, 196
Cotter, Robert Michael 'Bobb' 538
Couple of White Chicks Sitting Around Talking, A 591
Coward, Noël 103, 105, 108, 111, 113, 155, 156, 553, 628, 649
Crist, Judith 53, 123, 208
Cristal, Linda 24
Critic's Circle, The 635
Crosby, Gary 30, 31
Crosscurrent see *The Cable Car Murder*
Crowther, Bosley 24, 35, 67, 117
Culp, Robert 407, 410, 411
Cult Culture: The Poseidon Adventure 655
Currie, Finlay 103, 109, 116
Curtis, Dan 297, 299, 300, 305
Curtis, Tony 518-521, 619

Daddy-O see *High Time*
Dahl, Arlene 65, 92, 644
Dallas 291, 483, 484, 503, 516, 518, 521, 522, 649
Dallesandro, Joe 573
Daltrey, Roger 543, 544, 547
Damsker, Gary 474
Dance Fever 646
Danger Route 155-161
Darby, Kim 248, 249, 259, 265
Darin, Bobby 54, 162, 293, 355, 364, 365, 623
Dark Tower 542-548, 565
Dash of Spirits, A 527
David Frost Show, The 623
David Frost's Night Out in London 155,
Davis, Don 562
Dawson, Curt 403

Day of the Locust 356
Day, Robert 382, 384, 387
Death Stalk xxiii, xxxiv, 365, 382-390, 512
Dee, Sandra x, xxviii-xxxi, 4, 7, 14, 18, 24, 35, 47, 90, 95, 125, 127, 163, 268, 430, 432, 497, 594, 608
Dee Time 621
Delatiner, Barbara 617
Democratic National Telethon, The 624
Dennis, Sandy 403, 404
Derleth, August 132, 133
deRuelle, Gene ix, 241, 244, 245
deWilde, Brandon 31, 32, 34, 39, 325, 609, 616
deWilde, Fritz 403
Dick Powell Theatre, The 60, 61
Dick Richards Show, The 627
Dickinson, Angie 35, 407, 593, 613, 615, 624
Dillman, Bradford 11, 63, 168, 169
Dinah! 482, 637
Dinah's Place 630
DiOrio, Al 364
Disney, Walt 11-13, 27, 613
Dobbs, Marlin x, 276, 346, 396, 397, 593, 594
Dr. Ruth Show, The 648
Donahue, Troy xxxi, 40, 201, 617
Donner, Richard 311, 313, 314
Dotson, Matt ix, 576-581, 584, 585, 595
Douglas, Illeana 588
Douglas, Kirk 43-47, 268, 478, 614
Doyle, David 517, 638
Driscoll, Edgar, Jr. 160, 260
Drowning on Dry Land 58
Druxman, Michael B. 539
Duke, Patty 74, 148, 161
Dullea, Keir 101-106, 110, 111, 113, 118, 119, 123, 124, 501
Dunaway, Faye xxxiv, 63, 163
Dunwich Horror, The 268
DuPont Show of the Month 17
Duval, Jose 71

E! Mysteries and Scandals 654
E! True Hollywood Story 653, 654
Earle Doud Radio Show, The 626
Easter Seal Telethon 641
Ebert, Roger 330
Eder, Shirley 527
Edwards, Randall 530, 532, 533
Edwards, Vince 15, 382-384, 386, 387, 389, 441

Elam, Jack 45
Elevator, The 365, 372, 375-379
Emmy Awards 60, 240, 305
Empathy 633
Enders, Robert 217, 218, 231
Estevez, Luis 198, 199
Estrada, Erik 571, 572
Everybody's Talking 618
Evil Touch, The xxii, xxiii, xxxv, 292, 294, 359, 365-372

F.B.I., The 178-180
Fabian 36, 37, 40
Falcon Crest 522
Falk, Peter 60, 61, 644
Fantastic Voyage 96
Fantasy Island (TV-movie) 65, 406, 429-435, 451, 596
Fantasy Island (TV series) xxiii, xxxiv, 365, 396, 435-449, 467, 501, 511, 655
Farentino, James xiv, 365, 375-377
Farrow, Mia xxiii, 90, 148, 177, 207, 402, 527, 619, 642
Fatal Attraction (stage play) 566
Faye, Alice 397
Fell, Norman 382, 385, 386, 639
Fellini, Federico 89, 163
Ferrer, Jose 53, 282, 283
Ferrer, Lupita 521, 522
Filerman, Michael 504, 505
Film Daily's Famous Fives 24, 35
Finder of Lost Loves 538
Five Easy Pieces 268, 269
Flannery, Susan 394
Flood xxiii, 365, 406-413, 589
Flower, George "Buck" 415
Flypaper 588
Fonda, Henry 55, 622, 624
Fonda, Jane xxxiv, 99, 101, 148, 161, 594, 644
Fonda, Peter xxxi, 268
Fontaine, Joan 30, 41, 626, 647
Ford, President Gerald 401
Ford, John 127
Forster, Robert 404, 523-525
Four Deuces, The 379-382, 413, 414, 491
Fox, Edward 454, 458, 460
Fox Mystery Theater 535
Fox, Sonny 622
Franciosa, Anthony 82, 87, 538
Francis, Freddie 543-546, 548
Franklin, Joe 648-650

Freeman, Alex 161, 163
Freeman, Everett 217, 218, 230
Freeman, Stephen G. 520
Friendly, Ed 224, 511, 515
Frost, David xx, 106, 107, 293, 405, 484, 485, 617-619, 623, 640, 644, 652
Frost, Mark 570
Fujimoto, Tak 415, 417, 418, 421
Funicello, Annette xxxi, 47, 74, 607, 613
Future Cop 473, 474

Gallico, Paul 316, 393
Gardella, Kay 238, 239
Garland, Judy 93, 94
Garroni, Andrew 523, 524
Gazzara, Ben 128, 130, 131, 617
Gelmis, Joseph 146
General Electric Theatre xxx, 38
George, Christopher 233, 235-241, 243, 244
Gerani, Gary 371
Gerber, Gail 292, 507
Gibson, Alan 361, 364
Gilford, Gwynne 287, 288
Girl Talk 89, 613, 616
Glass, Paul 111, 120, 309
Glass, Ron 517
God Told Me To 404
Godzilla vs. the Cosmic Monster 382
Goff, John ix, 415-419, 422
Golden Globe Awards 24, 35, 72, 110, 340
Good Morning America 640
Goodwin, Laurel 8
Goodyear Playhouse 9
Gordon, Richard 452-458, 460, 463-465
Gorman, Cliff 467, 469, 470
Gourmet Gala Cook-Off 636
Gourmet Show, The 616, 617
Graduate, The 161
Graham, Sheila 153
Graham, Virginia 613
Grauman, Walter 539
Graves, Peter 508, 510
Great Gatsby, The 356
Greatest Show on Earth, The 644
Greene, David xxxv, 134, 135, 140, 144, 146, 150, 311
Greene, Graham 10
Greenspun, Roger 215
Griffin, Merv 609, 614

SELECT INDEX

Guest, Val 311, 535, 538, 545
Gulager, Clu 57, 588
Gunn, James 233, 234, 238, 239, 241, 245
Gutteridge, Lucy 543, 544

Haber, Joyce 229, 335, 629
Hackman, Gene 191, 192, 316, 321, 325, 331-334, 339-341, 348, 349, 553, 625, 628, 629
Hagman, Larry 162, 285, 286, 288-291, 483, 484, 516
Haley, Jack, Jr. xx, 248, 249, 251-254, 260, 262-265, 293, 311, 430, 642, 644
Hall, Michael Keys 550, 555, 563
Hamilton, Tony 268
Hammer House of Mystery & Suspense 530, 534, 538
Harareet, Haya 41
Harford, Margaret 67, 79
Harlow xix, xxx, 93-95, 97, 119, 161, 196, 380, 470, 614, 649
Harmetz, Aljean 351
Harrington, Curtis 62
Harris, Jack H. 285, 286
Harrison, Joan 14, 180-182, 185
Harrison, Noel 527
Hart, Dolores 54, 63
Hart, Moss 6
Hart to Hart 501, 517
Harvard Lampoon Movie Worst Awards 47, 229, 342
Haunted House of Horror, The 147, 268
Having Babies II 467-470
Hawaii 5-O 472, 473
Hawn, Goldie 219, 224
Haworth, Jill 63, 74, 111, 268
Hay, Alexandra 92, 270, 534
Heartfelt 573, 650
Heiss, Carol 41
Helicopter Spies 171, 172
Hemingway, Ernest 507
Henderson, Florence 517, 629, 632, 639
Henreid, Monika ix, 31
Henreid, Paul 30, 31
Henry Fonda and the Family 55, 154
Here's Hollywood 609
Hershey, Barbara 407, 409, 411, 412, 589
Heston, Charlton 490, 522, 617, 619, 624
Hewitt, Celia 140
High Time 40
Highsmith, Patricia 203
Hill, Phyllis 6, 7
Hiller. Wendy 453-459, 463, 466

717

Hillyer, Sharyn 167
Hirschhorn, Joel 326, 327, 655
Holden, William 637, 644
Holiday for Lovers 30, 31, 628
Hollywood '65 614
Hollywood and the Stars 610
Hollywood Deb Star 13, 120
Hollywood Goes to a World Premiere 613
Hollywood Profiles 635
Hollywood Squares, The xix, 483, 620, 631, 638, 641
Holt, Seth 157, 159, 160
Honeymoon Hotel 40
Hooks, Robert 282
Hopper, Hedda 35, 68, 98, 127, 612
Horwitz, Howie 240, 245
Hotel 528, 529
Hound-Dog Man xxviii, xxx, 36, 37
Howard, Sandy 542-544, 546
Howling VI: The Freaks 572, 573
Hudson, Rock 43-47
Huestis, Mark 345-347
Hugo Awards 240
Hunt, Martita 103, 105, 107, 114
Hunt, Peter 476, 478, 482
Hussey, Olivia ix, 454, 456-459
Hyde-White, Wilfrid 454, 455, 458, 463, 466
Hyer, Martha 206, 207, 210, 213, 215, 218

I've Got a Secret 608
"If It's a Man, Hang Up!" xxxiv, 365, 394-401, 596
Iglesias, Julio 498, 499
Immortal, The xxiii, xxxiv, 213, 233-240, 294, 297, 470, 596
Immortal, The (TV series) 240-245, 270
"In Possession" 365, 534-539, 596
Inge, William 14, 62, 526, 527
Inside Edition 655
Invaders, The xxiii, xxxiv, xxxv, 172-178, 180, 235
It Takes a Thief 196-200, 470

Jackson, Sherry 92, 188, 189, 242
Jacobs, David 484
Jacobs, John 359
Jancovich, Mark xxiii,
Jenseits von Hollywood 656
Joan Fontaine Show, The 647
Joan Quinn Etc. 3, 539, 650, 651
Joe Franklin Show, The 648-650

Joey Adams, Show, The 634
Joey Bishop Show, The 224, 621
John, Errol 183
Johnson, Laura 522
Johnson, Richard 156, 157, 160
Jones, Cyril (Carol's father) 1, 354
Jones, Carolyn 25, 518
Jones, Dean 64, 75, 617, 624
Jones, Doug 545
Jones, Francis (Carol's mother) 1, 3, 4, 6, 9, 45, 73, 74, 354, 355, 650
Jones, James Earl 390, 391, 404, 633
Journey to the Unknown xxiii, 125, 180-186, 359
Judgement Day ix, 511-516
Junior Almost Anything Goes! 637
Junior Miss 17, 18

Kaiser Aluminum Hour 9
Kanaly, Steve 518, 520, 521
Kasha, Al 326, 327
Kazanjian, Howard ix, 203-209, 216
KCET Auction 621
Keith, Brian 82, 84, 613
Kenney, Margaret ix, 2
Kersh, Kathy 167
Kibbe, Tom ix, 418
Kidder, Margot 311, 642
Kirkland, Sally 503-505, 595, 648, 649
Kissinger, Henry 402
Kleiner, Dick 293, 325, 500
Knot's Landing 484
Kohner, Susan 24
Kojak 423-426
Kolbe, Marc ix, 575-581, 585
Kolchak Papers, The 294
Kolchak Tapes, The see *The Night Stalker*
Kopell, Bernie 517
Kuehn, Andrew J. 324, 625
Künstler, Mort 332
Kupcinet, Karyn 654
Kwan, Nancy 54

La Plante, Laura xxxvii, 451
Landgard, Janet 163
Lang, Richard 431
Langdon, Harry, Jr. ix, 275-278, 357-359, 363, 401, 492, 499, 595
Lange, Hope 24, 32, 49
Larch, John 514, 516

Last Summer at Bluefish Cove 527
Last Sunset, The 42-48, 53
Lawford, Peter 430-432, 434
Lawrence of Arabia 610
Le Mesurier, John 359, 361, 362
Lee, Daniel Jones ix, 1-4, 6, 8-10, 12, 19, 32, 45, 51, 73, 74, 91, 355
Lehmann, Beatrix 454, 457-459
Leigh, Vivien 105, 164
Lemmon, Jack 63-66, 72, 268, 624, 644, 652
Levi, Alan J. ix, 507, 511-516
Light in the Forest, A 589
Light in the Forest, The 12-13, 19-26, 607
Lilian Reynolds Show, The 626
Lindsey, Mayor John 334
Linney, Laura 571
Littlest Hobo, The 518
Lloyd, Norman 57, 154, 180
Lo Bianco, Tony 404
Lockwood, Gary 415-418, 420-422
Logan, Joshua 14, 18, 637
Lombard 539
Lombard, Carole 6, 404, 539
Lorenz, Isa 498
Louise, Tina 24
Love Boat, The 501, 517
Love Machine, The 265
Lovecraft, H.P. 132, 133, 148-150
Loy, Myrna 365, 375-378, 623
Luna, BarBara 507, 595
Lustig, William 523, 524, 526
Lynde, Paul 55, 66, 483, 632, 633, 638, 639, 641
Lyon, Sue xxviii, xxxii, 9. 90, 127, 161, 268, 330, 534, 594

MacArthur, James 12, 19, 22, 39, 472
MacGraw, Ali 249, 256, 642
Magician, The 365, 372-375, 476
Magnotto, Ernie 498
Maharis, George 98, 271, 648, 649
Majors, Lee 187, 235, 273-275, 567
Malone, Dorothy 45, 47
Maltese Bippy, The 213, 217-233, 269, 289, 403, 621
Maltin, Leonard 160, 190
Man from U.N.C.L.E., The xxiii, xxxiv, 165-172, 193
Man Who Loved Cat Dancing, The 356
Mankiewicz, Tom 131, 311
Mann, Roderick 490
Manners, Dorothy 251, 328

Mannix xxxv, 275, 278-281, 293, 623
March of Dimes National Telethon 647
Marquette, Jacques 209
Marshall, Peter 620, 641
Martin, Anne Marie see Eddie Benton
Martin, Dick 217-219, 221-225, 228-232, 621
Martin, Jared 504, 505
Martin, Mary 286, 637
Martin, Pamela Sue 317, 333-335, 339, 345, 350, 656
Martin, Quinn 173, 180
Marvin, Lee 614, 637
Masciarelli, Michael 542
Massey, Anna 103, 107, 114, 456
Massey, Daniel 455-459, 466
Massey, Raymond 490
Masters, George 65, 624
Matheson, Richard 295, 297, 304, 305
Matter of Innocence, A 156
Mayes, Wendell 316, 650
McBain, Diane xxviii, xxxii, 8, 91, 92, 163, 166, 269, 273, 594
McCallum, David 166, 167
McCowan, George 447, 489, 491
McDowall, Roddy 76, 78, 80, 111, 196, 199, 200, 317, 323, 333, 334, 348, 365, 375-378, 407, 410, 436, 441, 442, 449, 511-513, 515, 516, 613, 633, 655, 656
McEnery, Peter 455, 457-459
McGavin, Darren 292, 294, 297, 300, 301, 305
McGovern, Maureen 327, 389
McGrady, Mike 87
McKay, Gardner 82, 84, 85, 128
McNair, Barbara xxxviii, 92, 575, 576, 578, 580, 581, 584
Meadows, Jayne 608, 617
Media Funhouse 436, 655
Merv Griffin Show, The 111, 623, 624
Metalious, Grace 49, 53
Metzger, Radley 452, 454-456, 458, 460, 464-466, 526
Mickey Mouse Club, The 607
Mike Douglas Show, The 331, 483, 615, 626, 639
Miles, Joanna 553, 556
Mills, Hayley 54, 74, 156, 161
Milne, Tom 172, 291
Milner, Martin 407, 409-412
Mimieux, Yvette xx, xxviii, xxx, xxxii, 35, 95, 161-163, 265, 271, 272, 357, 413, 497, 501, 534, 567, 594, 646
Mineo, Sal 26, 201, 611
Mission: Impossible 270, 311, 314
Mitchell, Charles P. 132, 139, 148, 149, 411
Modell, Merriam see Evelyn Piper

Monsters 567-570
Montalbàn, Ricardo 430, 434, 435, 441, 445, 449
Moore, Gary 608
Moorehead, Agnes 27-29, 38, 622
Morheim, Lou 235, 240
Moriarty, Michael 544, 547
Moross, Jerome 72, 73
Morrow, Vic 292, 382-389, 617
Morse, Barry 487, 490, 492, 493, 497
Morse, Robert 9, 111
Mortiner, John 99
Mortimer, Penelope 99, 159
Most Deadly Game, The xxxiii, 270, 271, 649
Movie Game, The 622
Movie Talk 633
Moxey, John Llewellyn 294, 299, 304
Munro, Caroline 522
Munro, Janet 35
Murder on the Orient Express 449, 464, 465
Murder, She Wrote 539, 574, 650
Murray, Don 188-190, 650, 656
Musante, Tony 523, 565
My Blood Runs Cold 40, 41, 201

Namath, Joe 247, 249, 255, 256, 259, 260, 263, 264, 527
Narrow Chute, The see *Cotter*
Nathan Paul 249, 251-254
Natwick, Mildred 220, 221, 226, 229
NBC Wednesday Night Movie 193
NBC World Premiere Movie 153
Neame, Ronald xiv, 311, 316-318, 321-323, 325, 328, 625, 655
Needham, Hal 241
Negulesco, Jean 81, 84, 87
Neilson, James 27, 38
Neon Signs xxxviii, 575-585, 595
Nettleton, Lois 272-274
New CBS Friday Night Movie, The 282
New with Nelson 653
Newman, Paul 54, 185
Newmar, Julie 221, 222, 226, 229, 232, 574
Nicholson, Jack 268, 269
Nielsen, Leslie 13, 317, 333, 334
Night Gallery xxiii, 294, 306-310, 314
Night Heat 565, 566
Night Stalker, The xix, xxiii, xxxiv, xxxvii, 294-306, 353, 356, 596
Norwood 177, 247-265, 267, 291, 296
Not for Women Only 635

SELECT INDEX

Nuyen, France 24, 166
Nye, Louis 622, 637

O'Brian, Hugh 430, 432, 434
O'Brien, Joan 41
O'Connell, Arthur 317, 334
O'Connell, Helen 609
O'Grady, Gail 550, 552, 553, 555, 563
O'Neal, Ryan 101, 617
O'Neill, James xxxvii, 400, 466
Oakland, Simon 282, 283, 301, 305
Of Mice and Men 390-392, 404, 633
Off the Menu: The Last Days of Chasen's 652
Olivier, Laurence 96, 97, 103, 105, 106, 108, 111, 114, 117, 121-123, 268, 553, 608, 617, 628, 649
Olson, Eric 407, 410
Omnibus 645
On Stage: Nelson's World 652, 653
On the Town with Mike Farah 651
Once You Kiss a Stranger 177, 201-216, 296, 411, 439, 567, 581
Oppenheimer, Peer J. 74
Oringer, Barry 174, 177
Orson Welles' Great Mysteries xxxv, 125, 359-364, 366, 631
Other Side of the Stars, The 625
Out of Control see *Bad Georgia Road*

Page, Geraldine xxi, 403, 404, 649
Palance, Jack 379, 380, 382, 487, 489, 490, 493, 497, 641
Paluzzi, Luciana 51-53, 166
Panama, Norman 218, 224, 230
Paradise, Hawaiian Style 95, 248
Parker, Eleanor 51, 430, 432
Parker, Fess 19, 22
Parker, Suzy 30, 49, 99
Parkins, Barbara 528
Parsons, Gram 292, 293
Parsons, Louella 39, 40, 82, 91
Password 611
Patten, Luana 41
Paul, Louis xxii
Paul Ryan Show, The 638
Perkins, Millie 35, 99, 128
Perry, Frank 317
Pesce, Frank 523
Pettet, Joanna 92, 148
Peyton Place xx, 49, 131, 177, 233
Piper, Evelyn 97, 111

Play It As It Lays 317
Playboy (magazine) xxx, 90-92, 94, 164
Pleasure Seekers, The xxviii, xxx, 74, 75, 81-88, 91, 219, 261, 405
Pleshette, Suzanne 74, 90, 161, 632, 652
Poe, Edgar Allan 311, 313
Polakof, James ix, 518-522
Polanski, Roman 89, 111, 148
Police Woman 406, 407
Pollard, Michael J. 55, 154, 194
Portis, Charles 247, 248
Poseidon 350
Poseidon Adventure, The x, xi, xiii, xvii-xxii, xxiv, xxv, xxxiii, xxxv, 17, 150, 268, 270, 282, 291, 294, 315-351, 353, 355-357, 379, 389, 393, 405, 407, 408, 411, 413, 438, 451, 465, 475, 522, 591, 597, 625-630, 651, 655
Poseidon Adventure, The (2005 TV-movie) 349, 350
Poseidon Adventure Premiere, The 626
Poseidon Adventure, The – The Cast Looks Back 656
Potting Shed, The 10, 11
Powers, Stefanie 63, 517
Preminger: Academy of a Filmmaker 650
Premonition 507
Preminger, Otto xxxii, 59, 63, 64, 68-72, 97-99, 101, 103-112, 116-119, 121, 122, 124-127, 268, 295, 306, 311, 610, 611, 614, 615, 650, 656
Prentiss, Paula 54, 111, 468, 469
Presley, Elvis xx, xxx, 36, 37, 40, 41, 95, 97. 223, 248, 261, 317
Pretty Polly 155
Princess Margaret 162
Prisoner: Cell Block H 503
Prize Performance 3, 607
Project '68 619, 620
Prowse, Juliet 54, 128
Pulleine, Tim 497
Pursuit 26

Quayle, Anthony 366
Quest of Quests 643
Quincy, M.E. 406
Quinn, Joan 539, 650, 651

Radford, James x, 272, 324, 327
Rainmaker, The 527
Ray, Fred Olen 571
Redford, Robert 63, 76, 98, 356
Reed, Oliver xiv, 133-138, 141, 142, 144, 147, 149, 150, 269, 293, 405, 478, 629
Reed, Robert 221, 226, 279, 617
Reflets de Cannes 614
Reiner, Carl 612, 639

Reisner, Alan 472, 473
Reluctant Debutante, The 13, 14, 24
Remick, Lee xxiii, 32, 49, 90, 98, 161
Repulsion 89
Return of the Movie Movie, The 325, 625
Return to Fantasy Island 435
Return to Peyton Place xxviii, 38, 49-54, 65, 432
Reynolds, Burt 190, 356, 644
Reynolds, Debbie 75, 624
Rice, Jeff 294, 299, 304, 305
Richard Thomas American Dance Foundation Benefit 646
Richey, Jeremy R. xxxv, 151
Richie Brockleman, Private Eye 475
Rist, Robbie 468-470
Riva, Michael 416
Road Show 567
Roberts, Marguerite 248, 249, 257, 261, 262, 265
Roberts, Meade 62, 157
Robbins, Cindy 35, 41
Robinette, Dale 436, 445, 476, 478, 479, 481
Robson, Flora 133, 138, 142, 148, 454
Rod Serling's Night Gallery see *Night Gallery*
Rogers, Ginger 94, 95, 396, 614, 642
Roman, Ruth 503-505
Romantic Comedy 527
Rosemary's Baby 147, 148
Rosenberg, Max J. 157
Ross, Helen 51
Ross, Katherine xxiii, 161, 317, 357, 522
Ross, Lillian 51
Roud, Richard 71, 159, 172
Rowan, Dan 217-219, 221-225, 228-232, 621
Run for Your Life xxxv, 128-131, 193
Russell, Ken 133, 134
Russell, Rosalind 68
Ryan's Hope 530

Sagal, Boris 166
Salzman, Bert 530, 531
Sand Pebbles, The 127, 128
Sanders, Denis 76, 78, 79
Santa Claus Lane Parade, The 625
Sapinsley, Alvin 306, 307
Sargent, Bill 90, 93, 614
Sargent, Joseph 233, 235, 240, 311
Saric, Lazar 575, 578
Sarris, Andrew 117

Savalas, Telly 423-426, 642
Saxon, John 69, 76, 98, 271, 436, 443
Scacchi, Greta 536
Scheuer, Philip K. 47
Schneider, Romy 69, 72, 74
Schulman, Paul H. 371
Schwartz, Tony 510
Scott, Vernon 120, 162, 267
Sea Gull: The Hampton: 1990, The 570, 571
Selleck, Tom 470-472
Selsman, Jill 56, 88, 293, 501, 596
Selsman, Mike 48, 51, 73
Serf, Bennett 207
Serling, Rod 306, 307
Shadow on the Land 191-193, 232
Shain, Percy 60, 185, 238, 244, 275, 284, 379
Shales, Tom 505
Shape of Things to Come, The 365, 447, 476, 486-498
Shaw, Artie 627-629
Shaw, Rose Tobias 454 455
Shea, Eric 317, 326, 333-335, 339
Sheehan, David 484
Shepherd, Jack 359, 361, 362
Sherman, Allan 612
Shirley Temple's Storybook xxx, 26-29
Shock Treatment xxx, 75-81, 196
Shore, Dinah 621, 637
Shuttered Room, The xx, xxxii, xxxiii, xxxv, xxxvii, 125, 132-151, 160, 201, 271, 549, 596
Sidewalks of New York, The 3
Sidney, Sylvia 404
Siegel, Don 36, 37
Silliphant, Stirling 316
Sinatra, Frank xiv, 207, 650
Sinatra, Nancy 248, 249
Sinatra, Tina ix, 64, 65, 430-432, 435
Siskel, Gene 260
Sixth Sense, The xxxiv, 294, 310-314
Slade, Bernard 527, 566
Sly Fox 484
Smith, Cecil 38, 60, 284
Smith, Liz 570
Smith, William 575, 576, 578-580, 583
Smugglers, The xxii, 153, 154, 192-196
Snow White and the Three Stooges 41
Sommer, Elke 74, 90, 91, 401
Son of Blob see *Beware! The Blob*
Sour Apple Award 54

Southern, Terry 292
Sparkes, Jane 523
Sparr, Robert 201, 203-205, 209, 210
Specht, Robert 233, 234, 238, 240, 245
Spelling, Aaron 429-431, 435, 467, 484, 500, 511, 517, 518, 522, 528, 538
Spinell, Joe 523, 524
Spirits 571-573
Spy Who Came in from the Cold, The 120
Staenberg, Zacj 562
St. John, Jill 17, 24, 30, 74, 90, 111, 646
Stallone, Sage 587, 588
Stanley, Paul 188, 196
Star's Table 648
Starcrash 498
Stark, Koo 487
Steel Magnolias 527
Stefano, Joseph 549, 551
Stephenson, Skip 517
Sterling, Tisha 249, 259, 260
Steve and Judy Show, The 634
Stevens, Connie xxviii, xxx, xxxi, 24, 47, 54, 74, 90, 125, 163, 613, 624, 641
Stevens, Stella 35, 91, 99, 316, 320, 323-325, 331-336, 345, 346, 348, 438, 541, 591, 655, 656
Stevenson, McLean 629, 635, 638, 639
Stoddard, Brandon 429
Stollof, Victor 470, 472
Strangers on a Train 201, 209
Strasberg, Susan 163, 534
Stripper, The 62, 154, 157, 512
Stump the Stars 609
Subotsky, Milton 157, 159
Sudden Death see *Once You Kiss a Stranger*
Sullivan, Barry 93, 196, 199, 200, 233, 236, 239, 470-472, 511, 513, 516
Sullivan, Susan 467
Sunrise 656
Supernatural 594
Sweeney, D.B. 571
Swimmer, The 163
Sword of Justice 476
Syna, Sy 571
Szwarc, Jeannot 306, 307, 309

Talbot, Nita 218, 249
Tales of the Unexpected xxxiv, 125, 365, 530-534
Tanchuck, Nathaniel 133, 271
Taraborelli, J. Randy 207
Tarantino, Quentin 160, 389, 390, 592

Taylor, Robert (film critic) 260
Tenser, Tony 268
Things to Come 486, 490, 493
Thinnes, Roy 173-176
Third New York Big Laff Off, The 647
Thomas, Bob 55
Thomas, Kevin 290, 304, 387, 388, 434, 470, 481, 496
Thomas, Philip Michael 479, 481
Thomas, Thom 528
Thomas, Tony 619, 620
Thompson, Howard 79, 160, 260
Thorndike, Dame Sybil 10, 268, 593, 649
Thorpe, Jerry 281
Thriller 125, 394, 400, 401
Tierney, Gene 30, 82, 85, 86, 654, 655
Tiffin, Pamela xx, 63, 82-84, 87, 95, 128, 161, 616
Tilton, Charlene 483
Time Express 511
Tinee, Mae 47
To Catch a Thief 645
To Wong Foo, Thanks for Everything, Julie Newmar 574
Todos los dias, un dia 498-500
Tonight Show Starring Johnny Carson, The xi, 219, 224, 268, 331, 340, 359, 392, 610, 621, 623-625, 627-631, 635
Toppers, The 634
Torn, Rip xiv, 9, 188, 189
Towering Inferno, The 343, 394, 411
Towers, Harry Alan 486, 487, 498, 542
Travelin' see *Road Show*
Travilla 62, 63
Troupe, Tom 527
Trumbo, Dalton 43, 44, 47, 48, 98
Tryon, Tom 59, 63, 69-72, 104, 613, 650
Turman, Lawrence 161
TV Guide Television 654
TV Scout 122, 171, 187, 275, 284, 313, 379, 407
Twin Peaks 570

Under the Yum Yum Tree xxx, 63-68, 72, 74, 75, 91, 219, 610, 627

Vallee, Rudy 622
Valley of the Dolls 85, 88
Van Ark, Joan 484
Van Horne, Harriet 510
Varsi, Diane 24, 30, 32, 49
Vaughn, Robert 165-167
Vic 587, 588

Vigilante 522-526
Vilanch, Bruce 7, 8
Vilar, Esther 630
Villechaize, Hervé 430, 435, 436, 445, 449
Virginian, The 59

Wade, David 616, 617
Wagner, Lindsay 590
Wagner, Robert 30, 31, 131, 196-198, 200, 282-284, 393, 478, 517, 621
Wald, Jerry 36, 38, 41, 48-50, 53, 62
Walken, Christopher 423-426
Walker, Robert 208, 215
Walker, Robert, Jr. 208, 286-288, 290
Wallis, Hal B. 206, 247-254, 256, 260-264
Washington Affair, The 470-472, 491
Waterman, Dennis 181-185
Waters, John 592
Weaver, Fritz xxi, 220, 226, 229, 403
Webber, Robert 382-384, 386, 389, 511-514, 516
Weekend of Terror xxiii, 272-275
Weingott, Owen 369, 370
Weisbart, David 81, 88
Welch, Raquel xx, xxi, xxxi, xxxiv, 96, 202, 501, 594, 642
Weld, Tuesday xiv, xxviii, xxix, xxxii, xxxv, 4, 7, 9. 35, 40, 41, 47, 51, 54, 63, 90, 95, 127, 128, 148, 161, 163, 201, 317, 330, 497, 594, 650
Weldon, Michael J. 572
Welles, Orson 359, 361, 363, 366, 430
Wells, H.G. 486, 497, 498
Wendkos, Paul 174, 177
Westmore, Perc 204
Wexler, Howard ix, 577, 578
Whatever Happened to Baby Jane? 591
Whitman, Stuart 25, 36, 37, 63, 76, 80, 81, 436, 440
Wide World of Entertainment 394
Wide World of Mystery 394, 400, 401
Wiederhorn, Ken 543
Wilcox, Larry 382, 385, 386
Wild in the Country 40, 41, 51
Willard, John 451, 452
Williams, Cindy 287, 288, 646
Williams, John 333, 336, 340, 342
Williamson, Fred 523, 524
Willow B: Women in Prison 503-506
Wilmington, Michael 563
Wilson, Anthony 240, 241
Wilson, Barbara 326
Wilson, Earl 111, 156, 161, 330, 356, 423, 628

Winters, Shelley xxxvii, 317, 320, 323, 325, 331, 333, 334, 340, 342, 345, 349, 350, 624, 626, 641
Wise, Robert 128
Wolf, Jeffrey ix, 567, 570
Wong, B.D. 647
Wood, Natalie xxxiv, 54, 161, 642, 653
Wright, Teresa 375, 377, 378, 407, 410
Wyatt, Jane 272, 274, 275
Wyman, Jane 30, 31, 652
Wynant, H.M. 169

Yarnall, Celeste 317, 487
York, Francine 273, 407, 409, 411
York, Susannah 566
You Can't Win 'Em All see *Once You Kiss a Stranger*
You Don't Say! 89, 611
Young, Freddie 610
Young, Gig 133, 135-141, 144-147, 149, 649
Young Lovers, The 40
Young, Robert M. 242, 245
Young Set, The 615

Zanuck, Darryl F. 62, 75
Zanuck, Richard 75, 76, 82
Zarem, Bobby 330, 626
Zastupnevich, Paul 318, 340, 409
Zimbalist, Efrem, Jr. 93, 95, 178, 179, 613, 615
Zimmerman, Jill 8
Zombies, The 103, 121

www.ingramcontent.com/pod-product-compliance
Lightning Source LLC
Chambersburg PA
CBHW051551230426
43668CB00013B/1811